**Keep this book. You will
need it and use it throughout
your career.**

About the American Hotel & Lodging Association (AH&LA)

Founded in 1910, AH&LA is the trade association representing the lodging industry in the United States. AH&LA is a federation of state lodging associations throughout the United States with 11,000 lodging properties worldwide as members. The association offers its members assistance with governmental affairs representation, communications, marketing, hospitality operations, training and education, technology issues, and more. For information, call 202-289-3100.

LODGING, the management magazine of AH&LA, is a "living textbook" for hospitality students that provides timely features, industry news, and vital lodging information.

About the American Hotel & Lodging Educational Institute (EI)

An affiliate of AH&LA, the Educational Institute is the world's largest source of quality training and educational materials for the lodging industry. EI develops textbooks and courses that are used in more than 1,200 colleges and universities worldwide, and also offers courses to individuals through its Distance Learning program. Hotels worldwide rely on EI for training resources that focus on every aspect of lodging operations. Industry-tested videos, CD-ROMs, seminars, and skills guides prepare employees at every skill level. EI also offers professional certification for the industry's top performers. For information about EI's products and services, call 800-349-0299 or 407-999-8100.

About the American Hotel & Lodging Educational Foundation (AH&LEF)

An affiliate of AH&LA, the American Hotel & Lodging Educational Foundation provides financial support that enhances the stability, prosperity, and growth of the lodging industry through educational and research programs. AH&LEF has awarded millions of dollars in scholarship funds for students pursuing higher education in hospitality management. AH&LEF has also funded research projects on topics important to the industry, including occupational safety and health, turnover and diversity, and best practices in the U.S. lodging industry. For information, go to www.ahlef.org.

ACCOUNTING for HOSPITALITY MANAGERS

Educational Institute Books

UNIFORM SYSTEM OF ACCOUNTS FOR THE LODGING INDUSTRY
Tenth Revised Edition

WORLD OF RESORTS: FROM DEVELOPMENT TO MANAGEMENT
Third Edition
Chuck Yim Gee

PLANNING AND CONTROL FOR FOOD AND BEVERAGE OPERATIONS
Eighth Edition
Jack D. Ninemeier

UNDERSTANDING HOSPITALITY LAW
Fifth Edition
Jack P. Jefferies/Banks Brown

SUPERVISION IN THE HOSPITALITY INDUSTRY
Fifth Edition
Jack D. Ninemeier/Raphael R. Kavanaugh

MANAGEMENT OF FOOD AND BEVERAGE OPERATIONS
Fifth Edition
Jack D. Ninemeier

MANAGING FRONT OFFICE OPERATIONS
Ninth Edition
Michael L. Kasavana

MANAGING SERVICE IN FOOD AND BEVERAGE OPERATIONS
Fourth Edition
Ronald F. Cichy/Philip J. Hickey, Jr.

THE LODGING AND FOOD SERVICE INDUSTRY
Seventh Edition
Gerald W. Lattin

SECURITY AND LOSS PREVENTION MANAGEMENT
Third Edition
David M. Stipanuk/Raymond C. Ellis, Jr.

HOSPITALITY INDUSTRY MANAGERIAL ACCOUNTING
Seventh Edition
Raymond S. Schmidgall

PURCHASING FOR FOOD SERVICE OPERATIONS
Ronald F. Cichy/Jeffery D Elsworth

MANAGING TECHNOLOGY IN THE HOSPITALITY INDUSTRY
Sixth Edition
Michael L. Kasavana

HOTEL AND RESTAURANT ACCOUNTING
Seventh Edition
Raymond Cote

ACCOUNTING FOR HOSPITALITY MANAGERS
Fifth Edition
Raymond Cote

CONVENTION MANAGEMENT AND SERVICE
Eighth Edition
Milton T. Astroff/James R. Abbey

HOSPITALITY SALES AND MARKETING
Fifth Edition
James R. Abbey

MANAGING HOUSEKEEPING OPERATIONS
Revised Third Edition
Aleta A. Nitschke/William D. Frye

HOSPITALITY TODAY: AN INTRODUCTION
Seventh Edition
Rocco M. Angelo/Andrew N. Vladimir

HOSPITALITY FACILITIES MANAGEMENT AND DESIGN
Third Edition
David M. Stipanuk

MANAGING HOSPITALITY HUMAN RESOURCES
Fifth Edition
Robert H. Woods, Misty M. Johanson, and Michael P. Sciarini

RETAIL MANAGEMENT FOR SPAS

HOSPITALITY INDUSTRY FINANCIAL ACCOUNTING
Third Edition
Raymond S. Schmidgall/James W. Damitio

INTERNATIONAL HOTELS: DEVELOPMENT & MANAGEMENT
Second Edition
Chuck Yim Gee

QUALITY SANITATION MANAGEMENT
Ronald F. Cichy

HOTEL INVESTMENTS: ISSUES & PERSPECTIVES
Fifth Edition
Edited by Lori E. Raleigh and Rachel J. Roginsky

LEADERSHIP AND MANAGEMENT IN THE HOSPITALITY INDUSTRY
Third Edition
Robert H. Woods/Judy Z. King

MARKETING IN THE HOSPITALITY INDUSTRY
Fifth Edition
Ronald A. Nykiel

UNIFORM SYSTEM OF ACCOUNTS FOR THE HEALTH, RACQUET AND SPORTSCLUB INDUSTRY

CONTEMPORARY CLUB MANAGEMENT
Third Edition
Edited by Joe Perdue and Jason Koenigsfeld for the Club Managers Association of America

RESORT CONDOMINIUM AND VACATION OWNERSHIP MANAGEMENT: A HOSPITALITY PERSPECTIVE
Robert A. Gentry/Pedro Mandoki/Jack Rush

ACCOUNTING FOR CLUB OPERATIONS
Raymond S. Schmidgall/James W. Damitio

TRAINING AND DEVELOPMENT FOR THE HOSPITALITY INDUSTRY
Debra F. Cannon/Catherine M. Gustafson

UNIFORM SYSTEM OF FINANCIAL REPORTING FOR CLUBS
Sixth Revised Edition

HOTEL ASSET MANAGEMENT: PRINCIPLES & PRACTICES
Second Edition
Edited by Greg Denton, Lori E. Raleigh, and A. J. Singh

MANAGING BEVERAGE OPERATIONS
Second Edition
Ronald F. Cichy/Lendal H. Kotschevar

FOOD SAFETY: MANAGING WITH THE HACCP SYSTEM
Second Edition
Ronald F. Cichy

UNIFORM SYSTEM OF FINANCIAL REPORTING FOR SPAS

FUNDAMENTALS OF DESTINATION MANAGEMENT AND MARKETING
Edited by Rich Harrill

ETHICS IN THE HOSPITALITY AND TOURISM INDUSTRY
Second Edition
Karen Lieberman/Bruce Nissen

SPA: A COMPREHENSIVE INTRODUCTION
Elizabeth M. Johnson/Bridgette M. Redman

HOSPITALITY 2015: THE FUTURE OF HOSPITALITY AND TRAVEL
Marvin Cetron/Fred DeMicco/Owen Davies

REVENUE MANAGEMENT: MAXIMIZING REVENUE IN HOSPITALITY OPERATIONS
Gabor Forgacs

FINANCIAL MANAGEMENT FOR SPAS
Raymond S. Schmidgall/John R. Korpi

ACCOUNTING for HOSPITALITY MANAGERS

Fifth Edition

Raymond Cote

American Hotel & Lodging Educational Institute

Disclaimer

This publication is designed to provide accurate and authoritative information in regard to the subject matter covered. It is sold with the understanding that the publisher is not engaged in rendering legal, accounting, or other professional service. If legal advice or other expert assistance is required, the services of a competent professional person should be sought.

    —From the Declaration of Principles jointly adopted by the American Bar Association and a Committee of Publishers and Associations

The author, Raymond Cote, is solely responsible for the contents of this publication. All views expressed herein are solely those of the author and do not necessarily reflect the views of the American Hotel & Lodging Educational Institute (the Institute) or the American Hotel & Lodging Association (AH&LA).

Nothing contained in this publication shall constitute a standard, an endorsement, or a recommendation of the Institute or AH&LA. The Institute and AH&LA disclaim any liability with respect to the use of any information, procedure, or product, or reliance thereon by any member of the hospitality industry.

©2007
By the AMERICAN HOTEL & LODGING
EDUCATIONAL INSTITUTE
2113 N. High Street
Lansing, Michigan 48906-4221

The American Hotel & Lodging
Educational Institute is a nonprofit
educational foundation.

Printed in the United States of America
   7 8 9 17 16 15 14 13

ISBN 978-0-86612-297-9

Editor: Priscilla J. Wood

Contents

About the Author

Raymond Cote

FOLLOWING AN accomplished business career, Raymond Cote became an educator and achieved the rank of full professor at a major hospitality university in the United States. For 18 years, Professor Cote taught undergraduate and graduate courses in hospitality accounting, hospitality financial management, taxation, and advanced accounting subjects. His teaching experience includes setting up hospitality accounting courses in the United States and abroad for an international hospitality college.

In the private sector, he has held the positions of vice president, controller, MIS director, and chief accountant for a major food and lodging corporation. As an entrepreneur, he was president of several business conglomerates consisting of a food and beverage operation, retail and service companies, and a consulting/certified public accounting firm.

Professor Cote is a graduate of the undergraduate and graduate schools of Suffolk University and Burdett College, both located in Boston, Massachusetts. The professional credentials of Raymond Cote have included Certified Public Accountant (CPA), Certified Computer Professional (CCP), Enrolled Agent (EA) authorized to practice before the Internal Revenue Service, and an Accreditation in Accountancy by the American Council for Accountancy. His civic and professional positions were President of a Chamber of Commerce and Vice President and Director of Education for the Florida Accountants Association.

Professor Cote has written four hospitality accounting textbooks and supporting material for the Educational Institute: Basic Hotel and Restaurant Accounting, Accounting for Hospitality Managers, and the prior versions of these two books, Understanding Hospitality Accounting I and Understanding Hospitality Accounting II. Previous works include another text, College Business Math (1984-1988, PAR, Inc.), and numerous training and procedures manuals for private industry.

Preface

PREMIER HOSPITALITY COMPANIES want to attract management candidates who know financial management principles and how to apply them, and who have taken the usual specialty courses in purchasing, menu planning, and so on. A hospitality manager or executive is expected to be results-oriented and to have exceptional financial decision-making skills. *Accounting for Hospitality Managers* provides the information and tools a student or professional needs to become a successful executive in the hospitality industry.

Instructors require an up-to-date, authoritative text that offers relevant supplementary materials. Students deserve a text that is easy to read, meaningful, and useful in the real world of hospitality. As an author of hospitality accounting and managerial texts, I view the customer market as made up of more than teachers and students: it includes hospitality employers, who play an integral role in the professional cycle. My obligation as an author is to provide a product to academia that will help a job candidate develop in a manner satisfactory to the hospitality employment market. *Accounting for Hospitality Managers* is a pragmatic hospitality managerial accounting text based on industry prerequisites.

This fifth edition of *Accounting for Hospitality Managers* is a significant change from the fourth edition; it upgrades chapters, adds three essential chapters, and features many innovations. For example:

- Each chapter closes with a case study relevant to the chapter material.

- Each chapter lists Internet sites that can serve as reference sources for students who wish to research and study the topics further. In addition, instructors may wish to assign research projects based on material presented on the sites.

- Chapter 5, Hospitality Payroll Accounting, continues its unprecedented comprehensive coverage. It is updated and now includes an appendix containing research reports I've prepared on labor laws for employers, teen labor laws for employers, overtime rules, and tip reporting.

- Many revisions result from suggestions and comments made by valued customers and hospitality executives.

Other revisions and updates to the text include the following:

- RevPAR receives substantial presentation in Chapter 8.

- The Sarbanes-Oxley Act, the SEC, and the 10-K Report are covered extensively in Chapter 12.

- Numerous exhibits have been updated to reflect today's technology.

- The basic front office accounting procedures have been revised to relate to computerized processing.

The three new chapters in this edition address cash management and planning, casino accounting, feasibility studies, expense allocation, fair value accounting, and present and future value calculations for single cash flows and annuities. The cash management and planning chapter discusses not only cash management procedures, but also cash float, lockbox systems, zero balance accounts, sweep accounts, EBITDA, and free cash flow. The casino accounting chapter includes a brief history of gaming, casino industry demographics, descriptions of several casino games, the role of accounting in casinos, and important financial principles pertaining to casino accounting and internal control and casino financial accounting.

This fifth edition of *Accounting for Hospitality Managers* continues to address the needs of the hospitality industry and academia. It uses an organized writing style that students easily understand, yet is sufficiently comprehensive to provide the vocabulary and financial information required to achieve success.

Author's Website Information:

The author owns and maintains a website at www.raymondcote.com. The website, updated frequently during the school term, offers up-to-date hospitality news and special hospitality research reports prepared by the author. The author also owns the domain www.raymondcote.us.

A Special Thank You from the Author

Accounting for Hospitality Managers owes its existence to the greatest customers in the world. Thank you.

I sincerely thank the editing and production staff of the Educational Institute, who do a remarkable job of producing this text. My gratitude goes to Tim Eaton, the senior director of publications, who, no matter how preoccupied, is always liberal with his time and guidance during the arduous production process.

I further give unequivocal thanks to Vice President of Academic Programs Mari Behrendt and her staff for their proficient, speedy, and courteous responses to my numerous customer service requests.

I dedicate this work to the cherished memory of my mother and father, Alice and Raymond Cote, with love, honor, and gratitude.

Chapter 1 Outline

Revenue Centers
  Categories of Revenue Centers
  Revenue Centers and Financial
    Reports
  Minor Revenue Centers
Fundamental Revenue Concepts
  Revenue Accounts
  Net Revenue
  Gross Profit
Trade Discounts
Cash Discounts
  ROG
  EOM
  Transportation Charges
Recording Invoices and Discounts
  Gross Method
  Net Method
Internal Control for Food and Beverage
  Sales
  Guest Checks—Manual System
  Guest Checks—Automated System
  Debit and Credit Cards
  Guest Charges
  Accounting for Charged Tips
Accounting Personnel and Front Office
  Functions
  The Accounts Receivable Clerk
  The Cashier
  The Night Auditor
  A Summary of Front Office
    Accounting
Cash and Data Collection

Competencies

1. Define revenue centers, identify examples of revenue centers in a hospitality business, and explain their roles in financial reporting. (pp. 4–6)

2. Define revenue accounts, identify examples of revenue accounts for a hospitality business, and explain net revenue and gross profit. (pp. 6–9)

3. Identify what is meant by trade discounts and cash discounts, and explain their relevance to a hospitality business. (pp. 9–12)

4. Describe two methods for recording invoices involving discounts and two procedures for recording cash discounts. (pp. 12–15)

5. Explain the common internal control forms and procedures involved in food and beverage sales. (pp. 15–21)

6. Describe the difference between the guest ledger and the city ledger. (pp. 21–22)

7. Identify three front office personnel who report to the accounting department, and describe the roles they play in providing hospitality accounting information. (pp. 22–26)

8. Describe the system used for cash and data collection in a hospitality business. (pp. 26–32)

1

Hotel Revenue Accounting

In ACCOUNTING, there is an important distinction between the terms "revenue" and "income." Revenue is an exchange process represented by sales of merchandise, sales of services, and/or interest and dividends. It results from a business transaction, which is the exchange of goods, property, or services for cash or an account receivable (the customer's promise to pay).

In a hotel,* the major sources of revenue are rooms department sales and food and beverage department sales. Additional hotel revenues come from other operating departments, interest from savings and money market accounts, dividends from investments, concessions fees, commissions, and discounts earned for timely payment of invoices from suppliers. Because the largest source of revenue is sales, accounting professionals frequently use the terms "revenue" and "sales" synonymously.

Income is the result of revenue being greater than all the hotel's expenses. Income can be shown as:

Revenue (Sales) − All Expenses = Income

A hotel's generation of revenue requires good control procedures to record and process transactions involving cash, credit cards, and accounts receivable. Documents associated with revenue accounting provide internal control benefits for both the operation and its employees. All employees appreciate sound internal control procedures; such procedures allow employees to prove that they are performing their duties with efficiency and integrity.

In addressing the topic of revenue accounting and controls, this chapter will answer such questions as:

1. How does revenue accounting for operated departments differ from accounting for leased departments?
2. What is the relationship of net revenue to gross profit?
3. How are purchase discounts handled in the accounting records?
4. What front office activities do accounting department personnel perform?
5. How are computers used in modern property management systems?

---

*As it is used here, *hotel* is a broad generic term for all types of lodging operations, including luxury hotels, motels, motor inns, and inns.

This chapter presents various **revenue centers** and revenue accounts used by hospitality properties. The recommendations given by the Committee on Financial Management of the American Hotel & Lodging Association (AH&LA) form the basis for the revenue accounts discussed here. Operated and leased departments are discussed in terms of how the results of their operations are presented on financial statements.

Purchase discounts receive comprehensive coverage through explanations of the gross and net methods. Revenue and nonrevenue procedures for the treatment of discounts are also discussed.

The role of internal control forms for revenue in an accounting system is explained through discussion and examples. In addition, the relationship between the front office and the accounting department is examined.

Finally, since a hotel generates cash and revenue from many remote activities and departments, the fundamentals of cash and data collection at a central source are important topics of discussion.

Revenue Centers

For purposes of financial reporting and data collection, departments may be classified as revenue centers or support centers. Simply stated, revenue centers generate revenue through sales of products and/or services to guests; revenue centers are also referred to as operated departments. Support centers provide services to revenue centers. For ease of discussion, we will use the terms "center" and "department" interchangeably.

Categories of Revenue Centers

Revenue centers may be further categorized as major revenue centers and minor revenue centers. The three major revenue centers for a hotel are:

- Rooms
- Food
- Beverage

The scope of ancillary revenue centers depends on the number of services the hotel sells. The following are revenue centers if the hotel owns and operates the service:

- Telecommunications
- Garage and Parking
- Golf Course
- Golf Pro Shop
- Guest Laundry
- Health Center
- Swimming Pool

- Tennis
- Tennis Pro Shop
- Other Operated Departments

The departmental statement Other Operated Departments combines those revenue centers whose sales are minor and an individual report would not be practical. For example, any number of the above ancillary revenue centers might be combined into Other Operated Departments.

Revenue Centers and Financial Reports

The design of a financial information system will determine the number of individual reporting areas at a particular establishment. Most operated departments issue financial reports known as supporting schedules or departmental income statements. For example, a separate departmental income statement is produced for the rooms, food and beverage, and telecommunications departments. Some operated departments are considered incidental operations because their sales volumes and operating expenses are not significant. These departments may together form a single financial reporting category called Other Operated Departments.

Each revenue department receives credit for its share of sales regardless of where the sales are made. For example, any food or beverages sold to guests in their rooms would be reported by the food and beverage department, not the rooms department.

A hospitality establishment may use more than one account for food sales in order to isolate the separate contributions of various segments of its operations. For instance, food sales accounts may be set up for each of the following areas:

- Dining room
- Coffee shop
- Banquets
- Room service (food sales)
- Lounge (food sales)

Similarly, separate accounts to record sales of beverages (alcoholic drinks) may be established for the following areas:

- Bar
- Dining room
- Banquets
- Room service (beverage sales)

Minor Revenue Centers

Minor revenue centers perform functions vital to the operation of a hospitality establishment. Any minor revenue center that is hotel-operated requires a specific section in a hotel's chart of accounts to properly record sales, cost of sales, payroll, and other applicable operating expenses.

The functions associated with some minor revenue centers, rather than being performed by hotel-operated departments, may instead be leased to a **concessionaire.** This arrangement is common for barbershops and beauty salons as well as laundry and valet services. Separate income statements are not produced for concessions leased by the hotel because concessions are not hotel-operated departments. The income derived from leased shops or services appears on a hotel's schedule of **rentals and other income.** The responsibility area addressed by this schedule is considered another revenue center.

Telecommunications. The telecommunications department is responsible for providing telecommunications services for the hotel and its guests. If an electronic communications system is not installed, charges to guests for billable calls must be entered on a log or voucher. These charges must be promptly forwarded to the accounts receivable clerk in the front office. (In fact, any services that guests may charge to their room accounts will require a system to communicate such billings promptly to the accounts receivable clerk.)

Laundry. Laundry services for guests may be performed by the hotel or by an outside laundry. If the work is done by an outside laundry, the hotel usually receives a commission based on charges to the guests. The income from commissions will appear on the hotel's schedule of rentals and other income.

Other Minor Departments. Valet services may include pressing, cleaning, and repairing guests' clothes, as well as shoe shining. This service area may be hotel-operated or handled by a local vendor.

Similarly, a hotel barbershop, beauty salon, or newsstand may be either hotel-operated or leased to a concessionaire. These types of shops often transact business on a cash-only basis; such transactions do not require any provisions for charges to guests' accounts.

A recreation department oversees the use of such facilities as swimming pools, health clubs, golf courses, and tennis courts. These facilities may be free to registered guests or available at an extra charge. Such facilities may be hotel-operated or leased to a concessionaire.

Fundamental Revenue Concepts

As noted earlier, the definition of a business transaction is *the exchange of goods, property, or services for cash or a promise to pay.* Revenue results from the sales of goods and services to guests in exchange for cash or a promise to pay. The amount of a sale is exclusive of any sales taxes or tips.

The realization principle states that a sale is recognized only after services and/or products have been delivered and accepted. It is at this point—called the *point of sale*—that a sale should be recognized, regardless of the method by which the customer pays.

Deposits for services or products to be provided in the future do not constitute sales. For example, the receipt of a $500 deposit from a customer to reserve banquet facilities cannot be recorded as a sale because the services and products have not yet been delivered. The receipt of cash under such circumstances represents a liability broadly categorized as unearned revenue.

The receipt of a deposit results in a debit (increase) to the cash account and an offsetting credit to another account. The account to be credited depends on the hotel's accounting system. It may be Accounts Receivable, Banquet Deposits, or some other appropriate account. Generally, accounts of this type are summarized and shown as a liability on the balance sheet. They may appear as Unearned Revenue, or Deposits and Credit Balances.

Revenue Accounts

The revenue accounts a hotel uses depend on the type of business activities it conducts, the size of the business, and the amount of detailed information that management requires in its financial reporting system.

Definitions of the following revenue accounts comply with the recommendations of the Committee on Financial Management of the American Hotel & Lodging Association.

Room Sales. Rentals of guestrooms and apartments are credited to this account. Separate charges for housekeeper or linen service should be included. If meals are included in the room rate, a distinction should be made between rooms and food to properly account for room and food sales.

Room Allowances. This is a contra-revenue account that represents rebates and refunds allowed after room sales were initially recorded.

Hospitality businesses sometimes grant these and other types of **allowances** to guests in the interest of maintaining good customer relations. Most allowances involve disputed charges, price adjustments, correction of overcharges, and adjustments for unsatisfactory service.

Food Sales. Sales of food and non-alcoholic beverages served with meals are credited to this account. There may be several food sales accounts classified by facility (for example, dining room, room service, lounge, and banquets).

Employees' meals and officers' checks should be excluded from the food sales account. Officers' checks are guest checks signed by a hotel's corporate officers in lieu of payment for food and beverages.

Sales of grease, bones, and other kitchen by-products are credited to cost of sales, not to this revenue account.

Food Allowances. This is a contra-revenue account that represents rebates and refunds allowed after food sales were initially recorded.

Beverage Sales. Beverage sales may be separated into wines, liquor, beer, or any other category helpful in sales analysis and inventory control. Beverage sales may be further classified according to source, such as dining room, room service, banquets, and lounge. Officers' checks should be excluded from this revenue account.

Beverage Allowances. This is a contra-revenue account that represents rebates and refunds allowed after beverage sales were initially recorded.

Other Income—Food and Beverage Department. The other income—food and beverage account is used to record sales of merchandise not related to food and beverage service. Sales recorded to this account are for sales of items *not* sold from vending machines. For example, the dining room may sell items such as gum, cigars, cigarettes, candy, and novelty items. The lounge may sell peanuts, popcorn, and other snack items. Cover and minimum charges should also be recorded to this account.

These miscellaneous departmental sales are excluded from Food Sales and Beverage Sales to permit a gross profit analysis, that is, comparisons of the sales of food and beverages against their respective costs.

Telecommunications Sales. Revenue received from guests for use of telecommunications services and any commissions earned from pay phones are included in this account. Sales may be classified as local calls, long-distance calls, service charges, and commissions.

Telecommunications Allowances. This is a contra-revenue account that represents rebates and refunds allowed after sales were initially recorded.

Other Accounts for Income Earned by the Hotel. This is a general revenue classification consisting of many different revenue accounts; the revenue associated with this classification is not credited to any specific department. For purposes of financial reporting, a hotel's other income is treated as coming from a separate revenue center.

Items fitting this classification will appear on a hotel's schedule of rentals and other income. These items include:

- Interest income

- Dividend income

- Rental income (stores, offices, and clubs)

- Concessions income

- Commissions income

- Vending machines income (less the cost of merchandise sold)

- Cash discounts earned (purchase discounts)

- Salvage income

Minor gain or loss on sale of fixed assets may also appear on a hotel's schedule of rentals and other income. If the total gain or loss is significant, however, it should be separately shown on the hotel's summary income statement.

Net Revenue

Net revenue is not a bookkeeping account for revenue. It is a term that represents sales less allowances. Net revenue reflects the billable activities of a facility. For example, assume that room sales total $100,000 and room allowances total $1,500. The net revenue on room sales realized by the rooms department would be $98,500. For financial statement purposes, this is shown as follows on the rooms department income statement:

Revenue	
Room Sales	$100,000
Room Allowances	1,500
Net Revenue	$ 98,500

The term "net revenue" is sometimes referred to as net sales. This net amount is significant in financial statement analysis because it is used as a common divisor in computing percentage relationships of various items to net sales.

Gross Profit

Like net revenue, **gross profit** is not a bookkeeping account; rather, it is a line item on financial statements. It is a term that represents net revenue less cost of sales. Gross profit reflects the profit made on the sale of merchandise before deducting any expenses associated with operating a facility.

The calculation of gross profit depends in part on the type of department in question. Some departments may be described as merchandising facilities. Merchandising facilities sell goods or products and, therefore, have cost of sales expenses.

The rooms department is not a merchandising facility. Therefore, its net revenue and gross profit are identical. If a rooms department has a net revenue figure of $75,000, its gross profit also equals $75,000.

By contrast, the food and beverage department *is* a merchandising facility. Assume its food sales are $80,450, food allowances $450, and cost of food sold $25,000. The gross profit for food sales would appear on the departmental income statement as follows:

Revenue	
Food Sales	$80,450
Food Allowances	450
Net Revenue	$80,000
Cost of Food Sold	25,000
Gross Profit	$55,000

A department's gross profit must be sufficient to cover payroll and other operating expenses and produce a departmental income. The total of all the departmental incomes in turn must be large enough to cover undistributed expenses and fixed charges in order to produce a net income for the hotel.

Trade Discounts

Trade discounts are reductions to those prices indicated on a vendor's price list. Vendors sometimes use trade discounts as a convenience in making price changes without printing new catalogs or price lists.

Trade discounts are never recorded as such. The amount paid is entered without indicating that it is a trade discount. Trade discounts do not depend upon payment within a given time period.

Vendors' invoices normally show the gross amount, trade discount, and net billing; therefore, computation of trade discounts is generally not required. For example, kitchen equipment with a list price of $5,000 purchased at a 40 percent trade discount will be billed at a net invoice price of $3,000. The purchase of this asset is recorded as $3,000. Any applicable cash discounts are computed on the $3,000 net price.

Exhibit 1   Explanation of Discount Terms

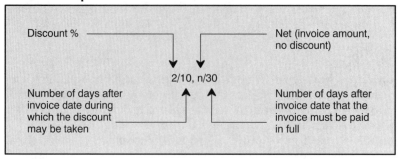

Cash Discounts

Some vendors offer a discount for payment of an invoice before its due date. Early collection from customers provides a vendor with one clear benefit: better cash flow to cover expenditures or to make investments. To encourage prompt payment, vendors may offer an incentive called a **cash discount,** also referred to as a purchase discount.

Unlike trade discounts, cash discounts depend upon payment *within a specified time period.* Cash discount terms are usually shown in abbreviated form such as 2/10, n/30. This format is interpreted in Exhibit 1.

For example, a $100 invoice dated October 16 with cash discount terms of 2/10, n/30 may be paid anytime between October 16 and October 26 to take advantage of the two percent discount. If payment is made during the discount period, the amount of the check in payment of this invoice is $98, computed as follows:

Invoice amount	$100
2% cash discount	− 2
Check amount	$ 98

This example uses terms of payment called ordinary dating. The payment period under ordinary dating payment terms begins with the date of an invoice. Cash discounts can also be given under other payment terms. Some vendors modify the discount terms by adding a suffix such as ROG (receipt of goods) or EOM (end of month) to the discount format. This suffix changes the date of the discount period, and initiates a form of extended dating.

ROG

The term "ROG" (receipt of goods) means the cash discount ending period is computed from the date goods are received—not the invoice date. This form of dating is used by vendors when goods are delivered a relatively long time after the invoice has been sent. Assume an invoice is dated March 5 with terms of 2/10, n/30 ROG. If the goods are received on March 10, the discount period is from March 10 to March 20.

To understand this concept further, review the following example. Assume a delivery of goods is received on August 15. The invoice amount for merchandise is $700, the invoice date is August 2, and terms are 1/10, n/30 ROG. Payment is made on August 24; the one percent cash discount is good until August 25. The payment is calculated as follows:

Invoice amount (merchandise)	$700
1% discount	− 7
Check amount	$693

EOM

The term "EOM" (end of month) signifies that the cash discount period begins after the end of the month in which the invoice is dated. If an invoice is dated June 8 with terms of 2/10, n/30 EOM, the discount period ends on July 10. The determination is simple: the month of the invoice date in this case is June; there are ten discount days and the following month is July; therefore, the discount period is good until July 10.

In a further example, an invoice is dated May 25, its terms are 4/15, n/30 EOM, and the invoice amount for merchandise is $600. Since the month of the invoice is May, the cash discount period extends to June 15. If the payment is made on or before June 15, it is calculated as follows:

Invoice amount (merchandise)	$600
4% discount	− 24
Check amount	$576

According to business practice, if an invoice with EOM terms is dated on or after the 26th day of a month, the cash discount period extends to the *second* month after the month of the invoice date. In essence, the invoice is treated as if it were dated for the beginning of the next month. Thus, any invoices dated May 26 through the end of the month are treated as if they are June 1 billings. The discount period will therefore extend into July.

For example, assume an invoice is dated May 26, credit terms are 4/15, n/30 EOM, and the invoice amount is $600. The month of the invoice is May but the date is on the 26th day of the month. In this case, the invoice is treated as a June 1 billing; the cash discount period extends to July 15 (15 days into the next month of the billing period). If the payment is made any time up to July 15, it is calculated as follows:

Invoice amount (merchandise)	$600
4% discount	− 24
Check amount	$576

Sometimes the abbreviation *Prox.* is used in offering extended dating terms. *Prox.* stands for *proximo,* which means "next month." The procedures for computing discounts with credit terms of Prox. are identical to those used for EOM.

Transportation Charges

Discounts on freight charges are generally not permitted. Cash discounts should be calculated on the invoice amount exclusive of any freight (delivery) charges. For example, assume a $271.95 invoice consisting of merchandise ($250.00) and freight charges ($21.95) is dated October 17 with discount terms of 2/10, n/30. If payment is made during the discount period, it is calculated as follows:

Invoice amount	$271.95
Cash discount (2% × $250)	− 5.00
Amount of check	$266.95

Recording Invoices and Discounts

A small hospitality business will usually record invoices only as they are paid. If financial statements are required, the accountant will prepare an adjusting journal entry for all unpaid invoices to comply with the matching principle. This procedure, while acceptable for a small business, is not good management practice for larger hospitality companies because of its poor internal control.

In a small restaurant, the owner or manager does the ordering, verifies the receipt of the product, and authorizes the invoice for payment; in fact, he or she might actually write the check. In a large hotel or restaurant operation, each of these functions is performed by different individuals.

Large hospitality businesses process all invoices through an accounts payable system or voucher register system as they are received, regardless of when the invoices are to be paid. A voucher system is a system used to control accounts payable and payments with the objective of safeguarding cash. In a payables or voucher system, the invoice is immediately recorded upon receipt regardless of whether it is to be paid now or at a future date. The entry is always a debit to a specific account for the purchase and a credit to Accounts Payable.

Some invoices involve discounts. There are two methods in accounting that are used to record these invoices:

- Gross method
- Net method

The *gross method* records the full amount of purchase to Accounts Payable upon receipt; the discount is recorded only upon actual payment of the invoice. The *net method* anticipates that the discount will be taken and records the net amount (amount after discount) to Accounts Payable immediately upon receipt of the invoice. The net method can be used only by hospitality businesses that have ample cash flow and are in a position to pay all discount invoices within the time period required to take advantage of the discount terms.

In addition to selecting a method for recording invoices, management must decide how to treat discounts for financial statement reporting purposes. The treatment of discounts is an important decision. For example, assume that food provisions are purchased for the restaurant operation of a hotel. Should the food cost be reduced by the discount or should the discount be recorded as other income of the hotel?

To answer this question, let's analyze why suppliers offer discounts. A supplier offers a discount as an incentive to receive payment within a timely period. However, the cost of this incentive has been "built into" the selling price; the discount is considered a cost of doing business. Therefore, the price paid after the discount really reflects the true price. It is likely that if the supplier did not have to offer a discount, the selling price might be lower.

There are two procedures for the recording of cash discounts:

- Revenue procedure
- Nonrevenue procedure

The *revenue procedure* records the discount as other income for the hotel in an account called Cash Discounts Earned. The Cash Discounts Earned account appears on a hotel's schedule of rentals and other income. Advocates of the revenue procedure believe that cash discounts are earned from the availability of funds and the proper management of cash and payment of accounts payable. The revenue procedure is recommended in the *Uniform System of Accounts for the Lodging Industry.*

The *nonrevenue procedure* treats the discount as a reduction of the cost of the item originally purchased. Advocates of the nonrevenue procedure believe that a department should be charged only for the net cost of a purchase since it represents a true cost.

Regardless of the procedure used, the treatment of the discount produces the same net income for the hotel; the only difference between the procedures is which department will get credit for the discount.

The procedure for recording discounts does not depend on whether the gross method or net method of recording invoices is used; either method may employ the revenue or nonrevenue procedure. The gross and net methods relate to the *amount* recorded to accounts payable. The discount procedures relate to *which account* will get the credit for the cash discount.

Gross Method

The gross method (also called the gross recording method) is a popular way to record invoices in the hospitality industry. The invoice is recorded at the full purchase price. The discount is not anticipated; it is recorded only when the invoice is timely paid and the actual discount is taken. The supporting principle for this method is that the hotel does not always know whether sufficient cash will be available for all discounts to be realized.

Recording an Invoice Upon Receipt. Assume that an invoice for the purchase of $500 of uniforms has just been received. The invoice is dated March 1 with terms of 2/10, n/30. Under the gross method, the journal entry to record the invoice is:

Uniforms	500	
Accounts Payable		500

The discount will not be recorded until the invoice is timely paid. Remember that the treatment of discounts can be either revenue or nonrevenue.

Revenue treatment of discount. Using the above example, assume the invoice is timely paid to take advantage of the two percent discount; the discount of $10 (2% × $500) allows the $500 liability to be discharged with a cash outlay of only $490. Under the revenue procedure, the entry is:

Accounts Payable	500	
Cash		490
Cash Discounts Earned		10

Nonrevenue treatment of discount. Again using the above example, assume the invoice is timely paid to take advantage of the two percent discount; under the nonrevenue procedure, the entry is:

Accounts Payable	500	
Cash		490
Uniforms		10

The nonrevenue procedure requires referencing the original account charged for the purchase so that the cash discount can be properly credited to the correct account.

Net Method

A major disadvantage of the gross method is that it does not reveal the amount of discounts that are lost because of poor cash flow or poor management of the payments operation. Another criticism of the gross method is that the accounts payable amount could be inflated for a hospitality business that is able to continually take most or all cash discounts within its normal accounts payable cycle.

The net method is suitable for those hospitality businesses that want to measure discounts lost and generally have the funds available to take advantage of cash discounts. (The net method is also referred to as the net purchases recording method.) In the net method, the cash discount is anticipated; that is, the hospitality business assumes that when the invoice will be paid, funds will be available to take advantage of the cash discount. Therefore, upon receipt of an invoice, the amount recorded is the purchase minus any potential discount. Upon payment, any discounts lost are recovered and recorded to an expense account called Discounts Lost.

Recording an Invoice Upon Receipt. To illustrate the net method, we will again use the invoice for the purchase of $500 of uniforms, dated March 1 with terms of 2/10, n/30. Under the net method, it is anticipated that the $10 discount will definitely be taken when the invoice is paid; the discount is "netted" upon receipt of the invoice. The journal entry to record the invoice is:

Uniforms	490	
Accounts Payable		490

If the invoice is timely paid within the discount period, the entry to record the payment is:

Accounts Payable	490	
Cash		490

Exhibit 2   Sample Allowance Voucher

464856	**ALLOWANCE**	

DEPARTMENT _____

DATE _____ 20 _____

NAME _____   ROOM OR ACCT. NO. _____

DATE	SYMBOL	AMOUNT

DO NOT WRITE IN ABOVE SPACE

EXPLANATION

AMERICAN HOTEL REGISTER CO., NORTHBROOK, IL 60062-7798
AHW 4211   SIGNED BY _____

Source: American Hotel Register Company.

If the invoice is not timely paid within the discount period, the entry to record the payment is:

Accounts Payable	490	
Discounts Lost	10	
Cash		500

Internal Control for Food and Beverage Sales

Cost control through proper handling of cash discounts is only one of the critical factors important to profitable operations. Sales control is an equally important requirement for profitability. Sales control relates to the set of controls and forms designed to enable management to monitor the revenue of a business. Sales control makes certain all sales are recorded and that all sales are made at the correct prices.

The audit of restaurant sales is accomplished by reviewing guest checks, servers' signature books, cashiers' documents, and cash register readings. The actual audit procedures for internal control purposes depend on the size of the establishment, its operating procedures, the design of its forms, and the use of automated equipment.

Allowances should be entered on an allowance voucher such as the sample form shown in Exhibit 2. Before these vouchers are processed, the amounts appearing on them must be approved by an employee designated by management.

Discussion of detailed control procedures is best reserved for specialized courses such as front office and food and beverage control. However, in learning hospitality accounting concepts, one should have a fundamental knowledge of procedures associated with the following:

- Guest checks—manual system
- Guest checks—automated system
- Debit and credit cards
- Guest charges
- Front office operations
- Daily room reports
- Housekeepers' reports

Guest Checks—Manual System

The **guest check** (Exhibit 3) serves a dual purpose: it initiates the food and beverage order taken from the guest, and eventually represents the invoice given to the guest. Guest checks are prenumbered and usually tinted so that any erasure can be detected. Guest checks are also called servers' checks.

There are a wide variety of procedures associated with the internal control of guest checks. One procedure is to keep them in locked storage and in numerical order, and issue them to servers when servers report for duty. Under this system, each server receives a specified quantity of consecutively numbered checks. As the checks are issued, the server's identification number or name is entered in a servers' signature book (Exhibit 4), along with an entry recording the first and last numbers of the checks issued. The server then signs the book and must account for the checks at the end of his or her shift.

When the server goes off duty, unused checks are returned and the last check number issued by the server is recorded. Unused checks are filed in numerical order and may be re-issued or taken out of circulation. Any outstanding checks should be accounted for under internal control procedures. Properly approved voided checks must also be submitted and substantiated for validity. The management policy regarding lost checks varies from operation to operation, and may depend upon state payroll laws.

The income auditor compares the servers' signature book to the checks returned to the cashier. In this way, the income auditor ensures that all used checks listed in the book have been recorded as sales.

Servers' checks may be in duplicate to provide a control at the point an order is taken. In a duplicate system, the guest's order is recorded on a special check that simultaneously produces a duplicate. Food can be ordered by the server from the kitchen only with this duplicate. The prenumbered duplicates are retained in the kitchen and later compared with guest checks from the cashier's station to determine whether all sales have been recorded and paid.

There are other types of control systems as well, but any control system must fit the particular needs of an operation. A good control system is one that achieves its objective with a minimum of delay and interference with customer service.

Exhibit 3   Sample Guest Check

Courtesy of the Viking Hotel and Motor Inn

Exhibit 4   Sample Servers' Signature Book

SERVERS' SIGNATURE BOOK					Date: _____ 20_____					
		CHECKS ISSUED			Last Check Used	CHECKS RETURNED			Total	Missing
Svr. No.	Signature	From	To	Total Issued		Unused	Void	Per Cashier		

Cash Control in the Dining Room. When a guest has finished dining, the server must price and total the guest check unless that function has been automatically performed by point-of-sale equipment. The server receives payment from the guest and delivers the guest check and payment to the cashier.

The cashier keys each item listed on the check into the register. The register tallies each item and imprints the total on the check for verification with the server's total. The cashier also keeps a record of checks charged to room numbers; amounts from these guest checks are communicated promptly to the front office for posting to guest accounts.

At the end of a shift, the cashier's cash drawer and supporting documents are accounted for. Cash register readings are taken and summarized. The cash, credit card vouchers, room charges, and any miscellaneous paid-outs are then reconciled with the cash register readings using a daily cashiers report.[1]

Cash Control in the Lounge. Internal control for beverage sales presents a greater challenge than internal control for dining room sales. The same person (a bartender) may take the customer's order, prepare and serve the drink, receive the cash, and record the sale. While no universal system of beverage control can be described, there are common procedures and rules found throughout the hospitality industry.

One common procedure is to require the bartender to ring each sale as it is made. Since the bartender also acts as the cashier, a safeguard is necessary to prevent the reuse of checks after they have been paid. One such safeguard is to require the bartender to insert each paid check into a locked box.

The control of cash and cashiering functions has great importance to sales control. Cashiering procedures should require that the cash register drawer never remain open, even for a short period of time. An operation that has cocktail servers in the lounge should not allow servers to first pay the bartender in cash and then collect from customers. This procedure may tempt servers to overcharge customers.

Controlling guest checks in the lounge operation is similar to controlling guest checks in the dining room operation. If for some reason it is totally impractical to use guest checks, the register should have a receipt tape that is given to the customer in lieu of a guest check.

Bartenders should not be allowed to take register readings or reconcile their own cash at the end of their shifts. Special procedures are necessary to guard against "voids" and "no sale" rings that may allow embezzlement. The reconciling for beverage sales may be prepared on a form similar to the daily cashiers report, which can be custom designed for a particular operation.

Automated beverage dispensing systems provide a new dimension in the control of liquor sales. Since these systems are costly, however, they are not justifiable for all operations.

Guest Checks—Automated System

Point-of-sale (POS) systems represent the new generation of order entry, billing, and internal control systems. Simply stated, a POS terminal is a computerized replacement for cash registers and manual guest checks. The system's computer

Exhibit 5   Sample Guest Check—POS System

```
                 Welcome
   5/12/2006                    11:35
   =====================
   Check:  2112710
   Server: Leah
   Terminal: 237
   =====================
     4  Soda Bar            7.00
        @ 1.75
        Lemonade
        Iced Tea
     1  WB Fiji Large       6.00
     3  Chicken Sandwich   48.00
        @ 16.00
              Subtotal     61.00
              Gratuity      9.06
   Service Charge           2.26
                 Total     72.32


              Gratuity
              _____

              Total
              _____

              Room Number
              _____


   Print Name
   _____

   Signature
```

interface is optimized for high-speed order input and communication between the dining room and the kitchen. Guest billing can be customized, and guests can pay with cash, credit cards, debit cards, or checks. The POS system records and tracks guest orders, prepares the billing, and manages inventory. Generally, a POS terminal uses a computer that contains the application programs and stores all menu items in a database that staff can access. POS terminals can feature touch-screen menus for quick, accurate order entry. Pricing errors and handwritten guest checks are virtually eliminated. (Exhibit 5 shows an automated guest check generated by a POS system.)

Debit and Credit Cards

Debit or ATM cards have an important characteristic that sets them apart from credit cards. The use of a debit card results in an instant reduction of the cash balance in the cardholder's bank account. The customer's funds are immediately transferred and deposited into the checking account of the hospitality business. Therefore, debit card transactions are treated like cash and processed similarly.

In comparison, the use of a credit card does not immediately affect the cardholder's bank account. Rather, the credit card company pays the retailer, and later the cardholder pays the credit card company upon receipt of a monthly statement. The popular credit cards are MasterCard, VISA, Discover, American Express, Carte Blanche, and Diners Club. Their treatment by a hospitality business depends on whether the card is classified as a bankcard.

Exhibit 6   Sample American Express Draft

Cardmember Acct. No.	
Cardmember	Approval Code
	Check or Bill No.
Service Establishment Date of Charge	Any delayed charges are listed below
Merchandise/Services	Type of Delayed Chg.
Taxes	Amt. of Delayed Chg.
Tips/Misc.	Revised Total

Establishment agrees to transmit to American Express Travel Related Services Co., Inc. or Authorized Representative for payment. Merchandise and/or service purchased on this card shall not be resold or returned for cash refund.

Cardmember Signature

X

Total

Amexco Use Only

Equivalent Amount

Invoice Number

AMERICAN EXPRESS

482095

Please Print Firmly Service Establishment Copy

Record of Charges

ROC Form 20249-SR-Rev. 12-82 Printed in USA 12-82

Source: American Express Company.

MasterCard and VISA are called bankcards because a business may deposit the credit card drafts directly into its checking account just like cash and personal checks. These cards are very popular in the hospitality industry because a business has instant access to the funds. There is no waiting period. *Therefore, a sale made to a guest using a bankcard is recorded as a cash transaction.*

A business may deposit Discover credit card drafts directly into its bank account. However, unlike the procedure used with bankcards, the bank grants use of the funds only after the drafts are approved by Discover. This approval may be granted as quickly as within 24 hours. In any case, a credit card deposit cannot be recorded as cash if the bank does not treat it like cash. Therefore, in cases where such approval is required, the credit card sale is recorded as an account receivable.

American Express, Carte Blanche, and Diners Club represent nonbank credit cards. Sales made to guests using a nonbank credit card or a "house" credit card are treated as accounts receivable transactions. In the case of nonbank credit cards, businesses must forward copies of credit card drafts and wait to be reimbursed. "House" credit cards require that the business bill the customer directly before funds can be collected. Exhibit 6 is a sample American Express draft.

Guest Charges

Certain guests may have charge privileges (i.e., open accounts) with the business. They may purchase services or products by merely signing a guest check or invoice. These transactions are recorded as accounts receivable transactions. The business then sends the customer a bill or statement requesting payment. Open account privileges may include extended credit terms whereby the hotel sends a monthly statement to the guest.

Accounting for Charged Tips

When a guest pays the server a cash tip, no accounting procedures are required since the tip is made directly to the server. Instead of paying the server a cash tip, however, a guest using a credit card or charge account may enter a tip on the credit card draft or guest check.

When tips are entered on credit card drafts or guest checks, the business becomes involved. In a sense, it is now acting as a collection agent for the server; charged tips are a liability of the business until the server is paid. Ultimately, the business will collect the tip portion from the credit card company or, in the case of guest charges, from the guest.

A tip policy should be established to provide a consistent accounting treatment for tips. For instance, a tip policy may state that the credit card fee applicable to the tip portion should not be deducted from the server's tip. A tip policy should also outline when a server will be paid his or her charged tips. Depending on a company's tip policy, a server may be paid for charged tips immediately or only at the end of the shift.

Accounting Personnel and Front Office Functions

The most visible area in a property is the front office, the initial contact point between guests and hotel personnel. It is the center of activities for processing guest reservations, arranging guest accommodations, providing information, checking out guests, and maintaining the guest ledger.

The guest ledger comprises individual records for each of the hotel's registered guests. During a guest's stay, the front office is responsible for summarizing all guest charges for goods and services and recording guest payments. These summaries are made on guest records, called folios, that collectively make up the guest ledger. Exhibit 7 presents a sample **guest folio.**

Guest ledger accounting, also referred to as front office accounting, includes the accumulation of guest charges, credits, and payments. There are two accounts receivable subsidiary ledgers for recording guest transactions: the guest ledger and the city ledger. The guest ledger is the accounts receivable subsidiary ledger for guests who are still registered at the hotel. It is maintained by room number in the front office.

By comparison, the city ledger is the accounts receivable subsidiary ledger for all nonregistered guests. The billings for guests who have checked out and charged their bills are transferred from the guest ledger to the city ledger. The city ledger is maintained alphabetically in the accounting department.

The accounting department is responsible for recording the results of front office activities, maintaining the city ledger, accounting for credit card receivables, paying vendors, handling payroll, preparing financial statements, budgeting, and other accounting functions. The controller, as head of the accounting department and a member of the executive committee, is responsible for timely communication

Exhibit 7   Sample Guest Folio

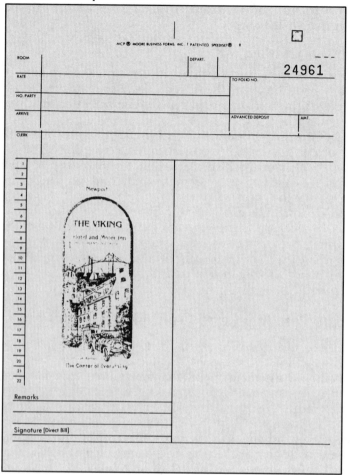

Courtesy of the Viking Hotel and Motor Inn

of financial information, participation in decision-making, interpretation of proposals, forecasting (short-term), and budgeting (long-term). Other responsibilities of accountants may include controlling and monitoring revenues, providing management advisory services, communicating to various departments, and organizing financial control systems.

Accounts receivable clerks, cashiers, and the night auditor report to the accounting department. These three categories of front office personnel play significant roles in providing hospitality accounting information.

The Accounts Receivable Clerk

The accounts receivable clerk posts charges to guest accounts for food, beverages, and other miscellaneous items. These guest charges are represented by charge vouchers, which are prenumbered for internal control purposes. Since the precise

Exhibit 8   Sample Charge Voucher

097261	**MISCELLANEOUS CHARGE**

DEPARTMENT _____

DATE _____ 20 _____

NAME _____   ROOM OR ACCT. NO. _____

DATE	SYMBOL	AMOUNT

DO NOT WRITE IN ABOVE SPACE

EXPLANATION

AMERICAN HOTEL REGISTER CO., NORTHBROOK, IL 60062-7798
AHW 4208

SIGNED BY _____

Source: American Hotel Register Company.

time a guest will check out is not known, it is important that all vouchers be posted immediately. Exhibit 8 presents a sample charge voucher; charges may be made for telephone use, laundry and valet services, and incidentals charged to the guest's folio.

The use of computerized systems is rapidly changing the form of many charge vouchers. For example, recent progress in automating the telecommunications department has permitted direct entry of charges to the guest folio, supported by a log of guest charges or an automated voucher, as shown in Exhibit 9.

The Cashier

The cashier receives payments from guests and, if allowed, will make payments on behalf of guests for such items as theater tickets, COD charges, and other incidental charges. The cashier may also be permitted to cash personal checks as a convenience to guests. The cashier is supplied with a fixed sum of money called a *bank*, usually maintained on an imprest system. With an imprest system, an accounting is made of receipts and payments at the end of each shift, and the bank is restored to its original, fixed amount.

The Night Auditor

The night auditor is primarily responsible for processing all room charges, and ensuring that all vouchers have been accounted for and properly posted to each

Exhibit 9   Sample Automated Telephone Voucher

Date	Time	Room No.	Telephone No.	State	Duration	Charge
10/27	10:46	0101	15175551276	MI	5.3	03.27
10/27	11:12	0028	5553600	RI	10.7	01.32
10/27	11:14	0072	13135554829	MI	7.4	04.25
10/27	11:25	0129	16145553882	OH	22.5	13.47
10/27	11:26	0053	5554731	RI	12.4	01.92

guest folio. One method of determining room charges is to examine the room rack. The room rack may consist of a card index system, which is constantly updated to reflect occupied and vacant rooms. When a guest registers, a multi-part form is prepared. Part of this form is a room card showing the room number, room rate, and number of guests. This room card is then inserted in the room rack.

In the evening, the room rack contains forms for only those *registered* guests remaining for the night who are to be charged for rooms. A list of rooms occupied by registered guests can be prepared from the room rack; this list is called a **daily room report** (Exhibit 10). As a convenience, the rates per room may be preprinted on the daily room report.

The daily room report is compared to the **housekeeper's report** (Exhibit 11), which is prepared from information supplied by individual housekeepers. This procedure identifies skippers and sleepers. A **skipper** is a guest who leaves the hotel without paying for charges incurred. A **sleeper** is a room shown as occupied that is actually vacant, usually occurring when the front office staff fails to update a room's status after a guest has settled his or her account. A major purpose of the housekeeper's report is to detect errors or intentional omissions from room sales. This report should be forwarded directly to the income auditor, not the front office.

Another duty of the night auditor is to verify food and beverage charges made by guests and charged to their rooms. This is accomplished by comparing the *transfer-in total* with the totals transferred out by the restaurant and lounge. Voucher charges from other departments are verified in a similar manner.

Overcharges and errors in guest billings are corrected by the use of allowance vouchers, which are posted to a separate allowance journal. This journal may affect either the guest ledger or the city ledger, depending on the status of the guest.

A Summary of Front Office Accounting

When front office personnel post transactions to the guest ledger, they perform a part of the accounting process. The design and form of the journals used in the front office depend on the accounting system and the hotel's size, and whether the procedures are manual, semi-automated, or computerized.

When the front office receives cash from guests, this acts as a debit to the house bank. When the front office pays out cash, the result is a credit to the bank.

Exhibit 10 Sample Daily Room Report

DAILY ROOM REPORT

Date: *March 2* 20 *X2*

Floor: 1

No.	Rate S/D	No. of Guests	Code	Room Charge
101	60/80	2		80.00
102	60/80		V	
103	55	1	S	40.00
104	60/80	2		80.00
105	75/95	2		95.00
106	75/95	2		95.00
107	60/80		OOO	
108	70		V	
109	60/80	2	C	—
110	55	1	E	55.00
111	55	1	H	—

C: Complimentary   E: Tax Exempt

H: House Staff   OOO: Out of Order

S: Special Rate   V: Vacant

Exhibit 11 Sample Housekeeper's Report

HOUSEKEEPER'S REPORT   Date: *November 14* 20 *X2*

Status Codes

LCO: Late Check-Out   OOO: Out of Order

V: Vacant   X: Occupied

Room	Status Code	Room	Status Code	Room	Status Code	Room	Status Code
101	V	201	X	301	X	401	X
102	V	202	X	302	X	402	X
103	X	203	X	303	X	403	V
104	X	204	X	304	X	404	V
105	X	205	X	305	V	405	X
106	X	206	X	306	V	406	X
107	OOO	207	V	307	V	407	V
108	V	208	V	308	X	408	V
109	X	209	X	309	X	409	X
110	X	210	X	310	X	410	X
111	X	211	V	311	X	411	X

Exhibit 12   Sample Front Office Cash Receipts and Disbursements Journal

		CASH RECEIPTS			CASH DISBURSEMENTS				
							Other		
NAME	Room No.	Bank dr	Guest cr	City cr	Guest dr	City dr	Amount (dr)	Account	Bank cr

FRONT OFFICE CASH RECEIPTS AND DISBURSEMENTS JOURNAL   Date: _____

Either of these transactions may affect the guest or city ledgers. Exhibit 12 shows a sample front office cash receipts and disbursements journal, in which front office employees record cash-in and cash-out transactions. The journal is verified by the night auditor and forwarded to the general cashier.

Each evening at a set time, the night auditor runs a computer program that enters the daily room charges, allowances, and voucher charges for each occupied guestroom. The night auditor verifies the results of this process by analyzing a computer-generated daily transcript report (shown in Exhibit 13), which summarizes all activity posted on the guest ledger.

Cash and Data Collection

Each operated department generates its individual daily cashiers report as an internal control procedure to reconcile revenue and receipts. These daily cashiers reports (one from each operated department) require a summary at a central point to control and verify sales, receivables, and bank deposits.

All cashiers (including those from the front office, restaurant, bar, and other operated departments) must compute their net receipts, place them in an envelope along with a cashier's deposit slip (Exhibit 14), and forward the envelope to the general cashier. (Sometimes the deposit slip form is printed directly on the envelope itself.)

The general cashier confirms the contents of each cashier's deposit envelope in the presence of the cashier. After confirmation is complete, the general cashier prepares a general cashier's deposit summary (Exhibit 15). This summary should list each operating department separately and by shift.

Note the column on the general cashier's deposit summary report labeled "due back" (sometimes called "due bank"). At the end of a shift, the house bank is *due back* any dip in the imprest of the house bank. A dip, also known as a difference, results when the front office pays out more cash in a day than it receives. For instance, with prior approval, the front office may cash checks for guests or make

Exhibit 13　Sample Daily Transcript Report

DAILY TRANSCRIPT REPORT								Date:			
		CHARGES TO GUEST FOLIO						CREDITS TO GUEST FOLIO			
Room No.	Previous Balance	Room	Tax	Restaurant	Lounge	Telephone	Other	Payment	Allowances	Transfer to City Ledger	Ending Balance

cash advances. Keep in mind that sales involving credit cards or checks do not add to the cash (actual currency) of the house bank.

Using a form similar to the one shown in Exhibit 15, the general cashier is allowed to take cash from the total receipts of the day and settle the due backs before depositing funds in the checking account of the business. Some hotel controllers prefer that all receipts of the day be deposited intact into the checking account of the business and that the cashier draw an exchange check for the due backs.

An income auditor confirms the sales and cash as reported by each department. After the audit is completed, the income auditor summarizes all sales and other pertinent data on a daily report of revenue, which usually forms the basis for the daily entry in a sales journal. The form and content of the daily report of revenue will depend on the amount of information management requires on a daily basis. Exhibit 16 presents a portion of a daily report of revenue. Additional items on this particular report not shown in the exhibit include the following: debits, guest and city ledgers, rentals and other income, accounts payable, room statistics, food statistics, and other information such as amounts of officers' checks and employee meals.

Information from the daily report of revenue may be used to prepare a departmental revenue report and a summary **sales and cash receipts journal.** The departmental revenue report is basically a sales log. It is individually prepared for each department, but is not used for input to the general ledger. The main purpose of the departmental revenue report is to summarize data that will be useful to management. Exhibit 17 presents a sample departmental revenue report for a main dining room. At the end of the month, the columns of each departmental revenue report are totaled and various sales analysis reports and statistics are prepared from the information.

Information from the daily report of revenue, daily transcript report, general cashier's deposit summary, and other documents is used to prepare a summary sales and cash receipts journal (Exhibit 18), which is the input journal to the general ledger. At the end of the month, the columns are totaled and posted to the general ledger. Exhibit 19 shows a possible route for the flow of forms presented previously.

Exhibit 14   Sample Cashier's Deposit Slip

```
                    CASHIER'S
                   DEPOSIT SLIP

   DATE _____

   CASHIER _____

   DEPARTMENT _____

            A.M.                        A.M.
   TIME     P.M.          TO            P.M.

                              AMOUNT      ✓

   CURRENCY

        FIFTIES & OVER

        TWENTIES

        TENS

        FIVES

        ONES AND TWOS

   COINS

        DOLLARS

        HALF-DOLLARS

        QUARTERS

        DIMES

        NICKELS

        PENNIES

   PETTY CASH VOUCHERS

   TOTAL CASH ENCLOSED


   REGULAR CHECKS

   TRAVELER'S CHECKS


   TOTAL DEPOSITS

   NET RECEIPTS


   DUE BACK


   FOR RESTAURANT CASHIERS

        TOTAL CASH/CHECKS

        LESS TIPS

        NET DEPOSIT OR (DUE BACK)
```

The summary sales and cash receipts journal shown in Exhibit 18 is designed for a small hotel. In this example, operated departments are not allowed to pay vendors out of the cash drawer; all petty cash payments are routed through the

Exhibit 15 Sample General Cashier's Deposit Summary

| Station | BREAKDOWN FROM ENVELOPES | | | | Due Back | Cash Deposit to Checking Account |
	Cash	Checks	MC/VISA	Total		
Front Office						
AM						
PM						
Night						
Subtotal						
City Ledger						
Total						
Restaurant						
Bar						
Gift Shop						
Recreation						
Garage						
Total						

Date: _____ 20 _____

front desk. A larger operation will require a more extensive journal to provide management with useful information on financial statements. For example, the sales accounts may be expanded as follows:

Food Sales	Beverage Sales	Telecommunications Sales
Dining Room	Lounge	Local
Lounge	Dining Room	Long-Distance
Banquets	Banquets	Service Charges
Coffee Shop		

Exhibit 20 is an allowances journal that shows any voucher adjustments processed to guestrooms. Observe that columns are assigned debits and credits in an opposite manner to those of the summary sales and cash receipts journal. Hotels using this form would require that any cash refunds be processed through the disbursements procedure.

Endnote

1. For further information on daily cashiers reports, see Raymond Cote, *Basic Hotel and Restaurant Accounting*, 6th ed. (East Lansing, Mich.: Educational Institute of the American Hotel & Lodging Association, 2006), Chapter 9.

Exhibit 16   Sample Daily Report of Revenue

SHERATON GRAND ON CAPITOL HILL	**DAILY REPORT—REVENUE JOURNAL**	FRS NO. 283
DAY	DAY OF Date _____ 20 _____	

SECTION I—REVENUE	ACCT. NO.	TODAY	ALLOW TODAY	NET TODAY	NET TO DATE THIS MONTH	POST	FORECAST TO DATE THIS MONTH	LAST YEAR TO DATE THIS MONTH
ROOMS—TRANSIENT—REG.	009 001 000							
TRANSIENT—GROUP	009 003 000							
PERMANENT	009 004 000							
EXTRA EARNINGS	009 005 000							
AIRLINES	009 006 000							
TOTAL ROOMS REVENUE								
FOOD—THE CAFE	030 019 000							
ROOM SERVICE	030 011 000							
SIGNATURE ROOM	030 020 000							
THE BAR	030 021 000							
WINE BAR	030 022 000							
MINI BAR	030 023 000							
HOSPITALITY	030 024 000							
SUB-TOTAL OUTLETS								
BANQUETS—LOCAL	030 029 001							
BANQUETS—GROUP	030 029 002							
MISC. S&W—TAX	030 199 001							
—NON TAX	030 199 002							
MISC. INC.—TAX	030 199 003							
—NON TAX	030 199 004							
PUBLIC RM. RENTAL	030 199 005							
TOTAL FOOD REVENUE								
BEVERAGE—THE CAFE	050 019 000							
ROOM SERVICE	050 011 000							
SIGNATURE ROOM	050 020 000							
THE BAR	050 021 000							
WINE BAR	050 022 000							
MINI BAR	050 023 000							
HOSPITALITY	050 024 000							
SUB-TOTAL OUTLETS								
BANQUETS—LOCAL	050 029 001							
BANQUETS—GROUP	050 029 002							
CASH BAR	050 030 000							
MISC. S&W—TAX	050 199 001							
—NON TAX	050 199 003							
MISC. INC.—TAX	050 199 003							
—NON TAX	050 199 004							
TOTAL BEVERAGE REVENUE								
MINOR OPERATED DEPARTMENT								
TELEPHONE—LOCAL	061 081 001							
L/DISTANCE	061 081 002							
TOTAL TELEPHONE								
GUEST LAUNDRY	061 082 000							
GUEST VALET	061 083 000							
PARKING	061 084 000							
CONCIERGE SALES	061 088 000							
TOTAL MINOR REVENUE								
RENT & OTHER INCOME								
TOTAL REVENUE								

Exhibit 17   Sample Departmental Revenue Report

MAIN DINING ROOM								
Date	Day	Breakfast	Lunch	Dinner	Total Food	Liquor	Other	Total Revenue

Exhibit 18   Sample Summary Sales and Cash Receipts Journal

SUMMARY SALES AND CASH RECEIPTS JOURNAL							Month:_____	
Date	Checking Account	Guest Ledger	City Ledger	Room Sales	Food Sales	Telephone Sales	Sales Tax	OTHER
								Amount / Account
	dr	dr	dr	cr	cr	cr	cr	cr

🔑 Key Terms

allowances—A contra-revenue account for sales allowances such as rebates or price adjustments made after billing. On the income statement, this account is deducted from gross sales (gross revenue) to arrive at net sales (net revenue).

cash discount—A discount offered for a specific time period by a seller on the amount of an invoice in order to encourage prompt payment. Also referred to as a purchase discount.

concessionaire—An individual or company given the right by the hotel to operate special sales activities on the premises.

daily room report—Listing of rooms occupied by registered guests. Also called the room rack report.

Exhibit 19   Sample Flowchart of Reports

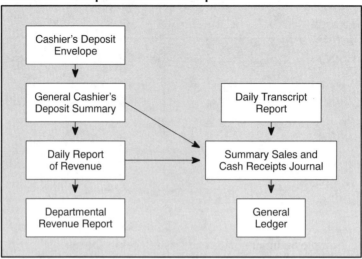

Exhibit 20   Sample Allowances Journal

DATE	NAME	Voucher Number	Room Number	Guest Ledger cr	City Ledger cr	Room Sales Allowance dr	Food Sales Allowance dr	Telephone Sales Allowance dr	Sales Tax dr	OTHER Amount dr	OTHER Account

ALLOWANCES JOURNAL   Month: _____

daily transcript—A documentation of guest ledger activity that serves as an essential reconciliation and audit tool.

gross profit—The profit on the sale of material or merchandise excluding labor and other operating expenses. It is computed as follows: net sales less cost of sales.

guest check—A document used for sales control designed to record a customer's order, requisition merchandise from the kitchen or bar, and serve as the guest bill.

guest folio—A statement of the guest's account that records guest transactions and shows a perpetual balance.

housekeeper's report—A report prepared each morning on the basis of reports from each room attendant; one of its purposes is to prevent intentional omissions from room sales. The status of a room (occupied, out of order, baggage, etc.) is shown in symbols on the housekeeper's report.

net revenue—The result of sales less any allowances; also referred to as net sales.

other income—food and beverage—An account representing sales other than food and beverage items. This account is used in the food and beverage department to record sales of candy, popcorn, postcards, and other nonfood or nonbeverage items.

rentals and other income—This report shows revenue not associated with any particular department. Examples of revenue accounts appearing in this report are: interest income, dividends income, rental of store or office space, concessions fee income, commissions income, cash discounts, salvage sales, and other similar revenue items.

revenue—Revenue results from the sale of goods or services and is measured by customer or client billings. Revenue also includes items such as interest, dividends, and commissions.

revenue center—An area within the hospitality operation that generates revenue; a facility that sells goods or services to customers. It can also be a data collection report in which miscellaneous revenue is listed.

sales and cash receipts journal—A special journal used to record sales activity (cash or on account) and the cash receipts for the day.

skipper—A hotel guest who leaves the hotel without paying or checking out.

sleeper—A room shown as occupied that is actually vacant, usually occurring when the front office staff fails to update a room's status after a guest has settled his or her account.

trade discount—A reduction on an item listed on a vendor's price list. The discount is not dependent on the date of payment.

 Review Questions ───────────────────────────────

1. Which revenue bookkeeping account is used to record each of the following activities?
   a. Sales of coffee, tea, and milk
   b. Sales of alcoholic beverages
   c. Rentals of guestrooms
   d. Price adjustment on a food tab, granted because of a customer's complaint
   e. A complimentary room provided to a guest
   f. Room service: sale of food

2. Which bookkeeping account is credited for each of the following activities? (Assume a debit to cash.)
   a. Sales of gum and novelty items in the dining room
   b. Interest income

    c. Sales of grease and bones from the kitchen

    d. Separate charges for housekeeping or linen service

    e. Concessions fees

3. What are the two major methods of recording invoices and treating cash discounts?

4. Which internal control document is used to record each of the following activities?

    a. Guest checks issued to servers

    b. Price adjustments

    c. Detection of errors or intentional omissions from room sales

    d. Issuance of food by the kitchen to the server

5. Which bookkeeping account is debited for each of the following activities? (Assume a credit to a sales account.)

    a. Payment by personal check

    b. Payment by a bankcard

    c. Payment by a nonbank credit card

    d. Guest signs the tab using open account privileges

6. Which accounts receivable subsidiary ledger(s) will be affected by the following situations? Specify whether the posting will be a debit or a credit.

    a. Sale of a room to a registered guest who will stay for several days

    b. Payment by a registered guest

    c. A guest who checks out and charges his or her bill with an American Express card

    d. A company that rents a conference room on an open account

7. Which member of the front office is responsible for each of the following functions?

    a. Posting of food and beverage guest charges to the guest ledger

    b. Posting of room charges to the guest ledger

8. Which departments are responsible for maintaining each of the following ledgers? In what sequence are the ledgers maintained?

    a. City ledger

    b. Guest ledger

Internet Sites

For more information, visit the following Internet sites. Remember that Internet addresses can change without notice. If the site is no longer there, you can use a search engine to look for additional sites.

Revenue Explained
http://beginnersinvest.about.com/cs/investinglessons/l/blrevenue.htm

Examples of Revenue Accounts
www.accountinginfo.com/study/fs/revenue-101.htm

Cash and Trade Discounts
www.ucop.edu/ucophome/policies/acctman/d-371-23.pdf

Different Types of Debit and Credit Cards
www.nolo.com/article.cfm/objectID/6A15A5E8-C7D8-47A5-B981ADB8C35CACFA/
213/208/230/ART/

Credit vs. Debit Cards
www.kiplinger.com/personalfinance/columns/fitness/archive/2001/ff20010808.htm?
http://search.about.com/fullsearch.htm?TopNode=%2F&terms=credit+vs.+debit+cards

Hotel Front Office Job Details
http://jobguide.thegoodguides.com.au/text/jobdetails.cfm?jobid=869

Problems

Problem 1

Specify whether each of the following statements is true (T) or false (F).

_____ 1. Rooms, food and beverage, and marketing are revenue centers.

_____ 2. Food sold in the course of room service is credited to Room Sales.

_____ 3. Other Income—Food Department and Other Income on the schedule of rentals and other income are the same items.

_____ 4. If food sales are $2,000 and food allowances are $25, net food sales are $1,975.

_____ 5. If food sales are $2,000, food allowances are $25, and cost of food sold is $600, gross profit is $1,375.

_____ 6. The gross method refers to a method for recording discounts.

_____ 7. The nonrevenue procedure refers to a procedure for recording invoices.

_____ 8. A sale to a guest using a credit card such as VISA is recorded to Accounts Receivable.

Problem 2

Indicate on which statement the following sales will occur:

	Beverage	Food	Rentals and Other Income
1. Commission from vending machine company	_____	_____	_____
2. Cash discounts earned	_____	_____	_____
3. Coffee, tea, milk	_____	_____	_____

Problem 3

A $200 invoice for storeroom food provisions is received with terms of 2/10, n/30. The invoice is paid within the discount period. What is the amount of the cash discount?

Problem 4

A hospitality operation purchases new tables and chairs at a list price of $12,000 and a trade discount of 25 percent. What amount will be recorded in the Furniture and Equipment account?

Problem 5

Give the latest date that the discount may be taken for each of the following invoices:

    a. Dated April 27, terms 3/15, n/30 EOM

    b. Dated April 20, terms 2/10, n/30 ROG, goods received May 31

    c. Dated September 26, terms 5/10, n/11 Prox.

Problem 6

Calculate the amount of the check remitted to pay for each of the following invoices:

    a. Dated June 7, terms 2/10, n/30, invoice amount $200, payment made on June 17

    b. Dated June 8, terms 1/10, n/30, invoice amount $200, payment made on June 20

    c. Dated July 14, terms 2/10, n/30 EOM, invoice amount $500, payment made on August 4

    d. Dated August 26, terms 2/10, n/30, invoice amount $60, payment made on September 10

    e. Dated September 5, terms 5/10, n/60, invoice amount $150, payment made on September 14

    f. Dated July 14, terms 3/10, n/30 Prox., invoice amount $400, payment made on August 4

Problem 7

For a given period, a hospitality operation has recorded the following amounts: food sales $50,000; food allowances $400; cost of sales $15,000; chef and kitchen labor $4,000; servers' payroll $3,200; and other operating expenses $18,000. Calculate the net food sales and the gross profit on food.

Problem 8

Assume a hospitality operation uses the gross method for recording invoices and treats discounts as revenue items. It uses the periodic inventory system. An invoice for storeroom food provisions totaling $700 is received. The credit terms are 2/10, n/30.

    a. Record the receipt of the invoice.

    b. Record the payment of the invoice if paid after the discount period.

    c. Record the payment of the invoice if paid within the discount period.

Problem 9

Assume a hospitality operation uses the gross method for recording invoices and treats discounts as nonrevenue items. It uses the periodic inventory system. An invoice for storeroom food provisions totaling $700 is received. The credit terms are 2/10, n/30.

a. Record the receipt of the invoice.

b. Record the payment of the invoice if paid after the discount period.

c. Record the payment of the invoice if paid within the discount period.

Case Study

Sales Reporting and Internal Control for a Pizza Restaurant

Pizza restaurant operations are cash intensive, and, in some cases, employees can remove currency from the register before sales are recorded. In many smaller and family-owned pizza restaurants, documentation of income and expenses may be lacking.

The Pizza Villa is a small restaurant selling pizza for delivery and to walk-in customers. There are no facilities for consumption on the premises. Cash and credit cards are accepted. Ninety percent of the transactions are on the cash basis.

The Pizza Villa operates 7 days a week, from 11 A.M. to 2 A.M. One person owns the business. Therefore, it is impossible to monitor operations at all times. The restaurant staff consists of relatives, friends, and other employees. The Pizza Villa is extremely popular and profitable.

Sales are rung on a cash register, and readings are taken daily. Cash is deposited daily after it is reconciled with the sales readings. No employees are paid with cash; instead, all employees are paid by check. Vendors are paid by check. A petty cash fund is maintained for incidentals. A voucher must support any paid-outs.

Challenge

1. Identify the areas that make theft attractive and possible.

2. Describe how cash could be stolen.

3. Explain whether and why the owner should be concerned that friends and relatives might steal cash from him.

4. Identify some basic requirements of internal control for cash.

5. Explain several procedures the owner could use to examine the validity of sales.

Chapter 2 Outline

Competencies

1. Define business segmentation, and describe its relevance to a hospitality corporation comprising multiple hotels. (pp. 39–46)

2. Define the term "financial reporting center," and give examples of the major classifications of financial reporting centers. (pp. 46–48)

3. Explain responsibility accounting, identify four broad categories of expenses, and describe the difference between direct and indirect expenses. (pp. 48–49)

4. Describe the cost of sales category of expense accounts, and identify the kind of departments to which this category applies. (pp. 49–52)

5. Describe the payroll and related expenses category of expense accounts, and identify the departments to which this category applies. (p. 52)

6. Identify the typical bookkeeping accounts used to record expenses for the various departments in a hotel property. (pp. 52–61)

7. Describe the special considerations involved in accounting for credit card fees, and differentiate between recording fees for bankcards and non-bank credit cards. (pp. 61–62)

8. Describe two major methods of accounting for bad debts. (pp. 62–67)

2

Hotel Expense Accounting

WHILE ACCOUNTING FOR **expenses** at the level of the business enterprise as a whole may be suitable for restaurant accounting, it is not satisfactory for hotel accounting. Hotel accounting requires that expenses be accounted for on the basis of specific responsibility areas. Often, these responsibility areas are departments within the hotel. Management decides how a hotel's departments are to be organized into responsibility areas. A hotel's accounting system reflects the organization of responsibility areas in its chart of accounts, which identifies the categories of expenses charged to each department.

The proper identification and departmentalization of expenses allows hotels to segment operating statements into separate departmental reports and schedules. These reports enable management to measure the efficiency of each responsibility area. Managers and supervisors can then be held accountable for the operating results of their assigned areas.

This chapter considers expense accounting from a hotel's perspective and addresses such questions as:

1. How are hotel operations departmentalized for purposes of expense accounting?

2. What are the functions of a hotel's various departments, and how are these departments staffed?

3. How does accounting for credit card fees differ depending on the type of credit card involved?

4. Why do hotels make estimates of potentially uncollectible accounts receivable?

5. What methods are used to record an uncollectible account receivable?

This chapter presents an in-depth analysis of hotel expense accounts.[1] It introduces the topic of responsibility accounting through discussion of business segmentation, direct and indirect expenses, and departmental functions and personnel.

Specialized topics include accounting procedures for credit card fees and uncollectible accounts. The chapter presents the allowance method for estimating bad debts as well as an alternative way to record uncollectibles—the direct write-off method.

Exhibit 1   Segmentation of the Somnus Corporation

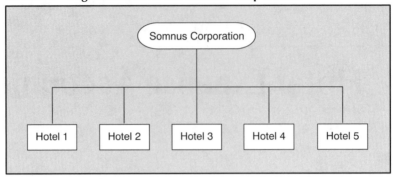

Business Segmentation

Business segmentation refers to the division of work into specialized areas of responsibility. Various accounting reports reflect the efficiency and/or profitability of each specific area of responsibility.

Business segmentation starts at the top echelons of a corporation and extends downward to the most detailed aspects of its operations. For example, assume that a hospitality company called the Somnus Corporation comprises five hotels (Exhibit 1). The first level of accounting reports for the Somnus Corporation combines the operating results of these five hotels. First-level accounting reports show the results of the corporation as a whole.

Accounting reports of this kind, however, are of very little use in measuring the performance of the individual hotels that compose the corporation. To achieve this second level of reporting, corporate operations must be segmented into individual hotels. For example, the top management of the Somnus Corporation assigns an executive or general manager to each of the five hotels. This individual is held responsible for the hotel's operation. Separate financial statements are produced to measure the performance of the general manager of each hotel.

In turn, the general manager of a hotel requires financial information to measure the efficiency of various areas of responsibility within the hotel. To achieve this third level of reporting, these areas of responsibility are identified as departments or other financial reporting centers. For our purposes, a financial reporting center is defined as an area of responsibility for which separate cost information must be collected and reported. Some of these financial reporting centers are considered departments, usually when top management assigns an individual to be the manager of the area's operations.

Management determines the extent to which each hotel function is divided into various reporting centers. A large hotel may organize its business into the following financial reporting centers:

- Rooms
- Food
- Beverage

- Telecommunications

- Administrative and general

- Marketing

- Property operation and maintenance

- Information systems

- Human resources

- Transportation

- Utility costs

- Fixed charges

The following sections discuss these departments and other financial reporting centers typically found within a hotel. Positions within each of these areas of responsibility are identified.

Rooms. Many rooms department personnel come into direct contact with guests. Rooms personnel register guests, maintain and clean guestrooms, provide information, handle guest complaints, and perform other services throughout the guest's stay. The rooms department may include the following positions:

- Management positions—supervisory personnel responsible for the overall operation of the rooms department

- Front office positions—front office manager, room clerks, information clerks, and mail clerks

- Housekeeping positions—house attendants, janitors, housekeepers, linen keepers, and room attendants

- Service positions—concierge, door attendants, bell staff

- Security positions—security officers, patrollers, and guards

Exhibit 2 presents a sample organization chart for the rooms department of a large hotel. There are many other organizational possibilities, depending on an operation's size, the guest services it offers, and additional factors. In small lodging operations, the front office, telecommunications, guest information, and reservations functions may be performed by as few as one or two persons.

Food and Beverage. The food and beverage departments are often referred to as F&B. Personnel in these departments are associated with the preparation and service of food and beverages. These departments may include the following positions:

- Management positions—supervisory personnel responsible for the overall operations of the food and beverage department

- Kitchen positions—chefs and assistants, preparation staff, runners, dishwashers, and utility persons

Exhibit 2   Sample Rooms Department Organization Chart for a Large Hotel

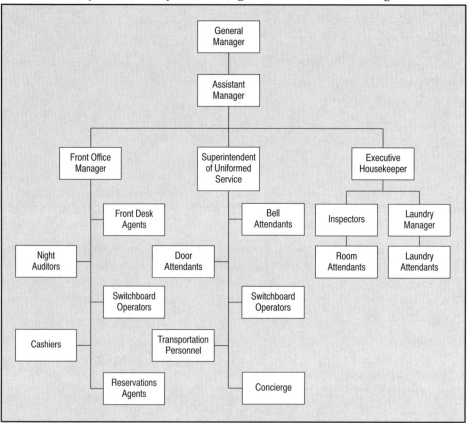

Source: Michael L. Kasavana and Richard M. Brooks, *Managing Front Office Operations*, 7th ed. (Lansing, Mich.: Educational Institute of the American Hotel & Lodging Association, 2005), p. 53.

- Service positions—hosts/hostesses, captains, servers, dining room attendants, and personnel involved in room service, banquet service, and beverage service

- Other positions—cashiers, checkers, food and beverage cost controllers, stewards, food and beverage purchasers, and entertainment managers

Exhibit 3 presents a sample organization chart for the food and beverage department of a medium-sized hotel, but a specific hotel's organization depends on its services and facilities. For instance, some large hotels separate the food and beverage department into several different revenue centers with separate managers or directors. Small hotels may not find this practical because of the joint costs (shared employees and common expenses) involved in various areas of operations.

Telecommunications. The telecommunications department handles in-house, local, and long-distance calls. The telecommunications department may consist of the following personnel:

Exhibit 3   Sample Organization Chart for the Food and Beverage Department of a Medium-Sized Hotel

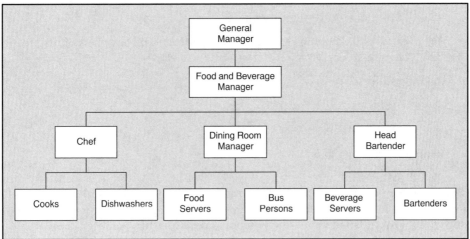

- Chief operator
- Supervisors
- Operators
- Messengers

Technical advances in communications equipment have greatly influenced accounting for telecommunications services. A property using a state-of-the-art communications system can separate the costs incurred by guests from the costs incurred by the business. With this type of system, the business usage costs may be charged to the user departments.

For some properties, it may not be practical or possible to separate telecommunications costs incurred by the business from those incurred by guests. In that case, all telecommunications expenses are charged to the telecommunications department. Unless telecommunications costs are divided between guest usage and business usage, a loss may result from operations of the telecommunications department. This loss represents the hotel's net telecommunications cost.

Administrative and General. The administrative and general department is commonly referred to as A&G. It may be separated into several separate financial reporting centers in large hotels. Included as administrative and general personnel are executives of the hotel and other employees involved with executive and financial activities. This department may include the following positions:

- Manager's office positions—managing director, general manager, resident manager, executive or first assistant manager (not on floor duty), secretaries, clerks, and receptionists

- Accounting office positions—controller and assistants, general cashier, paymaster, accountants, income auditors, payroll clerks, file clerks, and secretaries

- Credit office positions—credit manager and assistants

- Front office bookkeeping positions—front office bookkeeper, accounts receivable clerks, cashiers, voucher clerks, and file clerks

- Night auditors

- Receiving clerks

- Information systems staff

- Human resources staff

If the costs of the information systems and human resources functions are significant, these areas are not included in the administrative and general department but are instead established as separate departments. The human resources department may also be called the personnel department.

Marketing. The marketing department is the sales and public relations center of a hotel. It conducts research aimed at developing sources of potential sales, plans group and convention sales, and maintains a network of travel agent contacts. The department also designs "package programs" to attract weekend or off-season business. It actively promotes the hotel's facilities for weddings, business meetings, and gatherings of professional organizations. This department may include the following positions:

- Director of marketing

- Sales manager

- Convention service manager

- Sales representatives

Exhibit 4 shows a sample organization chart for the marketing department of a large hotel. As is true with any other department, the specific levels of responsibility and authority depend upon the special needs of the hotel. Some hotels may include the guest entertainment function within this department. However, if guest entertainment expenses are substantial, it may be better to establish a separate financial reporting center to monitor these expenses.

Property Operation and Maintenance. This department, abbreviated POM, is concerned with the appearance and physical condition of the building, the repair and maintenance of equipment, and rubbish removal. Personnel in this department may include:

- Management positions—chief engineer and first assistant

- Engineer positions—watch engineers, boiler room engineers, oilers, elevator engineers, and air conditioning control personnel

Exhibit 4   Sample Marketing Department Organization Chart for a Large Hotel

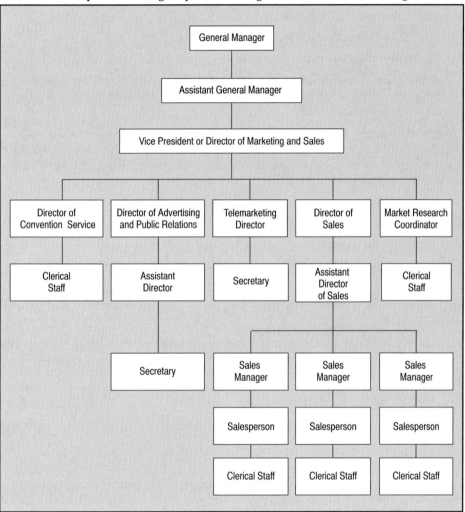

- Grounds positions—gardeners, laborers, and other landscaping personnel
- Office and storeroom positions—engineer's storeroom clerk, secretaries and clerks in the engineer's office, cleaners, yard attendants, and incinerator attendants
- Other positions—electricians, mechanics, plumbers, painters, upholsterers, and various repair personnel

Information Systems. Establishments with a significant investment in computer equipment and staff may set up a separate department to report expenses. The information systems department may include the following positions:

- Information systems manager
- Supervisors and systems analysts
- Systems personnel and programmers
- Operators and data entry personnel

If the costs of the information systems facility are not large, the expenses for staff, supplies, and other items may be part of the administrative and general department, as shown earlier.

Human Resources. Establishments that incur a significant expense for employee housing, employee relations, recruiting, and training may set up a separate department to report on these expenses. The human resources department may include the following positions:

- Director of human resources
- Human resources manager
- Training assistants
- Secretaries and clerks

If the costs of the human resources function are not large, the expenses for staff, supplies, and other items may be part of the administrative and general department, as shown earlier.

Transportation. Establishments that incur a significant expense for the transportation of guests may set up a separate department to report on these expenses. This department may include the following positions:

- Transportation manager
- Drivers
- Mechanics
- Secretaries and clerks

If the costs of this guest service are not large, the expenses associated with it may be recorded in a rooms department account called Guest Transportation.

Financial Reporting Centers

A financial reporting center is an area of responsibility for which separate cost information must be collected; this information is then used to prepare financial reports. Financial reporting centers may be classified as revenue centers, support centers, and other financial reporting centers. The number and types of revenue centers varies from one hotel to another. Every departmental statement incurs processing expense and requires the analytical time of busy management.

It may not be practical or possible to issue separate statements for the Food Department and the Beverage Department because of shared personnel, costs, and space. Smaller hotels might decide to combine Food and Beverage into one reporting center. For example, one hotel might have the following revenue centers:

- Rooms

- Food and beverage

- Telecommunications

- Gift shop

- Garage and parking

- Other operated departments

- Rentals and other income

Support centers are those departments that have minimal guest contact and do not produce sales. Support centers provide services to revenue centers which, in turn, provide goods and services to guests. The following are typical support centers in the hotel industry:

- Administrative and general

- Marketing

- Property operation and maintenance

- Information systems

- Human resources

Certain departments may not be large enough to warrant a separate responsibility area and, regardless of their physical locations, may be combined with other departments. For example, the information systems and human resources functions may be combined with other hotel functions to form the financial reporting center called administrative and general.

Other financial reporting centers include utility costs and fixed charges. A separate center for utility costs may be created as a means of centralizing all utility costs in a single reporting center. One or more separate centers for fixed charges may be used to consolidate expenses such as rent, property taxes, insurance, interest expense, and depreciation and amortization.

To facilitate the collection of financial information on the various responsibility areas, each financial reporting center is assigned an identification number. A hotel may choose any numbering configuration that it finds meaningful. For instance, the following numbering system could be assigned:

Financial Reporting Center	Identification No.
Rooms	11
Food and beverage	15
Telecommunications	17
Administrative and general	31
Marketing	36
Property operation and maintenance	38
Utility costs	41
Fixed charges	51

In this example, the high-order (left-most) digit indicates the type of financial reporting center. A high-order 1 represents a revenue center, a high-order 3 represents a support center, a high-order 4 represents utility costs, and a high-order 5 represents fixed charges.

Responsibility Accounting

The purpose of responsibility accounting is to provide financial information useful in evaluating the effectiveness of managers and department heads. Managers should be judged on the basis of revenues and expenses directly under their control. For this reason, only direct expenses are charged to specific departments. Any cost not associated with a specific department is charged to the hotel as a whole.

Expenses

Expenses include the day-to-day costs of operating a business, the expired costs of assets through depreciation and amortization, and the "write-off" of prepaid items. For purposes of financial reporting, expenses may be separated into four broad categories: cost of sales, operating expenses, fixed charges, and income taxes. Cost of sales and **operating expenses** can be classified as direct expenses. Fixed charges can be classified as indirect expenses. Income taxes are a separate class of expenses.

Direct Expenses. Direct expenses are costs incurred solely for the benefit of a particular department. A department is charged for only those expenses that can be identified as specifically associated with that department. Such expenses are within the responsibility area and control of the department head or manager.

Direct operating expenses include the following types of expenses:

- Cost of sales
- Payroll
- Payroll-related costs
- Operating supplies
- China, glassware, silver, and linen
- Laundry and dry cleaning

Indirect Expenses. Indirect expenses are incurred for the benefit of the hotel as a whole, and cannot be identified with any particular department. These expenses are not controllable by any single department head or manager and are the responsibility of top management.

Some indirect expenses are fixed charges (also called fixed costs or fixed expenses). A fixed charge is one that is incurred whether the hotel is open or closed and is independent of sales volume. Examples of fixed charges are:

- Insurance
- Interest expense
- Property taxes

- Rent expense

- Depreciation and amortization

Depreciation is the allocation of the cost of a tangible long-lived asset over its useful life. Amortization is a procedure similar to depreciation except it involves leaseholds, leasehold improvements, and other long-lived intangible assets.

For purposes of financial reporting, fixed charges are considered a financial reporting center and are reported on a separate supporting schedule. Information from this schedule is brought forward to the hotel's summary income statement.

Income Taxes. Income taxes expense is neither a fixed charge nor an indirect expense. Income tax appears as a separate line item on a hotel's summary income statement.

Departmental Expense Accounting

The presentation of expenses on the hotel financial statements and supporting schedules should be in a prescribed sequence. For the present, the sequence of expense accounts is not considered.

The expense accounts appearing in a chart of accounts depend on the size of the hotel, the number of financial reporting centers, and the level of detail that management requires in the financial reports. To collect information useful for departmental reporting, management needs to establish separate departmental accounts for various types of revenue and expenses. For example, one account for payroll would not be sufficient in meeting the demands of departmental reporting, which requires a separate payroll account for each responsibility area.

Exhibit 5 lists some expenses that are typically found in a hotel. Note that this list is not a chart of accounts and therefore may not relate to the actual names of the bookkeeping accounts. Also, the indication of the departments charged for these expenses is a representation. Determining which departments to charge for various expenses will depend on a hotel's size, type of operation, and accounting system.

Some expenses are temporarily recorded as one lump-sum amount in a non-departmental expense account and later are allocated to specific departments. Types of allocated expenses include payroll taxes, workers' compensation insurance, and other employee benefits. Allocations to specific departments are made by distribution formulas derived from an analysis of various criteria. For example, payroll taxes are paid based on the total payroll of the hotel. A department's share of the payroll taxes expense may be determined by analyzing the relationship of its payroll to the hotel's total payroll.

Examples of Hotel Expense Accounts

The number and types of bookkeeping accounts used by any given department or financial reporting center depend on the size of a property and the design of its management information system. The accounts to be discussed are representative of those used in most hotel properties.

Exhibit 5   Typical Expenses Classified by Responsibility Area

Account Name	Rooms	F&B	Tel.	A&G	Mktg.	POM	Utility	Fixed
Cost of Food Sales		X						
Cost of Beverage Sales		X						
Cost of Calls			X					
Salaries and Wages	X	X	X	X	X	X		
Payroll Taxes	X	X	X	X	X	X		
Employee Meals	X	X	X	X	X	X		
Workers' Compensation Insurance	X	X	X	X	X	X		
Employee Group Plans	X	X	X	X	X	X		
Commissions	X							
Reservation Expense	X							
Contract Cleaning	X	X						
Laundry and Dry Cleaning	X	X						
Guest Transportation	X							
Linen	X							
Guest Supplies	X	X						
Cleaning Supplies	X	X				X		
Printing and Stationery	X	X	X	X	X	X		
Uniforms	X	X				X		
China, Glassware, Silver, and Linen		X						
Kitchen Fuel		X						
Licenses		X						
Music and Entertainment		X						
Paper Supplies		X						
Bar Supplies		X						
Menus		X						
Utensils		X						
Credit Card Commissions				X				
Cash Short or Over				X				
Dues and Subscriptions				X	X			
Contributions				X				
Human Resources				X				
Postage and Telegrams				X	X			
Professional Fees				X				
Bad Debts				X				
Travel and Entertainment				X				
Direct Mail Advertising					X			
Outdoor Advertising					X			
Print Advertising					X			
Radio and Television Advertising					X			
In-House Graphics					X			
Point of Sale Material					X			
Selling Aids					X			
Advertising Agency Fees					X			
Franchise Fees					X			
Other Fees and Commissions					X			
Travel and Entertainment				X	X			
Repairs and Maintenance						X		
Removal of Waste Matter						X		
Electricity							X	
Fuel							X	
Steam							X	
Water							X	
Rent								X
Property Taxes								X
Insurance								X
Interest Expense								X
Depreciation Expense								X
Amortization Expense								X

Cost of Sales

A cost of sales account is required for each merchandising center of a hotel. The cost of sales accounts should have the same classifications as the accounts for revenue to permit a gross profit analysis of each merchandising facility.

Cost of Food Sales. This account represents the **food cost**: the cost of food served to guests in the revenue process. Cost of Food Sales is also called Cost of Food Sold. Employee meals are excluded from cost of food sold.

The food cost includes delivery charges. It is reduced by any trade discounts or any sales of grease and bones. According to the revenue procedure (which is advocated in the *Uniform System of Accounts for the Lodging Industry* [or *USALI*]), food cost is not reduced by cash discounts because these discounts should be recorded to Cash Discounts Earned on the hotel's schedule of rentals and other income.

Food cost is an important amount because it is used for menu planning and to measure the efficiency of the food operation. **Gross profit** measures the profit made on food used in the sales process. It is calculated as follows:

Food sales (net)	xxx
Minus cost of food sold	xxx
Gross profit	xxx

The cost of food sold amount is readily available if a **perpetual inventory accounting system** is used. A perpetual system requires the recording of every receipt and issue for each inventory item. While a perpetual system is best for inventory management because a daily balance is provided, it also incurs expense for clerical and computer processing.

Some food operations may instead elect to use a **periodic inventory accounting system** because it does not incur expensive clerical or computer expenses. A periodic system does not furnish any inventory balances, and the bookkeeping system does not have a cost of food sold account.

Because there is no cost of food sold bookkeeping account if the periodic inventory accounting system is used, it is necessary to compute the cost of food sold. The procedure to compute the direct cost of food sold is as follows:

	Beginning food inventory
+	Food purchases for the period
=	Cost of food available
−	Ending inventory
=	Cost of food used
−	Employee meals
=	Cost of food sold (also called cost of food sales or net food cost)

The procedure for computing cost of beverage sold is similar to that for cost of food sold. The cost of sales for food and the cost of sales for beverage are computed separately for proper presentation on the F&B departmental income statement.

Cost of Beverage Sales. This account represents the cost of wines, liquors, and beer, as well as the cost of mineral water, syrups, sugar, bitters, and other ingredients used in the preparation of mixed drinks. Costs include invoice amounts (less any trade discounts) plus transportation, storage, and delivery charges.

According to the revenue treatment, cash discounts are not used to reduce beverage cost; rather, cash discounts are credited to the hotel's other income account called Cash Discounts Earned.

Cost of Calls. This telecommunications department account includes the total cost of local and long-distance calls. Separate accounts should be established for Cost of Calls—Local, and Cost of Calls—Long Distance.

Payroll and Related Expenses

Any department having one or more employees requires bookkeeping accounts to record expenditures for payroll and related expenses. Hotel-operated departments (such as rooms, food and beverage, administrative and general, marketing, and property operation and maintenance) must be assigned payroll and payroll-related accounts.

Payroll and related expenses do not appear on the schedule of rentals and other income or on the schedule of fixed charges. These financial reporting centers are merely sources of data and have no physical existence or personnel.

Salaries and Wages. This account may also be called Payroll Expense. It includes salaries, wages, overtime pay, and any employee bonuses and commissions. Separate accounts should be established to record vacation pay and holiday pay if they are treated as employee benefits.

Payroll Taxes. This account includes social security taxes (employer's portion), and federal and state unemployment taxes.

Employee Meals. This account includes the cost of food furnished to employees as a convenience to the employer.

Workers' Compensation Insurance. This account includes the expense of workers' compensation insurance.

Employee Group Plans. This account includes life and health insurance, and other forms of employee group-plan fringe benefits. Separate accounts may be established for Group Health, Group Life, Group Retirement, and other such benefits if the costs are to be separately identified.

Rooms Department Expenses

Housekeeping labor costs and wages for room clerks, mail clerks, concierge, door attendants, and other rooms operations personnel are significant expenses in the rooms department. The rooms department expenses also include housekeeping supplies and other expenses related to rooms operations. There is no cost of rooms sold account because the rental of a room is not a merchandising transaction. In addition to payroll and related expenses, the rooms department has the following expense accounts.

Commissions. This account is used to record payments to authorized agents for rooms business secured for the hotel, including commissions to travel agents. Commissions also include amounts paid to rental agents for permanent rooms business which may involve leases. In the case of leases, the payment is expensed to this account over the term of the lease.

Reservation Expense. This account includes the cost of reservation services including telephone, teletype, reservation computer, and any telecommunications expenditures that can be directly related to the rooms department.

Contract Cleaning. This account includes any costs of contracting outside companies to clean areas of the rooms department. This may include washing windows, exterminating pests, and disinfecting.

Laundry and Dry Cleaning. This account includes outside laundry and dry-cleaning costs applicable to the rooms department. For work done by the property's laundry, all costs are assigned to a separate financial reporting center (House Laundry) and allocated to the user departments.

Guest Transportation. This account includes the cost of transporting guests to and from the property. If these costs are significant, a separate financial reporting center may be established.

Linen. This account includes the allocated costs of linen owned or rented by the hotel (including towels, facecloths, blankets, sheets, and similar items).

Guest Supplies. This account includes the cost of guest supplies and amenities that the rooms department provides to a property's guests on a gratis basis. The following is a partial list of guest supplies and amenities:

Newspapers	Guest stationery	Shoe cloths
Coffee	Writing supplies	Toilet requisites
Flowers	Hangers	Matches
Ice	Candy	Other favors

Cleaning Supplies. This account includes the cost of cleaning supplies applicable to the rooms department. The following is a partial list of items charged to this account:

Brooms	Soaps and polishes	Cleaning cloths
Mops	Cleaning chemicals	Dusters
Brushes	Insecticides	Dustpans
Pails	Disinfectants	Cleaning accessories

Printing and Stationery. Expenses included in this account are for printed forms, office supplies, service manuals, and similar items used by employees of the rooms department. Examples include:

Binders	Floor plans	Pencils and pens
Vouchers	Rack cards	Reports
Desk pads	Envelopes	

Uniforms. This account includes the expense of repairing, renting, or cleaning uniforms for employees of the rooms department. If uniforms are purchased, the cost is usually recorded to an asset account and then periodically allocated to the uniforms account based on the estimated useful life of the uniforms or other criteria.

F&B Department Expenses

The food and beverage department is a merchandising center and, therefore, has accounts for the cost of food sales and the cost of beverage sales. In addition to the cost of sales accounts and departmental accounts for payroll expenses, the food and beverage department has the following expense accounts.

China, Glassware, Silver, and Linen. This expense account should not be confused with the asset account of a similar name. The asset account is used to record the original purchase of new stock. The expense account contains the allocated adjustments for breakage, disappearance, deterioration based on age and condition, or depreciation based on estimated useful life.

Contract Cleaning. This account includes any costs of contracting outside companies to clean areas of the food and beverage department. This may include washing windows, exterminating pests, and disinfecting.

Kitchen Fuel. Fuel used for cooking is charged to this account rather than to utilities expense. If electric cooking units are used, separate metering is recommended. Otherwise, an allocation is required to separate kitchen fuel expense from electric expense. When the use of electricity for cooking purposes is only incidental, it is more practical to forgo any attempts to monitor the electricity used for cooking.

Laundry and Dry Cleaning. This account includes outside laundry and dry-cleaning costs applicable to the food and beverage department. For work done by the property's laundry, all costs are assigned to a separate financial reporting center (House Laundry) and allocated to the user departments.

Licenses. All federal, state, and municipal licenses, special permits, and inspection fees are charged to this account.

Music and Entertainment. This account includes costs for orchestras, musicians, entertainers, music services, piano rental, films, records, sheet music, royalties, booking agent fees, and courtesy meals served to entertainers.

Guest Supplies. This account includes expenses for complimentary guest items provided by the food and beverage department. Examples include:

Boutonnieres	Souvenirs	Newspapers
Corsages	Matches	Other favors

Cleaning Supplies. This account includes the expense of items used to keep the food and beverage areas and equipment clean and sanitary. The same types of items listed under the cleaning supplies account for the rooms department are included in this account.

Paper Supplies. This account includes the expense of paper supplies used by the food and beverage department, such as the following:

Wax paper	Paper napkins	Wrapping paper
Pastry bags	Paper plates	Twine
Filter paper	Soufflé cups	Straws

Bar Supplies. This account includes the expense for items such as the following:

Corkscrews	Swizzle sticks	Knives
Mixers	Toothpicks	Spoons
Strainers	Drink decorations	

Menus. This account includes the expense for menu design and printing.

Utensils. Included in this account are expenses for replacing all tools needed in the process of food preparation. Utensils may include kitchen tools, pots, pans, kettles, mixing bowls, beaters, can openers, and other small utensils.

Printing and Stationery. Expenses included in this account are for printed forms, office supplies, service manuals, and similar items used by employees of the food and beverage department. The following are examples:

Servers' books	Vouchers	Desk pads
Adding machine tapes	Guest checks	Staplers and staples
Pencils and pens	Rubber bands	Other office supplies

Uniforms. This account includes the expense of repairing, renting, or cleaning uniforms. If uniforms are purchased, the cost is usually recorded to an asset account and then periodically allocated to this expense account based on the estimated useful life of the uniforms or other criteria.

A&G Department Expenses

Unlike the rooms or food and beverage departments, the administrative and general department is a support center. In addition to accounts for payroll and related expenses, this department has such expense accounts as the following.

Credit Card Commissions. All credit card fees are charged to this administrative and general departmental account.

Cash Overages and Shortages. Cash shortages and overages of cashiers are charged to this account of the administrative and general department.

Dues and Subscriptions. This account includes the cost of representing the property in business organizations and the cost of subscribing to periodicals for use by employees. Dues and subscriptions related to marketing are charged to the marketing department's Dues and Subscriptions account.

Donations. This account is charged for charitable donations and contributions.

Human Resources. This account includes the expense of recruiting, relocating, and training personnel. If human resources expenditures are significant, the related staffing and operating expenses should be removed from the administrative and general department. In this case, a separate human resources department would be established with individual expense accounts identifying various expenditures.

Postage. This account includes postage costs, but excludes amounts that apply to the marketing department.

Professional Fees. This account includes the cost of attorneys, public accountants, and professional consultants.

Provision for Doubtful Accounts. This account represents the expense for accounts receivable that are judged uncollectible. Other names for this account are Uncollectible Accounts Expense and Bad Debts Expense.

Travel. This account includes the cost of travel and reimbursable expenses of hotel employees (except marketing department employees) traveling on business.

Printing and Stationery. Expenses included in this account are for printed forms, office supplies, service manuals, and similar items used by employees of the administrative and general department.

Marketing Department Expenses

The marketing department is a support center. In addition to accounts for payroll and related expenses, this department has the following expense accounts.

Direct Mail Advertising. This account includes the cost of mailing lists, writing letters, addressing envelopes or cards, postage, and other work of this type performed by outside companies.

Outdoor Advertising. Included here are the expenses for posters, billboards, and other signs used to merchandise hotel facilities.

Print Advertising. This account includes expenses for newspaper, magazine, and directory advertising.

Radio and Television Advertising. This account includes the cost of advertising on radio and television, and associated production costs.

In-House Graphics. Included in this account are expenses for directories, signs, brochures, and similar items used to merchandise services within the hotel.

Point-of-Sale Material. This account includes expenses for special tent cards, menu fliers, and other displays to stimulate sales.

Selling Aids. This account includes the expense of selling aids such as salespersons' kits, maps, floor plans, and similar material used to describe products and services of the hotel.

Advertising Agency Fees. Included in this account are fees paid to advertising and/or public relations agencies.

Other Fees and Commissions. This account includes additional marketing fees and commissions not provided for in other bookkeeping accounts.

Printing and Stationery. Expenses included in this account are for printed forms, office supplies, service manuals, and similar items used by employees of the marketing department.

Dues and Subscriptions. This account includes membership fees and the costs of subscriptions to papers, magazines, and books for members of the marketing department.

Postage. This account includes postage costs incurred by the marketing department.

Travel. This account includes the cost of travel and reimbursable expenses related to marketing functions.

Franchise Fees

This account includes all fees charged by the franchisor such as royalty fees and advertising charges. The *USALI* no longer includes franchise fees as part of the Marketing Department. Instead it is listed as a separate line item on the hotel's income statement. The line item Franchise Fees immediately follows the line item Marketing Department.

POM Department Expenses

The property operation and maintenance department is a support center. With the exception of outside cleaning contracted by the rooms and food and beverage departments, this department is charged for the cost of services and contracts relating to all repairs and maintenance work. In addition to accounts for payroll and related expenses, this department has the following expense accounts.

Repairs and Maintenance. According to *USALI*, repairs and maintenance expenses should be assigned to the following accounts instead of to a single account for all repairs and maintenance.

Building Supplies is an account charged with the cost of materials and contracts associated with the repair and maintenance of the building, both interior and exterior.

Electrical and Mechanical Equipment is an account charged with the cost of materials and contracts associated with repairing equipment. The term "equipment" includes ventilating systems, air conditioning systems, kitchen equipment, plumbing and heating systems, elevators, refrigeration systems, and general electrical and mechanical equipment.

Engineering Supplies is an account charged with supplies used in maintaining the property, such as small tools, water treatment chemicals, greases and oils, solvents, fuses, and light bulbs.

Furniture, Fixtures, Equipment, and Decor is an account charged for the cost of materials and contracts associated with the repair of curtains, floor coverings, and furniture, as well as painting and redecorating.

Grounds and Landscaping is an account charged for materials and contracts associated with the maintenance of grounds.

Swimming Pool is an account charged for all maintenance costs associated with swimming pools.

Removal of Waste Matter. This account is charged for the expense of the hotel's rubbish removal and the expense of operating an incinerator.

Uniforms. This account includes the expense of repairing, renting, or cleaning uniforms used by employees of the property operation and maintenance department. If uniforms are purchased, the cost is usually recorded to an asset account and then periodically allocated to this expense account based on the estimated useful life of the uniforms or other criteria.

Utility Costs

The financial reporting center termed "utility costs" has no physical existence or facility; it is simply a means of consolidating a property's utility costs for purposes of reporting on a separate statement. With the exception of energy used for cooking, all utility expenses are charged to this center.

Electricity. This account is charged for the hotel's total electricity cost. The cost should exclude any charges pertaining to electricity used for cooking unless such use is considered incidental. If electricity for cooking is a significant cost, it should be charged to the food and beverage department.

Fuel. This account is charged for the hotel's total heating fuel cost. The cost should exclude fuel used for cooking unless such use is considered incidental. If the cost of fuel used for cooking is significant, it should be charged to the food and beverage department.

Steam. The cost of steam purchased from outside producers is charged to this account.

Water. This account is charged with the cost of water and sewage services purchased from outside companies. This account should include water especially treated for circulating ice water systems or purchased for drinking purposes.

Fixed Charges

The financial reporting center termed **fixed charges** does not have a physical existence or facility. The purpose of this financial reporting center is to consolidate those expenses that are incurred whether the property is open or closed. These expenses are independent of sales volume. A department head cannot control these expenses; they are the responsibility of top management and are chargeable to the hotel as a whole. The following accounts are classified as fixed charges. These expenses can be reported on a single schedule, but *USALI* spreads them over three schedules: Rent, Property Taxes, and Insurance; Interest Expense; and Depreciation and Amortization.

Rent—Land and Buildings. This account is charged for the expense associated with renting land or buildings.

Rent—Information Systems Equipment. This account is charged with the rental or operating lease expense of computer equipment. Any items on a capital lease should be recorded to an asset account.

Rent—Telecommunications Equipment. This account is charged with the rental or operating lease expense of telecommunications equipment. Any items on a capital lease should be recorded to an asset account.

Rent—Other Property and Equipment. Other rentals would include the cost of renting any other major items which, had they not been rented, would be purchased as fixed assets.

Rental of miscellaneous equipment (copiers, projectors, and sound equipment) for a specific function, such as a banquet, should not be charged to this account; such expenses should be charged to the specific user department.

Any items on a capital lease should be recorded to an asset account.

Property Taxes. The following accounts may be used for taxes other than income and payroll taxes.

Real Estate Taxes is an account charged with taxes assessed on real property. Assessments for public improvements are not charged to this expense account; they are recorded as fixed assets.

Personal Property Taxes is an account charged for personal property taxes.

Utility Taxes is an account charged for sewer taxes and other utility taxes.

Business and Occupation Taxes is an account charged for business and occupation taxes imposed on the establishment. Such taxes are for gross receipts taxes on room sales or food and beverage sales and cannot be passed on to customers.

Property Insurance. This account is charged for the cost of insuring the building and its contents against financial loss due to destruction by fire, weather, and other casualties.

General Insurance. This account includes expenses for liability insurance, theft insurance, and fidelity bonds. This account does not include workers' compensation insurance or fire insurance on buildings and contents. Examples of the types of insurance that are charged to this account are:

Burglary	Fraud	Parcel post
Business interruption	Holdup	Products liability
Elevator liability	Public liability	Fidelity bonds
Forgery	Lost/damaged goods	Robbery

Interest Expense. This account includes all interest expense on mortgages, promissory notes, and other forms of indebtedness. If the interest expense is significant, separate accounts should be established that indicate the source of the principal indebtedness on which the interest is incurred. For example, the following accounts may be used:

- Interest Expense—Mortgages

- Interest Expense—Notes Payable

- Interest Expense—Capital Leases

Depreciation Expense. This account is charged with the periodic allocation of the cost of depreciable fixed assets. Separate accounts should be used to identify the principal source of the depreciation expense. For example, the following accounts may be used:

- Depreciation—Buildings and Improvements

- Depreciation—Furnishings and Equipment

- Depreciation—Capital Leases

Amortization Expense. This account is charged with the periodic allocation of the cost of leaseholds, leasehold improvements, and other purchased intangible assets. For example, the following accounts may be used:

- Amortization—Leaseholds and Improvements

- Amortization—Preopening Expenses

- Amortization—Goodwill

Income Taxes

The income taxes category includes the expenses charged for taxes imposed on the income of the business by federal, state, and, in some cases, municipal taxing authorities. Separate accounts should be maintained for each type of income tax.

Accounting for Employee Meals

A cost of sales account should reflect only that merchandise actually used to generate revenue. To meet this requirement, the cost of employee meals must be excluded from the net cost of food used (cost of sales). Otherwise, the cost of employee meals would inflate the cost of sales account.

Employee meals may be accounted for by keeping a log of meals served to employees. Each employee's meals should be charged to his or her department. Some hotels charge the actual cost of a meal, but small properties may not have the information or staff readily available to maintain such detailed records. In such a case, the cost of a typical employee meal may be averaged to arrive at a standard cost for each type of meal: breakfast, lunch, and dinner.

In a perpetual inventory system, the approach used to remove the cost of employee meals from the cost of food sold is to debit (increase) the various departmental expense accounts for employee meals and to credit (decrease) the cost of food sales account. This approach is illustrated by the following journal entry:

Employee Meals Expense—(F&B Department)	60	
Employee Meals Expense—(Rooms Department)	80	
Employee Meals Expense—(A&G Department)	50	
Cost of Food Sales		190

Officers' checks should be deducted from the cost of sales figure and charged to employee meals or entertainment accounts as appropriate. Accounting for employee meals and officers' checks under the periodic inventory system requires an entirely different procedure.

Accounting for Credit Card Fees

Credit card companies generally impose a fee for their services. This fee is considered an expense of doing business and is charged to an expense account called Credit Card Commissions within the A&G department. Until the credit card fee is provided for in the financial records, it represents a hidden expense to the hotel.

Two generally accepted accounting principles may influence a company's decision about how to treat credit card fees. The matching principle states that all expenses must be recorded in the same accounting period as the revenue that they helped to generate. The materiality principle, however, provides that the recording of an event may depend on its magnitude and surrounding circumstances, and whether its omission on financial statements would make a difference in the decision process of a reasonable user of those statements.

From a practical viewpoint, the estimation of credit card fees as they occur may result in time-consuming and tedious bookkeeping procedures. Since credit card fees are usually processed and reported within a short period of time, the unrecorded expense at the end of any month may be insignificant. Unless the volume of a hotel's credit card business is large, it is easier to simply record credit card fees upon receiving notice from the credit card company.

Whether a hotel records credit card fees at the time of billing from the credit card company or at the time of sale depends on the business's accounting policy. For purposes of this discussion, credit card fees will be recorded at the time of notification from the credit card company. This procedure is popular with small hotels as well as hotels whose outstanding credit card fees at the end of the accounting month are not considered significant.

The recording of credit card fees also depends on whether the fee relates to a bankcard or a nonbank credit card.

Credit Card Fees on Bankcards

At the end of each day, a hotel totals the bankcard drafts and deposits them with cash items into the hotel's checking account. Assuming that the hotel's credit card drafts total $1,000, the entry made at the time of deposit is:

Cash—Checking Account	1,000	
Sales		1,000

Banks usually deduct credit card fees directly from the checking account balance of the hotel and report them on the hotel's monthly bank statement. Many banks will mail a charge memo notifying the business of this action on the day the fee is charged. Assume that on this initial $1,000 deposit, the credit card company charges a four percent fee totaling $40 (4% × $1,000). Upon receipt of the bank's charge memo or bank statement, the entry made to record the credit card fee is:

Credit Card Commissions	40	
Cash—Checking Account		40

Once posted, this entry increases the expense account Credit Card Commissions and decreases the asset account for cash.

Nonbank Credit Card Fees

When nonbank credit card drafts are received from customers at the point of sale, they are summarized and recorded as accounts receivable. Assume that the total of nonbank credit card drafts is $1,000; the entry is:

Accounts Receivable	1,000	
Sales		1,000

These drafts are then forwarded to the credit card company. The credit card company will not remit a check for the full amount of the drafts; it will deduct its credit card fee and remit a check for the net balance.

For example, assume that the credit card company in this case charges a fee of four percent. After processing, the credit card company will send the hotel a check for $960; upon receipt and deposit of the check, the entry is:

Cash—Checking Account	960	
Credit Card Commissions	40	
Accounts Receivable		1,000

Although only $960 in cash was received, the balance of Accounts Receivable is credited for $1,000. The receipt of $960 represents payment in full for the $1,000 credit card charges. The difference of $40 was deducted by the credit card company as a fee.

Bad Debts

A business that sells goods or services on credit to its customers will usually incur **bad debts** regardless of how effectively its credit department evaluates its guests and customers. Bad debts are also called "uncollectible accounts" or "uncollectible receivables." A bad debt affects the general ledger account Accounts Receivable and the subsidiary ledger (the city ledger or possibly the guest ledger).

Bad debts occur when an account receivable cannot be collected. An account receivable originates when a sale is made on open account to a customer. A sale would never be made to a specific customer whose ultimate payment of the receivable would be doubtful. However, it is probable that collection of 100 percent of a receivable will not be possible because of the following:

- Customer bankruptcy
- Customer death
- A disagreement with the customer
- A faulty credit check
- Customer fraud

    There are two methods of accounting for bad debts:

- Direct write-off method

- Allowance method

Under the **direct write-off method,** bad debt losses are recorded when they occur. Under the **allowance method,** an estimate of potential bad debts is made before a specific customer's account is uncollectible.

Direct Write-Off Method

The direct write-off method can be used only by companies that have small amounts of accounts receivable; thus, the potential for any bad debt losses is not significant. The direct write-off method, also called the direct charge-off method, is a simple procedure that records a loss on an uncollectible account immediately as it occurs. The entry upon realization of a bad debt is:

Provision for Doubtful Accounts	xxx
Accounts Receivable	xxx

In this entry an expense account, Provision for Doubtful Accounts, is debited, and the general ledger account, Accounts Receivable, is credited. This entry will remove the uncollectible amount from the books. In addition, the uncollectible account is removed from the subsidiary ledger (city ledger or guest ledger).

Companies that have large amounts of accounts receivable are more likely to realize significant bad debt losses. Therefore, they cannot use the direct write-off method; they must use the allowance method.

Allowance Method

If a company has a large amount of sales on accounts receivable, generally accepted accounting principles mandate that the company estimate the expected bad debts that might occur because of the following requirements:

- The conservatism principle requires that assets not be overstated.

- The matching principle requires that expenses are to be recorded in the period incurred.

While it is not known exactly who will not pay their open account balance when sales are made, a representative dollar amount of bad debt losses can be estimated based on the company's experience. A review of prior years will usually show a relationship of bad debts to sales volume or to the age of an open account.

Recording Estimated Bad Debts. The allowance method *forecasts* potential bad debts before they occur. At the time the forecast is made, the estimated bad debts are "expensed"; that is, they are charged to the expense account Provision for Doubtful Accounts.

The estimated amount of potential bad debts that may occur in the future is maintained in an account called **Allowance for Doubtful Accounts.**

When the original forecast is made, the journal entry is:

Provision for Doubtful Accounts	xxx
Allowance for Doubtful Accounts	xxx

Keep in mind that the actual bad debts have not occurred. This is a prediction that is contained in the Allowance for Doubtful Accounts. This allowance account is increased by a credit entry because it is a contra-asset account.

Recording Actual Bad Debts. When a bad debt does occur, an expense account cannot be charged because the bad debt loss was expensed during the forecast entry. Remember that Allowance for Doubtful Accounts contains the estimate; therefore, the actual bad debts will be charged off against this estimate.

When a bad debt actually does occur, the journal entry is:

Allowance for Doubtful Accounts	xxx	
Accounts Receivable		xxx

Accounts Receivable is credited to remove the account that cannot be collected. Allowance for Doubtful Accounts is debited, which reduces the amount of potential bad debts expected in the future.

Presentation on the Balance Sheet. The current assets section of the balance sheet shows the status of Accounts Receivable and the related amount of potential uncollectible accounts as follows:

Cash		$77,000
Accounts Receivable	$90,000	
Less Allowance for Doubtful Accounts	5,700	84,300

Procedures Used to Calculate the Estimate. Under the allowance method, two different procedures may be used to estimate bad debts:

- Percentage of sales
- Percentage of receivables

Percentage of sales procedure. The percentage of sales procedure is also called the income statement approach. It calculates the potential bad debts based on net sales volume, which is the total sales billed minus any allowances due to price adjustments. Net sales can be shown as:

$$\text{Sales} - \text{Allowances} = \text{Net Sales}$$

At this point, the use of the word "allowances" may be confusing. When "allowances" is used with sales, it refers to price adjustments. When "allowances" is used with Accounts Receivable, it refers to the Allowance for Doubtful Accounts.

A study of past sales and bad debt losses is performed to develop a percentage relationship of bad debts to sales volume. The resulting percentage is then consistently used. It is not changed unless it eventually proves to be unreliable.

The percentage of sales method can be explained by the following example.

1. A company has the following balance in its allowance account:

Allowance for Doubtful Accounts	
	Bal 2,200

2. Based on experience, the expected bad debts are forecasted at one percent of net sales.

3. The net sales for this period are $350,000.

4. The forecast is computed as follows:

$350,000 (net sales) × 1% = $3,500 (potential bad debts increase)

5. The journal entry is as follows:

Provision for Doubtful Accounts	3,500	
Allowance for Doubtful Accounts		3,500

IMPORTANT: *Under the percentage of sales procedure, the computed estimate is used to increase the existing balance in Allowance for Doubtful Accounts.*

6. The allowance account now appears as follows:

Allowance for Doubtful Accounts

	Bal	2,200
	AJE	3,500
	Bal	5,700

Percentage of receivables procedure. The percentage of receivables procedure is also called the balance sheet approach. This procedure also requires research into past sales and bad debt losses. However, the research is based upon the relationship of the age of an account to any bad debt losses.

The accounts receivable are "aged" and categorized as not yet due, 1 to 30 days past due, 31 to 60 days past due, etc. Aging an account requires an analysis of the invoice date and the billing terms. If the billing terms are net 10 days, an account 40 days old is 30 days past due; it does not belong in the 31- to 60-day aging.

Then the aging categories are analyzed to determine the percentage that actually became uncollectible. For example, assume research shows that over the last three years, $20,000 of accounts that were 31 to 60 days past due resulted in bad debt losses of $2,000.

The relationship of the uncollectible percentage to accounts receivable is calculated as follows:

$$\frac{\text{Actual Bad Debts}}{\text{Accounts Receivable}} = \frac{2,000}{20,000} = 10\%$$

The 10 percent would then be applied to the current amount of accounts aged 31 to 60 days to estimate the potential bad debts for that aging category. Other uncollectible percentages would be calculated and applied to their aging categories to arrive at the total estimated bad debts.

The percentage of receivables procedure can be explained by the following example.

1. A company has the following balance in its allowance account:

Exhibit 6   Estimating Bad Debts by an Aging of Accounts Receivable

Aging Category	Accounts Receivable	Percentage Considered Uncollectible	Estimated Uncollectible Accounts
Not yet due	$60,000	1%	$ 600
1 to 30 days past due	22,000	5%	1,100
31 to 60 days past due	5,000	10%	500
61 to 90 days past due	2,000	35%	700
Over 90 days past due	1,000	60%	600
Total	$90,000		$3,500

Allowance for Doubtful Accounts
	Bal 2,200

2. Based on experience, the expected bad debts based on an aging analysis showed the following:

Aging Category	Percentage Considered Uncollectible
Not yet due	1%
1 to 30 days past due	5%
31 to 60 days past due	10%
61 to 90 days past due	35%
Over 90 days past due	60%

3. The Accounts Receivable balance at the end of this period is $90,000.

4. Exhibit 6 shows the computation of the estimated bad debts. The $90,000 of accounts receivable at the end of this period are aged. Each amount in the various aging categories is multiplied by the percentage considered uncollectible. The result of the multiplication becomes the estimated bad debt for that aging category. All categories are added to arrive at the total of $3,500 in *estimated potential bad debts.*

5. The journal entry is as follows:

Provision for Doubtful Accounts	1,300	
Allowance for Doubtful Accounts		1,300

    IMPORTANT: *Under the percentage of receivables procedure, the computed estimate becomes the new balance in Allowance for Doubtful Accounts.*

6. The allowance account now appears as follows:

Allowance for Doubtful Accounts

	Bal	2,200
	AJE	1,300
	Bal	3,500

Recovery of a Bad Debt. Sometimes an account that has been written off to bad debts may later be paid by the customer. In these cases, the original entry that wrote off the account must be reversed to reinstate Accounts Receivable, and the collection is recorded in the usual way.

Remember that the entry to write off a bad debt using the Allowance Method is as follows:

Allowance for Doubtful Accounts	xxx	
Accounts Receivable		xxx

Later, if a customer remits an amount in part or in full, the recovery is recorded by the following entries:

(1)

Accounts Receivable	xxx	
Allowance for Doubtful Accounts		xxx

To reinstate an account receivable previously written off to bad debts.

(2)

Cash	xxx	
Accounts Receivable		xxx

To record the collection

Endnote

1. Defined in accordance with recommendations of the Committee on Financial Management of the American Hotel & Lodging Association.

Key Terms

Allowance for Doubtful Accounts—A contra-asset account providing an estimate of total potential bad debts. On the balance sheet, this amount is deducted from Accounts Receivable to show the amount expected to be collected in the future. Also called Allowance for Uncollectible Accounts.

allowance method—A method for estimating and recording bad debts before they are actually incurred. The estimate is recorded in Allowance for Doubtful Accounts and Uncollectible Accounts Expense. If the income statement approach is used, the estimate increases the Allowance for Doubtful Accounts balance. If the balance sheet approach is used, the estimated amount becomes the new balance in Allowance for Doubtful Accounts.

bad debts—Expenses incurred because of failure to collect accounts receivable.

direct expenses—Expenses directly related to the department incurring the expenses. Examples are cost of sales, payroll and payroll related expenses, and other expenses that can be readily identified as associated with a specific department.

direct write-off method—A method of accounting for uncollectibles in which bad debt expense is recorded only after a particular account has been judged worthless and is to be written off the books. Also called the direct charge-off method.

expenses—The cost of items consumed in the process of generating revenue or that expire due to the passage of time. Examples include cost of sales, payroll, taxes, supplies, advertising, utilities, repairs, rent, depreciation, and other operating and fixed expenses.

fixed charges—Expenses incurred regardless of sales volume of the hotel. Examples are rent, property insurance, interest, depreciation, and amortization. Also referred to as occupancy costs.

food cost—The cost of food used in the production of a menu item; the cost of food served to guests in the revenue process.

gross profit—The profit on the sale of material or merchandise excluding labor and other operating expenses. It is computed as follows: net sales less cost of sales.

indirect expenses—Expenses that cannot be related directly to any specific department; generally, indirect expenses benefit the hotel as a whole.

operating expenses—Expenses (other than the cost of goods sold) incurred in the day-to-day operation of a business.

periodic inventory accounting system—A system of accounting for inventory under which cost of goods sold must be computed. There are no perpetual inventory records, so a physical count of the storeroom is required to determine the inventory on hand.

perpetual inventory accounting system—A system of accounting for inventory that records the receipts and issues and provides a continuous record of the quantity and cost of merchandise in inventory.

Review Questions

1. What is the concept of responsibility accounting?
2. What is business segmentation?
3. What is a support center? What are some of the support centers found in a hotel?
4. How are the terms "direct expense" and "indirect expense" defined?
5. How is the term "fixed charges" defined? What kinds of expenses are classified as fixed charges?
6. What is included in the Cost of Food Sales account? Do these items increase or decrease the cost of food sold?
7. What types of items are considered Payroll and Related Expenses?

8. What accounts are commonly used to record repairs and maintenance expenses?

9. What is the major difference between the allowance method and the direct write-off method in terms of when a bad debt is recorded?

10. What is the major difference between the percentage of sales procedure and the percentage of receivables procedure in the recording of the *estimated* bad debts calculation under the allowance method?

Internet Sites

For more information, visit the following Internet sites. Remember that Internet addresses can change without notice. If the site is no longer there, you can use a search engine to look for additional sites.

Business Segmentation
http://marketing.about.com/cs/sbmarketing/a/smbizmrktseg.htm
www.projectalevel.co.uk/business/segmentation.htm

Responsibility Accounting
www.accountancy.com.pk/articles_students.asp?offset=80&id=55

Examples of Expense Accounts
www.accountinginfo.com/study/fs/expense-101.htm

Cost of Goods Sold Explained
http://beginnersinvest.about.com/cs/investinglessons/l/blcogs.htm

Operating Expenses Explained
http://beginnersinvest.about.com/cs/investinglessons/l/blopexpenses.htm

Bad Debts Accounting
www.toolkit.cch.com/text/P06_2900.asp

Problems

Problem 1

Specify whether each of the following statements is true (T) or false (F).

_____ 1. Dividing a corporation into reporting areas by hotel location is a form of business segmentation.

_____ 2. Dividing a particular hotel into reporting areas by department is a form of business segmentation.

_____ 3. The payroll expense for housekeepers is charged to the rooms department.

_____ 4. The salary of the general manager is charged to the A&G department.

_____ 5. The payroll expense for the night auditor and front office bookkeeper is charged to the A&G department.

_____ 6. Repairs to an oven located in the restaurant are charged to the F&B department.

_____ 7. The cost of food sold includes employee meals expenses.

_____ 8. Contracting with an outside maintenance company to clean the restaurant is charged to the F&B department.

_____ 9. The expense for water used by registered guests is charged to the rooms department.

_____10. The percentage of sales procedure and the percentage of receivables procedure are classified as allowance methods.

Problem 2

A hospitality business receives a bank memo regarding bankcard fees. The memo states that the bank has charged the business's checking account a fee of $175 for processing bankcard vouchers previously deposited in this account. Journalize the entry recorded upon receipt of the bank memo.

Problem 3

Nonbank credit card vouchers totaling $4,000 were remitted to a private credit card company. The entry at that time was a debit to Accounts Receivable for $4,000, and a credit to Sales for $4,000. A check is received from the credit card company for $3,800, representing payment in full for these vouchers less a $200 credit card fee. Journalize the entry recorded upon receipt of the check.

Problem 4

Assume that a hospitality company uses the direct write-off method. Show the journal entry used to record an uncollectible receivable of $210.

Problem 5

Assume that a hospitality company uses the allowance method. Show the journal entry used to record an uncollectible receivable of $210.

Problem 6

Assume that a hospitality company uses the allowance method. The contra-asset account Allowance for Doubtful Accounts has a credit balance of $1,200. Based on an aging of the accounts receivable subsidiary ledger, estimated uncollectible accounts total $1,800. Journalize the entry to adjust Allowance for Doubtful Accounts using the percentage of receivables procedure.

Problem 7

Assume that a hospitality operation uses the allowance method. The contra-asset account Allowance for Doubtful Accounts has a credit balance of $1,200. Based on an analysis of sales for the period, the estimate for uncollectible accounts equals $1,800. Journalize the entry to adjust Allowance for Doubtful Accounts using the percentage of sales procedure.

Problem 8

Compute the cost of food sold for the month of March from the following information. The food inventory on February 28 is $1,500. A physical count of the food inventory on March 31 shows a total of $1,200 in storage. Purchases of food for March were $1,000, and employee meals amounted to $20.

Problem 9

Compute the gross profit from the following information:

Sales	$90,000
Sales allowances	1,000
Cost of sales	24,000
All other expenses	60,000

Case Study

Investigative Fire Loss of Inventory

The Paradise Cove is a large-volume restaurant serving expensive meals. Its menu consists of prime rib, filet mignon, lobster, and other fine entrées. Its décor is sophisticated, and its serving staff is uniformed in tuxedo-style outfits. A dress code is required of customers. The Paradise Cove is famous for its highest-quality food, service, and ambiance. Despite its high prices, customers are very happy with the dining experience, and the majority continually return.

A fire on the morning of June 11 destroys the kitchen and stockroom. The Paradise Cove has a comprehensive fire insurance policy, including coverage for loss of inventory. The available accounting data is as follows:

Inventory May 31: $35,000
Purchases June 1 to June 10: $65,000
Sales June 1 to June 10: $200,000

Selected financial statement information January 1 to May 31

Sales	$1,500,000
Cost of Sales	420,000
Gross Profit	1,080,000

Challenge

Calculate the cost of the inventory destroyed by fire.

Chapter 3 Outline

Competencies

1. Explain the items typically classified as property and equipment. (p. 73)

2. Describe the determination of acquisition costs recorded for various types of property and equipment. (pp. 74–77)

3. Summarize the difference between accounting for building repairs and accounting for building improvements. (p. 76)

4. Describe the difference between operating leases and capital leases, and explain the four criteria for distinguishing capital leases from operating leases. (pp. 77–78)

5. Explain the purpose of depreciation, the affected accounts, the different types of values of assets, and how the preparation of tax returns affects depreciation. (pp. 78–80, 94–95)

6. Explain the difference between time-factor and use-factor methods of depreciation. (p. 80)

7. Describe the straight-line, declining balance, and sum-of-the-years-digits methods of depreciation. (pp. 80–84)

8. Identify accelerated depreciation methods. (pp. 84–85)

9. Explain the options for computing depreciation for partial time periods. (p. 86)

10. Describe the productive-output method of depreciation. (pp. 86–87)

11. Explain what special considerations apply to the depreciation of china, glassware, and silver. (pp. 87–88)

12. Explain amortization and the amortization of leaseholds and leasehold improvements. (pp. 88–89)

13. Explain the accounting considerations involved in the sale, disposal, or trade-in of property and equipment. (pp. 89–94)

3

Property and Equipment Accounting

THE TERM **property and equipment** refers to long-lived assets that are acquired for use in the operation of a business and are not intended for resale to customers in the normal course of business. Land, buildings, furniture and fixtures, vehicles, office equipment, and kitchen equipment are examples of items typically classified as property and equipment. These items are also referred to as **tangible assets** because they have physical substance. Intangible assets include such items as copyrights, trademarks, franchises, and purchased goodwill.

This chapter focuses on accounting methods applicable to the acquisition, depreciation, and disposal of tangible long-lived assets. Questions answered within the chapter include:

1. How is the acquisition cost of a fixed asset determined?

2. What is the difference between a capital lease and an operating lease?

3. What is depreciation, and what methods are used to compute it?

4. What is amortization, and how is it computed?

5. What accounting methods are used to record the disposal or exchange of assets?

The chapter begins by illustrating how the acquisition cost of various property and equipment items is determined. Computing the acquisition cost of a tangible asset is important because this amount is used as the basis for capitalizing the item to an asset account and for computing depreciation.

Depreciation spreads the cost of an asset over the term of its estimated useful life. Estimated **useful life** refers to the estimated economic service life of an asset. The chapter explains and compares several depreciation methods that are used for financial accounting purposes. Special accounting procedures for depreciating china, glassware, and silver are also examined.

In addition, the chapter addresses the amortization of leaseholds and leasehold improvements. Like depreciation, amortization involves the write-off of the cost of an asset over its estimated useful life.

The final sections of the chapter examine accounting methods used to record the disposal of tangible assets. Accounting for exchanges involving either like-kind assets or dissimilar assets is addressed in relation to both financial and tax accounting rules.

Exhibit 1 Computing the Cost of a Land Purchase

Purchase price	$200,000
Brokerage fee	12,000
Legal, title, and recording fees	2,000
Razing of existing building to prepare for the construction of a new building	20,000
Less salvage proceeds of razed building	(8,000)
Site grading	5,000
Total acquisition cost	$231,000

Acquisition Costs of Property and Equipment ————————

When a property or equipment item is purchased, it is generally recorded at its acquisition cost. Acquisition cost includes all expenditures necessary to acquire, install, and prepare an item for use. For example, in addition to the purchase price (including any sales tax), acquisition cost may consist of freight costs, the expense of insurance while the item is in transit, legal or brokerage fees, installation charges, and any costs required to make the asset ready for use.

If a property and equipment item is purchased with an installment note or mortgage, the interest is not part of the acquisition cost. An exception to this rule occurs when a company is constructing an asset for its own use. In this case, Financial Accounting Standards Board (FASB) Statement #34 states that interest costs during the construction period are considered part of the acquisition cost.

Land with Building to Be Demolished

When land is purchased with an existing building that will be demolished, the purchase may involve brokerage fees, recording fees, escrow fees, and title fees. Other expenses may involve fees for surveying, draining, grading, and clearing the property. All of these expenditures may be part of the acquisition cost. In addition, any delinquent taxes paid by the buyer are part of the acquisition cost.

Exhibit 1 illustrates the computation of the acquisition cost of land with a building that will be demolished. All of these expenditures are recorded in the Land account.

Land and Building for a Lump Sum

It is not uncommon for hospitality companies to purchase land with an existing building that will be used in the business. Generally, the selling price is stated as one lump sum for both the land and building. Land is a non-depreciable asset because it has an unlimited life in the normal course of business for hospitality companies; on the other hand, a building is a depreciable asset. When land and building are purchased with a lump sum, the acquisition cost must be allocated between two asset accounts, one entitled Land and another entitled Building. This allocation is usually computed on the basis of real estate appraisals or tax valuations.

For example, assume that land with a building is purchased for $350,000, but the real estate tax appraisals total $300,000 ($90,000 for the land, $210,000 for the building). The first step in determining amounts of the $350,000 purchase cost to allocate to the Land and Building accounts is to calculate allocation percentages on the basis of the appraisal values. This is accomplished by dividing the appraisal value of the land and the appraisal value of the building by the total appraisal value. The resulting allocation is as follows:

Land	$ 90,000	30%
Building	210,000	70%
Total appraisal	$300,000	100%

The allocation percentage for the cost of the land is 30 percent ($90,000 divided by $300,000), and the allocation percentage for the cost of the building is 70 percent ($210,000 divided by $300,000).

The next step is to apply the individual allocation percentages to the total acquisition cost of $350,000. The individual allocations, or cost bases, of the land and building are recorded in the general ledger accounts as follows:

Land ($350,000 × 30%)	$105,000
Building ($350,000 × 70%)	245,000
Total acquisition cost	$350,000

Equipment Requiring Special Installation

Certain equipment items (such as ovens, dishwashers, and air conditioning systems) may require special platforms or electrical wiring to make them ready for use. These special installation costs are considered part of the asset's acquisition cost.

Assume that a hospitality business purchases equipment that requires special wiring. The acquisition cost of the equipment would be calculated as follows:

Invoice price	$2,000
Freight	100
Sales tax	120
Installation	350
Special wiring	200
Total acquisition cost	$2,770

Land Improvements

Land improvements (such as driveways, parking lots, and fences) should not be charged to the Land account. Whether the land is owned or leased is a determining factor in how these improvements are recorded.

If the land is owned by the hospitality business, improvements may be charged to an account called Land Improvements and depreciated over the improvement's estimated useful life.

If the land is leased, improvements may be charged to an account called **Leasehold Improvements** and amortized over the improvement's estimated useful life or the life of the **lease,** whichever is shorter. The life of the lease may include renewable options if the probability of renewal is high. Most lease agreements state that any improvements made by the **lessee** (tenant) to the leased property become the property of the **lessor** (landlord) at the expiration of the lease.

Building Repairs and Improvements

After a building has been placed in use, the costs of ordinary repairs and maintenance are charged to the appropriate expense account. Ordinary repairs and maintenance costs are defined as recurring expenditures that are necessary in order to keep an asset in good operating condition. These costs include expenditures associated with routine repair and maintenance activities such as repairing broken windows and doors, cleaning, lubricating, and painting. These expenditures do not increase the future service potential of an asset. Instead, they allow the company to derive the intended benefits from the asset over the asset's estimated useful life. Therefore, ordinary repairs and maintenance expenditures are expensed.

Improvements to a building (sometimes called betterments) are capitalized. Improvements are expenditures that improve or increase the future service potential of an asset. For example, expenditures associated with replacing an old heating system with a more efficient heating system would be considered an improvement and not a repair. When an old building is purchased and requires extensive repairs and maintenance before it is ready for use, related expenditures should be capitalized to the Building asset account. Other kinds of expenditures that are treated as improvements and not as repairs are major reconditioning and overhaul expenditures that extend the asset's useful life beyond the original estimate. The term "addition" applies to a building expansion made to increase the building's service potential.

It is not always easy to distinguish between an improvement and a repair. However, it is important to be able to distinguish them because their accounting treatments are different: expenditures for repairs are expensed; expenditures for improvements are capitalized.

The amount capitalized to a fixed asset account depends on whether the building is owned or leased. **Capital expenditures** for a leased building should be charged to an asset account called Leasehold Improvements and amortized. Capital expenditures for an owned building should be charged to the Building account and depreciated.

China, Glassware, Silver, Uniforms, and Linen

There are several ways to account for the acquisition costs of china, glassware, and silver. Three common methods recommended by the American Institute of Certified Public Accountants (AICPA) are:

1. Capitalize/Depreciate/Expense

    a. Capitalize the acquisition cost.

    b. Depreciate the acquisition cost.

    c. Charge the cost of any replacements to an expense account.

2. Capitalize/Depreciate/Expense/Adjust

    a. Capitalize the acquisition cost.

    b. Depreciate the acquisition cost.

    c. Charge the cost of any replacements to an expense account.

    d. Adjust the asset account annually to correspond to a physical inventory.

3. Capitalize/Depreciate/Capitalize/Adjust

    a. Capitalize the acquisition cost.

    b. Depreciate the acquisition cost.

    c. Capitalize any replacements and adjust the cost basis accordingly.

    d. Adjust the asset account annually to correspond to a physical inventory.

Accounting for china, glassware, and silver is presented later in this chapter when depreciation is discussed in detail.

Hotels that rent uniforms or use a linen service simply record these expenditures as they are incurred, charging their costs to expense accounts entitled Uniforms Expense and Linen and Laundry Expense. If a hotel purchases its own uniforms and linen, such expenditures should be capitalized and depreciated.

Operating Leases and Capital Leases

A hotel may purchase its **fixed assets** or it may lease them. A hotel may lease land, building(s), office equipment, vehicles, or any other fixed asset through a leasing company.

A lease is a contract in which the lessor (landlord or leasing company) gives the lessee (tenant or user) the right to use an asset over a period of time in return for lease or rental payments. The lessor is the owner of the asset and the lessee is the person or company obtaining the right to use and possess the asset.

Real estate leasing contracts generally do not present any accounting problem because they are truly rental arrangements. However, leases of vehicles and other equipment items may be simple rental arrangements or may actually serve as long-term financing arrangements.

Operating leases are rental arrangements. An operating lease generally involves equipment that will be used by the lessee for a relatively short period of time. At the end of the lease term, the asset has a substantial remaining useful life and the lessor retains ownership rights. Operating leases do not offer bargain purchase options. A bargain purchase option provides the lessee with the right to buy the asset at the end of the lease term for a nominal amount or for an amount that is substantially less than the asset's fair market value. Unlike operating leases, some **capital leases** offer such options.

Capital leases are not simply rental arrangements: they actually serve as long-term financing arrangements that effectively transfer ownership of the leased asset from the lessor to the lessee at the end of the lease term. Even though title may not be transferred until the end of the lease, a capital lease is essentially regarded as the sale of an asset from the lessor to the lessee. In some cases, the term of a capital lease may be so long that the asset's economic life (period during which the asset has value) is nil at the end of the lease. These types of leases are also classified as capital leases even though the lessor retains ownership at the end of the lease term.

FASB Statement #13 provides criteria for distinguishing capital leases from operating leases for accounting purposes. According to the FASB, if any of the following four criteria are met, the lessee must classify and account for the lease as a capital lease:

1. The lease transfers ownership of the property to the lessee by the end of the lease term.

2. The lease contains a bargain purchase option.

3. The lease term is equal to 75 percent or more of the estimated economic life of the leased property.

4. The present value of the minimum lease payments is at least 90 percent of the fair market value of the leased property.

Based on FASB Statement #13, *only those leases that do not meet any of these criteria may be accounted for as operating leases.* In accounting for an operating lease, the lessee records the lease payments as a rental expense.

When equipment is acquired through a capital lease, the lessee should capitalize the cost to an asset account called Leased Equipment. In the same journal entry, a liability account called Lease Payment Obligation is credited for the present value of the future lease payments. The journal entry is as follows:

Leased Equipment	xxx	
Lease Payment Obligation		xxx

The asset account Leased Equipment is depreciated over the estimated useful life of the asset rather than the life of the lease.

When the lease payments are made, the following entry is recorded:

Lease Payment Obligation	xxx	
Interest Expense	xxx	
Cash		xxx

Depreciation of Property and Equipment

Depreciation spreads the cost of an asset over its estimated useful life. Except for land, all property and equipment is depreciated by gradually converting the cost of the asset into an expense in the periods during which the asset provides a service. With the exception of china, glassware, silver, uniforms, and linen, the entry to record depreciation is as follows:

Depreciation Expense	xxx	
Accumulated Depreciation		xxx

Depreciation Expense is an expense account containing the depreciation charges for the current year only. Separate depreciation expense accounts may be used for each type of depreciable asset. Since depreciation is based on estimation, depreciation expense may be rounded to the nearest dollar to avoid implying pinpoint accuracy.

Accumulated Depreciation is a contra-asset account and contains depreciation charges from the date of purchase (or from the date on which the asset is placed in service) to the present. These charges represent the expired cost of the asset. Assets may be purchased with the intent to use them several months after the purchase date. Since depreciation is the allocation of the cost of an asset over its estimated useful life, depreciation charges should commence only when the asset is put in use. Separate accumulated depreciation accounts may be used for buildings, furniture, equipment, and other depreciable assets.

It is important to stress that depreciating an asset is not an attempt to establish the market value of the asset. The market value is the value that the asset could bring if sold on the open market. Depreciation does not represent a decline in market value. The cost of an asset minus the amount of its accumulated depreciation is the net asset value, commonly called the "book value" of the asset.

The useful life may be estimated in terms of time or in terms of units of output. These concepts will be discussed later in the chapter. When estimating the useful life of an asset, the following factors must be considered:

- Past experience with similar assets
- Age of the asset when acquired
- Repair, maintenance, and replacement policies of the company
- Current technological trends
- Frequency of use
- Local conditions, such as weather

Salvage value, sometimes called residual value, refers to the estimated proceeds from the disposal of an asset less all removal and selling costs at the end of its useful life. Salvage values are usually subjective because they require estimates. Nominal salvage values may be ignored and assigned a value of zero. One approach is to set the salvage value of an asset at zero when the estimated salvage value amounts to 10 percent or less of the asset's original cost. It is possible for a building to actually have a salvage value of zero because the costs incurred in tearing down the building at the end of its useful life may approximate the sales value of the scrap materials.

When the book value of an asset equals the asset's estimated salvage value, the asset is fully depreciated and no further depreciation is recorded for that asset. As long as the asset remains in use, its original cost and fully accumulated depreciation remain on the books. When an asset is disposed of, entries are made to remove the original cost from the asset account and to remove its related accumulated depreciation from the accumulated depreciation account.

Several methods may be used to compute depreciation. Different depreciation methods may be used for different assets. For example, one method may be used to allocate the cost of a building and another method may be used to allocate the cost of a vehicle. Also, one method of computing depreciation may be used for allocating the cost of a particular vehicle and another method for allocating the costs of other vehicles. Moreover, the depreciation methods used for financial reporting purposes may differ from those used for tax reporting purposes.

While a company may use different depreciation methods for different assets, the generally accepted accounting principle of consistency requires that once a depreciation method is selected for a particular asset, it should be used throughout that asset's estimated useful life. However, a company may be justified in changing depreciation methods for a particular asset. Any changes must be disclosed in the footnotes to the financial statements as required by the disclosure principle.

Depreciation methods may be classified as time-factor methods or use-factor methods. Time-factor methods estimate useful life in terms of time. Use-factor methods estimate useful life in terms of units of output. Three time-factor methods used for financial accounting purposes are presented in this chapter: the straight-line method, the declining balance method, and the sum-of-the-years-digits method. An identical example is used for all three time-factor methods. The time-factor methods are then compared, and depreciation for partial periods is addressed. The section concludes with a discussion of a use-factor method: the productive-output method.

Straight-Line Method

The **straight-line method** of depreciation is the simplest and most popular time-factor method used in computing depreciation for financial reporting purposes. Under the straight-line method, an equal allocation of the cost of the asset less salvage value is assigned to each period. This spreads depreciation expense evenly throughout the asset's estimated useful life.

Annual straight-line depreciation is calculated by subtracting salvage value from the cost basis and dividing this amount by the estimated useful life. The computation of straight-line depreciation is expressed by the following formula:

$$\text{Annual Depreciation Expense} = \frac{\text{Cost} - \text{Salvage Value}}{\text{Years of Useful Life}}$$

For example, assume that a hospitality business buys equipment at the beginning of a year for \$3,500; the salvage value of the equipment is estimated at \$500; and its useful life is estimated to be five years. The straight-line method computes the annual depreciation expense as follows:

$$\text{Annual Depreciation Expense} = \frac{\text{Cost} - \text{Salvage Value}}{\text{Years of Useful Life}}$$

$$\text{Annual Depreciation Expense} = \frac{\$3,500 - \$500}{5 \text{ Years}} = \underline{\underline{\$600}}$$

Another approach to computing straight-line depreciation is to calculate an annual depreciation percentage by dividing 100 percent by the estimated useful life of the asset:

$$\text{Annual Depreciation Percentage} = \frac{100\%}{\text{Years of Useful Life}}$$

Multiplying the annual depreciation percentage by the asset's cost determines the annual depreciation expense. Given the same information as in the previous example, the annual depreciation percentage is 20 percent (100 percent divided by five years) and the annual depreciation expense is computed at \$600 (20% × \$3,000).

Exhibit 2 Depreciation Schedule: Straight-Line Method

Year	Computation	Depreciation Expense	Accumulated Depreciation	Cost	Book Value
	Upon Acquisition	—	—	$3,500	$3,500
1	1/5 × $3,000	$ 600	$ 600	3,500	2,900
2	1/5 × $3,000	600	1,200	3,500	2,300
3	1/5 × $3,000	600	1,800	3,500	1,700
4	1/5 × $3,000	600	2,400	3,500	1,100
5	1/5 × $3,000	600	3,000	3,500	500
		$3,000			

Exhibit 2 presents a depreciation schedule of the equipment purchased in the preceding example. The schedule illustrates the effect of straight-line depreciation over the useful life of the asset.

The matching principle requires that all expenses incurred during an accounting period be recorded in that accounting period. Since financial statements are generally issued on a monthly basis, depreciation expense must be recorded monthly. If the annual depreciation expense for a purchased equipment item is $600, the monthly depreciation expense would be $50 ($600 divided by 12 months). The entry to record this monthly depreciation is as follows:

Depreciation Expense	50	
Accumulated Depreciation		50

Declining Balance Method

The declining balance method is based on a percentage rate. Although any percentage rate may be used, the most common rate is twice the straight-line rate. The method associated with this doubled rate is called the **double declining balance method.** The double declining rate is computed by the following formula:

$$\text{Double Declining Rate} = \frac{100\%}{\text{Years of Useful Life}} \times 2$$

For example, assume again that a hospitality business purchases equipment at the beginning of a year for $3,500; the salvage value of the equipment is estimated at $500; and its useful life is estimated to be five years. The double declining rate is computed as follows:

$$\text{Double Declining Rate} = \frac{100\%}{5} \times 2 = 40\%$$

The declining balance method computes depreciation expense for the first year of an asset's estimated useful life by multiplying the annual depreciation rate by the cost of the asset. Each successive year's depreciation expense is determined by multiplying the annual depreciation rate by the beginning book value of the asset. With the declining balance method of computing depreciation, salvage value is not

Exhibit 3   Depreciation Schedule: Double Declining Balance Method

Year	Computation	Depreciation Expense	Accumulated Depreciation	Cost	Book Value
	Upon Acquisition	—	—	$3,500	$3,500
1	40% × $3,500	$1,400	$1,400	3,500	2,100
2	40% × $2,100	840	2,240	3,500	1,260
3	40% × $1,260	504	2,744	3,500	756
4	(See *Note*)	256	3,000	3,500	500
5	Not Applicable	0	3,000	3,500	500
		$3,000			

Note: The allowable $256 depreciation expense is determined by computing the difference between the prior book value of $756 and the salvage value of $500.

subtracted from the asset's cost; however, the book value may never fall below the salvage value. If depreciation computations result in a book value at the end of a year that is less than the asset's salvage value, depreciation expense is computed by subtracting the salvage value from the book value at the beginning of that year.

Exhibit 3 presents a depreciation schedule that illustrates the effect of declining balance depreciation over the estimated useful life of the asset. Depreciation expense for the first year is calculated at $1,400 (the double declining rate of 40% × $3,500 cost). The book value of the asset at the beginning of the second year is $2,100 ($3,500 cost − $1,400 accumulated depreciation); therefore, depreciation expense for the second year is calculated at $840 (40% × $2,100).

At the beginning of the fourth year, the book value of the asset is $756. When this amount is multiplied by the 40 percent annual depreciation rate, the resulting depreciation expense is $302. However, this amount cannot be used because the resulting book value for the end of the fourth year would be $454 ($3,500 cost − $3,046 accumulated depreciation), which is less than the asset's salvage value of $500. Therefore, the allowable depreciation expense for the fourth year is $256, which is computed by subtracting the salvage value ($500) from the book value at the beginning of that year ($756). The book value at the end of the fourth year becomes equal to the asset's salvage value ($3,500 cost − $3,000 accumulated depreciation). There is zero depreciation expense for the fifth year because, at the end of the fourth year, the asset's book value equals its salvage value.

Sum-of-the-Years-Digits Method

The **sum-of-the-years-digits method** uses a fraction in computing depreciation expense. The numerator of the fraction is the remaining years of the asset's estimated useful life. This figure changes with each year's computation of depreciation. The denominator of the fraction is the sum of the digits of the asset's estimated useful life. This figure remains constant with each year's computation of depreciation. Each year's depreciation expense is determined by multiplying this fraction by the asset's cost less its salvage value.

For example, assume again that a hospitality business purchases equipment at the beginning of a year for $3,500; the salvage value of the equipment is estimated at $500; and its useful life is estimated to be five years.

The numerator of the fraction used to compute depreciation expense changes each year to match the remaining years of the asset's estimated useful life. In the first year of the asset's five-year estimated useful life, the numerator is 5; in the second year, the numerator is 4, and so on. An easy way to determine the appropriate numerator for each year's computation of depreciation expense is to simply list the estimated years of the asset's useful life and then reverse them:

Year of Useful Life	Years Reversed (Numerator)
1	5
2	4
3	3
4	2
5	1

The denominator of the fraction used to compute depreciation expense remains constant and is the sum of the digits of the asset's estimated useful life. Since the asset's estimated useful life is five years, the denominator of the fraction is 15 (1 + 2 + 3 + 4 + 5). When the span of an asset's estimated useful life is short, the sum of the years' digits is easily computed. However, when longer time spans are involved, it may be easier to compute the sum of the years' digits by using the following procedure:

1. Square the number of years estimated as the asset's useful life.

2. Add the asset's useful life to the squared result.

3. Divide the resulting figure by 2.

For our five-year estimated useful life example, the procedure is as follows:

1. $5 \times 5 = 25$

2. $25 + 5 = 30$

3. 30 divided by 2 = 15 (the denominator)

Therefore, the fractions used to compute depreciation expense in our example are as follows:

Year 1: $5/15$
Year 2: $4/15$
Year 3: $3/15$
Year 4: $2/15$
Year 5: $1/15$

For any particular year, depreciation expense is computed by using the following formula:

$$\text{Deduction Expense} = \frac{\text{Remaining Years of Useful Life}}{\text{Sum-of-the-Years-Digits}} \times (\text{Cost} - \text{Salvage Value})$$

Exhibit 4   Depreciation Schedule: Sum-of-the-Years-Digits Method

Year	Year Reversed	Computation	Depreciation Expense	Accumulated Depreciation	Cost	Book Value
		Upon Acquisition	—	—	$3,500	$3,500
1	5	5/15 × $3,000	$ 1,000	$ 1,000	3,500	2,500
2	4	4/15 × $3,000	800	1,800	3,500	1,700
3	3	3/15 × $3,000	600	2,400	3,500	1,100
4	2	2/15 × $3,000	400	2,800	3,500	700
5	1	1/15 × $3,000	200	3,000	3,500	500
	15		$ 3,000			

Exhibit 4 presents a depreciation schedule that illustrates the effect of the sum-of-the-years-digits depreciation over the useful life of the asset.

The previous computations assume that the asset was purchased at the beginning of the year. It is common for assets to be purchased throughout a year. If the sum-of-the-years-digits method is used, additional computations are necessary for any asset not purchased at the beginning of the year.

For example, assume that the equipment item was acquired on May 1. This means the asset will be in use for only 8 months in the first accounting period; therefore, only $8/12$ of the first year's depreciation calculation is allowed. In the second accounting year, the remaining $4/12$ of the first year's calculation is added to $8/12$ of the second year's calculation. A similar pattern is used for each accounting year during the asset's life. Exhibit 5 illustrates this procedure.

Comparison of Time-Factor Methods

The straight-line, double declining balance, and sum-of-the-years-digits methods are used to compute depreciation expense for financial accounting purposes. Exhibit 6 compares the results of these three time-factor methods for computing annual depreciation expense. The comparison is based on the preceding examples (depreciation for equipment purchased at the beginning of a year for $3,500, with an estimated salvage value of $500 and a useful life estimated at five years). Note that regardless of which depreciation method is used, the total depreciation expense amounts to $3,000 and the book value of the asset never falls below the asset's estimated salvage value. However, the methods differ in terms of the depreciation amounts computed for individual years.

The straight-line method results in equal depreciation charges each year of the asset's estimated useful life. The declining balance method and the sum-of-the-years-digits are called **accelerated depreciation methods** because they result in the highest depreciation charges in the first year, with lower and lower charges in successive years. These accelerated methods allocate the largest portion of an asset's depreciable cost to the early years of the asset's estimated useful life. As reflected in Exhibit 6, the double declining balance method generally results in the highest depreciation expense for the early years of an asset's estimated useful life.

Exhibit 5   Sum-of-the-Years-Digits Depreciation Method—Additional Computations

Year	Allocation	Carryover	Allowable Depreciation (Rounded)
20X1:	8/12 × $1,000		$ 667
	4/12 × $1,000	$ 333	
	Depreciation expense for 20X1		$ 667
20X2:	4/12 carryover		$ 333
	8/12 × $800		533
	4/12 × $800	$ 267	
	Depreciation expense for 20X2		$ 866
20X3:	4/12 carryover		$ 267
	8/12 × $600		400
	4/12 × $600	$ 200	
	Depreciation expense for 20X3		$ 667
20X4:	4/12 carryover		$ 200
	8/12 × $400		$ 267
	4/12 × $400	$ 133	
	Depreciation expense for 20X4		$ 467
20X5:	4/12 carryover		$ 133
	8/12 × $200		133
	4/12 × $200	$ 67	
	Depreciation expense for 20X5		$ 266
20X6:	4/12 carryover		$ 67
Total depreciation over life of asset			$3,000

Exhibit 6   Comparison of Depreciation Methods

	Straight-Line	Double Declining Balance	Sum-of-the-Years-Digits
Acquisition Cost	$3,500	$3,500	$3,500
Depreciation: Year			
1	$ 600	$1,400	$1,000
2	600	840	800
3	600	504	600
4	600	256	400
5	600	0	200
Total	$3,000	$3,000	$3,000
Book Value	$ 500	$ 500	$ 500

Depreciation for Partial Periods

The previous illustration of time-factor methods assumed that assets were purchased on the first day of the month. Of course, asset transactions may occur throughout a month. When these transactions occur, it is not necessary to carry depreciation precisely to the day or even the month because depreciation, after all, is not an exact science. The salvage value and the useful life used in depreciation calculations are not actual measurements, but simply estimates.

When an asset is purchased and a time-factor method is used to compute depreciation, company policy may state how depreciation for partial periods is to be determined. The following discussion presents possible options for depreciation involving partial periods.

Recognizing Depreciation to the Nearest Whole Month. Using this option, assets purchased from the 1st to the 15th of the month are depreciated as if they were purchased on the 1st of the current month. Any assets purchased from the 16th to the end of the month are treated as if they were purchased on the 1st of the following month.

Conversely, any assets sold from the 1st to the 15th of the month are not depreciated for that month. Any assets sold from the 16th to the end of the month are depreciated for the month.

Recognizing Depreciation to the Nearest Whole Year. Using this option, assets acquired during the first six months of the accounting year are considered held for the entire year. Assets acquired during the last six months are not depreciated in that accounting year.

Conversely, assets sold during the first six months of the accounting year are not depreciated for that year; those sold after the first six months are depreciated for the full year.

Other Options. Other options for depreciation involving partial periods are as follows:

- One-half year's depreciation is recognized on all assets acquired or sold during the year.

- No depreciation is recognized on any acquisitions during the year. Any asset sold during the year receives a full year's depreciation.

- A full year's depreciation is recognized on any acquisitions during the year. Any assets sold during the year receive no depreciation.

Productive-Output Method

This use-factor method allocates the depreciable cost of an asset on the basis of the asset's estimated useful output. When an asset is purchased, an estimate of its useful output is made. As expressed by the following formula, the cost of the asset minus its estimated salvage value is divided by its estimated useful output to arrive at depreciation per unit of output (unit depreciation factor):

$$\text{Unit Depreciation Factor} = \frac{\text{Cost} - \text{Salvage Value}}{\text{Estimated Useful Output}}$$

Depreciation expense is determined by multiplying the unit depreciation factor by the actual output of the asset during the depreciation period. This continues until the accumulated depreciation is the same as the asset's depreciable basis (cost minus salvage value).

Hospitality businesses may use the productive-output method to compute depreciation expense for vehicles. For example, assume that a vehicle is purchased for $25,000. The estimated output of the vehicle is 100,000 miles and its salvage value is estimated at $5,000. The unit depreciation factor is computed as follows:

$$\text{Unit Depreciation Factor} = \frac{\text{Cost} - \text{Salvage Value}}{\text{Estimated Useful Output}}$$

$$\text{Unit Depreciation Factor} = \frac{\$25,000 - \$5,000}{100,000 \text{ miles}}$$

$$\text{Unit Depreciation Factor} = 20\text{¢ per mile}$$

Assuming that the vehicle has traveled 1,500 miles in the current accounting month, the depreciation expense for the month would be $300 (1,500 miles times 20¢ per mile).

Depreciation of China, Glassware, and Silver

China, glassware, and silver may be depreciated using any of the depreciation methods presented earlier. However, no depreciation expense account or accumulated depreciation account is used to record the allocated acquisition costs of these assets. When depreciation is computed, the China, Glassware, and Silver asset account is directly reduced by the computed amount and the depreciation charge is made to the China, Glassware, and Silver expense account. The entry to record computed depreciation is as follows:

China, Glassware, and Silver (expense account)	xxx	
China, Glassware, and Silver (asset account)		xxx

The *Uniform System of Accounts for the Lodging Industry (USALI)* recommends that the initial purchase cost of china, glassware, and silver (and also uniforms and linen) be capitalized and then depreciated over a short period of time. Further, it states that all replacement purchases should be expensed.

For example, assume that a new restaurant purchases its original supply of china, glassware, and silver on April 1 at a cost of $9,000. The useful life is estimated at five years and the salvage value is estimated at $3,600. Assume further that straight-line depreciation has been selected to depreciate the acquisition cost.

The journal entry to record the purchase is as follows:

China, Glassware, and Silver (asset account)	9,000	
Cash (or Accounts Payable)		9,000

One month's depreciation is computed as follows:

$$\text{Monthly Depreciation Expense} = \frac{\text{Cost} - \text{Salvage Value}}{\text{Months of Useful Life}}$$

$$\text{Monthly Depreciation Expense} = \frac{\$9,000 - \$3,600}{60 \text{ Months}} = \underline{\underline{\$90}}$$

On April 30, the adjusting entry to record depreciation for the month is as follows:

China, Glassware, and Silver (expense account)	90	
China, Glassware, and Silver (asset account)		90

Since the restaurant has chosen to expense any replacements, these replacements do not affect the depreciation calculation for the life of this asset. For example, the purchase of replacements is recorded as follows:

China, Glassware, and Silver (expense account)	xxx	
Cash (or Accounts Payable)		xxx

For the purpose of illustration, the depreciations of china, glassware, and silver were combined. Since these assets may have different salvage values and depreciation periods, they may require separate computations.

Amortization of Leaseholds and Leasehold Improvements

Amortization is a means of allocating the costs of certain intangible assets to those periods that benefit from their use. Intangible assets are long-lived assets that are useful to a business but have no physical substance. Financial accounting rules require that certain intangible assets be amortized over their useful lives, with a maximum amortization period of 40 years. The useful life of some intangible assets may be limited by law, competition, or contract, in which case the amortization period may be less than the 40 years allowable under generally accepted accounting principles.

Unlike depreciation, amortization does not require an accumulated account for expense. The usual accounting entry for amortization is a debit to amortization expense and a credit directly to the asset account. Some accountants will credit an accumulated amortization account instead of reducing the basis of the asset, but this practice is not prevalent.

Examples of assets that are amortized are leaseholds, leasehold improvements, and certain types of intangible assets. According to *USALI*, leaseholds and leasehold improvements are classified as Property and Equipment on the balance sheet.

Leaseholds

The rights granted by a lease to the lessee (tenant or user) are called a **leasehold**. In addition to the periodic payments, some long-term leases require the lessee to make a substantial payment at the inception of the lease. This initial payment (if it is not a rental deposit) is recorded to a noncurrent asset account called Leasehold. The payment is amortized over the life of the lease for a period not to exceed 40 years.

For example, assume that on June 1 a hotel leases property for a 20-year period and makes an initial payment of $120,000 that is not considered a rental or security deposit. This payment is recorded as follows:

Leasehold	120,000	
Cash		120,000

The noncurrent asset account Leasehold is amortized over 20 years at the rate of $6,000 per year ($120,000 divided by 20 years). Therefore, the monthly amortization expense is $500 ($6,000 divided by 12 months). On June 30, the month-end entry is as follows:

Amortization Expense	500	
Leasehold		500

Sometimes a lease agreement requires an advance payment of the monthly rents. If the advance payments cover a period of one year or less, they are charged to Prepaid Rent and allocated to the proper accounting periods.

Security deposits are not classified as leaseholds; these deposits are recorded to a noncurrent asset that may be called Deposits or Security Deposits. These deposits remain on the books until refunded.

Leasehold Improvements

Any improvements made to leased property generally revert to the landlord (lessor) upon termination of the lease. Accordingly, the tenant (lessee) should record such improvements to a Leasehold Improvements account. Examples of leasehold improvements are expansion of a leased building, permanent partitions, or installation of any material fixtures that become a permanent part of the building.

A leasehold improvement should be amortized over its estimated useful life or over the remaining term of the lease (including renewal options that are highly likely to be exercised), whichever is shorter. However, the amortization period should not exceed 40 years.

Sale or Disposal of Property and Equipment

A business may sell its assets and receive cash from the transaction, or it may dispose of certain assets and receive no value in return. The gain or loss associated with such transactions is computed on the book value. As explained previously, the book value of an asset is the asset's cost less its accumulated depreciation. The book value of a fully depreciated asset with no salvage value would be zero, since its accumulated depreciation would equal its cost. The following sections explain how to account for the gain or loss on the sale of an asset.

Sale at a Price Above Book Value. Assume that equipment is sold for $2,000. Its original cost is $10,000 and its accumulated depreciation at the date of sale is $8,500. The gain is computed as follows:

Selling price	$2,000
Book value ($10,000 − $8,500)	1,500
Gain on disposal	$ 500

The entry to record the disposal of the equipment is as follows:

Cash	2,000	
Accumulated Depreciation—Equipment	8,500	
Equipment		10,000
Gain on Disposal of Equipment		500

Accumulated depreciation is a contra-asset account with a normal credit balance. It is credited with each period's computation of depreciation. When an asset is sold, it is necessary to remove all accumulated depreciation related to that asset with a debit entry. In the same entry, the asset account Equipment is credited to remove the original cost of the disposed asset from this account.

Sale at a Price Below Book Value. If the same asset had been sold for $1,200, the loss would be computed as follows:

Selling price	$1,200
Book value ($10,000 − $8,500)	1,500
Loss on disposal	$ 300

The entry to record the disposal of this asset would be as follows:

Cash	1,200	
Accumulated Depreciation—Equipment	8,500	
Loss on Disposal of Equipment	300	
Equipment		10,000

Sale at a Price Equal to Book Value. If the same asset had been sold for $1,500, there is neither a gain nor a loss:

Selling price	$1,500
Book value ($10,000 − $8,500)	1,500
Difference	$ 0

The entry to record the disposal of this asset would be as follows:

Cash	1,500	
Accumulated Depreciation—Equipment	8,500	
Equipment		10,000

Trade-In of Property and Equipment

New assets may be acquired by trading in old assets. Transportation equipment trade-ins are common in the hospitality industry. Accounting for trade-ins depends on the fair market value of the assets involved in the transaction. For our purposes, the basis for evaluating gain or loss on the trade-in of property and equipment will be the fair market value of the newly acquired asset.

Although uncommon, it is possible for a hospitality firm making a trade-in to receive cash (also called boot) in the transaction. This occurs when the asset traded in has a fair market value greater than the asset acquired. Whenever boot (cash) is involved, special procedures are necessary in computing gain or loss.

These procedures are beyond the scope of our discussion; interested readers are referred to intermediate accounting texts for specific explanations.

Trade-ins may involve the exchange of like-kind assets or the exchange of dissimilar assets. The trade-in of one automobile for another is an example of an exchange of like-kind assets. The trade-in of an automobile for a computer is an example of an exchange of dissimilar assets. The following sections address accounting for gain or loss on each of these types of exchanges.

Exchange of Like-Kind Assets

Certain types of depreciable assets, such as vehicles, computers, copying machines, and other equipment items, are customarily traded in for new assets of the same kind (like-kind). For example, the exchange of a van for another van is considered an exchange of like-kind assets. According to accounting rules, when a book gain results from the exchange of like-kind assets, the gain is not recognized through an entry involving a general ledger revenue account. Instead, the acquisition cost of the newly acquired asset is reduced by the amount of the book gain. However, when a material book loss results from the exchange of like-kind assets (due to a trade-in allowance that is substantially below the book value of the asset), the book loss must be recognized. The following sections explain these accounting rules and procedures in greater detail.

Nonrecognition of Book Gain. A book gain is not recognized when it results from an exchange of like-kind assets for two reasons:

1. It is difficult to objectively measure the realistic book gain because the list price of the asset to be acquired may be set artificially high, allowing the dealer to grant an inflated trade-in allowance.

2. The substitution of like-kind assets should not be a means of generating income.

For these reasons, no book gain is realized when a depreciable asset is traded in for another like-kind asset. Any computed gain is used to reduce the cost basis of the newly acquired asset. For example, assume that old equipment with an original cost of $10,000 and accumulated depreciation of $8,500 is traded in for similar equipment. The new equipment has a list price of $14,000 and the dealer grants a trade-in allowance of $2,000 on the old equipment. The balance of $12,000 is paid in cash. The nonrecognized gain is computed as follows:

Trade-in allowance on old equipment	$2,000
Book value of old equipment ($10,000 − $8,500)	1,500
Nonrecognized gain (to reduce cost basis of new equipment)	$ 500

The cost basis of the new equipment is computed as follows:

List price of new equipment	$14,000
Less: Nonrecognized gain on trade-in of old equipment	500
Recorded cost basis of new equipment	$13,500

The journal entry to record this transaction is as follows:

Equipment (new)	13,500	
Accumulated Depreciation—Equipment (old)	8,500	
Equipment (old)		10,000
Cash		12,000

Another method may be used to determine the cost basis of an asset acquired in a like-kind exchange resulting in a nonrecognition of gain. Using this method, the cost of the acquired asset may be computed as follows:

New Asset Cost = Book Value of Asset Exchanged + Cash Paid Out

This alternate method produces the same results and journal entries as the previous method. Using the information from the previous example, the cost basis of the new equipment would be computed as follows:

Book value of old equipment ($10,000 − $8,500)	$1,500
Add: Cash payment for new equipment	12,000
Cost basis of new equipment	$13,500

Recognition of Book Loss. In financial accounting, a material loss resulting from a trade-in allowance substantially below book value must be recognized. For example, assume that old equipment with an original cost of $10,000 and accumulated depreciation of $8,500 is traded in for similar equipment. The new equipment has a list price of $14,000 and the dealer grants a trade-in allowance of $1,200 on the old equipment, which has a book value of $1,500. The balance of $12,800 is paid in cash. The recognized loss is computed as follows:

Trade-in allowance on old equipment	$1,200
Book value of old equipment ($10,000 − $8,500)	1,500
Recognized loss	$ 300

The journal entry to record this transaction is as follows:

Equipment (new)	14,000	
Accumulated Depreciation—Equipment (old)	8,500	
Loss on Disposal of Equipment	300	
Equipment (old)		10,000
Cash		12,800

A small loss (as defined by management) may be accounted for in a manner similar to that described for the exchange of assets under tax rules, which is discussed later in this chapter.

Exchange of Dissimilar Assets

Examples of exchanges involving dissimilar assets are the exchange of equipment for a vehicle, or the exchange of inventory for equipment. When dissimilar assets are exchanged, any gain or loss is recognized immediately.

For example, assume that old equipment with an original cost of $10,000 and accumulated depreciation of $8,500 is traded in for supplies inventory. The inventory has a list price of $14,000 and the dealer grants a trade-in allowance of $2,000 on the old equipment. The balance of $12,000 is paid in cash. The recognized gain is computed as follows:

Trade-in allowance on old equipment	$2,000
Book value of old equipment ($10,000 − $8,500)	1,500
Recognized gain	$ 500

The cost basis of the supplies inventory is simply the list price of $14,000, assuming that this is the fair market value. The journal entry to record the transaction is as follows:

Inventory	14,000	
Accumulated Depreciation—Equipment	8,500	
Equipment		10,000
Cash		12,000
Gain on Disposal of Equipment		500

Sometimes there will be an even exchange of dissimilar assets. An even exchange raises the question, "Which asset represents the more reliable indicator of fair market value?" Assuming the acquired asset offers a more reliable indicator, this asset is recorded at its fair market value (current replacement cost in a market that is fair and reasonable in view of existing conditions); the resulting gain or loss is recognized as the difference between the fair market value of the new asset and the book value of the old asset.

For example, assume that equipment with an original cost of $25,000 and accumulated depreciation of $13,000 is exchanged for a vehicle having a fair market value of $12,500. The recognized gain is computed as follows:

Original cost of equipment traded in	$25,000
Less: Accumulated depreciation	13,000
Book value of equipment traded in	$12,000
Fair market value of vehicle received	12,500
Recognized gain	$ 500

The journal entry to record this transaction is as follows:

Autos and Trucks	12,500	
Accumulated Depreciation—Equipment	13,000	
Equipment		25,000
Gain on Disposal of Equipment		500

Tax Accounting for Exchange of Assets

Financial accounting records are used to prepare income tax returns. However, certain items require special treatment for reporting on tax returns. Exceptions resulting from tax accounting differences are not recorded in the financial records; they are accounted for either on the income tax returns or on supplementary schedules.

Differences between tax accounting and financial accounting affect the treatment of depreciation. A business may use one method of depreciation for financial statements and another method for income tax purposes. This may result in a different book value for an asset, which will affect the gain or loss when this asset is sold or exchanged.

For exchanges of dissimilar assets, the income tax rules are similar to the financial accounting rules. For exchanges of like-kind assets, however, the income tax rules do not allow the recognition of either gain or loss. A nonrecognized gain is treated similarly under both sets of rules, but financial accounting rules require the immediate recognition of any material loss. Tax accounting requires that any loss on a like-kind exchange be used to adjust the cost basis of the newly acquired asset.

For example, assume that old equipment with an original cost of $10,000 and accumulated depreciation of $8,500 is traded in for similar equipment. The new equipment has a list price of $14,000 and the dealer grants a trade-in allowance of $1,200 on the old equipment. The balance of $12,800 is paid in cash. The computation of nonrecognized loss is as follows:

Trade-in allowance on old equipment	$1,200
Book value of old equipment ($10,000 − $8,500)	1,500
Nonrecognized loss	$ 300

For income tax purposes, the loss is not deductible, but is instead used to increase the asset's cost basis. This adjusted cost, which will be the basis for depreciation, is computed as follows:

Book value of old equipment ($10,000 − $8,500)	$ 1,500
Add: Cash payment for new equipment	12,800
Cost basis of new equipment	$14,300

Another way to compute the cost basis of the new equipment for tax purposes is to add the unrecognized loss ($300) to the list price of the new equipment ($14,000). For income tax purposes, depreciation will be computed on the cost basis of $14,300; thus, the $300 loss will be prorated over the life of the equipment through higher depreciation charges.

In practice, many companies will not enter into a like-kind exchange that will result in a loss. Instead, they will sell the old asset first, then purchase the new asset. In this way, the loss will be deductible for tax purposes. On the other hand, if a like-kind exchange involves a gain, companies will make the trade so that the gain is not recognized or taxed.

The top half of Exhibit 7 summarizes the recognition of gain or loss for exchanges involving like-kind and dissimilar assets, based on Accounting Principles Board Opinion #29. The income tax rules regarding this area are slightly different from those of financial accounting. The bottom half of Exhibit 7 summarizes the income tax rules relating to the recognition of gain or loss for exchanges involving like-kind and dissimilar assets.

Depreciation and Income Taxes

The depreciation methods discussed thus far are supported by generally accepted accounting principles. They are also accepted in the hospitality industry and approved by the FASB. However, the accounting rules established by the FASB may differ from the rules established by the Internal Revenue Service (IRS). In preparing financial statements, hospitality businesses must conform to generally

Exhibit 7 Summary of Rules Relating to Like-Kind and Dissimilar Exchanges

	Financial Accounting	
	Like-Kind exchange	Dissimilar exchange
Gain on exchange	Not recognized, used to reduce basis of new asset	Recognized
Loss on exchange	Recognized	Recognized
	Tax Accounting	
	Like-Kind exchange	Dissimilar exchange
Gain on exchange	Not recognized, used to increase basis of new asset	Recognized
Loss on exchange	Not recognized, used to reduce basis of new asset	Recognized

accepted accounting principles; but, in preparing tax returns, they must follow tax rules and regulations.

Tax laws are complex and frequently change. Tax depreciation methods have changed several times over the last decade. IRS Publication 534 offers detailed information about tax depreciation methods.

Modified Accelerated Cost Recovery System

In the preparation of federal income tax returns, the Internal Revenue Code (IRC) requires that businesses use the straight-line depreciation method or a special accelerated depreciation method called **modified accelerated cost recovery system (MACRS).** MACRS is similar to the declining balance method except that salvage value is not taken into consideration. This means that the book value of an asset is fully depreciated down to zero. The Appendix to this chapter explains MACRS in more detail.

Key Terms

accelerated depreciation method—A depreciation method that produces relatively high depreciation expenses in the early years and smaller amounts in later years. However, at the end of the asset's useful life, total depreciation charges do not exceed the amount that the straight-line method would have produced. The double declining balance and sum-of-the-years-digits methods are both accelerated depreciation methods.

accumulated depreciation—A contra-asset account representing the depreciation on assets from the point at which they were acquired or first put into use until they are sold or disposed of.

capital expenditure—An expenditure recorded to an asset account and not directly to expense.

capital lease—A long-term financing arrangement that grants present or future ownership of the leased property to the lessee.

depreciation—The systematic transfer of part of a tangible long-lived asset's cost to an expense. The asset cost is generally not reduced, but is offset by an entry to the accumulated depreciation account that represents the depreciation recorded on an asset from the point at which it was acquired. Depreciation is usually associated with assets classified as property and equipment, but not with land.

double declining balance method—See accelerated depreciation method.

fixed assets—See property and equipment.

lease—A contract by which the use of property or equipment is granted by the lessor to the lessee.

leasehold—The right to use property or equipment by virtue of a lease.

leasehold improvements—Capital expenditures made by the lessee to improve leased property. The costs of these improvements are recorded in this account because the improvements become part of the leased property and thus revert to the lessor upon the lease's termination.

lessee—The person or company that uses leased property or equipment under the terms of a lease.

lessor—The person or company that leases property or equipment to a lessee.

modified accelerated cost recovery system—An accelerated depreciation method in which the book value of an asset is fully depreciated down to zero.

operating lease—A lease similar to a rental agreement without any appearance of present or future ownership of the leased property by the lessee.

property and equipment—A noncurrent asset category including assets of a relatively permanent nature that are tangible (such as land, buildings, and equipment) and are used in the business operation to generate sales; this category may be referred to as plant assets or fixed assets.

straight-line method—A depreciation method that allocates an equal amount of a depreciable asset's cost over the asset's estimated useful life.

sum-of-the-years-digits method—See accelerated depreciation method.

tangible assets—A business's assets that have physical substance, such as land, buildings, and equipment. Land is the only tangible asset not subject to depreciation because it does not wear out in the normal course of business.

useful life—The time period an asset is expected to be useful in the process of generating revenue for a company. An asset's useful life may be shorter than its actual life expectancy in terms of economic value or utility.

Review Questions

1. How are the following terms defined?
   a. Capital expenditure
   b. Revenue expenditure
   c. Acquisition cost
   d. Tangible asset
   e. Intangible asset

2. What is the major difference between a capital lease and an operating lease?

3. What is the major difference between the Depreciation account and the Accumulated Depreciation account?

4. What are three common time-factor depreciation methods?

5. What three common methods may be used to account for the acquisition and replacement of china, glassware, and silver?

6. Is the gain (or loss) recognized for the following transactions involving like-kind assets?

   a. For financial reporting purposes: a material loss on the exchange
   b. For tax reporting purposes: a loss on the exchange
   c. For financial reporting purposes: a gain on the exchange
   d. For tax reporting purposes: a gain on the exchange

7. Is the gain (or loss) recognized for the following transactions involving dissimilar assets?

   a. For financial reporting purposes: a loss on the exchange
   b. For tax reporting purposes: a loss on the exchange
   c. For financial reporting purposes: a gain on the exchange
   d. For tax reporting purposes: a gain on the exchange

Internet Sites

For more information, visit the following Internet sites. Remember that Internet addresses can change without notice. If the site is no longer there, you can use a search engine to look for additional sites.

Operating Leases
www.investorwords.com/3461/operating_lease.html

Operating Lease vs. Capital Lease
http://pages.stern.nyu.edu/~adamodar/New_Home_Page/AccPrimer/lease.htm

Depreciation—What Does it Mean?
www.bizhelp24.com/accounting/depreciation---what-does-it-mean.html

IRS Publication 946: How to Depreciate Property
www.irs.gov/publications/p946/index.html

FASB Statement 142: Amortization of Goodwill and Other Intangible Assets
www.fasb.org/st/summary/stsum142.shtml

IRS Publication 544: Sales and Other Dispositions of Assets
www.irs.gov/publications/p544/index.html

Problems

Problem 1

Compute the land acquisition cost from the following information:

Purchase price: $150,000

Legal fees: $1,500

Brokerage fees: $15,000

Site grading: $28,000

Delinquent taxes paid by buyer: $7,000

Removal of existing building: $12,000

Salvage proceeds from scrap of existing building: $2,000

Problem 2

Land and a building are purchased for a lump sum price of $500,000. According to county tax records, the real estate is appraised as follows: land, $99,000; building, $341,000. What cost basis will be entered in the general ledger for the land and the building?

Problem 3

An asset's cost is $10,000; its salvage value is estimated at $2,000; and its useful life is estimated at four years. Using each of the following depreciation methods, compute the depreciation, accumulated depreciation, and book value for each year of this asset's estimated useful life.

a. Straight-line method

b. Declining balance method using a double declining rate

c. Sum-of-the-years-digits method

Problem 4

A depreciation policy of the hospitality business in this example is to recognize depreciation to the nearest whole month. Compute the straight-line depreciation of the first and second months for the following assets:

	Date Acquired	Cost	Salvage Value	Useful Life Years
Asset A	3/15	$11,100	$1,500	8
Asset B	5/18	11,100	1,500	8

Problem 5

Journalize the following transactions:

   a. Depreciation on the building is $1,300.

   b. Depreciation on china and glassware is $275.

   c. Amortization of the leasehold is $300.

Problem 6

A truck is sold outright for $4,500. The financial records show that its cost was $12,500 and accumulated depreciation to the date of sale was $6,000. Journalize the entry to record the disposal of this asset. Trucks are recorded in an asset account called Transportation Equipment.

Problem 7

Journalize the entry for Problem 6 if the truck's accumulated depreciation to the date of sale was $9,200.

Problem 8

Journalize the entry for Problem 6 if the truck's accumulated depreciation to the date of sale was $8,000.

Problem 9

A computer with an original cost of $17,000 and accumulated depreciation of $15,000 is traded in for a new computer with a list price of $25,000. The dealer grants a trade-in allowance of $4,800 on the old computer. The balance of $20,200 is paid with $2,200 cash and a note for the balance. Journalize this transaction in accordance with generally accepted accounting principles. Computers are recorded in an asset account called Computer Equipment.

Problem 10

Journalize the entry for Problem 9 if the computer's accumulated depreciation was $10,000.

Problem 11

A computer with an original cost of $17,000 and accumulated depreciation of $15,000 is traded in for a new van with a list price of $25,000. The dealer grants a trade-in allowance of $4,800 on the old computer. The balance of $20,200 is paid with $2,200 cash and a note for the balance. Journalize this transaction in accordance with generally accepted accounting principles. Computers are recorded in the Computer Equipment account, and vans are recorded in the Transportation Equipment account.

Problem 12

Journalize the entry for Problem 11 if the computer's accumulated depreciation was $10,000.

Case Study

Rationale for Leasing, and the Effect of Operating and Capital Leases

The Hotel Opulent Corporation is a large multi-chain hotel company with hotels in over 40 locations. The company owns all locations; none are franchised. This prosperous company owes part of its success to the excellence of its furnishings and equipment, which are replaced with quality items at regular intervals so that the hotel's guests never suffer old or worn-out furnishings.

The new chief executive of the Hotel Opulent Corporation has reviewed a listing of various assets that include date of purchase and the auditor's opinion of quality. A meeting of corporate executives is planned. Hotel management, sales, and financial personnel will attend. The financial VP will conduct the meeting in an advisory capacity. The Hotel Opulent has never leased any furnishings, vehicles, or equipment.

The assets due for replacement are guestroom televisions sets, lobby furniture, and limousines at all 40 locations, consisting of hotels with room occupancy of 200 to 500 rooms. Each hotel has three to six limousines to provide a high level of customer service.

The financial VP is preparing a presentation on purchasing versus leasing. The presentation will educate the meeting participants so that they can decide in the best interests of operational quality, customer service, and financial reporting to stockholders.

Challenge

1. In one sentence, define a lease.

2. In one sentence, identify and define the parties to a lease.

3. Explain the basic difference between an operating lease and a capital lease.

4. Explain the accounting treatment of an operating lease and a capital lease, and explain the effect each lease has on the financial statements.

5. Explain the economic rationale (operational and financial) for an operating lease instead of an asset purchase.

6. Identify what an operating lease conceals on the balance sheet.

Appendix

Modified Accelerated Cost Recovery System (MACRS)

MACRS Rules

MACRS rules generally apply to tangible property placed in service after 1986. Property that cannot be depreciated using MACRS includes:

- Intangible property
- Motion picture film or videotape
- Sound recordings
- Property placed in service before 1987
- Property that the taxpayer chooses to exclude from MACRS because its depreciation method is not based on a term of years

Property Classes and Recovery Periods

Under MACRS, property is assigned to one of several property classes. Property classes designate the useful life (recovery period) of depreciable assets. Some examples of property classes are:

- **3-year property:** small tools, tractors
- **5-year property:** automobiles, computers, office machinery such as typewriters, calculators, and copiers
- **7-year property:** desks, files, safes, office furniture
- **10-year property:** vessels, barges, tugs
- **15-year property:** shrubbery, fences, roads, bridges
- **31.5-year property:** nonresidential real estate placed in service before May 13, 1993
- **39-year property:** nonresidential real estate placed in service after May 12, 1993

Conventions

Assets may be purchased throughout the year; therefore, depreciation calculations generally cannot be performed for an entire year unless an asset was purchased at the beginning of a tax year. The term "convention" describes a company's standard practice for treating depreciable assets purchased during the year.

The most common convention is the half-year convention. The half-year convention treats all property placed in service or disposed of during a tax year as placed in service or disposed of at the midpoint of that tax year. This means that in the year of purchase, a half year of depreciation expense is taken; when the asset is disposed of, another half year of depreciation expense is taken.

For example, an asset purchased on February 10 would have a half year of depreciation expense in the year of purchase. In subsequent years, a full year of depreciation expense would be taken. In the year of disposition, only a half year of depreciation expense would be allowed regardless of the month of disposition.

The same would be true for an asset purchased in December (assuming it is the last month of a tax year). In the year of purchase, a half year of depreciation expense would be taken. In subsequent years a full year of depreciation expense would be taken. If the asset were to be sold in January of a subsequent year, a half year of depreciation expense would be allowed for that year.

Calculating MACRS Depreciation

Depreciation expense is computed based on the tax basis (which is usually the cost) of a tangible asset. The straight-line method can be used for any property class. Other depreciation methods allowable for certain property classes under MACRS are:

- 200 percent declining balance method

- 150 percent declining balance method

Salvage values are ignored in calculating depreciation under MACRS. A depreciable asset is depreciated down to zero at the end of its recovery period.

MACRS Tables

The Internal Revenue Service (IRS) provides MACRS percentage tables that businesses can use instead of performing depreciation calculations. These tables are categorized by property recovery period and convention (half-year, mid-quarter, mid-month). IRS Publication 534 provides a complete set of MACRS tables.

For example, a 3-year recovery period, half-year convention table would provide the following depreciation percentages:

Year	Rate
1	33.33%
2	44.45%
3	14.81%
4	7.41%

Note that all the percentages for the recovery period add up to 100 percent; thus the asset is fully depreciated, leaving no salvage value. The four years in which the asset depreciates allow for the half-year convention. For a 3-year recovery period, the percentages have been computed using the 200 percent declining balance method.

To illustrate the use and effect of MACRS, the following example is provided.

Assume that assorted small tools amounting to $1,000 for the maintenance department of a new hotel are purchased in March of the current year.

Small tools are classified as 3-year recovery property. This hotel uses the half-year convention for all its depreciable assets.

Using the 3-year recovery period, half-year convention table, the depreciation expense over the life of this asset is computed as follows:

Year	Computation	Depreciation
1 (year of purchase)	(33.33% × $1,000)	$ 333
2	(44.45% × $1,000)	$ 445
3	(14.81% × $1,000)	$ 148
4	(7.41% × $1,000)	$ 74
Total		$1,000

Chapter 4 Outline

Intangible Assets
    Organization Costs
    Goodwill
    Franchises
    Trademarks and Tradenames
    Patents
    Copyrights
    Preopening Expenses
    Liquor Licenses
Cash Value Intangible Assets
    Security Deposits
    Cash Surrender Value of Life Insurance

Competencies

1. Define intangible assets, and list common intangible assets discussed in this chapter. (pp. 105–107)

2. Define organization costs, and describe how they are amortized. (p. 107)

3. Explain the accounting term "goodwill," and describe how goodwill is amortized. (pp. 107–108)

4. Explain franchise agreements, and describe how the costs of such agreements are amortized. (p. 108)

5. Define trademarks and tradenames, and describe how they are amortized. (p. 109)

6. Compare patents and copyrights, and describe how they are amortized. (pp. 109–110)

7. Define preopening expenses, and contrast them to organization costs. (pp. 110–111)

8. Describe the renewal and purchase of liquor licenses, and explain how their costs are amortized. (p. 111)

9. Define cash value intangible assets using security deposits as an example. (p. 112)

10. Describe the two basic kinds of life insurance, pointing out their similarities and differences. (pp. 112–113)

4

Other Noncurrent Assets Accounting

Long-lived assets that lack physical existence are called **intangible assets.** Some common examples of intangible assets are franchise rights, trademarks, trade-names, goodwill, copyrights, and patents. These intangible assets provide significant benefits to a business and may be a major reason for its success.

The acquisition cost of certain intangible assets is spread over the asset's useful life by the process of amortization. In comparison with the benefits derived from tangible assets such as property and equipment, the benefits derived from intangible assets are less certain and less well-defined. The real value of intangible assets depends on the earning power of the hospitality firm.

Intangible assets such as franchise rights, copyrights, and patents have a definite legal life. Frequently, the economic life of an intangible asset is shorter than its legal life; in such cases, the shorter life is used to compute amortization.

Some intangible assets do not have a limited legal life. For example, purchased goodwill may have a life that is beyond the scope of economic estimation. Generally accepted accounting principles require that the acquisition cost of intangible assets be allocated over a period not to exceed 40 years. Shorter periods are allowed for intangible assets with shorter economic or legal lives.

Sometimes an intangible asset will no longer have any economic value before the conclusion of its legal or useful life. In this case, the cost of the intangible asset should be written off when it is reasonably evident that the asset has become worthless. Some intangible assets continue to have value long after their legal or economic lives. Frequently, management decides that the amortization process will stop when the intangible asset's book value reaches one dollar. In these cases, the intangible asset's value is presented on the balance sheet as one dollar to serve as a reminder of the existence of an important but undervalued intangible asset of the business.

This chapter will address accounting for other noncurrent assets by answering such questions as:

1. How are the various intangible assets defined?

2. How is the acquisition cost of intangible assets determined?

3. How are intangible assets amortized?

4. What is a "covenant not to compete"?

The purpose of this chapter is to present accounting for the acquisition and amortization of intangible assets. The chapter begins by identifying common intangible assets and explains how they are recorded on the balance sheet. Next, each of these intangible assets is defined and the method of accounting for its acquisition and amortization is presented. The final section of the chapter discusses non-amortizable intangible assets such as security deposits, utility deposits, and the cash surrender value of life insurance.

Intangible Assets

Intangible assets are long-lived assets that are useful to a business but have no physical substance. All intangible assets provide benefits over the long term. Some intangible assets provide legal and economic rights by virtue of their ownership. Examples of intangible assets are:

- Organization costs
- Goodwill
- Franchises
- Trademarks and tradenames
- Patents
- Copyrights
- Preopening expenses
- Liquor licenses

Cost is used as the basis for recording intangible assets. Cost represents the acquisition cost of the asset. Some companies may have a valuable tradename or trademark that does not show on the financial records because it is the result of reputation or advertising, rather than a purchase transaction. Although a tradename and/or a trademark may be famous and valuable, neither of these intangible assets is recorded in the financial records or shown on the balance sheet unless an acquisition cost is involved.

Amortization is a means of allocating the costs of intangible assets to those periods that benefit from their use. While amortization and depreciation are similar in purpose, the salvage value of an asset is generally ignored in amortization computations. Also, an accumulated amortization account is generally not used. The amortized amount is generally a debit to amortization expense and a credit directly to the asset account. For example, the entry to amortize purchased goodwill is as follows:

Amortization Expense	xxx	
Goodwill		xxx

Financial accounting rules require that intangible assets be amortized over their useful lives, with a maximum amortization period of 40 years. The useful life of some intangible assets may be limited by law (as in the case of copyrights), by competition (as in the case of patents), or by contract (as in the case of franchise agreements). The useful life as limited by law, competition, or contract is used as the amortization period if it is less than the 40 years allowable under generally accepted accounting principles. However, some intangible assets (such as goodwill, tradenames, and trademarks) may have an indefinite useful life. In these cases, the amortization period may not exceed 40 years.

Long-term assets that cannot be classified as property, equipment, or investments are shown on the balance sheet in a section called Other Assets. This balance sheet section includes intangible assets. Sometimes intangible assets will be classified on the balance sheet as Deferred Charges instead of Other Assets. A deferred charge is an expenditure that will generate benefits over a long-term period and is amortized over its useful life. Deferred charges may include items such as remodeling expenditures, moving expenses, and bond issuance costs.

This chapter makes no distinction between Other Assets and Deferred Charges, since both of these balance sheet classifications are noncurrent assets representing costs that will benefit a business in the long run and are amortized in accordance with generally accepted accounting principles.

Organization Costs

Certain costs are incurred to form a corporation. These costs include state incorporation fees, attorneys' fees, costs of printing stock certificates, and other costs related to the formation of a corporate entity.

These costs of incorporating are recorded to a noncurrent asset account called **Organization Costs** and are amortized over a period not to exceed 40 years. Income tax rules require a minimum amortization period of five years, and many companies choose to amortize organization costs over this five-year period.

For example, assume that the total organization costs for a newly formed corporation were $6,000; the journal entry to record this expenditure is as follows:

Organization Costs	6,000	
Cash		6,000

The monthly amortization of the organization costs can be computed by dividing the cost ($6,000) by 60 months (5 years × 12 months). Therefore, at the end of the first accounting month, the amortization entry is as follows:

Amortization Expense	100	
Organization Costs		100

Goodwill

The term **goodwill** may mean one thing to the general public and quite a different thing to an accountant. The general public usually thinks of goodwill as the excellent reputation that a business has with its customers. To an accountant, goodwill means the potential of a business to earn a rate of return in excess of the average rate of return for similar businesses in that industry. Goodwill is the result of competitive advantages, customer recognition, a favorable location, outstanding management, excellent employee relations, and other factors that a successful company continuously develops.

Goodwill is recorded in the accounting records only if it is purchased. Any goodwill that a firm enjoys because of its reputation based on name recognition, product quality, or other factors is not recorded on the financial statements for accounting purposes. There are many well-known firms that do not show goodwill on their financial statements because it was not purchased in a business transaction.

When a business is purchased, the purchase price should stipulate the portion of the amount paid for assets purchased, for goodwill, and for any covenant not to compete. A covenant not to compete is an agreement by the seller not to operate a similar business in a certain geographical area for a specified number of years.

The *Uniform System of Accounts for the Lodging Industry (USALI)* recommends that goodwill be amortized over the period during which it is expected to benefit the business. Financial accounting standards specify that no intangible asset should be given a life of more than 40 years.

The purchase of goodwill is recorded as follows:

Goodwill	xxx	
Cash (or Notes Payable)		xxx

The monthly entry to amortize goodwill over its useful life is as follows:

Amortization Expense	xxx	
Goodwill		xxx

Franchises

A **franchise** is the exclusive right or privilege granted by the franchisor that allows the franchisee to sell certain services or products in a specified geographical area. A franchise agreement usually stipulates a period of time and establishes the conditions under which the franchise may be revoked. Examples of franchise operations include Ramada Inns, Sheraton Inns, McDonald's, Wendy's, Pizza Hut, and Dunkin' Donuts.

The cost of a franchise right includes the purchase price as well as legal fees and other costs associated with obtaining it. These costs may be substantial. The amortization period is based on the life of the franchise contract, but cannot exceed 40 years. The purchase of a franchise right is recorded as follows:

Franchise	xxx	
Cash (or Notes Payable)		xxx

The monthly entry to amortize the cost of a franchise right over its useful life is as follows:

Amortization Expense	xxx	
Franchise		xxx

A franchise right may be purchased for a lump sum plus periodic payments that may be based on sales volume or other criteria. In these cases, the initial lump sum is capitalized and amortized; the periodic payments are charged to an expense account called Franchise Expense.

Trademarks and Tradenames

The federal government provides legal protection for trademarks and tradenames if they are registered with the United States Patent Office. Once a trademark or tradename is registered, the company retains the right to it as long as it is continuously used. Distinctive trademarks and tradenames may be sold.

The cost of a trademark or tradename consists of the expenditures necessary to develop it as well as the filing and registry fees. If the costs are not material, they may be charged to an expense account. A purchased trademark or tradename is recorded at its purchase price.

Material costs associated with acquiring a trademark or tradename are capitalized to a noncurrent asset account called Trademarks and Tradenames. Even though a trademark or tradename may have an indefinite life, its cost must be amortized over its expected useful life, but for a period not to exceed 40 years. The purchase of a trademark or tradename is recorded as follows:

Trademarks and Tradenames	xxx	
Cash (or Notes Payable)		xxx

The monthly entry to amortize the cost of a trademark or tradename over its useful life is as follows:

Amortization Expense	xxx	
Trademarks and Tradenames		xxx

Patents

A **patent** is an exclusive right granted by the federal government to use, manufacture, sell, or lease a product or design. This right is granted for 17 years. The owner of a patent may sell a patent after it is granted. Patents that are purchased should be capitalized to a noncurrent asset account called Patents if the cost is material. (If the cost is not material, it should be charged to an expense account.) The cost of a patent is amortized over the course of either the 17-year legal life, the remaining years of its legal life, or the estimated useful life—whichever is shortest. The purchase of a patent is recorded as follows:

Patents	xxx	
Cash (or Notes Payable)		xxx

The monthly entry to amortize the cost of a patent over its useful life is as follows:

Amortization Expense	xxx	
Patents		xxx

The cost of a successful legal defense of patent rights may be capitalized to the cost of the patent and amortized over the remaining life of the patent. An unsuccessful defense might indicate that the patent is worthless, suggesting that the legal costs and unamortized patent costs should be expensed.

Copyrights

A **copyright** is an exclusive right granted by the federal government to produce and sell musical, literary, or artistic materials. The period of this right is equal to the life of the author plus 50 years.

The owner of a copyright may sell it after it is granted. Copyrights that are purchased should be capitalized to a noncurrent asset account called Copyrights if the cost is material. (If the cost is not material, it should be charged to expense.) The cost of a copyright is amortized over its useful life, but for a period not to exceed 40 years. The purchase of a copyright is recorded as follows:

Copyrights	xxx	
Cash (or Notes Payable)		xxx

The monthly entry to amortize the cost of a copyright over its useful life is as follows:

Amortization Expense	xxx	
Copyrights		xxx

The cost of a successful legal defense of a copyright may be capitalized to the cost of the copyright and amortized over its remaining life. An unsuccessful defense might indicate the copyright is worthless, suggesting that the legal costs and unamortized copyright costs should be expensed.

Preopening Expenses

Preopening expenses are costs associated with certain business activities that occur before a company is operational. They are sometimes called start-up costs. The following are examples of preopening expenses:

- Market and feasibility studies
- Travel costs for securing suppliers and customers
- Consultation fees
- Employee training costs
- Executive salaries
- Professional services
- Advertisements of the grand opening
- Labor costs associated with preparing for the grand opening

It is important to recognize the difference between organization costs and preopening expenses. While organization costs are expenditures incurred before a corporation legally exists, preopening expenses are expenditures incurred after the formation of a corporate entity but before it opens for business. Exhibit 1 illustrates the progression of a company's expenditures at various stages.

USALI recommends that preopening expenses be amortized over a period not to exceed one year. However, properties that are currently amortizing over a longer period would continue that procedure until the asset is fully amortized.

Exhibit 1   Progression of Business Expenditures

Organization Stage	→	Preopening Stage	→	Operations
• State incorporation fees • Legal fees—incorporation • Stock issuance costs		• Feasibility studies • Expenses prior to opening • Grand-opening advertising		• Sales and ordinary business expenses

Of particular note is that it may be acceptable for properties outside the United States to amortize preopening expenses over a number of years.

Expenditures for preopening expenses are recorded as follows:

Preopening Expenses	xxx	
Cash (or Notes Payable)		xxx

The monthly entry to amortize preopening expenses is as follows:

Amortization Expense	xxx	
Preopening Expenses		xxx

Liquor Licenses

Fees for the renewal of liquor licenses are generally recorded immediately to expense. Substantial annual fees should be recorded to a prepaid asset account. At the end of each month, an adjusting entry is recorded to expense the portion of the asset that has expired.

In some communities, liquor licenses may not be available from the local authority because of quota restrictions. In these cases, a business may have to purchase a liquor license from a current holder. This holder may be currently in business or may hold a license for sale.

In certain instances, liquor licenses have market values of $75,000 or more. Sometimes a company will purchase a going business for the sole purpose of acquiring this business's liquor license and transferring it to another location. In this case, the cost of the liquor license is the total purchase price of the business less any proceeds on the subsequent sale of the property and equipment.

If the acquisition costs of a liquor license are material, they are recorded to a noncurrent asset account; a separate account called Liquor License may be used. The cost is amortized over a period not to exceed 40 years. The purchase of a liquor license is recorded as follows:

Liquor License	xxx	
Cash (or Notes Payable)		xxx

The monthly entry to amortize the cost of the liquor license over its useful life is as follows:

Amortization Expense	xxx	
Liquor License		xxx

Cash Value Intangible Assets

Not all intangible assets are amortized over their useful lives. Some intangible assets represent future sources of cash. For example, when a hotel pays a security deposit to obtain a certain service, the deposit creates an intangible asset. Common intangible assets representing cash values are security deposits and the cash surrender value of life insurance.

Security Deposits

A hospitality operation may be required to pay a security deposit before a landlord will permit occupancy, before a leasing company will allow the use of rented equipment, or before utility companies will render services. These deposits are not an advance payment for occupancy, equipment, or services. A security deposit serves as reimbursement should any damages occur to the property or equipment, or as compensation should the depositor not pay for eventual services. Many utility companies refund a security deposit after one year while others may retain it indefinitely.

Although security deposits have characteristics in common with accounts receivable, they cannot be treated as such because: (1) they may not be collectible for as long as the leasing agreement or utility arrangement remains in effect, or (2) they may be refundable only at the option of the provider of the service. Therefore, security deposits are recorded in a noncurrent asset account and are not amortized. The account remains indefinitely until the deposit is refunded.

Cash Surrender Value of Life Insurance

Two basic kinds of life insurance are term life insurance and whole life insurance. Both provide a payment to the beneficiary if the insured person dies. Term life insurance does not build up any cash value and is worthless if it is canceled or if it is allowed to expire at the end of a specified termination date. On the other hand, whole life insurance (sometimes called permanent insurance) combines death benefits with a cash value. A portion of the premiums paid for whole life insurance is used to build up a cash value. The owner of the policy may redeem the policy for its cash value or may borrow against that value while the policy remains in force. Whole life insurance premiums are significantly higher than those for term life insurance, which is based solely on death benefit coverage. Therefore, if death benefits are the primary consideration, a $100,000 term life insurance policy may be a better buy than a $100,000 whole life policy.

Either the business will own the life insurance policy and be the beneficiary, or the employee will own the policy and have the right to name a beneficiary. When the employee owns the policy, this fringe benefit is an expense of the company. Under income tax rules, term life insurance (not exceeding a specified amount) is not considered compensation to the employee and therefore is not taxable income to the employee. However, whole life insurance provided as a fringe benefit to the employee is taxable income to the employee.

Fringe benefits are a business expense; for instance, any life insurance purchased for employees (who become the owners of these policies) is considered a business expense, not an asset of the business. However, in addition to life insurance purchased as fringe benefits to employees, it is not unusual for a company to insure the lives of its executives and retain ownership of the policies. For tax reporting, insurance premiums on company-owned policies are not a tax-deductible expense; on the other hand, the eventual collection of any death benefit or cash value is not taxable income. For financial reporting, insurance premiums are an expense and any collections are income.

Insurance premiums on company-owned whole life policies are separated into two parts:

1. The portion representing life insurance coverage is an expense.

2. The portion that builds up cash value is an asset.

Most whole life insurance policies provide for the payment of an annual cash dividend. Life insurance policy dividends are not income and should not be confused with dividends from investments. Life insurance policy dividends are really a return of the life insurance premium. In financial accounting, these dividends should be treated as a reduction in insurance expense.

Company-owned whole life insurance premiums may be paid monthly, quarterly, semi-annually, or annually. Any premiums paid in advance are recorded as follows:

Prepaid Insurance	xxx	
Cash		xxx

At the end of each month, an adjusting entry is recorded as follows to expense the portion of the asset that has expired:

Insurance Expense	xxx	
Prepaid Insurance		xxx

Insurance policies generally include a table showing cash values at various stages of the policy's life. The dividends may be guaranteed or stated as an expected dividend based on prior experience. The dividends may be left with the insurance company to accumulate and earn interest. This option will further increase the cash value of the policy.

There are several methods of accounting for the cash value of insurance policies and accounting for dividends. The end result of these methods is that the cash value of the life insurance is recorded as an intangible asset.

Key Terms

amortization—The systematic transfer of the partial cost of an intangible long-lived asset (such as purchased goodwill, franchise rights, trademarks, tradenames, and preopening expenses) to an expense. The asset cost is generally reduced and shown at its remaining cost to be amortized.

copyright—An exclusive right granted by the federal government to reproduce and sell an artistic or published work.

franchise—An agreement by which the franchisee undertakes to conduct a business or sell a product or service in accordance with methods and procedures prescribed by the franchisor; the franchise may encompass an exclusive right to sell a product or service or conduct a business in a specified territory.

goodwill—In simple terms, goodwill is an intangible asset that is recorded if a business is purchased at a price greater than the value of its property and equipment. The difference (or premium) is the amount recorded in goodwill.

intangible assets—Noncurrent assets that do not have physical substance; their value is derived from rights or benefits associated with their ownership. Examples include trademarks, patents, copyrights, purchased goodwill, and purchased franchise rights.

organization costs—Costs incurred before a business is incorporated. These costs include state incorporation fees, attorneys' fees, costs of printing stock certificates, and other costs related to the formation of a corporate entity.

patent—An exclusive right granted by the federal government to use, manufacture, sell, or lease a product or design. The right is granted for 17 years.

preopening expenses—Costs associated with certain business activities that occur before a company is operational. They are sometimes called start-up costs.

Review Questions

1. How are the following intangible assets defined?
    a. Preopening expenses
    b. Franchise cost
    c. Organization cost
    d. Liquor license cost
    e. Goodwill
    f. Covenant not to compete

2. What is the maximum write-off period for organization costs under generally accepted accounting principles?

3. What is the write-off treatment for goodwill under generally accepted accounting principles?

4. What is the major difference between term life insurance and whole life insurance?

5. In accounting for company-owned whole life policies, which of the following are expensed and which are capitalized?
    a. Portion of premium representing life insurance coverage
    b. Portion of premium that builds cash value
    c. Cash dividend earned on insurance policy

Internet Sites

For more information, visit the following Internet sites. Remember that Internet addresses can change without notice. If the site is no longer there, you can use a search engine to look for additional sites.

Errors in Lease & Leasehold Accounting
www.pwc.com/extweb/pwcpublications.nsf/DocID/
    18582BF4FF235E7B85256FA90055E985

FASB Statement 142: Amortization of Goodwill and Other Intangible Assets
www.fasb.org/st/summary/stsum142.shtml

Effect of Goodwill on Financial Statements
www.nysscpa.org/cpajournal/2004/1004/essentials/p30.htm

Goodwill: Pooling of Interest or Purchase
http://beginnersinvest.about.com/cs/investinglessons/l/blles3goodwill.htm

What Are Trademarks?
www.uspto.gov/web/offices/pac/doc/general/whatis.htm

U.S. Patent and Trademark Office
www.uspto.gov/

U.S. Copyright Office (Full Information on Copyrights)
www.copyright.gov/

Problems

Problem 1

Journalize the following expenditures:

    a. Purchase of $50,000 goodwill with cash
    b. Incorporation fees of $3,000
    c. Franchise right of $25,000
    d. Preopening expenses of $40,000

Problem 2

On July 1, goodwill was purchased for $60,000. This expenditure will be written off over 20 years.

    a. Journalize the July 31 adjusting entry.
    b. Journalize the August 31 adjusting entry.

Problem 3

On July 1, a new corporation was formed. The capitalized organization costs of $8,100 are to be written off over five years.

a. Journalize the July 31 adjusting entry.

b. Journalize the August 31 adjusting entry.

Problem 4

A $567 check is issued in payment of the employees' group insurance premium for the month. These policies are not company-owned. Journalize this expenditure.

Problem 5

The Prepaid Life Insurance account for company-owned policies shows a balance of $2,000. Of this balance, $300 represents a buildup of cash value and $800 represents expired premiums. Journalize the adjusting entry.

Problem 6

A $500 check representing an annual cash dividend on company-owned policies is received from the life insurance company. Journalize this transaction.

Case Study

Evaluating a Business Franchise Acquisition

Mike Brady is a graduate of a hospitality college and has worked for large restaurants in several capacities, including middle management. Mike's ambition has always been to run his own company. Mike prefers to have a well-known franchise operation because of the franchisor's quality support and high success rate. Name-brand franchises are costly, and Mike does not have the resources to handle it alone.

Mike has concluded that he will need investors in his business. Typically, investors will demand an ownership interest for their capital. Mike is comfortable with this arrangement and has limited his search for investors to colleagues he can trust. Mike is preparing a presentation to these potential investors. His presentation must cover the basics of franchising, including its advantages and disadvantages.

Challenge

1. Briefly define *franchising, franchise agreement, franchisor, franchisee*.

2. Name some of the services available from a franchisor.

3. Identify some of the benefits of franchising.

4. List some investigative questions the potential investors might ask about the franchisor.

5. List some particulars that might be included in the initial franchise package offered by a franchisor.

6. List any ongoing costs that could be paid to a franchisor.

7. Identify any other concerns the investors might express about the franchise right.

Chapter 5 Outline

The Fair Labor Standards Act (FLSA)
    Computing Time Worked
    Recording Time Worked
The Employer/Employee Relationship
Wages and Salaries
    Gross Pay and Net Pay
    Regular Pay and Overtime Pay
    Calculating Overtime Pay
Payroll Deductions
    Governmental Deductions
    Voluntary Deductions
    Federal Insurance Contributions Act
    Federal Income Tax
    State and City Income Tax
    State Temporary Disability Benefit
       Laws
Employer's Payroll Taxes
    FICA Tax Imposed on Employer
    IRS Form 941
    Unemployment Taxes
    IRS Form 940
    Depositing Payroll Taxes
The Payroll System
    Employee's Earnings Record
    Payroll Register
    Payroll Journal Entries
    Payroll Bank Account
    Computerized Payroll Applications
Payroll Accounting for Tipped Employees
    Service Charges
    Employee Tip Reporting
    FLSA Minimum Wage Rate
    FLSA Tip Credit
    Net Pay of Tipped Employees
    State Wage and Tip Credit Provisions
    Overtime Pay of Tipped Employees
The Eight Percent Tip Regulation
    Operations Affected by the Eight
       Percent Tip Regulation
Tip Shortfall Allocation Methods
    Gross Receipts Method
    Hours Worked Method
Appendix: Special Research Reports

Competencies

1. Describe areas covered under the Fair Labor Standards Act (FLSA) including how time worked is computed and recorded. (pp. 120–122)

2. Define the terms "employer" and "employee." (p. 123)

3. Differentiate the following sets of terms: wages and salaries; gross pay and net pay; and regular pay and overtime pay. (pp. 123–126)

4. Describe two methods of calculating overtime pay. (pp. 126–127)

5. Explain the major types of deductions affecting employee payroll. (pp. 127–130)

6. Describe the payroll taxes imposed on employers and the related forms and procedures. (pp. 130–131)

7. Explain the primary function of a payroll system and some of the forms, records, and procedures required to perform this function. (pp. 132–135)

8. Describe payroll accounting for tipped employees with respect to employee tip reporting, minimum wage, tip credit, net pay, and overtime pay. (pp. 135–137)

9. Explain the purpose of the eight percent tip regulation and its relationship to employee tip reporting. (pp. 138–140)

10. Recognize methods of allocating tip shortfall among directly tipped employees. (pp. 140–144)

Hospitality Payroll Accounting

PAYROLL IS A SIGNIFICANT EXPENSE in a hotel's budget. However, salaries and wages are not the only costs of labor. Additional expenses include payroll taxes and employee benefits. Because total labor costs are the largest single cost in hotel operations, they are a major concern of management and a first choice for cost cutting. However, cutting labor costs may prove self-defeating since a hotel is highly service-intensive. For example, a reduction in staff may produce poor service, which may lead to guest dissatisfaction, lost business, and a bad reputation.

Anyone responsible for human resource functions and/or payroll preparation should be knowledgeable about the most current employment and payroll laws and regulations—federal, state, and, in some cases, local. It is possible for federal and state payroll regulations to differ on the same issue. In this event, as a general rule, the employer must apply those standards, federal or state, that are the most beneficial to the employee. The issue is further complicated by contract law, such as union-negotiated rights. Contract rights prevail over federal and state laws if their provisions are more beneficial to the employee.

Maintaining a current knowledge of these laws is a never-ending effort. Significant changes may occur regarding minimum wages, income tax rates, Social Security taxes, and employment rights. These changes are regulated by both federal and state governments. In addition, certain cities have income tax withholding laws. Violations of payroll laws or labor regulations may bring civil and/or criminal penalties.

This chapter will discuss payroll accounting by addressing such questions as:

1. What are the major federal and state payroll laws?

2. How are weekly wages and annual salaries converted to an hourly rate?

3. How are governmental and voluntary deductions computed?

4. How is net pay for tipped and non-tipped employees computed?

5. What is the eight percent tip allocation regulation?

6. How are tips allocated for a payroll period using either the gross receipts method or the hours worked method?

After discussing the Fair Labor Standards Act (FLSA), the chapter addresses important payroll accounting concepts. Next, typical procedures for calculating time worked and gross pay are presented, followed by a discussion of federal and state payroll laws. The chapter closes with a detailed examination of payroll accounting for tipped employees. Operations and employees affected by the eight percent tip regulation are identified, and examples of tip shortfall allocation are discussed.

The Fair Labor Standards Act (FLSA)

The **Fair Labor Standards Act (FLSA),** commonly known as the federal wage and hour law, covers such areas as equal pay for equal work, child labor, recordkeeping requirements, minimum wage rate, and conditions defining **overtime pay.** The FLSA applies to most hospitality enterprises. However, certain small businesses with exceptionally low sales volumes may be exempt.

In addition to establishing a minimum wage rate, the FLSA requires that all hotel and motel employees covered by this act be paid at the rate of at least one and one-half times their regular hourly rate for all hours worked in excess of 40 hours per week. The FLSA makes no provisions for rest periods or coffee breaks. It also makes no provisions for vacation, holiday, severance, or sick pay. In addition, the FLSA does not require extra pay for work on Saturdays or Sundays.

For example, an employer is not required to pay employees one and one-half times their regular pay for any weekend or holiday hours worked during a week if the total hours worked do not exceed 40. Also, if an employee works 40 hours in a three-day workweek, the employee is not entitled to overtime pay according to FLSA provisions. However, custom, union contracts, and many states have established overtime provisions that are more generous to the employee. In these situations, the FLSA provisions are superseded.

States may have legislation that contradicts standards established by the FLSA. In cases where state and federal laws differ, the law offering the greater benefit to the employee prevails. For example, state laws may set a minimum wage rate that is greater than that set by federal law, and this higher minimum wage rate would prevail. State laws may also have provisions to regulate overtime pay, employee meals and lodging, tips, uniforms, and more.

Investigators stationed across the United States carry out enforcement of the FLSA. Under the FLSA, it is a violation to fire or in any other manner discriminate against an employee for filing a complaint or for participating in a legal proceeding.

The equal-pay provisions of the FLSA prohibit wage differentials between men and women employed in the same establishment performing similar occupations. The Equal Employment Opportunity Commission enforces these provisions, as well as other statutes prohibiting discrimination in employment.

Employers should be mindful of other labor laws in addition to the FLSA. For example, any business dealing with the federal government must be aware of legislation such as the Davis-Bacon Act, the Walsh-Healy Act, and the Service Contract Act.

There are also laws such as the Wage Garnishment Law, the Employee Polygraph Protection Act, the Family and Medical Leave Act, and the Immigration and Naturalization Act.

A complete presentation of labor laws is beyond the scope and purpose of this chapter.

Computing Time Worked

An employee must be paid for any work that is for the benefit of the employer, including productive work or any activity controlled or required by the employer for the employer's benefit. An employee's personal travel time to and from the job is generally not considered time worked. Exceptions apply to travel performed during the workday for the benefit of the employer.

The FLSA does not cover payment for time spent on coffee breaks or rest periods; however, custom, union contracts, or state laws may consider these periods time worked. Meal periods are not considered time worked unless an employee is required to perform some duty during the meal, whether active or inactive, for the benefit of the employer. Changing clothes or washing-up for the employee's own convenience is not considered time worked unless such activities are directly related to the nature of the employee's duties. Training sessions are considered time worked.

The FLSA requires that employees be paid for all time worked, including fractions of an hour. It is not necessary to compute time worked to the nearest minute if an employer adopts a consistent, equitable method of computation. For example, employers may adopt a practice of computing time worked to the nearest five minutes, to the nearest tenth of an hour, or to the nearest quarter of an hour.

The nearest tenth of an hour is based on the decimal system. Each hour is divided into 10 units of six minutes each. Six minutes would be recorded as .1, 12 minutes as .2, and 60 minutes as 1.0 or one hour. In using the decimal system, rounding techniques must be applied. Some companies use conventional rounding techniques and others always round up to the next highest time unit. For example, depending on company policy, seven minutes may be recorded as .1 (conventional rounding) or as .2 (rounding up). For our purposes, the conventional rounding method is used. The following example illustrates how the decimal system is used to compute time worked.

Assume that an employee worked five hours and 20 minutes and that time worked is recorded to the nearest tenth of an hour. The employee's time worked is computed by converting the five hours and 20 minutes into decimals. The five hours converts to 5.0; the 20 minutes converts to .3 (20 minutes divided by 60 minutes equals .3333 hours, or .3 rounded). The employee's total time worked would be recorded as 5.3 hours by conventional rounding.

Recording Time Worked

The FLSA requires that an employer maintain records of the time worked by hourly-paid employees. Time sheets or time cards are used to satisfy this time-keeping requirement. The form of records used depends on the size of a company and the type of payroll periods. Other factors determining the selection of a recordkeeping format are the use of time clocks and computerized systems.

Many businesses use a time card form (Exhibit 1). Entries to this form may be made either manually by designated personnel or mechanically by an electronic time-clock system. When time clocks are used, early arrival or wait time may create a problem. Some time clocks flag any "In" or "Out" times that vary from assigned shift hours. These few seconds or minutes are usually ignored when computing time worked because this time does not match the employees' assigned work hours.

We usually divide the day into two 12-hour periods. For example, 1 o'clock in the morning is 1 A.M. and 1 o'clock in the afternoon is 1 P.M. Another time system considers a day to be one period of 24 consecutive hours, beginning and ending at

Exhibit 1   Sample Employee Time Card

WEEK ENDING _____ 20 _____
Form No. 1212

No.

NAME

DAY	MORNING IN	NOON OUT	NOON IN	NIGHT OUT	EXTRA IN	EXTRA OUT	TOTAL

TOTAL TIME _____ HRS.

RATE _____

TOTAL WAGES FOR WEEK $ _____

midnight. This time system may be called the 24-hour time system, the continental system, or military time. Four digits are used to state time under this system, the first two representing the hour and the next two representing the minutes past the hour.

A simple technique by which to express time in the 24-hour time system is to convert the conventional time by placing a zero in front of any single digit A.M. hour and adding 1200 to any P.M. hour. The minutes are expressed in units of 00 to 59. Examples of converting conventional time to military time are as follows:

1 A.M.	=	0100 hours	1 P.M.	=	1300 hours
2 A.M.	=	0200 hours	2 P.M.	=	1400 hours
5:30 A.M.	=	0530 hours	5:30 P.M.	=	1730 hours
noon	=	1200 hours	midnight	=	2400 hours

The Employer/Employee Relationship

The Internal Revenue Service has issued technical regulations preventing employers from defining workers as independent contractors in order to evade payroll laws and related employer taxes. "Circular E, Employer's Tax Guide,"[1] a publication issued by the Internal Revenue Service, defines an employer/employee relationship that makes an employer subject to existing payroll laws and related employer taxes. An employer is defined as:

> *Generally … a person or organization for whom a worker performs a service as an employee. The employer usually gives the worker the tools and place to work and has the right to fire the worker. A person or organization paying wages to a former employee after the work ends is also considered an employer.*

An employee is defined as:

> *Anyone who performs services … if you, the employer, can control what will be done and how it will be done. This is so even when you give the employee freedom of action. What matters is that you have the legal right to control the method and result of the services.*

Circular E goes on to state that, if an employer/employee relationship exists, it does not matter what the employee is called. That is, it does not matter if the employer chooses to call workers by names other than employees. If an employer/employee relationship exists, workers who are called partners, agents, or independent contractors are *employees*—and the employer is subject to existing payroll laws and related employer taxes.

In addition, Circular E stresses that there are no class distinctions among employees:

> *An employee can be a superintendent, manager, or supervisor. Generally, an officer of a corporation is an employee, but a director is not. An officer who performs no services or only minor ones, and who neither receives nor is entitled to receive pay of any kind, is not considered an employee.*

Any person or organization considered an employer must file Form SS-4 with the Internal Revenue Service requesting an Employer Identification Number (EIN).

Similarly, any employee who is working in an employment covered by Social Security is supposed to have a Social Security card bearing the employee's Social Security account number. If an employer takes on an employee who does not have a Social Security card and number, according to the Federal Insurance Contributions Act (FICA), the employee is required to apply for an account number by filing Form SS-5 with the nearest District Office of the Social Security Administration.

Wages and Salaries

The terms "wages" and "salaries" are often used interchangeably. The term **wages** usually applies to payrolls computed on an hourly, weekly, or piecework basis. However, a fixed weekly pay may be called a **salary.** The term "salaries" usually applies to payrolls that are paid monthly, bimonthly, biweekly, or annually.

Generally, qualified supervisors and executives who receive a fixed amount each pay period (regardless of the number of hours worked) are considered salaried employees.

An employee who is paid a salary may or may not be paid for overtime hours worked. However, an employer cannot arbitrarily designate a salaried employee as exempt from overtime pay. Federal and state regulations must be satisfied in order to classify an employee as exempt from provisions regarding overtime pay. Under federal law, there are four types of exemptions from the overtime provisions of the Fair Labor Standards Act: executive, administrative, professional, and outside sales. In the hospitality industry, the most often used exemption is the executive exemption (although the administrative exemption sometimes applies to certain positions). Under the executive exemption, the employee's duties and salary must satisfy the following conditions:

1. The employee's primary duty must be that of managing.
2. The employee must customarily and regularly direct the work of a specified number of employees.
3. The employee can hire, fire, and suggest changes in the status of other employees.
4. The employee may exercise discretionary powers.
5. The employee's salary must be over an amount specified by law.

Gross Pay and Net Pay

Gross pay includes all of an employee's regular pay, overtime pay, commissions, and bonuses—before any payroll deductions. Gross pay may be calculated weekly, biweekly, bimonthly, monthly, daily, or over some other time period.

Salaried employees exempt from overtime do not require any special computation for gross pay because they are paid a fixed amount regardless of the actual number of hours worked. Tipped employees, on the other hand, require a special payroll computation, which is addressed in detail later in this chapter.

Net pay is the actual amount of an employee's paycheck. Net pay is the result of subtracting governmental and voluntary deductions from gross pay. Exhibit 2 illustrates a typical computation of net pay.

Regular Pay and Overtime Pay

The definition of regular pay varies because of different state laws, company policies, and contracts. However, under the FLSA, regular pay is based on a 40-hour workweek. The term "regular hourly rate" refers to the rate per hour that is used to compute regular pay.

The definition of overtime pay also varies because of different state laws, company policies, and contracts. According to the FLSA, overtime pay is required for any hours worked in excess of 40 hours in a week. The term "overtime hourly rate" refers to the rate per hour used to compute overtime pay. According to FLSA provisions, overtime is paid at the rate of 1.5 times the employee's regular hourly rate. The FLSA prescribes this rate regardless of the number of overtime hours worked and regardless of whether the overtime hours were worked on a weekend or on a legal holiday.

Exhibit 2   Computation of Net Pay

Gross Pay		$500.00
Less:		
FICA	$38.25	
FIT	89.00	
SIT	22.75	
TDI	7.90	
Union Dues	10.00	
Health Insurance	15.00	
TOTAL DEDUCTIONS		182.90
Net Pay (amount of check)		$317.10

In order to calculate the overtime pay for some employees, it may first be necessary to convert either a weekly wage or a monthly salary to an hourly rate.

Converting a Weekly Wage to an Hourly Rate. Some employees are hired at a stated weekly wage. This wage is generally fixed except for overtime pay and adjustments for absences. For these employees, it is often necessary to convert the weekly wage to a regular hourly rate. These calculations may require rounding. Actual practice varies as to the number of decimal places used in calculating a regular hourly rate. For our purposes, all hourly rates are rounded to the nearest cent.

The regular hourly rate is computed by dividing the weekly wage by the number of hours in a regular 40-hour workweek. For example, assume that an employee is hired at $320.00 per week for a regular workweek. The regular hourly rate for this employee is calculated as follows:

$$\text{Regular Hourly Rate} = \frac{\text{Weekly Wage}}{\text{No. of Hours in Regular Workweek}}$$

$$\text{Regular Hourly Rate} = \frac{\$320.00}{40 \text{ hours}} = \$8.00$$

Once an employee's regular hourly rate is known, an overtime hourly rate can be determined. Following FLSA provisions, overtime is paid at the rate of 1.5 times the employee's regular hourly rate. Therefore, the overtime hourly rate is simply 1.5 times the regular hourly rate:

$$\text{Overtime Hourly Rate} = \text{Regular Hourly Rate} \times 1.5$$
$$\text{Overtime Hourly Rate} = \$8.00 \times 1.5 = \$12.00$$

Converting a Monthly Salary to an Hourly Rate. As stated previously, some salaried employees may not be exempt from overtime pay. Therefore, it may be necessary to calculate an overtime hourly rate for some salaried employees. Since the number of pay weeks (and, therefore, the number of hours worked) varies from month to month, it is first necessary to annualize the monthly salary and then convert it to a weekly amount. Once the weekly amount is determined, the regular hourly rate and the overtime hourly rate can be computed by following the same procedure as in converting a weekly wage to an hourly rate.

For example, assume that an employee is hired at a monthly salary of $2,000.00 and that the employee is not exempt from overtime pay provisions. First, the monthly salary is annualized by multiplying the monthly salary by 12 months. Then, the weekly regular pay of the employee is calculated by dividing the annual salary figure by 52 weeks. These computations are summarized as follows:

$$\text{Annualized Salary} \ = \ \$2,000.00 \ \times \ 12 \ = \ \$24,000.00$$

$$\text{Weekly Rate} \quad = \quad \frac{\$24,000.00}{52} \ = \ \$461.54$$

The regular and overtime hourly rates of the salaried employee can now be determined by following the same procedure as in converting a weekly wage to a regular hourly rate.

$$\text{Regular Hourly Rate} \quad = \quad \frac{\$461.54}{40 \text{ hours}} \ = \ \$11.54$$

$$\text{Overtime Hourly Rate} \ = \ \$11.54 \ \times \ 1.5 \ = \ \$17.31$$

Calculating Overtime Pay

Two methods with which to compute an employee's overtime pay are the *overtime pay method* and the *overtime premium method*. These methods produce identical results with respect to gross pay. The major difference is in the classification of regular pay and overtime pay. According to the overtime pay method, all overtime hours are classified as overtime pay. According to the overtime premium method, overtime hours are separated into regular pay and overtime premium pay.

Overtime Pay Method. The overtime pay method computes overtime pay by multiplying the number of overtime hours by the employee's overtime hourly rate. In a state where FLSA provisions prevail, overtime hours are those hours worked in excess of 40 hours in a week. Using the overtime pay method, hours worked up to this 40-hour limit are the basis for computing regular pay. Any hours worked over the 40-hour limit are the basis for computing overtime pay.

Using the overtime pay method and assuming that FLSA provisions prevail, the gross pay for an employee is calculated by: (1) computing the employee's regular pay, (2) computing the employee's overtime pay, and (3) totaling the employee's regular and overtime pay. For example, assume that an employee receives a regular hourly rate of $8 and reports time worked of 46 hours. Using the overtime pay method, regular pay is computed on a basis *not to exceed 40 hours*. Multiplying 40 hours by the hourly rate of $8 results in $320 regular pay.

The employee's overtime pay is computed by first determining the employee's overtime hourly rate and then multiplying the overtime hourly rate by the number of overtime hours. Under the FLSA provisions used in this example, the employee's overtime hourly rate is $12 (1.5 times the regular hourly rate of $8). Since the employee worked 6 hours in excess of the 40-hour limit for regular pay, the employee's overtime pay is $72 (6 overtime hours multiplied by the $12 overtime hourly rate). The employee's gross pay can now be determined as follows:

Regular Pay (40 hours × $8)	$320.00
Overtime Pay (6 hours × $12)	72.00
Gross Pay	$392.00

Overtime Premium Method. The **overtime premium method** differs from the overtime pay method in two respects. First, the overtime premium method computes regular pay by multiplying the total hours worked (regular *and* overtime hours) by the employee's regular hourly rate. Second, the overtime premium method multiplies overtime hours by an overtime premium rate, which is half of the employee's regular hourly rate.

For example, using the overtime premium method and assuming that FLSA provisions prevail, the gross pay for an employee who receives a regular hourly rate of $8 and works 46 hours in one week is calculated by: (1) computing the employee's regular pay, (2) computing the employee's overtime premium, and (3) totaling the employee's regular pay and overtime premium. The employee's regular pay is computed by multiplying the 46 hours worked by the hourly rate of $8. The employee's overtime premium is computed by multiplying the 6 overtime hours by half the employee's regular hourly rate, or $4 (.5 times the regular hourly rate of $8). The employee's gross pay can now be determined as follows:

Regular Pay (46 hours × $8)	$368.00
Overtime Pay (6 hours × $4)	24.00
Gross Pay	$392.00

Payroll Deductions

An employee's gross pay is reduced by payroll deductions. Payroll deductions are classified as either governmental or voluntary deductions.

Governmental Deductions

Governmental deductions are mandatory deductions over which an employee has little control. These deductions consist of federal income taxes, FICA taxes, state income taxes, and other state taxes on employee earnings. These deductions are not an expense of the business because the employer merely acts as a collection agent for the government.

Voluntary Deductions

Voluntary deductions include premiums for health insurance group plans, life insurance group plans, retirement plans, savings plans, stock purchase plans, union dues, and contributions to charities. All voluntary deductions must be approved by the employee. Employees usually indicate approval by signing authorization forms. When the payroll check is processed, governmental deductions are subtracted before any voluntary deductions are made.

Federal Insurance Contributions Act

The **Federal Insurance Contributions Act**, commonly known as **FICA,** was enacted to provide workers with retirement and medical benefits. It is also referred to as Social Security and Medicare. The law requires (1) a tax upon the employer, and (2) a tax upon the employee that is deducted from the employee's paycheck. The FICA tax imposed on the employer will be discussed later in this chapter.

The retirement and medical benefits of this act also extend to self-employed persons under provisions of the Self-Employment Contributions Act. The self-employed person pays the FICA tax, which is computed from the profits of the business. This computation is performed on a special form that is part of the individual's personal income tax return.

Recent FICA tax rates (Social Security and Medicare) have not changed from year to year. Each of the FICA taxes is imposed at a single flat rate. However, the taxable wage ceiling for Social Security continually increases, while the Medicare taxable wage remains at no ceiling.

The FICA taxation of wages is as follows:

	Tax Rate	Computation of Tax
Social Security tax	6.2%	Limited to a dollar limit (ceiling)
Medicare tax	1.45%	Unlimited

The Social Security Web site (www.socialsecurity.gov) provides the current FICA tax rates and taxable earnings. Click on the subject "Taxes and Social Security," which is listed under Frequently Asked Questions. The information is also available in IRS Circular E, which can be viewed at www.irs.gov; to find it, type "Publication 15" in the Search field.

If a worker starts a new job during the year, the new employer is not allowed to include prior earnings in the calculation of the Social Security tax. If an employee has overpaid the Social Security tax at the end of the year because of having held more than one job or having switched jobs during the year, the overpayment can be claimed as a credit on his or her personal income tax return.

Federal Income Tax

The federal government requires employers to withhold income taxes from the wages and salaries of employees and pay these taxes directly to the federal government. This constitutes part of the system under which most persons pay their income tax during the year in which income is received or earned. For many employees whose entire income is wages, the amount withheld approximates the total tax due so that the employee will pay little or no additional tax at the end of the year. Circular E outlines the requirements for withholding income tax and includes tables showing the amounts to be withheld.

Before a newly hired employee starts to work, he or she should complete and sign an IRS Form W-4 (Exhibit 3). This form provides the employer with the employee's marital status (for tax withholding purposes), withholding allowances,

Exhibit 3   IRS Form W-4

Form **W-4**	**Employee's Withholding Allowance Certificate**	OMB No. 1545-0074
Department of the Treasury Internal Revenue Service	▶ **Whether you are entitled to claim a certain number of allowances or exemption from withholding is subject to review by the IRS. Your employer may be required to send a copy of this form to the IRS.**	2007

1	Type or print your first name and middle initial.	Last name		2	Your social security number

Home address (number and street or rural route)	3 ☐ Single ☐ Married ☐ Married, but withhold at higher Single rate. Note. If married, but legally separated, or spouse is a nonresident alien, check the "Single" box.
City or town, state, and ZIP code	4 **If your last name differs from that shown on your social security card, check here. You must call 1-800-772-1213 for a replacement card.** ▶ ☐

5	Total number of allowances you are claiming (from line **H** above **or** from the applicable worksheet on page 2)	5	
6	Additional amount, if any, you want withheld from each paycheck	6	$
7	I claim exemption from withholding for 2007, and I certify that I meet **both** of the following conditions for exemption.		

- Last year I had a right to a refund of **all** federal income tax withheld because I had **no** tax liability **and**
- This year I expect a refund of **all** federal income tax withheld because I expect to have **no** tax liability.

If you meet both conditions, write "Exempt" here . . . . ▶ | 7 |

Under penalties of perjury, I declare that I have examined this certificate and to the best of my knowledge and belief, it is true, correct, and complete.

Employee's signature (Form is not valid unless you sign it.) ▶   **Date** ▶

8	Employer's name and address (Employer: Complete lines 8 and 10 only if sending to the IRS.)	9 Office code (optional)	10 Employer identification number (EIN)

and other pertinent data. The employer retains this form, and the information is transferred to the employee's payroll record for future use in preparing the employee's paycheck.

An employee may submit a new Form W-4 whenever there is a change in his or her marital status or withholding allowances. For tax withholding purposes, marital status is designated as either single or married. A married employee may claim a single status in order to have larger amounts withheld from his or her paycheck. However, an unmarried employee may not claim a married status in order to have smaller amounts withheld.

Withholding allowances may be claimed by an employee in accordance with the rules provided with Form W-4. Generally, an employee may claim (1) an allowance called a personal allowance; (2) an allowance for each dependent the employee is entitled to claim on his or her federal income tax return; and (3) other special withholding allowances and tax credit allowances as described on Form W-4. An employee does not have to claim all the allowances to which he or she is entitled, but an employee may claim only valid allowances.

The amount to be withheld from an employee's gross pay for federal income taxes is computed by using income tax withholding tables or by using the income tax withholding percentage method. Both of these methods are explained in Circular E. Computerized payroll procedures usually involve the income tax withholding percentage method, while employees using manual payroll systems commonly find it more convenient to use the tax withholding tables. Circular E offers a full set of these tables.

Tax withholding tables are labeled in terms of an employee's marital status and the type of payroll period. A payroll period is generally determined by how frequently payroll checks are issued by the employer. Payroll periods may be weekly, biweekly, bimonthly, monthly, daily, or some other designation.

State and City Income Tax

Most states have a state income tax. The employer is responsible for withholding these taxes from the employee's gross pay and remitting them to the state as prescribed by law.

Computing the amount to be withheld from an employee's wages for state income taxes is generally similar to computing the withholding of federal income taxes. The state's division of taxation provides employers with the proper tax tables or withholding percentages. In some states, state income taxes are a "piggyback tax" on the federal income tax. For example, a state may impose its income tax at the rate of 25 percent of the federal income tax. Therefore, once the federal income tax is determined, the state income tax may be computed at 25 percent of the federal income tax.

The methods for computing withholdings for city income taxes are similar to the methods discussed for computing federal and state income tax withholdings.

State Temporary Disability Benefit Laws

A few states have passed tax laws to provide benefits for employees who are absent from employment because of illness or injury not connected with their jobs. This tax is sometimes referred to as a temporary disability insurance (TDI) tax. It is withheld from the employee's gross pay. In addition, certain states may require employers to contribute to this fund.

Generally, TDI is computed by multiplying an employee's gross pay by a percentage figure specified by the state. Amounts may be withheld from the employee's paycheck until a year-to-date ceiling is reached.

Employer's Payroll Taxes

The previous section discussed payroll taxes imposed on the employee. In these cases, the employer deducts governmental taxes from the employee's gross pay and remits them to the appropriate federal or state agency. Since these payroll taxes are levied on the employee, they are not an expense of the business.

In addition to payroll taxes imposed on employees, there are payroll taxes imposed on the employer. Such taxes are a business expense. The employer's payroll taxes discussed in this section are as follows:

- FICA taxes

- Federal unemployment taxes

- State unemployment taxes

FICA Tax Imposed on Employer

The Federal Insurance Contributions Act (FICA) imposes a separate Social Security and Medicare tax on the company's total taxable payroll. The rates and ceilings are identical to those previously discussed for employees. The employer's portion of FICA taxes will be the same as the amount for most employees, except for employees who receive tips below a certain amount per month.

Taxation of wages and withholdings is presented in Circular E, which can be viewed at www.irs.gov; to find it, enter "Publication 15" in the Search field.

IRS Form 941

IRS Form 941 is the *Employer's Quarterly Federal Tax Return,* which is used to report:

- Employee salaries and wages paid
- Tips received by employees
- Federal income tax withheld from employees
- Both the employer's and employees' FICA taxes

The initial return is filed for the quarter in which an employer first paid wages. Thereafter, Form 941 is filed every quarter even if there are no taxes to report. The form may be filed electronically. A sample Form 941 and instructions are available at www.irs.gov; enter "Form 941" in the Search field to find it.

Unemployment Taxes

The **Federal Unemployment Tax Act (FUTA)** imposes a tax on the taxable payroll of a business. Only the employer pays FUTA tax, which is based on the wages of each employee. Like FICA tax, FUTA tax is assessed at a given rate and subject to a ceiling. The federal government passes these collected taxes on to the state agency that administers the state's unemployment program.

Similarly, a state may have an unemployment insurance act (commonly referred to as SUTA). Generally, the SUTA tax is imposed on the employer based on the SUTA taxable portion of each employee's gross pay. However, some states impose this tax on both the employer and the employee.

IRS Form 940

Employers must use IRS Form 940 to report taxable wages covered under FUTA. A new simplified Form 940 replaced previous Form 940 for tax year 2006. Employers who filed Form 940-EZ before 2006 must also use the redesigned Form 940 to report FUTA taxes. A sample Form 940 and instructions are available at www.irs.gov; type "Form 940" in the Search field.

Form 940 is filed annually, but more frequent deposits might be required depending on the employer's tax liability. The form may be filed electronically.

Depositing Payroll Taxes

The rules for the timely deposit of payroll taxes are detailed and complicated, and applicable depending on the size of the taxable payroll and employer's tax liability. The Form 940 tax deposit requirements are separate from those of the Form 941 tax deposit requirements. The instructions for the applicable tax forms provide an explanation of the tax deposit schedules. The form used to deposit these taxes is IRS Form 8109-B, Federal Tax Deposit Coupon; the taxes are deposited at any federal reserve bank or authorized depositories. To view Form 8109-B at www.irs.gov, enter "Form 8109-B" in the Search field.

Exhibit 4　Sample Employee's Earnings Record

							Employee's Earnings Record							

NAME:
ADDRESS:
SOCIAL SECURITY NUMBER:

Pay Period Ending	EARNINGS				Wages for WH	Meals & Lodging	Wages for F.I.C.A.	DEDUCTIONS						NET PAY
	Regular	Overtime	Gross	Tips				F.I.C.A.	Fed. Income WH	St. Income WH	Ret. Cont.	Health Ins.		

The Payroll System

A primary function of a payroll system is to provide information necessary for computing employee payroll. An employee's earnings record serves as the basis for preparing his or her payroll check. Once the payroll checks have been prepared, they are recorded on a payroll register. From data in the payroll register, journal entries are prepared to record the payroll expense as well as the liability for payroll taxes. The net pay shown on the payroll register represents the cash demand that will be placed on the company's checking account. A payroll system comprises the forms, records, and procedures required to carry out these and other tasks.

Employee's Earnings Record

For each employee, an individual earnings record must be kept by calendar year. Exhibit 4 shows a sample employee's earnings record. The earnings record indicates gross wages earned and amounts withheld and deducted. Properties generally design the format of the earnings record to make it easy to conform with government reporting requirements. Also, for tax reporting purposes, it is important that earnings be entered in the proper payroll quarter; the determining date is the date of the payroll check, not the date of the workweek.

At the end of the year, an employee's earnings record is used to prepare IRS Form W-2, which is sent to federal and state agencies and to the employee. A sample IRS Form W-2 is shown in Exhibit 5. A new employee earnings record is started each calendar year.

Payroll Register

Another payroll accounting requirement is the preparation of reports for internal purposes. Management needs payroll cost information by department or area of responsibility. The accounting department supplies this information by maintaining a payroll register (Exhibit 6). The payroll register can also be used to reconcile the payroll checking account.

Exhibit 5   IRS Form W-2

22222	Void ☐	a Employee's social security number	For Official Use Only ▶ OMB No. 1545-0008		
b Employer identification number (EIN)			1 Wages, tips, other compensation		2 Federal income tax withheld
c Employer's name, address, and ZIP code			3 Social security wages		4 Social security tax withheld
			5 Medicare wages and tips		6 Medicare tax withheld
			7 Social security tips		8 Allocated tips
d Control number			9 Advance EIC payment		10 Dependent care benefits
e Employee's first name and initial	Last name	Suff.	11 Nonqualified plans		12a See instructions for box 12
		13 Statutory employee / Retirement plan / Third-party sick pay	12b		
		14 Other	12c		
			12d		
f Employee's address and ZIP code					
15 State Employer's state ID number	**16** State wages, tips, etc.	**17** State income tax	**18** Local wages, tips, etc.	**19** Local income tax	**20** Locality name

Form **W-2** Wage and Tax Statement   **2007**

Department of the Treasury—Internal Revenue Service
For Privacy Act and Paperwork Reduction Act Notice, see back of Copy D.

Copy A For Social Security Administration — Send this entire page with Form W-3 to the Social Security Administration; photocopies are **not** acceptable.

Cat. No. 10134D

Payroll Journal Entries

A payroll journal is used to record payroll expense, employee withholdings, and the employer's payroll tax liabilities. The journal entry to record the payroll register in Exhibit 6 is as follows:

Payroll Expense	1,520.35	
FICA Tax Payable		116.31
Federal Income Tax Withheld Liability		175.00
State Income Tax Withheld Liability		45.50
Group Insurance Withheld Liability		51.50
Cash—Checking Account		1,132.04

The credit to the cash account assumes that the payroll checks are issued at the same time the payroll register is prepared. If the checks are to be issued at a later date, the credit would be to Accrued Payroll; when the checks are issued, the payment is recorded by a debit to Accrued Payroll and a credit to the checking account.

The previous journal entry recorded the payroll expense and the employer's liability for taxes withheld from employees' wages. Another journal entry is required to record the employer's liability for those taxes imposed on the employer. Assume that the employer is liable for the following payroll taxes:

Employer's FICA tax	$116.31
Federal unemployment tax (FUTA)	68.42
State unemployment tax (SUTA)	12.16
Total payroll taxes imposed on employer	$196.89

Exhibit 6   Sample Payroll Register

		Earnings			Deductions					Net Pay	
Time Card No.	Name	Regular	Overtime	Gross	FICA Tax	Federal Income Tax	State Income Tax	Group Insurance	Check No.	Amount	
101	Deborah Stephens	320 00		320 00	24 48	34 00	9 00	10 00	386	242 52	
103	Roland Kenwood	208 00	32 40	231 40	17 70	30 00	7 75	15 75	387	160 20	
104	Thomas Lawton	222 30		222 30	17 01	28 00	7 25	10 00	388	160 04	
105	Robert Paul	188 00	21 15	209 15	16 00	21 00	5 50		389	166 65	
106	Steve Brentwood	537 50		537 50	41 12	62 00	16 00	15 75	390	402 63	
	Total	1 475 80	44 55	1 520 35	116 31	175 00	45 50	51 50		1 132 04	

PAYROLL REGISTER
For period ending: 3/10/XX

The journal entry to record these taxes is as follows:

Payroll Taxes Expense   196.89
    Accrued Payroll Taxes   196.89

Instead of one credit to Accrued Payroll Taxes, some accountants prefer to use separate liability accounts for each type of tax due.

Payroll Bank Account

Most hospitality businesses that pay their payroll by check establish a separate bank account for payroll. After the paychecks are prepared and the total disbursement is known, funds are transferred from the regular bank account to the payroll account. The separate account for payroll offers better control, since only sufficient funds to cover the current payroll are deposited. Furthermore, a separate bank statement is obtained that can be reconciled item by item with the payroll expenditures recorded in the payroll journal.

When an electronic funds transfer system (EFT) is used, employees do not receive payroll checks. Instead, they are given a statement of their gross pay, deductions, and net pay. The employer's bank receives a register of employees from the employer. This register indicates each employee's net pay, bank, and bank account number. The employer's bank then processes this information and deposits each employee's net pay into his or her bank account. (For those employees who do not maintain an account at the employer's bank, the employer's bank remits the pertinent information to an automated clearinghouse that transmits the information to each employee's bank shown on the register.)

Computerized Payroll Applications

Advances in computer technology have made computers affordable, practical, and cost-efficient for most hospitality operations. An operation lacking a sophisticated guest accounting system may still use a computer to prepare payroll checks, perform general ledger accounting, and carry out other tasks involving numerical computation and accumulation of data.

However, a small property may not be able to justify an in-house computer system. In this case, banks and computer service companies offer a low-cost alternative. They sell computer services such as payroll preparation and general ledger accounting for modest fees.

In a computerized payroll application, information such as employee number, pay rate, deductions, and earnings is not recorded on paper, but stored in a computer file. Computer files are usually maintained on magnetic disks, which allow random access of information. In computer terminology, the earnings records for all employees are called the *payroll master file* or *database*.

The payroll process begins when hours worked are entered into the payroll master file. The computer then processes each employee's hours worked in accordance with information on that employee's file record and instructions in the computer program. This process emulates the manual procedures previously discussed.

The output of a computerized payroll application is similar to that of a manual system, namely, the payroll register and the payroll checks. Each employee's record in the master file is updated during the payroll process to maintain current and year-to-date earnings information.

Payroll Accounting for Tipped Employees

Preparing the payroll for tipped employees is complex because tipped employees earn wages from two sources: the employer they work for and the guests they serve. A tip is considered payment by a guest to a hospitality employee for services rendered and must be included as part of the gross income reported by the employee on his or her personal income tax return. For purposes of determining tip income, tips include cash tips, charge tips, and tips on credit cards. If an employee splits tips among other employees, only the portion that the employee retains is included in his or her gross income. All income earned by an employee, whether received as wages or as tips, is taxable and subject to both federal and state income tax withholding provisions.

Service Charges

Some hospitality operations, especially in resort areas, may add service charges to guests' billings. These service charges are distributed to servers and other customarily tipped employees. A service charge is not considered a tip. Such charges are defined as wages by the IRS and are treated the same as other wages for purposes of tax withholding requirements.

Employee Tip Reporting

IRS Publication 531 provides information on tip income reporting and employers' responsibilities. It also includes sample tip reporting forms. This publication is available at www.irs.gov; to find it, enter "Publication 531" in the Search field.

Employees must report cash tips received from customers as well as charge or credit card tips the employer passed on to them. An employee may use IRS Form

Exhibit 7   IRS Form 4070

Form **4070** (Rev. August 2005) Department of the Treasury Internal Revenue Service	**Employee's Report** **of Tips to Employer**	OMB No. 1545-0074
Employee's name and address		Social security number
Employer's name and address (include establishment name, if different)		1 Cash tips received
		2 Credit and debit card tips received
		3 Tips paid out
Month or shorter period in which tips were received from , , to ,		4 Net tips (lines **1** + **2** - **3**)
Signature		Date
For Paperwork Reduction Act Notice, see the instructions on the back of this form.	Cat. No. 41320P	Form **4070** (Rev. 8-2005)

4070 (Exhibit 7) or a similar statement in reporting tips to the employer. A daily report or card showing the employee's name, cash tips received, and charge tips received is sufficient. Some employers require tipped employees to record their tips daily on the backs of their time cards.

FLSA Minimum Wage Rate

The FLSA mandates the minimum hourly wage rate for nonexempt employees and states that the overtime pay rate must be not less than 1.5 times the employee's regular rate of pay after the employee has worked 40 hours in a workweek.

The FLSA allows the payment of wage rates below the statutory minimum for certain types of individual workers. Such individuals include student-learners (full-time students in retail or service establishments or institutions of higher learning) and people whose earning or productive capacity is impaired by a physical or mental disability, such as incapacity related to age or injury, for the work to be performed. Any employer should check with the federal and state departments of labor to verify that the payment of sub-minimum wage is justifiable for a specific situation.

State labor regulations *supersede* those of the FLSA *if* the state employment laws regulating minimum wage or overtime are more generous to the employee than those provisions of the FLSA.

FLSA Tip Credit

Provisions of the FLSA allow employers to apply a tip credit toward the minimum wage of tipped employees. This tip credit effectively lowers the gross wages payable by the employer because tips may be treated as supplemental wages.

If an employee's tips are less than the FLSA maximum allowable tip credit, the employer may not use the FLSA tip credit. Instead, the actual tips received by the employee are used as the tip credit. This ensures that the employee does not earn less than the minimum hourly wage from the combined payments of the employer (in the form of a wage) and guests (in the form of tips).

Net Pay of Tipped Employees

A tipped employee's gross taxable earnings include the gross wages payable by the employer *and* the actual tips the employee receives from guests.

It is possible for the governmental and voluntary deductions of a tipped employee to exceed the gross wages payable by the employer for a payroll period. In this case, available amounts are first applied to FICA taxes, then to federal and state income taxes, and finally to voluntary deductions. However, an employee's paycheck may never be less than zero; if the gross wages payable by the employer are insufficient to cover an employee's governmental and voluntary deductions, the employee may pay over the deficiency to the employer. If the employer is unable to withhold FICA taxes, this fact is reported on the employee's W-2 form and is reported as taxes due on the employee's personal income tax return. It is not necessary to report any deficiency on withheld income taxes because any deficiency will be made up when the employee's total income tax liability is computed on his or her personal income tax return.

State Wage and Tip Credit Provisions

Many states have passed minimum wage legislation that is more generous to the employee than the federal minimum wage. In these cases, the state law takes precedence over the federal law. In addition, some employers voluntarily pay tipped employees at rates above federal and state minimum hourly wages.

Some states also limit the maximum tip credit that may be used against the minimum wage. For example, assume a state's minimum wage provision is identical to the federal provision. However, the employer's maximum tip credit is the lower of the state or federal tip credit.

Overtime Pay of Tipped Employees

Overtime pay for tipped employees is calculated in exactly the same manner as for non-tipped employees. However, in computing the gross wages payable by the employer, the federal or state tip credit is multiplied by the total hours worked (regular hours plus overtime hours) by the employee.

As stressed earlier, the definition of overtime pay varies because of different state laws, company policies, and contracts. Federal law requires that overtime be paid for any hours worked in excess of 40 in a payroll week. Thus, an employee who works ten-hour shifts for four days within a payroll week is not entitled to overtime under the FLSA. Some states require that employees receive overtime pay for any hours worked in excess of eight hours in a payroll day.

The Eight Percent Tip Regulation

The Tax Equity and Fiscal Responsibility Act of 1982 (TEFRA) established regulations affecting food and beverage operations with respect to tip reporting requirements. The intent of the regulation is for all tipped employees to report tips of at least eight percent of the gross receipts of the hospitality establishment. If tips reported by employees fail to meet this eight percent requirement for a particular period, the deficiency is called a tip shortfall. This shortfall will require allocation to those employees classified as directly tipped employees.

The eight percent tip regulation distinguishes between directly tipped employees and indirectly tipped employees. Directly tipped employees are those who receive tips directly from customers. Examples of directly tipped employees are servers, bartenders, and other employees, such as maître d's. Indirectly tipped employees are employees who do not normally receive tips directly from customers. These employees include buspersons, service bartenders, and cooks.

When a shortfall is allocated, the employer is required to provide each directly tipped employee with an informational statement showing the tips reported by the employee and the tips that should have been reported. An employer does not have to provide employees with tip allocation statements when the total tips reported for a period are greater than eight percent of the gross receipts for that period. For example, assume that a large food and beverage establishment records gross receipts of $100,000 for a particular period. If the actual tips reported by employees total more than $8,000 ($100,000 × 8%), the employer does not have to provide employees with tip allocation statements.

An employee's tip allocation for a calendar year is stated separately from any wages and reported tips appearing on the employee's W-2 form. Employees should maintain adequate records to substantiate the total amount of tips included in income. If possible, the employee should keep a daily record of his or her sales, cash tips, charge tips, and hours worked. To facilitate recordkeeping, a business may provide the employee with a multi-purpose form similar to the one shown in Exhibit 8.

Operations Affected by the Eight Percent Tip Regulation

The eight percent tip regulation does not apply to every food and beverage establishment. For example, cafeteria and fast-food operations are exempt from the eight percent tip regulation. Cafeteria operations are defined as food and beverage establishments that are primarily self-service and in which the total cost of food and/or beverages selected by a customer is paid to a cashier (or is stated on a guest check) before the customer is seated. Fast-food operations are defined as food and beverage establishments where customers order, pick up, and pay for their orders at a counter or window and then consume the items at another location, either on or off the premises. In addition to cafeteria and fast-food operations, food and beverage establishments are exempt from the eight percent tip regulation when at least 95 percent of their gross receipts include a service charge of 10 percent or more. As pointed out previously, service charges are not considered tips. Service charges are defined as wages by the IRS and are treated the same as other wages for purposes of tax withholding requirements.

Exhibit 8   Sample Employee Report of Daily Sales and Tips

Employee Report of Daily Sales and Tips

Business _____   Week Ending _____/_____/_____

                                                          (Month/Day/Year)

Employee _____

Enter day of the month	Date	Date	Date	Date	Date	Date	Date	
	Mon.	Tues.	Wed.	Thurs.	Fri.	Sat.	Sun.	Grand Total
SALES 1. Total sales to patrons 2. Charge sales in								
TIPS 1. Total cash and charge tips 2. Total charge tips in								
Total hours worked								

Check shift worked: ☐ Days   ☐ Evenings   ☐ Split

The eight percent tip regulation defines gross receipts as all receipts (both cash and charge sales) received for providing food and/or beverages. However, according to the eight percent tip regulation, the following are typically *not* considered part of an operation's gross receipts because tipping is not customary for these services:

- Complimentary hors d'oeuvres served at a bar
- Complimentary dessert served to a regular patron
- Complimentary fruit baskets placed in guestrooms
- Carry-out sales
- State or local taxes
- Services to which a ten percent (or more) service charge is added

An exception applies to gambling casinos. In casinos, the retail value of complimentary food and/or beverages served to customers is considered part of gross receipts because tipping is customary for this service.

Given these exemptions and exceptions, the eight percent tip regulation applies to food and beverage establishments that normally employ the equivalent of more than ten employees on a typical business day and are thus classified as *large*. The phrase "the equivalent of more than ten employees" means any combination of full- or part-time employees whose hours worked on a typical business day total more than 80 hours.

Employers can determine whether the eight percent tip regulation applies to their establishments by averaging the number of hours worked by employees during the best and worst months of the previous calendar year. For example, assume that an employer compiles the following statistics:

	Gross Receipts	Days Open	Employee Hours	Hours Worked per Day
Best month: July	$125,578	31	2,883	93
Worst month: February	$ 89,162	28	2,184	78

The number of hours worked by employees on a typical day for that calendar year can be determined by averaging the average hours worked per day in July and February:

$$\text{Typical Business Day} = \frac{\text{Hrs. Worked (July)} + \text{Hrs. Worked (February)}}{2}$$

$$\text{Typical Business Day} = \frac{93 + 78}{2} = \frac{171}{2} = 85.5 \text{ hrs. per day}$$

Since the result exceeds 80 hours per day, the employer's business is considered to have more than ten employees and is therefore subject to the eight percent tip regulation. For a new food and beverage business (one that did not operate in the previous year), the time periods used in the calculations may be any two consecutive months.

If an employer conducts business at more than one location, each location is considered a separate food and beverage establishment. This also applies to separate activities within a single building if records of receipts are kept separately. If employees work at multiple locations for an employer, the employer may make a good faith estimate of the number of hours these employees worked for each location.

If a food and beverage establishment is subject to the eight percent tip regulation, IRS Form 8027 (Exhibit 9) must be completed, whether or not a tip shortfall allocation is made. IRS Form 8027 is called Employer's Annual Information Return of Tip Income and Allocated Tips.

Tip Shortfall Allocation Methods

If, during a particular period, the total tips reported by directly and indirectly tipped employees fall short of eight percent of the establishment's gross receipts for that same period, the employer must: (1) determine the shortfall (the amount by which the total reported tips falls short of eight percent of the gross receipts), and (2) allocate the shortfall among *directly tipped employees*. After these computations have been completed, the tip shortfall allocations must be reported to each affected employee.

Exhibit 9   IRS Form 8027

Form **8027** Department of the Treasury Internal Revenue Service	**Employer's Annual Information Return of Tip Income and Allocated Tips** ▶ See separate instructions.	OMB No. 1545-0714 20**06**

Name of establishment		Type of establishment **(check only one box)**
Number and street (see instructions)	Employer identification number	☐ 1 Evening meals only ☐ 2 Evening and other meals
City or town, state, and ZIP code		☐ 3 Meals other than evening meals ☐ 4 Alcoholic beverages

Employer's name (same name as on Form 941)	**Establishment number** (see instructions)

Number and street (P.O. box, if applicable)	Apt. or suite no.

City, state, and ZIP code (if a foreign address, see instructions)

Does this establishment accept credit cards, debit cards, or other charges? ☐ Yes (lines 1 and 2 **must** be completed) ☐ No	Check **if:** Amended Return ☐ Final Return ☐

Attributed Tip Income Program (ATIP). See Revenue Procedure 2006-30 . . . . ▶ ☐

1	Total charged tips for calendar year 2006.	**1**
2	Total charge receipts showing charged tips (see instructions)	**2**
3	Total amount of service charges of less than 10% paid as wages to employees. . . .	**3**
4a	Total tips reported by indirectly tipped employees	**4a**
b	Total tips reported by directly tipped employees	**4b**
	Note. Complete the **Employer's Optional Worksheet for Tipped Employees** on page 6 of the instructions to determine potential unreported tips of your employees.	
c	Total tips reported (add lines 4a and 4b)	**4c**
5	Gross receipts from food or beverage operations (not less than line 2—see instructions) .	**5**
6	Multiply line 5 by 8% (.08) or the lower rate shown here ▶_____ granted by the IRS. (Attach a copy of the IRS determination letter to this return.)	**6**
	Note. If you have allocated tips using other than the calendar year (semimonthly, biweekly, quarterly, etc.), mark an **"X"** on line 6 and enter the amount of allocated tips from your records on line 7.	
7	Allocation of tips. If line 6 is more than line 4c, enter the excess here	**7**
	▶ This amount must be allocated as tips to tipped employees working in this establishment. Check the box below that shows the method used for the allocation. (Show the portion, if any, attributable to each employee in box 8 of the employee's Form W-2.)	
a	Allocation based on hours-worked method (see instructions for restriction) . . . . ☐	
	Note. If you marked the checkbox in line 7a, enter the average number of employee hours worked per business day during the payroll period. (see instructions) _____	
b	Allocation based on gross receipts method . . . . ☐	
c	Allocation based on good-faith agreement (Attach a copy of the agreement.). . . ☐	

8   Enter the total number of directly tipped employees at this establishment during 2006 ▶

Under penalties of perjury, I declare that I have examined this return, including accompanying schedules and statements, and to the best of my knowledge and belief, it is true, correct, and complete.

Signature ▶	Title ▶	Date ▶

For Privacy Act and Paperwork Reduction Act Notice, see page 6 of the separate instructions.   Cat. No. 49989U   Form **8027** (2006)

There are several acceptable methods by which to compute tip shortfall allocations for directly tipped employees. One method is through a good faith agreement. A good faith agreement is a written agreement between the employer and employees, consented to by two-thirds of the tipped employees at the time of the agreement. This agreement becomes the basis of allocating tip amounts to employees when the actual tips reported are short of the expected eight percent of gross receipts.

In the absence of a good faith agreement, the eight percent tip regulation provides tip allocation methods. For purposes of allocating the tip shortfall to directly tipped employees, these regulations permit the use of the gross receipts method or, under certain conditions, the hours worked method. The following examples explain and illustrate both methods.

Gross Receipts Method

The gross receipts method requires that gross receipts (food and beverage sales) and tip records be maintained for each directly tipped employee. Gross receipts are used as a basis for allocating each directly tipped employee's share of the tip shortfall. The tip shortfall allocation may be performed weekly, monthly, quarterly, annually, or at some other designated time period during the year. The following hypothetical example demonstrates the computations involved when the gross receipts method is used to allocate a tip shortfall among the directly tipped employees of Bruno's Restaurant.

Bruno's Restaurant is a food and beverage establishment with an equivalent of more than ten employees and, therefore, is subject to the government's eight percent tip regulation. Bruno's Restaurant had food and beverage sales of $100,000 for a particular period. According to the government's eight percent tip regulation, directly and indirectly tipped employees should have reported a minimum of $8,000 in tips for that period ($100,000 × 8% = $8,000); this amount will be referred to as "eight percent gross receipts." The tip records show that all employees reported total tips of only $6,200 for the period. Therefore, a tip shortfall of $1,800 ($8,000 − $6,200) has occurred.

Exhibit 10 presents information compiled by Bruno's management for this particular period, including the gross receipts (food and beverage sales) and tips reported by each directly tipped employee. It also shows that the total shortfall to be allocated is $1,800. This information will be used later in Exhibits 11 and 12 to compute tip shortfall allocations for directly tipped employees.

While directly tipped employees are required to account for the tip shortfall, the tips of indirectly tipped employees may be counted toward the "eight percent gross receipts" estimate of total tips that should have been reported. For Bruno's Restaurant, total tips that should have been reported by all employees are $8,000; the tips reported by indirectly tipped employees total $500. Therefore, the directly tipped employees' portion of eight percent gross receipts is $7,500.

Exhibit 11 uses the directly tipped employees' portion of eight percent gross receipts as the basis for calculating shortfall allocation ratios. The shortfall allocation ratios will be used to allocate the $1,800 tip shortfall among directly tipped employees. However, before tip shortfall allocation ratios can be computed, a method must be used to determine each employee's share of the $7,500 portion of tips that should have been reported by directly tipped employees. Each employee's share will be compared to the tips actually reported by the employee to determine if the employee reported tips above or below his or her share of the $7,500 portion of eight percent gross receipts.

Exhibit 10   Sales and Tips Analysis—Bruno's Restaurant

Directly Tipped Employee	Gross Receipts for Period	Tips Reported by Employees
1	$ 18,000	$1,080
2	16,000	880
3	23,000	1,810
4	17,000	800
5	12,000	450
6	14,000	680
Total	$100,000	5,700
Indirectly tipped employees		500
Total		$6,200

Tips that should have been reported ($100,000 × 8%)	=	$8,000
Actual tips reported	=	6,200
Shortfall to be allocated		1,800
Tips that should have been reported	=	8,000
Tips reported by indirectly tipped employees	=	500
Directly tipped employees' portion of 8% gross receipts	=	$7,500

Exhibit 11   Determining Shortfall Ratios—Bruno's Restaurant

Directly Tipped Employee	Total Portion of 8% Gross Receipts	Gross Receipts Ratio			Employee's Share of 8% Gross Receipts	Actual Tips Reported		Employee's Shortfall Numerator
1	7,500	×	18,000/100,000	=	$1,350	− $1,080	=	$ 270
2	7,500	×	16,000/100,000	=	1,200	− 880	=	320
3	7,500	×	23,000/100,000	=	1,725	− 1,810	=	0
4	7,500	×	17,000/100,000	=	1,275	− 800	=	475
5	7,500	×	12,000/100,000	=	900	− 450	=	450
6	7,500	×	14,000/100,000	=	1,050	− 680	=	370
Total					$7,500	$5,700		$1,885
								Shortfall Denominator

Exhibit 12   Allocation of the Tip Shortfall—Bruno's Restaurant

Directly Tipped Employee	Shortfall Ratio		Shortfall to Be Allocated		Tip Allocation
1	270/1,885	×	$1,800	=	$ 258
2	320/1,885	×	1,800	=	306
4	475/1,885	×	1,800	=	453
5	450/1,885	×	1,800	=	430
6	370/1,885	×	1,800	=	353
Total					$1,800

Under the gross receipts method, a gross receipts ratio is used to determine each employee's share of the $7,500. A gross receipts ratio is the proportion of gross receipts attributable to each employee in relation to the total gross receipts for the period. This ratio is multiplied by $7,500 (directly tipped employees' portion of eight percent gross receipts) to determine each directly tipped employee's share of this amount. Exhibit 11 illustrates these calculations for Bruno's Restaurant.

The actual tips reported by each employee are then subtracted from the employee's share of eight percent gross receipts. The resulting figure is the employee shortfall numerator. For Bruno's Restaurant, this subtraction process is possible for all employees except Employee #3. This employee reported tips greater than his or her share of the tips that should have been reported. Therefore, Employee #3 does not have a tip shortfall. The total shortfall ($1,800) must be allocated on a proportional basis among the remaining directly tipped employees.

Exhibit 12 shows how the $1,800 tip shortfall is allocated among directly tipped employees whose reported tips did not equal or exceed their share of the eight percent tip estimate. This proportional allocation is accomplished by the use of a shortfall ratio. The total of the employees' shortfall numerators, or $1,885, is used as the denominator of the shortfall ratio. Each employee's shortfall numerator, together with the shortfall denominator, form the shortfall ratio used to allocate his or her share of the tip shortfall.

Hours Worked Method

The use of the hours worked method is limited to those establishments with fewer than the equivalent of 25 full-time employees during the payroll period. The mathematical procedures in this method are identical to those explained for the gross receipts method. The only difference between the hours worked method and the gross receipts method is that employee hours worked are substituted wherever employee gross receipts were used in the previous method.

For example, Dot's Diner, a hypothetical food establishment employing fewer than the equivalent of 25 employees, elects to allocate the tip shortfall on the basis of hours worked. Exhibit 13 shows the hours worked and tips reported for the employees of this restaurant. Exhibit 14 shows the computation of the shortfall allocation ratios based on the hours worked. Exhibit 15 shows the allocation of the tip shortfall using the ratios developed in Exhibit 14.

Endnote

1. U.S. Department of Treasury, Internal Revenue Service, Publication 15, *Circular E, Employer's Tax Guide.* This publication can be obtained at an Internal Revenue Service office or found online at www.irs.gov.

Key Terms

Fair Labor Standards Act (FLSA)—A federal law that regulates such areas as minimum wage, overtime pay, and equal pay provisions. This federal law's provisions can be superseded by any state or contractual provision that is more generous to the employee. Also commonly known as the federal wage and hour law.

Exhibit 13   Sales and Tips Analysis—Dot's Diner

Directly Tipped Employee	Employee Hours for Period	Tips Reported by Employees
1	40	$1,080
2	35	880
3	45	1,810
4	40	800
5	15	450
6	25	680
Total	200	$5,700
Indirectly tipped employees		500
Total		$6,200

Tips that should have been reported ($100,000 × 8%)	=	$8,000
Actual tips reported	=	6,200
Shortfall to be allocated		1,800
Tips that should have been reported	=	8,000
Tips reported by indirectly tipped employees	=	500
Directly tipped employees' portion of 8% gross receipts	=	$7,500

Exhibit 14   Determining Shortfall Ratios—Dot's Diner

Directly Tipped Employee	Total Portion of 8% Gross Receipts		Employee Hours Ratio		Employee's Share of 8% Gross Receipts		Actual Tips Reported		Employee's Shortfall Numerator
1	$7,500	×	40/200	=	$1,500	−	$1,080	=	$ 420
2	7,500	×	35/200	=	1,312	−	880	=	432
3	7,500	×	45/200	=	1,687	−	1,810	=	0
4	7,500	×	40/200	=	1,500	−	800	=	700
5	7,500	×	15/200	=	563	−	450	=	113
6	7,500	×	25/200	=	938	−	680	=	258
Total					$7,500		$5,700		$ 1,923
									Shortfall Denominator

Exhibit 15   Allocation of the Tip Shortfall—Dot's Diner

Directly Tipped Employee	Shortfall Ratio		Shortfall to Be Allocated		Tip Allocation
1	420/1,923	×	$1,800	=	$ 393
2	432/1,923	×	1,800	=	404
4	700/1,923	×	1,800	=	656
5	113/1,923	×	1,800	=	106
6	258/1,923	×	1,800	=	241
Total					$1,800

Federal Insurance Contributions Act (FICA)—The federal law governing the national Social Security system, which imposes a payroll tax on the employee and the employer.

Federal Unemployment Tax Act (FUTA)—A federal law imposing a payroll tax on the employer for the purpose of funding national and state unemployment programs.

gross pay—The total amount of pay before any payroll deductions. Also referred to as gross earnings

net pay—Gross pay less all payroll deductions. Net pay is the amount of the payroll check. Also referred to as net earnings.

overtime pay—A term that indicates a premium paid for hours worked in excess of a specified total of hours as stated by the FLSA, state, or contractual provisions.

overtime pay method—A method of computing overtime pay in which overtime hours are excluded from regular hours (straight-time hours). The overtime hours are multiplied at a rate of 1.5 times the regular hourly rate. This overtime pay is added to regular pay to arrive at gross pay. This method results in the same amount of gross pay as the premium method.

overtime premium method—A method of computing overtime pay in which overtime hours are included in the computation of regular pay (straight-time pay). The total regular hours and overtime hours are multiplied by the regular rate to arrive at straight-time pay. Then the overtime premium is computed by multiplying only the overtime hours by a rate of one-half the regular hourly pay rate. The straight-time pay added to the overtime premium is the gross pay for the employee. This method results in the same amount of gross pay as the overtime pay method.

salary—A term that usually applies to payrolls paid monthly, bimonthly, biweekly, or annually. Generally, qualified supervisors and executives who receive a fixed amount each pay period (regardless of the number of hours worked) are considered salaried employees.

wages—A term that usually applies to payrolls computed on an hourly, weekly, or piecework basis. However, a fixed weekly pay may be called a salary.

 # Review Questions

1. What wage and salary areas are not covered by the Fair Labor Standards Act?

2. What are the major provisions of the following federal acts or laws?
   a. Fair Labor Standards Act
   b. Federal Insurance Contributions Act
   c. Federal Income Tax Withholding Law
   d. Federal Unemployment Tax Act

3. An employer is interviewing job candidates for a server's position. The employer states that the person hired will be considered self-employed by mutual agreement. Is this arrangement in accordance with federal payroll provisions? Justify your answer.

4. In each of the following situations, which federal form is required?

   a. A new business is formed and employees will be hired.
   b. A new employee is hired.
   c. An employee requests a change in withholding status.
   d. An employer reports annual wages and taxes withheld to employees.

5. What are two methods of computing overtime pay? Describe how each method calculates overtime pay.

6. A restaurant where tipping is customary has 15 employees who collectively work 70 hours per business day. Are the employees of the establishment subject to the minimum eight percent tip regulation? Explain your answer.

Internet Sites

For more information, visit the following Internet sites. Remember that Internet addresses can change without notice. If the site is no longer there, you can use a search engine to look for additional sites.

Fair Labor Standards Act
www.dol.gov/esa/whd/flsa/

U.S. Department of Labor, Wage & Hour Division
www.dol.gov/esa/minwage/q-a.htm

Overtime Regulations
www.dol.gov/esa/regs/compliance/whd/fairpay/main.htm

IRS Guide to Tip Reporting—Publication 1875
www.irs.gov/pub/irs-pdf/p1875.pdf

Allocated Tips
www.wwwebtax.com/income/allocated_tips.htm

IRS 8% Tip Regulation; Form 8027 Instructions
www.irs.gov/pub/irs-pdf/i8027.pdf

Youth Labor Laws
www.dol.gov/esa/programs/whd/state/nonfarm.htm
www.dol.gov/esa/regs/compliance/whd/whdfs34.htm.

IRS Circular E—Publication 15
www.irs.gov/pub/irs-pdf/p15.pdf

Social Security Administration
www.socialsecurity.gov

State Payday Requirements
www.dol.gov/esa/programs/whd/state/payday.htm

State Meal Period Requirements
www.dol.gov/esa/programs/whd/state/meal.htm

 **Problems**

Problem 1

Convert the following time worked to the nearest tenth of an hour:

a. 7 hours, 16 minutes

b. 4 hours, 37 minutes

c. 9 hours, 57 minutes

d. 7 hours, 50 minutes

Problem 2

Convert the following conventional times to military time:

a. 3 P.M.

b. 3 A.M.

c. 6:45 A.M.

d. 6:45 P.M.

Problem 3

Convert the following weekly wages to an hourly rate (to three decimal places). The workweek is 37.5 hours.

a. $416

b. $295

c. $325

Problem 4

Convert the following monthly salaries to an hourly rate (to three decimal places). The workweek is 37.5 hours.

a. $1,500

b. $1,200

c. $2,150

Problem 5

Compute the regular pay, overtime pay, and gross pay for an employee who worked 49 hours this week. The employee's hourly rate is $8.15. The state overtime provisions apply to any hours worked in excess of 40 in a week.

a. Use the overtime pay method.

b. Use the overtime premium method.

Problem 6

Use the overtime premium method to compute the regular pay, overtime pay, and gross pay for an employee who worked 45 hours this week. The employee's hourly rate is $12.00. The following is the employee's time report.

Sunday	5
Monday	8
Tuesday	12
Wednesday	12
Thursday	8
Friday	0
Saturday	0
Total	45

a. Assume that state law requires overtime to be paid for any hours worked in excess of eight hours in a day.

b. Assume that state overtime provisions apply to any hours worked in excess of 40 in a week.

Case Study

Planning a Computerized Hospitality Payroll System

The hospitality service industry has payroll needs unique to the industry that must be addressed and resolved before a payroll can be automated on a computer.

The Global Gourmet is a chain of casual-dining restaurants that offers a variety of international dishes for dining in and for takeout; delivery service is not available. The Global Gourmet started with one restaurant and now is expanding rapidly. The gross pay for each employee has traditionally been calculated manually and then sent to a service center for computer processing. The executive vice-president of finance has concluded that the gross pay calculations must be computerized.

Executives of the Global Gourmet have decided to buy their own computer system and are considering whether to: (1) buy payroll software "off the shelf" from a retail store or from an Internet supplier, or (2) hire a computer/software consultant to design and program the software to their specifications.

Challenge

List some components that make up the calculation of gross pay. How might these elements affect Global Gourmet's choice between off-the-shelf or custom-designed software?

Appendix

Special Research Reports

It should by now be clear that payroll and its related regulations are complex and ever-changing. Persistent vigilance is required to stay updated with federal and state changes in payroll laws.

The author provides periodic special research reports to customers and members of the hospitality academic community on his Web site, http://raymondcote.com. This appendix consists of reprints of select special research reports related to hospitality payroll and labor issues—specifically, to the following:

- Labor Laws for Employers
- Teen Labor Laws for Employers
- Overtime Rules
- Tip Reporting

LABOR LAWS FOR EMPLOYERS

This special report covers labor laws for the following areas:

- Employment of youth labor
- Family medical leave
- Employment eligibility
- State payday requirements
- State meal period requirements

Youth Labor

- Refer to special report previously issued on February 24, 2005 by Ray Cote and titled: Employing Youth in Restaurants and Quick-Service Establishments under the Fair Labor Standards Act (FLSA)

- For state youth rules refer to: http://www.dol.gov/esa/programs/whd/state/nonfarm.htm

The Family and Medical Leave Act of 1993

Covered employers
(http://www.dol.gov/dol/allcfr/ESA/Title_29/Part_825/29CFR825.104.htm)

must grant an eligible employee
(http://www.dol.gov/dol/allcfr/ESA/Title_29/Part_825/29CFR825.110.htm)

up to a total of 12 workweeks of unpaid leave during any 12-month period for one or more of the following reasons:

- for the birth and care of the newborn child of the employee;

- for placement with the employee of a son or daughter for adoption or foster care;

- to care for an immediate family member (spouse, child, or parent) with a serious health condition; or

- to take medical leave when the employee is unable to work because of a serious health condition.

Employment Eligibility

Citizens and nationals of the U.S. are automatically eligible for employment but they must present proof of employment eligibility and identity and complete an Employment Eligibility Verification form (Form I-9), see http://uscis.gov/graphics/formsfee/forms/I-9.htm

The federal Form I-9, Employment Eligibility Verification, is used by employers as a record of their basis for determining eligibility of an employee to work in the United States. The form is kept by the employer and made available for inspection by officials of the U.S. Immigration and Naturalization Service, the Department of Labor and the Office of Special Counsel for Immigration Related Unfair Employment Practices.

Citizens of the U.S. include persons born in Puerto Rico, Guam, the U.S. Virgin Islands, and the Northern Mariana Islands. Nationals of the U.S. include persons born in American Samoa, including Swains Island.

Form I-9 is completed only for people actually hired. For purposes of the I-9 rules, a person is "hired" when he or she begins to work for wages or other compensation; remuneration is anything of value given in exchange for labor or services rendered by an employee, including food and lodging.

An employee who fails to produce the required document(s), or a receipt for a replacement document(s) (in the case of lost, stolen or destroyed documents), within three (3) business days of the date employment begins may be fired. However, these practices must be uniformly applied to all employees. If an employee has presented a receipt for a replacement document(s), he or she must produce the actual document(s) within 90 days of the date employment begins.

An employer must examine the document(s) and, if they reasonably appear on their face to be genuine and relate to the person presenting them, you must accept them. To do otherwise could be an unfair immigration-related employment practice. If a document does not reasonably appear on its face to be genuine and to relate to the person presenting it, you must not accept it. Employees must present original documents. Photocopies are not acceptable; the only exception is an employee may present a certified copy of a birth certificate.

You cannot be charged with a verification violation if a Form I-9 is properly completed and the BICE discovers that the employee is not actually authorized to work. However, such employee cannot **continue** to be employed. What is my responsibility concerning the authenticity of document(s) presented to me?

State Payday Requirements
http://www.dol.gov/esa/programs/whd/state/payday.htm

State Meal Period Requirements
http://www.dol.gov/esa/programs/whd/state/meal.htm

TEEN LABOR LAWS FOR EMPLOYERS

All states have their own youth employment provisions and when state and federal rules differ, employers are held to the stricter standards. Visit the Youth Rules Website to learn about your state's provisions.

Employing Youth in Restaurants and Quick-Service Establishments under the Fair Labor Standards Act (FLSA)

(Effective February 14, 2005)

18 Years of Age: Not subject to the federal youth employment provisions.

16 & 17 Years of Age: May be employed for unlimited hours those declared hazardous such as hazardous power-driven meat processing machines (meat slicers, meat saws, patty forming machines, meat grinders, and meat choppers), commercial mixers and certain power-driven bakery machines. Also, they are not permitted to operate, feed, set-up, adjust, repair, or clean any of these machines.

17-year-olds, who meet certain specific requirements, may drive automobiles and trucks that do not exceed 6,000 pounds gross vehicle weight for limited amounts of time. They are prohibited from making time sensitive deliveries (such as pizza deliveries or other trips where time is of essence) and from driving at night. See http://www.dol.gov/esa/regs/compliance/whd/whdfs34.htm.

14 & 15 Years of Age: Fourteen- and 15- year-olds may be employed in restaurants and quick-service establishments outside school hours in a variety of jobs for limited periods of time and under specified conditions.

Under 14 Years of Age: May not be employed by food service establishments.

In addition to age regulations, there are also regulations that define the working hours and occupational duties.

Working Hours Standards for 14- and 15-Year-Olds

Child Labor Regulation No. 3, 29 CFR Part 570, Subpart C, limits the hours and the times of day that 14- and 15-year-olds may work:

- outside school hours;
- no more than 3 hours on a school day, including Fridays;
- no more than 8 hours on a nonschool day;
- no more than 18 hours during a week when school is in session;
- no more than 40 hours during a week when school is not in session;
- between 7 A.M. and 7 P.M. - except between June 1 and Labor day when the evening hour is extended to 9 P.M.

Occupational Duties Standards for 14- and 15-Year-Olds

Fourteen- and 15-year-olds may work in restaurants and quick-service food establishments, but only in certain jobs.

- **May not** cook over open flames
- **May not** operate NIEOC boilers, rotisseries, pressure cookers or fryolators
- **May not** perform any baking activities.
- **May not** operate, maintain, or repair power driven machines including food slicers, processors, or mixers.
- **May not** operate power lawn equipment, work in freezers or meat coolers, or load or unload goods from trucks or conveyors.
- **May not** operate microwave ovens having capacity to warm above 140° F.
- **May not** cook with deep fat fryers unless equipped with devices that automatically raise and lower the "baskets" into and out of the hot grease or oil.
- May perform cashiering, table service and "busing," and clean up work, including the use of vacuum cleaners and floor waxers.
- May work in preparing food and beverages, including the operation of devices such as dishwashers, toasters, milk shake blenders, warming lamps, and coffee grinders.
- May perform limited cooking duties using electric or gas grills (no open flames).
- May dispense food from cafeteria lines and steam tables
- May clean kitchen surfaces and non-power-driven equipment and dispose of cooking oil, but only when the temperature of the surface and oils do not exceed 100° F.

OVERTIME RULES

The federal Department of Labor (DOL) overtime regulation can be summarized as:

Almost All Employees Who Make Less Than $455 A Week ($23,660 A Year)
Are Eligible For Overtime Pay.

The new rule applies whether the employee is blue collar or white collar, or whether they supervise people of not. The exception for this rule is teachers, doctors and lawyers. They do not get overtime, no matter what they are paid.

Union workers covered by contracts will not be affected by the change.

Impact on the Restaurant Industry

Low-level and mid-level managers at restaurants who earn less than $23,660 a year will be newly eligible. However, employers can avoid paying them overtime by raising their salaries to the threshold amount.

State Laws. Eighteen states — including Wisconsin, New Jersey, Oregon and Kentucky — have separate state laws protecting overtime eligibility. In most states, employers must apply whichever regulation is more favorable to the employee. Legislative action is required in some states to make changes. Illinois became the first state to reject the new overtime rules.

DOL Rules. The 474-page rules change means that millions of low-wage workers will get overtime and millions of others may lose it. The Labor Department states that the law affects only salaried workers; hourly workers should continue to receive overtime.

There is plenty of confusion with the DOL rules. Here are some important rules to know:

- The new benchmark allows employers to designate certain workers as administrative, executive or professional, and exempt from overtime only if they are paid at least at least $455 a week, or $23,660 a year not including bonuses or commissions.

- Any employee who earns more than $100,000 a year is not eligible for mandated overtime for any reason.

- Any employee who earns between $23,660 and $100,000 a year, and who is in most executive, professional, or administrative positions, is not eligible for overtime. This does not, however, apply to salespeople. They are still eligible. Sales staff that regularly work outside of the employer's place of business are not eligible.

For more information:
U.S. Department of Labor—Employment Standards Administration Wage & Hour Division—http://www.dol.gov/esa/regs/compliance/whd/fairpay/main.htm

TIP REPORTING

Employers are not required to pay FICA tax (social security and medicare taxes) if an employee's tips are less than $20 per month or if his/her wages exceed the FICA annual wage base. A restaurant is responsible for paying FICA tax (7.65%) on taxable employee wages and tips. Employees are required to report tips on Form 4070 *Employee's Report of Tips to Employer* (or employer custom designed form) for proper withholding of employee income tax, FICA tax, and correct payment of the employer FICA tax. Noncash tips, such as tickets and passes, are not reported to the employer and not subject to FICA tax.

Professor Robert Ragsdale, CPA sent in an article from the Journal of Accountancy, July 2000 written by Lesli S. Laffie, JD. LLM, Technical Editor, The Tax Adviser. Following is an abstract of that article.

Under regulation section 31.3111-3, an employer must pay FICA taxes on tips as reported by employees. However, if the employee tips are under-reported, regulation 3121(q) comes into play. This regulation states that if the IRS ascertains that tips have been under-reported, a notice and demand payment can be sent to the restaurant owner for payment of FICA tax on those under-reported tips.

The unreported tip income is assessed by an IRS audit on the restaurant and not individual employees. The employer share of FICA is based on an aggregate amount of unreported tips using a method known as the aggregate method. Basically this method arrives at sales per hour number, which is then multiplied by each server's hours worked to determine yearly sales; this yearly sale is then multiplied by an average tip rate; the tips and sales charged on credit cards determine this tip rate.

Federal Circuit Courts of Appeal have upheld the IRS use of this indirect method. Some district courts have sided with restaurants. Those courts concluding in favor of restaurants have based their decisions on the following examples:

- Section 3121(q) allows the IRS to demand FICA tax on tips for unreported tips; it does not allow aggregation estimates.

- The aggregate method does not take into account the $20 de minimis rule.

- IRC Section 6053(c)(3) states that restaurant employers are to determine if the tips reported by employees are less than 8% of gross receipts. Reported tips not meeting that threshold are to be allocated among tipped employees in one of the following three methods:
  - (a) hours worked
  - (b) gross receipts
  - (c) good-faith agreement

Chapter 6 Outline

Hotel Financial Information Systems
    Classification of Hotel Departments
The Uniform System of Accounts
Basic Revenue and Support Center
    Statement Formats
Presentation of Payroll Expenses
Example of Hotel Departmental Statements
    Identification and Referencing of
        Departmental Statements
    Rooms Department Income Statement
    Food and Beverage Department
        Income Statement
    Telecommunications Department
        Income Statement
    Other Operated Departments Income
        Statement
    Schedule of Rentals and Other Income
    Administrative and General
        Department Statement
    Marketing Department Statement
    Property Operation and Maintenance
        Department Statement
    Schedule of Utility Costs
    Schedule of Fixed Charges
Income Statement
*Uniform System of Accounts for the Lodging
    Industry,* Tenth Revised Edition
Appendix: *USALI* Summary Operating
    Statement and Sample Departmental
    Statements

Competencies

1. Summarize the purposes and users of a hotel's departmental statements. (p. 159–162)

2. Differentiate between the general formats for financial statements for revenue and support centers. (p. 162)

3. List the information included in the standard reporting of departmental payroll expenses. (p. 163)

4. Recognize the ways in which financial statements are identified and referenced in relation to other statements. (pp. 163–164)

5. Describe the general formats used for a hotel's departmental financial statements. (pp. 164–167)

6. Explain how information from departmental statements is used to prepare a hotel's income statement. (pp. 167–175)

6

Hotel Departmental Statements

In HOTELS, departmental statements (also called internal financial statements) are an important part of any financial information system. Top managers require statements regarding the property as a whole, and middle and lower managers need detailed information about the departments for which they are responsible.

The purposes of these internal financial statements are to present information for management to monitor the profitability of operations and to be useful for long-range planning. Internal financial statements include numerous **supporting schedules** that provide significant detail about each department's operations and the financial affairs of the company. The appendix to this chapter presents samples of common supporting schedules.

Departmental statements are issued only to internal users, such as top management, department heads, and supervisors. Departmental statements are not issued to external users, such as stockholders, creditors, and potential investors.

In discussing hotel departmental statements, this chapter will address such questions as:

1. What is the basic format for a revenue center statement?

2. What is the basic format for a support center statement?

3. Why is the presentation of payroll information standardized for all departmental statements?

4. Which financial statements make up the set of internal financial statements used by management?

5. How is information from the departmental statements used to prepare the hotel's income statement?

Hotel Financial Information Systems

The foundation of a financial information system for a hotel consists of the financial reports issued to management. A hotel is a unique business institution. Unlike other retail operations, a hotel's operating environment is composed of several different revenue centers and numerous support centers. A hotel's management requires more than the typical **income statement** and **balance sheet** for the company as a whole. Hotel managers need financial statements for the major departments in order to measure the income and expenses of each responsibility area.

Classification of Hotel Departments

A hotel's departments can generally be classified as follows:

- Revenue centers
- Support centers
- Utility costs
- Fixed charges

Exhibit 1 illustrates this classification of the departments of a hotel. Small hotels may not have all of the listed departments, while large hotels may have more departments. For example, a large hotel may have several food and beverage facilities, such as a main dining room, patio, and cafeteria. Each of these areas would be shown separately.

Revenue Centers. A revenue center serves guests and generates sales but does not necessarily earn profits. The generation of sales, no matter how small, qualifies a facility as a revenue center. A departmental income statement is produced for each facility classified as a revenue center.

Typical revenue centers are:

- Rooms
- Food and beverage (F&B): dining room, cafeteria, patio, coffee shop, and the banquet operation.
- Telecommunications
- Other operated departments: gift shop, recreation, and any other department operated by the hotel and not by a concessionaire
- Schedule of rentals and other income: This is not an actual physical department. It is a schedule used to report revenue that is not attributable to any other revenue center. The schedule lists revenue such as interest income, dividend income, rentals of store and office space, concessions income, commissions, vending machine profits (if owned), cash discounts earned, and salvage income.

Support Centers. A support center provides services essential to the operation of revenue centers. A support center does not directly generate sales. A departmental statement is produced for each support center to show its expenses. A support center's departmental statement cannot be called an income statement because an income statement shows sales and expenses.

Many hospitality students mistakenly believe that the housekeeping function is a support center. From an operations standpoint, housekeeping does serve a revenue center; however, housekeeping is a service dedicated to the rooms department and does not provide a service to other revenue centers. All housekeeping expenses and wages are combined in the rooms department income statement.

Typical support centers are:

- Administrative and general (A&G)
- Marketing
- Property operation and maintenance

Exhibit 1   Hotel Financial Information System

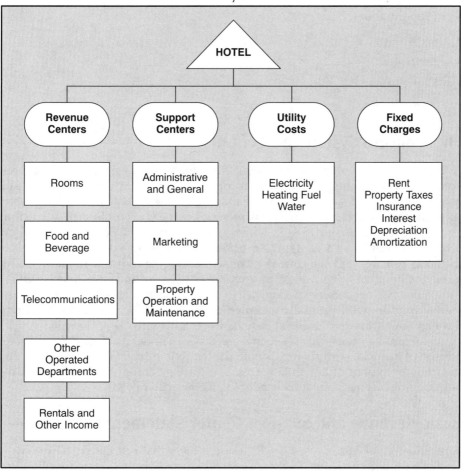

Utility Costs. In most hotels, this department has no physical presence. Because utility costs are significant, management needs a report that lists the utility costs of the hotel for:

- Electricity
- Heating fuel
- Water

Fixed Charges. This department has no physical presence. Fixed charges are important for management to track because fixed costs are incurred regardless of the volume of sales; in fact, they are incurred even when a hotel is closed.

The typical fixed charges are:

- Rent

- Property taxes

- Insurance

- Interest

- Depreciation

- Amortization

The Uniform System of Accounts

A uniform system of accounts provides standardized accounting procedures, account titles, and financial statement formats to guide in the preparation and reading of financial statements. In the lodging industry, the specialized industry standards are established by recommendations in the *Uniform System of Accounts for the Lodging Industry (USALI),* which is published by the Educational Institute of the American Hotel & Lodging Association. It is developed by professionals in the hotel industry and is a consensus of senior lodging industry financial executives, public accounting authorities, representatives of industry benchmarking companies, and academic experts. The *USALI* approach to external financial statements complies with generally accepted accounting principles (GAAP). With a few exceptions, internal financial statements comply with GAAP as well.

Standardized financial statements are easier to understand, and permit comparison of financial performance within the lodging industry. For new properties, the uniform system of accounts serves as a turnkey accounting system that the new lodging business can quickly adapt to its particular needs.

Basic Revenue and Support Center Statement Formats

A revenue center generates sales. Revenue centers that sell merchandise have a Cost of Sales account. After all expenses are deducted, the operating result for any revenue center is either departmental income or loss.

The basic format of a financial statement for revenue-producing departments is:

$$
\begin{array}{l}
\ \text{Revenue} \\
-\ \underline{\text{Allowances}} \\
\ \text{Net revenue} \\
-\ \underline{\text{Cost of sales}} \\
\ \text{Gross profit} \\
-\ \underline{\text{Expenses}} \\
\ \text{Departmental income (or loss)}
\end{array}
$$

A support center does not generate sales; thus it cannot have a gross profit resulting in departmental income or loss. Therefore, the departmental statement for a support center is a list of the expenses incurred for the period.

Presentation of Payroll Expenses

Because salaries and wages are a significant part of any department's expenses, management requires pertinent information on this important expense. Whether a department is a revenue or support center, the reporting of its payroll expense is standardized as follows:

- Salaries and wages

- Employee benefits

- Total payroll and related expenses

These three lines or lines that are similar to them are included on each departmental statement. See the Appendix to this chapter for the format currently presented in the newest *USALI*.

Example of Hotel Departmental Statements

A set of departmental statements for the fictitious Hotel DORO is presented in this chapter to serve as an example. These departmental statements are:

- Exhibit 2—Rooms Department Income Statement

- Exhibit 3—Food and Beverage Department Income Statement

- Exhibit 4—Telecommunications Department Income Statement

- Exhibit 5—Other Operated Departments Income Statement

- Exhibit 6—Schedule of Rentals and Other Income

- Exhibit 7—Administrative and General Department Statement

- Exhibit 8—Marketing Department Statement

- Exhibit 9—Property Operation and Maintenance Department Statement

- Exhibit 10—Schedule of Utility Costs

- Exhibit 11—Schedule of Fixed Charges

Identification and Referencing of Departmental Statements

Each departmental statement shows an identifier in the upper right corner. For example, the identifier for the rooms department income statement (Exhibit 2) is A1. These identifiers are used as references on the hotel's income statement, shown in Exhibit 12. In the operated departments section of this statement, the reference to A1 in the schedule column indicates that the corresponding information came from Schedule A1.

Observe that the Hotel DORO's income statement is identified as Schedule A. This indicates that it is a summary or master statement. The identifier for each supporting statement for Schedule A is preceded by A and followed by the supporting statement's sequential number. Because the statement for the rooms department is the first departmental statement that supports the summary hotel statement, it is assigned the identifier of A1.

Rooms Department Income Statement

Exhibit 2 presents the Hotel DORO's rooms department income statement, which is referenced as Schedule A1. Notice that the rooms department does not have a Cost of Sales account because it does not sell merchandise. (Sales from the honor bar in a guestroom are credited to the food and beverage department.) Since there is no Cost of Sales account, it is not necessary to show a gross profit line.

Some hotel managers prefer to have the rooms department income statement itemize the rooms revenue derived from transient guests, permanent guests, or other designations. The management of the Hotel DORO does not need this itemized information because all the hotel guests are transient.

The net revenue of $897,500 is the result of subtracting the allowances of $2,500 from the total billings of $900,000. The total payroll and related expenses of $143,140 represent the salaries and wages of $120,000 plus the employee benefits of $23,140. The total other expenses of $62,099 are arrived at by adding all the items listed under other expenses, from commissions down to other operating expenses in this case. The total expenses of $205,239 are arrived at by adding the total payroll and related expenses of $143,140 to the total other expenses of $62,099. *(Because the procedures explained above are similar for all departments, they will not be repeated in the analyses of the rest of the financial statements for the Hotel DORO in this chapter.)*

The departmental income (loss) of $692,261 is arrived at by subtracting the total expenses of $205,239 from the net revenue of $897,500. The amount of $692,261 is interpreted as departmental income because the amount is not enclosed in parentheses. *The departmental income (loss) line demonstrates an "accounting shorthand" labeling technique. The number on this line will be shown without any mathematical sign if the result is income; the number on this line will be shown in parentheses if the result is a loss.*

Food and Beverage Department Income Statement

Exhibit 3 presents the Hotel DORO's food and beverage department income statement, identified as Schedule A2. Notice that sales are shown for food, beverage, and "other." The other sales represent sales of souvenirs, postcards, candy, popcorn, and other nonvending-machine sales in the restaurant and lounge.

The Hotel DORO uses the periodic inventory accounting method to compute cost of sales. A supporting schedule detailing the food and beverage inventory activities would be attached to the department income statement. For example, the cost of food sales supporting schedule could appear as follows:

Hotel Doro, Inc.
Cost of Food Sales Supporting Schedule
For the year ended December 31, 20X2   **Schedule A2.1**

Beginning inventory	$	5,800
+ Purchases		145,600

	Cost of food available	151,400
−	Ending inventory	7,000
	Cost of food consumed	144,400
−	Employee meals credit	9,200
	Cost of food sales	$135,200

Observe that the food and beverage department income statement repeats the last three lines from the cost of food sales supporting schedule A2.1: the cost of goods consumed of $144,400 and the cost of all employee meals of $9,200 are subtracted from the cost of goods consumed to arrive at the $135,200 cost of sales.

Net other income of $3,800 is the result of other revenue of $6,400 less its respective cost of sales of $2,600.

The gross profit of $346,260 is arrived at by subtracting the $175,710 food and beverage cost of sales from the food and beverage net revenue of $518,170 and adding net other income of $3,800. The total expenses of $258,883 are subtracted from the gross profit of $346,260 to arrive at the **departmental income** of $87,377.

Telecommunications Department Income Statement

Exhibit 4 presents the Hotel DORO's telecommunications department income statement, identified as Schedule A3. There are several methods of accounting for the revenue and expenses of a hotel's telecommunications service.

With today's sophisticated computerized accounting systems, the telecommunications service for guests and for various hotel departments can be reported separately. Each department can be charged for its telecommunications usage, which would appear on each department's statement. The revenue and expenses pertaining to guests would be the only items appearing on the telecommunications department statement. An advantage of this accounting method is that it provides a means for evaluating the telecommunications department as a profit-making center.

The Hotel DORO has selected a different alternative. While the telecommunications department is a revenue center because it generates sales, management prefers to show all the expenses for telecommunications usage by guests and by all departments of the hotel on this departmental statement. Therefore, this statement shows 100 percent of the costs of the telecommunications system and costs for the hotel as a whole.

Management's philosophy is that the revenue from guests helps to defray the costs of the hotel's total telecommunications service. While Schedule A3 may appear to show a loss, management would instead interpret the results as follows: *The net cost of the total telecommunications service for the hotel was $27,623 for the year.*

In the body of the statement, the line item gross profit (loss) shows a loss of $8,904, indicated by the parentheses. This gross loss occurred because the cost of calls expense of $60,044 exceeded the net revenue of $51,140. Remember that this is not unusual for the Hotel DORO because the cost of calls includes the telecommunications usage of the guests and all departments of the hotel.

Because the $8,904 is a loss, it has the same effect as an expense; additional expenses of $18,719 increase the final loss to $27,623 for the year. This final loss is shown in parentheses on the departmental income (loss) line.

Other Operated Departments Income Statement

Exhibit 5 displays the Hotel DORO's **other operated departments** income statement, identified as Schedule A4. The format and line items on this schedule may vary according to the different kinds of goods and services sold to guests, such as items from the gift shop, apparel shop, or package store, recreation, and garage and parking (if guests are charged). Each operated department may be shown separately on its dedicated departmental statement so that each can be evaluated independently.

The Hotel DORO is a small hotel with minor sales from each of its other operated departments. Instead of having a report for each area, management has decided to combine all these reports into one statement until one or more individual departments have significant sales volume.

Schedule of Rentals and Other Income

Exhibit 6 shows the Hotel DORO's schedule of rentals and other income, identified as Schedule A5. This schedule reports revenue that is not attributable to any other revenue center. The schedule lists revenue from such sources as:

- Interest income
- Dividend income
- Rentals of store and office space
- Concessions income
- Commissions
- Vending machine profits (if owned)
- Cash discounts earned
- Salvage income

Minor gains or losses from the sale of fixed assets could also appear on this schedule. The Hotel DORO's management prefers that such gains or losses appear as a separate line item on the hotel's income statement.

Administrative and General Department Statement

Exhibit 7 presents the Hotel DORO's administrative and general (A&G) department statement, identified as Schedule A6. The statement for any support center does not include sections for sales or cost of sales because support centers do not generate revenue by the sales of services or merchandise.

The management of the Hotel DORO includes the following support services in the A&G department:

- General manager and staff
- Accounting

- Human resources
- Information systems

Some hotels prefer to have separate reports for each of these areas, especially human resources and data processing services.

Marketing Department Statement

Exhibit 8 features the Hotel DORO's marketing department statement, identified as Schedule A7. Costs associated with advertising, public relations, and research are shown on this statement.

Property Operation and Maintenance Department Statement

Exhibit 9 displays the Hotel DORO's property operation and maintenance department statement, identified as Schedule A8. This statement shows all maintenance and repair expenses for the equipment for all departments, grounds, and buildings of the hotel.

Schedule of Utility Costs

Exhibit 10 shows the Hotel DORO's schedule of utility costs, identified as Schedule A9. This statement reports the expenses for electricity, fuel, and water used by all departments of the hotel. However, utility costs associated with the cooking of food are shown on the food and beverage departmental income statement.

Schedule of Fixed Charges

Exhibit 11 presents the Hotel DORO's schedule of fixed charges, identified as Schedule A10. These expenses are important because they are incurred regardless of sales volume, even if the hotel is closed. Another characteristic of these fixed charges is that they benefit the hotel as a whole, not any specific department. Notice that the fixed charges are classified into six major areas:

- Rent
- Property taxes
- Insurance
- Interest expense
- Depreciation
- Amortization

Income Statement

All the results of the revenue centers, support centers, utility costs, and fixed charges are consolidated into one statement called the income statement. Information from each departmental statement is brought forward to prepare this statement. Departmental managers do not receive this statement; it is issued to top management and the board of directors.

Exhibit 12 shows the income statement for the Hotel DORO, identified as Schedule A, which indicates that it is a master schedule. The format illustrated is the long-form income statement.

The operated departments section includes information from the statements of each revenue center as indicated by the references shown in the schedule column. The information brought forward from the departmental statements is as follows:

- Net revenue

- Cost of sales

- Payroll and related expenses

- Total other expenses

- Departmental income (loss)

Refer to each departmental statement in Exhibits 2 through 11, and trace the amounts that were brought forward to this master statement. Keep in mind the following points:

- The total expenses should not be brought forward to the other expenses column. Rather, this column is the total of expenses exclusive of payroll and related expenses.

- The net revenue for the food and beverage department is computed from Schedule A2 as follows:

Food net revenue	$358,300
Beverage net revenue	+ 159,870
Other revenue	+ 6,400
Total net revenue	$524,570

- The cost of sales for the food and beverage department is computed from Schedule A2 as follows:

Food cost of sales	$135,200
Beverage cost of sales	+ 40,510
Other cost of sales	+ 2,600
Total cost of sales	$178,310

The Undistributed Operating Expenses section includes departments that cannot be charged to any revenue center, specifically support centers and utility costs. The expense of each department is shown in the income (loss) column because it will be deducted from operating income.

The income before fixed charges of $485,029 is arrived at by subtracting the total undistributed expenses of $340,915 from the total operating income of the revenue centers of $825,944.

The information for the fixed charges section comes from the schedule of fixed charges. The expenses for depreciation and amortization have been combined because both of these expenses are "noncash" expenses; that is, while they are a deduction from income, they did not and will not require any payment of cash.

The income before income taxes of $66,138 is the result of subtracting the total fixed charges of $418,891 from the income before fixed charges of $485,029.

Exhibit 12 is not a fully completed income statement for the Hotel DORO. Income taxes that are a hotel expense have not yet been entered. Also, there may be gains or losses from the sale of assets. The emphasis in this chapter is on individual departments and not the hotel as a whole.

Exhibit 2   Rooms Department Income Statement—Hotel DORO

	Hotel DORO, Inc.		
	Rooms Department Income Statement		
	For the year ended December 31, 20X2		**Schedule A1**
Revenue			
Lodging		$900,000	
Allowances		2,500	
Net Revenue			$897,500
Expenses			
Salaries and Wages		$120,000	
Employee Benefits		23,140	
Total Payroll and Related Expenses			143,140
Other Expenses			
Commissions		2,500	
Contract Cleaning		5,285	
Guest Transportation		10,100	
Laundry and Dry Cleaning		7,000	
Linen		11,000	
Operating Supplies		11,125	
Reservation Expense		9,950	
Uniforms		2,167	
Other Operating Expenses		2,972	
Total Other Expenses			62,099
Total Expenses			205,239
Departmental Income (Loss)			$692,261

Exhibit 3   Food and Beverage Department Income Statement—Hotel DORO

Hotel DORO, Inc.
Food and Beverage Department Income Statement
For the year ended December 31, 20X2   Schedule A2

	Food	Beverage	Total
Revenue	$360,000	$160,000	$520,000
Allowances	1,700	130	1,830
Net Revenue	358,300	159,870	518,170
Cost of Food and Beverage Sales			
Cost of Food and Beverage Consumed	144,400	40,510	184,910
Less Cost of Employees' Meals	9,200		9,200
Net Cost of Food and Beverage Sales	135,200	40,510	175,710
Other Income			
Other Revenue			6,400
Other Cost of Sales			2,600
Net Other Income			3,800
Gross Profit			346,260
Expenses			
Salaries and Wages	177,214		
Employee Benefits	26,966		
Total Payroll and Related Expenses		204,180	
Other Expenses			
China, Glassware, and Silver	7,779		
Contract Cleaning	3,630		
Kitchen Fuel	2,074		
Laundry and Dry Cleaning	5,182		
Licenses	800		
Music and Entertainment	16,594		
Operating Supplies	11,409		
Uniforms	2,568		
Other Operating Expenses	4,667		
Total Other Expenses		54,703	
Total Expenses			258,883
Departmental Income (Loss)			$ 87,377

Exhibit 4   Telecommunications Department Income Statement—Hotel DORO

Hotel DORO, Inc. Telecommunications Department Income Statement For the year ended December 31, 20X2		Schedule A3
Revenue		
Local	$ 9,740	
Long Distance	41,011	
Service Charges	514	
Total Revenue	51,265	
Allowances	125	
Net Revenue		$ 51,140
Cost of Calls		
Local	8,660	
Long Distance	51,384	
Total Cost of Calls		$ 60,044
Gross Profit (Loss)		(8,904)
Expenses		
Salaries and Wages	14,831	
Employee Benefits	2,301	
Total Payroll and Related Expenses	17,132	
Other Operating Expenses	1,587	
Total Expenses		18,719
Departmental Income (Loss)		$ (27,623)

Exhibit 5   Other Operated Departments Income Statement—Hotel DORO

Hotel DORO, Inc. Other Operated Departments Income Statement For the year ended December 31, 20X2		Schedule A4
Revenue		
Services	$40,005	
Sales of Merchandise	22,995	
Net Revenue		$63,000
Cost of Merchandise Sold		10,347
Gross Profit		52,653
Expenses		
Salaries and Wages	30,164	
Employee Benefits	3,112	
Total Payroll and Related Expenses	33,276	
Other Operating Expenses	6,731	
Total Expenses		40,007
Departmental Income (Loss)		$12,646

Exhibit 6   Schedule of Rentals and Other Income—Hotel DORO

Hotel DORO, Inc.
Schedule of Rentals and Other Income
For the year ended December 31, 20X2   **Schedule A5**

Space Rentals		
Stores	$25,474	
Offices	16,723	
Total Rental Income		$42,197
Concessions Income		9,862
Commissions		
Laundry	1,814	
Valet	1,017	
Vending Machines	1,265	
Total Commissions Income		4,096
Cash Discounts Earned		3,200
Interest Income		1,928
Total Rentals and Other Income		$61,283

Exhibit 7   Administrative and General Department Statement—Hotel DORO

Hotel DORO, Inc.
Administrative and General Department Statement
For the year ended December 31, 20X2   Schedule A6

Salaries and Wages	$85,718	
Employee Benefits	11,914	
Total Payroll and Related Expenses		$ 97,632
Other Expenses		
Credit Card Commissions	14,389	
Data Processing Expense	7,638	
Dues and Subscriptions	3,265	
Human Resources Expense	10,357	
Operating Supplies	9,784	
Postage and Telegrams	4,416	
Professional Fees	4,136	
Uncollectible Accounts	1,291	
Traveling and Entertainment	4,250	
Other Operating Expenses	7,023	
Total Other Expenses		66,549
Total Administrative and General Expenses		$164,181

Exhibit 8   Marketing Department Statement—Hotel DORO

Hotel DORO, Inc.
Marketing Department Statement
For the year ended December 31, 20X2   Schedule A7

Salaries and Wages	$31,418	
Employee Benefits	4,407	
Total Payroll and Related Expenses		$35,825
Advertising		
Outdoor	600	
Print	11,560	
Radio and Television	2,800	
Other	700	
Total Advertising		15,660
Fees and Commissions		
Agency Fees	1,500	
Commissions	11,250	
Total Fees and Commissions		12,750
Other Operating Expenses		3,633
Total Marketing Expense		$67,868

Exhibit 9   Property Operation and Maintenance Department Statement—Hotel DORO

Hotel DORO, Inc.
Property Operation and Maintenance Department Statement
For the year ended December 31, 20X2   Schedule A8

Salaries and Wages	$32,412	
Employee Benefits	4,505	
Total Payroll and Related Expenses		$36,917
Other Expenses		
Building Supplies	2,816	
Electrical and Mechanical Equipment	5,013	
Engineering Supplies	1,612	
Furniture, Fixtures, Equipment, and Decor	4,811	
Grounds and Landscaping	3,914	
Operating Supplies	1,018	
Removal of Waste Matter	2,416	
Swimming Pool	1,800	
Uniforms	137	
Other Operating Expenses	1,100	
Total Other Expenses		24,637
Total Property Operation and Maintenance		$61,554

Exhibit 10   Schedule of Utility Costs—Hotel DORO

Hotel DORO, Inc.	
Schedule of Utility Costs	
For the year ended December 31, 20X2	**Schedule A9**
Electric	$32,172
Fuel	10,509
Water	4,631
Total Utility Costs	**$47,312**

Exhibit 11   Schedule of Fixed Charges—Hotel DORO

Hotel DORO, Inc.		
Schedule of Fixed Charges		
For the year ended December 31, 20X2		**Schedule A10**
Rent		
Real Estate	$12,000	
Furnishings, Fixtures, and Equipment	7,500	
Total Rent Expense		$ 19,500
Property Taxes and Other Municipal Charges		
Real Estate Taxes	35,762	
Personal Property Taxes	7,312	
Utility Taxes	750	
Business and Occupation Taxes	1,500	
Total Property Taxes and Other Municipal Charges		45,324
Insurance		15,914
Interest Expense		192,153
Depreciation		
Buildings and Improvements	87,500	
Furnishings, Fixtures, and Equipment	56,000	
Total Depreciation Expense		143,500
Amortization		
Leasehold Improvements	1,000	
Preopening Expenses	1,500	
Total Amortization Expense		2,500
Total Fixed Charges		**$418,891**

Exhibit 12   Long-Form Income Statement—Hotel DORO

Hotel DORO, Inc.
Statement of Income
For the year ended December 31, 20X2   **Schedule A**

	Schedule	Net Revenue	Cost of Sales	Payroll and Related Expenses	Other Expenses	Income (Loss)
Operated Departments						
Rooms	A1	$ 897,500		$ 143,140	$ 62,099	$692,261
Food and Beverage	A2	524,570	$ 178,310	204,180	54,703	87,377
Telecommunications	A3	51,140	60,044	17,132	1,587	(27,623)
Other Operated Departments	A4	63,000	10,347	33,276	6,731	12,646
Rentals and Other Income	A5	61,283				61,283
Total Operated Departments		1,597,493	248,701	397,728	125,120	825,944
Undistributed Expenses						
Administrative and General	A6			97,632	66,549	164,181
Marketing	A7			35,825	32,043	67,868
Property Operation and Maintenance	A8			36,917	24,637	61,554
Utility Costs	A9				47,312	47,312
Total Undistributed Expenses				170,374	170,541	340,915
Income Before Fixed Charges		$1,597,493	$248,701	$568,102	$295,661	$485,029
Fixed Charges						
Rent	A10					28,500
Property Taxes	A10					45,324
Insurance	A10					6,914
Interest	A10					192,153
Depreciation and Amortization	A10					146,000
Total Fixed Charges						418,891
Income Before Income Taxes						66,138

Uniform System of Accounts for the Lodging Industry, Tenth Revised Edition

The *USALI* is periodically revised and is now in its tenth revised edition, which was issued in 2006. This edition contains a number of significant changes from the prior edition. The format and level of detail in the tenth edition were developed to meet the financial statement needs of management. The formats follow U.S. accounting standards; international users may find significant differences with accounting standards applicable in their countries.

The Appendix to this chapter contains the *summary operating statement* for internal users and samples of *internal departmental schedules* promulgated by the *USALI*, tenth revised edition.[1]

Endnote

1. *Uniform System of Accounts for the Lodging Industry,* Tenth Revised Edition (Lansing, Mich.: American Hotel & Lodging Educational Institute, 2006). For more information, or to order this reference, access the Educational Institute's website at www.ahlei.org.

⚿ Key Terms

balance sheet—A statement reporting on the financial position of a business by presenting its assets, liabilities, and equity on a given date.

departmental income—The difference between an operating department's revenue and direct expenses.

income statement—A financial statement of the results of operations that presents the sales, expenses, and net income of a business entity for a stated period of time. Also called statement of income.

other operated departments—A term used to represent incidental operating departments not including those departments operated by concessionaires.

supporting schedules—Schedules providing additional detail for the general ledger or the financial statements. For example, an accounts payable schedule lists all the vendors to which the company owes a balance on open account; the total should agree with the balance in the general ledger accounts payable account.

uniform system of accounts—A manual (usually produced for a specific segment of the hospitality industry) that defines accounts for various types and sizes of operations. A uniform system of accounts generally provides standardized financial statement formats, explanations of individual accounts, and sample bookkeeping documents.

⁇ Review Questions

1. Specify whether the following items are presented on the hotel income statement as Operated Departments, Undistributed Expenses, or Fixed Charges.

   a. Real Estate Rent Expense
   b. Administrative and General Department
   c. Depreciation
   d. Rentals and Other Income
   e. Food and Beverage Department
   f. Mortgage Interest Expense
   g. Telecommunications Department

2. How is net revenue computed on a departmental income statement?

3. How is gross profit computed on a departmental income statement?

4. What items are included as Total Payroll and Related Expenses on a departmental statement?

5. Which statement reports the revenue for vending machine sales of cigarettes in a public lobby?

6. What is the purpose of supporting schedules? Name some of these.

Internet Sites

For more information, visit the following Internet sites. Remember that Internet addresses can change without notice. If the site is no longer there, you can use a search engine to look for additional sites.

Financial Information System and XBRL
www.bcs.org/server.php?show=ConWebDoc.2709

Spa Revenue Center
www.hotelinteractive.com/index.asp?page_id=5000&article_id=5580

Revenue Explained
http://beginnersinvest.about.com/cs/investinglessons/l/blrevenue.htm

Examples of Revenue Accounts
www.accountinginfo.com/study/fs/revenue-101.htm

Operating Expense Explained
http://beginnersinvest.about.com/cs/investinglessons/l/blopexpenses.htm

Examples of Expense Accounts
www.accountinginfo.com/study/fs/expense-101.htm

Cost of Goods Sold
http://beginnersinvest.about.com/cs/investinglessons/l/blcogs.htm

Problems

Problem 1

All of the problems in this section are based on the fictional Village Hotel, Inc. The following information summarizes various general ledger accounts of the Village Hotel for the year ended December 31, 20X9. Prepare the departmental statements for this hotel, and save these results for the preparation of the hotel income statement in several formats

Prepare all the statements in accordance with the formats shown for the Hotel DORO's financial statements. *Any account information relating to employee benefits is to be consolidated and shown under the caption called Employee Benefits.*

1. Rooms Department:

	debit	credit
Room Sales		1,043,900
Allowances	2,700	
Salaries and Wages	159,304	
Payroll Taxes	18,716	
Employee Meals	3,450	
Other Employee Benefits	3,864	
Commissions	4,124	
Contract Cleaning	13,200	
Guest Transportation	12,494	

	debit	credit
Laundry and Dry Cleaning	11,706	
Linen	7,742	
Operating Supplies	12,619	
Reservation Expense	7,288	
Uniforms	3,032	
Other Operating Expenses	6,875	

2. Food and Beverage Department:

	debit	credit
Food Sales		442,471
Beverage Sales		183,929
Allowances—Food	600	
Allowances—Beverage	63	
Other Sales		1,070
Cost of Food Consumed	177,873	
Employee Meals Credit		12,832
Cost of Beverage Sales	43,407	
Other Cost of Sales	642	
Salaries and Wages	182,214	
Payroll Taxes	21,866	
Employee Meals	6,890	
Other Employee Benefits	7,562	
China, Glassware, and Silver	8,766	
Contract Cleaning	4,000	
Kitchen Fuel	2,505	
Laundry and Dry Cleaning	6,199	
Licenses	3,130	
Music and Entertainment	31,308	
Operating Supplies	12,523	
Uniforms	3,757	
Other Operating Expenses	7,271	

3. Telecommunications Department:

	debit	credit
Local		4,783
Long Distance		47,228
Service Charges		389
Allowances	372	
Local	4,587	
Long Distance	41,918	
Salaries and Wages	12,307	
Payroll Taxes	1,580	
Employee Meals	130	
Other Employee Benefits	300	
Other Operating Expenses	6,816	

4. Rentals and Other Income:

	debit	credit
Commissions: Vending Machines		1,500
Cash Discounts Earned		2,700
Interest Income		800

5. Administrative and General Department:

	debit	credit
Salaries and Wages	96,997	
Payroll Taxes	8,719	
Employee Meals	1,259	
Other Employee Benefits	3,500	
Credit Card Commissions	11,330	
Data Processing Expense	6,400	
Dues and Subscriptions	1,200	
Human Resources Expense	7,817	
Operating Supplies	7,805	
Postage and Telegrams	3,203	
Professional Fees	4,000	
Uncollectible Accounts	1,432	
Traveling and Entertainment	2,000	
Other Operating Expenses	3,022	

6. Marketing Department:

	debit	credit
Salaries and Wages	22,420	
Payroll Taxes	2,690	
Employee Meals	769	
Other Employee Benefits	1,121	
Outdoor Advertising	500	
Print Advertising	3,500	
Radio and Television Advertising	1,800	
Other Advertising	288	
Agency Fees	1,200	
Commissions	10,500	
Other Operating Expenses	3,421	

7. Property Operation and Maintenance Department:

	debit	credit
Salaries and Wages	27,790	
Payroll Taxes	3,335	
Employee Meals	334	
Other Employee Benefits	193	
Building Supplies	9,251	
Electrical and Mechanical Equipment	16,243	

	debit	credit
Engineering Supplies	2,311	
Furniture, Fixtures, Equipment, and Decor	14,177	
Grounds and Landscaping	4,414	
Operating Supplies	2,749	
Removal of Waste Matter	2,499	
Swimming Pool	2,500	
Uniforms	500	
Other Operating Expenses	2,000	

8. Utility Costs:

	debit	credit
Electric	29,012	
Fuel	44,638	
Water	7,770	

9. Fixed Charges:

	debit	credit
Rental Expense Accounts:		
Real Estate	100,225	
Furnishings, Fixtures, and Equipment	17,000	
Real Estate Taxes	44,950	
Personal Property Taxes	8,650	
Utility Taxes	850	
Business and Occupation Taxes	1,200	
Insurance	27,986	
Interest Expense (Notes Payable)	52,148	
Depreciation Accounts:		
Furnishings, Fixtures, and Equipment	85,272	
Amortization Accounts:		
Leasehold Improvements	30,588	

Problem 2

Using the departmental statements from Problem 1, prepare the preliminary statement of income for the Village Hotel. For your convenience, the following checkpoint amount is provided: the income before income taxes for the hotel is $140,424.

Problem 3

Management has requested an analysis of the employee meals expense for the Village Hotel. Prepare a supporting schedule showing the cost of employee meals for each department. For your convenience, the following checkpoint amount is provided: the total on this schedule must agree with the employee meals credit of $12,832 that appears on the food and beverage department income statement prepared in Problem 1.

Problem 4

Management has requested an analysis of the cost of food sold for the Village Hotel. Prepare a supporting schedule showing the cost of food sold. For your convenience, the following checkpoint amount is provided: The total on this schedule must agree with the $165,041 cost of food sales amount that appears on the food and beverage department income statement prepared in Problem 1.

You will need this information from the following partial section of a worksheet to complete the supporting schedule in this problem:

	Income Statement		Balance Sheet	
	debit	credit	debit	credit
Food Inventory			6,825	
Income Summary	5,570	6,825		
Food Purchases	179,128			
Employee Meals Credit		12,832		

Case Study ———————————————————————

Accounting System Function and Structure

The 100-room Domain Hotel has been operating for three years. Its market is value-minded travelers who enjoy comfortable rooms and a variety of complimentary services, including a hot breakfast with delicious offerings. The Domain's other amenities are high-speed Internet access in all rooms, wireless Internet access in the lobby and meeting rooms, 24-hour coffee in the lobby, local calls, and an in-room movie channel. The Domain Hotel is family owned. A close family friend, in public practice, serves as the hotel's accountant and has designed the hotel's financial reporting system. The friend has no hospitality experience or education.

The current system consists of two reporting segments: (1) a revenue center that includes rooms, restaurant, and gift shop (no liquor is sold on premises); and (2) a support center that includes marketing, administrative, maintenance, and utility costs. Income from vending machines is credited to the administrative department.

Essentially, the income statements prepared for the Hotel Domain's management are:

- The Hotel Income Statement
- One Revenue Center
- One Support Center

Challenge

1. Describe the major weaknesses of the practice of placing all revenue centers into one reporting segment.

2. Describe the major weaknesses of the grouping of all support centers into one reporting segment.

3. Comment on the handling of income from vending machines.

4. Explain how the departments should be structured for reporting in accordance with the *Uniform System of Accounts for the Lodging Industry.*

5. Summarize your explanation in #4 with a diagram of the reporting structure.

6. Explain whether the accountant should be retained.

7. Comment on other areas that might not be in compliance with the *Uniform System of Accounts for the Lodging Industry.*

Appendix: *USALI* Summary Operating Statement and Sample Departmental Statements

The Ninth Revised Edition of *USALI* included a *Summary Income Statement* for internal use. The Tenth Revised Edition of *USALI* has replaced that statement with a *Summary Operating Statement*. As the name change suggests, the new statement is not in fact a complete income statement, as it focuses on the net and adjusted operating income rather than on the operation's final net income. This statement is part of a financial reporting package that includes departmental schedules and other schedules to supplement the operating information provided to a hotel's management.

There are many differences between the previous edition's summary income statement and the new edition's summary operating statement. The most significant changes are as follows:

- Certain expenses normally found on an income statement, such as Interest, Depreciation, Amortization, and Income Taxes, are omitted, because they are usually not controllable by operating managers.

- A *Less: Replacement Reserves* line reduces net operating income. Many management contracts, loan agreements, and owners/operators specify the use of the reserves to accumulate funds for future fixed asset replacements or capital improvements. The amounts shown may not represent money actually set aside to fund the reserves.

- A *rigid designated format* for the Summary Operating Statement and each departmental schedule is mandated. *USALI* states: "Individual properties may delete irrelevant line items, but the Tenth Revised Edition does not provide for the addition or substitution of other revenue or expense line items. Rather, properties will now have to develop a sub-account/sub-schedule to provide more detail related to a particular revenue or expense item." *USALI* then provides the following reason: "This method of presentation will permit external users of financial statements to compare the financial position and operational performance of a particular property with similar types of properties in the lodging industry."

- The Summary Operating Statement includes only these *four sources of revenue*: rooms, food, beverage, and other operated departments. This means that the telecommunications department is summarized into the other operated departments. The food and beverage operations must be combined in the Summary Operating Statement; those properties desiring separate reporting may do so using supplementary schedules.

- The *net operating income* from the Summary Operating Statement *will not link* to actual net income because of the elimination of certain expenses, as previously explained. *USALI* presents this justification: "The revision committee believes that this approach is more informative for the owner or manager who is focused on operating cash flows."

- Various account titles and line titles have changed. Any reader interested in the full scope of these changes should refer to the *USALI*, Tenth Revised Edition.

Because of many of these changes, *USALI* acknowledges that the summary operating statement does not conform to generally accepted accounting principles (GAAP). Internal statements are prepared for management's benefit and need not comply with GAAP; however, they must be mathematically accurate and follow *USALI* guidelines.

This Appendix presents the following statements from the Tenth Revised Edition as representative samples:

- Summary Operating Statement
- Rooms Department Income Statement
- Food and Beverage Department Income Statement
- Administrative and General Department Statement
- Statement of Rent, Property and Other Taxes, and Insurance

Summary Operating Statement

	CURRENT PERIOD						YEAR-TO-DATE					
	ACTUAL		FORECAST		PRIOR YEAR		ACTUAL		FORECAST		PRIOR YEAR	
	$	%	$	%	$	%	$	%	$	%	$	%
REVENUE												
Rooms												
Food and Beverage												
Other Operated Departments												
Rentals and Other Income												
Total Revenue												
DEPARTMENTAL EXPENSES												
Rooms												
Food and Beverage												
Other Operated Departments												
Total Departmental Expenses												
TOTAL DEPARTMENTAL INCOME												
UNDISTRIBUTED OPERATING EXPENSES												
Administrative and General												
Sales and Marketing												
Property Operation & Maint.												
Utilities												
Total Undistributed Expenses												
GROSS OPERATING PROFIT												
MANAGEMENT FEES												
INCOME BEFORE FIXED CHARGES												
FIXED CHARGES												
Rent												
Property and Other Taxes												
Insurance												
Total Fixed Charges												
NET OPERATING INCOME												
LESS: REPLACEMENT RESERVES												
ADJUSTED NET OPERATING INCOME												

ROOMS—SCHEDULE 1

	CURRENT MONTH			YEAR-TO-DATE		
	ACTUAL	FORECAST	PRIOR YEAR	ACTUAL	FORECAST	PRIOR YEAR
	$ | %	$ | %	$ | %	$ | %	$ | %	$ | %
REVENUE						
Transient Rooms Revenue						
Group Rooms Revenue						
Contract Rooms Revenue						
Other Rooms Revenue						
Less: Allowances						
Total Rooms Revenue						
EXPENSES						
Payroll and Related Expenses						
Salaries, Wages, and Bonuses						
Salaries and Wages						
Bonuses and Incentives						
Total Salaries, Wages, and Bonuses						
Payroll-Related Expenses						
Payroll Taxes						
Supplemental Pay						
Employee Benefits						
Total Payroll-Related Expenses						
Total Payroll and Related Expenses						
Other Expenses						
Cable/Satellite Television						
Cleaning Supplies						
Commissions						
Commissions and Rebates—Group						
Complimentary Services and Gifts						
Contract Services						
Corporate Office Reimbursables						
Decorations						
Dues and Subscriptions						
Equipment Rental						
Guest Relocation						
Guest Supplies						
Guest Transportation						
Laundry and Dry Cleaning						
Licenses and Permits						
Linen						
Miscellaneous						
Operating Supplies						
Printing and Stationery						
Reservations						
Royalty Fees						
Telecommunications						
Training						
Travel—Meals and Entertainment						
Travel—Other						
Uniform Laundry						
Uniforms						
Total Other Expenses						
TOTAL EXPENSES						
DEPARTMENTAL INCOME (LOSS)						

FOOD AND BEVERAGE—SCHEDULE 2

	CURRENT MONTH			YEAR-TO-DATE		
	ACTUAL	FORECAST	PRIOR YEAR	ACTUAL	FORECAST	PRIOR YEAR
	$ | %	$ | %	$ | %	$ | %	$ | %	$ | %
REVENUE						
Outlet Food Revenue						
Outlet Beverage Revenue						
In-Room Dining Food Revenue						
In-Room Dining Beverage Revenue						
Banquet/Catering Food Revenue						
Banquet/Catering Beverage Revenue						
Mini Bar Food Revenue						
Mini Bar Beverage Revenue						
Other Food Revenue						
Other Beverage Revenue						
Less: Allowances						
Total Food and Beverage Revenue						
OTHER REVENUE						
Audiovisual						
Public Room Rentals						
Cover Charges						
Service Charges						
Miscellaneous Other Revenue						
Less: Allowances						
Total Other Revenue						
TOTAL REVENUE						
COST OF FOOD AND BEVERAGE SALES						
Cost of Food Sales						
Cost of Beverage Sales						
Total Cost of Food and Beverage Sales						
COST OF OTHER REVENUE						
Audiovisual Cost						
Miscellaneous Cost						
Total Cost of Other Revenue						
TOTAL COST OF SALES AND OTHER REVENUE						
GROSS PROFIT (LOSS)						
EXPENSES						
Payroll and Related Expenses						
Salaries, Wages, and Bonuses						
Salaries and Wages						
Bonuses and Incentives						
Total Salaries, Wages, and Bonuses						
Payroll-Related Expenses						
Payroll Taxes						
Supplemental Pay						
Employee Benefits						
Total Payroll-Related Expenses						
Total Payroll and Related Expenses						

(continued)

FOOD AND BEVERAGE—SCHEDULE 2 *(continued)*

	CURRENT MONTH			YEAR-TO-DATE		
	ACTUAL	FORECAST	PRIOR YEAR	ACTUAL	FORECAST	PRIOR YEAR
	$ %	$ %	$ %	$ %	$ %	$ %
Other Expenses						
Banquet Expense						
China						
Cleaning Supplies						
Complimentary Services and Gifts						
Contract Services						
Corporate Office Reimbursables						
Decorations						
Dishwashing Supplies						
Dues and Subscriptions						
Equipment Rental						
Flatware						
Glassware						
Ice						
Kitchen Fuel						
Laundry and Dry Cleaning						
Licenses and Permits						
Linen						
Management Fees						
Menus and Beverage Lists						
Miscellaneous						
Music and Entertainment						
Operating Supplies						
Paper and Plastics						
Printing and Stationery						
Royalty Fees						
Telecommunications						
Training						
Travel—Meals and Entertainment						
Travel—Other						
Uniform Laundry						
Uniforms						
Utensils						
Total Other Expenses						
TOTAL EXPENSES						
DEPARTMENTAL INCOME (LOSS)						

ADMINISTRATIVE AND GENERAL—SCHEDULE 5

	CURRENT MONTH			YEAR-TO-DATE		
	ACTUAL	FORECAST	PRIOR YEAR	ACTUAL	FORECAST	PRIOR YEAR
	$ %	$ %	$ %	$ %	$ %	$ %
EXPENSES						
Payroll and Related Expenses						
Salaries, Wages, and Bonuses						
Salaries and Wages						
Bonuses and Incentives						
Total Salaries, Wages, and Bonuses						
Payroll-Related Expenses						
Payroll Taxes						
Supplemental Pay						
Employee Benefits						
Total Payroll-Related Expenses						
Total Payroll and Related Expenses						
Other Expenses						
Audit Charges						
Bank Charges						
Cash Overages and Shortages						
Centralized Accounting Charges						
Complimentary Services and Gifts						
Contract Services						
Corporate Office Reimbursables						
Credit and Collection						
Credit Card Commissions						
Decorations						
Donations						
Dues and Subscriptions						
Equipment Rental						
Human Resources						
Information Systems						
Laundry and Dry Cleaning						
Legal Services						
Licenses and Permits						
Loss and Damage						
Miscellaneous						
Operating Supplies						
Payroll Processing						
Postage and Overnight Delivery Charges						
Printing and Stationery						
Professional Fees						
Provision for Doubtful Accounts						
Security						
Settlement Costs						
Telecommunications						
Training						
Transportation						
Travel—Meals and Entertainment						
Travel—Other						
Uniform Laundry						
Uniforms						
Total Other Expenses						
TOTAL EXPENSES						

RENT, PROPERTY AND OTHER TAXES, AND INSURANCE— SCHEDULE 10

	CURRENT MONTH			YEAR-TO-DATE		
	ACTUAL	FORECAST	PRIOR YEAR	ACTUAL	FORECAST	PRIOR YEAR
	$ | %	$ | %	$ | %	$ | %	$ | %	$ | %
RENT						
Land and Buildings						
Information Systems Equipment						
Telecommunications Equipment						
Other Property and Equipment						
Total Rent						
PROPERTY AND OTHER TAXES						
Real Estate Taxes						
Personal Property Taxes						
Business and Transient Occupation Taxes						
Other Taxes						
Total Property and Other Taxes						
INSURANCE						
Building and Contents						
Liability						
Total Insurance						
TOTAL RENT, PROPERTY AND OTHER TAXES, AND INSURANCE						

Chapter 7 Outline

Competencies

1. Describe the two groups who use a hotel income statement and the formats available for presenting data to them, and explain the elements and conventions used in preparing an income statement. (pp. 193–198)

2. Explain the preparation and purposes of common-size and comparative income statements, and describe their analysis and interpretation. (pp. 198–207)

3. Describe the purpose of and information reported on the statement of retained earnings. (pp. 207–208)

7

Hotel Income Statements

THE INCOME STATEMENT for a hotel shows the operating results of its departments and revenue from other sources. While all income statements present operating results, this information may be presented in a variety of formats. This chapter provides examples of different types of income statements so that the reader should be able to properly analyze any income statement issued by a hospitality business.

One reason for having various formats for financial statements is to best meet the needs of the two groups who use the statements: **internal users** and **external users**. Even users within these two groups have different requirements because some of them perform statistical analysis using percentages, comparative data, and ratios.

Internal financial statements are designed to include great detail and contain numerous supporting schedules to serve the needs of internal users like a company's board of directors, executives, managers, and supervisors.

External financial statements are designed to present information in a summarized format and emphasize company results. They are intended for external users like stockholders, creditors, and members of the investment community. These statements are reviewed or audited by independent certified public accountants.

In explaining hotel income statements, this chapter will address such questions as:

1. What are the basic elements and conventions used in the preparation of an income statement?

2. What is the difference between internal long-form and short-form hotel income statements?

3. What is an external income statement?

4. What is a common-size income statement?

5. What is a comparative income statement?

6. What is the relationship between an income statement and a statement of retained earnings?

Elements and Conventions

Over the years, the income statement has also been called the statement of operations, the profit and loss statement, and the earnings statement.

The purpose of the income statement is to report the results of operations of a hospitality business for a specific period of time. This period can be as short as one month or one quarter, but not longer than one year. The accounting cycle for a hospitality business that is legally organized as a corporation is any consecutive 12-month period, called a **fiscal year**. At the end of a fiscal year, income statement bookkeeping accounts (revenue and expenses) are closed and set to zero. The start of the new fiscal year begins with entries pertaining only to that accounting period.

The elements that form the basis for preparation of the income statement can be represented by the equation: Revenue − Expenses = Net Income.

Revenue. Revenue results from the sale of goods and services. Revenue also includes interest income, dividend income, and other items reported on the schedule of rentals and other income.

Expenses. Expenses are the costs of goods and services used in the process of creating revenue. Classifying expenditures as assets or expenses is critical to the proper measurement of income or loss for a period. Some expenditures are assets when purchased but become expenses as they are used (food inventory, for example). A one-year fire insurance policy is an asset when purchased; as time expires, part of its cost also expires and becomes an expense.

Dividends are not a business expense. The declaration of dividends is a reduction of retained earnings, which is a balance sheet item. Dividends are explained in more detail in the section on the statement of retained earnings.

Conventions. All revenue and expenses are recorded using **accrual basis accounting.** The income statement recognizes all sales and other revenue in the time period in which they are earned and not when cash is received. Likewise, all expenses are recognized in the time period in which they are incurred and not when they are paid.

The **realization principle** of accounting dictates that revenue is recorded when a sale has been made *and* earned. The **matching principle** dictates that all expenses associated with the earning of revenue be recorded in the same accounting period as the revenue they helped generate.

Hotel Income Statement Formats

The income statement for a hotel combines all the financial data from its revenue centers, support centers, utility costs, fixed costs, and other items that are not reported in any departmental reports or schedules. For instance, the expense for income taxes is not allocated to any specific department. Also, gains and losses from the sale of assets such as marketable securities, investments (subsidiaries), property, and equipment may have occurred during the reporting period.

Many formats are available for presenting financial data on a hotel income statement. The following formats are described in this chapter:

- Internal long-form format

- Internal short-form format

- External formats

Net Income Is Not Cash Flow

As stated earlier, **net income** represents revenue less expenses for a period. Revenue is generated from both cash sales and sales on account. Likewise, expenses either are paid during the period or may still be due. However, the net income of a business does not necessarily cause a corresponding increase in the business's cash account.

While net income is the result of revenue minus expenses, not all expenses require a cash payment. For example, depreciation is an expense that is merely the write-off of the cost of a fixed asset over its useful life. While depreciation expense appears on the income statement as a reduction of net income, it does not involve any cash payment. Amortization is another expense that does not require any cash payment but appears on the income statement as a reduction of net income. Therefore, to properly reflect cash flow, items such as depreciation and amortization must be "added back" to net income to reflect net income as a source of cash. (Net income on the income statement is *not* affected by this procedure.)

On the other hand, some items requiring cash payments do not appear on the income statement. For example, principal payments on debt require cash payments, but never appear on the income statement. These payments must be subtracted from net income to properly reflect cash flow.

The difference between net income and cash flow can be best explained using the following business transactions during a given month:

	Effect on:	
	Income Statement	Cash Balance
Cash sales	+ 100,000	+ 100,000
Sales on account	+ 400,000	0
Total	+ 500,000	+ 100,000
Expenses purchased on account	− 200,000	0
Payment of last month's accounts payable	0	− 270,000
Total	+ 300,000	− 170,000
Depreciation	− 120,000	0
Total	+ 180,000	− 170,000
New bank loan	0	+ 50,000
Total	+ 180,000	− 120,000

The Hotel DORO's Income Statement ——————————————

The fictitious Hotel DORO is used here to present the following example of an income statement for a hotel as a whole. To complete an income statement, it is necessary to include any gains or losses from the sale of assets and other items not related to revenue centers, support centers, utility costs, and fixed charges. Finally, income taxes must be entered to arrive at the net income for the hotel. During the reporting period under consideration, the Hotel DORO sold property, resulting in a gain of $10,500, and its income tax expense (state and federal) was $16,094.

Exhibit 1   Internal Long-Form Income Statement—Hotel DORO

Hotel DORO, Inc.
Statement of Income
For the year ended December 31, 20X2   Schedule A

	Schedule	Net Revenue	Cost of Sales	Payroll and Related Expenses	Other Expenses	Income (Loss)
Operated Departments						
Rooms	A1	$ 897,500		$ 143,140	$ 62,099	$ 692,261
Food and Beverage	A2	524,570	$ 178,310	204,180	54,703	87,377
Telecommunications	A3	51,140	60,044	17,132	1,587	(27,623)
Other Operated Departments	A4	63,000	10,347	33,276	6,731	12,646
Rentals and Other Income	A5	61,283				61,283
Total Operated Departments		1,597,493	248,701	397,728	125,120	825,944
Undistributed Expenses						
Administrative and General	A6			97,632	66,549	164,181
Marketing	A7			35,825	32,043	67,868
Property Operation and Maintenance	A8			36,917	24,637	61,554
Utility Costs	A9				47,312	47,312
Total Undistributed Expenses				170,374	170,541	340,915
Income Before Fixed Charges		$1,597,493	$248,701	$568,102	$295,661	$485,029
Fixed Charges						
Rent	A10					28,500
Property Taxes	A10					45,324
Insurance	A10					6,914
Interest	A10					192,153
Depreciation and Amortization	A10					146,000
Total Fixed Charges						418,891
Income Before Income Taxes and Gain on Sale of Property						66,138
Gain on Sale of Property						10,500
Income Before Income Taxes						76,638
Income Taxes						16,094
Net Income						$ 60,544

Internal Formats

The following sections describe the two formats for internal income statements: the long form and the short form.

Long Form. The long-form income statement presents detailed information to the reader. Exhibit 1 illustrates the completed internal long-form income statement for the Hotel DORO. If there had been no gain on the sale of property, the line showing $66,138 would have been labeled as income before income taxes. Since there has been a gain on the sale of property, the line showing $66,138 must be labeled as income before income taxes and gain (loss) on sale of property. The $10,500 gain on the sale of property is added to the $66,138 to arrive at income before income taxes of $76,638. The income taxes of $16,094 are then subtracted to arrive at the $60,544 net income.

Exhibit 2   Internal Short-Form Income Statement—Hotel DORO

Hotel DORO, Inc.
Statement of Income
For the year ended December 31, 20X2   Schedule A

	Schedule		Income
Operated Departments			
Rooms	A1		$692,261
Food and Beverage	A2		$ 87,377
Telecommunications	A3		(27,623)
Other Operated Departments	A4		12,646
Rentals and Other Income	A5		61,283
Total Operated Departments			825,944
Undistributed Expenses			
Administrative and General	A6	164,181	
Marketing	A7	67,868	
Property Operation and			
Maintenance	A8	61,554	
Utility Costs	A9	47,312	
Total Undistributed Expenses			340,915
Income Before Fixed Charges			485,029
Fixed Charges			
Rent	A10	28,500	
Property Taxes	A10	45,324	
Insurance	A10	6,914	
Interest	A10	192,153	
Depreciation and Amortization	A10	146,000	
Total Fixed Charges			418,891
Income Before Income Taxes and			
Gain (Loss) on Sale of Property			66,138
Gain on Sale of Property			10,500
Income Before Income Taxes			76,638
Income Taxes			16,094
Net Income			$ 60,544

Short Form. Sometimes a brief income statement format is required. Exhibit 2 illustrates the short-form income statement, which shows only summary information for revenue and support centers. Aside from this difference, the long and short forms have the same general format; information appearing in the right-most column of the long-form income statement is identical to the information presented in the short-form version.

External Formats

The Securities and Exchange Commission (SEC) and the Sarbanes-Oxley Act of 2002 place critical requirements on the content, accuracy, and reliability of external financial statements issued to shareholders and the public. There is no single standard format for external income statements, but all external statements must comply with the pronouncements of the American Institute of Certified Public Accountants (AICPA) and the Financial Accounting Standards Board (FASB).

Exhibit 3   External Income Statement—Hotel DORO

Hotel DORO, Inc.
Income Statement
For the year ended December 31, 20X2   Schedule A

Net Revenue		
Rooms	$ 897,500	
Food and Beverage	524,570	
Telecommunications	51,140	
Other Operated Departments	63,000	
Rentals and Other Income	61,283	
Total Operated Departments		$ 1,597,493
Costs and Expenses		
Rooms	205,239	
Food and Beverage	437,193	
Telecommunications	78,763	
Other Operated Departments	50,354	
Administrative and General	164,181	
Marketing	67,868	
Property Operation and Maintenance	61,554	
Energy Costs	47,312	
Rent, Property Taxes, and Insurance	80,738	
Interest Expense	192,153	
Depreciation and Amortization	146,000	
Total Costs and Expenses		1,531,355
Income Before Gain on Sale of Property		66,138
Gain on Sale of Property		10,500
Income Before Income Taxes		76,638
Income Taxes		16,094
Net Income		$ 60,544

Exhibit 3 illustrates one type of external income statement for the Hotel DORO; this statement complies with generally accepted accounting principles. Its financial data can be traced back to Exhibit 1. The net revenue has been copied onto this statement, and each department's costs and expenses consist of the total of its cost of sales, payroll expenses, and other expenses from Exhibit 1.

Two additional popular ways to present financial information are common-size financial statements and comparative financial statements.

Common-Size Income Statement

While an income statement shows the operating results for a period, managers need more information to measure efficiency and investigate potential problem areas. To accommodate management, accountants have designed a common-size income statement.

A common-size financial statement shows the relationship of each item on the statement to a common base amount. Each dollar amount on the financial statement is converted to a percentage. In the case of the common-size income statement, the relationship of the items to net sales is expressed as a percentage.

Common-Size Analysis of an Income Statement. The importance of **common-size analysis** can be emphasized by the following example: If management has budgeted 1.0 percent of net sales for allowances (price adjustments), and the results for the period show allowances of 1.5 percent, there may be a quality control problem. The potential problem has been brought to light because the actual allowances have exceeded those budgeted.

The computation to arrive at common-size percentages is expressed by the following formula:

$$\frac{\text{Line Amount}}{\text{Net Sales}} = \text{Common-Size Percentages}$$

The dividend is the dollar amount for any line of the income statement. The divisor is always net sales. Since every item is divided by net sales, the net sales figure will always have a common-size figure of 100 percent.

Common-size analysis is also referred to as **vertical analysis** because computations are made from top to bottom on an income statement using the same divisor.

Common-size percentages can be rounded to a whole number or shown with any number of decimal places. For example, 5 divided by 3 can be shown as 2 (rounded to a whole number), 1.7 (shown with one decimal), or 1.67 (shown with two decimals). Regardless of the decimal places used, common-size percentage calculations require rounding. To illustrate this concept, the following data will be used.

Food sales	$250,000
Cost of food sold	−84,125
Gross profit	$165,875

The common-size percentages are computed and rounded to one decimal position as follows:

	Input	Calculator Display		Rounded
Food Sales	$\dfrac{\$250,000}{\$250,000}$ =	100.	=	100.0%
Cost of food sold	$\dfrac{\$84,125}{\$250,000}$ =	33.65	=	33.7%
Gross Profit	$\dfrac{\$165,875}{\$250,000}$ =	66.35	=	66.4%

Putting the results of these computations in proper form results in the following:

Food sales	$250,000	100.0%	
Cost of food sold	−84,125	−33.7	
Gross profit	$165,875	66.4%	← Problem:
			100.0 − 33.7 is not 66.4

Because of rounding, sometimes the technically accurate computations do not lend themselves to logical presentation. This is a problem that is resolved by different company policies.

Some companies follow a policy of *forcing* the computations as necessary to present logical results. One policy is to force the largest number (except sales or net income) up or down to accommodate the problems caused by rounding. Such a policy would produce the following results:

Food sales	$250,000	100.0%
Cost of food sold	−84,125	−33.7
Gross profit	$165,875	66.3%

Other companies have a policy of entering the computation regardless of any mathematical discrepancy. This policy is often used for computer-prepared statements since a computer cannot backtrack after it has printed a computed amount. *Any forced numbers presented in this chapter appear in bold print on the financial statements.*

Common-size analysis is useful beyond examining the percentages for signs of potential problems. It is also useful for forecasting sales and expenses for budget purposes. For example, if supplies expense currently shows a common-size percentage of 10 percent, a quick and simple method for forecasting supplies expense is to apply that percentage to the forecasted revenue for a period. That is, if the marketing department is forecasting sales of $200,000 for a future period, management could forecast the corresponding supplies expense to be $20,000.

Common-size percentages also provide data useful for preparing meaningful reports for management or for meetings. Generally, pictures depict outcomes or predictions better than words do. Common-size percentages can easily be converted into graphics, especially with the capabilities of today's computers and software. Graphic illustrations are very effective for delivering information in a dramatic fashion to emphasize highs, lows, and trends. One popular graphic device is the pie chart.

Pie charts. Pie charts quickly deliver an easy-to-understand message. Simply stated, a pie chart is a circle (called a "pie") that is divided into "slices." Each slice (item) represents a different portion of the pie. The larger the slice, the larger that portion is relative to the pie.

To construct a pie chart, one must know the relationship of each portion to the whole. Exhibit 4 shows an example of a pie chart, which shows that the Hotel DORO's food and beverage sales dollar generated a profit of about nine cents. (Refer to the food and beverage department income statement in Exhibit 5 to see how data there can be presented as the pie chart shown in Exhibit 4, including the impact of costs and expenses.)

Common-size analysis can be performed for the income statement of a hotel or individually for any department that has net sales, as explained in the following sections.

Common-Size Analysis—the Hotel DORO's Food and Beverage Department Income Statement. Exhibit 5 shows a common-size analysis of the Hotel DORO's food and beverage department income statement. Each dollar amount was divided

Exhibit 4   Pie Chart—Hotel DORO's Food and Beverage Sales Dollar

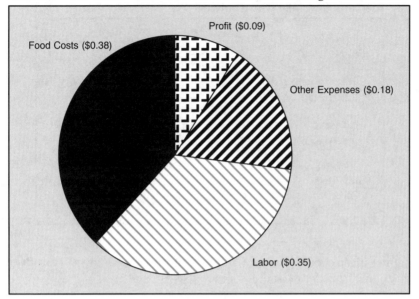

by the net sales amount of $50,000 to arrive at the common-size percentages. All percentages were rounded to one decimal place; none required forcing up or down. The technical answer for each computation was entered, and the column footings were checked as follows:

100.7%	−	.7%	did equal	100.0%
100.0%	−	38.0%	did equal	62.0%
35.4%	+	18.0%	did equal	53.4%
62.0%	−	53.4%	did equal	8.6%

Interpretation of Common-Size Analysis—the Hotel DORO's Food and Beverage Department Income Statement. The data shown on a common-size income statement is interpreted in relationship to net sales. Interpretation can be simplified by restating the percentages as a component of the sales dollar (100 percent equaling one dollar).

Refer to Exhibit 5 to trace the following interpretation of the data:

• Allowances were less than one percent of net sales (.7 percent).

• Food cost was 38 percent, which can be restated as 38¢ on the food sales dollar (net sales).

• A 38 percent food cost resulted in a gross profit of 62 percent. This means that there was 62¢ left of the food sales dollar to cover payroll and all the other expenses.

• The total expenses amounted to 53.4 percent or about 53¢ on the food sales dollar. This means that the food cost and operating expenses of the food and beverage department totaled 91¢ (38¢ + 53¢) on the food sales dollar.

Exhibit 5   Common-Size Income Statement—Hotel DORO's Food and Beverage Department

Food Sales	$50,350	100.7%
Allowances	350	.7
Net Food Sales	50,000	100.0
Cost of Food Sold	19,000	38.0
Gross Profit	31,000	62.0
Expenses		
Payroll and Related Expenses	17,700	35.4
All Other Expenses	9,000	18.0
Total Expenses	26,700	53.4
Food Department Income	$ 4,300	8.6%

- The net income of 8.6 percent shows that the hotel enjoyed a profit of only about nine cents for each dollar of food sales.

Common-Size Analysis—the Hotel DORO's Income Statement. Exhibit 6 illustrates a common-size income statement for the Hotel DORO. A common-size analysis for a hotel income statement uses the same procedures previously explained. Again, net revenue is used as the common divisor. Each amount on the statement is divided by net sales to arrive at a common-size percentage.

Internal and external hotel income statements may contain common-size percentages. To provide management with further information, an accountant may supplement the internal income statement with budgeted ratios and/or industry ratios.

Interpretation of the Hotel DORO's Common-Size Income Statement. The income statement in Exhibit 6 shows that the rooms department generated 56.3 percent of the hotel's total revenues of $1,597,493. This department's expenses were only 12.8 percent of revenues.

Total costs and expenses of the hotel were 95.9 percent or 96 cents on the sales dollar. The gain on the sale of property added about one cent and income taxes took away one cent of the sales dollar. The final result was that the hotel was able to keep only about four cents (3.8 percent) of each sales dollar.

Comparative Income Statement

A comparative financial statement presents financial data for two or more periods. The comparative data can be shown in the form of dollar amounts or percentages that management finds useful in its planning and controlling functions. Because computations are made on a side-by-side basis, a **comparative analysis** is also known as a **horizontal analysis**. A comparative analysis does not use a common divisor. The divisor for each line is the prior period's data for that particular line.

A popular comparative income statement format is the following:

Exhibit 6 Common-Size Income Statement—Hotel DORO

Hotel DORO, Inc.
Income Statement
For the year ended December 31, 20X2

Net Revenue		
Rooms	$ 897,500	**56.3%**
Food and Beverage	524,570	32.8
Telecommunications	51,140	3.2
Other Operated Departments	63,000	3.9
Rentals and Other Income	61,283	3.8
Total Departmental Revenue	1,597,493	100.0
Costs and Expenses		
Rooms	205,239	12.8
Food and Beverage	437,193	27.4
Telecommunications	78,763	4.9
Other Operated Departments	50,354	3.2
Administrative and General	164,181	10.3
Marketing	67,868	4.2
Property Operation and Maintenance	61,554	3.9
Utility Costs	47,312	3.0
Rent, Property Taxes, and Insurance	80,738	5.1
Interest Expense	192,153	12.0
Depreciation and Amortization	146,000	9.1
Total Costs and Expenses	1,531,355	95.9
Income Before Gain on Sale of Property	66,138	4.1
Gain on Sale of Property	10,500	.7
Income Before Income Taxes	76,638	4.8
Income Taxes	16,094	1.0
Net Income	$ 60,544	3.8%

Current Year	Prior Year	$ Change	% Change

The method for preparing a comparative income statement is outlined in the following discussion.

	20X4	20X3	$ Change	% Change
Net sales	$210,000	$200,000		
Cost of sales	80,000	82,000		

After the current and prior years' data have been entered as shown above, the steps required to complete the comparative income statement are:

1. The *dollar change* is computed by entering the current year's amount in a calculator and then subtracting the prior year's amount. The proper mathematical sign (positive or negative) will be provided by the calculator.

$$
\begin{array}{r}
\$210{,}000 \\
-200{,}000 \\
\hline
\$\ 10{,}000
\end{array}
\qquad
\begin{array}{r}
\$80{,}000 \\
-82{,}000 \\
\hline
\$\ (2{,}000)
\end{array}
$$

2. The *percentage change* is computed by dividing the dollar change amount by the prior year's amount. The mathematical sign of the percentage change is always the same as that for the dollar change.

$$
\frac{10{,}000}{200{,}000} = 5.0\% \qquad \frac{(2{,}000)}{82{,}000} = (2.4)\%
$$

Once the dollar changes and percentage changes have been computed, they can be entered in the appropriate columns as shown below.

	20X4	20X3	$ Change	% Change
Net sales	$210,000	$200,000	$10,000	5.0%
Cost of sales	80,000	82,000	(2,000)	(2.4)%

The preceding example shows the current year in the left-most column. Some companies prefer to have the prior year in the left-most column. The following example shows the different presentation of the current and prior year's data. Notice that this format has no effect on the changes between the periods.

	20X3	20X4	$ Change	% Change
Net sales	$200,000	$210,000	$10,000	5.0%
Cost of sales	82,000	80,000	(2,000)	(2.4)%

Always read the date headings so that the math is performed as this year's amount less last year's amount; otherwise, it is easy to make a mistake in signing the change as an increase or decrease.

Comparative Income Statement for the Hotel DORO. Exhibit 7 illustrates a comparative income statement for the Hotel DORO. The dollar change for each line item (including any total) was independently computed horizontally. The $72,100 for all departments was also a horizontal computation. It is possible to verify the accuracy of the $72,100 by vertically adding each department's dollar changes. (This *cross-checking* of all columns is standard procedure for producing an accurate statement.)

Because the percentage changes are computed without a common divisor, it is not possible to add a column of percentages to verify any total percentage. For example, the 9.6 percent total change for the operating departments cannot be verified by adding the individual percentage changes for each department. Therefore, it is suggested that all percentage computations be rechecked for accuracy as follows:

- Verify that the mathematical sign of the percentage change is the same as that of the dollar change.

- Use a change of 10 percent as a mental guide when entering a percentage change. For example, the rooms department of the Hotel DORO had last year's income of $615,114. A 10 percent change is $61,511 (simply drop the last digit, moving the decimal point one position to the left). The actual dollar

Exhibit 7   Comparative Income Statement—Hotel DORO

	20X2	20X1	$ Change	% Change
Hotel DORO, Inc.				
Statement of Income				
For the years ended December 31, 20X2 and 20X1				
Income of Operated Departments				
Rooms	$692,261	$615,114	$77,147	12.5%
Food and Beverage	87,377	90,520	(3,143)	(3.5)
Telecommunications	(27,623)	(26,814)	(809)	(3.0)
Other Operated Departments	12,646	14,502	(1,856)	(12.8)
Rentals and Other Income	61,283	60,522	761	1.3
Total Departmental Income	825,944	753,844	72,100	9.6
Undistributed Expenses				
Administrative and General	164,181	140,812	23,369	16.6
Marketing	67,868	57,647	10,221	17.7
Property Operation and Maintenance	61,554	64,482	(2,928)	(4.5)
Utility Costs	47,312	42,114	5,198	12.3
Total Undistributed Expenses	340,915	305,055	35,860	11.8
Income Before Fixed Charges	485,029	448,789	36,240	8.1
Fixed Charges				
Rent	28,500	28,500	0	0
Property Taxes	45,324	33,421	11,903	35.6
Insurance	6,914	4,900	2,014	41.1
Interest	192,153	193,814	(1,661)	(.9)
Depreciation and Amortization	146,000	128,000	18,000	14.1
Total Fixed Charges	418,891	388,635	30,256	7.8
Income Before Income Taxes and Gain on Sale of Property	66,138	60,154	5,984	9.9
Gain on Sale of Property	10,500		10,500	—
Income Before Income Taxes	76,638	60,154	16,484	27.4
Income Taxes	16,094	14,030	2,064	14.7
Net Income	$ 60,544	$ 46,124	$14,420	31.3%

change amount was $77,147, which is slightly more than 10 percent. If you had entered a percentage change of 125 percent or 1.3 percent, you would know there is a calculation error.

*   Double-check the percentage change on those items that show a possible calculation error when the preceding procedure has been applied.

Interpretation of a Comparative Analysis. A specialized vocabulary is used to discuss changes in a comparative financial statement. If this year's data is larger than last year's data, the change is called an *increase* or simply stated as *up* or *upward;* it cannot be called a *gain* because a gain results from the sale of assets at a price exceeding book value. If this year's data is smaller than last year's data, the change is called a *decrease* or simply stated as *down* or *downward*; it cannot be called a *loss* because a loss results from the sale of assets at a price less than book value.

If this year's data is equal to last year's data, the situation is referred to as *no change*; it would be illogical to call it a zero change.

Sometimes it is impossible to calculate a *percentage change* because there is no last year's data, which means there is no divisor. In this case, the proper procedure is to indicate that the percentage change is *not measurable* by entering the symbol "—" or "n/m" in the applicable column.

When analyzing the changes, it is incorrect to concentrate only on the percentage changes because a large percentage change may not necessarily represent a large dollar change. The comparing of small numbers can produce a large percentage change for a minor dollar change. For example, a $50 change on last year's data of $20 results in a 250 percent change. Conversely, a small percentage change could represent a large dollar change. For example, if the dollar change is $500,000 on last year's data of $50,000,000, the percentage change is only one percent.

Interpretation of the Hotel DORO's Comparative Income Statement. The comparative income statement for the Hotel DORO in Exhibit 7 is used to make the following brief interpretation of its operating results based on a comparison of 20X2 (current year) with 20X1 (prior year).

- The resulting *increase* of 31.3 percent in net income is misleading because of the gain on the sale of property. Selling assets is not part of the hotel's normal business purpose. Ignoring the gain on the sale of property reveals that the hotel's normal course of business actually produced an *increase* of only 9.9 percent in profits before income taxes.

- The income for the rooms department showed an *increase* of 12.5 percent, but the food and beverage department had a *decrease* of 3.5 percent. This situation requires further study.

- The results of the telecommunications department are at first difficult to interpret. Consider that the income of an operating department is being analyzed. A larger loss this year causes a decrease to operating income. The $809 change is a *decrease* in income because this year's departmental loss of $27,623 is greater than last year's departmental loss of $26,814.

- At first glance, the 12.8 percent *decrease* in the income for the other operated departments is alarming. However, the dollar decrease is only $1,856. In any case, management would want to find out why this year's trend was *downward*.

- The rentals and other income increase of 1.3 percent appears to have followed the trend in rooms department income but at a lower rate.

- The administrative and general expenses had an increase of 16.6 percent. This increase needs management attention because it is out of proportion when compared with the 9.6 percent increase for the income of all revenue centers (operated departments).

- The increase in marketing expense might be related to the increase in room sales. Perhaps more money was spent on advertising, which increased room sales. In any case, management would investigate the reason for the marketing expense increase.

- The property operation and maintenance data is for an expense. If this year's expense is smaller than last year's expense, the change is a *decrease*.

- The data in the change column for rent expense is referred to as *no change*.

- The percentage change column for the gain on the sale of property cannot be computed because there is no divisor (no last year's data). Therefore, a dash is inserted.

Statement of Retained Earnings

The statement of retained earnings is prepared for any hospitality business legally organized as a corporation. The purpose of this statement is to provide updated information about the lifetime earnings retained by a corporation. These **retained earnings** represent the lifetime profits of a business that have not been declared as dividends to the shareholders.

Retained earnings are increased by the net income for the period and reduced by any dividends *declared* for the period. Dividends may be declared in one period and paid in the following period; thus, the distinction between *dividends declared* and *dividends payable* has important consequences for this statement.

Dividends are first declared by action of a corporation's board of directors. This declaration immediately becomes a reduction to retained earnings as shown by the following journal entry:

> Retained Earnings (or Dividends Declared)   xxx
>   Dividends Payable   xxx

When the dividends are paid, the entry now affects cash, as shown by the following journal entry:

> Dividends Payable   xxx
>   Cash   xxx

The statement of retained earnings may be prepared as a separate statement or combined with the income statement. In either case, the ending retained earnings are brought forward to the equity section of the balance sheet.

Statement of Retained Earnings for the Hotel DORO

Exhibit 8 illustrates a separate statement of retained earnings for the Hotel DORO. Because the statement of retained earnings is generally prepared after the income statement, it is designated as Schedule B.

The computations for the statement of retained earnings are relatively simple. The beginning retained earnings are those of prior years, which represent the lifetime profits (net income) of the corporation less lifetime dividends declared as of the beginning of the period. For the Hotel DORO, retained earnings at the start

Exhibit 8   Statement of Retained Earnings—Hotel DORO

Hotel DORO, Inc. Statement of Retained Earnings For the year ended December 31, 20X2	Schedule B
Retained Earnings at beginning of year	$278,118
Net Income for the year (Schedule A)	60,544
Total	338,662
Less Dividends Declared during the year	20,000
Retained Earnings at end of year	$318,662

of the year are $278,118. To this amount is added the net income for the period, $60,544, resulting in a total of $338,662. Dividends declared during the year, $20,000, are subtracted to arrive at the retained earnings of $318,662 at the end of the period. This amount will be carried over to the Hotel DORO's balance sheet.

Statement of Income and Retained Earnings for the Hotel DORO

Exhibit 9 illustrates retained earnings data combined with the income statement. This is a popular statement format because it readily shows the net income incrementing the retained earnings in one statement. In this combined statement, called the statement of income and retained earnings, the net income is not double-underlined. Instead it is added to the beginning retained earnings, and then the dividends declared are subtracted to arrive at ending retained earnings. End-of-year retained earnings are double-underlined to indicate the end of the statement.

Uniform System of Accounts for the Lodging Industry, Tenth Revised Edition

The tenth revised edition of the *Uniform System of Accounts for the Lodging Industry (USALI)* states, "The degree of detail presented in the [external income] statement is discretionary, although captions for revenue, expense, interest, depreciation, and income taxes are included unless the amounts are insignificant. To the extent that any individual revenue or expense item is significant, separate disclosures are made."

USALI states that "The [income] statement presented to external users is typically relatively brief, providing only summary detail about the results of operations."

Generally accepted accounting principles, the FASB, and the SEC govern the reporting of financial information and statements to the investing public. Therefore, *USALI* cannot state any modifications that will be in conflict with these accounting principles, governing standards, and governmental agencies. A certified public accounting firm will audit the records of a hotel company and issue audited financial statements in conformity with the standards of the certified public accounting professional requirements.

Exhibit 9   Statement of Income and Retained Earnings (External)—Hotel DORO

Hotel DORO, Inc.
Statement of Income and Retained Earnings
For the year ended December 31, 20X2

Net Revenue

Rooms	$ 897,500	
Food and Beverage	524,570	
Telecommunications	51,140	
Other Operated Departments	63,000	
Rentals and Other Income	61,283	
Total Departmental Revenue		$1,597,493

Costs and Expenses

Rooms	205,239	
Food and Beverage	437,193	
Telecommunications	78,763	
Other Operated Departments	50,354	
Administrative and General	164,181	
Marketing	67,868	
Property Operation and Maintenance	61,554	
Utility Costs	47,312	
Rent, Property Taxes, and Insurance	80,738	
Interest Expense	192,153	
Depreciation and Amortization	146,000	
Total Costs and Expenses		1,531,355
Income Before Gain on Sale of Property		66,138
Gain on Sale of Property		10,500
Income Before Income Taxes		76,638
Income Taxes		16,094
Net Income		60,544
Retained Earnings at beginning of year		278,118
Less Dividends Declared during the year		20,000
Retained Earnings at end of year		$ 318,662

Exhibits 10 and 11 provide a sample external income statement and sample statement of stockholders' equity recommended by *USALI* and in compliance with professional and governmental standards and regulations. The income statement for external users is based on generally accepted accounting principles. This particular format does not show change to the equity accounts. If net income or loss is the only change to the equity accounts, it is permissible to reconcile the change in retained earnings at the bottom of the statement of income as shown in this chapter.

The statement of stockholders' equity for external users is separately prepared if there is significant activity in the equity accounts during the reporting period. Significant activity warrants a comprehensive statement showing the cumulative amounts for additional paid-in capital, retained earnings, and total stockholders' equity.

Exhibit 10   Sample External Income Statement Format

STATEMENT OF INCOME

	Period	
	Current Year	Prior Year
REVENUE		
Rooms	$	$
Food and Beverage		
Other Operated Departments		
Rentals and Other Income		
Total Revenue		
EXPENSES		
Rooms		
Food and Beverage		
Other Operated Departments		
Administrative and General		
Sales and Marketing		
Property Operation and Maintenance		
Utilities		
Management Fees		
Rent, Property Taxes, and Insurance		
Interest Expense		
Depreciation and Amortization		
Loss or (Gain) on the Disposition of Assets		
Total Expenses		
INCOME BEFORE INCOME TAXES		
INCOME TAXES		
Current		
Deferred		
Total Income Taxes		
NET INCOME	$	$

Source: *Uniform System of Accounts for the Lodging Industry,* Tenth Rev. Ed. (Lansing, Mich.: American Hotel & Lodging Educational Institute, 2006), p. 18.

🔑 Key Terms

accrual basis accounting—System of reporting revenue and expenses in the period in which they are considered to have been earned or incurred, regardless of the actual time of collection or payment.

common-size analysis—An analytical procedure in which each item amount is stated as a percentage of a base amount. The base amount for a common-size income statement is net sales (net revenue), and that for a common-size balance sheet is total assets. Also called vertical analysis because comparisons on common-size financial statements are made from top to bottom.

Exhibit 11   Stockholders' Equity Statement Format

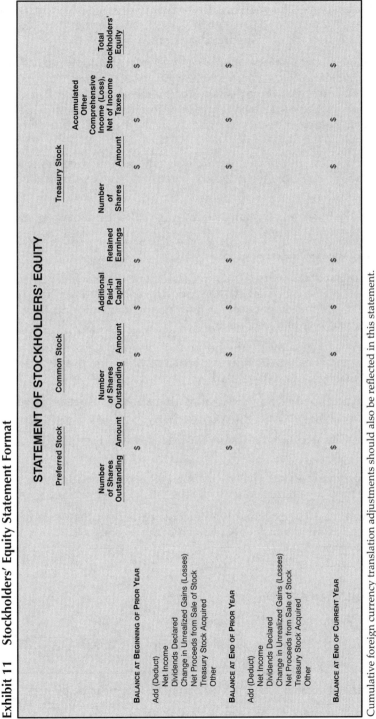

STATEMENT OF STOCKHOLDERS' EQUITY

Cumulative foreign currency translation adjustments should also be reflected in this statement.

Source: *Uniform System of Accounts for the Lodging Industry*, Tenth Rev. Ed. (Lansing, Mich.: American Hotel & Lodging Educational Institute, 2006), p. 20.

comparative analysis—An analytical procedure performed on comparative statements showing the actual and percentage change from the prior period. Also called horizontal analysis because comparisons are made from left to right.

external financial statements—Statements designed to inform outside parties of the results of operations (as reported by the income statement), the financial position of the company as a whole (as reported by the balance sheet), or other pertinent information. These statements present information in a summarized format and emphasize company results. They are typically audited and certified by independent CPAs.

external users—Groups outside the business who require accounting and financial information; external users include suppliers, bankers, stockholders, and investors.

fiscal year—The business year; it may or may not differ from the calendar year but is always a 12-month period.

horizontal analysis—See comparative analysis.

internal financial statements—Financial statements intended for internal users. These statements present detailed information on each responsibility area and the hotel as a whole. Management uses the information in monitoring the profitability of operations and in long-range planning.

internal users—Groups inside the hospitality business who require accounting and financial information, such as the board of directors, the general manager, department managers, and other staff.

matching principle—The principle stating that all expenses must be recorded in the same accounting period as the revenue that they helped to generate.

net income—The excess of revenue earned over expenses for the accounting period.

realization principle—The principle stating that revenue resulting from business transactions should be recorded only when a sale has been made *and* earned.

retained earnings—The portion of net income earned by the corporation that is not distributed as dividends, but is retained in the business.

vertical analysis—See common-size analysis.

 # Review Questions

1. What is the purpose of the income statement?

2. What are some other names used for the income statement?

3. What are the components of revenue for a hotel?

4. What are the financial components of a hotel income statement?

5. Why is net income *not* the same as cash flow?

6. What is a common-size income statement?

7. What is a comparative income statement?

8. What is the purpose of the statement of retained earnings?

9. What is a statement of income and retained earnings?

Internet Sites

For more information, visit the following Internet sites. Remember that Internet addresses can change without notice. If the site is no longer there, you can use a search engine to look for additional sites.

Financial Statements Slideshow
www.business.gsw.edu/busa/faculty/jkooti/Finance/Pres/Chapt3/sld025.htm

Common-Size Financial Statements
www.netmba.com/finance/statements/common-size/

Benchmarks and Ratios
http://bizstats.com/ (Instructions: In first window, scroll to Other Services—
  Hotels & Inns; enter the business total revenue amount, and press compute.)

Trends, Benchmarks, Prices, and More
www.pkfc.com/store/Download_Samples.aspx

Problems

Problem 1

Prepare an internal short-form income statement based on the following data for Hotel Sivad, Inc.

The data is for the year ended September 30, 20XX.

Income of Revenue Centers:	
Rooms	$776,786
Food and Beverage	119,726
Telecommunications	(15,610)
Vending Machine Commissions	1,500
Cash Discounts Earned	2,700
Interest Income	800
Expenses of Support Centers:	
Administrative and General	158,684
Marketing	48,209
Property Operation and Maintenance	88,296
Other Expenses:	
Utility Costs	81,420
Rent	135,225
Property Taxes	55,650

Insurance	9,986
Interest	52,148
Depreciation and Amortization	115,860
Income Taxes	48,707

Problem 2

Prepare a statement of retained earnings based on the following data for Hotel Carbob, Inc.

The data is for the year ended June 30, 20X9.

Dividends paid this year	$ 40,000
Dividends declared this year	60,000
Income before income taxes	140,424
Income taxes	48,707
Retained earnings July 1, 20X8	122,930

Problem 3

Prepare a common-size income statement for The Garden Bistro, Inc. The rules for rounding are as follows:

a. Show all answers to one decimal, rounded (for example, 7,900 divided by 170,000 equals 4.6 percent).
b. If a series of computed percentages do not add up to the computed total, force the largest number in the series up or down as necessary.
c. The net income percentage is not to be forced up or down.

The Garden Bistro, Inc.
Income Statement
For the Year Ended December 31, 20X8

REVENUE	
Food Sales	$ 171,000
Allowances	1,000
Net Revenue	170,000
Cost of Food Sold	53,000
Gross Profit	117,000
OPERATING EXPENSES	
Payroll	55,000
Payroll Taxes and Employee Benefits	7,900
China, Glassware	300
Kitchen Fuel	900
Laundry and Dry Cleaning	2,100
Credit Card Fees	1,500
Operating Supplies	5,000
Advertising	2,000
Utilities	3,800
Repairs and Maintenance	1,900
Total Operating Expenses	80,400
Income Before Fixed Charges and Income Taxes	36,600
FIXED CHARGES	
Rent	6,000
Property Taxes	1,500

Insurance	3,600
Interest	3,000
Depreciation	5,500
Total Fixed Charges	19,600
Income Before Income Taxes	17,000
Income Taxes	2,000
Net Income	$ 15,000

Problem 4

Prepare a comparative analysis from the following income statement. Show all percentages to one decimal, rounded.

The Garden Bistro, Inc.
Income Statement
For the Years Ended December 31, 20X8 and 20X7

	20X8	20X7	$ Change	% Change
REVENUE				
Food Sales	$171,000	$160,800		
Allowances	1,000	800		
Net Revenue	170,000	160,000		
Cost of Food Sold	53,000	51,000		
Gross Profit	117,000	109,000		
OPERATING EXPENSES				
Payroll	55,000	56,000		
Payroll Taxes and Employee Benefits	7,900	7,500		
China, Glassware	300	300		
Kitchen Fuel	900	600		
Laundry and Dry Cleaning	2,100	1,800		
Credit Card Fees	1,500	0		
Operating Supplies	5,000	5,200		
Advertising	2,000	1,400		
Utilities	3,800	3,000		
Repairs and Maintenance	1,900	1,000		
Total Operating Expenses	80,400	76,800		
Income Before Fixed Charges and Income Taxes	36,600	32,200		
FIXED CHARGES				
Rent	6,000	6,000		
Property Taxes	1,500	1,200		
Insurance	3,600	3,600		
Interest	3,000	2,800		
Depreciation	5,500	4,700		
Total Fixed Charges	19,600	18,300		
Income Before Income Taxes	17,000	13,900		
Income Taxes	2,000	1,600		
Net Income	$ 15,000	$ 12,300		

Problem 5

Determine the effects on an income statement and cash flow from the following data. Show the effect of each item and indicate the total effect.

		Effect on:	
		Income Statement	Cash Balance
Cash sales	$200,000		
Sales on account	500,000		
Expenses purchased on account	300,000		
Payment of last month's accounts payable	200,000		
Depreciation	80,000		
Amortization	15,000		
New bank loan	25,000		
Payment of mortgage principal	60,000		

Problem 6

You have been asked to perform forensic accounting to discover financial information missing due to fraud within a company. It has been determined that sales for the period were $791,000. Your assignment is to determine the following items based on the average common-size percentages typical for this company. Round your answers to the nearest dollar.

Cost of sales	61.9%
Selling expenses	22.8
Administrative and general expenses	6.8

Format your answer as follows:

Sales	_____
Cost of sales	_____
Gross profit	_____
Selling expenses	_____
Administrative and general expenses	_____
Income before income taxes	_____

Problem 7

Due to destruction of certain records by fire, you have been hired by a firm to perform forensic accounting to discover missing financial information. Fill in the following blanks based on the information provided.

20X9	20X8	$ Change	% Change
_____	20,269	16,231	80.1
3,450	_____	733	27.0
_____	2,100	(200)	(9.5)
3,000	_____	0	0
4,000	_____	4,000	n/m
48,000	_____	1,807	_____
_____	50,000	_____	10.0

Problem 8

Computer Assignment: Prepare a pie chart showing the disposition of the sales dollar based on the following information.

Net food sales	100.0%
Cost of food sold	32.0
Labor costs	37.0
Other operating costs	13.2
Fixed costs	13.3
Income taxes	.8
Net income	3.7

Case Study

Purpose and Preparation of a Pro Forma Income Statement

A pro forma income statement is an income statement that projects the future or an anticipated result instead of reporting the past. It shows what a company might achieve if it asks a "what if" question.

When applying for a bank loan, a start-up business might use pro forma income statements to project its income for the coming several years. An established business might also apply for financing and prepare pro forma income statements to show how an acquisition, a new location, or a new product line might affect its earnings.

The Coastal Motel has enjoyed a booming occupancy due to its beachside location in a tropical area that is immensely popular with tourists year round. Guests loyally return, praising the motel's management, clean well-equipped rooms with outstanding amenities, and excellent customer service. Guests may stay for several days or up to several weeks. The motel does not have restaurant facilities. Management has decided to open a restaurant in a section of its unused facilities based on the motel's history of high occupancy, returning guests, and average length of stay.

A bank loan will be required for this expansion to maintain the financial integrity of the rooms operation. The bank has requested a pro forma income statement for the restaurant operation. Management retains a consultant to determine the menu composition, menu prices, equipment and staffing requirements, and anticipated operating expenses. Due to licensing regulations, the restaurant will not sell alcoholic beverages.

The restaurant will not serve dinner because of the competitive dining environment; the area has many fine restaurants with high-quality chefs, liquor, and outstanding entertainment. Based on occupancy, walk-in traffic, and seat turnover, it is estimated that the daily traffic count will be 200 guests for breakfast with an average check of $8.00. The lunch crowd will be smaller than the breakfast crowd because of the nature of the tourist attractions. However, the motel expects that beach enthusiasts will buy 70 take-out lunches at $9.00, and sit-down guests will number 80 at an average check of $12.00. The restaurant will be open seven days per week. It is not necessary to provide for allowances and returns because the amount is negligible.

After reviewing the menu mix and vendor pricing, the consultant estimates a 28 percent food cost. Based on staffing schedules and local labor costs, the consultant estimates that payroll and related expenses will total 34 percent. The consultant further estimates that restaurant equipment depreciation will total $20,000 annually, and that all other expenses will total 20 percent, based on regional common-size percentages.

Challenge

1. Prepare a pro forma income statement for the proposed restaurant venture for its first full year of operation.

2. Comment on the omission of income taxes.

3. Assume the bank will not lend funds unless the operation will realize a 10 percent return on sales before any provision for income taxes. Based only on this standard, appraise the bank's likelihood of approving the motel's bank loan application.

Chapter 8 Outline

Competencies

1. Explain the use of ratios in the analysis of a hospitality business income statement, and list the advantages and limitations of their use. (pp. 222–223)

2. Summarize the general categories of popular income statement ratios. (pp. 223–225, 241–242)

3. List the ratios typically used to analyze a hotel rooms department, and describe their formulas and interpretation. (pp. 225–229)

4. List the ratios typically used to analyze a food and beverage department, and describe their formulas and interpretation. (pp. 229–236)

5. List the ratios typically used to analyze a hotel, and describe their formulas and interpretation. (pp. 236–241)

8

Ratio Analysis of the Income Statement

$\mathbf{A}$ DETAILED ANALYSIS of an income statement is important because the long-term success of a hospitality business depends upon the realization of profits. Common-size and comparative analysis of an income statement is not sufficient because the results cannot be compared against standard or expected criteria.

The volume of sales reflects the dynamic activity of a hospitality business. An increase in sales volume is not necessarily favorable for profits, and a decrease in sales volume may not be unfavorable in the measurement of profits. The analysis of an income statement requires an in-depth study of the relationships between sales and expenses and a comparison of these relationships with benchmarks.

Ratios express a direct relationship between two relevant items for a period; they are calculated by dividing one figure by another, both for the same accounting period. The use of ratios makes it possible to convert an absolute dollar amount to a number that can be used as a basis to measure against benchmarks of prior years, industry standards, and management goals. The goals of management are interpreted by the use of forecasts and budgets. The proper use of ratios requires an understanding of the advantages and limitations of ratio analysis.

Ratio analysis has many advantages:

- Ratios are easy to compute and use.

- Ratios provide a basis of comparison against benchmarks established by management and industry studies.

- Ratios can point to problem areas.

- Ratios provide a basis for establishing trends.

    The limitations of ratio analysis include the following:

- A ratio standing alone cannot be properly evaluated.

- Ratios do not solve problems.

- Ratios must be properly interpreted.

- Income statements contain estimates that may influence results.

- A change in accounting procedures may influence ratios.

Any single management tool has limitations; therefore, financial analysis requires the use of dollar income statements that show only absolute amounts, data of prior periods, percentages, and ratios. This chapter presents information about ratios based on financial information from the fictitious Hotel DORO, and answers the following questions:

1. What are ratios, and how are they used?
2. What are the advantages and limitations of prior-period ratios, trade association ratios, and budgeted ratios?
3. Which ratios are most commonly used to analyze an income statement?
4. What is RevPAR?

Ratio Analysis of the Income Statement

Good financial management requires more than common-size or comparative income statements. Therefore, in addition to these different income statements, the accountant provides managers with a number of ratios that will assist them in studying the results of operations.

A ratio is the relationship of one item to another expressed as a number. For example, the relationship of food sales of $358,300 and food covers (customers) of 37,716 results in a $9.50 average food check ($358,300 ÷ 37,716 = $9.50). Ratios may be expressed as percentages, decimals, dollars and cents, or other indices customary to the hospitality industry.

Ratios are a critical part of financial analysis because they point to potential problem areas. A ratio by itself does not give a complete picture. For example, knowing that the average food check is $9.50 is insufficient unless another comparative ratio is provided. When ratios are interpreted, the determination of a favorable or unfavorable condition cannot be made unless there are other measuring devices or standards of comparison. Meaningful ratios that can be used for comparisons are:

- Prior-period ratios
- Industry and trade association ratios
- Budgeted ratios

Prior-Period Ratios

Prior-period ratios provide a basis for comparison with the current period's ratio. For example, assume that the average food check ratios for a business are as follows:

	20X2	20X1	20X0
Average food check	$9.50	$9.45	$9.48

At first glance, the assumption might be that everything is normal. However, what if there had been five-percent menu price increases in 20X1 and 20X2? This would mean that the average food check actually is declining. This example illustrates one danger of using results of prior periods for comparisons: the inefficiencies of prior periods may be carried over from one period to the next and remain undetected.

Industry and Trade Association Ratios

Hospitality industry ratios and statistics are published by PKF Consulting, Andersen, Smith Travel Research, and the National Restaurant Association (for stand-alone restaurants).

Hospitality industry ratios are useful because they represent the average of similar businesses and provide management with uniform ratios that can be used as another measurement tool.

However, industry ratios are not meant to be relied upon as a "yardstick." The timeliness of industry ratios is affected by the delay in collecting the data, then the extensive time for assembling the data, publishing, and distribution.

Furthermore, some members of the industry are in excellent financial condition and have favorable operating results, while others are not. Industry ratios come from composite statements and might be affected by the extreme figures of the most successful and unsuccessful companies unless these wide swings are eliminated. (For example, if five companies have a net income of $100,000 each and five other companies have a net income of $10,000 each, the average net income is $55,000. However, only half of the companies are very profitable, and the other half are barely surviving.) Finally, the use of these standards is affected by geographic and demographic factors.

Budgeted Ratios

Budgeted ratios represent the goals of management. They are developed as part of the planning process and are used to measure against actual results. Budgeted ratios are the best form of measurement when they are properly developed.

The validity of budgeted ratios depends on the source of data used in preparing the budget. If only prior years' averages are used, the inconsistencies of the prior periods will be built into the budget. The proper development of a budget requires a study of operating results and up-to-date forecasting techniques and data. Some companies use a budgeting process called **zero base budgeting.** Under this concept, all expenditures are reviewed and must be justified from a starting point of zero. But even zero base budgeting has limitations because of its large volume of paperwork and the difficulties in describing and identifying resources and activities.

Popular Income Statement Ratios

Many ratios are used to analyze the results of operations for operating departments and a hotel as a whole. Some ratio formulas are applicable to all areas (for example, the profit margin ratio) while others can be used only in one department (for example, average room rate). There are differences in the form in which a ratio is expressed, but this dissimilarity does not affect the accuracy or usage of ratio analysis.

The use of a ratio to evaluate items on an income statement requires knowledge of what a ratio measures. Ratios relative to the income statement are used to measure profitability, activity, and operations. The following sections classify ratios according to what they measure and list some of the popular ratios in each classification.

Profitability Ratios

Profitability ratios reflect the effectiveness of management in producing income. Two of the popular ratios used to measure profitability in the hospitality industry are:

- Profit margin ratio (net income to net sales ratio)
- Return on equity ratio

Activity Ratios

Activity ratios measure the effectiveness with which management uses the assets of a hospitality business. Activity ratios are also called *asset management ratios*. Two of the popular ratios used to measure asset management in the hospitality industry are:

- Inventory turnover ratio
- Days' inventory on hand ratio

Operating Ratios

Operating ratios measure the effectiveness with which management controls expenses and the efficiency of operations. Some of the popular ratios used to measure operating efficiency in the hospitality industry are:

- Average room rate
- Occupancy percentage
- RevPAR
- Food cost percentage
- Labor cost percentage
- Prime cost percentage
- Average food check

Occupancy Ratios

Occupancy ratios measure the success of rooms management in selling the primary product of the hotel or motel. Occupancy ratios can be computed for *paid occupancy, complimentary occupancy, average occupancy,* and *multiple occupancy.* For our purposes, this chapter will work with the paid occupancy ratio and call it *occupancy percentage.*

Stock Valuation Ratios

Stock valuation ratios are used by investors to determine if they should buy, hold, or sell the stock of a hospitality corporation. Sometimes these ratios are classified as profitability ratios. However, they are classified separately in this chapter because they apply only to corporations and are used by the investment community. Department managers and executive managers do not use these ratios in their planning, organizing, and controlling functions.

Exhibit 1   Rooms Department Income Statement—Hotel DORO

Hotel DORO, Inc.
Rooms Department Income Statement
For the year ended December 31, 20X2

Revenue			
Room Sales		$900,000	
Allowances		2,500	
Net Revenue			$897,500
Expenses			
Salaries and Wages	$120,000		
Employee Benefits	23,140		
Total Payroll and Related Expenses		143,140	
Other Expenses			
Commissions	2,500		
Contract Cleaning	5,285		
Guest Transportation	10,100		
Laundry and Dry Cleaning	7,000		
Linen	11,000		
Operating Supplies	11,125		
Reservation Expense	9,950		
Uniforms	2,167		
Other Operating Expenses	2,972		
Total Other Expenses		62,099	
Total Expenses			205,239
Departmental Income (Loss)			$692,261

Investors use many tools in deciding the merits of investing in any stock listed on a major stock exchange. The two popular measurements of a stock's value are:

- Earnings per share ratio
- Price earnings ratio

Rooms Department Ratios

The rooms department ratios in this chapter are computed from the Hotel DORO's departmental income statement shown in Exhibit 1. The popular ratios used in analyzing any rooms department are:

- Profit margin ratio
- Labor cost percentage
- Average room rate

- Occupancy percentage
- RevPAR

Profit Margin Ratio

The profit margin ratio, also called the **net income to sales ratio**, is used as a measure of profitability. It provides the net income on each sales dollar. It is computed by dividing the net income by net sales and is expressed as a percentage.

Formula. The profit margin ratio is computed as follows:

$$\frac{\text{Departmental Income}}{\text{Net Sales}}$$

The profit margin ratio for the Hotel DORO's rooms department is computed as follows:

$$\frac{\$692,261}{\$897,500} \ = \ 77.1\%$$

Interpretation. The average dollar of sales in the rooms department is generating a profit of 77.1 percent, or it could be stated that the rooms department income is 77¢ on the sales dollar. This profit might seem high, but be aware that building depreciation is charged to the schedule of fixed charges, building maintenance is charged to the property operation and maintenance department, and electricity, water, and heat are charged to the utility costs reporting department.

This ratio should be compared with a benchmark profit margin ratio. If this ratio is equal to or greater than the benchmark, a preliminary and general assumption is that the condition appears *favorable*. For example, comparing the result of 77.1 percent with a budgeted profit margin ratio of 75 percent would indicate that the rooms department has generated the desired profit margin return and has done slightly better.

Labor Cost Percentage

One of the largest expenses for hotels and motels is labor. Labor expense includes total payroll costs and all related expenses, such as benefits and payroll taxes. The **labor cost percentage** is used as a measure of *operating* efficiency and provides the labor cost on each sales dollar.

Formula. The labor cost percentage is computed as follows:

$$\frac{\text{Total Payroll and Related Expenses}}{\text{Net Sales}}$$

The labor cost percentage for the Hotel DORO's rooms department is computed as follows:

$$\frac{\$143,140}{\$897,500} \ = \ 15.9\%$$

Interpretation. The average labor cost in the rooms department is 15.9 percent of the sales dollar, or it could be stated that 16¢ of the sales dollar is used to pay labor costs.

This ratio should be compared with a benchmark labor cost ratio. If this ratio is equal to or less than the benchmark, a preliminary and general assumption is that the condition appears *favorable*. For example, comparing the result of 15.9 percent with a budgeted ratio of 16 percent would indicate that the desired goal for operating efficiency has been achieved.

Average Room Rate

While room rates vary depending on the type of room, number of guests, and other factors, it is important to measure the *average selling price*, which is also called **average room rate (ARR)** or **average daily rate (ADR)**. This ratio provides the average rate charged per paid room occupied. The ARR is used as a measure of *operations*.

Formula. The ARR is computed as follows:

$$\frac{\text{Net Room Sales}}{\text{Paid Rooms Occupied}}$$

An income statement is not sufficient to calculate ARR. Statistics not appearing on the income statement must be maintained separately for the paid rooms occupied during the related period. The Hotel DORO had 17,950 total paid rooms occupied during the year 20X2. The ARR for the Hotel DORO's rooms department is computed as follows:

$$\frac{\$897,500}{17,950} = \$50$$

Interpretation. Taking all rooms into consideration, the average selling price was $50.00, with some rooms selling for more and others for less.

This ratio should be compared with a benchmark ratio. If this ratio is equal to or greater than the benchmark, a preliminary and general assumption is that the condition appears *favorable*. For example, comparing the result of $50.00 with a budgeted ratio of $48.00 would indicate that the average selling price has improved; this could be attributable to factors such as less discounting, selling more higher-priced rooms, better economic conditions, and other factors.

Occupancy Percentage

The **occupancy percentage** is important because it measures rooms sales in terms of the hotel's capacity to generate rooms sold. This occupancy percentage requires a hotel or motel to keep separate statistical information during a period for data such as rooms available to sell, complimentary rooms, and paid rooms occupied.

Formula. The paid occupancy percentage is computed as follows:

$$\frac{\text{Paid Rooms Occupied}}{\text{Rooms Available}}$$

The Hotel DORO is a 75-room hotel. All these rooms were available for sale during the year. The hotel is not a resort hotel. Its operations calendar is 365 days. There were 17,950 paid rooms occupied for the hotel during the year 20X2. The paid occupancy percentage for the Hotel DORO's rooms department is computed as follows:

$$\frac{17,950}{75 \times 365} = 66\%$$

Interpretation. The result shows that the Hotel DORO rented 66 percent of its room nights available. As with any average calculation, care must be taken in interpreting the information. The occupancy percentage of any hotel varies from day to day and month to month. Any average statistical information tends to disguise these variations.

This ratio should be compared with a benchmark ratio. If this ratio is equal to or greater than the benchmark, a preliminary and general assumption is that the condition appears *favorable.* For example, comparing the result of 66 percent with a budgeted ratio of 60 percent would indicate that occupancy has improved. This could be due to an effective advertising program, local special tourist attractions, better economic conditions, and other factors.

RevPAR

RevPAR is an acronym for *revenue per available room.* This ratio is one of the most important in the hotel industry, because it is the basic measure of industry success. The purpose of the ratio is to evaluate if the inventory of rooms is being most advantageously managed in relation to its maximum revenue potential.

Formula. RevPAR measures how well the hotel has been able to fill its rooms, measured in dollars per room. According to the *Uniform System of Accounts for the Lodging Industry (USALI)*, the formula is:

$$\text{RevPAR} = \frac{\text{Rooms Revenue}}{\text{Rooms Available for Sale}}$$

USALI does not include out-of-order rooms or rooms reserved for corporate use in the denominator *Rooms Available for Sale.* Including those rooms will typically lower a hotel's RevPAR.

Hotel DORO has 75 daily rooms available for sale. Assume it does not have any rooms reserved for corporate use and its skilled maintenance staff expediently remedies any room problems, successfully avoiding out-of-order rooms for the period. Therefore, the denominator is 27,375 (75 × 365). RevPAR for Hotel DORO, using information available in Exhibit 1, is calculated as follows:

$$\text{RevPAR} = \frac{\$897,500}{27,375} = \$32.79$$

Interpretation. This result means the hotel generated room revenue of $32.79 for every room it had available for sale. RevPAR is more useful and revealing than just the average room rate or the occupancy percentage ratio alone. A high average room rate may look good on its own, but it may present a misleading picture

Exhibit 2   Food and Beverage Department Income Statement—Hotel DORO

Hotel DORO, Inc.
Food and Beverage Department Income Statement
For the year ended December 31, 20X2

	Food	Beverage	Total
Revenue	$360,000	$160,000	$520,000
Allowances	1,700	130	1,830
Net Revenue	358,300	159,870	518,170
Cost of Sales:			
Beginning Inventory	5,800	3,000	
Purchases	145,600	40,310	
Available	151,400	43,310	
Ending Inventory	7,000	2,800	
Cost of Goods Used	144,400	40,510	184,910
Cost of Employee Meals	9,200		9,200
Cost of Goods Sold	135,200	40,510	175,710
Net Other Income			3,800
Gross Profit			346,260
Operating Expenses:			
Total Payroll and Related Expenses			204,180
Total Other Operating Expenses			54,703
Departmental Income			$ 87,377

of the hotel's financial condition if the hotel has only 30 percent occupancy. Similarly, a 90-percent occupancy may look much better than it is if those rooms were all filled at steep discounts. By combining occupancy and room rate into a single statistic, RevPAR permits more meaningful comparison with a hotel's competitors. For example, suppose one hotel has paid occupancy of 80 percent and an average daily rate of $70, while a competitor has paid occupancy of 75 percent and an average daily rate of $80. Which hotel has the better situation? ADR points one way, occupancy percentage the other. RevPAR provides a more useful comparison.

RevPAR does not take into account revenue from other hotel services, such as restaurants, spas, golf courses, marinas, casinos, and so on. RevPAR reflects only rooms revenue, which is heavily influenced by factors managers cannot control, such as business travel and the general economy.

Food and Beverage Department Ratios

The food and beverage (F&B) department ratios in this chapter are computed from the Hotel DORO's departmental income statement shown in Exhibit 2. The popular ratios used in analyzing any F&B department are:

- Profit margin ratio

- Labor cost percentage

- Food cost percentage

- Prime cost percentage

- Beverage cost percentage

- Average food check

- Average beverage check

- Average total check

- Inventory turnover ratio

- Days' inventory on hand ratio

Profit Margin Ratio

The profit margin ratio for the F&B department is calculated in the same manner as that discussed for the rooms department and provides the same measurement of profitability. However, net sales of the F&B department needs definition. Does net sales include only food and beverage sales, or should it also include other revenue such as cover charges, souvenirs, and candy? It is not important how net sales is defined as long as the definition is used consistently and the benchmarks are composed of the same elements.

Formula. The profit margin ratio is computed as follows:

$$\frac{\text{Departmental Income}}{\text{Net Sales}}$$

The Hotel DORO excludes other revenue from its F&B departmental net sales. The profit margin ratio for the hotel's F&B department is computed as follows:

$$\frac{\$87,377}{\$518,170} \ = \ 16.9\%$$

Interpretation. The average dollar of sales in the F&B department is generating a profit of 16.9 percent, or it could be stated that F&B departmental income is 17¢ on the sales dollar. This profit cannot be measured against a stand-alone restaurant because an independent restaurant operation has the following expenses on its income statement: depreciation, repairs and maintenance, electricity, water, heat, administrative and general (A&G), marketing, and fixed charges.

This ratio should be compared with a benchmark profit margin ratio. If this ratio is equal to or greater than the benchmark, a preliminary and general assumption is that the condition appears *favorable*. For example, comparing the result of 16.9 percent with a budgeted profit margin ratio of 16 percent would indicate that the F&B department has generated the desired profit margin return and has done slightly better.

Labor Cost Percentage

The labor cost percentage for the F&B department is calculated in the same manner as that discussed for the rooms department and provides the same operating measurement.

Formula. The labor cost percentage is computed as follows:

$$\frac{\text{Total Payroll and Related Expenses}}{\text{Net Sales}}$$

The Hotel DORO excludes other revenue from its departmental net sales. The labor cost percentage for the hotel's F&B department is computed as follows:

$$\frac{\$204,180}{\$518,170} = 39.4\%$$

Interpretation. The average labor cost in the F&B department is 39.4 percent of the sales dollar, or it could be stated that 39¢ of the sales dollar is used to pay labor costs.

This ratio should be compared with a benchmark labor cost ratio. If this ratio is equal to or less than the benchmark, a preliminary and general assumption is that the condition appears *favorable.* For example, comparing the result of 39.4 percent with a budgeted ratio of 40 percent would indicate that the desired goal for operating efficiency has been achieved.

Food Cost Percentage

The **food cost percentage** for the F&B department is calculated in nearly the same manner as the labor cost percentage except that food cost is the numerator in the formula. The food cost ratio excludes beverage costs and beverage sales.

This ratio shows the cost of food per dollar of sales. It is a key operating ratio popular with most food service managers for evaluating and controlling food costs.

Formula. The food cost percentage is computed as follows:

$$\frac{\text{Cost of Food Sold}}{\text{Net Food Sales}}$$

The food cost percentage for the Hotel DORO's F&B department is computed as follows:

$$\frac{\$135,200}{\$358,300} = 37.7\%$$

Interpretation. The average cost of food used to serve guests is 37.7 percent of the sales dollar, or it could be stated that 38¢ of the sales dollar is used to pay for food prepared for guest consumption.

This ratio should be compared with a benchmark food cost ratio. If this ratio is equal to or less than the benchmark, a preliminary and general assumption is that the condition appears *favorable.* For example, comparing the result of 37.7 percent with a budgeted ratio of 38 percent would indicate that the desired goal for operating efficiency has been achieved.

However, caution is necessary when judging if results are favorable or unfavorable. It is possible for this ratio to be manipulated even if the actual sales volume is identical to the forecasted sales volume. Substituting a lower-quality product or reducing portion size will lower the food cost ratio. A high food cost ratio could be the result of poor portion control, poor purchasing practices at high costs, spoilage, or theft. Another factor affecting the food cost ratio is menu pricing. With no changes in quality or food costs, the food cost ratio can be reduced merely by increasing menu prices.

Prime Cost Percentage

Prime costs refer to the total labor and materials used in the production or selling process. Prime costs for the F&B department are total labor costs and total cost of sales. This operating measurement is more meaningful if it is prepared separately for food prime costs. However, this is not always possible because of the difficulties of separating labor applicable to food from labor applicable to beverages.

The Hotel DORO does not separate food labor from beverage labor. However, the consistent application of this percentage will lend itself to proper measurement and interpretation for the hotel.

Formula. The prime cost percentage is computed as follows:

$$\frac{\text{Total Cost of Sales } + \text{ Total Payroll and Related Expenses}}{\text{Net Sales}}$$

The prime cost percentage for the Hotel DORO's F&B department is computed as follows:

$$\frac{\$175,710 + \$204,180}{\$518,170} = 73.3\%$$

Interpretation. The prime costs for labor and food used to provide guest service are 73.3 percent of the sales dollar, or it could be stated that 73¢ of the sales dollar is used to pay prime costs, leaving 27¢ of the sales dollar to cover kitchen fuel, laundry, menus, uniforms, china, and other operating expenses.

This ratio should be compared with a benchmark ratio. If this ratio is equal to or less than the benchmark, a preliminary and general assumption is that the condition appears *favorable*. For example, comparing the result of 73.3 percent with a budgeted ratio of 75 percent would indicate that the desired goal for operating efficiency has been achieved.

Beverage Cost Percentage

The **beverage cost percentage** is calculated in the same manner as the food cost percentage, except that only costs and sales applicable to beverages are in the formula. This *operating* measurement for beverage cost does not include any food costs or food sales.

Formula. The beverage cost percentage is computed as follows:

$$\frac{\text{Cost of Beverages Sold}}{\text{Net Beverage Sales}}$$

The beverage cost percentage for the Hotel DORO's F&B department is computed as follows:

$$\frac{\$40,510}{\$159,870} = 25.3\%$$

Interpretation. The average cost of beverages used to serve guests is 25.3 percent of the sales dollar, or it could be stated that 25¢ of the sales dollar goes to materials used in preparing guest beverages.

This ratio should be compared with a benchmark beverage cost ratio. If this ratio is equal to or less than the benchmark, a preliminary and general assumption is that the condition appears *favorable*. For example, comparing the result of 25.3 percent with a budgeted ratio of 26 percent would indicate that the desired goal for operating efficiency has been achieved.

The cautions involved in interpreting the food cost percentage also apply to this ratio. Quality is a factor in the preparation of alcoholic beverages because of the wide price variation between well brands (lower-cost, lesser-known brands of liquor) and call brands (higher-priced and specifically ordered by the guest). Portion control is also an important issue in a bar operation and an integral part of any food and beverage operations management course.

Average Food Check

The **average food check** for a food service operation represents the average sale per **cover**. The term "covers" refers to the number of guests served in a food service operation during a specific period. This *operating* ratio should be computed separately for the dining room, cafeteria, snack bar, and other facilities because of the wide variations in menu prices at these locations within a hotel.

Formula. The average food check is computed as follows:

$$\frac{\text{Net Food Sales}}{\text{Covers}}$$

The number of guests served during 20X2 in the Hotel DORO's food service operation was 37,716. The average food check for the hotel is computed as follows:

$$\frac{\$358,300}{37,716} = \$9.50$$

Interpretation. The average food check for the period was $9.50, which did not include any alcoholic beverage sales.

This ratio should be compared with a benchmark ratio. If this ratio is equal to or greater than the benchmark, a preliminary and general assumption is that the condition appears *favorable*. For example, comparing the result of $9.50 with a budgeted ratio of $9.25 would indicate that the desired goal for operating efficiency has been achieved. This could be due to menu price increases or to guests selecting more expensive menu items.

Average Beverage Check

The procedure for computing the average beverage check is identical to that explained for the average food check except that beverage sales is substituted for food sales.

Average Total Check

The average total check includes the sales of food and beverages for a cover. Its computation is identical to that explained for the average food check except that the total of food and beverage sales is substituted for food sales.

Inventory Turnover Ratio

The **inventory turnover ratio** indicates how fast inventory moves through a hospitality business. The inventory turnover ratio shows *activity* by measuring the number of times inventory turns over relative to demand, and is a good asset management tool. Turnover should be computed separately for the food inventory and the beverage inventory.

The food inventory turnover is an average turnover of all items such as perishables, canned goods, and frozen foods. Since some of these products move faster than others, an average inventory turnover may seem high for some items and low for others. However, this limitation can be overcome by comparing this period's turnover with prior-period ratios, budgeted ratios, and industry standards.

Similarly, the separately computed beverage turnover is an average turnover of all alcoholic beverages, including expensive wines that might not move as rapidly as beer, house wines, and liquor.

The inventory turnover ratio is an indication of how well the funds invested in food and beverage inventories are being managed. A decrease in inventory turnover might indicate that the size of the inventory relative to sales is increasing unnecessarily. Having an inventory larger than required to meet sales demand ties up funds and may also increase food cost due to spoilage and other factors.

Formula. The inventory turnover ratio formula uses an average of the inventories for the period. The average inventory is computed by adding the beginning and ending inventories and then dividing this total by two. If the beginning and ending inventories are not shown on the F&B department income statement, it will be necessary to find these on the cost of sales supplementary schedule, balance sheet, or footnotes to the balance sheet. In using inventory figures, one must be careful to ensure that the food inventory amount is stated separately from the beverage inventory amount. The F&B department income statement shown in Exhibit 2 shows the required inventory data.

If *cost of food used* is not available, the *cost of food sold* may be used. Because employee meals are a small part of food used, either number may be used without distorting the inventory turnover for a period. Regardless of which number is used, it should be used consistently.

The average food inventory turnover ratio is computed as follows:

$$\frac{\text{Cost of Food Used}}{\text{Average Food Inventory}}$$

The food inventory turnover ratio for the Hotel DORO's F&B department is computed as follows:

$$\frac{\$144,400}{(\$5,800 + \$7,000) \div 2} = 23 \text{ Times}$$

The beverage inventory turnover ratio for the Hotel DORO's F&B department is computed as follows:

$$\frac{\text{Cost of Beverages Used}}{\text{Average Beverage Inventory}}$$

$$\frac{\$40,510}{(\$3,000 + \$2,800) \div 2} = 14 \text{ Times}$$

Interpretation. Notice that the inventory turnover figures have a label of "Times." The term "times" refers to the number of times the *complete* inventory, on average, has been *purchased* and *used* (sold). It takes both the purchase and use to equal a cycle of one time.

Interpreting any inventory turnover ratio requires careful attention to the time period involved. One must know if the data used results in an inventory turnover ratio for a month, year, or other period.

In the case of the Hotel DORO, the data was from the year ended; therefore, the ratios represent the average food and beverage inventory turnovers for the current year. The annual beverage inventory turnover of 14 times divided by 12 converts to an average monthly turnover of roughly one time.

If management requests information about a specific month's turnover, the computation is performed by dividing the food used for that month by the average of the inventories (beginning inventory for that month plus the ending inventory of the period divided by two).

Generally, a high inventory turnover ratio indicates a favorable condition because it shows that less investment in the inventory is required. However, a high turnover might also mean that too little inventory is carried and frequent stock-outs will occur. A stock-out results in poor guest service, and in the long run may prove costly because of loss of repeat business. A low turnover might mean that excessive stock is on hand relative to sales demand, resulting in unnecessary use of cash and possibly increased spoilage.

What is the best inventory turnover ratio? The answer depends on the type of food service operation, management's policy on customer service, and the use of fresh goods versus canned and frozen goods. Therefore, budgeted ratios based on these factors appear to be the best benchmarks for any particular hospitality business. A new restaurant operation might refer to industry standards, also called "norms," as a guide in setting turnover goals.

Hospitality Industry Turnover Norms. The Hotel DORO's food inventory turnover of 23 times for the year converts to a turnover of two times per month. At first glance, one might consider this turnover too low. However, the hotel's management has a policy of quality service and quality food at its fine-dining restaurant. A ratio of two times per month falls within the low end of the industry norm.

Fine dining restaurants will have low turnovers. A quick-service restaurant will have extremely high food inventory turnovers, sometimes in excess of 200 times in a year (17 times a month). The industry norms for hotels having several types of restaurants are as follows:

	Per Year	Per Month
Food inventory turnover	48	4
Beverage inventory turnover	15	1

These turnovers are generally considered satisfactory to maintain sales levels at reasonable cost. However, there are always exceptions. In addition to type of service, type of menu, and customer service policies, another factor a food service operation must consider is the frequency of delivery by suppliers. This is especially true of remote resort locations and franchised operations.

Days' Inventory on Hand Ratio

This ratio measures the average number of days that inventory is on hand before being used. This ratio is calculated simply by dividing 365 days (or less for seasonal operations) by the annual inventory turnover ratio. The days' inventory on hand ratio provides another way to evaluate inventory activity for proper asset management.

Formula. The days' inventory on hand ratio is computed as follows:

$$\frac{365 \text{ Days}}{\text{Annual Inventory Turnover Ratio}}$$

The average number of days the food inventory was in stock for the Hotel DORO can be calculated by referring to the annual food inventory turnover previously calculated and computing as follows:

$$\frac{365}{23} = 16 \text{ Days}$$

Interpretation. Generally, a low number of days' inventory on hand is desired. However, the same considerations discussed for the inventory turnover ratio apply to the measurement of the days' inventory on hand ratio.

Hotel Ratios

A hotel may be only one of several properties that make up a business corporation. There are ratios to measure the activities of a single property and other ratios to measure the activities of a corporation (the sum of all its locations). Ratios used to measure corporate activities cannot be applied to a single property because it is the corporation that issues stock.

The popular ratios used in analyzing any single hotel property are the profit margin ratio and the labor cost percentage. The popular ratios used in analyzing any hotel corporation are:

- Profit margin ratio
- Return on equity ratio

Exhibit 3   Long-Form Income Statement—Hotel DORO

Hotel DORO, Inc.
Statement of Income
For the year ended December 31, 20X2

	Schedule	Net Revenue	Cost of Sales	Payroll and Related Expenses	Other Expenses	Income (Loss)
Operated Departments						
Rooms	A1	$ 897,500		$ 143,140	$ 62,099	$ 692,261
Food and Beverage	A2	524,570	$ 178,310	204,180	54,703	87,377
Telephone	A3	51,140	60,044	17,132	1,587	(27,623)
Other Operated Departments	A4	63,000	10,347	33,276	6,731	12,646
Rentals and Other Income	A5	61,283				61,283
Total Operated Departments		1,597,493	248,701	397,728	125,120	825,944
Undistributed Expenses						
Administrative and General	A6			97,632	66,549	164,181
Marketing	A7			35,825	32,043	67,868
Property Operation and Maintenance	A8			36,917	24,637	61,554
Utility Costs	A9				47,312	47,312
Total Undistributed Expenses				170,374	170,541	340,915
Income Before Fixed Charges		$ 1,597,493	$ 248,701	$ 568,102	$ 295,661	$ 485,029
Fixed Charges						
Rent	A10					28,500
Property Taxes	A10					45,324
Insurance	A10					6,914
Interest	A10					192,153
Depreciation and Amortization	A10					146,000
Total Fixed Charges						418,891
Income Before Income Taxes and Gain on Sale of Property						66,138
Gain on Sale of Property						10,500
Income Before Income Taxes						76,638
Income Taxes						16,094
Net Income						$ 60,544

- Earnings per share ratio
- Price earnings ratio

The Hotel DORO is a single property in a one-property corporation. Therefore, our discussion will cover all of the listed single-property and corporate ratios. The ratios for the Hotel DORO will be computed from its income statement, shown in Exhibit 3.

Profit Margin Ratio—Hotel

The profit margin ratio for a hotel is computed in a procedure identical to those previously discussed for individual departments. In the case of a hotel, the ratio provides a mixed measure of profitability because it is based on sales of all revenue centers, and its income is the result of all departments of the hotel.

Formula. The profit margin ratio for a hotel is computed as follows:

$$\frac{\text{Net Income}}{\text{Net Sales}}$$

The profit margin ratio for the Hotel DORO is computed as follows:

$$\frac{\$60,544}{\$1,597,493} = 3.8\%$$

Interpretation. The hotel's average dollar of sales from all revenue centers is generating a profit of 3.8 percent, or it could be stated that the hotel keeps about 4¢ of each sales dollar. Unlike the amount in a departmental analysis, this amount is after income taxes.

This ratio should be compared with a benchmark profit margin ratio. If the ratio is equal to or greater than the benchmark, a preliminary and general assumption is that the condition appears *favorable*.

Profit Margin Ratio—Corporation

The profit margin ratio for a corporation is computed using the same formula as for a hotel. Since the Hotel DORO is a single-property corporation, the hotel profit margin ratio and corporate profit margin ratio would be identical.

Labor Cost Percentage

One of the largest expenses for hotels and motels is labor. Labor expense includes total payroll costs and all the related expenses such as benefits and payroll taxes. The labor cost percentage for a hotel is computed using a procedure identical to that previously discussed for the individual departments. In the case of a hotel, the ratio gives a mixed measure of labor costs because it is based on sales of all revenue centers, and its labor cost is the result of all departments of the hotel.

Formula. The labor cost percentage is computed as follows:

$$\frac{\text{Total Payroll and Related Expenses}}{\text{Net Sales}}$$

The labor cost percentage for the Hotel DORO includes the labor costs of revenue centers and support centers. It is computed as follows:

$$\frac{\$568,102}{\$1,597,493} = 35.6\%$$

Interpretation. The average labor cost for the hotel is 35.6 percent of the sales dollar, or it could be stated that 36¢ of the sales dollar is used to pay labor costs.

This ratio should be compared with a benchmark labor cost ratio. If this ratio is equal to or less than the benchmark, a preliminary and general assumption is that the condition appears *favorable*.

Return on Equity Ratio

The return on equity ratio measures the profit after taxes of the hospitality corporation relative to the equity of its owners (shareholders). **Equity** represents the

Exhibit 4   Condensed Balance Sheet—Hotel DORO

Hotel DORO, Inc. Condensed Comparative Balance Sheet December 31, 20X2 and December 31, 20X1		
	20X2	**20X1**
Current Assets	$ 147,888	$ 147,654
Property & Equipment (net)	3,095,524	3,139,217
Other Noncurrent Assets	4,000	5,500
Total Assets	$ 3,247,412	$ 3,292,371
Current Liabilities	$ 123,750	$ 139,253
Long-Term Debt	2,055,000	2,125,000
Total Liabilities	2,178,750	2,264,253
Shareholders' Equity		
Common Stock Issued	50,000	50,000
Additional Paid-In Capital	700,000	700,000
Retained Earnings	318,662	278,118
Total Shareholders' Equity	1,068,662	1,028,118
Total Liabilities and Shareholders' Equity	$ 3,247,412	$ 3,292,371

retained earnings of the corporation and proceeds from its sale of stock (common stock issued + paid-in capital). The equity amount comes from the balance sheet. Therefore, the computation of this ratio requires both an income statement and a balance sheet.

Formula if Common Stock Is Issued. The formula for this ratio depends on the capitalization of the corporation, which might consist of both common and preferred stock. If only common stock is issued, the following formula is used:

$$\frac{\text{Net Income}}{\text{Average Equity}}$$

Average equity is the equity at the beginning of the year added to the equity at the end of the year, divided by two. Remember that balance sheet data at the end of a year becomes the beginning data for the next condensed comparative year.

The equity section of the Hotel DORO's condensed balance sheet is shown in Exhibit 4. It is used with the net income shown in Exhibit 3, the corporation's income statement. The return on equity ratio for the hotel is computed as follows:

$$\frac{\$60,544}{(\$1,068,662 \ + \ \$1,028,118) \ \div \ 2} = 5.8\%$$

Interpretation. The rate of return after taxes using shareholders' equity is 5.8 percent. This amount is after taxes. If a comparison is made to money market rates, the stated money market rates must be reduced by the effect of income taxes (state and federal).

This ratio should be compared with a benchmark profit margin ratio. Like any other type of profitability ratio, if this ratio is equal to or greater than the benchmark, a preliminary and general assumption is that the condition appears *favorable.*

Formula if Preferred Stock Is Issued. If preferred stock is issued, the formula is modified to measure the *return on common stockholders' equity*. The formula is modified as follows:

$$\frac{\text{Net Income Less Preferred Dividends}}{\text{Average Common Shareholders' Equity}}$$

The Hotel DORO has only common stock issued, and this calculation is not necessary.

Earnings per Share Ratio

The **earnings per share (EPS) ratio** is a corporation's net income divided by the number of common shares issued and outstanding. For the moment, the EPS ratio will be discussed in its simplest form.

Formula. The EPS is computed as follows:

$$\frac{\text{Net Income}}{\text{Average Common Stock Outstanding}}$$

The Hotel DORO's common shares issued represent common stock outstanding because there is no treasury stock. Also, the common stock outstanding has not changed between January 1, 20X2 and December 31, 20X2 (see the equity section of the balance sheet shown in Exhibit 4). The hotel's common stock is $1 par value; thus, there are 50,000 common shares issued and outstanding.

The EPS for the Hotel DORO is computed as follows:

$$\frac{\$60,544}{50,000} = \$1.21$$

Interpretation. Each share of the Hotel DORO's stock earned $1.21 after taxes. Investors expect a *growth* company to have increasing EPS in each successive reporting period. The significance of the use of EPS in measuring a stock's value will become apparent when the price earnings ratio is discussed.

Complications in Computing. Computing EPS for the Hotel DORO is quick and easy because it has a *simple capital structure*, meaning that the corporation has no convertible preferred stock, convertible bonds, or options. If the holders of convertible securities and options exercise their conversion privileges, the number of outstanding common shares will increase. Corporations that have convertible securities or options have a *complex capital structure*.

A corporation with a complex capital structure will eventually incur a dilution to its EPS because more common stock will eventually be issued. Therefore, the EPS formula must be modified to account for diluted earnings per share. These calculations are very technical, lengthy, and complex. Their computation is best left to the professional accountant.

Price Earnings Ratio

The **price earnings (PE) ratio** is a popular ratio used by the investment community to evaluate whether a stock is reasonably priced. This ratio is computed for both current earnings and forecasted earnings. Investment reports, financial periodicals, and financial sections of newspapers widely use and display the PE ratio.

Formula. The PE ratio is computed as follows:

$$\frac{\text{Market Price per Share}}{\text{Earnings per Share}}$$

Previously, the EPS for the Hotel DORO was computed at $1.21 per share. Assume the stock is listed on a major stock exchange at $15.00 per share. The PE ratio for the hotel's stock is computed as follows:

$$\frac{\$15.00}{\$1.21} = 12$$

Interpretation. While not conclusive, any PE ratio higher than that of other companies in the same industry might indicate that a stock is fully priced or possibly overpriced. In the case of the Hotel DORO, if the stocks of other similar companies listed on the stock exchange are selling at a PE ratio of 15, the hotel might be considered an attractive *buy* situation, assuming there is a growth pattern to earnings or other fundamental factors that might benefit earnings.

The EPS and PE ratios are only two of the measurements used by investment analysts and investors. Even though the use of these ratios might prove attractive, investing in the stock market requires specialized knowledge of technical factors and other considerations.

Considerations in Calculating. Typically, net income should exclude extraordinary items that are not recurring in the normal course of business. In the case of the Hotel DORO, earnings were inflated by the gain on the sale of property. Therefore, the investment community would calculate the EPS and PE ratios in the following ways:

- Based on total net income
- Based on income before extraordinary items

The allocation of income taxes becomes a problem in these computations, and the necessary technical procedures are best left to the professional accountant.

Other Income Statement Ratios

The study of ratios can be never-ending because ratios are the relationships between two numbers. This chapter has presented the more popular and common ratios. However, the chapter would not be complete if it did not present other ratios used in evaluating the income statement.

Number of Times Interest Earned Ratio

The **number of times interest earned ratio** shows the number of times the interest expense is covered by earnings. Although a business may be heavily financed by debt, its earnings may be adequate to pay the interest expense.

Formula. This ratio is computed as follows:

$$\frac{\text{Net Income } + \text{ Income Taxes } + \text{ Interest}}{\text{Interest}}$$

The number of times interest earned ratio for the Hotel DORO is computed as follows:

$$\frac{\$60,544 \ + \ \$16,094 \ + \ \$192,153}{\$192,153} = 1.4 \text{ Times}$$

Interpretation. A ratio of less than one would indicate that the current earnings are not sufficient to meet interest expense.

Return on Assets Ratio

The **return on assets (ROA) ratio** measures how productively the assets have been used to generate net income.

Formula. This ratio is computed as follows:

$$\frac{\text{Net Income}}{\text{Average Total Assets}}$$

The total assets from the balance sheet (not shown) for the Hotel DORO are $3,292,371 on December 31, 20X1 and $3,247,412 on December 31, 20X2. The ROA would be calculated as follows:

$$\frac{\$60,544}{(\$3,292,371 \ + \ \$3,247,412) \div 2} = 1.9\%$$

Interpretation. The corporation generates a profit after taxes of 1.9 percent for each dollar of its assets (at book value). Depreciation policies will affect the comparability of this ratio because total assets is a base. This ratio should be compared with prior-period ratios or budgeted ratios.

Reference List of Ratio Formulas

The following list shows the major ratios and their formulas and is intended to be a convenient reference.

Average Food Check

$$\frac{\text{Net Food Sales}}{\text{Covers}}$$

Average Room Rate

$$\frac{\text{Net Room Sales}}{\text{Paid Rooms Occupied}}$$

Days' Inventory on Hand Ratio

$$\frac{365 \text{ Days (or operating year)}}{\text{Annual Inventory Turnover Ratio}}$$

Earnings per Share Ratio

$$\frac{\text{Net Income}}{\text{Average Common Stock Outstanding}}$$

Food Cost Percentage

$$\frac{\text{Cost of Food Sold}}{\text{Net Food Sales}}$$

Food Inventory Turnover Ratio

$$\frac{\text{Cost of Food Used}}{\text{Average Food Inventory}}$$

Beverage Inventory Turnover Ratio

$$\frac{\text{Cost of Beverages Used}}{\text{Average Beverage Inventory}}$$

Labor Cost Percentage

$$\frac{\text{Total Payroll and Related Expenses}}{\text{Net Sales}}$$

Number of Times Interest Earned Ratio

$$\frac{\text{Net Income } + \text{ Income Taxes } + \text{ Interest}}{\text{Interest}}$$

Occupancy Percentage

$$\frac{\text{Paid Rooms Occupied}}{\text{Rooms Available}}$$

Price Earnings Ratio

$$\frac{\text{Market Price per Share}}{\text{Earnings per Share}}$$

Prime Cost Percentage

$$\frac{\text{Cost of Sales } + \text{ Payroll and Related Expenses}}{\text{Net Sales}}$$

Profit Margin Ratio

$$\frac{\text{Net Income (or Departmental Income)}}{\text{Net Sales}}$$

Return on Assets Ratio

$$\frac{\text{Net Income}}{\text{Average Total Assets}}$$

Return on Equity Ratio

$$\frac{\text{Net Income}}{\text{Average Equity}}$$

RevPAR

$$\frac{\text{Rooms Revenue}}{\text{Rooms Available for Sale}}$$

🔑 Key Terms

average daily rate (ADR)—A key rooms department operating ratio obtained by dividing rooms revenue by number of rooms sold. Also called average room rate.

average food check—A ratio comparing the revenue generated during a meal period with the number of guests served during the period. It is calculated by dividing total food revenue by number of food covers sold during a period. This ratio should be calculated for different dining areas and/or meal periods.

average room rate (ARR)—See average daily rate (ADR).

beverage cost percentage—A ratio that shows beverage cost as a percentage of beverage sales; calculated by dividing the cost of beverages sold by beverage sales.

cover—A meal served in a restaurant or at a food function; term used when counting the volume of business.

earnings per share (EPS) ratio—A ratio that serves as a general indicator of corporate profitability by the comparison of net income of the corporation with the average common shares outstanding. If preferred stock has been issued for the operation, preferred dividends are subtracted from net income before EPS is calculated. Calculated by dividing net income by average common shares outstanding.

equity—The claims of owners to assets of the business; equity represents the residual amount after liabilities are deducted from assets.

food cost percentage—A ratio calculated by dividing cost of food sales by net food sales. Food cost percentages vary from company to company depending on such factors as service level, menu prices, and food quality.

inventory turnover ratio—The average number of days the inventory is on hand. Any turnover ratio can be converted to a turnover period by dividing 365 days by the number of turnover times in a year.

labor cost percentage—Often referred to as labor cost to sales ratio, the percentage of sales that is used to pay labor, including salaries, wages, bonuses, payroll taxes, and fringe benefits. Calculated by dividing total labor costs by total revenue. This ratio should be calculated for each operated department. Sometimes used by international hotels to measure comparative operational advantages among properties in different countries.

net income to sales ratio—A ratio computed by dividing net income by net sales. It gives the amount of net income on each sales dollar and is expressed as a percentage. The net income to sales ratio is also called the profit margin ratio.

number of times interest earned ratio—A solvency ratio expressing the number of times interest expense can be covered. Calculated by dividing earnings before interest and taxes by interest expense.

occupancy percentage—A ratio indicating management's success in selling its "product." (1) Among lodging properties, occupancy percentage is also referred to as the occupancy rate and is calculated by dividing the number of rooms sold by the number of rooms available. (2) In food service operations, occupancy percentage is referred to as seat turnover and is calculated by dividing the number of people served by the number of seats available.

price earnings (PE) ratio—A profitability ratio used by financial analysts to show investors the relative value of an investment; calculated by dividing market price per share by earnings per share.

prime costs—The cost of food sold plus payroll cost (including employee benefits). These are a restaurant's largest costs.

ratio—The mathematical relationship of two figures.

return on assets (ROA) ratio—A ratio that provides a general indicator of the profitability of a hospitality operation by comparing bottom line profits with total investment; in accounting terms, ROA is net income divided by total assets; in finance terms, ROA is the rate of discount that makes the weighted average cost of capital approach to net present value (NPV) equal zero.

RevPAR—A ratio that measures how effectively a hotel is able to fill its rooms, calculated as room revenue per available room.

zero base budgeting—An approach to preparing budgets that requires the justification of all expenses; this approach assumes that each department starts with zero dollars and must justify all budgeted amounts.

Review Questions

1. What is a ratio?
2. What are the advantages and limitations of ratio analysis?
3. How can a ratio be used to determine if a condition is favorable or unfavorable?
4. Which specific ratios can be used by a rooms department manager to evaluate profitability, operational efficiency, and asset management?
5. Which specific ratios can be used by a food service manager to evaluate profitability, operational efficiency, and asset management?
6. Which two ratios are most frequently used to measure a stock's value?
7. How is a rooms department profit margin ratio of 72 percent interpreted?
8. How is a food cost percentage of 30 percent interpreted?
9. What do the acronyms "ARR" and "ADR" represent?
10. What factors may reduce a food cost percentage?
11. What are prime costs?
12. What are covers?
13. What is the monthly inventory turnover for a food service operation that has had an annual inventory turnover ratio of 60 times?
14. What is the formula for each of the following ratios as applicable to a rooms department analysis?

    Average room rate
    Labor cost percentage
    Occupancy percentage
    Profit margin ratio

15. What is the formula for each of the following ratios as applicable to a food service department analysis?

    Average food check
    Inventory turnover ratio
    Days' inventory on hand ratio
    Food cost percentage

Labor cost percentage
Prime cost percentage
Profit margin ratio

16. What is the formula for each of the following ratios as applicable to a corporate income statement analysis?

Earnings per share ratio
Price earnings ratio
Profit margin ratio
Return on equity ratio

17. Which of the following ratios is expressed as a percentage?

Average food check
Average room rate
Days' inventory on hand ratio
Earnings per share ratio
Food cost percentage
Inventory turnover ratio
Labor cost percentage
Occupancy percentage
Price earnings ratio
Profit margin ratio
Return on equity ratio

Internet Sites

For more information, visit the following Internet sites. Remember that Internet addresses can change without notice. If the site is no longer there, you can use a search engine to look for additional sites.

Common-size Financial Statements
www.netmba.com/finance/statements/common-size/

Financial Ratios
http://beginnersinvest.about.com/od/financialratio/

Return on Equity Ratio Analyzed
http://beginnersinvest.about.com/cs/investinglessons/l/blreturnequity.htm

Earnings per Share Analyzed
http://stocks.about.com/od/evaluatingstocks/a/eps1.htm

Diluted Earnings per Share
http://beginnersinvest.about.com/cs/newinvestors/l/bldilutedeps.htm

Price Earnings Ratio Analyzed & Interpreted
http://stocks.about.com/od/evaluatingstocks/a/pe.htm
http://economics.about.com/cs/finance/l/aa030503a.htm

Problems

Problem 1

Compute the food cost percentage (with two decimals) from the following information:

Food sales	$345,000
Allowances	3,000
Cost of food sold	95,000

Problem 2

Compute the beverage cost percentage (with two decimals) from the following information:

	Food	Beverage
Sales	$596,000	$150,000
Allowances	3,000	1,000
Cost of sales	170,000	30,000

Problem 3

Compute the food inventory turnover ratio (with one decimal) from the following information:

Food sales	$345,000	
Allowances		3,000
Net sales		342,000
Cost of food sold:		
Beginning inventory	$ 2,800	
Purchases	105,000	
Available	107,800	
Ending inventory	1,600	
Food used	106,200	
Employee meals	2,200	
Cost of food sold		104,000
Gross profit		$238,000

Problem 4

What was a hotel's current labor expense if its labor cost percentage was 40 percent and its net sales were $800,000?

Problem 5

What was the gross profit percentage if a food service operation had a food cost of 28 percent?

Problem 6

What was a hotel's current net income if its profit margin ratio was eight percent and its net sales were $2,000,000?

Problem 7

The following supplementary information and income statement is provided for The Garden Bistro, Inc. for its year ended December 20X8.

Supplementary Information
Food covers: 21,250
Common stock issued and outstanding: 25,000 shares (all year)
Common stock quotation, end of year: $12.00 per share
Inventory 12/31/X7: $2,100
Inventory 12/31/X8: $2,400
Shareholders' equity 12/31/X7: $83,000
Shareholders' equity 12/31/X8: $98,000

The Garden Bistro, Inc.
Income Statement
For the year ended December 31, 20X8

Net Food Sales		$170,000
Cost of Food Used	$54,000	
Employee Meals	1,000	
Cost of Food Sold		53,000
Gross Profit		117,000
Operating Expenses:		
Payroll	55,000	
Payroll Taxes and Benefits	7,900	
Laundry	2,100	
Supplies	1,500	
Advertising	2,000	
Utilities	3,800	
Repairs	1,900	
Other	6,200	
Total Operating Expenses		80,400
Income Before Fixed Charges		
and Income Taxes		36,600
Fixed Charges		19,600
Income Before Income Taxes		17,000
Income Taxes		2,000
Net Income		$15,000

Instructions:

1. Compute the following ratios.

2. Unless the ratio result is stated in dollars and cents, show the computed result with one decimal, properly rounded (xx.x).

Average food check	Inventory turnover ratio
Food cost percentage	Days' inventory on hand ratio
Labor cost percentage	Earnings per share ratio
Prime cost percentage	Price earnings ratio
Profit margin ratio	
Return on equity ratio	

Problem 8

A 120-room hotel with a 365-day year sold 25,864 rooms (paid occupancy of $1,463,902) for the year. Compute its occupancy ratio (as a whole number) and average room rate for that year.

Problem 9

A hotel had 400 rooms available for sale on February 21. The paid room occupancy was $18,077 on 289 rooms sold for that evening. Compute the following ratios for February 21:

Occupancy percentage (show answer as a whole number)
Average room rate

Problem 10

In July, a hotel had a daily capacity of 540 rooms available for sale. The paid room occupancy was $506,340 on 8,730 room nights sold. Compute the occupancy percentage (as a whole number) based on rooms available to sell for July.

Problem 11

Executive managers of the Dermonel National Hotels, Inc. have completed analyzing the income statement for the current period. Compare the results against the budgeted goals and indicate whether the results are favorable or unfavorable. Do not consider any other factors but the ratio numbers provided.

	Actual	Budget
Average room rate	$120.00	$118.00
Occupancy percentage	68%	72%
Average food check	$12.00	$11.15
	Actual	Budget
Food cost percentage	31%	32%
Labor cost percentage	34%	34%
Inventory turnover ratio	48	41
Profit margin ratio	12%	10%
Return on equity ratio	18%	22%

Problem 12

Hotel Blue Moon has 300 guestrooms. Management has requested an analysis of RevPAR for the periods shown below, as well as the annual RevPAR figure. The analysis is to be performed in accordance with *USALI*. Show each quarterly RevPAR and the annual RevPAR in dollars and cents format.

	Days in Period	Days Rooms Out of Order	Days Rooms Reserved for Corporate	Rooms Sales
First quarter of year	90	5	0	$2,976,199
Second quarter of year	91	0	5	3,141,655
Third quarter of year	92	3	2	3,155,764
Fourth quarter of year	92	6	4	3,099,185

Case Study

Critique of Hotel Income Statement

The executives of the Hotel Quantum are reviewing and analyzing a comparative income statement for a two-year period. No supporting schedules are provided with the statement, which is shown below.

Hotel Quantum, Inc.
Comparative Income Statement
For the years ended December 31, 20X9 and 20X8

	20X9	20X8	Change	%
Income from rooms department	$ 900,000	$ 890,000	$ 10,000	1.1
Income from F&B departments	120,000	119,000	1,000	0.8
Income from other departments	5,000	5,650	(650)	-11.5
Total income	1,025,000	1,014,650	10,350	1.0
Administrative department	160,000	130,000	30,000	23.1
Maintenance department	60,000	35,000	25,000	71.4
Utility costs	40,000	39,000	1,000	2.6
Other support center costs	50,000	49,500	500	1.0
Total expenses of support centers	310,000	253,500	56,500	22.3
Income before fixed charges	715,000	761,150	(46,150)	-6.1
Fixed charges	420,000	380,000	40,000	10.5
Income before other items	295,000	381,150	(86,150)	-22.6
Loss on sale of property	124,000	100	123,900	123,900.0
Income before income taxes	171,000	381,050	(210,050)	-55.1

At the beginning of the current year, management increased room rates by 10 percent. Management also increased food menu prices and liquor prices. Staffing has remained relatively stable. Hotel Quantum owns its property and does not incur rental expenses. During the year, it sold property that had been intended for expansion.

The hotel president, general manager (GM), and revenue center directors are examining the income statement and have expressed various comments. The president is very disturbed that income before income taxes is down by $210,050.

The rooms department director boasts that his department's income rose by $10,000.

The F&B director states that his department maintained its profitability and even enjoyed a modest increase in profits from the previous year.

The GM declares that the Hotel Quantum actually has had very profitable operations. The operational profit number is distorted by the loss on sale of property, which is not an operational issue. In fact, the hotel's operational income before this loss was actually $295,000, not the $171,000 shown on the last line of the statement. The GM sums it up by saying, "All in all, we had a very good year."

The president has decided to have you, the hotel's chief accountant, comment on the financial statements. The president meets with you to inform you of the various comments made at the meeting. The president wants to get at the true meaning of the numbers in order to initiate corrective management action as necessary.

Challenge

As chief accountant, you must respond to the comments expressed at the meeting. The president also expects you to further analyze the financial statement's line items. In addition to commenting as directed below, you are expected to provide any recommendations for statistical analysis.

1. Comment on the boast that the rooms department income is up $10,000 from the previous year.

2. Comment on the F&B director's claim of maintaining profitability.

3. Comment on the GM's true conclusion that the loss on the sale of property distorts the "bottom line"; comment also on the GM's assertion that the income before the loss was $295,000.

4. Comment on the income from other departments being down 11.5 percent.

5. Comment on each of the support centers.

6. Comment on the fixed charges.

7. Comment on the exclusion of an income tax line to arrive at a true "bottom line."

Chapter 9 Outline

Elements and Conventions
Assets
    Current Assets
    Noncurrent Assets
Liabilities
    Current Liabilities
    Long-Term Liabilities
Equity
Hotel Balance Sheet Formats
The Hotel DORO's Balance Sheet
    Common-Size Balance Sheet
    Comparative Balance Sheet
The Statement of Retained Earnings

Competencies

1. Describe the purpose, general content, and users of a hotel balance sheet, and explain the elements and conventions used in preparing a balance sheet. (pp. 253–254)

2. Explain assets, and identify current and noncurrent assets. (pp. 254–256)

3. Explain liabilities, and identify current and long-term liabilities. (pp. 256–257)

4. Describe the items that might appear in the equity section of a balance sheet. (pp. 257–258)

5. Differentiate between the account and report formats and the internal and external formats for a balance sheet. (pp. 258–260)

6. Explain the preparation and purposes of common-size and comparative balance sheets, and describe their analysis and interpretation. (pp. 260–267)

7. Explain the relationship between the statement of retained earnings and the balance sheet. (p. 267)

9

Hotel Balance Sheets

THE BALANCE SHEET shows a hotel's assets, liabilities, and owner's equity for a particular date. The balance sheet is a property or corporate statement; it is not a financial tool directed to supervisors and departmental managers. It is useful to executives, the board of directors, shareholders, creditors, and the investment community.

The content of all balance sheets is fairly consistent because of the reporting requirements established by the Financial Accounting Standards Board (FASB) and generally accepted accounting principles (GAAP). This standardization results in very similar formats. Like hotel income statements, balance sheets can be prepared in internal or external formats.

A balance sheet is very important because it presents the "financial health" of a company on a certain date. An income statement shows what happened in the past but does not give an indication of the company's ability to continue in business.

The income statement shows the profit for a period of time, while the balance sheet shows what a company *owns* and *owes* on a given date. It is possible that a profitable company could go out of business because of its debt service load.

In presenting the hotel balance sheet, this chapter will address the following questions:

1. What are the basic elements and conventions used in the design of a balance sheet?

2. What is the difference between internal and external balance sheets?

3. What is a common-size balance sheet?

4. What is a comparative balance sheet?

5. What is the relationship between the balance sheet and the statement of retained earnings?

Elements and Conventions

The balance sheet is also called the *statement of financial position*. Its purpose is to report a company's resources and commitments as of a specified date. For example, a balance sheet dated December 31 does not cover the month or the year ended December 31; it reports financial balances as of the close of business for the day ended December 31. To clarify, a company issuing its annual statements on a calendar basis would use the following headings on its financial reports:

253

Katygard Motel, Inc.	Katygard Motel, Inc.
Income Statement	Balance Sheet
For the year ended December 31, 20XX	December 31, 20XX

Elements. The basic elements of the balance sheet are represented by the following accounting equation:

$$\text{Assets} = \text{Liabilities} + \text{Equity}$$

Because liabilities and equity are claims on the assets of the business, the equation can be stated as follows:

$$\text{Assets} = \text{Claims}$$

The accounting equation can be restated in the form of a financial equation as follows:

$$\text{Assets} \quad = \quad \begin{array}{c}\text{Claims of} \\ \text{Creditors} \\ \uparrow \\ \text{Liabilities}\end{array} \quad + \quad \begin{array}{c}\text{Claims of} \\ \text{Owners} \\ \uparrow \\ \text{Equity}\end{array}$$

Conventions. The *going concern principle* and *historical cost principle* dictate that assets be shown at amounts not greater than their cost; this allows the reader to measure the use of resources. In the case of accounts receivable, inventories, marketable securities, and investments, the *principle of conservatism* dictates that these assets be shown at the lesser of their cost or current market value.

Assets

An **asset** is anything of monetary value that is owned by a business. To qualify as an asset, an item must provide future economic benefit or provide certain rights or claims. For example, the acquisition of a franchise right is capitalized (recorded as an asset instead of an expense) because the "right" will be a benefit over an extended period of time. The assets of a hospitality business can be classified as current and noncurrent assets.

Current Assets

Current assets include cash and other assets that will be converted to cash within 12 months of the balance sheet date. Also included in current assets are prepayments of expenditures expected to benefit operations over the next 12 months from the balance sheet date. Current assets are listed on the balance sheet in descending order of liquidity and consist of:

- Cash
- Short-term investments (also called marketable securities)
- Accounts receivable
- Inventories
- Prepaid expenses

Cash. Cash consists of cash in checking and savings accounts, cash in house banks, and certificates of deposit. However, money held in a bank account that has a *restricted use* is shown as a noncurrent asset and listed under the other assets classification.

Short-Term Investments. Short-term investments are securities that are readily marketable and can be converted into cash. With marketable securities, management's intention is to invest in other companies for potential gain and not for control of or affiliation with these companies.

Accounts Receivable. In a hotel operation, accounts receivable include the guest ledger and the city ledger. An *Allowance for Doubtful Accounts* is used to estimate potential bad debts. This allowance is listed as a deduction from the face value of the receivables.

Inventories. Inventories include food, beverages, guestroom supplies, office supplies, cleaning supplies, and other reserve stocks of operating supplies that are on hand on the balance sheet date.

Prepaid Expenses. Prepaid expenses are expenditures paid in advance for services that will benefit the hospitality company for a period up to 12 months from the balance sheet date. Typical examples of prepaid expenses are insurance, interest, property taxes, rent, and service contracts.

Noncurrent Assets

Noncurrent assets are those assets that will not be converted to cash within 12 months of the balance sheet date. Categories of noncurrent assets include noncurrent receivables, investments, property and equipment, and other assets.

Noncurrent Receivables. Noncurrent receivables represent accounts and notes that are not expected to be collected during the next 12 months. Amounts due from owners, officers, employees, and affiliated entities should be shown separately, unless insignificant. If any noncurrent receivables are estimated to be uncollectible, an allowance for doubtful noncurrent receivables should be established.

Investments. In accounting, the term "investments" applies to investments in other companies that are made with an objective of control or affiliation. Investments do not meet any or all of the conditions of marketable securities.

Property and Equipment. Assets grouped under property and equipment are long-lived, tangible assets that may also be called fixed assets. These assets include land, buildings, vehicles, china, glassware, silver, linen, uniforms, machinery, rooms department furniture, food and beverage department furniture, and all other furniture and equipment necessary for a hotel to do business.

Also included in property and equipment are leaseholds, leasehold improvements, construction in progress, and assets held under a capital lease (a lease that is in essence a purchase of an asset).

Accumulated depreciation, the sum of all depreciation charges over a period of time, is subtracted from cost to arrive at the net book value of the assets in this category. (Land is not depreciated in the hospitality industry.)

Other Assets. This noncurrent asset classification includes intangible assets and deferred charges. Examples of intangible assets in this category are organization costs, preopening expenses, franchise rights, goodwill, trademarks, tradenames, security deposits, patents, copyrights, and cash surrender value of officers' life insurance.

These intangible assets must have been *acquired*. They are carried at cost and *amortized* over their expected life (not to exceed 40 years). Amortization reduces the book value of the intangible asset, and the amortization expense appears on the income statement.

Deferred charges are similar to prepaid expenses since both are temporary assets that become expenses over a period of time. However, while a prepaid expense benefits the next 12 months, a deferred expense has a benefit beyond 12 months. For example, assume a hotel signs up for a three-year service contract to get a discounted rate. At any time, 12 months of contract costs are a prepaid expense and any remaining contract costs are a deferred expense.

Liabilities

Liabilities represent amounts owed to creditors. They are classified as current and long-term liabilities.

Current Liabilities

Current liabilities are liabilities that must be paid within 12 months of the balance sheet date. Current liabilities include the current portion of long-term loans such as bank loans and mortgages. Also included in current liabilities are *deferred credits.* Two examples of deferred credits are unearned revenue and deferred income tax.

Unearned revenue results when a hotel collects room deposits or banquet deposits from guests before any services have been rendered. Unearned revenue may appear on the balance sheet under other names such as advance deposits, deposits and credit balances, or customer deposits.

Deferred income tax represents the amount of a hotel's potential income tax obligation that results from differences in financial reporting and income tax reporting. This situation is not uncommon. For example, some depreciation methods approved by the FASB are not accepted by the Internal Revenue Service. Therefore, there will be a difference between book income and taxable income. This can be shown as follows:

	Books	Tax Return
Sales	$100,000	$100,000
Expenses before depreciation	− 70,000	− 70,000
Income before depreciation	30,000	30,000
Depreciation	3,000	10,000
Income for tax computation	27,000	20,000
Income tax at 30%	8,100	6,000

In filing its income tax return, the company will have a tax liability of $6,000. However, its financial statements will show a tax liability of $8,100 based on its book income. The above data is recorded by the following journal entry:

Income tax expense	8,100	
Income tax payable		6,000
Deferred income tax		2,100

Deferred income taxes relating to a specific asset or liability are usually classified as current or long-term depending on the classification of the asset or liability. Deferred income taxes relating to depreciation are generally classified as long-term liabilities.

Deferred income taxes arise because accounting for income and expenses under generally accepted accounting principles generally differs from income tax procedures and regulations. It is not unusual for the taxable income on the financial statements to be different from the taxable income on the income tax return. These differences are classified as *permanent differences* and *timing differences*.

A **permanent difference** occurs when a revenue or expense appears on the income statement but does not appear on the income tax return. For example, qualifying municipal bond interest income is recorded on the books as income but receives favorable tax treatment in that it is never taxed.

Timing differences, also called temporary differences, occur when revenue or expense amounts on the income statement differ from the amounts entered on the income tax return for a given year; but, over a period of several years, the totals of these amounts will eventually be equal. A timing difference occurs when the tax depreciation method differs from the book depreciation method. While the depreciation expense may vary from year to year, the *total* expense at the end of the asset's life is the same.

Permanent differences do not cause deferred income taxes. A deferred tax liability is attributable to nontaxable temporary differences. The calculation of deferred income taxes is technical and complex; it is a task best left to a professional accountant. ← HA! WTF...

Long-Term Liabilities

Long-term liabilities are debts and commitments that are due beyond 12 months of the balance sheet date.

Equity

The equity section of a corporation is called *shareholders' equity* or *stockholders' equity*. Its content depends on the type of equity transactions that have occurred. Some corporations have simple capital structures while others have complex structures. The types of items that might appear in the equity section of a balance sheet are:

- Common stock issued
- Preferred stock issued
- Additional paid-in capital
- Retained earnings
- Donated capital
- Treasury stock

Common Stock Issued. This item represents the amount of common stock issued shown at par value.

Preferred Stock Issued. This item represents the amount of preferred stock issued shown at par value.

Additional Paid-In Capital. When stock is issued at an amount in excess of par value, the stock has been issued at a premium that is recorded as additional paid-in capital.

Retained Earnings. This item includes the net income and net losses of the business since its inception, reduced by any *dividends declared* since inception.

Donated Capital. Sometimes corporations receive assets (such as land) as gifts from states, cities, or private benefactors to increase local employment or encourage business activity in a locality. In such cases, the asset is recorded (debited) to its proper asset account, and, instead of crediting cash or a liability, the donated capital account is credited for the asset's fair market value (FMV) on the date of the gift.

Treasury Stock. A corporation may reacquire shares (at market price) of its previously issued stock to reduce the number of outstanding shares. When stock is reacquired, it is called **treasury stock**. The possession of treasury stock does not give the corporation any voting rights. Some common reasons a corporation may acquire its own stock are as follows:

- To increase earnings per share by reducing outstanding shares

- To reduce outside ownership

- To block takeover attempts

Treasury stock is not an asset. The purchase cost of treasury stock is shown as a contra item in the equity section. However, the amount of issued and outstanding stock is generally not changed.

Hotel Balance Sheet Formats

The balance sheet can be designed in either the *account format* or the *report format.* The **account format** lists the asset accounts on the left side of the statement and the liabilities and equity accounts on the right side. The more popular balance sheet design is the **report format,** which lists the assets, liabilities, and owners' equity sequentially in a vertical presentation. Exhibit 1 shows a balance sheet in the report format.[1]

The Hotel DORO's Balance Sheet

Exhibit 2 shows an internal balance sheet, and Exhibit 3 shows an external balance sheet for the fictitious Hotel DORO. Compared with the internal format, the external format is more condensed. For example, notice the differences for cash, accounts receivable, and long-term debt. In any case, these slight format differences do not have any effect on the mathematical result of the balance sheet.

Exhibit 1   Balance Sheet—Report Format

BALANCE SHEET

Assets

	Current Year	Prior Year
CURRENT ASSETS		
Cash		
House Banks	$	$
Demand Deposits		
Temporary Cash Investments		
Total Cash		
Restricted Cash		
Short-Term Investments		
Receivables		
Accounts Receivable		
Notes Receivable		
Current Maturities of Non-current Receivables		
Other		
Total Receivables		
Less Allowance for Doubtful Accounts		
Net Receivables		
Due To/From Owner, Management Company,		
or Related Party		
Inventories		
Operating Equipment		
Prepaid Expenses		
Deferred Income Taxes—Current		
Other		
Total Current Assets		
NON-CURRENT RECEIVABLES, Net of Current Maturities		
INVESTMENTS		
PROPERTY AND EQUIPMENT		
Land		
Buildings		
Leaseholds and Leasehold Improvements		
Furnishings and Equipment		
Construction in Progress		
Total Property and Equipment		
Less Accumulated Depreciation and Amortization		
Net Property and Equipment		
OTHER ASSETS		
Intangible Assets		
Cash Surrender Value of Life Insurance		
Deferred Charges		
Deferred Income Taxes—Non-current		
Operating Equipment		
Restricted Cash		
Other		
Total Other Assets		
TOTAL ASSETS	$	$

(continued)

Exhibit 1 *(continued)*

	BALANCE SHEET		
	Liabilities and Owners' Equity		
		Current Year	**Prior Year**
CURRENT LIABILITIES			
Notes Payable			
Banks		$	$
Others			
Total Notes Payable			
Due To/From Owner, Management Company			
or Related Party			
Accounts Payable			
Accrued Expenses			
Advance Deposits			
Income Taxes Payable			
Deferred Income Taxes—Current			
Current Maturities of Long-Term Debt			
Other			
Total Current Liabilities			
LONG-TERM DEBT, Net of Current Maturities			
Mortgage Notes, other notes, and similar liabilities			
Obligations Under Capital Leases			
Total Long-Term Debt			
OTHER LONG-TERM LIABILITIES			
DEFERRED INCOME TAXES—Non-current			
COMMITMENTS AND CONTINGENCIES			
OWNERS' EQUITY			
____% Cumulative Preferred Stock, $ ____ par value, authorized ____ shares; issued and outstanding ____ shares		$	$
Common Stock, $____ par value, authorized ____ shares; issued and outstanding ____ shares			
Additional Paid-In Capital			
Retained Earnings			
Accumulated Other Comprehensive Income (Loss), Net of Income Tax			
Less: Treasury Stock, ____ shares of Common Stock, at cost			
Total Stockholders' Equity		$	$
TOTAL LIABILITIES AND OWNERS' EQUITY		$	$

Source: *Uniform System of Accounts for the Lodging Industry,* 10th Rev. Ed. (Lansing, Mich.: American Hotel & Lodging Educational Institute, 2006).

Common-Size Balance Sheet

While a balance sheet reports a company's financial position on a given data, management needs more information to measure financial growth and determine

Exhibit 2   Balance Sheet (Internal)—Hotel DORO

Hotel DORO, Inc.
Balance Sheet
December 31, 20X2   **Schedule C**

ASSETS

Current Assets			
Cash—House Banks	$ 3,500		
Cash—Demand Deposits	55,000		
Total Cash		$ 58,500	
Short-Term Investments		25,000	
Accounts Receivable	41,216		
Less Allowance for Doubtful Accounts	1,020	40,196	
Inventories		11,000	
Prepaid Expenses		13,192	
Total Current Assets			$ 147,888
Property and Equipment			
Land		850,000	
Building		2,500,000	
Furniture and Equipment		475,000	
Total		3,825,000	
Less Accumulated Depreciation		775,000	
Total		3,050,000	
Leasehold Improvements (net)		9,000	
China, Glassware, and Silver (net)		36,524	
Total Property and Equipment			3,095,524
Other Noncurrent Assets			
Security Deposits		1,000	
Preopening Expenses (net)		3,000	
Total Other Assets			4,000
Total Assets			$3,247,412

LIABILITIES

Current Liabilities			
Accounts Payable		$ 13,861	
Current Portion of Long-Term Debt		70,000	
Federal and State Income Taxes Payable		16,545	
Accrued Payroll		11,617	
Other Accrued Items		7,963	
Deposits and Credit Balances		3,764	
Total Current Liabilities			$ 123,750
Long-Term Debt			
Mortgage Payable		2,125,000	
Less Current Portion		70,000	
Total Long-Term Debt			2,055,000
Total Liabilities			2,178,750

SHAREHOLDERS' EQUITY

Common Stock, par value $1, authorized			
and issued 50,000 shares		50,000	
Additional Paid-in Capital		700,000	
Retained Earnings		318,662	
Total Shareholders' Equity			1,068,662
Total Liabilities and Shareholders' Equity			$3,247,412

Exhibit 3   Balance Sheet (External)—Hotel DORO

<table>
<tr><td colspan="3" align="center">Hotel DORO, Inc.
Balance Sheet
December 31, 20X2</td><td align="right">Schedule C</td></tr>
<tr><td colspan="4" align="center">ASSETS</td></tr>
<tr><td colspan="4">Current Assets</td></tr>
<tr><td>Cash</td><td></td><td align="right">$ 58,500</td><td></td></tr>
<tr><td>Short-Term Investments</td><td></td><td align="right">25,000</td><td></td></tr>
<tr><td>Accounts Receivable (net)</td><td></td><td align="right">40,196</td><td></td></tr>
<tr><td>Inventories</td><td></td><td align="right">11,000</td><td></td></tr>
<tr><td>Prepaid Expenses</td><td></td><td align="right">13,192</td><td></td></tr>
<tr><td> Total Current Assets</td><td></td><td></td><td align="right">$ 147,888</td></tr>
<tr><td colspan="4">Property and Equipment</td></tr>
<tr><td>Land</td><td></td><td align="right">850,000</td><td></td></tr>
<tr><td>Building</td><td></td><td align="right">2,500,000</td><td></td></tr>
<tr><td>Furniture and Equipment</td><td></td><td align="right">475,000</td><td></td></tr>
<tr><td>Total</td><td></td><td align="right">3,825,000</td><td></td></tr>
<tr><td>Less Accumulated Depreciation</td><td></td><td align="right">775,000</td><td></td></tr>
<tr><td>Total</td><td></td><td align="right">3,050,000</td><td></td></tr>
<tr><td>Leasehold Improvements</td><td></td><td align="right">9,000</td><td></td></tr>
<tr><td>China, Glassware, and Silver (net)</td><td></td><td align="right">36,524</td><td></td></tr>
<tr><td> Total Property and Equipment</td><td></td><td></td><td align="right">3,095,524</td></tr>
<tr><td colspan="4">Other Noncurrent Assets</td></tr>
<tr><td>Security Deposits</td><td></td><td align="right">1,000</td><td></td></tr>
<tr><td>Preopening Expenses (net)</td><td></td><td align="right">3,000</td><td></td></tr>
<tr><td> Total Other Assets</td><td></td><td></td><td align="right">4,000</td></tr>
<tr><td>Total Assets</td><td></td><td></td><td align="right">$3,247,412</td></tr>
<tr><td colspan="4" align="center">LIABILITIES</td></tr>
<tr><td colspan="4">Current Liabilities</td></tr>
<tr><td>Accounts Payable</td><td></td><td align="right">$ 13,861</td><td></td></tr>
<tr><td>Current Portion of Long-Term Debt</td><td></td><td align="right">70,000</td><td></td></tr>
<tr><td>Federal and State Income Taxes Payable</td><td></td><td align="right">16,545</td><td></td></tr>
<tr><td>Accrued Payroll</td><td></td><td align="right">11,617</td><td></td></tr>
<tr><td>Other Accrued Items</td><td></td><td align="right">7,963</td><td></td></tr>
<tr><td>Unearned Revenue</td><td></td><td align="right">3,764</td><td></td></tr>
<tr><td> Total Current Liabilities</td><td></td><td></td><td align="right">$ 123,750</td></tr>
<tr><td colspan="4">Long-Term Debt</td></tr>
<tr><td>Mortgage Payable, less current portion</td><td></td><td></td><td align="right">2,055,000</td></tr>
<tr><td>Total Liabilities</td><td></td><td></td><td align="right">2,178,750</td></tr>
<tr><td colspan="4" align="center">SHAREHOLDERS' EQUITY</td></tr>
<tr><td>Common Stock, par value $1, authorized
  and issued 50,000 shares</td><td></td><td align="right">50,000</td><td></td></tr>
<tr><td>Additional Paid-in Capital</td><td></td><td align="right">700,000</td><td></td></tr>
<tr><td>Retained Earnings</td><td></td><td align="right">318,662</td><td></td></tr>
<tr><td> Total Shareholders' Equity</td><td></td><td></td><td align="right">1,068,662</td></tr>
<tr><td>Total Liabilities and Shareholders' Equity</td><td></td><td></td><td align="right">$3,247,412</td></tr>
</table>

potential problem areas. To accommodate management, accountants have designed a **common-size balance sheet** to measure the relationship of each item on the balance sheet to *total assets*. The relationship of the components of the balance sheet to total assets is expressed as a percentage.

Since every item on the balance sheet is divided by total assets, the percentage listed next to total assets will always be 100 percent. Also, since the total liabilities and shareholders' equity line is always the same as total assets, that line will likewise be 100 percent. The computation to arrive at common-size percentages can be expressed by the following formula:

$$\frac{\text{Line Amount}}{\text{Total Assets}} = \text{Common-Size Percentage}$$

As with any *vertical analysis,* the components of a series can be added to cross-check the computed percentages for their total. Because these computations are rounded, it might be necessary to "force" certain results. *In the exhibits in this chapter, forced numbers are shown in bold print.*

Either an internal or external balance sheet may contain common-size percentages. To provide management with further information, an accountant may supplement the internal balance sheet with budgeted and/or industry ratios.

Interpretation of Hotel DORO's Common-Size Balance Sheet. The balance sheet in Exhibit 4 tells us that the claims on the assets are as follows:

Assets	=	Liabilities	+	Owners' Equity
100%	=	67.1%	+	32.9%

Obviously, the Hotel DORO has substantial debt because about 67 percent of its assets have creditor claims. However, financial decisions should not be based on one ratio alone. In addition to comparing any ratio with budgeted ratios and industry ratios, it is necessary to determine if the company is using its debt favorably to generate earnings growth. Therefore, a complete ratio analysis requires a reader to study both the income statement and the balance sheet.

Further interpretations of the common-size balance sheet are made possible through a study of the components of the various subdivisions of the balance sheet. For example, cash represents about 2 percent of assets; current assets represent 4.6 percent of assets. While this might seem minor, notice that the current liabilities are only 3.8 percent of assets. It is not unusual for fixed assets to compose the largest percentage of assets.

Comparative Balance Sheet

A **comparative balance sheet** presents financial data for two or more periods. The comparative data can be in the form of dollars or percentages that management finds useful in its planning and controlling functions. Because computations are made on a side-by-side basis, a comparative analysis is also known as a *horizontal analysis.*

A popular comparative balance sheet is in the following format:

Current Year	Prior Year	$ Change	% Change

After the current and prior years' data have been entered, the steps to complete a comparative statement are as follows:

Exhibit 4 Common-Size Balance Sheet—Hotel DORO

Hotel DORO, Inc.
Balance Sheet
December 31, 20X2

ASSETS

Current Assets		
Cash	$ 58,500	1.9%
Short-Term Investments	25,000	.8
Accounts Receivable (net)	40,196	1.2
Inventories	11,000	.3
Prepaid Expenses	13,192	.4
Total Current Assets	147,888	4.6
Property and Equipment		
Land	850,000	26.2
Building	2,500,000	77.0
Furniture and Equipment	475,000	14.6
Total	3,825,000	117.8
Less Accumulated Depreciation	775,000	23.9
Total	3,050,000	93.9
Leasehold Improvements	9,000	.3
China, Glassware, and Silver (net)	36,524	1.1
Total Property and Equipment	3,095,524	95.3
Other Noncurrent Assets		
Security Deposits	1,000	—
Preopening Expenses (net)	3,000	.1
Total Other Assets	4,000	.1
Total Assets	$3,247,412	100.0%

LIABILITIES

Current Liabilities		
Accounts Payable	$ 13,861	.4%
Current Portion of Long-Term Debt	70,000	2.2
Federal and State Income Taxes Payable	16,545	.5
Accrued Payroll	11,617	.4
Other Accrued Items	7,963	.2
Unearned Revenue	3,764	.1
Total Current Liabilities	123,750	3.8
Long-Term Debt		
Mortgage Payable, less current portion	2,055,000	63.3
Total Liabilities	2,178,750	67.1

SHAREHOLDERS' EQUITY

Common Stock, par value $1, authorized		
and issued 50,000 shares	50,000	1.5
Additional Paid-in Capital	700,000	21.6
Retained Earnings	318,662	9.8
Total Shareholders' Equity	1,068,662	32.9
Total Liabilities and Shareholders' Equity	$3,247,412	100.0%

1. The *dollar change* is computed by entering the current year's amount in a calculator and then subtracting the prior year's amount. The proper mathematical sign (positive or negative) will be provided by the calculator.

2. The *percentage change* is computed by dividing the dollar change amount by the *prior year's amount*. The sign of the percentage change (either positive

or negative) is always the same as that for the dollar change. A comparative analysis does not use a common divisor. The divisor for each line is the prior period's data for that particular line item.

Exhibit 5 presents a comparative balance sheet for the Hotel DORO. The dollar change for each line item is independently computed using a horizontal process. The $234 for the total dollar change is also a horizontal computation. It is possible to verify the accuracy of the $234 by adding the dollar changes of each current asset. The cross-checking of all columns is a standard procedure that produces an accurate statement.

After the dollar changes are computed and cross-checked, the next step is to compute the percentage changes. This is accomplished by dividing the dollar change by the prior year's amount. For example, the change for cash of $(3,006) is divided by the 20X1 amount of $61,506 to arrive at a (4.9) percent change.

Because the percentage changes are computed without a common divisor, it is not possible to add a column for percentages to verify any total percentage. Therefore, it is suggested that all percentage computations be rechecked for accuracy.

Interpretation of a Comparative Analysis. A specialized vocabulary is used to discuss changes in a comparative financial statement. If this year's data is larger than last year's data, the change is called an *increase* or simply stated as *up* or *upward*; it cannot be called a *gain* because a gain results from the sale of assets at a price exceeding book value. If this year's data is smaller than last year's data, the change is called a *decrease* or simply stated as *down* or *downward*; it cannot be called a *loss* because a loss results from the sale of assets at a price less than book value.

If this year's data is equal to last year's data, the situation is referred to as *no change*; it would be illogical to call it a zero change.

Sometimes it is impossible to calculate a *percentage change* because there is no last year's data, which means there is no divisor. In this case, the proper procedure is to indicate that the percentage change is *not measurable* by entering the symbol "—" or "n/m" in the applicable column.

When analyzing the changes, it is incorrect to concentrate only on the percentage changes because a large percentage change may not necessarily represent a large dollar change. The comparing of small numbers can produce a large percentage change for a minor dollar change. For example, a $50 change on last year's data of $20 results in a 250 percent change. Conversely, a small percentage change could represent a large dollar change. For example, if the dollar change is $500,000 on last year's data of $50,000,000, the percentage change is only one percent.

Interpretation of the Hotel DORO's Comparative Balance Sheet. The balance sheet for the Hotel DORO in Exhibit 5 is used to make the following interpretation of its financial position from a comparison of data on December 31, 20X2 with data on December 31, 20X1.

1. The decrease to cash of 4.9 percent might first be a subject of concern. However, notice that current liabilities have decreased by 11.1 percent. This looks especially favorable because it was accomplished without any new long-term debt, bank financing, or secondary issuance of common stock.

Exhibit 5 Comparative Balance Sheet—Hotel DORO

Hotel DORO, Inc.
Comparative Balance Sheet
December 31, 20X2 and December 31, 20X1

ASSETS	20X2	20X1	$ Change	% Change
Current Assets				
Cash	$ 58,500	$ 61,506	$ (3,006)	(4.9)%
Short-Term Investments	25,000	25,000	0	0
Accounts Receivable (net)	40,196	38,840	1,356	3.5
Inventories	11,000	10,143	857	8.4
Prepaid Expenses	13,192	12,165	1,027	8.4
Total Current Assets	147,888	147,654	234	.2
Property and Equipment				
Land	850,000	792,000	58,000	7.3
Building	2,500,000	2,500,000	0	0
Furniture and Equipment	475,000	427,814	47,186	11.0
Total	3,825,000	3,719,814	105,186	2.8
Less Accumulated Depreciation	775,000	640,000	135,000	21.1
Total	3,050,000	3,079,814	(29,814)	(1.0)
Leasehold Improvements	9,000	10,000	(1,000)	(10.0)
China, Glassware, and Silver	36,524	49,403	(12,879)	(26.1)
Total Property and Equipment	3,095,524	3,139,217	(43,693)	(1.4)
Other Noncurrent Assets				
Security Deposits	1,000	1,000	0	0
Preopening Expenses (net)	3,000	4,500	(1,500)	(33.3)
Total Other Assets	4,000	5,500	(1,500)	(27.3)
Total Assets	$3,247,412	$3,292,371	$(44,959)	(1.4)
LIABILITIES				
Current Liabilities				
Accounts Payable	$ 13,861	$ 18,642	$ (4,781)	(25.6)%
Current Portion of Long-Term Debt	70,000	70,000	0	0
Federal and State Income Taxes	16,545	24,619	(8,074)	(32.8)
Accrued Payroll	11,617	9,218	2,399	26.0
Other Accrued Items	7,963	10,899	(2,936)	(26.9)
Unearned Revenue	3,764	5,875	(2,111)	(35.9)
Total Current Liabilities	123,750	139,253	(15,503)	(11.1)
Long-Term Debt				
Mortgage Payable	2,055,000	2,125,000	(70,000)	(3.3)
Total Liabilities	2,178,750	2,264,253	(85,503)	(3.8)
SHAREHOLDERS' EQUITY				
Common Stock Issued	50,000	50,000	0	0
Additional Paid-In Capital	700,000	700,000	0	0
Retained Earnings	318,662	278,118	40,544	14.6
Total Shareholders' Equity	1,068,662	1,028,118	40,544	3.9
Total Liabilities and Shareholders' Equity	$3,247,412	$3,292,371	$(44,959)	(1.4)%

2. Receivables are up 3.5 percent. If the income statement were provided, it would show that sales are up over last year, which might justify the increase in accounts receivable.

3. Inventories are up 8.4 percent. This matter should be investigated because the food and beverage department income decreased from last year.

Exhibit 6   Statement of Retained Earnings—Hotel DORO

Hotel DORO, Inc. Statement of Retained Earnings For the year ended December 31, 20X2	Schedule B
Retained Earnings at beginning of year	$278,118
Net Income for the year (Schedule A)	60,544
Total	338,662
Less Dividends Declared during the year	20,000
Retained Earnings at end of year	$318,662

4. The increase in prepaid expenses could be due to increases in insurance premiums and taxes, which are typical from year to year.

5. The company has increased its land and furniture and equipment holdings. The reasons for these acquisitions should be explained.

6. Preopening expenses have decreased because of amortization. Unlike fixed assets, intangible assets do not have an accumulated depreciation account. The amortization expense appears on the income statement, and it is used to directly reduce the book value shown on the balance sheet. In time, the preopening expenses will be fully amortized and will no longer appear on the balance sheet.

7. The company has managed its resources to reduce all of its current liabilities and long-term debt.

8. The increase to retained earnings is due to the income from operations less any dividends declared. The company's net profit for the year was $60,544 and dividends declared were $20,000; thus retained earnings increased by $40,544.

The Statement of Retained Earnings

This statement was prepared with the income statement and serves as a "connecting link" between the income statement and balance sheet because it brings the computed retained earnings amount over to the balance sheet.

Exhibit 6 shows the statement of retained earnings that was prepared after the income statement was completed. Notice that the final amount representing retained earnings for the year just ended is brought over to the retained earnings line item of the balance sheet as of the end of the same period.

Endnote

1. The format in Exhibit 1 is taken from the *Uniform System of Accounts for the Lodging Industry*, Tenth Revised Edition (*USALI*), published in 2006. The examples in the rest of this chapter do not necessarily reflect all of the elements of this new format. Changes

in the Tenth Revised Edition affect the presentation of operating equipment and the reporting of amounts due to (or due from) owners, management companies, or other related entities. Operating equipment includes assets such as china, glassware, silver, linen, and uniforms. Any operating equipment with a life of one year or less is shown in the Current Assets section of the balance sheet; operating equipment with a life exceeding one year is shown under Other Assets. When a hotel implements this edition of *USALI*, it should expense the balance of any remaining linen, china, glassware, silver, or uniforms in its bookkeeping accounts. *USALI* states: "The number and types of accounts that appear on the Balance Sheet will vary according to the needs and requirements of the business. Accordingly, appropriate modification should be made to the suggested format to accommodate the individual requirements of the business, while remaining consistent with GAAP."

Key Terms

account format—An arrangement of a balance sheet that lists the asset accounts on the left side of the page and the liability and owners' equity on the right side.

asset—Anything a business owns that has commercial or exchange value.

common-size balance sheet—A balance sheet in which each line item is shown as a percentage of the dollar total of assets. The analytical procedure is called a vertical analysis.

comparative balance sheet—A balance sheet in which each line item is compared from one period to a base period and the change for that line item is expressed in dollars and as a percentage. The analytical procedure is called a horizontal analysis.

current assets—Cash or assets that are convertible to cash within 12 months of the balance sheet date; to be considered a current asset, an asset must be available without restriction for use in payment of current liabilities.

current liabilities—Those liabilities expected to be satisfied by the use of a current asset or to be replaced by another current liability within 12 months of the balance sheet date.

deferred income taxes—When the income taxes on the statement of income exceed the amount of liability to government tax agencies for the year, the business records the excess as deferred income taxes. This difference generally represents timing differences with respect to payment dates of taxes.

liabilities—The claims of outsiders (such as creditors) to assets of the business; liabilities are sometimes called creditors' equities.

long-term liabilities—Debts *not* due within 12 months of the balance sheet date.

noncurrent assets—Assets that are *not* to be converted to cash within 12 months of the balance sheet date.

permanent difference—Occurs when a revenue or expense appears on the income statement but does not appear on the income tax return.

report format—An arrangement of a balance sheet that lists the assets first, followed by liabilities and owners' equity.

timing difference—Occurs when revenue or expense amounts on the income statement differ from the amounts entered on the income tax return for a given year. Over a period of several years, the totals of these amounts will eventually be equal.

treasury stock—Stock that has been reacquired by the company and is no longer considered issued and outstanding.

unearned revenue—The offset for cash received for services before they are rendered.

 ## Review Questions ——————————————————

1. What is the purpose of a balance sheet?

2. What is the time period covered by a balance sheet?

3. How can the accounting equation be restated to a financial equation?

4. What are the three major sections of a balance sheet?

5. How are the different assets of a hospitality business classified on a balance sheet?

6. What is the definition of a current asset? List the five major current assets in their descending order of liquidity.

7. What is the difference between short-term investments and investments on a balance sheet?

8. What is the difference between a prepaid expense and a deferred charge on a balance sheet?

9. What is unearned revenue on a balance sheet?

10. What does the line item Deferred Income Tax represent on a balance sheet?

11. What is a common-size balance sheet?

12. What is a comparative balance sheet?

Internet Sites ——————————————————

For more information, visit the following Internet sites. Remember that Internet addresses can change without notice. If the site is no longer there, you can use a search engine to look for additional sites.

Balance Sheet Accounts
www.loadledger.com/support/HTML-Java/htm/balancesheetaccounts.htm
www.sedonaoffice.com/WebHelp/General_Ledger/Getting_Started/Balance_
  Sheet_Accounts.htm

Assets Defined
http://sbinfocanada.about.com/od/accounting/g/assets.htm

Liabilities Defined
www.investopedia.com/terms/l/liability.asp

Shareholders' Equity Defined
www.answers.com/topic/shareholders-equity

Balance Sheet
www.toolkit.cch.com/text/P06_1574.asp
www.sec.gov/investor/pubs/begfinstmtguide.htm
www.investopedia.com/articles/04/031004.asp

Problems

Problem 1

A newly formed corporation issues 40,000 shares of its $1 par value common stock for $90,000. How will this appear on the balance sheet?

Problem 2

A hospitality corporation has some issued and outstanding common stock of $100,000. It recently reacquired 1,000 shares of its own stock for $20,000. What will be the amount of issued and outstanding common stock after this acquisition of treasury stock?

Problem 3

A company recently purchased land with a mortgage of $50,000, which will require monthly payments on the principal of $1,000. What will be the amount of long-term debt before any payments are made?

Problem 4

Prepare a balance sheet using the internal format for the Village Hotel, Inc. as of its year ended December 31, 20X9. The following are selected accounts from the worksheet necessary to prepare this statement.

	Balance Sheet	
	dr	cr
Cash—House Banks	10,000	
Cash—Regular Checking	37,148	
Cash—Payroll Checking	500	
Short-Term Investments	10,000	
Guest Ledger (debit balances)	41,221	
City Ledger	20,616	
Allowance for Doubtful Accounts		1,523
Food Inventory	6,825	

Beverage Inventory	3,614	
Supplies Inventory	8,726	
Prepaid Insurance	12,819	
Prepaid Rent	3,000	
Furniture	475,000	
Equipment	450,000	
Allowance for Depreciation: Furniture		125,000
Allowance for Depreciation: Equipment		150,000
Leasehold Improvements	475,000	
China, Glassware, and Silver	42,119	
Security Deposits	2,500	
Accounts Payable		36,972
Income Taxes Payable		15,212
Accrued Payroll		21,316
Other Accrued Items		34,918
Guest Ledger Credit Balances		4,500
Notes Payable (see Note 1)		425,000
Common Stock (see Note 2)		30,000
Additional Paid-In Capital		600,000
Retained Earnings (as of 12/15/X9)		62,930

The following notes must be taken into account when preparing the balance sheet:

1. The item referred to as Notes Payable is a ten-year note. Of the $425,000 unpaid balance, $25,000 is due in the next 12 months.

2. There are 50,000 shares of $1 par common stock authorized; 30,000 shares have been issued.

3. The retained earnings of $62,930 are not the retained earnings as of the period ended December 31 and should be ignored. To compute the retained earnings for December 31, the following data is provided:

Retained earnings 1/1/X9	$122,930
Net income for the year ended 12/31/X9	91,717
Dividends declared during the year	60,000

4. For your convenience, a checkpoint amount for total assets is provided: $1,322,565.

Problem 5

Prepare a common-size income statement for The Garden Bistro, Inc. as of December 31, 20X8. The rules for rounding are as follows:

a. Show all answers to one decimal, rounded (for example, 7,900 divided by 170,000 equals 4.6 percent).

b. If a series of computed percentages do not add up to the computed total, force the largest number in the series up or down as necessary.

The Garden Bistro, Inc.
Balance Sheet
December 31, 20X8

ASSETS

CURRENT ASSETS	
Cash	$ 34,000
Accounts Receivable	4,000
Food Inventory	2,400
Supplies Inventory	2,600
Prepaid Expenses	2,000
Total Current Assets	45,000
PROPERTY AND EQUIPMENT	
Land	30,000
Building	60,000
Furniture and Equipment	52,000
China, Glassware, and Silver	8,000
Total	150,000
Less Accumulated Depreciation	40,000
Net Property and Equipment	110,000
OTHER ASSETS	
Security Deposits	1,500
Preopening Expenses (net)	2,500
Total Other Assets	4,000
TOTAL ASSETS	$159,000

LIABILITIES

CURRENT LIABILITIES	
Accounts Payable	$ 11,000
Sales Tax Payable	1,000
Accrued Expenses	9,000
Current Portion of Long-Term Debt	6,000
Total Current Liabilities	27,000
LONG-TERM LIABILITIES	
Mortgage Payable, net of current portion	34,000

SHAREHOLDERS' EQUITY

Paid-In Capital:	
Common Stock, par value $1, authorized	
50,000 shares, issued 25,000 shares	25,000
Additional Paid-in Capital	15,000
Total Paid-in Capital	40,000
Retained Earnings, December 31, 20X8	58,000
TOTAL LIABILITIES AND SHAREHOLDERS' EQUITY	$159,000

Problem 6

Prepare a comparative analysis from the following balance sheet. Show all answers to one decimal, rounded.

The Garden Bistro, Inc.
Balance Sheet
December 31, 20X8 and December 31, 20X7

ASSETS

	20X8	20X7
CURRENT ASSETS		
Cash	$ 34,000	$ 36,500
Accounts Receivable	4,000	3,450
Food Inventory	2,400	2,100
Supplies Inventory	2,600	1,900
Prepaid Expenses	2,000	2,600
Total Current Assets	45,000	46,550
PROPERTY AND EQUIPMENT		
Land	30,000	30,000
Building	60,000	60,000
Furniture and Equipment	52,000	48,000
China, Glassware, and Silver	8,000	8,300
Total	150,000	146,300
Less Accumulated Depreciation	40,000	35,000
Net Property and Equipment	110,000	111,300
OTHER ASSETS		
Security Deposits	1,500	1,500
Preopening Expenses (net)	2,500	3,000
Total Other Assets	4,000	4,500
TOTAL ASSETS	$159,000	$162,350

LIABILITIES

	20X8	20X7
CURRENT LIABILITIES		
Accounts Payable	$ 11,000	$ 25,400
Sales Tax Payable	1,000	950
Accrued Expenses	9,000	7,000
Current Portion of Long-Term Debt	6,000	6,000
Total Current Liabilities	27,000	39,350
LONG-TERM LIABILITIES		
Mortgage Payable, net of current portion	34,000	40,000

SHAREHOLDERS' EQUITY

	20X8	20X7
Paid-In Capital:		
Common Stock, par value $1, authorized		
50,000 shares, issued 25,000 shares	25,000	25,000
Additional Paid-In Capital	15,000	15,000
Total Paid-In Capital	40,000	40,000
Retained Earnings, December 31, 20X8	58,000	43,000
TOTAL LIABILITIES AND SHAREHOLDERS' EQUITY	$159,000	$162,350

Case Study

Critique of a Balance Sheet

Executives of the Grande Hotel meet to review the hotel's most recent (and much-neglected) balance sheet. Management has focused its attention and effort on improving profitability, because the hotel has been only marginally profitable for the last several years. Indeed, the balance sheet as a financial statement can sometimes be underrated when owners and managers concentrate on sales, expenses, and profits. However, a business's financial strength and survival depend on its financial condition as represented by the balance sheet.

The three important financial statements managers must analyze are the balance sheet, the income statement, and the cash flow statement. The balance sheet presents a company's resources, how much it owes, and what is left for the owners. The income statement measures the business's profitability. The cash flow statement shows where cash came from and where it was spent. All three statements play an important role in the management of any business.

The Grande has not purchased any new or replacement property and equipment, nor has it sold any property and equipment. The company uses straight-line depreciation for financial reporting.

The executives have been given a copy of the most recent comparative balance sheet, which appears in a condensed format below. The general manager declares that the financial condition of the hotel has improved because cash funds have increased by $20,000, or 33.3 percent.

	20X2	20X1	$ Change	% Change
CURRENT ASSETS				
Cash	$ 80,000	$ 60,000	$ 20,000	33.3
Receivables	30,000	50,000	(20,000)	(40.0)
Inventories	5,000	9,000	(4,000)	(44.4)
Prepaid Items	8,000	7,600	400	5.3
Total Current Assets	123,000	126,600	(3,600)	(2.8)
Property & Equipment,				
Net of Depreciation	900,000	950,000	(50,000)	(5.3)
Other Noncurrent Assets	2,000	1,950	50	2.6
Total Assets	$1,025,000	$1,078,550	$(53,550)	(5.0)
CURRENT LIABILITIES				
Accounts Payable	$ 18,000	$ 10,000	$ 8,000	80.0
Loans Payable	30,000	10,000	20,000	200.0
Other Liabilities	5,000	4,800	200	4.2
Total Current Liabilities	53,000	24,800	28,200	113.7
Net Long-Term Debt		3,000	(3,000)	(100.0)
Stockholders' Equity	972,000	1,050,750	(78,750)	(7.5)
Total Liabilities and Equity	$1,025,000	$1,078,550	$(53,550)	(5.0)

Challenge

At the meeting, the president asks you to conjecture about what might have caused any significant changes in the balance sheet. In your responses to the challenges below, state which additional financial statements, if any, you will need to support your conclusions.

1. Comment on the general manager's claim that the company's financial strength has improved due to the significant increase in cash this year.
2. Furnish possible reasons for the increase in cash.
3. Provide possible reasons for any significant changes in any other assets.
4. Suggest possible reasons for any significant changes in liabilities.
5. Suggest possible reasons for the change in stockholders' equity.

Chapter 10 Outline

Ratio Analysis of the Balance Sheet
    Liquidity
    Asset Management
    Debt Management
Ratio Analysis of the Hotel DORO's
    Balance Sheet
Current Ratio
    Bank Standard
    Composition
Quick Ratio
    Bank Standard
Accounts Receivable Turnover Ratio
Average Collection Period Ratio
Inventory Turnover Ratio
Fixed Asset Turnover Ratio
Debt-to-Equity Ratio
Assets-to-Liabilities Ratio
Working Capital
    Computation of Working Capital
    Composition of Working Capital
    The Importance of Adequate Working
        Capital
    Causes of Inadequate Working Capital
    Causes of Excess Working Capital
    Factors Affecting Working Capital
        Requirements
Reference List of Ratio Formulas

Competencies

1. Describe the use of ratios in the analysis of a hospitality business balance sheet. (pp. 277–278)

2. Explain the purpose and use of the current ratio, and describe its formula and interpretation. (pp. 278–282)

3. Explain the purpose and use of the quick ratio, and describe its formula and interpretation. (p. 282)

4. Explain the purpose and use of the accounts receivable turnover ratio, and describe its formula and interpretation. (pp. 282–283)

5. Explain the purpose and use of the average collection period ratio, and describe its formula and interpretation. (pp. 283–284)

6. Identify the formulas for food and beverage inventory turnover. (p. 284)

7. Explain the purpose and use of the fixed asset turnover ratio, and describe its formula and interpretation. (p. 285)

8. Explain the purpose and use of the debt–to–equity ratio, and describe its formula and interpretation. (pp. 285–286)

9. Explain the purpose and use of the assets–to–liabilities ratio, and describe its formula and interpretation. (pp. 286–287)

10. Describe the computation, composition, and importance of working capital. (pp. 287–289)

10

Ratio Analysis of the Balance Sheet

Ratio analysis of a hotel's balance sheet is very useful to the hotel's board of directors, management, shareholders, and creditors, and to the investment community. Unlike the income statement, the balance sheet is not oriented toward departmental use; a balance sheet shows the overall financial condition of a hospitality property or corporation. It is important to know the financial condition of any business to determine its ability to stay in business.

The balance sheet uses historical costs to measure a hospitality company's use of its resources. While there is some debate over the use of market values on the balance sheet, these values can be achieved only if the company is sold. This value concept is contrary to the purpose of a going concern.

Balance sheet ratios are tools for analyzing and interpreting the financial soundness of a hospitality company. *Analysis* involves the calculating of percentages and ratios; *interpretation* involves comparing percentages and ratios to determine the meaning and significance of the analysis. Ratios that can be used in an interpretation are prior-period ratios, industry and trade association ratios, and budgeted ratios.

This chapter will answer the following questions:

1. What do balance sheet ratios measure?

2. What are some of the popular ratios used in the analysis of a balance sheet?

3. What is working capital?

4. What is the significance of adequate and inadequate working capital?

Ratio Analysis of the Balance Sheet

Ratios are a critical part of financial analysis because they point to symptoms or potential problem areas when compared with budgeted ratios, prior-period ratios, and industry and trade association ratios. Hospitality industry ratios and statistics are published by PKF Consulting, Smith Travel Research, and the National Restaurant Association (for stand-alone restaurants).

Balance sheet ratios are used to measure liquidity, asset management, and debt management.

Liquidity

A company's ability to pay its current liabilities is a measurement of **liquidity**. Creditors and the investment community are especially interested in knowing whether a company can pay its current obligations without needing to borrow money not intended to finance future growth. Liquidity ratios assume that current assets are the major source of funds to pay current liabilities. The two most popular ratios in evaluating liquidity are the current ratio and the quick ratio.

Asset Management

The financial soundness and success of a company depend on how the company's assets are managed. Asset management involves controlling the level of assets according to company policies and sales volume. As a business grows, it is not uncommon to find growth in its accounts receivable, inventory, and fixed assets. However, sales growth should not produce unjustified increases in these assets. The most popular ratios in evaluating asset management are:

- Accounts receivable turnover ratio

- Average collection period ratio

- Inventory turnover ratio

- Fixed asset turnover ratio

Debt Management

In addition to measuring its liquidity, a company must determine its ability to service its total debt (short-term and long-term). Debt management is a measure of **solvency,** which refers to a company's ability to meet its long-term obligations. A hotel, motel, or other hospitality business is solvent when its assets are greater than its liabilities. The most popular ratios in evaluating the solvency of a company are the debt-to-equity ratio and the assets-to-liabilities ratio.

Ratio Analysis of the Hotel DORO's Balance Sheet ———

The Hotel DORO's balance sheet depicted in Exhibit 1 will be used, as well as information in Exhibits 2 and 3, to explore the ratios that measure liquidity, asset management, and debt management. Each ratio presentation will include a brief description of the ratio, its formula, and its specific application to the Hotel DORO.

At the conclusion of each ratio discussion will be an interpretation of the results of that specific ratio and other factors critical to its application in the actual business environment.

Current Ratio ———

The current ratio shows the relationship of current assets to current liabilities. It is also called the *working capital ratio* because working capital is the excess of current assets over current liabilities. The current ratio is one of the most popular ratios used in the banking industry and investment community.

Exhibit 1   The Hotel DORO's Balance Sheet

Hotel DORO, Inc.
Comparative Balance Sheet
December 31, 20X2 and December 31, 20X1

	20X2	20X1	$ Change	% Change
ASSETS				
Current Assets				
Cash	$ 58,500	$ 61,506	$ (3,006)	(4.9)%
Short-Term Investments	25,000	25,000	0	0
Accounts Receivable (net)	40,196	38,840	1,356	3.5
Inventories	11,000	10,143	857	8.4
Prepaid Expenses	13,192	12,165	1,027	8.4
Total Current Assets	147,888	147,654	234	.2
Property and Equipment				
Land	850,000	792,000	58,000	7.3
Building	2,500,000	2,500,000	0	0
Furniture and Equipment	475,000	427,814	47,816	11.0
Total	3,825,000	3,719,814	105,186	2.8
Less Accumulated Depreciation	775,000	640,000	135,000	21.1
Total	3,050,000	3,079,814	(29,814)	(1.0)
Leasehold Improvements	9,000	10,000	(1,000)	(10.0)
China, Glassware, and Silver	36,524	49,403	(12,879)	(26.1)
Total Property and Equipment	3,095,524	3,139,217	(43,693)	(1.4)
Other Noncurrent Assets				
Security Deposits	1,000	1,000	0	0
Preopening Expenses (net)	3,000	4,500	(1,500)	(33.3)
Total Other Assets	4,000	5,500	(1,500)	(27.3)
Total Assets	$3,247,412	$3,292,371	$ (44,959)	(1.4)%
LIABILITIES				
Current Liabilities				
Accounts Payable	$ 13,861	$ 18,642	$ (4,781)	(25.6)%
Current Portion of Long-Term Debt	70,000	70,000	0	0
Federal and State Income Taxes	16,545	24,619	(8,074)	(32.8)
Accrued Payroll	11,617	9,218	2,399	26.0
Other Accrued Items	7,963	10,899	(2,936)	(26.9)
Unearned Revenue	3,764	5,875	(2,111)	(35.9)
Total Current Liabilities	123,750	139,253	(15,503)	(11.1)
Long-Term Debt				
Mortgage Payable	2,055,000	2,125,000	(70,000)	(3.3)
Total Liabilities	2,178,750	2,264,253	(85,503)	(3.8)
SHAREHOLDERS' EQUITY				
Common Stock Issued	50,000	50,000	0	0
Additional Paid-In Capital	700,000	700,000	0	0
Retained Earnings	318,662	278,118	40,544	14.6
Total Shareholders' Equity	1,068,662	1,028,118	40,544	3.9
Total Liabilities and Shareholders'				
Equity	$3,247,412	$3,292,371	$ (44,959)	(1.4)%

Formula. The current ratio formula is as follows:

$$\frac{\text{Current Assets}}{\text{Current Liabilities}}$$

Exhibit 2   Condensed Income Statement—Hotel DORO

Hotel DORO, Inc.
Condensed Income Statement
For the year ended December 31, 20X2

Net Revenue	$1,597,493
Costs and Expenses	1,531,355
Income Before Gain on Sale of Property	66,138
Gain on Sale of Property	10,500
Income Before Income Taxes	76,638
Income Taxes	16,094
Net Income	$ 60,544

Exhibit 3   Food & Beverage Department Condensed Income Statement—Hotel DORO

Hotel DORO, Inc.
F&B Department Condensed Income Statement
For the year ended December 31, 20X2

	Food	Beverage	Other	Total
Revenue	$360,000	$160,000	$6,400	$526,400
Allowances	1,700	130		1,830
Net Revenue	358,300	159,870	6,400	524,570
Cost of Sales:				
Cost of Goods Consumed	144,400	40,510	2,600	187,510
Less Cost of Employees' Meals	9,200			9,200
Cost of Sales	135,200	40,510	2,600	178,310
Gross Profit	223,100	119,360	3,800	346,250
Payroll and Related Expenses				204,180
Other Expenses				54,703
Total Expenses				258,883
Departmental Income				$ 87,377

The Hotel DORO's current ratio for 20X2 is calculated as follows:

$$\frac{\$147,888}{\$123,750} = 1.20$$

Interpretation. The current ratio is 1.20 to 1; it is sometimes expressed as follows:

1.20:1

This result indicates that there is $1.20 of current assets for every $1 of current liabilities. Another way of stating the result is: The current assets are 1.2 times larger than the current liabilities.

The larger the current ratio, the less difficulty a company should have in paying its current obligations. Therefore, a *favorable* condition prevails when the ratio is equal to or greater than prior-period or budgeted ratios.

The current ratio can be manipulated by borrowing long-term funds. The cash would become a current asset and the bank loan would not appear as a current liability.

Bank Standard

Banks generally require a current ratio of 2.0 as a prerequisite for the approval of loans. While this bank standard of 2.0 is arbitrary, the investment community has also adopted it as a standard of measure.

This bank standard was developed in the evaluation of retail stores and manufacturing companies, which are characterized by large amounts of inventory and receivables. Hotels and restaurants do not require large amounts of inventory with a low turnover; therefore, their current assets are generally more liquid. The receivables of hotels and restaurants are mostly from credit cards that are more dependable for collection than the high customer billings common in many other types of industries.

Composition

The interpretation of the current ratio requires more than comparison with other ratios and the bank standard. Two different companies can have identical current ratios, and yet one company's assets will not be as liquid as the other's. The following example shows how identical current ratios can be deceiving when two different companies are compared.

	Company A	Company B
Cash	$100,000	$ 20,000
Short-term investments	25,000	0
Accounts receivable	20,000	75,000
Inventories	40,000	90,000
Prepaid expenses	15,000	15,000
Total current assets	$200,000	$200,000
Total current liabilities	$100,000	$100,000
Current ratio	2:1	2:1

Even though both companies have 2:1 current ratios, Company A is in a better liquid position with larger amounts of cash and short-term investments. Company B is burdened by its heavy commitment in accounts receivable and inventories.

To overcome this limitation of the current ratio, the quick ratio was developed. This ratio does not use inventories and prepaid expenses in the evaluation of liquidity.

Quick Ratio

The quick ratio, also called the **acid-test ratio**, is a more refined version of the current ratio. In the quick ratio, the numerator includes only highly liquid current assets that are more quickly converted to cash. It excludes the less liquid current assets such as inventories and prepaid expenses.

Formula. The quick ratio formula is as follows:

$$\frac{\text{Cash + Short-Term Investments + Receivables (Net)}}{\text{Current Liabilities}}$$

Hotel DORO's quick ratio for 20X2 is calculated as follows:

$$\frac{\$58,500 + \$25,000 + \$40,196}{\$123,750} = 1.00$$

Interpretation. The quick ratio is 1.00 to 1; it is sometimes expressed as follows:

1.00:1

This result indicates that there is $1 of highly liquid (quick) assets for every $1 of current liabilities. Another way of stating the result is: The quick assets are equal to the current liabilities.

The larger the quick ratio, the less difficulty a company should have in paying its current obligations. Therefore, a favorable condition exists when the ratio is equal to or greater than prior-period or budgeted ratios.

Relationship of Current Ratio Results to Quick Ratio Results. The current ratio for the Hotel DORO is 1.2 and its quick ratio is 1.0; the ratios are very close. This is typical for companies in the hospitality industry because of the industry's low inventory requirements.

Bank Standard

Banks generally require a quick ratio of 1.0 as a prerequisite for the approval of loans. When the Hotel DORO is analyzed, its quick ratio of 1.0 is satisfactory under the bank standard even though its current ratio fails the 2.0 bank standard. These contradictory results emphasize the importance of not making any decisions on the basis of analyzing a limited number of ratios.

Accounts Receivable Turnover Ratio

The accounts receivable turnover ratio measures the number of times that, on average, receivables are collected during a period. The data used in calculating this ratio are *sales* and *accounts receivable.* This ratio would not apply to a hospitality company whose sales are entirely on cash or bank credit cards. In those cases where a company sells for cash and credit, only the sales on credit should be used. If the separation of cash and credit sales is not possible, the accounts receivable turnover ratio will be of value if its basis for calculation is consistent. A low receivables-to-sales ratio is the result for any hospitality company that has mostly cash sales.

The accounts receivable turnover ratio requires the use of two financial statements: the income statement (to provide the sales figure) and the balance sheet (to provide the beginning and ending balances of the accounts receivable). The accounts receivable (after subtracting the allowance for doubtful accounts) are averaged by adding the beginning and ending balances for the period and dividing by two.

Formula. The accounts receivable turnover ratio formula is as follows:

$$\frac{\text{Net Revenue}}{\text{Average Accounts Receivable (Net)}}$$

As shown in Exhibit 2, the net sales for the Hotel DORO in 20X2 were $1,597,493. The hotel's accounts receivable turnover ratio for 20X2 is calculated as follows:

$$\frac{\$1,597,493}{(\$38,840 + \$40,196) \div 2} = 40 \text{ Times}$$

Interpretation. The accounts receivable have turned over 40 times on average. This high number indicates that the Hotel DORO's sales are mostly on bankcards and cash. A favorable condition occurs when the ratio is equal to or greater than prior period or budgeted ratios.

The ratio takes on more meaning when it is restated in days; the conversion is made possible by computing the average collection period ratio.

Average Collection Period Ratio

The average collection period ratio can be used to evaluate a company's credit and collection policy. If the policy states that all billings are payable in 30 days, the average collection period result should reflect that policy.

The accounts receivable turnover ratio can be converted to days (average collection period) by dividing the business year stated in days by the turnover.

Formula. The accounts receivable average collection period ratio formula is as follows:

$$\frac{365}{\text{Accounts Receivable Turnover}}$$

The average collection period for the Hotel DORO in 20X2 is calculated as follows:

$$\frac{365}{40} = 9 \text{ Days}$$

Interpretation. The average collection period for accounts receivable was nine days, or approximately every week. Another interpretation is that the accounts receivable balance consists of nine days of sales.

A favorable condition occurs when the ratio is equal to or less than prior period or budgeted ratios.

Inventory Turnover Ratio

The **inventory turnover ratio** measures how quickly the inventory of a hospitality business was bought and sold. The buy-and-sell cycle represents one inventory turnover, also referred to as one *time*. This turnover is an average of fast-moving items and slower items such as canned goods, frozen goods, and expensive wines. The inventory turnovers for food, beverage, gift shop, and other merchandising operations must each be computed separately; otherwise, the averages will be subject to deceptive results.

Generally, a progressively higher number indicates an improved turnover. However, a hospitality business must attain a balance between high and low turnover. A high turnover may result in out-of-stock conditions, while a low turnover may result in inventory spoilage or an excess of inventory that ties up the business's limited cash resources.

Formula. The food inventory turnover formula is as follows:

$$\frac{\text{Cost of Food Used}}{\text{Average Food Inventory}}$$

If Cost of Food Used is not available, use Cost of Food Sold. The average inventory is computed as follows:

$$\frac{\text{Beginning Inventory} + \text{Ending Inventory}}{2}$$

The beverage inventory turnover formula is similar. Often the balance sheet does not provide sufficient information to compute inventory turnovers because the inventories are shown in total on one line item, as in Exhibit 1. Using Exhibit 3, which shows the food and beverage activities, the inventory turnovers can be calculated as follows:

$$\frac{\text{Cost of Food Used}}{\text{Average Food Inventory}} = \frac{\$144,400}{(\$5,800 + \$7,000) \div 2} = 23 \text{ Times}$$

$$\frac{\text{Cost of Beverages Used}}{\text{Average Beverage Inventory}} = \frac{\$40,510}{(\$3,000 + \$2,800) \div 2} = 14 \text{ Times}$$

The unique wine list provided to Hotel DORO's distinguished clientele results in a low average beverage turnover. However, management justifies its unique wine list because of its appeal to guests and its marketing advantage.

Fixed Asset Turnover Ratio

The fixed asset turnover ratio measures management's effectiveness in using fixed assets (property and equipment) to generate revenue. This ratio requires the use of two financial statements: the income statement (to provide the sales figure) and the balance sheet (to provide the average of the fixed assets).

Formula. The fixed asset turnover ratio formula is as follows:

$$\frac{\text{Net Revenue}}{\text{Average Fixed Assets}}$$

The Hotel DORO's fixed asset turnover ratio for 20X2 is calculated as follows:

$$\frac{\$1,597,493}{(\$3,139,217 + \$3,095,524) \div 2} = 0.5 \text{ Times}$$

Interpretation. The Hotel DORO's revenue was less than one time its average total fixed assets for the period. A favorable condition exists when the ratio is equal to or greater than prior-period or budgeted ratios.

Limitation. Any ratio that uses fixed assets or total assets is subject to wide variations because of the effect of depreciation. In the case of the fixed asset turnover ratio, the fixed assets are at net of accumulated depreciation. Therefore, newer hotels or hotels with conservative depreciation policies will have lower fixed asset turnover ratios.

Fixed assets are a significant part of any hotel company. The fixed asset turnover ratio ignores the market value of assets. As a result, the ratio could unfairly penalize newer hotels that were built at higher costs.

Debt-to-Equity Ratio

The debt-to-equity ratio compares the total debt of a hotel company with the total equity of its shareholders (owners). It shows the extent to which the company has borrowed from suppliers and banks and reveals whether the creditors or owners are financing most of the corporate assets. Creditors are interested in this ratio because it provides an indicator of risk: the higher the ratio, the higher the risk for those extending credit to the company.

Formula. The debt-to-equity ratio formula is as follows:

$$\frac{\text{Total Liabilities}}{\text{Total Equity}}$$

The Hotel DORO's 20X2 debt-to-equity ratio for 20X2 is calculated as follows:

$$\frac{\$2,178,750}{\$1,068,662} = 2.04$$

Interpretation. A favorable condition exists when the ratio is equal to or less than prior-period or budgeted ratios. The result of 2.04 tells us that the creditors have financed $2.04 for every $1 the company (owners) has invested in the assets. A ratio higher than 1.00 indicates that the hotel is using debt financing more than equity financing to operate or expand its business. This is known as using **financial leverage.**

The significance of this leverage can be more clearly illustrated with the application of the financial equation to the Hotel DORO as follows:

Assets	=	Claims of Creditors	+	Claims of Owners
$3.04	=	$2.04	+	$1.00

The financial equation can be restated in percentages to show the proportion of who is financing most of the assets. This is done by dividing each claim by the total assets of $3.04, and results in the following:

Assets	=	Claims of Creditors	+	Claims of Owners
100%	=	67%	+	33%

Creditors have financed 67 percent of the assets, while shareholders are bearing only 33 percent of the risk.

Significance. Each corporation has its own optimal credit and debt structure. Properly used financial leverage can maximize growth. Therefore, a high debt ratio is not necessarily unfavorable as long as the company is capable of servicing its debt (paying the interest and principal).

A high ratio could indicate the probability of a company becoming insolvent, especially if the company cannot service its debt. If a bank feels that a company has a high debt ratio, it may demand a higher rate of interest on any new loans and/or collateral to support the loans in case of default by the company.

Assets-to-Liabilities Ratio

The assets-to-liabilities ratio is also called the **solvency ratio.** It compares total assets to total liabilities. A hospitality business gives the appearance of being solvent when its assets are greater than its liabilities. Therefore, the result of this ratio should be greater than 1.00.

Formula. The assets-to-liabilities ratio formula is as follows:

$$\frac{\text{Total Assets}}{\text{Total Liabilities}}$$

The Hotel DORO's assets-to-liabilities ratio for 20X2 is calculated as follows:

$$\frac{\$3,247,412}{\$2,178,750} = 1.49$$

Interpretation. A favorable condition exists when the ratio is equal to or greater than prior-period or budgeted ratios. The result of 1.49 tells us that there is $1.49 of assets for each $1 of liabilities.

This ratio is more meaningful if the financial equation is applied as follows:

Assets	=	Claims of Creditors	+	Claims of Owners
$1.49	=	$1.00	+	$.49
100%	=	67%	+	33%

Notice that, when this ratio is converted to percentages, it gives the same result as the debt-to-equity ratio percentages.

Variation of the Assets-to-Liabilities Ratio. There are several variations of ratios used to measure solvency, but they all produce the same result. For example, some analysts use a ratio called the *debt-to-assets ratio* (or liabilities-to-assets ratio), which would produce the following result when applied to the Hotel DORO:

$$\frac{\text{Total Liabilities}}{\text{Total Assets}} = \frac{\$2,178,750}{\$3,247,412} = 67\%$$

The use of one or more solvency ratios depends on management's particular likes or dislikes. The analyst or accountant will select those ratios that management favors and has used to evaluate solvency.

Working Capital

A study of working capital is important because of its close relationship to day-to-day operations. Working capital as a topic often does not get the attention it deserves in schools, texts, and seminars, in large part because business executives tend to dwell on cash. Yet management of working capital is necessary for business survival, financial efficiency, and satisfactory profitability. One of the leading causes of business failures is the mismanagement of working capital.

Computation of Working Capital

Working capital is computed as follows:

$$\begin{array}{l} \text{Current Assets} \\ - \ \underline{\text{Current Liabilities}} \\ \text{Working Capital} \end{array}$$

If current liabilities exceed current assets, a net working capital *deficit* occurs. Working capital cannot be manipulated by loans from banks or extension of credit by suppliers. The immediate availability of working capital depends upon the composition of its current assets, especially cash, short-term investments, and receivables.

Composition of Working Capital

In addition to comparing the amount of current assets to current liabilities, the components of working capital can be converted to percentages by dividing each current asset by the total current assets. In the example below, each current asset of Company A was divided by $200,000.

	Company A	
Cash	$ 100,000	50.0%
Marketable securities	25,000	12.5
Accounts receivable	20,000	10.0
Inventories	40,000	20.0
Prepaid expenses	15,000	7.5
Total current assets	$ 200,000	100.0%
Total current liabilities	$ 100,000	
Working capital	$ 100,000	

The Importance of Adequate Working Capital

Working capital should be sufficient to enable a company to conduct its business and meet emergencies without danger of financial disaster. Adequate working capital:

- Makes it possible to take advantage of cash discounts.
- Permits the company to pay all interest and debt when due.
- Maintains the company's good credit rating.
- Permits the carrying of inventories at quantities that will provide the highest level of customer service.
- Enables the company to extend credit on open account to expand sales growth.
- Allows the company to operate more efficiently because there are no delays in receiving goods or services, and items are not delivered C.O.D. (collect on delivery).
- Provides a margin of safety for the company during economic recessions.

Causes of Inadequate Working Capital

It is not necessary to have a working capital deficit to suffer inadequate working capital. A common ailment of companies is to have a working capital balance that is positive but inadequate for the company's needs. Inadequate working capital may be caused by the following:

- Large or numerous operating losses because of lower sales volume and/or increased costs
- Losses due to theft or casualty losses that were uninsured or under-insured
- Failure of management to obtain the necessary funds
- Excessive investment in fixed assets

Causes of Excess Working Capital

Adequate working capital is desirable, but excess working capital may result if:

- Fixed assets were purchased with excessive borrowings or issuance of capital stock. (These tactics permit the company to purchase long-term assets without using current funds.)
- Fixed assets were sold and not replaced.
- Shareholders are deprived of their fair share of earnings in the form of dividends.

Factors Affecting Working Capital Requirements

Many factors affect working capital requirements. The hospitality industry, which is characterized by small inventories and minor sales on open account, can survive on smaller working capital than the manufacturing industry. The following are some determinants of working capital requirements:

- Time from purchase of goods to sale (inventory turnover)
- Profit margins (return on assets, return on equity)
- Credit policies (receivables turnover)
- Debt load (debt to equity, assets to liabilities)

Reference List of Ratio Formulas

This list shows the major balance sheet ratios and their formulas and is intended to be a convenient source of reference.

Accounts Receivable Turnover Ratio $$\frac{\text{Net Revenue}}{\text{Average Accounts Receivable (Net)}}$$

Assets-to-Liabilities Ratio $$\frac{\text{Total Assets}}{\text{Total Liabilities}}$$

Average Collection Period Ratio $$\frac{365}{\text{Accounts Receivable Turnover}}$$

Beverage Inventory Turnover $$\frac{\text{Cost of Beverages Used}}{\text{Average Beverage Inventory}}$$

Current Ratio $$\frac{\text{Current Assets}}{\text{Current Liabilities}}$$

Debt-to-Assets Ratio $$\frac{\text{Total Liabilities}}{\text{Total Assets}}$$

Debt-to-Equity Ratio $$\frac{\text{Total Liabilities}}{\text{Total Equity}}$$

Fixed Asset Turnover Ratio $$\frac{\text{Net Revenue}}{\text{Average Fixed Assets}}$$

Food Inventory Turnover $$\frac{\text{Cost of Food Used}}{\text{Average Food Inventory}}$$

Quick Ratio $$\frac{\text{Cash + Short-Term Investments + Receivables (Net)}}{\text{Current Liabilities}}$$

Key Terms

acid-test ratio—A more refined version of the current ratio. The denominator is the same (current liabilities), but the numerator is made up of only those current assets that are relatively liquid: cash, short-term investments, and net receivables. The acid-test ratio is often called the quick ratio.

financial leverage—The use of debt in place of equity dollars to finance operations and increase the return on the equity dollars already invested.

inventory turnover ratio—A ratio representing the number of times inventory is turned over (sold and replaced) during the period under consideration. This ratio is calculated by dividing the cost of sales by average inventory on hand.

liquidity—The ability of a hospitality operation to meet its short-term (current) obligations by maintaining sufficient cash and/or investments easily convertible to cash.

quick ratio—See acid-test ratio.

solvency—The extent to which a hospitality operation is financed by debt and is able to meet its long-term obligations. An operation is solvent when its assets exceed its liabilities.

solvency ratio—A ratio that measures the extent of a business's debt financing and ability to meet long-term obligations.

Review Questions

1. What is the difference between the terms "analysis" and "interpretation"?

2. What do the terms "liquidity," "asset management," and "debt management" mean?

3. Which ratios are used to measure liquidity?

4. Which ratios are used to evaluate asset management?

5. Which ratios are used to evaluate debt management?

6. How would a current ratio result of 3.12 be interpreted?

7. How would a quick ratio result of 1.55 be interpreted?

8. What is financial leverage?

9. What are the formulas for the following ratios?

    a. Current ratio
    b. Quick ratio
    c. Accounts receivable turnover
    d. Average collection period
    e. Food inventory turnover ratio
    f. Fixed asset turnover
    g. Debt-to-equity ratio
    h. Assets-to-liabilities ratio

10. How is working capital computed?

11. What is the importance of adequate working capital?

12. What are some causes of inadequate working capital?

13. What are some causes of excess working capital?

14. What are some factors affecting working capital requirements?

Internet Sites

For more information, visit the following Internet sites. Remember that Internet addresses can change without notice. If the site is no longer there, you can use a search engine to look for additional sites.

Financial Ratios
www.netmba.com/finance/financial/ratios/

Balance Sheet Analyzed
www.investopedia.com/articles/04/031004.asp

Current Ratio & Quick Ratio Analyzed
www.bankrate.com/brm/news/biz/bizcalcs/ratiocurrent.asp
www.investorwords.com/4008/quick_ratio.html
www.americancentury.com/servlet/GlossaryManager/acb.americancentury.com/
  ilQ.htm

Working Capital and Working Capital Calculator
www.investorwords.com/5334/working_capital.html
www.planware.org/workingcapital.htm
www.dinkytown.net/java/Capital.html

Problems

Problem 1

The result of a debt-to-equity ratio is .75 at the end of a hospitality corporation's current year.

a. State this result in the form of the financial (accounting) equation.

b. Restate this result using percentages (rounded to a whole number) in the financial equation.

c. Who is financing most of the assets?

Problem 2

The result of an assets-to-liabilities ratio is 2.33 at the end of a hospitality corporation's current year.

a. State this result in the form of the financial (accounting) equation.

b. Restate this result using percentages (rounded to a whole number) in the financial equation.

c. Who is financing most of the assets?

Problem 3

Compute the percentage composition of the current asset section of the Pikalou Hotel from the information provided below. Carry your answers to one decimal.

Cash	$150,000
Short-term investments	40,000
Accounts receivable	12,000
Inventories	20,000
Prepaid expenses	5,000
Total current assets	$227,000

Problem 4

Executive management of the Dav-Elen National Hotel have completed analyzing the hotel's balance sheet for the current period. Compare the results against the budgeted goals and indicate whether the results are favorable or unfavorable. Do not consider any other factors but the ratio numbers provided.

	Actual	Budget
Current ratio	3.5	3.9
Quick ratio	1.6	1.2
Accounts receivable turnover ratio	25.3	30.0
Fixed asset turnover ratio	3.0	2.5
Debt-to-equity ratio	2.5	2.2
Assets-to-liabilities ratio	1.4	1.5

Problem 5

Compute the following ratios and working capital for 20X8 from The Garden Bistro's balance sheet and supplementary information presented below. Show all ratio results carried to two decimals, rounded.

a. Current ratio

b. Quick ratio

c. Accounts receivable turnover ratio

d. Average collection period ratio

e. Fixed asset turnover ratio

f. Debt-to-equity ratio

g. Assets-to-liabilities ratio

h. Working capital

Supplementary Information:

Selected information from the income statement for the 365-day operating year ended December 31, 20X8:

Sales	$171,000
Allowances	− 1,000
Net Sales	$170,000

The Garden Bistro, Inc.
Balance Sheet
December 31, 20X8 and December 31, 20X7

ASSETS

CURRENT ASSETS	20X8	20X7
Cash	$ 34,000	$ 36,500
Accounts Receivable	4,000	3,450
Food Inventory	2,400	2,100
Supplies Inventory	2,600	1,900
Prepaid Expenses	2,000	2,600
Total Current Assets	45,000	46,550
PROPERTY AND EQUIPMENT		
Land	30,000	30,000
Building	60,000	60,000
Furniture and Equipment	52,000	48,000
China, Glassware, and Silver	8,000	8,300
Total	150,000	146,300
Less Accumulated Depreciation	40,000	35,000
Net Property and Equipment	110,000	111,300
OTHER ASSETS		
Security Deposits	1,500	1,500
Preopening Expenses	2,500	3,000
Total Other Assets	4,000	4,500
TOTAL ASSETS	$ 159,000	$ 162,350

LIABILITIES

CURRENT LIABILITIES		
Accounts Payable	$ 11,000	$ 25,400
Sales Tax Payable	1,000	950
Accrued Expenses	9,000	7,000
Current Portion of Long-Term Debt	6,000	6,000
Total Current Liabilities	27,000	39,350
LONG-TERM LIABILITIES		
Mortgage Payable, net of current portion	34,000	40,000
TOTAL LIABILITIES	61,000	79,350

SHAREHOLDERS' EQUITY

Paid-In Capital:		
Common Stock, par value $1,		
authorized 50,000 shares,		
issued 25,000 shares	25,000	25,000
Additional Paid-In Capital	15,000	15,000
Total Paid-In Capital	40,000	40,000
Retained Earnings, December 31, 20X8	58,000	43,000
TOTAL SHAREHOLDERS' EQUITY	98,000	83,000
TOTAL LIABILITIES AND SHAREHOLDERS' EQUITY	$ 159,000	$ 162,350

Case Study ──────────────────────

Working Capital Management

The president of Daisy Hospitality Enterprises is holding a special meeting on working capital. She introduces the following statements for discussion and elaboration during the meeting.

- The definition of *working capital management* as management of current assets and current liabilities is correct, but it is not generally meaningful to managers.

- Economist John Maynard Keynes explains why any business holds cash: (1) for the purpose of speculation, (2) for the purpose of precaution, and (3) for the purpose of making transactions.

- A business cannot let excess working capital remain without proper executive decision and action.

Challenge

During the meeting, the president asks everyone to:

1. Provide a more specific, informative definition of *working capital management* than "the management of a company's current assets and current liabilities."

2. Provide examples of what Mr. Keynes might have meant by the purposes of speculation, precaution, and making transactions when he explained why businesses hold cash.

3. Provide some examples of what a company can do with its excess working capital.

Chapter 11 Outline

Competencies

1. Explain the purpose and use of the statement of cash flows. (pp. 297–298)

2. Summarize how and why items may be treated as cash in preparing a statement of cash flows. (pp. 298–299)

3. Identify the general format for a statement of cash flows. (p. 299)

4. Differentiate between income and cash flow from operating activities, and explain the preparation of the operating activities section of a statement of cash flows. (pp. 299–305, 308–312)

5. Explain the preparation of the investing activities section of a statement of cash flows. (pp. 305–306, 312–313)

6. Explain the preparation of the financing activities section of a statement of cash flows. (pp. 306–307, 313)

7. Describe the use of footnotes and disclosures on a statement of cash flows. (pp. 307–308, 314)

11

Statement of Cash Flows

Every hospitality business needs to predict **cash flow** to ensure that it has sufficient funds to finance its current operations and growth. The income statement, balance sheet, and statement of retained earnings are not designed to provide information about cash inflows and cash outflows. These financial statements are prepared using the accrual basis of accounting, in which all revenues are recorded when realized and all expenses are recorded when incurred, whether or not cash was involved at the time of the business transaction.

The income statement and balance sheet provide information that can be used to prepare another statement called the statement of cash flows (SCF). The SCF reflects the cash inflows and outflows of a business for a period of time.

The procedures for preparing the SCF are relatively simple, but obtaining certain information requires a complex analysis of the general ledger and journal entries. An accounting department is responsible for performing the analysis and preparing the SCF. The responsibility of a hospitality professional is to understand how an SCF is prepared and know how to read and interpret the SCF in order to make intelligent management decisions. It is not necessary to be an expert in the analytical effort.

In order to provide the hospitality professional with sufficient background to read an SCF, this chapter uses a unique approach to explain the preparation of the SCF:

- The format of the SCF is described.

- The information for preparing the SCF is provided.

- The procedures for preparing the SCF are explained.

- For those desiring more knowledge about the accountant's approach to the SCF, the Appendix to this chapter describes how the data is obtained.

    This chapter also answers such questions as:

1. What is the purpose of the SCF?
2. What is the relationship of the SCF to the other major financial statements?
3. What is the format of the SCF?
4. How are cash inflows and outflows classified?
5. How is the SCF prepared?

The Purpose of the Statement of Cash Flows

The major purpose of the **statement of cash flows** is to provide relevant information about the cash receipts and cash payments of a hospitality business for a stated period of time. The time period covered by the SCF is identical to that of the accompanying income statement.

The Financial Accounting Standards Board (FASB) is responsible for establishing standards of financial accounting and reporting. Its major function is to study accounting issues and produce Statements of Financial Accounting Standards (SFAS or FAS). The FASB has issued SFAS 95 (FAS 95), which mandates that the SCF be included with the income statement, balance sheet, and statement of retained earnings as part of the information a company provides to external users. The income statement reports on the results of operations, the balance sheet reveals the financial position, and the SCF shows the sources and uses of cash. The SCF answers such questions as:

1. How much cash was generated from operations?

2. How much cash was received from borrowings?

3. How much cash was received from the issuance of common stock or sale of treasury stock?

4. How much cash was received from the sale of property, equipment, investments, and marketable securities?

5. What amount of cash was used to pay back current loans and long-term debt?

6. What amount of dividends were paid?

7. What amount of cash was used to acquire property and equipment?

8. What amount of cash was used to make investments?

The major users of the SCF are management, creditors, and investors. Management uses the SCF to judge the company's ability to meet its debt obligations, estimate future borrowings, invest excess funds, plan for growth of facilities or locations, and determine dividend policy. Creditors and investors use the SCF to judge the company's abilities to meet its debt obligations and pay dividends, and to assess the company's financial soundness.

Cash and Cash Equivalents

Because the SCF explains the changes in cash for a period of time, it is important to define which items represent cash. Company management must establish a policy outlining which items are to be treated as cash in preparing the SCF. In addition to cash in savings and checking accounts, there are certain types of financial instruments that can be equivalent to cash even though they are not in the form of cash.

To qualify as a cash equivalent, a financial instrument must be (1) readily convertible to cash, and (2) so near its maturity that there is virtually no risk of decline in value due to changes in the market interest rates. Cash equivalents are highly liquid investments such as United States treasury bills, commercial paper, and money market funds.

U.S. treasury bills are borrowings by the United States government from investors. In the investment community, they are called U.S. T-bills or simply T-bills. T-bills are issued weekly at public auction through regional federal reserve banks. They can also be purchased through commercial banks and brokers for a small processing fee. The minimum T-bill purchase is $10,000, with the amount increasing in $1,000 increments. The minimum maturity period is 13 weeks from the date of original issue. There is a secondary market for selling these T-bills for holders who find that they cannot wait for the maturity date.

Commercial paper is unsecured short-term obligations of major corporations issued through brokers or directly by the corporations.

A **money market fund** is a mutual fund that invests primarily in U.S. T-bills, commercial paper, and other financial instruments offering attractive interest rates. Investors in money market funds may redeem their holdings directly through the mutual fund or a broker.

Funds in marketable securities such as common and preferred stock of other companies are not classified as cash equivalents because these securities do not have a maturity date and may be subject to significant fluctuations in market value.

Format of the Statement of Cash Flows

Cash flow is the net result of cash receipts and cash payments. If cash receipts are greater than cash payments, the result is a positive cash flow, also called a **cash inflow**. A negative cash flow, also called a **cash outflow**, is the result of cash payments being greater than cash receipts.

Exhibit 1 shows the major sections of an SCF. The cash flows are classified in three major activities:

- Operating activities
- Investing activities
- Financing activities

If the cash inflows exceed the cash outflows, the net total of the section is labeled *net cash provided by (name of activity)*. If the cash outflows exceed the cash inflows, the net total of the section is labeled *net cash used in (name of activity)*.

The amount entered on the line labeled *increase (decrease) in cash for the period* is the net total of the three activities sections.

The beginning cash balance is the ending balance from the previous period's SCF. As an alternative, the appropriate comparative balance sheet also provides the beginning cash balance for the SCF.

The ending cash balance for the period results from totaling the increase (decrease) in cash for the period and the beginning cash balance for the period. The ending cash balance on the SCF must agree with the amount shown on the balance sheet for the same date.

Income from Operating Activities

Operating activities are a hospitality company's primary revenue-generating activities. For a hotel, revenue from all its operating centers less expenses of operating centers, support centers, energy costs, and fixed charges is classified as income

Exhibit 1   Format of the Statement of Cash Flows

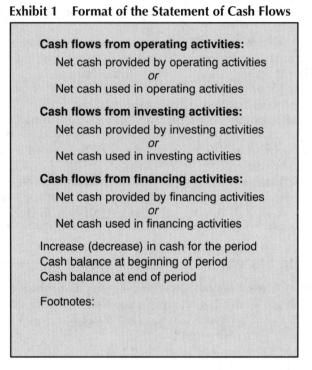

> **Cash flows from operating activities:**
>   Net cash provided by operating activities
>   *or*
>   Net cash used in operating activities
>
> **Cash flows from investing activities:**
>   Net cash provided by investing activities
>   *or*
>   Net cash used in investing activities
>
> **Cash flows from financing activities:**
>   Net cash provided by financing activities
>   *or*
>   Net cash used in financing activities
>
> Increase (decrease) in cash for the period
> Cash balance at beginning of period
> Cash balance at end of period
>
> Footnotes:

from operating activities. Interest income and dividends income are also included in income from operating activities.

Income from operating activities, also called income from operations, can be summarized as follows:

$+$ Sales: revenue centers
$+$ Interest income
$+$ Dividends income
$-$ Expenses: revenue centers
$-$ Expenses: support centers and utility costs
$-$ Fixed charges
$-$ Income taxes
$=$ Income from operations

Cash flows from the sale of property, equipment, and long-term investments are not considered to result from operating activities because these transactions are not part of a hotel's primary business purpose or day-to-day operations.

Marketable Securities

Showing the cash flows from the sale of marketable securities as an operating activity depends upon how the securities are categorized according to SFAS 115 (FAS 115). The classification criteria are technical and are explained in the Appendix to this chapter.

Exhibit 2   Condensed Hotel Income Statement (Example)

Room sales	$600,000
Food and beverage sales	100,000
Interest and dividends income	1,000
Total revenue	701,000
Less depreciation	50,000
Less other expenses	450,000
Income before income taxes and gain on sale of investments	201,000
Gain on sale of investments	10,000
Income before income taxes	211,000
Income taxes	60,000
Net income	$151,000

Under SFAS 115, cash flows from the sale of marketable securities categorized as *trading securities* should be included in the operating activities section of the SCF. Trading securities are characterized by frequent and heavy trading. If the marketable securities are not categorized as trading securities, the cash flows are shown in the investment activities section of the SCF, which is explained later in this chapter.

It is unlikely that a busy general manager of a hotel attending to its critical and demanding day-to-day management has the time to devote to heavy trading of securities. Therefore, this chapter will not classify marketable securities as trading securities.

> *Cash flows from the sale of marketable securities appear in the investing activities section of the statement of cash flows throughout this chapter.*

A typical hotel income statement in condensed form is shown in Exhibit 2. The $151,000 net income amount is not income from operating activities because it includes a $10,000 gain from the sale of investments. Since the $10,000 was originally added to the hotel's income, nonoperating income of this type must be subtracted to eliminate the effect of a gain.

Net income	$151,000
Less gain on sale of investment	10,000
Income from operations	$141,000

Cash Flow from Operating Activities

While the $141,000 (as adjusted) is *income from operations,* it is not the *cash flow from operations.* Remember that the SCF is based on cash transactions and not on accrual accounting for income and expenses. The reason the $141,000 is not cash flow from operating activities is that not all sales were for cash and not all expenses were paid in the period reported. To understand this, review the following summary of accrual accounting:

- Sales can be for cash or on account (accounts receivable).
- Purchases can be for cash or on account (accounts payable).
- Expenses such as depreciation and amortization never require a cash outlay because this type of expense is derived from adjusting entries that merely allocate the historical cost of a long-lived asset over an estimated useful life.

There are two methods for computing the cash flows from operating activities: the direct method and the indirect method.

Direct Method

One approach to preparing the operating activities section of the SCF is the direct method. Under the direct method, a thorough analysis of various general ledger accounts is required to determine cash receipts and cash disbursements from operations. A logical account to start with is the Cash account because all cash receipts and disbursements flow through this account. However, there are two major complications:

1. The volume of transactions posted to the Cash account is substantial, making it impractical to analyze all of them.
2. The individual postings to the Cash account and other accounts generally do not contain a sufficient description of the transaction.

Most hospitality companies do not use the direct method; instead they elect the faster, easier indirect method. Both methods produce the same amount to represent cash flows from operating activities. Therefore, this chapter concentrates on the indirect method. The Appendix to this chapter offers more information on the direct method for interested readers.

Indirect Method

The indirect method for preparing the operating activities section of the SCF is simple and efficient because it utilizes the existing income statement and balance sheet. The indirect method begins with net income as shown on the income statement, adjusts net income for noncash items, continues with the elimination of nonoperating gains and losses, and concludes with the conversion from accrual accounting to cash basis accounting. This conversion is accomplished by adding or subtracting changes in certain current asset and current liability accounts.

Adjustments for Noncash Items. Under the indirect approach, cash flows from operating activities are determined in part by adjusting the net income shown on the income statement for any items that appear in it but do not have an effect on cash. Depreciation expense and amortization expense are noncash expenses that never affect cash flows. Since they are deducted from revenue on the income statement to arrive at net income, these noncash expenses must be added back. Thus, the procedure to adjust operating net income to operating cash flow begins as follows:

Net income
+ Depreciation and amortization

Exhibit 3 Accrual Accounting versus Cash Basis Accounting

Transaction: Cash sales are $100,000.

Cash	Accounts Receivable	Sales
100,000		100,000

Transaction: Additional sales of $20,000 were on account.

Cash	Accounts Receivable	Sales
100,000	20,000	100,000
		20,000
		120,000

Result:

Accrual accounting shows sales of:	$120,000
However, cash received is:	$100,000

Reconciliation to cash received:

Total sales	$120,000
Less: Increase in accounts receivable	(20,000)
Cash received	$100,000

Adjustments for Nonoperating Gains and Losses. The gains and losses from the sale of assets are the result of selling or disposing of property, equipment, investments, and marketable securities. Since a gain had previously increased net income as shown on the income statement, it must now be subtracted to eliminate this transaction. Conversely, losses were deducted to arrive at net income; thus, the elimination adjustment requires adding back the amount of loss. The procedure to adjust operating net income to operating cash flow continues as follows:

> Net income
> + Depreciation and amortization
> − Gains from sale of assets
> + Losses from sale of assets

Adjustments for Changes in Current Assets and Current Liabilities. Adjustments are necessary to convert from accrual basis accounting to cash basis accounting. Some of the sales on the income statement may not have been cash sales, and certain expenses may not yet be paid. Exhibit 3 shows how sales of $120,000 actually result in only $100,000 of cash received. This is because, of the $120,000 total sales, $20,000 were on accounts receivable and $100,000 were cash sales.

Eliminating the need to analyze many ledger accounts, the indirect method employs logic to adjust accrual accounting to cash basis accounting. Exhibit 3 shows that it is possible to "squeeze" the amount representing cash sales using logic. Notice that sales and accounts receivable increased. Accounts receivable is a result of the selling process. Therefore, an increase to accounts receivable results in an increase to sales without a corresponding increase to cash. Accordingly, the increase of $20,000 in accounts receivable is subtracted from the total sales of $120,000 to arrive at cash sales of $100,000.

To present the basis of the logic involved, we will analyze three items that usually appear on a balance sheet: accounts receivable, inventory, and accounts payable.

Assume a balance sheet shows the following comparative data for accounts receivable.

Accounts receivable:
This year's ending balance	$40,000
Last year's ending balance	30,000
Increase to accounts receivable	$10,000

An increase to accounts receivable delays a sale's conversion to cash. It could be stated that the customers of the company are using its money. Refer again to Exhibit 3, and notice that the increase to accounts receivable was used as a deduction from sales to arrive at cash received.

Assume a balance sheet shows the following comparative data for inventory.

Inventory:
This year's ending balance	$3,000
Last year's ending balance	2,000
Increase to inventories	$1,000

An increase to inventory is equivalent to a cash outflow because the increase is due to purchases that ultimately require cash payment.

Observe that *increases* in these *current asset* accounts caused a *decrease* to *cash flow*. Therefore, it is logical to assume that increases in a current asset account are a cash outflow and, conversely, decreases in a current asset account result in a cash inflow. (Note that the increase or decrease effects in *cash* and *marketable securities* are ignored for purposes of the operating activities section because these accounts are presented elsewhere in the SCF.)

The procedure to adjust operating net income to operating cash flow continues as follows:

Net income
+ Depreciation and amortization
− Gains from sale of assets
+ Losses from sale of assets
− Increases to certain current asset accounts
+ Decreases to certain current asset accounts

Our analysis of the logic used in the cash conversion procedure now turns to current liabilities. Assume a balance sheet shows the following comparative data for accounts payable.

Accounts payable:
This year's ending balance	$25,000
Last year's ending balance	18,000
Increase to accounts payable	$ 7,000

An increase to accounts payable is equivalent to a *cash inflow* because the use of credit to purchase inventory and other items results in the use of "other people's money," which is similar to borrowings of cash.

Using logic regarding accounts payable, we can conclude that increases in current liability accounts are a cash inflow. Increases in current liabilities preserve cash in the business. Conversely, decreases in a current liability account result in a cash outflow. *Notice that the increases and decreases to current liabilities are exactly the opposite of those stated for current assets.* This adds validity to the logic, because liabilities always have an effect opposite to that of assets, including the selection of debits and credits to record these transactions. (Note, however, that the increase or decrease effects in *loans due to cash borrowings, dividends payable,* and *current portion of long-term debt* are ignored for purposes of the operating activities section because these accounts are presented elsewhere in the SCF.)

The procedure to adjust operating net income to operating cash flow can now be completed as follows:

>   Net income
> + Depreciation and amortization
> − Gains from sale of assets
> + Losses from sale of assets
> − Increases to certain current asset accounts
> + Decreases to certain current asset accounts
> + Increases to certain current liability accounts
> − Decreases to certain current liability accounts

Procedures reference chart. The various steps in the indirect method for adjusting net income from operations to cash flows from operating activities are listed in the procedures reference chart in Exhibit 4. This exhibit is a comprehensive procedures chart that can be used to prepare all sections of the SCF. Refer to the operating activities section of this chart, which summarizes how to convert net income to cash flow from operations.

Investing Activities

The investing activities section is the second cash activities section of the SCF. Investing activities generally involve cash transactions that affect marketable securities and noncurrent assets such as investments and property, plant, and equipment.

The purchase of these assets is a decrease to cash flow (cash outflow) for the amount of cash disbursed at the time of acquisition. The proceeds from the sale of these assets is an increase to cash flow (cash inflow) whether there was a gain or a loss in the selling transaction. The following comparison explains why the emphasis is on *proceeds* (selling price) instead of on the gain or loss.

	Investment A	Investment B
Proceeds (cash received)	$100,000	$100,000
Cost basis	80,000	120,000
Gain (loss)	$ 20,000	$ (20,000)

Regardless of the gain or loss, the sale of either investment generated a cash inflow of $100,000, which is classified as an investing activity. The gain or loss is not relevant to the SCF.

Purchases of property and expensive equipment are seldom transacted with only a cash payment. Quite often, a cash down payment and debt such as a mortgage payable or note payable are used to complete the purchase. For example, land might be purchased as follows:

Acquisition cost	$80,000
Mortgage	60,000
Cash down payment	$20,000

The SCF reflects only cash inflows and cash outflows. Therefore, only the $20,000 cash payment will appear in the investing activities section of the SCF. Because this transaction also involves noncash investing and financing activities, it would be fully disclosed in the footnotes to the SCF. (Footnotes and disclosures are discussed later in this chapter.)

The items entered in the investing activities section of the SCF can be summarized as follows:

Cash inflows:
Proceeds from sale of marketable securities
Proceeds from sale of investments
Proceeds from sale of property and equipment

Cash outflows:
Cash used to acquire marketable securities
Cash used to acquire investments
Cash used to acquire property and equipment

While the investing activities section is relatively simple to complete, obtaining the data requires a thorough knowledge of accounting and bookkeeping procedures. Since the readers of this chapter are probably not accountants, the procedures for obtaining the data are explained in the Appendix for those interested.

The steps for preparing the investing activities section are summarized in the procedures chart in Exhibit 4.

Financing Activities

The financing activities section is the third and final cash activities section of the SCF. The financing activities section deals with equity and debt transactions. It explains how cash was obtained from investors (equity financing) and from creditors (debt financing). For example, cash can be obtained by issuing capital stock or borrowings. These financing activities ultimately require paying the debt principal, paying dividends, and possibly reacquiring stock (treasury stock).

The items entered in the financing activities section of the SCF can be summarized as follows:

Cash inflows:
Issue capital stock (common or preferred)
Issue bonds

Sell treasury stock
Cash borrowings

Cash outflows:
Payment of dividends
Purchase of treasury stock
Payment of principal on debt (mortgages, loans, bonds)

While the financing activities section is relatively simple to complete, obtaining the data requires a thorough knowledge of accounting and bookkeeping procedures. Since the readers of this chapter are probably not accountants, the procedures for obtaining the data are explained in the Appendix for those interested in that knowledge.

The steps for preparing the financing activities section are summarized in the procedures chart in Exhibit 4.

Footnotes and Disclosures

Since the three activities sections of the SCF present only those activities that are cash-basis oriented, it is usually necessary to provide disclosures either in narrative form or summarized in a schedule. These disclosures and **footnotes** may be on the same page as the SCF or reported on an attachment page. Footnotes and disclosures are required for the following transactions:

- Income taxes and interest paid in the period
- Accounting policy regarding cash
- Noncash investing and financing transactions

Income Taxes and Interest Paid

The FASB requires that the amount paid for income taxes and interest be disclosed on the SCF if the indirect method of presenting cash flow from operating activities is used. This information is generally not found on the income statement because these expenses are recorded on the accrual basis. Therefore, an analysis of the bookkeeping accounts for income taxes expense and interest expense is necessary. The cash expenditure for income taxes and interest is most conveniently shown as a footnote on the SCF as follows:

Interest paid for the period	$xxx
Income taxes paid for the period	$xxx

Accounting Policy Regarding Cash

The footnote for the *disclosure of accounting policy* explains the reporting of cash flows based on cash, cash equivalents, and cash on hand.

Noncash Investing and Financing Transactions

Noncash investing and financing transactions are transactions during a period that affect long-term assets, equity, or debt but do not result in cash receipts or payments.

Examples of noncash investing and financing transactions are converting debt to equity, acquiring assets by part cash and part mortgage, obtaining an asset by entering into a capital lease, and the exchange of noncash assets or liabilities for other noncash assets or liabilities. Some specific examples of these transactions are:

- Issuing stock to settle a note payable

- Executing a new note to settle a note that became due

- Acquiring an auto via a three-year lease

- Exchanging vacant land for vacant land owned by another party

- Purchasing an asset with a cash down payment and the balance financed by a mortgage or note payable. In this case, only the cash down payment would appear in the investing activities section of the SCF. This transaction would require disclosure, which might take the following form:

Acquisition cost of land	$80,000
Cash down payment	20,000
Balance financed by mortgage	$60,000

Demonstration Problem

Now that the logic and principles underlying the SCF have been presented, they can be applied to perform the procedure shown in Exhibit 4, the procedures reference chart for the SCF. This chart will be used along with Exhibit 5, which presents the financial statements (income statement and comparative balance sheet) of the Demonstration Hotel. The results of assembling this information are presented in Exhibit 6, which is the completed SCF.

The SCF will be prepared in the following sequence:

1. Operating activities section
2. Investing activities section
3. Financing activities section
4. Computation of ending cash balance
5. Footnotes and disclosures

Preparing the Operating Activities Section

Preparing the operating activities section requires an analysis of the balance sheet and the income statement. The objectives of this section are to convert net income, which has been computed on the accrual basis, to cash flow income, and also to eliminate nonoperating gains and losses to arrive at cash flows from operations.

The starting point in preparing the operating activities section of the SCF is the net income of $9,000. To this amount are added back the $18,000 depreciation and $500 amortization noncash expenses.

Next are the adjustments to reconcile (convert) net income to net cash flows from operating activities. The nonoperating gains and losses are eliminated; the $1,000 gain is subtracted and the $1,200 loss is added back.

Exhibit 4   Procedures Reference Chart—Statement of Cash Flows

Operating Activities Section

	Effect
Net income (starting point)	+
Adjustments for noncash items:	
Depreciation	+
Amortization	+
Adjustments for nonoperating gains and losses:	
Gain on sale of assets	−
Loss on sale of assets	+
Adjustments for changes in current assets:	

	Increase	Decrease
Cash	NA	NA
Marketable securities	NA	NA
Receivables	−	+
Inventories	−	+
Prepaids	−	+
Adjustments for changes in current liabilities:		

	Increase	Decrease
Loans for cash borrowings	NA	NA
Dividends payable	NA	NA
Current portion of long-term debt	NA	NA
Accounts payable	+	−
Accrued liabilities	+	−
Other current liability accounts	+	−

> **LEARNING TIP**
>
> The mathematical signs of the changes in current liabilities stay the same on the SCF. For example, a change that is an increase (+) is also an increase (+) on the SCF. It then follows that the changes in current assets would be reversed.

Investing Activities Section

	Effect
Proceeds from sale of marketable securities	+
Proceeds from sale of investments	+
Proceeds from sale of property and equipment	+
Cash used to acquire marketable securities	−
Cash used to acquire investments	−
Cash used to acquire property and equipment	−

Financing Activities Section

	Effect
Issue capital stock	+
Issue bonds	+
Sell treasury stock	+
Cash borrowings	+
Payment of dividends	−
Purchase of treasury stock	−
Payment of principal on debt	−

NA = Not applicable

Exhibit 5   Demonstration Problem—Income Statement and Balance Sheet

Income Statement
Demonstration Hotel
For the year ended 12/31/X2

Sales		$310,000
Depreciation	$ 18,000	
Amortization	500	
Other expenses	277,300	
Total expenses		295,800
Income before nonoperating gains (losses)		14,200
Gain on sale of equipment		1,000
Loss on sale of marketable securities		(1,200)
Income before income taxes		14,000
Income taxes		5,000
Net income		$ 9,000

Balance Sheet
Demonstration Hotel
12/31/X2 and 12/31/X1

	20X2	20X1	Increase (Decrease)
Cash	$ 39,000	$ 45,000	$ (6,000)
Marketable securities	0	5,000	(5,000)
Accounts receivable (net)	28,000	18,500	9,500
Inventories	10,000	12,000	(2,000)
Prepaid expenses	3,000	2,000	1,000
Total current assets	$ 80,000	$ 82,500	$ (2,500)
Property and equipment (net)	190,000	130,000	60,000
Other assets (net)	5,000	5,500	(500)
Total assets	$275,000	$218,000	$ 57,000
Accounts payable	$ 88,000	$ 89,500	$ (1,500)
Sales tax payable	2,000	1,200	800
Accrued expenses	6,000	7,300	(1,300)
Dividends payable	3,000	0	3,000
Current portion of mortgage	5,000	0	5,000
Total current liabilities	$104,000	$ 98,000	$ 6,000
Mortgage payable (net)	27,000	0	27,000
Note payable due 2/1/X4	30,000	0	30,000
Capital stock issued (no par)	117,000	108,000	9,000
Treasury stock	(20,000)	0	(20,000)
Retained earnings	17,000	12,000	5,000
Total liabilities and equity	$275,000	$218,000	$ 57,000

Exhibit 6 Demonstration Problem—Statement of Cash Flows

Statement of Cash Flows
Demonstration Hotel
For the year ended 12/31/X2

Cash Flows from Operating Activities:

Net income		$ 9,000
Adjustments to reconcile net income to net cash flows from operating activities:		
Depreciation expense	18,000	
Amortization expense	500	
Gain on sale of equipment	(1,000)	
Loss on sale of marketable securities	1,200	
Increase in accounts receivable	(9,500)	
Decrease in inventories	2,000	
Increase in prepaid expenses	(1,000)	
Decrease in accounts payable	(1,500)	
Increase in sales tax payable	800	
Decrease in accrued expenses	(1,300)	8,200
Net cash provided by operating activities		17,200
Cash Flows from Investing Activities:		
Proceeds from sale of equipment	6,000	
Proceeds from sale of marketable securities	3,800	
Purchase of equipment	(43,000)	
Down payment on purchase of land	(8,000)	
Net cash used in investing activities		(41,200)
Cash Flows from Financing Activities:		
Cash proceeds from note payable due 2/1/X4	30,000	
Proceeds from issuance of no par capital stock	9,000	
Dividends declared and paid this year	(1,000)	
Purchase of treasury stock	(20,000)	
Net cash provided by financing activities		18,000
Increase (decrease) in cash for the year		(6,000)
Cash at the beginning of the year		45,000
Cash at the end of the year		$ 39,000

Supplemental Disclosures of Cash Flow Information

Cash paid during the year for:

Interest	$ 1,000
Income taxes	$ 2,000

Supplemental Schedule of Noncash Investing and Financing Activities

A parcel of land was purchased in December 20X2 as follows:

Acquisition cost of land	$40,000
Cash down payment	8,000
Balance financed by mortgage	$32,000

Disclosure of Accounting Policy

For purposes of the statement of cash flows, the Company considers all highly liquid debt instruments purchased with a maturity of three months or less to be cash equivalents.

The final step to complete the operating activities section of the SCF is using the balance sheet to enter the increases and decreases in certain current asset and current liability accounts. These increases and decreases are processed as follows:

- *Increases* in current assets are *subtracted.*

- *Increases* in current liabilities are *added.*

It then follows that decreases in current assets and current liabilities require mathematical functions that are the opposite of those stated for increases.

The current asset accounts for cash and marketable securities are bypassed because these items are processed elsewhere in the SCF. The $9,500 increase in accounts receivable is subtracted, the $2,000 decrease in inventories is added, and the $1,000 increase in prepaid expenses is subtracted.

The current liability accounts are now processed. The $1,500 decrease in accounts payable is subtracted, and the $800 increase in sales tax payable is added. The current liability accounts for dividends payable and current portion of mortgage are bypassed because these items are processed elsewhere in the SCF.

The adjustments total $8,200, which is added to the net income of $9,000. This results in a positive cash flow of $17,200, which is labeled *net cash provided by operating activities.*

Preparing the Investing Activities Section

The objective of the investing activities section is to show cash receipts and payments involving marketable securities and noncurrent assets such as investments, property, plant, and equipment.

Obtaining the information for the investing activities section requires technical accounting knowledge. Otherwise, analyzing the balance sheet changes can result in misleading information. For example, the balance sheet shows a $60,000 increase to property and equipment. It would be erroneous to assume that this increase applies only to a purchase of property and equipment. In actuality, the $60,000 increase is a combination of many transactions as follows:

Equipment purchased ($43,000 cash paid)	$43,000
Land purchased ($8,000 cash paid)	40,000
Equipment disposed of ($6,000 cash proceeds)	(8,000)
Accumulated depreciation (adjusting entry)	(18,000)
Accumulated depreciation (disposed asset)	3,000
Net change	$60,000

The analysis required to obtain the information for this section is provided in the Appendix to this chapter for those readers interested in the detailed and technical expertise required in the process. We will be concerned here only with the types of cash transactions that are entered in the investing activities section as listed in the reference chart.

The investing activities section for the Demonstration Hotel shows a net cash outflow of $41,200, which is labeled *net cash used in investing activities.* This cash outflow is the result of the following cash investing transactions:

- $6,000 proceeds from the sale of equipment

- $3,800 proceeds from the sale of marketable securities

- $43,000 cash purchase of equipment

- $8,000 down payment for the purchase of land. The land acquisition cost was $40,000, but only the $8,000 cash paid is entered because the balance was financed by a mortgage (a noncash investing activity that is explained in the footnotes and disclosures section of the SCF).

Preparing the Financing Activities Section

The objective of the financing activities section is to show how cash was obtained from investors and creditors and how cash was used to pay the debt principal and dividends and purchase treasury stock.

Obtaining the information for this section involves the same degree of complexity mentioned in the investing activities section. We will be concerned here only with the types of cash transactions that are entered in the financing activities section as listed in the reference chart.

The financing activities section for the Demonstration Hotel shows a net cash inflow of $18,000, which is labeled *net cash provided by financing activities*. This cash inflow is the result of the following cash financing transactions:

- $30,000 proceeds from borrowings by a note payable to a bank

- $9,000 proceeds from the sale of no-par stock

- $1,000 cash payment for dividends declared and paid this year

- $20,000 cash paid out to reacquire its own stock to buy out a dissident shareholder

Areas that should be studied are the current portion of long-term debt and long-term debt lines shown on the balance sheet. In the demonstration problem, the current portion of the mortgage payable is $5,000 and the long-term portion is $27,000. These amounts are not shown in two bookkeeping accounts. There is only one bookkeeping account called Mortgage Payable. In this case, its balance would be $32,000, which is allocated by the accountant into its current and long-term portions. The general ledger account and presentation of this "mixed" debt is shown in Exhibit 7.

The debit side of the mortgage payable or other liability account generally indicates the payments on this debt. These payments are verified by their reference to a cash disbursements entry.

Computing the Ending Cash Balance

The $17,200 cash inflow from the operating activities section, the $41,200 cash outflow from the investing activities section, and the $18,000 cash inflow from the financing section result in a $6,000 *decrease* in cash for the year.

The balance sheet shows that the cash balance on 12/31/X1 was $45,000, which became the beginning cash balance on 1/1/X2. Subtracting the decrease of $6,000 results in a cash balance of $39,000 at the end of the year. This number is verified by the balance sheet, which also shows cash on 12/31/X2 of $39,000.

Exhibit 7   Current and Long-Term Portion Presentation

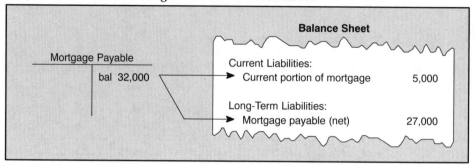

Preparing the Footnotes and Disclosures

It is necessary to show the amounts paid for interest expense and income taxes. The amounts shown on the income statement are accounted for on the accrual basis and do not necessarily reflect the actual cash paid. The cash payments of $1,000 for interest expense and $2,000 for state and federal income taxes were determined by analysis of the respective general ledger bookkeeping accounts.

Transactions that affect assets, liabilities, or equity but did not involve cash are disclosed in a supplemental schedule called noncash investing and financing activities. The acquisition of land by cash and mortgage by the Demonstration Hotel has been explained earlier.

To comply with the disclosure on accounting policy, the Demonstration Hotel describes its cash and cash equivalents policy.

Key Terms

cash flow—A stream of receipts (inflows) and disbursements (outflows) resulting from operational activities or investments.

cash inflow—Cash received by the hospitality organization during the accounting period.

cash outflow—Cash disbursed by the hospitality organization during the accounting period.

commercial paper—Unsecured short-term securities or promissory notes issued by the largest and strongest corporations in our economy. Generally has a maturity of less than 270 days.

footnotes—Notes of explanation that provide financial information not easily presented in financial statements. Also called notes to the financial statements.

money market fund—A mutual fund that invests primarily in commercial paper, U. S. T-bills, and other financial instruments offering attractive interest rates. Investors in money market funds may redeem their holdings directly through the mutual fund or a broker.

statement of cash flows—A financial statement that explains the change in cash for an accounting period by showing the effects on cash of a business's operating, investing, and financing activities for the accounting period.

U.S. treasury bills—Securities issued by the U. S. government for fairly short periods. Usually considered riskless.

Review Questions

1. What is the purpose of the statement of cash flows (SCF)?

2. What kinds of questions are answered by the SCF?

3. How does the management of a hotel use the SCF?

4. What are some examples and brief descriptions of cash equivalents?

5. Why aren't marketable securities considered cash equivalents in the SCF?

6. What are the three sections of the SCF?

7. What does the term "operating activities" mean?

8. Why aren't gains and losses from the sale of property, equipment, and investments considered a part of operating activities?

9. Why can't the net income from the income statement be used as cash flow from operating activities?

10. What are the two major noncash expenses?

11. What are nonoperating gains and losses?

12. What kinds of transactions would be entered in the investing activities section of the SCF?

13. What kinds of transactions would be entered in the financing activities section of the SCF?

14. What are three types of transactions that can appear in the footnotes and disclosures section of the SCF?

15. How would the acquisition of land at a cost of $100,000, purchased with a $30,000 down payment and the balance financed with a mortgage, be shown in the SCF?

Internet Sites

For more information, visit the following Internet sites. Remember that Internet addresses can change without notice. If the site is no longer there, you can use a search engine to look for additional sites.

Statement of Cash Flows
www.investopedia.com/articles/04/033104.asp
www.va-interactive.com/inbusiness/editorial/finance/ibt/cash_flow.html

FASB 95
www.fasb.org/st/summary/stsum95.shtml

U.S. Treasury Bills
www.treasurydirect.gov/indiv/products/prod_tbills_glance.htm

Commercial Paper
www.investopedia.com/terms/c/commercialpaper.asp
http://beginnersinvest.about.com/od/commercialpaper/Commercial_Paper.htm
www.ge.com/en/company/investor/fixed_income/fi_commercial_paper.htm

Money Market Funds
www.investorwords.com/3107/money_market_fund.html
www.sec.gov/answers/mfmmkt.htm
http://mutualfunds.about.com/cs/buildingblocks/a/moneymarket.htm

Marketable Securities
www.investorwords.com/5917/marketable_securities.html
www.investorguide.com/igu-article-816-stock-basics-introduction-to-stocks.html

✏️ Problems

Problem 1

Indicate the section of the statement of cash flows (SCF) in which the following items would be entered. Assume the operating activities section is prepared according to the indirect method.

	Operating Activities	Investing Activities	Financing Activities
Amortization	_____	_____	_____
Proceeds from sale of marketable securities	_____	_____	_____
Payment of principal on debt	_____	_____	_____
Cash used to acquire investments	_____	_____	_____
Depreciation	_____	_____	_____
Gain on sale of assets	_____	_____	_____
Increase or decrease in accrued liabilities	_____	_____	_____
Cash borrowings	_____	_____	_____
Proceeds from sale of property and equipment	_____	_____	_____
Increase or decrease in prepaid expenses	_____	_____	_____
Issue of capital stock	_____	_____	_____
Cash used to acquire marketable securities	_____	_____	_____
Loss on sale of assets	_____	_____	_____
Increase or decrease in receivables	_____	_____	_____
Net income	_____	_____	_____
Payment of dividends	_____	_____	_____
Proceeds from sale of investments	_____	_____	_____
Increase or decrease in inventory	_____	_____	_____
Purchase of treasury stock	_____	_____	_____
Proceeds from sale of treasury stock	_____	_____	_____

Cash used to acquire property and equipment _____ _____ _____
Increase or decrease in accounts payable _____ _____ _____

Problem 2

Indicate the mathematical function (+ or −) in the proper activities section of the SCF for the following items. Assume the operating activities section is prepared according to the indirect method.

	Operating Activities	Investing Activities	Financing Activities
Amortization	_____	_____	_____
Proceeds from sale of marketable securities	_____	_____	_____
Payment of principal on debt	_____	_____	_____
Cash used to acquire investments	_____	_____	_____
Depreciation	_____	_____	_____
Gain on sale of assets	_____	_____	_____
Increase in accrued liabilities	_____	_____	_____
Decrease in accrued liabilities	_____	_____	_____
Cash borrowings	_____	_____	_____
Proceeds from sale of property and equipment	_____	_____	_____
Increase in prepaid expenses	_____	_____	_____
Decrease in prepaid expenses	_____	_____	_____
Issue capital stock	_____	_____	_____
Cash used to acquire marketable securities	_____	_____	_____
Loss on sale of assets	_____	_____	_____
Increase in accounts receivable	_____	_____	_____
Decrease in accounts receivable	_____	_____	_____
Net income	_____	_____	_____
Payment of dividends	_____	_____	_____
Proceeds from sale of investments	_____	_____	_____
Increase in inventory	_____	_____	_____
Decrease in inventory	_____	_____	_____
Purchase of treasury stock	_____	_____	_____
Proceeds from sale of treasury stock	_____	_____	_____
Cash used to acquire property and equipment	_____	_____	_____
Increase in accounts payable	_____	_____	_____
Decrease in accounts payable	_____	_____	_____

Problem 3

Prepare the operating activities section of the SCF for the Davdeg Motel using the indirect method.

Income Statement		
Sales		$500,000
Depreciation	$ 40,000	
Other expenses	400,000	440,000
Operating income		60,000
Loss on sale of equipment		(12,000)
Gain on sale of investments		5,000
Net income		$ 53,000

Changes in balance sheet accounts:	Increase (Decrease)
Cash	$ 20,000
Accounts receivable	(10,000)
Inventories	3,000
Prepaid expenses	1,000
Property and equipment	36,000
Accounts payable	7,000
Taxes payable	(1,000)
Current portion of long-term debt	3,000
Long-term debt	9,000
Equity accounts	32,000

Problem 4

Prepare the operating activities section of the SCF for the Lizdale Bistro using the indirect method.

Income Statement		
Sales		$200,000
Depreciation	$ 10,000	
Other expenses	170,000	180,000
Income from operations		20,000
Gain on sale of equipment		2,000
Gain on sale of marketable securities		3,000
Net income		$ 25,000

Changes in balance sheet accounts:	Increase (Decrease)
Cash	$ (7,000)
Marketable securities	4,000
Accounts receivable	15,000
Inventories	(2,000)
Prepaid expenses	(1,000)
Property and equipment	(9,000)
Accounts payable	(8,000)
Accrued payables	3,000
Dividends payable	3,000
Current portion of long-term debt	(5,000)
Long-term debt	(6,000)
Equity accounts	13,000

Problem 5

Prepare the operating activities section of the SCF for the Bessdoon Restaurant using the indirect method.

Income Statement		
Sales		$300,000
Depreciation	$ 8,000	
Other expenses	284,000	292,000
Operating income		8,000
Loss on sale of equipment		(1,000)
Loss on sale of marketable securities		(2,000)
Net income		$ 5,000

Changes in balance sheet accounts:	Increase (Decrease)
Cash	$ 10,000
Marketable securities	(5,000)
Accounts receivable	18,000
Inventories	5,000
Prepaid expenses	(2,000)
Property and equipment	10,000
Accounts payable	(6,000)
Accrued payables	1,000
Dividends payable	2,000
Current portion of long-term debt	12,000
Long-term debt	24,000
Equity accounts	3,000

Problem 6

Prepare the operating activities section of the SCF for the Walkam Ristorante using the indirect method.

Income Statement	20X2	
Sales	$900,000	
Cost of sales	300,000	
Gross profit	600,000	
Depreciation	80,000	
Amortization	10,000	
Other expenses	430,000	
Operating income	80,000	
Gain on sale of investments	4,000	
Income before income taxes	84,000	
Income taxes	30,000	
Net income	$ 54,000	

Balance Sheet	20X2	20X1
Cash	$ 30,000	$ 42,000
Marketable securities	10,000	0
Accounts receivable	120,000	90,000
Inventories	50,000	55,000
Prepaid expenses	7,000	9,000
Total current assets	$217,000	$196,000
Property and equipment (net)	500,000	420,000
Total assets	$717,000	$616,000
Accounts payable	$110,000	$90,000
Wages payable	30,000	37,000
Current maturities of long-term debt	24,000	12,000
Total current liabilities	$164,000	$139,000
Long-term debt	200,000	178,000
Total liabilities	$364,000	$317,000
Shareholders' equity	353,000	299,000
Total liabilities and equity	$717,000	$616,000

Problem 7

Shown below are totals of the three sections from the SCF for the Sivad Motel for the year just ended. Analyze this information and prepare a report indicating your opinion regarding its sources and uses of cash and their impact on the future of the company. Your conclusions and recommendations should be supported with proper explanations and assumptions.

Statement of Cash Flows

Net cash provided by operating activities	$10,000
Net cash used by investing activities	(15,000)
Net cash used by financing activities	(5,000)
Decrease in cash for the year	(10,000)
Cash at beginning of year	15,000
Cash at end of year	$ 5,000

Problem 8

Shown below are totals of the three sections from the SCF for the Nanood Motel for the year just ended. Analyze this information and prepare a report indicating your opinion regarding its sources and uses of cash and their impact on the future of the company. Your conclusions and recommendations should be supported with proper explanations and assumptions.

Statement of Cash Flows

Net cash provided by operating activities	$ 5,000
Net cash used by investing activities	(50,000)
Net cash provided by financing activities	$100,000
Increase in cash for the year	55,000
Cash at beginning of year	15,000
Cash at end of year	$ 70,000

Problem 9

Shown below are totals of the three sections from the SCF for the Nanged Motel for the year just ended. Analyze this information and prepare a report indicating your opinion regarding its sources and uses of cash and their impact on the future of the company. Your conclusions and recommendations should be supported with proper explanations and assumptions.

Statement of Cash Flows

Net cash provided by operating activities	$ 505,000
Net cash provided by investing activities	150,000
Net cash used by financing activities	(50,000)
Increase in cash for the year	605,000
Cash at beginning of year	500,000
Cash at end of year	$1,105,000

Problem 10

Shown below is the SCF for the Nimak Steakhouse Chain for the year just ended. Analyze this statement and prepare a report indicating your opinion regarding its sources and uses of cash and their impact on the future of the company. Your conclusions and recommendations should be supported with proper explanations and assumptions.

Statement of Cash Flows

Cash Flows from Operating Activities		
Net income		$ 4,000
Adjustments to reconcile net income to net cash flow:		
Depreciation	$ 6,000	
Loss on sale of equipment	10,000	
Decrease in accounts receivable	25,000	
Decrease in inventories	3,000	
Decrease in prepaid expenses	1,000	
Increase in accounts payable	18,000	63,000
Net cash provided by operating activities		$ 67,000
Cash Flows from Investing Activities		
Proceeds from sale of store equipment	$32,000	
Proceeds from sale of office equipment	5,000	
Net cash provided by investing activities		37,000
Cash Flows from Financing Activities		
Cash borrowings	$20,000	
Payment on cash borrowings	(5,000)	
Net cash provided by financing activities		15,000
Increase in cash for the year		$119,000
Cash at beginning of year		3,000
Cash at end of year		$122,000

Case Study

Statement of Cash Flows

You are engaged to prepare an SCF and make a presentation to the executives of the Empire Steakhouse. The following information is provided:

Income Statement	20X2
Sales	$780,000
Cost of sales	250,000
Gross profit	530,000
Depreciation	50,000
Other expenses	445,000
Operating income	35,000
Gain on sale of investments	30,000
Income before income taxes	65,000
Income taxes	25,000
Net income	$ 40,000

Balance Sheet	December 31		
	20X2	20X1	Change
Cash	$ 32,000	$ 50,000	$ (18,000)
Marketable securities	40,000	35,000	5,000
Accounts receivable	140,000	90,000	50,000
Inventories	30,000	35,000	(5,000)

Prepaid expenses	3,000	2,000	1,000
Total current assets	$245,000	$212,000	$ 33,000
Property and equipment (net)	299,000	330,000	(31,000)
Total assets	$544,000	$542,000	$ 2,000
Accounts payable	$ 60,000	$ 70,000	$ (10,000)
Wages payable	10,000	8,000	2,000
Bank loan payable	15,000	0	15,000
Current maturities of long-term debt	14,000	14,000	0
Total current liabilities	$ 99,000	$ 92,000	$ 7,000
Long-term debt	65,000	100,000	(35,000)
Total liabilities	$164,000	$192,000	$ (28,000)
Shareholders' equity	380,000	350,000	30,000
Total liabilities and equity	$544,000	$542,000	$ 2,000

Supplementary information:

1. Marketable securities transactions during the year were as follows: sold securities with original cost of $15,000 for $45,000; cash purchase of new securities at a cost of $20,000.

2. Sold old equipment with a basis of $13,000 for $13,000; cash purchase of new equipment for $32,000.

3. In the last month of the year, transacted a cash borrowing of $15,000, which is classified as a bank loan payable in the balance sheet.

4. Cash payments of $35,000 were made on the long-term loan.

5. Dividends of $25,000 were declared and paid this year.

6. Treasury stock was purchased at a cost of $3,000.

7. The issuance of no-par common stock resulted in $18,000 being received.

Challenge

1. Describe the three major sections of the SCF to the executives.

2. Present an SCF for the year ended December 31, 20X2, using the indirect method for preparing the operating activities section.

Appendix: Additional Preparation Information

The purpose of this appendix is to provide additional information regarding the preparation of the statement of cash flows (SCF). The material is arranged by topics and concludes with a presentation of the direct method of preparing the operating activities section of the SCF.

Cash and Cash Equivalents. Generally, the maturity date of cash equivalents must be three months or less from the date of purchase. For example, a three-month treasury bill and a three-year treasury note purchased three months from maturity qualify as cash equivalents.

Commercial Paper. These corporate short-term promissory notes are generally issued in minimum units of $25,000. Finance companies such as General Motors Acceptance Corporation (GMAC) issue commercial paper directly instead of going through banks or brokers; this type of paper is called finance paper or direct paper. The commercial paper that is issued through dealers is called dealer paper.

Treasury Bills. These U.S. government issues mature in one year or less and are issued in three-month, six-month, and one-year maturities. The minimum purchase is $10,000, with the size increasing in $1,000 increments. Typically, the longer the maturity, the higher the interest rate paid to the holder. T-bill interest comes "up front." For example, a $10,000 T-bill selling at 6 percent discount means that the buyer pays $9,400 to purchase the T-bill and collects $10,000 at maturity.

Treasury Notes. These U.S. government issues are typically sold with maturities of two, three, five, and ten years. The two- and three-year notes have a $5,000 minimum investment, with $1,000 increments above that level. There is a $1,000 minimum investment for five- and ten-year notes, which generally pay interest twice a year.

Treasury Bonds. These U.S. government issues have maturities of more than ten years. It is not unusual for them to have a maturity of 30 years. They may be purchased in multiples of $1,000, with interest paid twice a year.

Marketable Securities

Statement of Financial Accounting Standards (SFAS) 115 arranges debt and equity investments into three categories:

- Trading securities
- Available for sale securities
- Held to maturity securities

Trading Securities. These are bought primarily to sell in the short term; they reflect active and frequent buying and selling. If marketable securities do not meet these requirements, they are treated as available for sale securities.

Available for Sale Securities. These are securities that are not classified as trading securities or held to maturity securities.

Held to Maturity Securities. These can consist only of debt securities because, unlike equity securities, they are characterized by a maturity date. However, if management has a positive intent to dispose of a debt security prior to its maturity, the debt security can be classified as available for sale.

SFAS 115 specifies the treatment of these three categories of securities as follows:

Trading securities	Operating activity
Available for sale securities	Investing activity
Held to maturity securities	Investing activity

Cash Flows from Investing Activities

According to SFAS 95 (FAS 95) issued by the Financial Accounting Standards Board, additional cash inflows that could appear in this section are receipts from collection or sales of loans by the enterprise and other entities' debt instruments (other than cash equivalents and certain debt instruments that are acquired specifically for resale) that were purchased by the enterprise.

Cash outflows would be the result of disbursements for loans made by the enterprise and payments to acquire debt instruments of other entities (other than cash equivalents and certain debt instruments that are acquired specifically for resale).

Cash Flow per Share

Financial statements shall not report an amount of cash flow per share. Neither cash flow nor any component of it is an alternative to net income as an indicator of an enterprise's performance, as reporting per share amounts might imply. [FAS 95, ¶33]

Foreign Currency Cash Flows

A statement of cash flows of an enterprise with foreign currency transactions or foreign operations shall report the reporting currency equivalent of foreign currency cash flows using the exchange rates in effect at the time of the cash flows. An appropriately weighted average exchange rate for the period may be used for translation if the result is substantially the same as if the rates at the dates of the cash flows were used. The statement shall report the effect of exchange rate changes on cash balances held in foreign currencies as a separate part of the reconciliation of the change in cash and cash equivalents during the period. [FAS 95, ¶25]

Obtaining Data for the Investing Activities Section

Preparation of the investing activities section requires an analysis of the long-term asset accounts and also any transactions affecting short-term investment accounts (marketable securities). Specifically, any account that contains any transactions for the sale or purchase of property, equipment, investments, and marketable securities requires careful scrutiny.

For example, analyzing investment transactions requires an analysis of the Investments account and related journal entries. The following explains the basic procedure:

Investments		
beg bal 8,000	J1 Sale 8,000	
J2 Pur 5,000		
end bal 5,000		

The beginning balance in the account was $8,000. All these investments were sold. The investing activities section is not concerned with gain or loss. The proceeds from the sale, which represent a cash inflow, can be determined only by referring to J1. Later, the company made additional investments that cost $5,000, which represents a cash outflow.

J1:	Cash	12,000	
	Investments		8,000
	Gain on sale of securities		4,000

Analyzing Journal 1 shows that the cash inflow from the sale of investments was $12,000, which would be entered in the investment activities section of the SCF.

It is necessary to analyze Journal 2 to ascertain that the $5,000 purchase of new investments was indeed paid in cash and did not involve a noncash exchange of other assets or the company's stock.

J2:	Investments	5,000	
	Cash		5,000

Analyzing Journal 2 shows that the cash outflow from the purchase of investments was $5,000, which would be entered in the investment activities section of the SCF.

Obtaining Data for the Financing Activities Section

Preparation of the financing activities section requires an analysis of any account that contains transactions for short-term borrowings, long-term debt, and stockholders' equity accounts. Cash dividends paid may be determined by analyzing their declaration as a debit to retained earnings and tracing their ultimate payment as a debit to dividends payable.

The activity for dividends may be analyzed as follows:

Retained Earnings		Dividends Payable	
J4 Dec 2,000	beg bal 50,000	J5 Pay 2,000	beg bal 0
J5 Dec 3,000	end bal 45,000		J4 Dec 2,000
			J5 Dec 3,000
			end bal 3,000

Dividends declared total $5,000, as indicated by the debits to retained earnings and credits to dividends payable. However, the debit to dividends payable shows that only $2,000 of the dividends have been paid. Thus, $2,000 would be entered as a cash outflow in the financing activities section of the SCF.

Direct Method for Preparing the Operating Activities Section

The procedure for preparing the operating activities section of the SCF using the direct method differs from that using the indirect method. Under the direct method, the operating activities section does not begin with net income; instead, it shows cash collected from customers and cash used for various operating expenses.

Obtaining cash basis information requires an analysis of the transactions of each income and expense account or a conversion of year-end information from the accrual basis to cash basis accounting.

A typical operating activities section prepared under the direct method might appear as follows:

Statement of Cash Flows

Cash Flow from Operating Activities:	
Cash receipts	
from customers	$xxx
from interest and dividends	xxx
Cash payments	
to suppliers	$xxx
for operating expenses	xxx
for interest expense	xxx
for income taxes	xxx
Net cash provided (used) by operating activities	$xxx

Preparing the investing and financing activities sections is the same whether the direct or indirect method is used for the operating activities section.

When the direct method of reporting cash flows from operating activities is used, a separate schedule must be provided to reconcile the net income to net cash flow from operating activities. This supporting schedule is prepared according to the indirect method.

Chapter 12 Outline

Role of the Independent Certified Public
    Accountant
Audit Service
    Purpose of an Audit
    Scope of an Audit
    Auditor's Report
Review Service
    Purpose of a Review
    Scope of a Review
    Review Report
Compilation Services
    Purpose of a Compilation
    Scope of a Compilation
    Compilation Report
Consolidated Financial Statements
    Minority Interest
    Purpose of Consolidated Financial
        Statements
    Intercompany Transactions
    Investment in Subsidiary Account
    Consolidated Worksheet
Governmental Authority on Reporting by
    Public Companies
    The SEC
    The Sarbanes-Oxley Act of 2002
    The 10-K Report
Annual Report to Shareholders
    Letter to the Shareholders
    Financial Statements
    Notes to the Financial Statements
    Management Assessment of Internal
        Controls
    Report of Independent Public
        Accountants
    Certification of the Annual Report by
        Company Executives
    How to Read an Annual Report
    Financial Statements in an Annual
        Report
    Conclusion of an Annual Report
    Investor Relations Department

Competencies

1. Summarize the role of and criteria for an independent certified accountant. (pp. 329–330)

2. Explain the purpose and scope of an audit, and describe an auditor's report. (pp. 330–332)

3. Explain the purpose and scope of a review, and describe a review report. (pp. 332–334)

4. Explain the purpose and scope of a compilation, and describe a compilation report. (pp. 334–335)

5. Describe the purpose and preparation of consolidated financial statements. (pp. 335–338)

6. Summarize the federal government's authority regarding reporting by public companies, and discuss the SEC, the Sarbanes-Oxley Act, and the 10-K report. (pp. 338–341)

7. List and describe the major components of the annual report to shareholders and explain its purpose. (pp. 341–346)

12

Interim and Annual Reports

CORPORATIONS THAT HAVE ISSUED STOCK to the public and are listed on a major stock exchange are required to keep their shareholders informed of the company's financial status. This is accomplished by issuing condensed financial statements during the year **(interim reports)** and a comprehensive information package at the end of the year (annual report). The Securities and Exchange Commission (SEC) requires that annual reports be audited by an independent certified public accounting firm. Because audits are very time-consuming and expensive, interim reports do not require an audit; however, they must be reviewed by an independent certified public accountant.

Interim and annual reports are also issued to creditors, especially when a company is seeking a bank loan. Not all creditors require audited financial statements. Many accept financial statements that have been reviewed or compiled by an independent certified public accountant.

Corporations generally produce extravagant annual reports because the reports also serve as marketing tools to the investment community. Expensive annual reports are printed on glossy paper, feature many color photos, and have as many pages as a small magazine.

The annual report is designed and arranged based on its "selling" philosophy and not for the convenience of the analyst. An annual report can be intimidating to a reader who is not familiar with the report's financial data, letters, and illustrations.

In presenting interim and annual reports, this chapter will address the following questions:

1. What is the role of a certified public accountant in the issuance of reports to shareholders, creditors, and other third parties?

2. What are the differences among the audit, review, and compilation services provided by certified public accountants?

3. What are consolidated financial statements?

4. What is the content of an annual report?

5. How does one read an annual report?

6. How does governmental legislation affect annual reports?

7. What is the SEC?

8. What is the Sarbanes-Oxley Act of 2002?

9. What is a 10-K report?

Role of the Independent Certified Public Accountant ———

An independent certified public accountant (CPA) is in public practice and is expected to perform all services with impartiality. The demonstration of bias toward any client may influence the independence of the CPA. To provide guidelines for the independence of CPAs, the American Institute of Certified Public Accountants (AICPA) has established a *Code of Professional Conduct.* Violation of the code can result in the revocation of a license or suspension from public practice. The following are some of the criteria used to judge whether a CPA is independent:

- The CPA cannot be an employee of the client.

- The CPA must be free of any substantial financial interest in the client.

- The CPA must be free of any obligation to the client.

- The CPA must avoid any situation that may lead outsiders to doubt his or her independence. (For example, a presumption that independence is impaired arises from a significant financial interest, directorship, or close kin relationship with the client firm.)

When interim or annual reports are issued to shareholders, creditors, or other third parties, the financial statements are accompanied by a letter from the independent CPA explaining the *scope* of the service performed and the degree of responsibility assumed by the CPA.

The CPA may attach to the financial statements a letter called an **accountant's report.** The report varies based on whether the service provided was an *audit,* a *review,* or a *compilation.*

Audit Service ————————————————————

Auditing is the most recognized service that CPAs provide. Publicly owned companies are required to issue annual financial statements audited by an independent CPA. Audits are performed in accordance with *generally accepted auditing standards,* which are technical guidelines established by the AICPA in cooperation with the SEC. These standards ensure that an audit is conducted competently, ethically, and professionally.

Purpose of an Audit

The purpose of an audit is to ensure that financial statements *present fairly* and are *in conformity with generally accepted accounting principles.*

The phrase "present fairly" means that:

- The accounting principles used by the company have general acceptance.

- The financial statements and accompanying notes are informative and not misleading as to their use, understanding, and interpretation.

- The financial information is neither too detailed nor too condensed.

- The financial data is within a range of acceptable limits that are reasonable and practicable to attain in the preparation of any financial statements.

- The financial statements represent the financial position, results of operations, and cash flows for the period.

Generally accepted accounting principles (GAAP) is a technical accounting term that includes broad guidelines and detailed procedures relating to the conventions and rules that define the accepted accounting practice of a particular industry and the certified public accounting profession.

An audit is not designed to express judgment on the competence of management, the merits of investing in the company, or extending the company any credit; it is the responsibility of the reader to interpret the financial data and make these evaluations. The auditing process might also detect fraud or illegal acts, but there is no guarantee that all *irregularities* will be discovered. (CPA services do provide specialized audits solely for the purpose of detecting fraud and other irregularities.)

Scope of an Audit

Before an audit begins, the independent CPA must have or obtain a working knowledge of the client company and its industry. During the audit, the CPA will investigate and examine account balances and certain transactions. Not all accounts or transactions are examined; instead, samples are randomly selected and tested.

An audit is the only service that is a comprehensive investigation and examination of the items that appear on the financial statements and the accompanying footnotes (notes). The following are some functions that a CPA must perform during an audit:

- Observe the physical inventory-taking by the client company and test the reliability of the counts, condition, and cost valuation of the inventory.

- Confirm the receivables with the company's customers.

- Confirm the payables with the company's creditors.

- Verify the existence of the marketable securities and their valuation at market.

- Review the minutes of the corporate meetings.

- Communicate with management, the board of directors, and outside legal counsel of the company.

After completing an audit, the independent CPA expresses an *opinion* as to the fairness of the financial statements; this opinion is called the **auditor's report.** The report is in letter form and will accompany the financial statements.

Auditor's Report

The auditor's report (letter) should be read carefully because it states the conclusion of the auditor as to the fairness of the financial statements and the consistent application of GAAP.

The standard auditor's report consists of three paragraphs. The first paragraph introduces the financial statements that were audited. The second paragraph

Exhibit 1   Auditor's Report for the Hotel DORO

To Hotel DORO, Inc., The Board of Directors, and Shareholders:

We have audited the accompanying balance sheet of Hotel DORO, Inc. as of December 31, 20X2 and the related statements of income, retained earnings and cash flows for the year then ended. These financial statements are the responsibility of the Company's management. Our responsibility is to express an opinion on these financial statements based on our audits.

We conducted our audits in accordance with generally accepted auditing standards. Those standards require that we plan and perform the audit to obtain reasonable assurance about whether the financial statements are free of material misstatement. An audit includes examining, on a test basis, evidence supporting the amounts and disclosures in the financial statement. An audit also includes assessing the accounting principles used and significant estimates made by management, as well as evaluating the overall financial statement presentation. We believe that our audits provide a reasonable basis for our opinion.

In our opinion, the financial statements referred to above present fairly, in all material respects, the financial position of Hotel DORO, Inc. as of December 31, 20X2 and the results of its operations and its cash flows for the year then ended in conformity with generally accepted accounting principles.

describes what an audit is, and the third paragraph presents the auditor's opinion regarding the fairness of the financial statements and consistent application of GAAP.

The auditor's opinion is an important part of the auditor's report. A favorable opinion is called a "clean opinion." A clean opinion clearly states that the financial statements are presented fairly and in accordance with GAAP.

An example of a standard auditor's report for the fictitious Hotel DORO is shown in Exhibit 1. Notice that the report states a clean opinion. The different types of opinions that may be expressed by a public accountant are discussed later in this chapter.

Review Service

An audit of financial statements is expensive and time-consuming for the client company's staff. Physical inventories can disrupt operations, customers are contacted, staff is interviewed, and the company's accounting department is constantly asked to supply financial records. It is not unusual for an audit to take several months, starting well in advance of the date of the financial statements. Because the auditing process is a burden on a company's finances and operations, the audit of quarterly (interim) statements is not required. To ensure that interim financial statements provide shareholders with timely, relevant financial information, the SEC has approved the issuance of *reviewed* financial statements during the year.

Reviews are performed in accordance with *standards for accounting and review services*, which are technical standards for *unaudited* financial statements. Established by the AICPA, these standards ensure that a review is conducted competently, ethically, and professionally.

Purpose of a Review

The objective of a review differs significantly from the objective of an audit, which is to express an opinion. The purpose of a review is to express *limited assurance* that no material changes to the financial statements are necessary for them to be consistent with GAAP.

Scope of a Review

Before a review begins, the independent CPA must have or obtain a working knowledge of the client company and its industry. A review does not require a comprehensive investigation of the company's financial records. Instead, the CPA makes inquiries and performs analytical procedures to form a reasonable basis for expressing limited assurance.

The following are some examples of the CPA's inquiries and analytical procedures:

- Inquiries concerning the client company's accounting principles, practices, and methods
- Inquiries regarding the procedures for classifying and recording business transactions
- Analytical procedures for business transactions, account balances, or other items that appear to be unusual
- Inquiries concerning actions taken at meetings of shareholders, the board of directors, or other committees that may affect the financial statements
- Reading financial statements

A review is not designed to express an opinion as to the fairness of the financial statements. The CPA does not confirm receivables or payables, observe the inventory, seek other corroborative evidential matter, or perform the other tests demanded of an audit service. A review may bring to the CPA's attention significant matters affecting the financial statements, but its procedures are not designed to provide assurance that the CPA will become aware of these matters.

Review Report

After completing a review, the independent CPA does not express an opinion but gives what is called a level of *negative assurance*. In other words, in the CPA's view, no modifications to the financial statements are necessary. This *limited assurance* is part of the review report that is in letter form and will accompany the financial statements.

The review report comprises three paragraphs. The first paragraph introduces the financial statements that were reviewed. The second paragraph describes what a review is, and the third paragraph presents the CPA's level of assurance as to the conformity of the financial statements with GAAP. A favorable third paragraph in a review report would include a "clean review" absent of any "except for" statements or other qualifying statements.

Exhibit 2   Review Report for the Hotel DORO

> To Hotel DORO, Inc., The Board of Directors, and Shareholders:
>
> We have reviewed the accompanying balance sheets of Hotel DORO, Inc. as of December 31, 20X2 and the related statements of income, retained earnings and cash flows for the year then ended in accordance with standards established by the American Institute of Certified Public Accountants. All information included in these financial statements is the representation of the management of Hotel DORO, Inc.
>
> A review consists principally of inquiries of company personnel and analytical procedures applied to financial data. It is substantially less in scope than an examination in accordance with generally accepted auditing standards, the objective of which is the expression of an opinion regarding the financial statements taken as a whole. Accordingly, we do not express such an opinion.
>
> Based on our review, we are not aware of any material modifications that should be made to the accompanying financial statements in order for them to be in conformity with generally accepted accounting principles.

An example of a standard review report for the Hotel DORO is shown in Exhibit 2. Notice that the report gives a clean level of assurance.

Compilation Services

Even though reviewed financial statements are less expensive than audited financial statements, the review services performed by a CPA are still costly. As a result, a lesser alternative might be acceptable to creditors or other third parties. Compiled financial statements, also referred to as *compilations,* are the least expensive and lowest level of financial statement services provided by a CPA.

Compilations are performed in accordance with *standards for accounting and review services,* which are technical standards for *unaudited* financial statements. These standards, established by the AICPA, ensure that a compilation is conducted competently, ethically, and professionally.

Purpose of a Compilation

The purpose of a compilation is to present in the form of financial statements information that is the representation of client company management. The CPA does not express an opinion or any level of assurance on the statements.

Scope of a Compilation

Before a compilation begins, the independent CPA must have or obtain a working knowledge of the client company and its industry. A compilation does not require the CPA to make inquiries or perform other procedures to verify or review information supplied by the client company.

In a compilation, the CPA becomes familiar with a company's bookkeeping procedures and then compiles the financial data into a professional format.

The CPA should possess a general understanding of the company's business transactions, its form of accounting records, and the qualifications of its accounting personnel. Based on this understanding, the CPA might consider it necessary

Exhibit 3 Compilation Report for the Hotel DORO

> To Hotel DORO, Inc., The Board of Directors, and Shareholders:
>
> We have compiled the accompanying balance sheets of Hotel DORO, Inc. as of December 31, 20X2 and the related statements of income, retained earnings and cash flows for the year then ended in accordance with standards established by the American Institute of Certified Public Accountants.
>
> A compilation is limited to presenting, in the form of financial statements, information that is the representation of management.
>
> We have not audited or reviewed the accompanying financial statements and, accordingly, do not express an opinion or any other form of assurance on them.

to perform other services such as assistance in determining adjusting entries or consulting on accounting matters for the proper presentation of the financial statements.

Compilation Report

After completing a compilation, the independent CPA does not express an opinion as to the fairness of the financial statements or express any level of assurance.

The compilation report comprises three paragraphs. The first paragraph introduces the financial statements that were compiled. The second paragraph describes what a compilation is, and the third paragraph simply states that the financial statements were prepared on the basis of information provided by management without audit or review and disclaims any level of assurance by the CPA.

A favorable third paragraph would include a "clean compilation" absent of any "except for" statements or other qualifications. However, since a compilation is a very limited service, the absence of any qualifications should provide little certainty.

An example of a standard compilation report for the Hotel DORO is shown in Exhibit 3.

Consolidated Financial Statements

The big-business environment is characterized by large corporations operating in many locations. To further expand their earning power, corporations may seek acquisitions. By acquisition, a corporation may own 100 percent of another corporation's voting stock or own a majority (more than 50 percent) of the voting stock of another corporation. The company owning the controlling interest is called the **parent company** and the controlled company is called a **subsidiary.**

A parent-subsidiary relationship does not affect the issued and outstanding common stock. Each corporation's stock remains issued and listed on any stock exchange as it was before the parent company purchased the stock of the subsidiary.

Minority Interest

When a parent corporation owns less than 100 percent of a subsidiary's stock, the portion of the outstanding shares not owned is considered owned by a **minority interest**.

Because they are separate corporations, the parent and its subsidiaries maintain separate accounting records. The parent must issue **consolidated financial statements,** which include the financial data of the parent and its subsidiaries. It should be noted that when a minority interest exists, financial statements for the subsidiary must be issued separately because consolidated statements rarely present specific information useful to minority interest shareholders.

Purpose of Consolidated Financial Statements

Consolidated financial statements are issued so that investors and other interested parties get complete information about all resources and operations under the control of the parent company. Consolidated financial statements combine the parent and subsidiaries into a single reporting economic entity.

All the financial data from these separate corporations is combined on a consolidated worksheet; entries are not made in the general ledger of any company.

Intercompany Transactions

An **intercompany transaction** is any transaction between a parent and any of its subsidiaries, or transactions among the subsidiaries of the parent. Before any amounts from the parent and its subsidiaries are combined on the consolidated financial statements, all intercompany transactions must be eliminated so that the parent and subsidiaries are represented as one economic entity.

Even though intercompany transactions do in fact occur, they must be eliminated from the financial statements because it would not be logical for a single entity to buy and sell from itself, especially since these transactions inflate the true sales of the single reporting entity. For example, if a parent sells $100,000 of merchandise to its subsidiary, the following book transactions occur:

Books of Parent
Sales $100,000

Books of Subsidiary
Purchases $100,000

When the consolidated income statement is prepared, the intercompany sales and purchases are offset (eliminated) to properly reflect the operating results of a single economic unit.

Intercompany transactions involving the lending or borrowing of money between a parent and subsidiary are likewise eliminated from the financial statements because it is not logical for a single entity to borrow from itself and owe itself. For example, if a parent loans $50,000 to its subsidiary, the following book transactions occur:

Books of Parent
Loan receivable from subsidiary $50,000

Books of Subsidiary
Loan payable to parent $50,000

When the consolidated balance sheet is prepared, the loan receivable from the subsidiary is offset (eliminated) by the loan payable to the parent.

Investment in Subsidiary Account

The parent company's purchase cost of the subsidiary's stock is recorded to an account called *Investment in Subsidiary*. For consolidated financial statement purposes, this cost is eliminated by allocating it against the subsidiary's common stock, retained earnings, and possibly some assets and liabilities. The allocation procedure is determined by whether the parent purchased the stock at book value or at fair market value. Very few companies are purchased at book value. *Eliminating the investment in subsidiary accounts is the first elimination entry on the consolidated worksheet.*

Consolidated Worksheet

The preparation of consolidated worksheets is highly technical and very complex. For example, a purchase at fair market value may generate goodwill, which requires tedious computations and special processing on the worksheet; there are several different methods used to eliminate the investment in subsidiary accounts on the worksheet; the existence of any minority interest complicates the worksheet procedures because the parent does not own 100 percent of the subsidiary; and there are alternate accounting procedures to perform the elimination allocation, in addition to many other technical accounting procedures.

A different kind of accounting arises depending on the stock purchase. If the stock purchase involves, among other factors, an exchange of the parent's stock, it qualifies for "pooling" accounting. Stock purchases can also be accounted for under the purchase method of accounting.

Because the consolidated worksheet is so complex, several chapters would be necessary to present the levels of worksheet preparation. Therefore, this chapter will provide only basic information about preparing a consolidated worksheet. To simplify the discussion, the following conditions will be established:

- The parent has only one subsidiary.

- The parent owns 100 percent of the subsidiary.

- The parent purchased the subsidiary's stock at book value.

- The purchase of the subsidiary's stock was a cash purchase.

- The parent method of accounting will be used.

- No dividends have been declared by the parent or subsidiary.

- There are no intercompany sales or purchases.

In addition, the example that follows will use a partial trial balance including only selected accounts necessary to explain the consolidation procedures.

Exhibit 4 shows the separate trial balances of the parent and subsidiary before consolidation begins. Exhibit 5 shows the first step in the consolidation process. This step involves entering the trial balance information on a consolidated worksheet. (Instead of debit or credit columns, credits will be indicated by parentheses.)

Exhibit 4   Trial Balances of the Parent Subsidiary

Trial Balance of Parent:

	Debit	Credit
Cash	$100,000	$ 30,000
Accounts receivable	80,000	40,000
Receivable from subsidiary	20,000	
Investment in subsidiary	70,000	
Common stock		80,000
Retained earnings		140,000
Sales		500,000

Trial Balance of Subsidiary:

	Debit	Credit
Cash	$30,000	
Accounts receivable	40,000	
Payable to parent		20,000
Common stock		30,000
Retained earnings		40,000
Sales		200,000

The next step is to perform the elimination entries. These are shown in Exhibit 6. The first elimination entry is to allocate the $70,000 in the *investment in subsidiary account*. In this example, this is very simple since the subsidiary was purchased at book value; the $70,000 is allocated to the subsidiary's common stock of $30,000 and retained earnings of $40,000. The effect of this entry is to eliminate the parent's cost and the subsidiary's equity section.

Next, the intercompany loan transaction is eliminated. The receivable of $20,000 from the subsidiary and the $20,000 payable to the parent by the subsidiary are eliminated since they cancel each other under the single economic entity concept.

After all elimination entries are completed, the trial balance and elimination entry columns of the worksheet are combined and entered in the consolidated column as shown in Exhibit 6. The consolidated worksheet is then used to prepare the consolidated financial statements.

Governmental Authority on Reporting by Public Companies

Understanding the annual report to shareholders requires readers to have a basic understanding of:

- The Securities and Exchange Commission
- The Sarbanes-Oxley Act of 2002
- The 10-K report

Exhibit 5   Starting the Consolidated Worksheet

	Parent	Subsidiary	Elimination	Consolidated
Cash	$100,000	$ 30,000		
Accounts receivable	80,000	40,000		
Receivable from subsidiary	20,000			
Investment in subsidiary	70,000			
Payable to parent		(20,000)		
Common stock	(80,000)	(30,000)		
Retained earnings	(140,000)	(40,000)		
Sales	(500,000)	(200,000)		

Exhibit 6   Completing the Consolidated Worksheet

	Parent	Subsidiary	Elimination	Consolidated
Cash	$100,000	$ 30,000		$130,000
Accounts receivable	80,000	40,000		120,000
Receivable from subsidiary	20,000		(20,000)	-
Investment in subsidiary	70,000		(70,000)	
Payable to parent		(20,000)	20,000	-
Common stock	(80,000)	(30,000)	30,000	80,000
Retained earnings	(140,000)	(40,000)	40,000	140,000
Sales	(500,000)	(200,000)		(700,000)

Publicly listed companies must fulfill many governmental filing requirements. The **Securities and Exchange Commission (SEC)** has requirements that under penalty of law must be followed. Numerous reports must be filed with the SEC and other governmental agencies. The SEC plays the major role in the governmental regulation of the securities markets and the reporting that is required of publicly held companies.

The **Sarbanes-Oxley Act of 2002** places additional requirements on a company's management and auditing firm. This act is very important legislation affecting corporate governance, financial disclosure, and the practice of public accounting.

The SEC requires that a company create two types of annual reports: the **10-K report** (also referred to as the Form 10-K report), which is filed with the SEC, and the company's annual report to shareholders. We will cover these topics in the following sections.

The SEC

Before the Great Stock Market Crash of 1929, most government regulators and financial investors did not perceive any need for federal regulation of the securities market. The rare recommendations that the federal government require financial disclosure by companies and enact laws to prevent the fraudulent sale of company stock were never seriously considered.

The SEC was created because of an economic catastrophe that remains notorious to this day. When the stock market crashed in October 1929, many investors lost fortunes. Banks also were great losers in the Crash, because they had invested heavily in the stock markets. During the Crash, people feared that banks might not be able to pay back the money in their accounts. A run on the banking system caused many bank failures. In response to the crisis, Congress passed the Securities Act of 1933 and the Securities Exchange Act of 1934. These laws were designed to restore investor confidence, regulate the securities market, and regulate shareholder-reporting requirements.

The SEC is a government agency concerned with the securities industry. Its effectiveness is due in large part to its enforcement authority. The primary mission of the SEC is to protect investors and maintain the integrity of the securities markets. One reason this agency is so necessary is that (unlike in the banking world where deposits are guaranteed by the federal government) stocks, bonds, and other securities can lose their value. This makes government oversight more important. The laws and rules that govern the securities industry in the United States are derived from this concept: "All investors, whether large institutions or private individuals, should have access to certain basic facts about an investment prior to buying it." To achieve this goal, the SEC requires public companies to disclose meaningful financial (and other) information to the public.

In addition to monitoring publicly held companies, the SEC oversees stock exchanges, broker-dealers, investment advisors, mutual funds, and public utility holding companies.

The Sarbanes-Oxley Act of 2002

In spite of the SEC, corporate scandals, deceptions, and bankruptcies continued. Especially conspicuous was the period from 2000 to 2002:

- 2000: 176 public companies with assets of $95 billion filed for bankruptcy
- 2001: 257 public companies with assets of $259 billion filed for bankruptcy
- 2002: 189 public companies with assets of $382 billion filed for bankruptcy

Two of the most infamous corporate bankruptcies and scandals during this period occurred at Enron Corporation and WorldCom, Inc. Tyco International, Ltd., was also involved in a scandal, but bankruptcy was not imminent. Although there were several other notable bankruptcies and scandals during these years, information on these three companies will provide an overview of the types of problems that led to the passage of the Sarbanes-Oxley Act of 2002.

Enron Corporation had 21,000 employees and was one of the world's leading electricity, natural gas, and communications companies. In 2001, Enron filed for bankruptcy—the second largest bankruptcy in U.S. history. This corporate collapse caused big financial losses for creditors, and thousands of employees lost their life savings, because their 401(k) plans were tied to Enron's stock. In 2002, WorldCom (at that time, the nation's No. 2 long-distance phone company, with 60,000 employees) filed for Chapter 11 bankruptcy after it revealed that it had improperly booked $3.8 billion in expenses. WorldCom's bankruptcy is the largest in U.S. history, dwarfing that of Enron Corp. Again, shareholders and creditors were saddled with huge financial losses. In 2002, Tyco's former management was charged with improper and illegal activities, including nearly $100 million in unauthorized payments to them or associates.

The fall of these three mega-companies, as well as other corporate catastrophes, caused public confidence in corporate reporting and in the reliability of the public accounting profession to sink to critically low levels. The stock market downturn during 2000–2002 was widespread. The technology bubble burst in March 2000 was another factor that contributed to the volatility of the stock market.

The Sarbanes-Oxley Act of 2002 was passed by Congress to protect investors from the potential of fraudulent accounting activities by publicly held corporations. This legislation improves the accuracy and reliability of corporate disclosures under securities laws. It contains criminal provisions applicable to a company's management and its public auditing firm. These provisions strengthen criminal sanctions for violators by creating new federal criminal offenses and increasing penalties for existing federal criminal offenses.

The Sarbanes-Oxley Act is arranged into 11 "titles." The more important sections relative to compliance within these titles are sections 302, 401, 404, 409, and 802. The topics covered in these sections are as follows:

- Section 302: Corporate Responsibility for Financial Reports

- Section 401: Disclosures in Periodic Reports

- Section 404: Assessment of Internal Controls

- Section 409: Disclosures

- Section 802: Criminal Penalties

The 10-K Report

The 10-K report is the official annual business and financial report filed by public companies with the SEC. Companies with at least 500 shareholders of one class of stock and at least $5 million in assets are required to file this report with the SEC. This document contains comprehensive information about the company, including financial statements and other financial information; a business summary; and a list of properties, subsidiaries, legal proceedings, and other information not usually found in the annual report to shareholders.

Annual Report to Shareholders

Annual reports give a detailed picture of a company's financial condition and the results of its operations. Annual reports include management's discussion of the previous year, an analysis of important company events, the company's stock price history, and financial data presented quantitatively on the income statement, balance sheet, and statement of cash flows. Statistics and graphs often accompany these statements.

Under Section 409 of the Sarbanes-Oxley Act, issuers of financial statements are required to disclose information on material changes in their financial condition or operations. These disclosures should be supported by graphic presentations as appropriate.

The SEC requires that audited financial reports be sent to the company's shareholders at the end of a company's fiscal year. In addition to the financial statements, a description of the company's operations and future outlook is required. Many companies go to considerable expense when creating the annual report, using high-quality, glossy paper and colorful pictures to make their report a showcase for the company.

The content of the annual report will vary somewhat from one company to another. Some companies will include their 10-K report, since it contains all of the financial statements and other shareholder information required for the annual report as well. Regardless of the differences in the production quality and reporting style, all annual reports to shareholders should contain the following:

- Letter to the shareholders

- Financial statements

- Notes to the financial statements

- Management assessment of internal controls

- Report of independent public accountants

- Certification of the annual report by company executives

We'll take a look at each of these elements in the following sections.

Letter to the Shareholders

The shareholders' letter highlights the company's activities during the past year, especially its acquisitions and the opening of new outlets. Typically, the letter discusses the company's growth activities and accomplishments. Financial highlights and graphs often are an integral part of the letter. The letter usually ends with upbeat plans for the future. The company's chief executive officer (CEO) signs the letter.

Financial Statements

The financial statements are written reports describing the financial health of a company and its operating results in quantitative terms. The financial statements include a balance sheet, an income statement, and a statement of cash flows. The financial statements are prepared and certified by a certified public accounting firm (the auditor).

Notes to the Financial Statements

The notes are an integral part of the financial statements because they provide valuable information; the absence of this information might make the financial statements incomplete or misleading. Notes serve as **disclosures** for items on the financial statements by doing the following:

- Explaining the composition of certain line amounts on the financial statements

- Explaining the meaning or calculation of certain line items on the financial statements

- Explaining critical company facts that cannot be conveniently shown in the body of statements due to limitations of financial statement formats

- Explaining critical events that have affected or might affect the company

The disclosure of information must be sufficient so that the reader can make an informed judgment or decision. Disclosure is not limited only to financial statement data. Any fact that would affect the reader's judgment must be disclosed. For example, if a company has lost a customer that represented a significant portion of its sales, that information must be disclosed. The disclosure must state the percentage of business represented by that customer and its potential effect on the business.

Sometimes the numbers shown on the financial statements do not provide complete information. For example, the balance sheet may show accounts receivable on one line at net realizable value. The notes will disclose the amount the company has estimated for bad debts (allowance for doubtful accounts) so that the reader is properly informed.

Notes to the financial statements may consist of several pages; it is not unusual for notes to constitute more of an annual report than the financial statements. Notes cover a variety of items, including the following.

Accounting policies. This should be the first note. A description of all significant accounting policies such as depreciation and amortization methods, inventory valuation, and accounting principles specific to the industry must be disclosed.

Lease information. Financial statements do not indicate the long-term dollar commitment of operating lease contractual obligations. Therefore, this type of note discloses the lease period and payments required under the leases.

Discontinued operations. This type of note discloses any business segment that has been disposed of or is the subject of a formal plan for disposal. The particular business segment may be a product line or a subsidiary.

Contingent liabilities. This type of note explains an existing condition, situation, or circumstance involving uncertainty as to possible loss which cannot be determined until a future event occurs or fails to occur. Some examples of **contingent liabilities** that may need disclosure are pending lawsuits, possible tax assessments, future commitments, and loan guarantees.

Contingent liabilities for which the amount can be *estimated* and the loss is *probable* are shown in the financial statements and also explained in this type of note.

Liabilities for which the amount cannot be estimated and the loss is probable or *possible* are explained in the notes but do not appear in the financial statements.

If a contingency is *remote*, it is not shown in the financial statements and there is no requirement for disclosure in the notes to the financial statements unless the contingency applies to a loan guarantee. Sometimes a company may enter into a contract that guarantees payment of a loan for another company. This other company could be a subsidiary, supplier, or favored customer. This type of guarantee obligates the guarantor to pay the loan should the borrower default. Even if the likelihood of the borrower not paying the note is remote, disclosure is required.

Management Assessment of Internal Controls

Under Section 404 of the Sarbanes-Oxley Act, publicly held companies are required to publish information in their annual reports concerning:

- The scope and adequacy of the company's internal control structure.

- The company's procedures for financial reporting.

- A statement assessing the effectiveness of the company's internal controls and procedures.

Report of Independent Public Accountants

The independent accountants' report is often called the Accountant's Letter or Auditor's Report. The auditor or auditing firm certifies that the financial statements meet the requirements of GAAP, and that the auditor's examination complied with mandatory auditing standards. In some cases, the auditor may give a certification with restrictions, or no certification at all. Each of these certifications is referred to as an "opinion." The term "opinion" regarding financial statements has legal significance and can be used only by certified public accountants. The "opinion" can be in the form of a(n):

- Unqualified opinion

- Qualified opinion

- Adverse opinion

- No opinion

An **unqualified opinion** is given when the financial statements fairly present, in all material respects, a company's financial position, results of operations, and cash flows in conformity with GAAP. An unqualified opinion is also called a "clean opinion" and, from the company's viewpoint, is the most desirable form of opinion. A **qualified opinion** is given when, except for a certain specific issue (as described by the auditor or auditing firm), the financial statements fairly present the company's financial position, results of operations, and cash flows in conformity with GAAP. An **adverse opinion** is given when a company's financial statements are not fairly presented, or the company's system of internal controls has deficiencies. In extreme cases, the auditor may express **no opinion** on the financial statements, especially if the scope of the audit was insufficient or impeded by the company's management or staff.

In addition to the auditor's opinion of the financial statements, Section 404 of the Sarbanes-Oxley Act requires that the public accounting firm, in its auditor's report, assess and report on the effectiveness of the company's internal control system and procedures for financial reporting. Under Section 802 of the Sarbanes-Oxley Act, the accountant or accounting firm that knowingly and willfully violates the requirement that all audit or review papers be maintained for a period of five years will face fines and/or imprisonment of up to ten years.

Certification of the Annual Report by Company Executives

Two certifications of the annual report are required. One relates to the 10-K report and is usually signed by the CEO. The other certification relates to the annual report and is usually signed by the CEO and chief financial officer (CFO).

Under Section 302 of the Sarbanes-Oxley Act, executives must certify their company's financial statements. This certification signifies that:

- The signing officers have reviewed the report.

- The report does not contain any misleading or materially untrue statements or material omissions.

- The financial statements and related information fairly present the company's financial condition and results of operations.

- The signing officers are responsible for internal controls and have evaluated these internal controls within the previous 90 days.

- The officers have provided a list of all deficiencies in the internal controls and information on any fraud that involves employees who are involved with internal activities.

- The signing officers have disclosed whether or not there were any significant changes in internal controls or in other factors that could negatively affect the internal controls, and any corrective actions taken.

Pursuant to Section 401 of the Sarbanes-Oxley Act, financial statements are required to be accurate, containing no incorrect statements.

Under Section 802 of the Sarbanes-Oxley Act, penalties of fines and/or up to 20 years imprisonment are imposed for altering, destroying, mutilating, concealing, or falsifying records with the intent to obstruct, impede, or influence a legal investigation.

How to Read an Annual Report

Many people have trouble understanding annual reports because they attempt to read them as they would read a book. The information in annual reports is scattered, and there is no standard format or sequence. The annual report of one company may be totally different from the report of another company.

Starting Point. The experienced reader *starts* with the *auditor's report*. The auditor's report is usually found just after the footnotes and just before the back cover of the annual report. The reader may proceed immediately to the third paragraph and look for a *clean opinion*. A paragraph with "except for" or other qualifying statements might signal serious trouble. Auditors are sometimes reluctant to use straightforward, strong language because of the client relationship. While they do make the qualification, they often use a subtle approach. Therefore, if the third paragraph does not present a clean opinion, it may be a warning, and care should be taken in studying the complete annual report.

The President's Letter. Some experienced readers save reading the president's letter until they are nearly finished with the annual report. Others prefer to read it before proceeding to the financial statements because they feel it serves as a prelude to what the statements might reveal. A careful reading of this letter can be useful because the president reviews the past year, unveils new products or new company developments, or discusses the targeting of new markets.

Financial Statements in an Annual Report

The set of audited statements and accompanying footnotes tells the story of the company's financial success or failure. Some experienced readers claim that they get more from the financial statements if they first read the footnotes and then the financial statements. Other readers prefer to move back and forth between the financial statements and the footnotes. The method of reading an annual report is a matter of personal preference. In any case, it is probably not advisable to concentrate solely on the financial statements without referring to the footnotes.

Conclusion of an Annual Report

The annual report may provide trends for the last five or ten years and selected statistical information that requires careful reading. The sequence of reading this data varies with the skills and interests of the reader.

If key ratios are not provided, the reader will need to calculate the ratios and interpret the results.

After studying an annual report and analyzing ratios, it is not unusual for a reader to go back and read the report again. Reading the report a second time allows the reader to focus more on individual details and content.

Investor Relations Department

Most corporations make a sincere effort to communicate with their shareholders and the investment community. They will gladly send copies of their annual reports, answer questions, advise of the next shareholders' meeting, and respond to other investor-related concerns. The address and telephone number of the corporation's investor relations department is usually found on the inside of the back cover of the annual report.

References

www.soxlaw.com/introduction.htm

www.soxlaw.com/s404.htm

www.thelenreid.com/articles/article/art_138_idx.htm

www.investopedia.com/

www.investopedia.com/terms/s/sarbanesoxleyact.asp

www2.lib.udel.edu/subj/bsec/resguide/annual10.htm

www.sec.gov/about/whatwedo.shtml

www.aicpa.org/members/glossary/u.htm

www.sec.gov/about/laws/soa2002.pdf

www.cnn.com/SPECIALS/2002/enron/

www.money.cnn.com/2002/07/19/news/worldcom_bankruptcy/

www.bofabusinesscapital.com/resources/capeyes/a04-03-155.html

www.boston.com/business/articles/2004/06/15/ama_cites_mass_malpractice_
premiums?pg=2

🔑 Key Terms

accountant's report—See auditor's report.

adverse opinion—A statement in an auditor's report given when a company's financial statements are not fairly presented, or the system of internal controls has deficiencies.

annual report—A comprehensive report on a publicly held company's financial operations over the previous year. It includes audited financial statements. The SEC requires that it be sent to the company's shareholders.

auditor's report—A report, prepared by an independent auditor, that accompanies the financial statements and explains the degree of responsibility assumed by the auditor for those financial statements. Also referred to as the *accountant's report.*

consolidated financial statements—Financial statements that present the combined financial data of a company and its controlled subsidiaries as if they were a single business entity; that is, the combined assets and liabilities of the companies are reported on one balance sheet, their combined revenues and expenses are reported on one income statement, and their combined cash flows are reported on one statement of cash flows.

contingent liabilities—Liabilities that are conditioned upon a future occurrence that may or may not take place.

disclosure—An explanation of a financial statement item or any fact about a company's financial condition.

generally accepted accounting principles (GAAP)—Professional accounting standards that have received substantial authoritative support and approval from professional accounting associations and governmental agencies.

intercompany transaction—A transaction between a parent company and any of its subsidiaries.

interim report—A condensed financial statement issued during the period between annual reports. Also called an *interim statement.*

minority interest—The equity interest in a subsidiary that is not owned by the parent, or the portion of a subsidiary's net assets owned by outsiders other than the parent.

no opinion—A statement in an auditor's report given when the scope of the audit was insufficient or impeded by the company's management or staff.

parent company—A company that exercises control over another company through ownership of all, or a majority of, the other company's voting stocks.

qualified opinion—A statement in an auditor's report given when, except for a certain specific issue as described therein, the financial statements are fairly presented.

Sarbanes-Oxley Act of 2002—An act that places additional requirements on management and the auditor or auditing firm regarding financial reporting and disclosures.

Securities and Exchange Commission (SEC)—A government agency regulating the securities industry.

subsidiary company—A company that is controlled by another company.

10-K report—The official annual business and financial report filed by public companies with the Securities and Exchange Commission; also called a Form 10-K report.

unqualified opinion—A statement in an auditor's report given when a company's financial statements are fairly presented. It is also called a "clean opinion" and is the most desirable form of opinion from the company's viewpoint.

Review Questions

1. What is an interim financial statement?

2. What does the term *independent certified public accountant* mean?

3. What professional standards does the CPA use to perform an audit service?

4. What is the purpose of an audit?

5. What is the scope of an audit?

6. What is an auditor's report? Describe each paragraph of the auditor's report.

7. What professional standards does the CPA use to perform a review service?

8. What is the purpose of a review?

9. What is the scope of a review?

10. What professional standards does the CPA use to perform a compilation service?

11. What is the purpose of a compilation?

12. What is the scope of a compilation?

13. Under what conditions are consolidated financial statements required?

14. What are some of the disclosures that might appear in the notes to the financial statements?

15. What is a contingent liability? Give examples.

16. What two types of annual reports does the SEC require?

17. What kind of agency is the SEC? What is its primary mission?

18. What is the significance of October 1929?

19. Why was the SEC created?

20. What is the importance of the Sarbanes-Oxley Act of 2002? Of what significance are sections 302, 401, 404, 409, and 802 of the act?

21. What is a 10-K Report?

22. What types of opinions can a certified public accounting firm give in its auditor's reports?

23. What is the standard content of an annual report to shareholders?

Internet Sites

For more information, visit the following Internet sites. Remember that Internet addresses can change without notice. If the site is no longer there, you can use a search engine to look for additional sites.

AICPA Code of Conduct
www.aicpa.org/about/code/index.html

Annual reports—free downloads
www.annualreportservice.com
www.irin.com/cgi-bin/main.cgi?index=main
www.reportgallery.com

Audit: description and slide show
www.busn.ucok.edu/cknapp/Auditing%20PPT/ch_01/sld005.htm

Consolidated Financial Statements
http://insurance.cch.com/rupps/consolidated-financial-statement.htm
www.dummies.com/WileyCDA/DummiesArticle/id-2840.html

Financial Statements description and slide show
www.business.gsw.edu/busa/faculty/jkooti/Finance/Pres/Chapt3/sld001.htm

Form 10-K
www.sec.gov/answers/form10k.htm

Sample annual report: Northampton Group, Inc.
www.nhgi.com/MS/MS1/page.php?p=19

Sarbanes-Oxley Act of 2002
www.sec.gov/about/laws/soa2002.pdf

Securities and Exchange Commission
www.sec.gov

SEC documents that public companies must file
www.sec.gov/edgar.shtml

SEC's Office of Investor Education and Assistance
www.sec.gov/investor.shtml

Problems ──────────────────────────────

Problem 1

Complete a consolidated worksheet from the following supplementary information and worksheet data:

1. The period is for the year ended 12/31/X9.

2. The parent company's name is Don-Bess, Inc., and the subsidiary's name is Deb-Mar, Inc.

3. The parent owns 100 percent of Deb-Mar's voting stock. There is no preferred stock.

4. The subsidiary was purchased for cash in 20X9 at the book value of its assets and liabilities.

5. There were no sales and purchase transactions between the parent and subsidiary in 20X9.

6. No dividends were declared by either the parent or subsidiary.

	Parent	Subsidiary	Elimination	Consolidated
Cash	$ 70,000	$ 10,000		
Accounts receivable	50,000	20,000		
Inventories	30,000	15,000		
Receivable from subsidiary	10,000			
Prepaid expenses	3,000	1,000		
Investment in subsidiary	90,000		(1) (90,000)	
Land	70,000	30,000		
Building	150,000	92,000		
Equipment	30,000	20,000		
Accounts payable	(10,000)	(23,000)		
Payable to parent		(10,000)		
Accrued items	(8,000)	(6,000)		
Current portion of long-term debt	(20,000)	(12,000)		
Long-term debt (net of CP)	(60,000)	(30,000)		
Stock issued	(200,000)	(50,000)	(1) 50,000	
Retained earnings 1/1	(95,000)	(40,000)	(1) 40,000	
Sales	(400,000)	(100,000)		
Cost of sales	100,000	28,000		
Labor cost	120,000	32,000		
Other operating expenses	40,000	10,000		
Fixed expenses	28,000	12,000		
Income taxes expense	2,000	1,000		
Total	0	0		

Problem 2

Using the completed worksheet from Problem 1, prepare the three consolidated financial statements: income statement, statement of retained earnings, and balance sheet.

Case Study

Preparation of an Annual Report to Shareholders

ETOC Hotels, Inc., is a corporation listed on a major stock exchange; its market capitalization is over $900 million, and its common stockholders number in excess of 700,000. The company's fiscal year ends on December 31. In April, after the close of the fiscal year, the company's chief executive officer and chief financial officer are preparing the annual report to shareholders and a 10-K to file with the SEC. The CEO and CFO are also preparing for a meeting with their certified public accounting firm next week.

The CEO and CFO have decided the following issues:

- The annual report to shareholders will not include color pictures, because they are too costly to print.

- They will insert a copy of the 10-K report in the annual report, in lieu of a separate set of financial statements.

- The annual report will not contain any graphs, since they are too costly to prepare.

A review of the company's financial reports and system of internal control reveals that:

- The financial statements are in compliance with generally accepted accounting principles, and all material representations are included.

- The company installed an internal system of controls and procedures, but the system is insufficient to determine if any irregularities occurred. However, the CEO and CFO are confident that fraud or irregularities did *not* occur during the year.

During the fiscal year just ended, ETOC Hotels, Inc., made its first acquisition, of YAR, Inc. (a hotel amenities sales company) by purchasing 90 percent of YAR's common stock. The CEO prefers not to include YAR's financial data in ETOC's annual report because ETOC has held YAR's stock for less than a full year. In any case, the CEO will concur with the CFO's decision in this regard.

Challenge

Based on this information, compose a critique of ETOC's annual report, with references to sections of the Sarbanes-Oxley Act and/or the SEC, as applicable. Specifically:

1. Analyze and comment on the three decisions made by the CEO and CFO.

2. Decide what the auditor's opinion will be of the annual report—that is, will the auditor give the company an unqualified opinion, a qualified opinion, an adverse opinion, or a no opinion—regarding the company's financial statements and system of internal controls. Explain why the other types of opinions might not be proper in this instance.

3. Decide whether the CFO should choose to include the financial data of YAR, Inc., in the annual report of ETOC Hotels, Inc. Explain why or why not.

4. Analyze and comment on any other item that requires further consideration.

Chapter 13 Outline

Responsibility Accounting
Action Traits of Expenses
Variable Expenses
    Strategies for Budgeting Variable
        Expenses
Fixed Expenses
Semi-Variable Expenses
    High-Low Method
    Regression Analysis Method
Breakeven Point
Contribution Margin
Profit Target
Effects of Volume and Price Increases
Appendix: Regression Analysis

Competencies

1. Define responsibility accounting and explain how it affects a manager's role and duties. (p. 355)

2. Define and create budgets for variable, fixed, and semi-variable expenses. (pp. 356–363)

3. Determine breakeven points, contribution margins, and profit targets. (pp. 363–365)

4. Describe the effects of a price increase on costs. (pp. 365–366)

13

Budgeting Expenses

Hospitality financial managers make decisions and use strategies to accomplish the ultimate business goal, which is to maximize the owners' wealth. Successful managers coordinate technology, guest service principles, human resources, and financial management to accomplish this goal. Forecasting sales and budgeting expenses are important steps in planning the future prosperity of a company.

This chapter will concentrate on the budgeting of expenses. It will answer such questions as:

1. What effect does volume have on the action traits of variable, semi-variable, and fixed expenses?

2. How can knowledge of these action traits be used to budget expenses?

3. What is the high-low method?

4. What is regression analysis?

5. How are the action traits of expenses put to use in the analysis of breakeven point and profit goals?

6. What is contribution margin?

7. How do volume increases and price increases affect costs?

Responsibility Accounting

A cost is any expense of doing business. Costs include labor, cost of sales, supplies, and the many other expenses incurred in operating a hospitality business.

The hospitality industry uses the concept of responsibility accounting. Under this concept, only those costs that a manager can control are charged to the manager's department. That manager has the responsibility for and corresponding authority and control over the department's expenses.

Some managers think that the way to increase profits is to reduce costs. Cutting costs is a fundamental approach to budgeting and is not a very sophisticated solution to cost management. Cost-cutting is not practical when any further reduction would result in a significant decrease in customer service or product quality or quantity. Drastic reductions in quality and quantity may cause guest dissatisfaction, lower sales volume, perhaps even business failure.

Today's hospitality manager is expected to be sufficiently educated in financial areas to make superior profit-making decisions that unite the best interests of both the company and its guests.

Exhibit 1   Graphic Presentation of Variable Expense

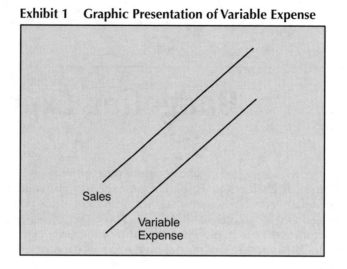

Action Traits of Expenses

The term **action trait** refers to how an expense reacts to changes in volume. Some expenses move incrementally with volume, while other expenses are not affected by volume. Covers, rooms, guests, and sales dollars are measurements of volume. Fundamentally, any expense can be categorized according to its reaction to volume as being *variable*, *semi-variable*, or *fixed*.

A useful equation that can be used to determine cost is as follows:

$$\text{Total Cost} = \text{Variable Cost} + \text{Fixed Cost}$$
$$\text{TC} = \text{VC} + \text{FC}$$

If two components of this equation are known, the equation can be easily manipulated to determine the unknown component as follows:

$$\text{TC} = \text{VC} + \text{FC}$$
$$\text{VC} = \text{TC} - \text{FC}$$
$$\text{FC} = \text{TC} - \text{VC}$$

Variable Expenses

Variable expenses are the only expenses that have a direct relationship with volume, as shown graphically in Exhibit 1. If the quantity sold goes up by one unit, the variable expense also goes up by one unit of expense. Stated another way, a variable cost is the additional or marginal cost a business incurs when it produces one more unit of whatever it sells. This association is called a *linear* relationship.

The action trait of a variable expense and its relationship to volume is demonstrated as follows.

Unit Sales	Sales $	Variable Expense	% of Sales $
0	$ 0	$ 0	--
1	10	3	30%
2	20	6	30%
10	100	30	30%
50	500	150	30%

Each unit sale of $10 creates a corresponding $3 unit of variable expense. Note that, while the total *dollar* cost of the variable expense changes, the unit *percentage* remains the same. Also note that there is no variable expense if there is no sales volume.

Typical variable expenses in the hospitality industry include cost of food sold, cost of beverage sold, and any cost of sales.

Budgeting is not an exact science. Menu changes and seasonal purchase cost changes affect the best-laid plans. As hospitality managers use budgets, they get better at it. Managers learn that it is not always easy to define expenses neatly as variable, semi-variable, or fixed. Quite often, professional judgment must also be used to classify expenses. In this context, guest supplies and other supplies are often classified as variable expenses as well.

Some critics argue that volume purchasing can be used to change the relationship of variable expenses to volume. The rebuttal to this argument is that the linear relationship is based on a **relevant range.** That is, the linear relationship is based on normal operations. The business is assumed to be purchasing quantities that are suitable for its sales volume. Unessential increases in purchasing volumes can result in spoilage, possible disappearance, and the ill-advised use of funds. Any significant change in relevant range merely requires a new analysis to determine the changed relationship.

Strategies for Budgeting Variable Expenses

Variable expenses are simple to budget because the variable expense percentage remains constant. If food cost is 34 percent at one level of sales dollar volume, it will be 34 percent at any level of sales dollar volume. This static percentage will be true as long as menu prices do not change. (The effect of price changes will be discussed later.)

Assume that an income statement shows the following:

Net Food Sales	$100,000
Cost of Food Sales	34,000

The food cost percentage is 34 percent, computed by dividing the $34,000 cost of sales by the $100,000 net sales volume. If management forecasts that the next period's food sales will be $125,000, the food cost for the period is calculated as follows:

$ 125,000	Food Sales
× 34%	Food Cost Percentage
$ 42,500	Forecasted Food Cost

The food cost budget is estimated at $42,500. Since food cost is a variable expense, the percentage can be used at any volume within a relevant range.

Exhibit 2   Graphic Presentation of Fixed Expense

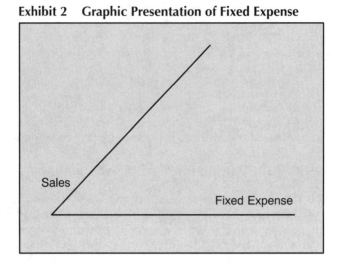

Fixed Expenses

Fixed expenses are sometimes imprecisely defined as those expenses that stay the same regardless of volume. The more precise and accurate definition is that *fixed expenses are those expenses that are not affected by volume.* The relationship of a fixed expense to volume is shown graphically in Exhibit 2. When volume goes up by one or more units, the fixed expense is not affected.

The action trait of a fixed expense and its relationship to volume is demonstrated below.

Unit Sales	Sales $	Fixed Expense	% to Sales $
0	$ 0	$50	--
1	10	50	500%
2	20	50	250%
10	100	50	50%
50	500	50	10%

Examples of fixed expenses for a hospitality business are depreciation, amortization, rent, interest, property taxes, and insurance. Unlike variable expenses, fixed expenses are incurred even if volume is zero. However, a fixed expense remains fairly constant as volume increases.

Fixed expenses are simple to budget because the expense *dollar* remains relatively constant. If the daily fixed expense is $50, it will be $50 at any sales level. The percentage of a fixed cost cannot be used to budget expenses because there is no linear relationship of a fixed expense to volume.

A new analysis of fixed expense is required if the hospitality business expands or changes its relevant range of operations.

Exhibit 3 Graphic Presentation of Semi-Variable Expense

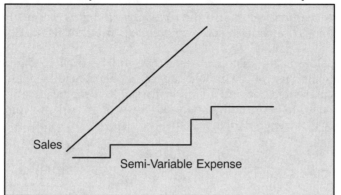

Semi-Variable Expenses

Semi-variable expenses consist of mixed elements: one portion is variable and another is fixed. Unlike variable and fixed expenses, semi-variable expenses do *not* have a predictable reaction to volume. The pattern of a particular semi-variable expense might look like a series of steps, as shown in Exhibit 3. If volume goes up one or more units, the semi-variable expense does not have any direct relationship to it that can be stated in dollars or a percentage. The semi-variable expenses include payroll and related expenses and any expense that is not variable or fixed.

The action trait of labor, a semi-variable expense, and its relationship to volume is demonstrated below. Payroll and related expenses rank with food cost as the largest operating expenses in the hospitality industry. Expenses related to payroll are employee-related costs such as fringe benefits, payroll taxes, and employee meals. Regardless of the volume level, there is no consistent percentage or dollar relationship.

Unit Sales	Sales $	Semi-Variable Expense	% to Sales $
0	$ 0	$ 20	--
1	10	20	200%
2	20	30	150%
10	100	60	60%
50	500	100	20%

A semi-variable expense cannot be precisely estimated unless it is separated into its fixed and variable components. Since a variable expense has a predictable percentage and a fixed expense has a predictable dollar amount, separating these mixed expenses allows accurate budgeting of a semi-variable expense.

Two methods that can be used to separate a semi-variable cost into its variable and fixed components are the high-low method and the regression analysis method.

High-Low Method

The **high-low method**, also called the *maximum-minimum method*, is a fast, easy procedure used to separate a semi-variable expense into its variable and fixed components.

Listed below is the historical data that will be used to demonstrate this method. Note: Because of the limited capacity of hand-held business calculators, the amounts presented here are intentionally small. Also, the 12 previous months are normally used to perform this analysis. However, to keep our computations to a minimum, we present only five months.

Month	Rooms Volume	Semi-Variable Expense
1	160	$75
2	140	65
3	150	60
4	220	90
5	180	85

Step 1: Set up a working paper as follows:

	Expense	Volume
High volume month		
Low volume month		

Step 2: Next, enter the high and low volumes:

	Expense	Volume
High volume month		220
Low volume month		140

Step 3: Enter the semi-variable expenses associated with the respective volumes:

	Expense	Volume
High volume month	$90	220
Low volume month	65	140

Step 4: Subtract to get the variance between the high and low amounts:

	Expense	Volume
High volume month	$90	220
Low volume month	65	140
Variance	$25	80

Step 5: Divide the *expense variance* by the *volume variance* to arrive at a variable rate per unit:

$$\frac{\text{Expense variance}}{\text{Volume variance}} = \frac{\$25}{80} = \$.3125 \text{ unit variable rate}$$

Step 6: Use the basic total cost equation to determine the variable and fixed portions of the cost: TC = VC + FC. Recall that when we know two components of this equation, we can manipulate it to determine the third. We know total cost. VC is computed by multiplying the volume by the unit variable rate. *Either the high or low volume can be used in this step.* Each will result in the same answer.

$$VC = 220 \times \$.3125$$
$$= \$69$$

$$TC - VC = FC$$
$$\$90 - \$69 = \$21$$

Interpretation of result: For the high month, the fixed cost is $21. Since fixed costs are not affected by volume, it can be stated that the fixed cost for *any* month is $21. Therefore, in this case, the fixed cost portion of this semi-variable expense is stated as $21 per month, or $252 for a year.

In this example, the high-low method produced a variable rate per room of $.3125 and a fixed cost per year of $252. If the marketing department forecasts that rooms volume will be 3,000 rooms sold next year, the estimated budget for this semi-variable expense for next year is determined as follows:

$$TC = VC + FC$$
$$= (3,000 \times \$.3125) + \$252$$
$$= \$1,190$$

The forecasted annual budget for this particular semi-variable expense is $1,190.

Limitations of the High-Low Method. The high-low method uses two points: the high volume and low volume for the period. If volume fluctuates significantly from month to month, the fixed cost result might not be as precise as desired. The high-low method is very useful because it is easy and fast to use. For significant semi-variable expenses, however, it might be more suitable to use a refined method such as regression analysis.

Regression Analysis Method

The **regression analysis method**, also called the *least squares method*, is a more accurate method than the high-low method because it correlates all the data for a period instead of using just two points.

The manual procedure for regression analysis (shown in the Appendix to this chapter) is tedious and complex. This disadvantage can be easily overcome through use of a computer spreadsheet application. After the data (volumes and expenses) are entered, the software can quickly calculate the fixed and variable elements of a semi-variable expense. The user does not need to remember any formulas or perform any tedious mathematical functions. Much time can be saved when analyzing several semi-variable expenses because, once the data for volume is entered, it can be used again for each semi-variable expense.

The actual processes of setting up the calculations may vary somewhat from one software program to another, but they are often quite similar. The following discussion is based on the Excel program.

Computing the Fixed Portion of a Semi-Variable Expense. The first step is to prepare the computerized spreadsheet as follows:

Exhibit 4   Regression Analysis Computerized Spreadsheet

	A	B	C	D	E	F
1	Month	Volume (X)	SV Expense (Y)			
2	1	160	75			
3	2	140	65			
4	3	150	60			
5	4	220	90			
6	5	180	85			

Explanation:

Columns are labeled with a letter, A through Z. Columns beyond Z use two letters.

Rows are labeled with a number, starting with 1.

Cells contain the data and information. Each cell is referenced by an address that is a combination of its column letter and row number. In this case, the quantity of 160 in the volume column is referenced as cell B2; and the quantity of 220 in the volume column is referenced as cell B5.

Range of cells refers to a series of data. The format is to enter the first cell, a colon, and then the last cell. In this case, to perform a mathematical function on all volume quantities, the range of cells is identified as B2:B6.

1. Set up two columns, one labeled *X* and the other labeled *Y*.

2. Enter the volume (called the independent variable) in the *X* column. Enter the semi-variable expense in the *Y* column. Refer to Exhibit 4 for the completed worksheet.

3. Click *fx* (the *Paste Function* button at top of screen).

4. Highlight *Statistical* in Function Category and highlight *Intercept* in Function Name. Click OK.

5. In the Intercept frame, enter the cell range for *Y* and *X*. In the example shown in Exhibit 4, the entry for *Y* is C2:C6 and the entry for *X* is B2:B6.

After the cell ranges are entered, the program automatically computes and shows the result. In this case, the result is 13.375, which is rounded to 13. This result means the fixed cost for any month is $13, or $156 for one year.

Computing the Variable Rate of a Semi-Variable Expense. The data previously entered in the *X* and *Y* columns of the spreadsheet is used again without any need for further entries.

Once again the Paste Function button is employed. The procedure is identical, except that this time *Slope* is highlighted as the function name instead of *Intercept*. The cell ranges are repeated for *X* and *Y*. Using the data in Exhibit 4, the variable rate is $.3625 (related to volume).

Forecasting Expenses from Regression Analysis Results. In the previous examples, the components for a particular semi-variable expense were as follows:

> Annual fixed expense $156
> Variable rate of $.3625 (associated with units of volume)

If the marketing department forecasts rooms volume at 3,000 rooms sold next year, the estimated budget for this semi-variable expense for the same period is determined as follows:

$$
\begin{aligned}
\text{TC} \quad &= \quad \text{VC} + \text{FC} \\
&= \quad (3,000 \times \$.3625) + \$156 \\
&= \quad \$1,244
\end{aligned}
$$

The forecasted annual budget for this particular semi-variable expense is $1,244.

Limitations of Regression Analysis. As with any statistical methodology, regression analysis provides only an estimate. The real number may be more or less than the computed result. Also, any forecasting method requires the user to ascertain that a relationship does indeed exist between the expense and volume.

However, no substitute exists for having an objective target based on careful analysis and proven methodology. Regression analysis is a feasible method because it correlates numerous data, and its results have been determined to be dependable through many years of usage.

Breakeven Point

The **breakeven point** is the level of sales at which there will be no profit or loss before income taxes. The property breaks even. The zero profit or loss is *not* the breakeven point. The following example clarifies this distinction:

Sales	$100,000	← *Breakeven point*
Variable Costs	70,000	
Contribution Margin	30,000	
Fixed Costs	30,000	
Income (Loss)	$ 0	← *Breakeven*

The computation of a breakeven point requires that all expenses be listed on a working paper and grouped as variable or fixed, as shown in Exhibit 5. This analysis can be performed using the previous year's financial data or the current year's budget. The semi-variable expenses require separation into their variable or fixed elements by use of the high-low method, regression analysis, or professional judgment. Once all expenses are grouped, a total is taken to arrive at variable costs and fixed costs. The variable cost percentage is computed by dividing the total variable expenses by the sales dollars.

After the working paper is completed, the data can then be applied to the breakeven point formula. The formula to compute breakeven point (sales volume) is as follows:

Exhibit 5   Worksheet to Group Costs

Forecasted Sales		$200,000			
Budgeted Expense	**Type**	**TC**	**VC**	**FC**	**Comments**
Cost of food sold	V	$ 61,000	$ 61,000		
Payroll & related	SV	58,000	36,000	$ 22,000	Regression analysis
Guest supplies	V	3,000	3,000		
Operating supplies	V	8,000	8,000		
Utilities	SV	9,000	7,000	2,000	High-low method
Other variable cost	V	10,000	10,000		} In actual practice,
Other fixed costs	F	12,000		12,000	} each expense is
Other SV costs	SV	7,000	5,000	2,000	} listed individually.
Total expenses	SV	$168,000	$130,000	$ 38,000	
IBIT		$ 32,000			

$$\text{Variable Cost \%} = \frac{VC}{\text{Sales}} = \frac{\$130,000}{\$200,000} = 65\%$$

$$\text{Breakeven point} = \frac{\text{Fixed Costs}}{100\% - \text{Variable Cost \%}}$$

often condensed as

$$\text{BEP} = \frac{FC}{100\% - VC\%}$$

Applying the breakeven formula with the information in Exhibit 5 results in the following:

$$\text{BEP} = \frac{\$38,000}{100\% - 65\%} = \$108,571$$

The breakeven point formula indicates that the company in Exhibit 5 will incur no profit and no loss at a sales volume of about $108,571. This breakeven point can be verified by the following procedure:

Sales	$108,571	← *Breakeven point*
VC ($108,571 × 65%)	70,571	
CM	38,000	
FC ($38,000 at any volume)	38,000	
Income Before Income Tax	$ 0	← *Breakeven*

It is a common custom to round variable cost percentages to whole percentages and to round the computed breakeven sales volume and all monetary calculations to whole dollars. This is done to condense the data and to avoid the implication that any planning formula produces exactness. These formulas produce approximate and very useful numbers, not precisely accurate forecasts.

Contribution Margin

Contribution margin is the amount of sales revenue that is contributed toward fixed costs and/or profit. It is calculated by subtracting variable costs from sales.

Sales	$ xxx
Variable Costs	(xxx)
Contribution Margin	xxx
Fixed Costs	(xxx)
IBIT	$ xxx

The abbreviation IBIT is a common business usage meaning *Income Before Income Taxes*. The abbreviation EBIT, meaning *Earnings Before Income Taxes*, is also commonly used in the profit-before-taxes line.

Profit Target

A hospitality business does not set a goal of breaking even. Instead, a more useful management tool is one that answers this question: What sales volume is required so we can achieve a specific profit? Profit planning is a primary goal for any successful hospitality business. Planning for profits can be accomplished by using a modification of the breakeven formula as follows:

$$\text{Sales \$} = \frac{\text{FC} + \text{Profit Objective}}{100\% - \text{VC}\%}$$

Assume the company has a profit goal of $40,000 before income taxes. The data in Exhibit 5 provide this solution:

$$\text{Sales \$} = \frac{\$38,000 + \$40,000}{100\% - 65\%}$$

$$= \$222,857$$

The result indicates that a sales volume of $222,857 is required to achieve a profit goal of $40,000. This conclusion can be confirmed as follows:

Sales	$222,857	← *sales point*
VC ($222,857 × 65%)	144,857	
CM	78,000	
FC ($38,000 at any volume)	38,000	
IBIT	$ 40,000	← *profit target*

Effects of Volume and Price Increases

To this point, the chapter has presented principles of cost management that assumed that any increase in sales dollars was caused by an increase to sales volume. Regardless of quantity sold, the variable expense percentage remains the same. What if the increase in sales dollars is instead caused by a *price* increase?

A change in menu price has no effect on actual variable, semi-variable, or fixed costs. However, menu price changes do affect both sales dollars and variable cost *percentages*. To illustrate, consider the following example:

	1 Unit
Menu Price	$10.00
Food Cost	3.50
Food Cost %	35%

Increasing the menu price by $.75 changes the food cost percentage as follows:

	1 Unit
Menu Price	$ 10.75
Food Cost	3.50
Food Cost %	32.6% ($3.50 ÷ $10.75)

A menu price increase results in a decrease in food cost percentage, but there is no change to unit food *dollar* cost. Increasing menu price is one technique management can apply to reduce food cost percentage without affecting quality or quantity.

A menu price change requires a new computation of percentage relationship to sales for all variable costs and semi-variable costs. Since the relationship to sales for fixed costs is based on fixed cost dollars, the fixed costs are not affected.

🔑 Key Terms

action trait—A term referring to the way in which an expense reacts to changes in volume. Some expenses are incremental with volume, while other expenses are not affected by volume.

breakeven point—The level of sales at which there will be no profit or loss.

contribution margin—The amount of sales that contributes toward fixed costs and/or profits. It is computed by subtracting variable costs from sales.

fixed expenses—Expenses that are not affected by volume. Examples include depreciation, amortization, rent, interest, and property taxes.

high-low method—A fast, easy procedure used to separate a semi-variable expense into its variable and fixed components. Also called the *maximum-minimum method*.

regression analysis method—A procedure used to separate a semi-variable expense into its variable and fixed components. It is a more accurate method than the high-low method because it correlates all the data for a period instead of using just two points. Also called the *least squares method*.

relevant range—The normal range of business a company conducts, using the resources suitable for its sales volume.

semi-variable expenses—Expenses consisting of both variable and fixed portions. Semi-variable expenses are not directly related to volume. Examples include payroll and related expenses.

variable expenses—Expenses that move in direct linear relationship with unit volume.

Review Questions

1. What is the concept of responsibility accounting?

2. What are the three possible action traits of expenses? Can any individual expense possess all three action traits? What is the action trait of a variable expense? a fixed expense? a semi-variable expense?

3. What equation can be used to determine the components of total cost?

4. What major expense in a restaurant is a variable expense?

5. What are the six fixed expenses in the hospitality industry?

6. What major expense in a restaurant is a semi-variable expense?

7. What two methods can be used to determine the fixed component of a semi-variable expense?

8. What is the definition of breakeven point?

9. What is the definition of contribution margin?

10. What is IBIT?

Internet Sites

For more information, visit the following Internet sites. Remember that Internet addresses can change without notice. If the site is no longer there, you can use a search engine to look for additional sites.

Small Business Forecasting and Budgeting Tips
www.score.org/5_tips_s_cs_5.html
www.score.org/5_tips_bp_4.html
www.score.org/pdf/12%20Month%20Sales%20Forecast1.pdf

Budgeting Slide Show
www.aaasc.org/membership/documents/FRIA9amTritinger
   AAAHC2006Budgeting101.ppt

Fixed and Variable Expenses
www.small-business-dictionary.org/default.asp?term=VARIABLE+COST
www.entrepreneur.com/encyclopedia/term/82266.html
http://business.enotes.com/small-business-encyclopedia/fixed-variable-expenses

Breakeven Point
www.accountingcoach.com/online-accounting-course/01Xpg01.html
http://connection.cwru.edu/mbac424/breakeven/BreakEven.html
www.businesstown.com/accounting/projections-breakeven.asp

High-Low Method
www.accd.edu/sac/slac/ppointshows/acct/high_low.htm

Regression analysis
http://en.wikipedia.org/wiki/Regression_analysis
http://elsa.berkeley.edu/sst/regression.html

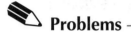 **Problems** ――――――――――――――――――――――――――

Problem 1

Compute the food cost percentage if sales are $200,000 and food cost is $65,000.

Problem 2

Budget the food cost if forecasted sales are $200,000 and the food cost percentage is 34 percent.

Problem 3

The rent expense is $1,000 at a sales level of $100,000. Budget the rent expense at a sales level of $200,000.

Problem 4

Budget the labor expense for a forecasted sales level of $200,000 from the following data:

Historical sales level: $100,000
Historical semi-variable: $30,000 (TC $30,000   =   VC $25,000 + FC $5,000)

Problem 5

Compute the monthly and annual fixed portion of the following semi-variable expense using the high-low method:

Month	Rooms Volume	Labor Cost
1	175	$100
2	125	80
3	128	79
4	200	120
5	150	90

Carry the unit variable rate to four decimals. Round the final answers to whole dollars.

Problem 6

Use the data in Problem 5 to compute the monthly fixed portion, annual fixed portion, and variable rate of this semi-variable expense using regression analysis. Round the fixed cost to whole dollars. Show the variable rate in decimal format, carried to four decimals properly rounded.

Problem 7

Assume that a certain semi-variable expense has an annual fixed portion of $58,000 and a variable rate of $4 per unit. Determine the budget for this semi-variable expense if volume is estimated at 30,000 annual units.

Problem 8

Complete the following working paper to separate costs into their variable and fixed amounts. Compute IBIT and the variable cost percentage.

Forecasted Sales $150,000

Budgeted Expense	Type	TC	VC	FC	Comments
Cost of food sold	V	45,000			
Payroll & related	SV	42,000			F=$7,000
Guest supplies	V	2,200			
Operating supplies	V	5,100			
Utilities	SV	7,000			F=$5,000
Other variable costs	V	6,200			
Other fixed costs	F	9,000			
Other SV costs	SV	7,000			F=$2,000
Total expenses		$123,500	$	$	

IBIT = $_____

VC% = _____%

Problem 9

Compute the breakeven point and verify it from the following data:

Fixed Costs: $140,000
Variable Cost Percentage: 60 percent

Problem 10

Compute the sales level and verify it to achieve a profit target of $200,000 from the data in Problem 9.

Problem 11

Compute the sales and food costs for the volumes below from the following data:

Menu Price $12.00
Food Cost   3.60

Covers	Sales	Food Cost
1		
10		
50		

Problem 12

Compute the food costs from the data in Problem 11, except assume that the menu price has changed to $12.75. Carry the food cost percentage to three decimal positions.

Covers	Sales	Food Cost
1		
10		
50		

Problem 13

Complete the working paper below and compute the breakeven point.

Forecasted Sales $200,000

Budgeted Expense	Type	TC	VC	FC	Comments
Cost of food sold		44,000			
Payroll & related		48,000			Use high-low method
Guest supplies		3,600			
Operating supplies		5,000			
Utilities		9,000			F=$6,000
Other variable cost		5,000			
Other fixed costs		6,000			
Other SV costs		7,000			F=$4,000
Total expenses		$127,600			
IBIT		$ 72,400			

The following information is provided for the high-low method:

	Volume	Expense
Jan	2,100	$ 3,000
Feb	2,200	3,000
Mar	2,300	3,000
Apr	3,000	4,000
May	3,400	5,000
Jun	4,500	5,000
Jul	7,000	6,000
Aug	4,500	5,000
Sep	4,000	5,000
Oct	2,400	3,000
Nov	2,300	3,000
Dec	2,000	3,000
Total		$48,000

Case Study

Budgeting Expenses and Breakeven Analysis

The Dotco Restaurant has been in business for two years but has never prepared a budget or used breakeven analysis as part of its management tools. The company will soon be in its third year of operation. Management realizes that it is not operating at optimum efficiency and profit levels.

You have been engaged as a consultant to the company. Management has provided you with historical data that you have analyzed. You have applied regression analysis as necessary to develop variable cost percentages and fixed costs data. Your results are shown on the following pro forma income statement working paper.

Dotco, Inc.
Pro forma Income Statement Workpaper

		$400,000	$500,000
Annual forecasted sales			
Expenses:			
Cost of sales	35% VC	_____	_____
Payroll & related	20% VC, $12,000 Fixed	_____	_____
Operating supplies	8% VC	_____	_____
Utilities	2% VC, $5,000 Fixed	_____	_____
Rent	$18,000 Fixed	_____	_____
Property insurance	$3,000 Fixed	_____	_____
Depreciation	$12,000 Fixed	_____	_____
Other	10% VC, $5,000 Fixed	_____	_____
Total expenses		_____	_____
IBIT		_____	_____
% of IBIT to sales (IBIT ÷ Sales)		_____	_____

Challenge

1. Prepare a typed report to management.

   a. Explain any assumptions, limitations, or other information that affect the scope of your engagement and calculations.

   b. Comment on whether budgeting and breakeven analysis are/are not exact sciences. Support your answer.

   c. Explain the advantages of budgeting and breakeven analysis.

   d. Include any suggestions to management.

2. Use the working paper above to prepare budgets for sales levels of $400,000 and $500,000.

3. Prepare a breakeven analysis with supporting mathematical proof that the breakeven sales volume will indeed result in a zero profit/loss.

Appendix: Regression Analysis

Regression analysis is based on the following formula:

$$\frac{(\Sigma y)(\Sigma x^2) \ - \ (\Sigma x)(\Sigma xy)}{n(\Sigma x^2) \ - \ (\Sigma x)^2}$$

The various symbols and characters in this formula are defined as follows:

Symbol	Meaning
Σ	Sum of or Total of.
Σy	Total of Expenses for all periods.
Σx	Total of Volume for all periods.
$(\Sigma x)^2$	Total of Volume for all periods, which is then squared.
(Σx^2)	Each period's Volume is squared, then totaled.
Σxy	Each period's Volume and Expense are multiplied, then totaled.
n	Number of periods (months, quarters, etc.).

The procedure for solving any formula is to replace the symbols with numbers. Neighboring parentheses and/or symbols are multiplied. For example, $(4)(5) = 20$ or $4(5) = 20$. Once all symbols are replaced, the basic math functions of add, subtract, multiply, and divide are used.

The five-month data from the example in the chapter will be used to demonstrate how the regression analysis formula is applied. The following is a step-by-step explanation. The entire result is shown in the illustration at the end of this procedure.

Step 1: Enter the volumes in a column labeled x and the expense data in a column labeled y.

	x	y
1	160	75
2	140	65
3	150	60
4	220	90
5	180	85
$n=5$		

Step 2: Total the x and y columns.

	x	y
1	160	75
2	140	65
3	150	60
4	220	90
5	180	85
	850	375
$n=5$	Σx	Σy

Step 3: Calculate the xy values and x^2 values. For each month, multiply the amount in column x by the amount in column y to get xy. For each month, multiply the x amount by itself to get x^2.

	x	y	xy	x^2
1	160	75	12000	25600
2	140	65	9100	19600
3	150	60	9000	22500
4	220	90	19800	48400
5	180	85	15300	32400
	850	375		
$n=5$	Σx	Σy		

Step 4: Total the xy and x^2 columns.

	x	y	xy	x^2
1	160	75	12000	25600
2	140	65	9100	19600
3	150	60	9000	22500
4	220	90	19800	48400
5	180	85	15300	32400
	850	375	65200	148500
$n=5$	Σx	Σy	Σxy	$\Sigma x2$

Step 5: Apply the regression analysis formula. Replace the symbols with the computed values. Complete the math process.

$$\text{Fixed Cost} = \frac{(\Sigma y)(\Sigma x^2) - (\Sigma x)(\Sigma xy)}{n(\Sigma x^2) - (\Sigma x)^2}$$

$$= \frac{(375)(148,500) - (850)(65,200)}{5(148,500) - (850)^2}$$

$$= 13.375$$

$$= 13 \text{ (rounded)}$$

Interpretation of result: The fixed cost portion of this semi-variable expense is stated as $13 per month, or $156 for a year.

Chapter 14 Outline

Competencies

1. Define and apply the concept of price elasticity of demand in a hospitality setting. (p. 375)

2. Identify the elements of revenue and describe how changes in one element may affect revenue. (pp. 376–377)

3. Describe and apply the moving average method and the percentage method of revenue forecasting. (pp. 377–379)

4. Describe and apply several statistical models that can be used to forecast rooms, food, and beverage sales. (pp. 379–386)

5. Use CVP analysis to forecast both revenue and unit sales. (pp. 387–392)

14

Forecasting Sales

ACCURATE SALES FORECASTS are an important element in planning and achieving a hospitality company's financial prosperity. Sales volume is the primary factor to consider when budgeting variable and semi-variable expenses. Forecasting sales is more difficult than budgeting expenses because sales revenue is not something a manager can control. Weather, competition, changing appetites, economic conditions, and other factors influence the demand for a hospitality service or product.

A mature hospitality business has a distinct advantage in forecasting sales compared with a start-up venture or rapidly expanding company. Fully developed hospitality operations have consistent historical results that might be used as a dependable basis in forecasting procedures.

In some cases, food and lodging companies may be affected by **price elasticity of demand,** the changes in demand due to price sensitivity. A small change in price followed by large changes in demand is called **elastic demand** and is of more concern to fast-service food operations and budget motels. A price change followed by no significant change in demand is called **inelastic demand;** it is more related to resorts, luxury hotels, and fine dining establishments. Competition, advertising, reputation, and other factors affect the elasticity of demand. Each hospitality business must determine whether price elasticity of demand is a factor in its sales volume.

This chapter will answer such questions as:

1. What are the elements of revenue?

2. Which will result in larger profits, a price increase or a volume increase?

3. What methods are available for forecasting sales?

4. What forecasting models are used in the food and lodging industry?

5. Why does forecasting liquor sales introduce issues that forecasting food and rooms sales does not?

6. How is average room rate calculated without any sales data?

7. What is the Hubbart formula?

8. What are the definitions of the terms *contribution margin* and *sales mix*?

9. How is CVP analysis used to forecast sales dollars and quantities?

Revenue Elements

Sales dollars (or revenue) are a consequence of two elements, *volume* and *price*. The potential interrelationships of volume and price are demonstrated by the following examples.

Revenue will go up if a price increase has no effect on volume. For example:

	Before	After
Volume	1,000	1,000
Menu Price	$5.00	$5.25
Sales	$5,000	$5,250

Revenue can go up despite a price decrease when linked with an increase in volume. For example:

	Before	After
Volume	1,000	1,100
Menu Price	$5.00	$4.80
Sales	$5,000	$5,280

Revenue can also go up after a price increase despite a decrease in volume. For example:

	Before	After
Volume	1,000	980
Menu Price	$5.00	$5.25
Sales	$5,000	$5,145

However, revenue can also go down after a price increase because of a decrease in volume. For example:

	Before	After
Volume	1,000	900
Menu Price	$5.00	$5.25
Sales	$5,000	$4,725

Similarly, revenue can go down after a price decrease despite an increase in volume. For example:

	Before	After
Volume	1,000	1,050
Menu Price	$5.00	$4.60
Sales	$5,000	$4,830

These examples present the elements behind some fundamental marketing questions: should prices be changed, and, if so, how? Will price increases generate increased profits? Will price decreases raise profits by creating enough of a volume increase to offset increased costs? Successful hospitality operations answer these questions by carefully examining their market conditions, competition, and price elasticity.

Interestingly, a given percentage increase applied to either price or volume produces the same increase to sales dollars. For example:

	Before	After 5% Price Increase	After 5% Volume Increase
Menu Price	$5.00	$5.25	$5.00
Volume	1,000	1,000	1,050
Sales $	$5,000	$5,250	$5,250

Are these situations identical? Assuming no change in volume, which increase will contribute to bigger profits? To answer this, recall that variable costs are incremental. The following analysis can be made:

	Before	5% Volume Increase	5% Price Increase
Sales	$200,000	$210,000	$210,000
VC	120,000 (60%)	126,000 (60%)	120,000 (57%)
CM	80,000	84,000	90,000
FC	60,000	60,000	60,000
IBIT	$ 20,000	$ 24,000	$ 30,000

A volume increase raises variable costs because of the incremental costs of the additional units sold. However, a price increase does not affect variable costs because there is no change in quantities sold. (Note also that price increases reduce the percentage of variable costs to sales.) Clearly, a price increase of a given percentage will boost profits more than an equivalent percentage volume increase.

Sales Forecasting Methods

There are many methods available for forecasting sales, ranging from simplistic to very sophisticated. The choice of any forecasting method should be based on whether it yields accurate forecasts rather than its sophistication.

Some forecasting techniques can be used for any time period. Forecasts can be made for one day, one month, or any period of time usually not exceeding one business year.

Forecasting deals with the future, which always has an element of uncertainty. Professional judgment and experience play an important part in the forecasting process.

This chapter covers the following forecasting methods:

- Moving average method
- Percentage method
- Statistical models
- CVP (cost-volume-profit) analysis

Moving Average Method

This method is more suitable for short-term than long-term forecasting. The moving average formula is:

$$\frac{\text{Volume in Base Period}}{\text{Weeks in Base Period}}$$

For example, assume that a hospitality establishment has selected a four-week base period as its moving average. As each new week's data becomes available, it is added to the total, and the oldest base week is deleted.

The following data illustrates how the moving average is computed for a restaurant operation using a four-week base period. The first base period is weeks one to four.

Weeks 1–4	Guests Served
1	750
2	760
3	740
4	800
Total	3,050

Forecasting the guest volume for week five is done as follows:

$$\frac{\text{Volume in Base Period}}{\text{Weeks in Base Period}} = \frac{3,050}{4} = 763 \text{ Estimated Guest Volume for Week Five}$$

The moving average forecast estimated a volume of 763 guests for the upcoming week 5.

Assume the actual volume for week five is 780. The manager then updates the actual weekly volume by deleting week one and adding week five to the four-week base period.

Weeks 2–5	Guests Served
2	760
3	740
4	800
5	780
Total	3,080

The forecast for week six is calculated as follows:

$$\frac{\text{Volume in Base Period}}{\text{Weeks in Base Period}} = \frac{3,080}{4} = 770 \text{ Estimated Guest Volume for Week Six}$$

As each week is ended, the oldest week is dropped and the most recent week is added to continue with a four-week base period moving average.

A hospitality operation may use any number of weeks in its base period. Using more weeks in a base period helps to smooth out the randomness in data. However, too many weeks will require tedious recordkeeping and calculations.

The moving average may not be appropriate for an operation with dramatic swings in volume. Caution is required for seasonal deviations or one-time volume increases due to special events.

Percentage Method

The percentage method is the simplest to use, and it gives accurate results. It is commonly used for year-to-year estimates. A percentage may be applied to volume, price, or both of these revenue elements.

This approach uses a base period and increases it by an expected growth percentage. For example, if sales for last year were $900,000 and sales growth is forecasted at 10 percent, the forecasted sales next year are estimated at $990,000.

Sales growth by way of volume or price increase does not necessarily fall within a company's normal business year. Assume that the following company has a calendar business year and plans a 10 percent menu price increase that will become effective in March. The company's seasonal business starts in May, and management expects a 20 percent volume increase from May to the end of the year. The forecasted sales for the first six months are computed as follows:

	Sales Last Year	Planned Price Increase	Expected Volume Increase	Forecasted Sales	
January	$ 50,000			$ 50,000	
February	60,000			60,000	
March	70,000	10%		77,000	(70,000 × 110%)
April	100,000	10%		110,000	(100,000 × 110%)
May	150,000	10%	20%	198,000	(150,000 × 110% × 120%)
June	200,000	10%	20%	264,000	(200,000 × 110% × 120%)

The forecast for the remainder of the year is continued accordingly until the sales for the 12 months are estimated.

Statistical Models

Statistical models can be used to forecast sales for a day or for any period up to one year. The data used in the forecasting model may be last year's data or, in the case of a new business, a combination of industry averages and known factors such as room rates or menu prices.

Rooms Revenue Statistical Model

The statistical model formula used to compute the revenue from rooms sales is as follows:

Rooms × Occupancy Percentage × Average Room Rate × Days Open

A motel expecting to sell 60 percent of its 200 rooms available for sale at an average daily rate of $50 for April forecasts its April sales as follows:

$$200 \times 60\% \times \$50 \times 30 = \$180,000$$

Accurate results from statistical models are easily obtained if the calculations are separately performed for each season or for cyclical business swings. These individual calculations can then be added to arrive at a sales forecast for the next year's period.

Food Revenue Statistical Model

The statistical model formula used to compute revenue from food sales is as follows:

$$\text{Seats} \times \text{Turnover} \times \text{Average Food Check} \times \text{Days Open}$$

Accurate use of a statistical model requires individual calculations for breakfast, lunch, and dinner because there are variations in turnover, average check, and, often, seats and days a meal is served.

For example, assume a restaurant has 100 seats available for breakfast and 150 seats for lunch and dinner. Breakfast and lunch are not served on Saturday and Sunday. Using its estimated turnover and average check data, the March food sales are forecasted as follows:

	Seats	×	Turnover	×	Average Food Check	×	Days Open	=	
Breakfast	100	×	4.0	×	$ 4	×	23	=	$ 36,800
Lunch	150	×	2.5	×	8	×	23	=	69,000
Dinner	150	×	2.0	×	14	×	31	=	130,200
Total									$236,000

A hospitality business can easily and accurately forecast its food sales using this statistical model.

Beverage Revenue Statistical Model

The forecasting of beverage sales using a variation of the food statistical model may not yield accurate results. A guest occupying one seat in the dining room has only one meal but may have several drinks or none at all. Some guests may prefer to stand and drink at the bar or in the lounge. An experienced hospitality manager might develop a model using statistical data based on the history of the particular operation.

Instead of using a model similar to that for food, a manager may decide to use historical averages and percentages. A percentage of liquor sales to food sales may prove to be a reasonable predictor of beverage sales for dining room guests. Daily averages might be good predictors of liquor sales in the bar and lounge. For instance, it is not unusual for bar/lounge sales to follow patterns that vary by the day of the week. Therefore, a model used to forecast beverage sales could be as follows:

Beverage Percentage × Food Sales	[for liquor sales in dining room]
+ Comparable Day's Sales	[for liquor sales in bar/lounge]
= Total Beverage Sales	

For example, suppose a restaurant recently performed a historical analysis of dining room sales and discovered that its liquor sales typically equal 30 percent of food sales. Assume a similar analysis of its day-to-day liquor sales in the bar and lounge shows the following:

Day	Bar/Lounge Liquor Sales
Monday	$1,000
Tuesday	1,200
Wednesday	1,800
Thursday	2,200
Friday	4,000
Saturday	3,400
Sunday	800

The total liquor sales for a Thursday with estimated food sales of $5,000 and a 30 percent food/liquor relationship in the dining room is computed as follows:

Dining Room: Beverage Percentage × Food Sales = 30% × $5,000	=	$1,500
Bar/Lounge: usual sales on a Thursday	=	2,200
Forecasted liquor sales for Thursday	=	$3,700

Average Room Rate

A lodging business offers different rates for various types of rooms and for different types of customers (corporate, group, tourist). Day of week and time of day may also affect room rates. Therefore, the rack rates (essentially the hotel's list prices) may not represent an average room rate.

A lodging business with historical sales data can compute its average room rate (ARR), also called average daily rate (ADR), by dividing room revenue by the number of paid rooms occupied. For example, the ARR for a hotel with $130,000 of rooms revenue that sold 2,000 rooms during that period is calculated as follows:

$$\frac{\$130,000}{2,000} = \$65 \text{ ARR}$$

A new lodging business could use forecasted sales data by substituting as follows:

$$\frac{\text{Forecasted Sales Dollars}}{\text{Forecasted Rooms Sold}}$$

Often, average room rate must be calculated without the luxury of having historical or forecasted sales data. Two methods that do not rely on historical or forecasted data are the weighted average method and the Hubbart formula.

Weighted Average Method. An average room rate is often necessary for planning purposes and sales forecasting. The only information available may be the planned rates by type of room. For example:

Room Type	Rooms	Room Rate
Single	20	$50.00
Double	50	80.00

A simple average ($50 + $80 ÷ 2) gives an ARR that will be incorrect unless an equal number of single and double rooms is sold. A more accurate procedure applies a weighted average as follows:

1. Multiply the rooms quantity by the room rate for each type of room to arrive at hypothetical daily sales.

2. Total the rooms quantity and hypothetical sales.

3. Divide the hypothetical sales by the rooms quantity to arrive at average daily rate.

Using the data given, the weighted average procedure is demonstrated as follows:

Room Type	Rooms	Room Rate	Hypothetical Daily Sales
Single	20	$50.00	$1,000
Double	50	80.00	4,000
Total	70		$5,000

$5,000 ÷ 70 = $71.43 Average Room Rate

This demonstration assumes that the occupancy percentage will be identical for each type of room. The calculations used 100 percent occupancy, but any equal occupancy percentage will produce the same result of $71.43.

If the expected occupancy percentage is different for each type of room, the weighted average procedure may be refined accordingly for those establishments desiring more precise data. For example:

Type	Rooms	Occupancy	Rooms Sold	Room Rate	Hypothetical Daily Sales
Single	20	70%	14	$50.00	$ 70
Double	50	80%	40	80.00	3,200
Total			54		$3,900

$3,900 ÷ 54 = $72.22 Average Room Rate

Hubbart Formula. The Hubbart formula is a method that is independent of planned or existing room rates. It is called a bottom-up approach to pricing because it starts with the data line called *income before income taxes,* which is near the bottom of the income statement. Next, the departmental data is entered until the rooms revenue required to achieve the stated goal is determined. The computed rooms revenue is then divided by the forecasted rooms sales to arrive at a theoretical average room rate required to achieve an intended profit.

The average room rate calculated by use of the Hubbart formula may be ideal and impractical because it ignores competitive rates. However, the rate determined by this formula can be useful in determining the feasibility of constructing a new lodging property.

The data used in the Hubbart formula can be listed in detail or in summary totals. For example, fixed charges such as interest, depreciation, amortization, property taxes, property insurance, and rents could be listed separately or shown as one line item called fixed charges. Support centers such as A&G, marketing, and property operation and maintenance could be listed separately or shown as one line item called support centers. This chapter will use summary line items to more concisely present the concept of the formula. In actual practice, supporting schedules accompany the working paper to provide the detail for each summary line item.

The basic procedure used in the Hubbart formula is as follows:

1. Enter the desired pretax income (income before income taxes) necessary to achieve a desired return on investment.

2. Add the fixed charges, utility costs, and support centers.

3. Take a total. This total represents the desired IBIT plus expenses of non-revenue centers before any income from revenue centers.

4. Enter the departmental income from the revenue centers *excluding* the rooms department.

5. Subtract the total income of the revenue centers (Step 4) from the total in Step 3. This new total represents the IBIT plus all departmental results with the exception of the rooms department.

6. Add in only the expenses for the rooms department.

7. Take a total. This new total represents the sales required by the rooms department to achieve the desired profit determined in Step 1.

8. Divide the required rooms sales dollars (Step 7) by the forecasted rooms sales. The result is the average room rate.

Consider the following example. Hotel DORO Enterprises is thinking about constructing a new 75-room hotel with an expected occupancy of 65.57 percent that translates to forecasted annual sales of 17,950 rooms (365 × 75 × 65.57%). An income before income taxes (pretax profit) of $66,138 is needed to generate the desired return on the owners' investment. Using this information and given departmental financial data, the procedure for completing the Hubbart formula is shown in Exhibit 1.

The $50.00 average room rate in Exhibit 1 is an average for all types of rooms. Further computations are necessary to assign different room rates to the various types of rooms. A simple way is to assign the resulting rate from the Hubbart formula to the lowest class of room and increase it accordingly with a fixed rate differential for the upper-class rooms. This approach would ensure that the realized room rate would never be below the Hubbart formula rate. In the case of Hotel DORO, a single room would have a rate of $50. If double rooms were to be stated at a $15 difference, the double room rate would be $65. This approach ignores competition and may not be achievable.

An alternative is to be more precise and compute differential rates that would mathematically produce a true average room rate of $50. The procedure is performed as follows:

1. Compute the rooms that will be sold daily.

2. Calculate the daily total sales.

3. Determine the occupancy percentage for double rooms.

4. Calculate the double rooms sold daily.

5. Calculate the single rooms sold daily.

Exhibit 1   Hubbart Formula for Hotel DORO

Supplementary Data:

Daily rooms available to sell: 75
Forecasted occupancy %:   65.57%
Forecasted rooms sold for the year: 17,950 (365 × 75 × 65.57%)

Desired pretax profit (IBIT): $66,138

Hubbart Formula Procedure:

1.	Desired pretax profit	$ 66,138
2.	Add:	
	Fixed charges	418,891
	Utility costs	47,312
	Support centers	293,603
3.	Total	825,944
4.	Less: Income from revenue centers, excluding rooms	133,683
5.	Net expenses before rooms department	692,261
6.	Rooms department expenses	205,239
7.	Total sales required by Rooms department	897,500
8.	Average room rate	$ 50.00
	($897,500 ÷ 17,950 forecasted room sales)	

6. Determine the price differential between room types.

7. Apply the following formula to compute the *single room rate*:

(Total Rooms Sold × Single Rate) + (Double Rooms Sold × Differential) = Daily Sales

8. The double room rate is single room rate plus differential.

Hotel DORO expects that 60 percent of its rooms will be occupied as double rooms. Since Hotel DORO is a 75-room hotel with an expected occupancy of 65.57 percent, this means that daily sales of 49 rooms are forecasted. The calculation of single and double rates for Hotel DORO is performed in Exhibit 2. The formula produces a single room rate of $41.12. The results of the formula can be verified as follows:

Single rooms sales	=	20 × $41.12	=		$822.40
Double rooms sales	=	29 × $56.12	=		1,627.48
Total					$2,449.88
Average Room Rate		$50 × 49 Rooms	=		$2,450.00

The minor difference is due to the rounding of calculations.

Contribution Margin

Contribution margin (CM) is defined as the portion of revenue that contributes to fixed costs and/or profit. It is computed by subtracting variable costs from sales.

Exhibit 2   Assigning Single and Double Rates for Hotel DORO

Supplementary Data:

Average room rate:	$ 50.00
Daily rooms available to sell:	75
Forecasted occupancy %:	65.57%
Rooms rate differential:	$15 more for double room

Calculating Single/Double Room Rates Procedure:

1. 75 rooms × 65.57% occupancy = 49 rooms sold daily.
2. 49 daily rooms × $50 average room rate = $2,450 daily sales.
3. Management estimates that 60% of the total rooms sold will be double rooms.
4. 49 rooms sold × 60% = 29 double rooms sold.
5. 49 total rooms − 29 double rooms = 20 single rooms sold.
6. Management decides that the double room rate will be $15 higher than the single room rate.
7. Daily Rooms Sold × Single Rate + Double Rooms × Differential = Daily Sales

   49(Single Room Rate) + 29($15) = $2,450 (See Step 2)
   49(Single Room Rate) + $435   = $2,450
            49(Single Room Rate) = $2,450 − $435
                Single Room Rate = $2,015
                                   ———
                                    49
                                 = $41.12

8. | Single room rate | $41.12 |
   |---|---|
   | Differential | 15.00 |
   | Double room rate | $56.12 |

Exhibit 3 shows the contribution margin for each department of a restaurant and for the restaurant as a whole. Subtracting the fixed costs of $12,000 from the total contribution margin of $33,000 results in a $21,000 surplus called Income Before Income Taxes (IBIT).

The contribution margin percentage (CM%) is computed by dividing the contribution margin dollars by sales dollars. Exhibit 3 shows the contribution margin percentage for each department of a restaurant and the hospitality business as a whole. The 16.5 percent contribution margin percentage for all revenue centers is also called a *weighted contribution margin percentage (CM%$_w$)*.

Sometimes the food and beverage departments may share personnel and other costs. These shared costs are called **joint costs**. Variable and semi-variable joint costs should be properly allocated to each department to arrive at a reasonable estimate of contribution margins. Allocation of joint costs may be done on a percentage of sales or other representative basis. Shared fixed costs do not require allocation since they are not used to compute contribution margin.

Exhibit 3   Contribution Margin and Sales Mix

	Food Department		Beverage Department		Company	
Sales	$180,000	100%	$ 20,000	100%	$200,000	100.0%
VC	153,000	85%	14,000	70%	167,000	83.5%
CM	$ 27,000	15%	$ 6,000	30%	33,000	16.5%
FC					12,000	
IBIT					$ 21,000	

Computation of CM%:

$$\text{Food CM\%} = \frac{\text{Food CM\$}}{\text{Food Sales}} = \frac{\$27,000}{\$180,000} = 15\%$$

$$\text{Beverage CM\%} = \frac{\text{Beverage CM\$}}{\text{Beverage Sales}} = \frac{\$6,000}{\$20,000} = 30\%$$

$$\text{CM\%}_w = \frac{\text{Total CM\$}}{\text{Total Sales}} = \frac{\$33,000}{\$200,000} = 16.5\%$$

Computation of Sales Mix:

$$\text{Food Sales Mix} = \frac{\text{Food Sales}}{\text{Total Sales}} = \frac{\$180,000}{\$200,000} = 90\%$$

$$\text{Beverage Sales Mix} = \frac{\text{Beverage Sales}}{\text{Total Sales}} = \frac{\$20,000}{\$200,000} = 10\%$$

Sales Mix

Sales mix is the proportion of each revenue center's sales to total sales. It is computed by dividing the departmental sales dollars by the total sales dollars for the business. Using the data in Exhibit 3, the sales mix is as follows:

	Sales	Sales Mix %
Food Department	$180,000	90%
Beverage Department	20,000	10%
Total	$200,000	100%

Sales mix plays an important role in forecasting and profit planning because each revenue center has a different contribution margin. Using Exhibit 3, the following conclusion can be stated: The food department's sales are 90 percent of the total sales with each food sales dollar generating a 15 percent contribution margin. The beverage department's sales are only 10 percent of the total, but its sales dollar generates a much better contribution margin percentage of 30 percent.

CVP Analysis

CVP is an acronym for cost-volume-profit. The CVP method is a management tool that brings together the interrelationship of cost, volume, and profit to forecast sales volume in dollars or units such as rooms or covers. The CVP method is useful for forecasting the sales volume necessary to achieve a profit target and other monetary operating objectives.

The use of CVP requires listing all expenses on a working paper and grouping them as variable or fixed, and separating semi-variable expenses into their variable and fixed elements by use of the high-low method, regression analysis, or professional judgment. Once all expenses are grouped, the variable costs are totaled separately from the fixed costs. The variable cost percentage is computed by dividing the total variable expenses by the sales dollars.

All statistical and forecasting models have built-in assumptions. The ordinary assumptions in the CVP method are as follows:

1. Variable costs and sales maintain their linear relationship.

2. Fixed costs remain stable during the forecasting period.

3. Semi-variable costs have been properly separated into their variable and fixed elements.

Forecasting Sales Dollars

The CVP method can be used to forecast sales dollars for a single-product or multiple-product hospitality business. The numerator is composed of fixed costs plus any objectives such as profit goals and any costs committed for a specific purpose. The denominator is composed of the contribution margin expressed as a percentage. Contribution margin percentage can be calculated by using 100 percent less the variable cost percentage. The formula for forecasting sales dollars uses fixed costs (FC) and the variable cost percentage (VC%) as follows:

$$\text{Sales} = \frac{\text{FC} + \text{Objectives}}{100\% - \text{VC}\%}$$

Recall that contribution margin (CM) is the result of sales less variable costs. The formula can be further abbreviated as follows:

$$\text{Sales} = \frac{\text{FC} + \text{Objectives}}{\text{CM}\%}$$

Both denominators produce the same result.

Dollar Forecasts for a Single-Product Business. Financial data for a single-product lodging business is shown in Exhibit 4. Assume that management requests a sales forecast that achieves a pretax profit (IBIT) of $40,000 after incurring an additional $10,000 in advertising expense. The sales forecast is computed as follows:

$$
\begin{aligned}
\text{Sales} &= \frac{\text{FC} + \text{Objectives}}{100\% - \text{VC}\%} \quad or \quad \frac{\text{FC} + \text{Objectives}}{\text{CM}\%} \\
&= \frac{\$38,000 + \$40,000 + \$10,000}{35\%} \\
&= \$251,429
\end{aligned}
$$

Exhibit 4   Single Product Lodging Business

Contributory Income Statement

Rooms Sales	$ 200,000	100%	
Total Variable Costs	130,000	65%	($130,000 ÷ $200,000)
Contribution Margin	70,000	35%	($70,000 ÷ $200,000)
Total Fixed Costs	38,000		
IBIT	$ 32,000		

The result means that a sales volume of $251,429 is required to achieve a profit (income before income taxes) goal of $40,000 after an additional $10,000 is spent for advertising. This conclusion can be confirmed as follows:

Sales	$251,429	← *forecasted sales*
VC ($251,429 × 65%)	163,429	
Additional advertising	10,000	← *advertising increase*
CM	78,000	
FC	38,000	
IBIT	$40,000	← *profit target*

Dollar Forecasts for a Multiple-Product Business. Many hospitality businesses sell multiple products or services. For example, a restaurant might sell food and beverages; a hotel might sell rooms, food, beverages, and other products or services. The CVP formula remains the same. However, because the denominator is a mix of all departments, the contribution margin percentage is called a *weighted* contribution margin percentage and the formula is sometimes shown as:

$$\text{Sales} = \frac{\text{FC} + \text{Objectives}}{\text{CM\%}_w}$$

Financial data for a multiple-product hospitality company is shown in Exhibit 5. Assume that management asks for a sales forecast that allows the hospitality business to break even. The sales forecast is computed as follows:

$$\text{Sales} = \frac{\text{FC} + \text{Objectives}}{\text{CM\%}_w}$$

$$= \frac{\$40,000 + 0}{62.5\%}$$

$$= \$64,000$$

Sales of $64,000 (breakeven point) are required to achieve breakeven (no profit, no loss). The $64,000 breakeven point can be verified as follows:

Exhibit 5   Multiple-Product Hospitality Company

	Food Department		Beverage Department		Company	
Sales	$ 90,000	100%	$ 30,000	100%	$ 120,000	100.0%
VC	36,000	40%	9,000	30%	45,000	37.5%
CM	$ 54,000	60%	$ 21,000	70%	$ 75,000	62.5%
FC					40,000	
IBIT					$ 35,000	

Sales Mix:

$$\text{Food} = \frac{90,000}{120,000} = 75\%$$

$$\text{Beverage} = \frac{30,000}{120,000} = 25\%$$

Sales:
Food ($64,000 × 75% sales mix)	$48,000	
Beverage ($64,000 × 25% sales mix)	16,000	
Total Sales		$64,000
Variable Costs:		
Food (40% × $48,000)	19,200	
Beverage (30% × $16,000)	4,800	
Total VC for departments		24,000
Contribution Margin		40,000
Fixed Costs		40,000
IBIT		$ 0

Forecasting Sales Units

The CVP formula used to determine sales *dollars* uses the contribution margin *percentage* as the denominator. If we modify the denominator to use the contribution margin itself (that is, the dollar value), the formula can be used to forecast *units* (rooms, guests) as follows:

$$\text{Units} = \frac{\text{FC + Objectives}}{\text{Price} - \text{Variable Cost}}$$

Price can be expressed as average room rate for the rooms department and average check (average menu price) for the food department.

Forecasting Rooms. Assume a lodging business has a profit goal of $40,000 before income taxes and will commit an additional $10,000 to advertising. Its fixed costs are $38,000, its ARR is $60, and its variable cost (based on a *VC% of* 65%) is $39. The forecasted rooms necessary to attain this objective is calculated as follows:

$$\text{Rooms} = \frac{\text{FC + Objectives}}{\text{ARR} - \text{VC}} \quad or \quad \frac{\text{FC + Objectives}}{\text{CM}}$$

$$= \frac{\$38,000 + \$40,000 + \$10,000}{\$60 - \$39}$$

$$= \ 4{,}190$$

To meet management's objectives, 4,190 rooms must be sold. This result can be verified as follows:

Sales (4,190 × $60 ARR)	$251,400
VC (4,190 × $39)	163,410
Additional Advertising	10,000
CM	77,990
FC	38,000
IBIT	$ 39,990
Original Goal	$ 40,000

The difference of $10 is due to rounding of calculations.

Forecasting Food Covers. Assume a restaurant has a profit goal of $20,000 before income taxes. Its fixed costs are $12,000, its average check (or average menu price) is $10, and its variable cost per food cover (at 40 percent) is $4. The forecasted covers figure necessary to attain this objective is calculated as follows:

$$\text{Covers} \ = \ \frac{\text{FC} + \text{Objectives}}{\text{Average Check} - \text{VC}} \quad or \quad \frac{\text{FC} + \text{Objectives}}{\text{CM}}$$

$$= \ \frac{\$12,000 + \$20,000}{\$6}$$

$$= \ 5{,}333$$

In other words, 5,333 meals must be sold to achieve a pretax profit of $20,000. This result can be verified as follows:

Sales (5,333 × $10)	$53,333
VC (5,333 × $4)	21,332
CM	32,001
FC	12,000
IBIT	$20,001

The extra dollar is due to rounding.

Income Tax Considerations

Up to now, sales dollars and units have been forecasted to achieve a given *IBIT* (income before income taxes). Management might ask: What sales dollars will attain a given *net income*?

The CVP formula can be modified to forecast sales dollars to achieve a desired net income. However, a simpler approach is to use a two-step process featuring a formula previously discussed. First, compute the IBIT necessary to get the desired net income:

$$IBIT = \frac{\text{Desired Net Income}}{100\% - \text{Income Tax Rate}}$$

Then insert this IBIT into the CVP formula as usual.

This two-step procedure is demonstrated by the following example. Assume a restaurant has a profit goal of $16,000 net income. Its fixed costs are $12,000 and the anticipated income tax rate is 20 percent. Its average menu price is $10 and its variable cost per cover is $4. The forecasted covers figure necessary to attain the income objective is calculated as follows:

Step 1: Compute IBIT:

$$IBIT = \frac{\text{Desired Net Income}}{100\% - \text{Income Tax Rate}}$$

$$= \frac{\$16,000}{100\% - 20\%}$$

$$= \$20,000$$

Step 2: Use the applicable CVP formula:

$$\text{Covers} = \frac{\text{FC} + \text{Objectives}}{\text{CM}}$$

$$= \frac{\$12,000 + \$20,000}{\$6}$$

$$= 5,333$$

Forecasting Without Financial Statements

Until now, this chapter has demonstrated CVP for a hospitality business acting as though financial statements were readily available. Quite often, management will need to forecast sales using only estimated sales mix percentages and contribution margin percentages for each separate revenue center. In this case, the weighted contribution margin percentage for the business as a whole is not readily available.

The formula used to forecast sales dollars remains as follows:

$$\text{Sales} = \frac{\text{FC} + \text{Objectives}}{\text{CM\%}_w}$$

The CVP denominator to arrive at the weighted contribution margin percentage for multiple products is the sum of each department's sales mix percentage multiplied by that department's contribution margin percentage. The CVP denominator for a hotel would require the weighting of its numerous revenue centers, and a full illustration of its CVP formula would be tedious. A restaurant selling only food and beverage is easier to illustrate; its CVP denominator would be as follows:

(Food Sales Mix % × Food CM%) + (Beverage Sales Mix % × Beverage CM%)

Exhibit 6   Fixed Costs, Sales Mix, and Contribution Margin Percentage for a Multiple-Product Business

---

Fixed Costs for the Restaurant: $40,000

Sales Mix Percentages:

	Sales	÷	Total Sales	=	Sales Mix %
Food Department	= $90,000	÷	$120,000	=	75%
Beverage Department	= $30,000	÷	$120,000	=	25%
Proof:			Total	=	100%

Contribution Margin Percentages:

Food Department: 60%
Beverage Department: 70%

Exhibit 6 demonstrates the use of a multiple product CVP formula that is not accompanied by financial statements.

Assume a restaurant sells food and beverage. Management wants to know the minimum sales dollars required to break even. Exhibit 6 shows that fixed costs are $40,000, food sales mix is 75 percent with a contribution margin percentage of 60 percent, and beverage sales mix is 25 percent with a contribution margin percentage of 70 percent. The breakeven point is calculated as follows:

$$\text{Sales} = \frac{\text{FC} + \text{Objectives}}{\text{CM\%}_w}$$

$$= \frac{\text{FC} + \text{Objectives}}{(\text{Food Sales Mix \%} \times \text{Food CM\%}) + (\text{Beverage Sales Mix \%} \times \text{Beverage CM\%})}$$

$$= \frac{\$40,000 + \$0}{(75\% \times 60\%) + (25\% \times 70\%)}$$

$$= \$64,000$$

🔑 Key Terms

contribution margin (CM)—The amount of sales that is applied to fixed costs and/or profit. It is computed by subtracting variable costs from sales.

elastic demand—A change in demand that exceeds the size of the change in price that caused it; likely to be found in fast-service food operations and budget motels.

inelastic demand—Demand that changes relatively little in relation to a price change; more likely to be found in resorts, luxury hotels, and fine dining establishments.

joint costs—Personnel and other costs shared by the food and beverage departments.

price elasticity of demand—A measure of the changes in demand caused by price sensitivity.

sales mix—The proportion of each revenue center's sales to total sales. It is computed by dividing the departmental sales dollars by the total sales dollars for the business.

 # Review Questions

1. What does *elastic demand* mean?

2. What are the two elements of revenue?

3. Ignoring elasticity of demand, does a five-percent price increase have a better effect on profits than a five-percent volume increase? Why or why not?

4. What is the formula for the moving average sales forecasting method?

5. What is the formula for the statistical model for forecasting rooms revenue? food revenue? Why might a statistical method similar to forecasting food revenue not be suitable for forecasting beverage revenue?

6. What is the formula for calculating average room rate if the sales dollars are available?

7. What is the procedure for calculating the average room rate using the weighted average method?

8. Starting with a given pretax income, what basic procedure can be used to calculate the average room rate using the Hubbart Formula?

9. How is a desired rate of return calculated?

10. What formula can be used to compute pretax profit if only the net income and tax rate are known?

11. What is contribution margin percentage? How is it computed?

12. What are joint costs?

13. What is sales mix? How is it computed?

14. What are the built-in assumptions of the CVP method?

15. What is the CVP formula for forecasting sales dollars? rooms unit sales? food covers?

16. What is the CVP denominator for forecasting sales dollars for a multiple-products company selling food and beverage when only each department's sales mix and contribution margin percentages are available?

Internet Sites

For more information, visit the following Internet sites. Remember that Internet addresses can change without notice. If the site is no longer there, you can use a search engine to look for additional sites.

Sales Forecasting
http://sbinfocanada.about.com/od/cashflowmgt/a/salesforecast.htm
http://sbinfocanada.about.com/b/a/093169.htm?terms=forecasting+financial+statements
www.cbsc.org/servlet/ContentServer?cid=1102940227898&pagename=OSBW%
  2FCBSC_WebPage%2FCBSC_WebPage_Temp&c=CBSC_WebPage

Moving Average Method
www.marketingprofs.com/Tutorials/Forecast/movingaverage.asp

Contribution Margin
http://retailindustry.about.com/od/merchandisemanagement/g/contrib_margin.htm
www.toolkit.cch.com/text/P06_7520.asp

Sales Mix
www.restaurantedge.com/index.phtml?catid=1257
www.evtpc.org/tutor/archive/originals/menucountsactivity.doc

CVP Slide Show
www.course.com/downloads/newperspectives/officexp/Excel_2002_tut09_edited.ppt

Cost-Volume-Profit Analysis
www.middlecity.com/ch20.shtml

Problems

Problem 1

Compute the sales mix percentages for the following:

Room Sales	$850,000
Food Sales	120,000
Beverage Sales	30,000

Problem 2

Compute the contribution margin percentages for the following:

	Sale	Variable Cost
Rooms Department	$850,000	$127,500
Restaurant	120,000	54,000
Bar & Lounge	30,000	10,500

Problem 3

Compute the pretax profit (income before income taxes) if the net income is $140,000 and the income tax rate is 30 percent.

Problem 4

Compute the contribution margin dollars if volume is 20,000 units, price is $10 per unit, and variable costs are 60 percent of revenue.

Problem 5

Use the data in Problem 4 to compute the contribution margin dollars if volume increases by 10 percent.

Problem 6

Use the data in Problem 4 and compute the contribution margin dollars if price increases 10 percent.

Problem 7

Forecast the upcoming Week 8's volume if a food operation uses a five-week base period.

Week	Covers
1	1020
2	1080
3	1060
4	1100
5	1160
6	1170
7	1160

Problem 8

A lodging operation has a calendar business year. Room rates will increase five percent starting March 1 next year. Management expects volume to increase ten percent starting April 1 next year. Forecast the sales for the first six months of next year using the percentage method on last year's data as follows:

January	$150,000
February	200,000
March	200,000
April	220,000
May	240,000
June	250,000

Problem 9

Use the rooms revenue statistical model to forecast sales dollars for a 300-room hotel with an occupancy percentage of 75 percent and an average room rate of $70 for a 31-day month.

Problem 10

Use the food revenue statistical model to forecast food sales for a restaurant that serves breakfast, lunch, and dinner for a 30-day month that has five Sundays and five Saturdays. Breakfast and lunch are not served on Saturday. The restaurant is closed on Sunday. Use the following data:

	Seats	Turnover	Average Check
Breakfast	50	2.0	5.00
Lunch	100	1.5	8.00
Dinner	100	1.0	25.00

Problem 11

Forecast the beverage sales for a Wednesday from the following data: This restaurant serves only dinner. Historically, beverage sales are 30 percent of food sales. Historical daily beverage sales in the lounge:

Sunday	(closed)
Monday	(closed)
Tuesday	4,000
Wednesday	2,000
Thursday	3,000
Friday	6,000
Saturday	4,000

Forecasted food sales for this Wednesday: $30,000

Problem 12

Compute the average room rate for a hotel that had room sales of $400,000 with a paid rooms occupancy of 6,154 rooms for the month.

Problem 13

Use the weighted average to compute the average room rate from the following data:

	Rooms	Rate
Single	33	$ 60
Double	75	79
Suite	18	105

Problem 14

Use the Hubbart formula to compute the average room rate of all rooms for the Village Hotel. The owners of the Village Hotel desire a pretax profit (IBIT) of $140,424. They have forecasted sales of 17,500 rooms and estimated the following departmental data:

Fixed charges	$368,869
Utility costs	81,420
Support centers	295,189
Income from revenue centers except rooms	109,116
Expenses of rooms department	264,414

Problem 15

Assume an average room rate of $80 was estimated from applying the Hubbart formula. Compute the single and double room rates from the following information:

Daily rooms to sell: 280
Forecasted occupancy: 75%

Estimated double rooms sold: 70%
Rooms rate differential: Double room is $20 higher than a single room.

Problem 16

Use CVP and compute the sales revenue (dollars) to achieve an IBIT of $420,000 from the forecasted information provided below. Prove the accuracy of your answer.

Sales	$900,000	100%
VC	360,000	48%
CM	$540,000	52%
FC	300,000	
IBIT	$240,000	

Problem 17

Use CVP and compute the rooms sales to achieve breakeven for a single-product motel with total fixed costs of $40,000, an average room rate of $80, and a variable cost per room of $30. Prove the accuracy of your answer.

Problem 18

Use CVP and compute the food covers necessary to achieve breakeven for a single-product restaurant with total fixed costs of $16,000, an average check of $15, and a variable cost per cover of $7. Prove the accuracy of your answer.

Problem 19

Use CVP and compute the rooms sales necessary to achieve a net income of $156,000 for a single-product motel with total fixed costs of $180,000, an average room rate of $50, and a variable cost per room of $20. The motel's income tax rate is 35 percent. Prove the accuracy of your answer.

Problem 20

Use CVP and compute the sales revenue necessary to achieve an IBIT of $162,000 for a multi-product restaurant from the information below.

	Food	Beverage	Total	
Sales	$240,000	$160,000	$400,000	100%
VC	144,000	48,000	192,000	48%
CM	96,000	112,000	208,000	52%
FC			150,000	
IBIT			58,000	

Problem 21

Use CVP and compute the sales revenue necessary to achieve an IBIT of $162,000 for a multi-product restaurant with total fixed costs of $150,000 from the information below.

	Sales Mix	Contribution Margin
Food	60%	40%
Beverage	40%	70%

Case Study

Forecasting Beverage Sales

The Signature Restaurant has been using a method of forecasting sales that has proven unreliable. Management has engaged your services to use a better method that will improve sales forecasts, which, in turn, will provide information for better staff scheduling and inventory control.

The method you select to forecast liquor sales uses historical averages and percentages, and involves a two-step process that computes liquor sales in the dining room independent of liquor sales in the lounge.

1. For the Dining Room: You will determine and apply food/liquor relationships. You explain to management that there usually is a correlation between food and liquor sales in the dining room.

2. For the Lounge: You will use liquor sales activity based on daily sales for a corresponding month last year. You explain to management that it is not unusual for lounge sales to follow patterns that vary by each day of the week within a particular month.

Management has provided you with the following historical data.

Dining room sales for August last year:

	Food Sales	Beverage Sales
Lunch	$10,000	$1,000
Dinner	20,000	4,000

Lounge sales for August last year:

	Beverage Sales
Sunday	(closed)
Monday	$100
Tuesday	400
Wednesday	200
Thursday	300
Friday	600
Saturday	400

Forecasted dining room activity for August this year:

	Food Sales
Lunch	$12,000
Dinner	24,000

Number of weekdays for August this year:

Five each of Sundays, Mondays, Tuesdays
Four each of Wednesdays, Thursdays, Fridays, Saturdays

Challenge

1. Prepare working papers showing the computational sequence of your forecast. Label your steps with proper headings and show your computations for each step.
2. Prepare a report explaining the advantages and limitations of the method you used.
3. Prepare a report explaining conclusions that should be considered about the forecasting method.

Chapter 15 Outline

Budget Planning and Preparation
    Budgeting Fixed Costs
Budget Reports
    Budget Variances
Master and Flexible Budgets
Variance Analysis
    Manager's Budgetary Working Papers
    Analyzing Variances to Ascertain
        Causes
Capital Budgeting Synopsis

Competencies

1. Identify various kinds of budgets and the role they play in planning and operating a hospitality operation. (pp. 401–402, 414–415)

2. Describe the kinds of information used in preparing a budget and how this information varies depending on whether revenues, expenses, or fixed costs are being budgeted. (pp. 402–403)

3. Create budget reports and determine budget variances. (pp. 404–405)

4. Distinguish between master budgets and flexible budgets and use each appropriately. (pp. 405–409)

5. Analyze sales and expense variances to determine their causes. (pp. 409–414)

15

Budgetary Reporting and Analysis

Every successful hospitality business has a master plan integrating the activities of all revenue centers, support centers, and other departments. This master plan sets forth objectives, human resource policies, organizational hierarchy, steps stating how to achieve the goals, and methodology to monitor the progress of every component of the organization. Master plans take many forms but they all include one common element: *budgets*. The forecasted sales and expenses become a budget stated in monetary terms that sets the business's operating goals. The master plan also includes budgets expressed in non-monetary terms such as rooms, covers, and hours worked.

Managers at all levels must participate in the preparation and planning of budgets if the monetary plan is to be useful and attainable. A large company may have a budget committee composed of top executives who provide guidance and coordination of the budgeting phase. A budget director, usually an upper-level accountant, supervises the mechanical processing of the budget. The accounting department plays a major role by providing historical data, other financial data, and assistance to department managers and executives for the forecasting of revenue and expenses.

Budgets that are forced on department managers without their participation may foster hostility toward budgetary controls. Excellent sales forecasts and expense budgeting result from cooperative effort among executives, managers, and the accounting department. The expertise of these professionals contributes to successful budget planning and preparation. After the budget is installed, teamwork is essential for proper control and evaluation of the progress toward the goals of the master plan.

This chapter will answer such questions as:

1. What are the major reasons to have budgets?
2. What is zero-base budgeting?
3. What is an operations budget?
4. How is a budget report read and interpreted?
5. What are budget variances?
6. What is the difference between master and flexible budgets?
7. What are the causes of budget variances?

8. How is a budget variance analyzed?

9. What is a capital budget?

While preparing and monitoring budgets can be costly, the benefits exceed the cost. Budgets are more than a means of controlling expenditures. When they are properly prepared, budgets are strategic plans, and planning is a major function of management. Financial planning plays a large role in the success of any hospitality business. The budgeting process forces managers to think about and anticipate the future. Resources such as assets and labor can then be allocated to their most productive and profitable uses. The budget also serves as a control tool that provides a standard of comparison against which to measure actual results. Managers are accountable for deviations from the plan.

A hospitality business uses many types of budgets. It uses a **capital budget** to plan and control the purchase of major assets. It uses a **cash budget** to monitor cash and plan for borrowings as necessary. It uses an **operations budget** to budget sales and expenses in order to achieve a desired profit. The operations budget is the primary focus of this chapter. Although this is only one kind of budget required for a hospitality business, it is the most common and well known. When most people think of budgets, they think of budgeting sales and expenses. The operations budget is a profit plan that incorporates all revenue and expenses of the business. In its final format, it is identical to an income statement except that the amounts are **pro forma,** meaning that the numbers are estimates and not actual in form.

The operations budget is forecasted for the year and then appropriated into monthly plans, which become the standards against which the actual monthly results will be measured.

Preparing the operations budget first requires that departmental sales and expenses be forecasted and approved by the budget committee. The accounting department then reviews these preliminary departmental plans for mathematical accuracy and completeness. After review, the accounting department merges the departmental budgets into a consolidated budget.

Budget Planning and Preparation

The preparation of budgets is an organizational effort. Executives, managers, and accountants work together for the best interests of the hospitality business. They use financial statistics, financial methods, and professional judgment in planning revenue and expenses. Budget planning meetings are frequently held for effective planning and efficient use of time. The agenda for these meetings might feature:

- A review of historical operations.

- A review of current operations and finances.

- Analysis of local and national economic data.

- Projections of occupancy, covers, and other revenue sources.

Sales projections are forecasted through the use of financial tools such as CVP (cost-volume-profit) analysis, statistical models, and the percentage method.

Revenue center expenses are budgeted through the use of a combination of such financial methods as:

- Study of historical relationships to volume.

- Classification of expenses as variable, semi-variable, or fixed.

- The high-low or regression analysis methods.

- Analysis of the effect of price and volume increases.

Non-revenue centers do not have sales volume and, accordingly, their expenses are not directly related to sales. The common non-revenue centers are the undistributed expenses of a hotel, such as administrative and general (executives, accounting, data processing, payroll, human resources), marketing, property operations and maintenance, and utility costs. While historical statistics are often valuable in the budgeting process, the use of historical statistics might result in unknowingly repeating the wrongdoing of the past. A popular solution to budgeting expenses for support centers and utility costs is to use a "fresh start" by applying the zero-base budgeting approach. **Zero-base budgeting (ZBB)** is not a method; it is a philosophy. The ZBB approach requires that non-revenue department managers prepare a budget from zero and cost-justify each expense item. For example, the manager of the information systems department would have to justify all payroll, supplies, and other expenses in the operations of that department. This approach is designed to guarantee that every expense yields a benefit greater than its cost. Even though the zero-base budgeting process is time-consuming, it offers a major advantage: it forces managers to identify inefficient operations, overstaffing, duplication, and non-guest services that could be eliminated.

Budgeting Fixed Costs

A hotel's fixed costs include insurance, property taxes, rent, interest, depreciation, and amortization. ZBB is not used to budget fixed costs because these costs are imposed on the business as a result of past and present executive decisions regarding purchases of capital assets and related financing.

Insurance, property taxes, rent, interest, depreciation, and amortization are not within the control of any department manager. However, these fixed costs are easily estimated because of their source. For example:

- Insurance premiums are available from the insurer.

- The local town government readily provides tax rates and property valuation.

- Rents are stated in rental agreements.

- Interest on loans for the year can be computed manually or by computerized loan amortization software.

- Depreciation and amortization is based on present and planned acquisitions of capital assets. The calculations can be performed manually or with depreciation software.

Exhibit 1   Budget Variances

SAMPLE 1:

	Budget	Actual	Variance
Sales	50,000	55,000	5,000 favorable
Food Cost	15,000	17,000	2,000 unfavorable
Payroll	3,000	4,900	1,900 unfavorable
Supplies	1,500	1,300	200 favorable

SAMPLE 2:

	Budget	Actual	Variance
Sales	50,000	45,000	5,000 unfavorable
Food Cost	15,000	13,000	2,000 favorable
Payroll	3,000	2,500	500 favorable
Supplies	1,500	1,700	200 unfavorable

LOGIC TO DETERMINE VARIANCES:

More actual sales = favorable

More actual expenses = unfavorable

Budget Reports

Monthly income statements (for revenue centers) and expense statements (for non-revenue centers) will show actual financial data, the budget, and the difference between the budgeted and actual amount. A typical format of a report appears as follows:

	Month				Year-to-Date	
Budget	Actual	Difference		Budget	Actual	Difference

The monthly section is separate from the year-to-date section. The sections may, however, be on the same page. The listing of the budgetary and actual amounts allows the reader to compare the plan against what was actually accomplished.

Budget Variances

A **variance** is the difference between a budgeted amount and the actual amount. A variance is either *favorable* or *unfavorable*. A favorable variance is the result of the actual being better than the budget; a result is unfavorable if the actual is worse than the budget. The method of determining a favorable or unfavorable condition depends on whether we are analyzing a revenue item or an expense item. A sales variance is *favorable* if actual sales are greater than budgeted sales. An expense variance is *unfavorable* if actual expenses are greater than budgeted expenses. Exhibit 1 illustrates favorable and unfavorable variances.

Exhibit 2 Alternate Format to Display Budget Variances

	Budget	Actual	Variance*
Sales	50,000	55,000	5,000
Food Cost	15,000	17,000	(2,000)
Payroll	3,000	4,900	(1,900)
Supplies	1,500	1,300	200

*Positive numbers indicate a favorable variance. Negative numbers indicate an unfavorable variance.

There are no uniform rules for showing favorable and unfavorable variances. Companies may use different terms to reflect variance conditions. For instance, the label "Better" might be used to indicate a favorable variance and the label "Worse" to indicate an unfavorable variance.

One common practice is to show favorable variances as positive numbers and unfavorable variances as negative numbers (usually enclosed in parentheses). Exhibit 2 illustrates the use of this format. When using this format, keep in mind the fact that "positive" and "negative" variances do *not* equate with being "over" and "under" the budgeted amounts (or vice versa). That is, if an actual amount is less than a budgeted amount, this fact alone does not determine its favorableness. We must also know if the budgeted item is sales or an expense.

Master and Flexible Budgets

The **master budget** represents a company's primary financial planning tool. The annual master budget is prepared for each department and then divided into monthly amounts. The departmental budgets are combined to form an integrated plan for the organization as a whole.

The master budget is a short-run budget; that is, the activities are budgeted for one year or less. It is developed in accordance with a predetermined plan and is goal oriented. The main assumption in designing the master budget is that it predetermines the sales volume the organization must reach to make a desired profit.

The master budget is an excellent management tool for measuring progress toward attaining a specific profit goal. However, it is not useful as a financial tool for examining the operating efficiency of revenue centers when the actual sales volume is significantly different from the budgeted sales volume. Exhibit 3 shows the kinds of extreme variances that can occur when the sales goal from a master budget is significantly different from the actual sales. (Lower-than-expected sales could be due to circumstances such as an unrealistic original sales goal, unexpected competition, or unforeseen economic recession.) In this case, the master budget emphasizes that the original sales objective was not achieved (or surpassed), but the analysis of operating efficiencies yields absurd variances from the budget. Food cost and labor expense will almost invariably show favorable variances when actual sales are significantly lower than the budgeted sales volume.

Exhibit 3   Master Budget Variances when Actual Sales Radically Differ from Budgeted Sales

	Budget	**Actual**	**Variance**	**(comment)**
Sales	50,000	31,522	(18,478)	unfavorable
Food Cost	15,000	9,100	5,900	favorable
Payroll	13,000	8,500	4,500	favorable
Supplies	1,500	850	650	favorable

(Fixed expenses are not materially affected because these expenses are not affected by volume.)

Regardless of actual sales, the master budget will be issued to executives to measure progress (or lack of progress) toward fulfilling the master plan. A master budget is based on one level of sales volume to achieve a stated goal. For this reason, master budgets are not intended to reflect expenses at other levels of activity.

To make up for the master budget's shortcomings as a managerial tool for measuring efficiency when there is a wide variance in volume, an organization might use flexible budgets to augment the budgetary reporting process. **Flexible budgets** are designed for many different levels of sales volume. Management determines a series of probable sales volumes, and then establishes expense budgets for each of those levels.

For example, a restaurant in a motel might expect sales volumes of $30,000, $40,000, $50,000, or $60,000 throughout the year for any given month. A flexible budget is set up for each of these volumes to properly reflect expenses and operating performance. Exhibit 4 shows a series of flexible monthly budgets for these individual sales volumes. Each range of the flexible budget shown in Exhibit 4 was determined in accordance with the characteristics of variable, semi-variable, and fixed costs. Food cost and supplies were budgeted as variable costs with a relationship to sales, respectively, of 30 percent and 3 percent. A regression analysis for payroll expense indicated that this semi-variable expense is composed of two elements: a $2,000 fixed portion and a variable portion that amounts to 22 percent of sales. China, glassware, silver is considered fixed because the motel treats the original purchase as a capital asset, and the cost is depreciated over its useful life. (While most depreciation goes on a hotel's fixed cost schedule, the depreciation of china, glassware, silver is an exception and is charged to the user department.) Contract cleaning is fixed because of its contractual nature. The other expenses are considered semi-variable, and regression analysis studies for this particular motel show that it can reliably use two percent of sales plus a $400 fixed element in estimating these expenses.

Master budgets and flexible budgets are created during the budget planning and preparation stages. Unlike the master budget, the flexible budget to be used for budgetary reporting purposes in any given month is *unknown* until the current month is completed and the actual sales volume is known. When the actual sales

Exhibit 4 Flexible Budget for a Motel's Restaurant Operation

Sales (net)	$30,000	$40,000	$50,000	$60,000
Budgeted Expenses:				
Food cost	9,000	12,000	15,000	18,000
Payroll & related	8,600	10,800	13,000	15,200
Supplies	900	1,200	1,500	1,800
China, glassware, silver	300	300	300	300
Contract cleaning	500	500	500	500
Other expenses	1,000	1,200	1,400	1,600
Total expenses	20,300	26,000	31,700	37,400
Departmental Income	$ 9,700	$14,000	$18,300	$ 22,600

Budgeting data: **Expense**	**Type**	**Method used to calculate budget**
Food Cost	V	30% of sales
Payroll & Related	SV	$2,000 fixed + 22% of sales
Supplies	V	3% of sales
China, glassware, silver	F	$300
Contract cleaning	F	$500
Other expenses	SV	$400 fixed + 2% of sales

volume becomes reality, the flexible budget nearest to the actual sales volume is used in the budgetary report.

For example, assume that the above motel's restaurant experienced actual sales of $31,522 for the current month. Exhibit 4 shows that the nearest applicable flexible budget to actual sales is the $30,000 sales volume budget. (The series of flexible budgets in Exhibit 4 was established in $10,000 sales volume increments. Management might decide to establish a series of flexible budgets in smaller increments to provide more accurate expense comparisons of actual to budget.)

Exhibit 5 illustrates the use of the $30,000 budget from Exhibit 4 for budgetary reporting. There is a $1,522 favorable variance for sales, a $150 unfavorable total expense variance, and a $1,372 favorable variance for the departmental income. It is unclear whether the expenses that generated unfavorable variances are in fact over budget. The reason for this uncertainty is that the sales shown on the flexible budget rarely turn out exactly the same as the actual sales. Often, a comparison based on dollars alone is not sufficient to measure performance. Therefore, a relativity analysis using percentages as related to sales is usually a part of the budgetary report.

Exhibit 6 shows an alternative budgetary reporting format that uses a percentage comparison. The budgeted expenses are divided by the budgeted sales. The actual expenses are divided by the actual sales. This process shows expenses as they relate to volume and supplements the dollar analysis. The percentages

Exhibit 5   Flexible Budgetary Reporting for $31,522 Actual Sales

	Budget	Actual	Difference*
Sales	$30,000	$31,522	$1,522
Expenses:			
Food cost	9,000	9,100	(100)
Payroll & related	8,600	8,500	100
Supplies	900	850	50
China, glassware, silver	300	300	0
Contract cleaning	500	500	0
Other expenses	1,000	1,200	(200)
Total expenses	20,300	20,450	(150)
Departmental Income	$ 9,700	$ 11,072	$1,372

*Positive numbers indicate a favorable variance. Negative numbers indicate an unfavorable variance.

Exhibit 6   Flexible Budgetary Reporting with Percentages of Sales

	Budget		Actual		Difference**
	Amount	%	Amount	%	Amount
Sales	$30,000	100.0%	$31,522	100.0%	$1,522
Expenses:					
Food cost	9,000	30.0%	9,100	28.9%	(100)
Payroll & related	8,600	28.7%	8,500	27.0%	100
Supplies	900	3.0%	850	2.7%	50
China, glassware, silver	300	1.0%	300	1.0%	0
Contract cleaning	500	1.7%	500	1.6%	0
Other expenses	1,000	3.3%	1,200	3.8%	(200)
Total expenses	20,300	67.7%	20,450	64.9%*	(150)
Departmental Income	$ 9,700	32.3%	$11,072	35.1%	$1,372

* The column of percentages do not add to 64.9% due to rounding of individual line items.

** Positive numbers indicate a favorable variance. Negative numbers indicate an unfavorable variance.

in Exhibit 6 reveal that, even though the actual food cost dollars were higher than the budget, the expense was indeed properly controlled when related to sales volume. That is, the $100 unfavorable variance for food cost is misleading because the budgeted food cost percentage is 30.0 percent, while the actual food cost is 28.9 percent.

Fixed expenses with no dollar variance will always show actual percentages that are equal to or lower than the budgeted percentages when sales volume is higher than the budget. This condition is due only to the mathematics of having a higher divisor. Measuring the efficiency of fixed expenses based on volume is usually irrelevant; therefore, vigilance is constantly necessary when analyzing fixed expenses.

Variance Analysis

Merely knowing that a budget variance is favorable or unfavorable does not provide enough information to manage and control a hospitality operation. Even favorable variances (or no variances) might result from a hidden problem. A department manager should find out why a variance has occurred in order to manage the department efficiently and profitably while providing the level of guest service prescribed by company policy.

Manager's Budgetary Working Papers

Variance analysis is possible only if the supporting data used in preparing the budget has been retained and systematically indexed. For example, it is not enough to show that the budgeted sales were $30,000 for a month. It is important to show in the working papers that a $30,000 sales budget was computed using a $10 average check and 3,000 covers. Similar supporting detail should be retained for each budgeted expense. For example, the following computational notes may support a $9,000 food cost:

> 3,000 covers
> $3 average food cost (30% food cost $\times$ $10 average check)

Accurate variance analysis requires the maintenance of precise background data. A manager must properly interpret budget variances to perform appropriate corrective action.

Practically all budgeted sales and expenses will ultimately differ from the actual results, with perhaps the exception of certain fixed expenses. Variances occur because no budgeting method or procedure can precisely predict the future. An experienced hospitality manager generally recognizes which variances, large or small, should be investigated.

Generally, a *sales variance* is due to price, quantity, or both. *Price* is the product selling price such as average room rate or average check. *Quantity* is the sales volume stated in units, such as rooms or covers.

Variance analysis might show that a favorable sales variance is not necessarily a positive thing if actual sales are higher because of price increases coupled with lower customer volume. Higher prices might turn customers away, beginning an unfavorable trend.

An unfavorable sales variance might be due to a drop in customer volume or customers spending less because of economic conditions. Unfavorable rooms sales might result when too many rooms are out of order or an unrealistic average room rate is used in the forecasting process.

An *expense variance* is due to cost, quantity, or both. *Cost* is the unit purchase cost of an expense item. Again, *quantity* is the sales volume stated in units, such as rooms or covers.

A favorable expense variance could conceal future problems if the variance results from, for example, lower food cost because of buying lower quality, or lower-than-expected payroll costs because of understaffing. Lower purchase quality might be readily apparent to guests. Understaffing could lead to diminished guest service. These situations are critical to the success of any hospitality business because unsatisfied guests are not repeat guests.

An unfavorable expense variance could be due to overstaffing or staffing problems, excessive or unplanned overtime pay, and/or supplier cost increases. Finding the causes helps management take corrective action. The staffing and overtime problems might be due to unreliable staff or perhaps unsatisfactory supervision. Extraordinary supplier cost increases might be resolved by a meeting with the supplier or by a change in supplier.

Analyzing Variances to Ascertain Causes

Several methods may be used to determine causes of variances. The uncomplicated procedures are just as precise as the sophisticated techniques. Since financial management is results oriented, a simple method is most satisfactory.

Price is related to a sales variance, while cost is related to an expense variance. In either case, the quantity is always sales volume stated in covers, rooms, or other unit measurements. The same procedure can be used to determine the causes of sales variances and expense variances: the formula merely interchanges the terms *cost* and *price*.

This chapter suggests using the acronym **BAD PQ** to aid your recall of the variance analysis procedure. This memory aid associates the letters BAD PQ with the following:

> **B**udget
> **A**ctual
> **D**ifference (Variance)
> **P**rice (or Cost)
> **Q**uantity

The BAD PQ approach is formatted on the working paper as follows:

	Price	**Quantity**
Budget		
Actual		
Difference		

The next step involves entering the data in each field.

> **Price Column:**
> Enter the budgeted unit selling price (or cost).
> Enter the actual unit selling price (or cost).
> Subtract the actual from the budgeted price (or cost).

Quantity Column:
Enter the budgeted sales quantity (covers, rooms).
Enter the actual sales quantity (covers, rooms).
Subtract the actual from the budgeted quantity.

The causes of the variance may now be determined as follows:

Price Difference × Actual Quantity = Price Cause

Quantity Difference × Budgeted Price = Quantity Cause

The total of these two causes must agree with the total variance on the budgetary report.

Note that the rules of algebraic multiplication are followed in the multiplication process, as follows:

A positive number × a positive number = a positive result (favorable)

A positive number × a negative number = a negative result (unfavorable)

The next two sections of the chapter will demonstrate the variance analysis process.

Determining Causes of a Sales Variance. Assume a rooms department monthly departmental budgetary report shows, in part, the following:

	Budget	**Actual**	**Difference**
		Month	
Sales	$195,000	$206,500	$11,500 Favorable
Guest Supplies Expense	6,000	6,195	195 Unfavorable

At first glance, the favorable sales variance might seem to indicate that there is no need to analyze the variance. This example will reveal that even favorable variances might conceal a weakness that requires corrective action.

The manager's budget preparation working papers and current actual statistics from the accounting department are shown in Exhibit 7. The sales data from the manager's budgetary working papers and from the accounting department are then entered (using the BAD PQ format) as shown in Exhibit 8. The actual data is subtracted from the budgeted data to arrive at the differences. The differences need to be labeled as favorable or unfavorable, depending on whether sales or expenses are analyzed. When sales are analyzed, the following logic is used:

More customers than budgeted = Favorable

Higher selling price than budgeted = Favorable

Exhibit 8 shows a mixed result. The price difference of $5 is favorable because the actual average room rate exceeded the budgeted rate. The quantity difference of 50 rooms is unfavorable because the actual rooms sold were fewer than those budgeted.

These differences are used to explain the price and quantity components of the total variance. Exhibit 9 shows the completed sales variance analysis. The cause due to price is determined as follows:

Exhibit 7   Manager's Working Papers and Accounting Department Statistics

Information from manager's budget working papers:

Sales Forecast Computation:

Average Room Rate:	$65
Rooms Sold:	3,000
Budgeted Sales:	$195,000

Guest Supplies Expense Budget Computation:

Rooms Sold:	3,000
Unit Cost:	$2.00
Budgeted Guest Supplies:	$6,000

Current Month's statistics reported from the accounting department:

Average Room Rate:	$70
Rooms Sold:	2,950 ($70 × 2,950 = $206,500)
Guest Supplies Unit Invoice Cost:	$2.10 ($2.10 × 2,950 = $6,195)

Exhibit 8   Entering Price and Quantity Data for Sales Variance

	Price		Quantity	
Budget	$65	ARR	3,000	Rooms Sold
Actual	70		2,950	
Difference	$ 5	Favorable	50	Unfavorable

$$\text{Price Cause} = \text{Price Difference} \times \text{Actual Quantity}$$
$$= \$5 \times 2,950$$
$$= \$14,750 \text{ favorable}$$

The cause due to quantity is determined as follows:

$$\text{Quantity Cause} = \text{Quantity Difference} \times \text{Budgeted Price}$$
$$= (50) \times \$65$$
$$= \$(3,250) \text{ unfavorable}$$

The causes of the variance are then explained as follows:

Favorable variance due to Price	$14,750
Unfavorable variance due to Quantity	(3,250)
Net Favorable Variance	$11,500

The $11,500 favorable variance matches the sales variance shown earlier on the budgetary report.

Exhibit 9   Completed Sales Variance Analysis

	Price	**Quantity**
Budget	$65 ARR	3,000 Rooms Sold
Actual	70	2,950
Difference	$ 5 Favorable	(50) Unfavorable

**Determining the Reasons for (causes of)
the $11,500 Favorable Sales Variance**

Variance due to PRICE: **CAUSE**

Price Difference	×	Actual Quantity	=	$14,750 Favorable Price
$5	×	2,950		

Variance due to QUANTITY:

Quantity Difference	×	Budgeted Price		
(50)	×	$65	=	(3,250) Unfavorable Quantity

Total of Causes	$11,500 Favorable (net)
Proof: Variance on Budgetary Report	$11,500

Summation:

Favorable variance due to Price	$14,750
Unfavorable variance due to Quantity	(3,250)
Net Favorable Variance	$11,500

Determining Causes of an Expense Variance. Referring again to the above rooms department monthly departmental budgetary report, it may seem at first glance that the small ($195) unfavorable guest supplies expense is compensated for by the significant favorable sales variance. This example will again emphasize the importance of properly interpreting budgetary reports and carefully analyzing variances.

The manager's budget preparation working papers and current actual statistics from the accounting department were shown in Exhibit 7. The data from the manager's budgetary working papers and from the accounting department is then entered as shown in Exhibit 10. (Notice that the BAD PQ format has been altered to BAD CQ. The change simply reflects the terminology used in an expense analysis.) The actual data is then subtracted from the budgeted data to arrive at the differences. The differences must be labeled as favorable or unfavorable. When expenses are analyzed, the following logic is used:

More guests than budgeted = Unfavorable

Higher unit purchase cost than budgeted = Unfavorable

Exhibit 10   Entering Cost and Quantity Data for Expense Variance

	Cost		**Quantity**	
Budget	$ 2.00	Unit Cost	3,000	Rooms Sold
Actual	2.10		2,950	
Difference	$ (.10)	Unfavorable	50	Favorable

While more guests are desirable in a sales analysis, a higher guest figure has an opposite effect on an expense analysis. More guests imply an increase to expense; any increase to sales or profit is ignored when an expense variance is analyzed.

Exhibit 10 shows a mixed result. The cost difference of $.10 is unfavorable because the actual unit purchase cost exceeded the budgeted unit cost. The quantity difference of 50 rooms is favorable because the actual rooms sold were less than those budgeted. (Contrary to a sales analysis, a lower guest figure is favorable in an expense analysis.)

These differences are used to explain the price and quantity components of the total variance. Exhibit 11 shows the completed expense variance analysis. The cause due to cost is determined as follows:

$$\text{Cost Cause} = \text{Cost Difference} \times \text{Actual Quantity}$$
$$= \$(.10) \times 2,950$$
$$= \$(295) \text{ unfavorable}$$

A negative number multiplied by a positive number produces a negative result, which is translated as unfavorable. The cause due to quantity is determined as follows:

$$\text{Quantity Cause} = \text{Quantity Difference} \times \text{Budgeted Cost}$$
$$= 50 \times \$2$$
$$= \$100 \text{ favorable}$$

The causes of the variance are then explained as follows:

Unfavorable variance due to Cost	$ (295)
Favorable variance due to Quantity	100
Net Unfavorable Variance	$ (195)

The $195 unfavorable variance matches the guest supplies expense variance shown on the budgetary report.

Capital Budgeting Synopsis

The discussion of budgeting in this chapter has been based on budgeting of revenue and expenses. However, hospitality businesses also need to forecast the purchase of property and equipment. Capital budgets are balance sheet-related, and the planning emphasis is for the long run. Typically, capital budgets are fixed-asset

Exhibit 11 Completed Expense Variance Analysis

	Cost		Quantity	
Budget	$ 2.00	Unit Cost	3,000	Rooms
Actual	2.10		2,950	
Difference	$ (.10)	Unfavorable	50	Favorable

**Determining the Reasons for (Causes of)
the $195 Unfavorable Expense Variance**

Variance due to COST:			CAUSE	
Cost Difference	×	Actual Quantity	=	$(295) Unfavorable Cost
$(.10)	×	2,950		

Variance due to QUANTITY:				
Quantity Difference	×	Budgeted Cost	=	100 Favorable Quantity
50	×	$2		

Total of Causes	$(195) Unfavorable (net)
Proof: Variance on Budgetary Report	$(195)

Summation:

Unfavorable variance due to Cost	$(295)
Favorable variance due to Quantity	100
Net Unfavorable Variance	$(195)

oriented; the purchases of fixed assets require executive planning and approval because of such assets' significant costs and associated financing requirements.

In the capital budgeting process, managers are asked to submit a list of their present and future asset requirements. Top-level executives then perform long-range planning for the following:

- Replacement of present assets
- Addition of new assets
- Expansion of present facilities
- Acquisition of land for development
- Acquisition of other operating businesses

Management decides on the priorities of asset purchases. Those acquisitions that yield the best return for the company generally receive the higher rankings. A capital budget is then developed that will control the future purchase of assets.

A detailed examination of capital budgeting is beyond the scope of this chapter.

Key Terms ————————————————————————————

BAD PQ—An acronym for *budget, actual, difference, price,* and *quantity,* intended as a mnemonic aid in determining causes of sales and expense variances.

capital budget—A budget used to plan and control the purchase of major assets.

cash budget—A budget used to monitor cash and plan for borrowings as necessary.

flexible budgets—Budgets designed for the different levels of sales volume that an organization might expect in any given month; they augment master budgets.

master budget—A budget integrating individual departmental budgets; prepared for the organization as a whole. It represents the company's primary financial planning tool.

operations budget—A budget used to budget sales and expenses to achieve a desired profit. It is a profit plan that incorporates all revenue and expenses of a business. When completed, it is identical to an income statement except that the numbers listed are *pro forma.*

pro forma—Estimated or not actual in form.

variance—The difference between a budgeted amount and the actual amount; it may be favorable or unfavorable.

zero-base budgeting (ZBB)—A philosophy of budgeting (not a method) that requires that non-revenue department managers prepare a budget starting at zero and justify each expense item.

Review Questions ————————————————————————————

1. What financial methods are used to perform sales forecasting?
2. What financial methods are used to budget revenue center expenses?
3. What is zero-base budgeting?
4. What is cost justifying an expense?
5. What are the six fixed costs of a hotel?
6. What is an operations budget?
7. What does the term *pro forma* mean?
8. What is the typical format for a monthly budgetary report?
9. What is a budget variance?
10. What is a favorable variance?
11. What is a favorable sales variance?
12. What is an unfavorable expense variance?
13. What is a master budget?
14. What is the main assumption in the design of a master budget?

15. What is a flexible budget?

16. What are the two causes of a sales variance?

17. What are the two causes of an expense variance?

18. What formula determines the total price cause of a sales variance?

19. What formula determines the total quantity cause of a sales variance?

20. What formula determines the total cost cause of an expense variance?

21. What formula determines the total quantity cause of an expense variance?

22. What is a capital budget?

Internet Sites

For more information, visit the following Internet sites. Remember that Internet addresses can change without notice. If the site is no longer there, you can use a search engine to look for additional sites.

Budgeting
www.baranskyvaccaro.com/budget.html

Small Business Forecasting and Budgeting Tips
www.sba.gov/library/pubs/fm-8.txt

Budgeting Slide Show
www.aaasc.org/membership/documents/
   FRIA9amTritingerAAAHC2006Budgeting101.ppt

Zero-Base Budgeting
www.investopedia.com/terms/z/zbb.asp
www.caltax.org/ZeroBase.pdf
www.mackinac.org/article.aspx?ID=5928

Fixed and Variable Budgets
www.e-tba.com/flexible-budgeting.htm

Capital Budgeting and Methods
www.netmba.com/finance/capital/budgeting/
www.studyfinance.com/lessons/capbudget/index.mv?page=01
www.studyfinance.com/lessons/capbudget/index.mv?page=09
www.studyfinance.com/lessons/capbudget/index.mv?page=10

Problems

Problem 1

Determine the amount of the variance and whether it is favorable or unfavorable.

	Budget	Actual
Sales	$100,000	$90,000

Problem 2

Determine the amount of the variance and whether it is favorable or unfavorable.

	Budget	Actual
Cost of food sold	$35,000	$38,000

Problem 3

Determine the amount of the variance and whether it is favorable or unfavorable.

	Budget	Actual
Interest income	$1,000	$1,200

Problem 4

Identify the favorable budget variances from the following partial budgetary report:

	Variance
Food sales	$10,000
Beverage sales	(200)
Food cost	100
Supplies expense	(500)

Problem 5

Determine the causes of the following variance:

	Budget	Actual	Variance
Food sales	$18,000	$18,700	$700 favorable

Information from manager's budget working papers:

Sales Forecast Computation:

Average check:	$9
Covers:	2,000

Current month's statistics reported from the accounting department:

Average check:	$8.50
Covers:	2,200

Problem 6

Determine the causes of the following variance:

	Budget	Actual	Variance
Food sales	$35,000	$38,400	$3,400 favorable

Information from manager's budget working papers:

Sales Forecast Computation:

Average check:	$7
Covers:	5,000

Current month's statistics reported from the accounting department:

Average check:	$8
Covers:	4,800

Problem 7

Determine the causes of the following variance:

	Budget	Actual	Variance
Food sales	$48,000	$38,000	$(10,000) unfavorable

Information from manager's budget working papers:

Sales Forecast Computation:
Average check:	$12
Covers:	4,000

Current month's statistics reported from the accounting department:
Average check:	$10
Covers:	3,800

Problem 8

Determine the causes of the following variance:

	Budget	Actual	Variance
Food cost	$7,000	$7,480	$(480) unfavorable

Information from manager's budget working papers:
Covers:	2,000
Average food cost:	$3.50

Current month's statistics reported from the accounting department:
Covers:	2,200
Average food cost:	$3.40

Problem 9

Determine the causes of the following variance:

	Budget	Actual	Variance
Food cost	$20,000	$22,356	$(2,356) unfavorable

Information from manager's budget working papers:
Covers:	5,000
Average food cost:	$4.00

Current month's statistics reported from the accounting department:
Covers:	4,860
Average food cost:	$4.60

Problem 10

Determine the causes of the following variance:

	Budget	Actual	Variance
Food sales	$36,000	$44,450	$8,450 favorable

Information from manager's budget working papers: 6,000 covers. Current month's statistics from accounting: $7 average check.

Problem 11

Determine the causes of the following variance:

	Budget	Actual	Variance
Food cost	$16,800	$15,600	$1,200 favorable

Information from manager's budget working papers:

Average check:	$12
Covers:	4,000
Food cost %:	35%

Current month's statistics reported from the accounting department:

Covers:	3,900
Average food cost:	$4.00

Problem 12

Compute the percentages of sales from the following budgetary report. Show the percentages with one decimal (xx.x%).

	Budget Amount	%	Actual Amount	%
Sales	$50,000		$55,000	
Expenses:				
Food cost	16,000		18,150	
Payroll & related	15,000		15,950	
Supplies	800		935	
China, glassware, silver	200		200	
Contract cleaning	500		500	
Other expenses	1,000		1,280	
Total expenses	33,500		37,015	
Departmental Income	$16,500		$17,985	

Problem 13

Prepare a flexible budget from the following information:

Food sales:	$100,000
Food cost:	38% variable
Payroll & related:	$4,000 fixed, 25% variable
Supplies:	8% variable
China, glass, silver:	$400 fixed
Contract cleaning:	$600 fixed
Other expenses:	$2,000 fixed, 12% variable

List the sales and each expense, and show total expenses and departmental income.

Problem 14

Prepare a series of flexible budgets from the following information:

Food sales:	$100,000
Food cost:	38% variable
Payroll & related:	$4,000 fixed, 25% variable

Supplies:	8% variable
China, glass, silver:	$400 fixed
Contract cleaning:	$600 fixed
Other expenses:	$2,000 fixed, 12% variable

1. The series of budgets are to be in $10,000 increments starting with $100,000 sales and ending with $140,000 sales.

2. List the sales, expenses, and total expenses, and show departmental income.

3. Show a percentage of departmental income to sales for each level. Carry the percentage to one decimal position (xx.x%).

Problem 15

Perform Problem 13 using a computer spreadsheet application.

Case Study

Budget Installation: A Management Critique

The Rogers Hotel is a subsidiary of a major corporation. The hotel has experienced minimal profits or losses for the last five years. The corporate home office recently replaced the hotel's general manager, marketing manager, and controller. The new executives are highly experienced professionals recognized as elite in their field.

The hotel's new executives have discovered that the hotel never did any forecasting or budgeting. They have decided to develop a master budget. The sales and expenses are established at levels that will yield a profit satisfactory to the home office.

To achieve this profit level, the new executives have developed the master budget as follows:

1. The marketing manager forecasted sales for all revenue centers that was subsequently approved by the general manager.

2. The controller prepared the expense budget for all revenue centers that was subsequently approved by the general manager.

3. The non-revenue department managers prepared their expense budgets. Management instructed them to use zero-base budgeting in preparing their departmental budgets, which were subsequently approved by the general manager.

4. The controller prepared the budget for the hotel's fixed costs that was subsequently approved by the general manager.

The revenue and non-revenue managers, collectively among themselves, have heavily criticized management's approach to budgeting and are hostile to the budget reporting process.

The new general manager, marketing manager, and controller are concerned with the animosity shown by the department managers because the latter are qualified professionals who conscientiously perform their responsibilities.

Challenge

You have been engaged by the Rogers Hotel to review the budget planning and preparation process, and also any other important issues critical to effective budgetary management. Your report should include, at a minimum, the following:

- A critique that identifies the commendable actions and the inadvisable actions management took in the installation of the master budget.
- An examination of the budgetary system's planning and preparation process.
- An analysis of the reaction of the department managers.
- Advice to management.
- Limitations of your report.
- Unexplored issues.

Chapter 16 Outline

Competencies

1. Determine whether a seasonal business should remain open during the off-season. (pp. 426–429)

2. Describe the many factors and elements that should be examined as part of a decision to acquire a business. (pp. 429–438)

3. Identify the advantages and disadvantages of buying a franchise. (pp. 438–439)

4. Explain the terms of realty leases and how to choose between variable and fixed leases. (pp. 439–440)

5. Explain the terms of automobile leases and identify when such leases may be appropriate. (pp. 440–443)

6. State the purpose of capital budgeting and demonstrate two simple capital budgeting methods. (pp. 443–446)

16

Financial Decision-Making

PLANNING IS an important management function. The professional hospitality manager must possess knowledge and experience sufficient for making operational and financial decisions in a highly competitive business environment. A successful hospitality business is measured by its profitability, and managers are evaluated on their departments' contribution to profits. Managers who consistently make financial decisions that increase the owners' wealth tend to reach executive ranks with all the accompanying perquisites and remuneration.

Financial decision-making relates to the future and is concerned with alternative courses of action. Financial decision-making must consider both *quantitative* and *qualitative* factors. Quantitative factors are those that can be measured in monetary terms. A decrease of $500 in guest supplies expense is a quantitative factor. Qualitative factors cannot be expressed in monetary terms since it is impossible to measure them with any degree of accuracy; for instance, it is speculative to quantify the benefits of goodwill with any sureness of estimation. Although they cannot be measured precisely, qualitative factors can play a significant role in decision-making.

This chapter uses a pragmatic approach to financial decision-making based primarily on quantitative factors. Though the focus is on quantitative factors, keep in mind that qualitative factors *do* have an effect on decision-making.

This chapter will answer such questions as:

1. Should a hospitality business close or remain open for the off-season?

2. What qualitative factors should be examined in a business acquisition venture?

3. What hazards are involved in using a seller's financial statements?

4. In a business acquisition, what is the difference between a common stock purchase and an asset purchase?

5. What impact do the seller's salary and buyer's needs have on the forecasting of profits when a change of ownership takes place?

6. What critical area requires special scrutiny when the purchase of a family-operated business is considered?

7. What is the impact of financing in a business acquisition?

8. Which enterprise is the best buy among a number of choices?

9. What are the advantages and disadvantages of buying a franchise?

Exhibit 1   Contributory Income Statement Format

Sales	$200,000
Variable Costs	130,000
Contribution Margin	70,000
Fixed Costs	38,000
Income Before Income Taxes	$ 32,000

The contributory income statement is commonly shown in its abbreviated format as follows:

Sales	$200,000
VC	130,000
CM	70,000
FC	38,000
IBIT	$ 32,000

10. What factors must be examined in leasing realty?
11. What are the buy-versus-lease considerations for automobiles?
12. What methods are used to make decisions in the capital budgeting process?

Off-Season Analysis

A financial management tool useful in performing quantitative analysis is the *contributory income statement format* shown in Exhibit 1. The use of this format first requires that all expenses be identified as variable, fixed, and semi-variable. The next step is a cost analysis that determines all variable costs, including the variable portion of semi-variable costs; all fixed costs, including the fixed portion of semi-variable costs; and the variable cost percentage. The data in a cost analysis can be historical or forecasted. A sample cost analysis is shown in Exhibit 2.

Closing for the off-season is a traditional practice for many resorts and tourist-related hospitality businesses. Many times, such businesses close for the off-season primarily because it is the customary action for a seasonal business. The contributory income statement format is useful in determining (from a quantitative viewpoint) whether a hospitality company should close for the off-season or not.

Quantitative Analysis

The first column of figures in Exhibit 3 shows historical data for the Autry Resort. The general manager must decide whether to continue a 12-month operation or close for the off-season.

After the historical information is collected, the next step is to refine the 12-month data by separating it into the in-season and off-season periods. The accounting department easily prepares this information. Refer again to Exhibit 3,

Exhibit 2   Cost Analysis to Determine Variable and Fixed Costs

Forecasted Sales		$200,000			
Budgeted Expense	**Type**	**TC**	**VC**	**FC**	**Comments**
Cost of Food sold	V	$ 61,000	$ 61,000		
Payroll & related	SV	58,000	36,000	$ 22,000	Regression analysis
Guest supplies	V	3,000	3,000		
Operating supplies	V	8,000	8,000		
Utilities	SV	9,000	7,000	2,000	High-low method
Other variable cost	V	10,000	10,000		} In actual practice,
Other fixed costs	F	12,000		12,000	} each expense is
Other SV costs	SV	7,000	5,000	2,000	} listed individually.
Total expenses	SV	$168,000	$ 130,000	$ 38,000	
IBIT		$ 32,000			

$$\text{Variable Cost \%} = \frac{VC}{Sales} = \frac{\$130,000}{\$200,000} = 65\%$$

Exhibit 3   Autry Resort: In-Season and Off-Season Data

	Last Year (12 Months)	In-season (9 Months)	Off-season (3 Months)	Comments
Sales	$1,100,000	$1,000,000	$100,000	
VC	660,000	600,000	60,000	60%
CM	$ 440,000	$ 400,000	$ 40,000	
FC	240,000	180,000	60,000	See footnote
IBIT	$ 200,000	$ 220,000	$ (20,000)	

Footnote:

$240,000 FC ÷ 12 = $20,000 allocated equally to each month.

In-season = $20,000 × 9 months = $180,000 FC
Off-season = $20,000 × 3 months = $60,000 FC
                  12 months = $240,000 FC

which shows a 9-month in-season and a 3-month off-season. The exhibit reveals a $220,000 profit for the in-season and a loss of $20,000 for the off-season, netting a $200,000 profit for the year.

Would the Autry Resort enjoy a $220,000 profit for the year if it closed for the three-month off-season and eliminated the $20,000 loss?

As disclosed in Exhibit 4, the answer is no. In fact, the profits of the Autry Resort would decline to $160,000. How can staying open for the off-season and incurring a $20,000 loss actually *improve* profits? The answer centers on fixed costs,

Exhibit 4   Pro forma Autry Resort Income Statement if Closed for the Off-Season

	12 Months	Comments
Sales	$1,000,000	Sales are for 9 months
VC	600,000	60%
CM	$ 400,000	
FC	240,000	$240,000 per year
IBIT	$ 160,000	

which exist regardless of the sales level and are incurred even when the resort is closed. The off-season's value is its **contribution margin.** Observe that, while the off-season has an operating loss, it also has a contribution margin of $40,000; the contribution margin is the amount necessary to cover fixed costs (and, after fixed costs are paid, operating profit).

In this case, fixed costs were $60,000, and the contribution margin covered $40,000 of these costs. If the Autry Resort closed for the off-season, the fixed costs would have to be absorbed by a shorter operating year. The significance of the contribution margin to the Autry Resort can be explained as follows:

Profit if open 12 months	$200,000
Contribution margin lost if closed for off-season	40,000
Profit if open for only 9 months	$160,000

The Autry Resort is an unsophisticated model for making an open/close decision for the off-season. There are some variable and fixed costs that might change when the resort closes for the off-season. However, if one attempts to be uncompromisingly precise in quantitative analysis, the financial decision-making process may never end. A flawless analysis would be costly and time consuming, and yet produce a similar conclusion. Pragmatism advocates the use of financial decision models that can easily be employed in the actual world of business to produce timely and effective business decisions.

Qualitative Considerations

A decision-making model cannot evaluate qualitative factors in the final decision-making process because of the personal and isolated considerations inherent in this decision. Nevertheless, there are many qualitative factors that might be significant to an open-or-close decision.

For example, community relations may be important. There may possibly be negative reaction in the community to a business that enjoys profits only in prosperous times, but does not serve residential citizens all year. There may be significant loss of goodwill to local competitors who stay open. There may be local political considerations as well.

As for employee considerations, there might be a demoralizing effect on employees and uncertain availability of qualified personnel to hire when reopening. Closing may also introduce a greater need for ongoing training and retraining. On the other hand, an owner/manager who has worked 60 to 80 hours a week and endured a stressful period might look forward to this extended vacation.

When qualitative factors agree with quantitative factors, the decision is straightforward. When they point in opposite directions, it becomes necessary to weigh them against each other in the attempt to find the best course of action.

Acquiring a Business

Entrepreneurs and executives of major corporations may face a common financial decision at some point: Which business should be purchased? While this chapter cannot provide comprehensive coverage of all the qualitative and quantitative factors critical in buying a business, it can provide a useful introduction.

Qualitative Considerations

Again, qualitative factors will not be quantified or evaluated in our decision-making models. However, the purchase of a business raises some engaging questions, such as the following:

1. How will guests react to a new ownership?
2. Will essential key personnel remain with the new ownership?
3. What is the condition of the property and equipment?
4. How many times has the business been sold in the past?
5. Has there been a recent change in competition?
6. Is new formidable competition coming in the future?
7. If the property is leased, is the lease short term? Is the lease due for renewal? Does the lease have unreasonable escalation clauses?
8. If this is a franchise, is the franchise readily transferable? Are the franchise terms expiring?

Many authoritative sources advise prospective buyers to ask the seller: Why are you selling the business? The answer must be carefully appraised, since not many sellers would truthfully say, "I am selling because the future looks terrible for my business."

Covenant Not to Compete

During the negotiation process of acquiring a business, a buyer wants assurance that the seller will not continue to operate a similar business. A **covenant not to compete** is an agreement made by the seller not to operate a similar business in a certain geographical area for a specified period of time. In some cases, a seller may negotiate an extra payment for this agreement. A payment for a covenant not to compete is treated as the purchase of an intangible asset that must be amortized over a 15-year life, regardless of its useful life (mandated by Section 197 of the Internal Revenue Code).

Using the Seller's Financial Statements

A prospective buyer of a business must study the business's financial records in order to gather relevant financial data. Financial statements audited by a certified public accountant impart credibility to the fairness of financial information. However, most small businesses have never had their financial statements audited because owners and managers find audits unnecessary and tremendously expensive. A potential buyer should ascertain the authenticity of any financial data before relying on its representation. For instance, a buyer could study copies of income tax returns to verify the seller's financial data.

Some sellers of small businesses might claim that the profits of the business are understated because of their practice of "skimming," the owner's embezzlement of sales by pilferage to circumvent the record-keeping system. Is this skimming alleged or real? First, note that skimming is illegal. Second, it is poor management because the resulting lower historical profits may hinder getting future financing due to "weak" financial statements. How much trust can you place in the owner's character, records, and statements? Perhaps this is not the business that warrants your attention and risk of capital.

Assuming that the authenticity of the financial records is proven, a next step involves forecasting the profits of the business. It is important to realize that the financial needs of the previous owner and the new owner are separate and distinct. Some critical questions a prospective buyer must ask when using a seller's financial statements to project profits include the following:

1. Is the buyer purchasing the common stock from the seller, or, instead, is this an asset purchase?

2. Is the seller drawing a salary that reflects the buyer's personal needs?

3. Is this a family-operated business?

4. What effect will financing have on profits and cash flow?

Seller's Legal Form of Organization

The legal form of the seller's business plays a major role in the negotiations. The two most common legal forms of business organization in the hospitality industry are the *proprietorship* (an unincorporated business owned by one person) and the *corporation*. Because of personal liability concerns, most hospitality businesses are incorporated (corporations).

If the seller's business form is a proprietorship, a buyer purchases *the assets* of the business at a negotiated price. The legal form of the business is *not* purchased. While the buyer may retain the original business name, he or she is required to start a new business entity, which could be in any legal form, such as a proprietorship or corporation.

In contrast, the owners (stockholders) of a corporation own the business, but the corporation owns its own assets.

When purchasing a proprietorship, a buyer must use the asset method (discussed later in this chapter) to account for the assets acquired. When purchasing an incorporated business, a buyer can choose between two alternatives for the method of acquisition:

1. Purchase only the assets from the corporation and not its legal organization. In this case, the asset method is used.

2. Purchase the common stock from the stockholder (owner).

If an existing corporation is acquired via the purchase of corporate stock from the stockholders, *it is the legal form of the business that is purchased,* and the buyer becomes a new shareholder in the existing corporation. While there is a change in ownership, there is no change made to the accounting records of the corporation. When common stock is purchased from a seller, the transaction is solely a change in control (stock ownership) of the business. The corporation continues in business, keeping its legal form of business organization. Some accounting and legal considerations are as follows:

1. The bookkeeping records remain with the corporation and continue unaffected by the change in ownership.

2. Depreciation of existing assets is not affected because the assets remain at their original cost with respective accumulated depreciation. (However, any purchased covenant not to compete will set up a new asset to be depreciated.)

3. Recorded liabilities remain with the business.

4. The business will be responsible for any unknown liabilities. (The buy/sell agreement should contain provisions for this contingency, holding the seller legally liable.)

Since the purchase of common stock represents a business acquisition, the depreciation of existing assets is not affected. However, the acquisition may create new assets such as a covenant not to compete. For example, assume a target company has the following assets on its books:

	Cost	Accumulated Depreciation
Land	$200,000	
Building	500,000	$175,000
Furniture & equipment	$100,000	30,000

The corporate stock is to be purchased for $1,500,000. Furthermore, the seller adds $40,000 for a covenant not to compete.

The remaining allowable depreciation and amortization for the assets under a stock purchase is computed as follows:

Land	$ 0	
Building	325,000	($500,000 − $175,000)
Furniture & equipment	70,000	($100,000 − $30,000)
Covenant not to compete	40,000	
Total remaining depreciation & amortization	$435,000	

Land is an asset that is not depreciated. The remaining depreciation on the building and furniture and equipment is computed by subtracting the accumulated depreciation (depreciation taken in prior periods) from the cost of the assets. The covenant not to compete creates a new intangible asset, which must be amortized over 15 years. The $1,500,000 is not a factor because the purchase is for the corporate stock; the existing assets and liabilities accompany the stock at book value.

Purchasing common stock might bring a tax disadvantage to the buyer because the purchase price cannot be depreciated since the price paid represents the cost basis of the stock, similar to purchasing stock on the New York Stock Exchange. Consequently, the cost is not recoverable until the stock is sold.

Depreciation is a non-cash expense that is tax deductible, thereby reducing the company's tax liability. Acquiring a business by purchase of the seller's stock usually means the buyer (by losing the ability to depreciate) is paying a premium for the business that is not reflected in the basis of the assets. Quite often, the seller offers a lower acquisition price as an incentive when the basis of the buy/sell agreement is a stock purchase rather than an asset purchase.

The Asset Method. The asset method is used when the target company is a proprietorship and when a corporation's assets are purchased rather than its common stock. The newly purchased assets are then capitalized at the buyer's cost and depreciated over their useful lives. The buyer may select any form of business organization for his or her new business.

The target company's books showing the asset costs and accumulated depreciation are not a factor for the buyer. The seller will retain the accounting records of the pre-sale company, and the buyer will set up a new set of accounting records.

To properly depreciate the assets, the buyer will need to obtain the fair market value (FMV) of the assets. This FMV will become the new basis for depreciation. In addition, goodwill and any covenant not to compete create new intangible assets, which must be amortized over 15 years. Fundamentally, goodwill is the excess price paid above the FMV of the assets.

For example, the following assets of a company are to be purchased for $1,500,000. Furthermore, the seller adds $40,000 for a covenant not to compete. A market evaluation of the assets is as follows:

	FMV
Land	$ 300,000
Building	600,000
Furniture & equipment	200,000
Total	$1,100,000

The remaining allowable depreciation and amortization for the assets under an asset purchase is computed as follows:

Land	$ 0
Building	600,000
Furniture & equipment	200,000
Covenant not to compete	40,000
Goodwill	400,000
Total remaining depreciation and amortization	$1,240,000

Exhibit 5   Business Acquisition via Purchase of Assets: Impact of Depreciation

	Seller (a)	Buyer (b)
Sales	$ 400,000	$ 400,000
Cost of sales	120,000	120,000
Gross profit	$ 280,000	$ 280,000
Operating Expenses:		
Payroll & Related	150,000	150,000
Depreciation	10,000	40,000 (c)
Other expenses	100,000	100,000
Total expenses	260,000	290,000
IBIT	$ 20,000	$ (10,000)

(a) Last year's data. Also represents typical operating year.

(b) Seller's sales and expenses as modified are used to forecast buyer's first year of operations.

(c) The building and equipment are depreciated at the buyer's cost over an estimated useful life. The purchase price of the land must be separately identified because land is not depreciated in the hospitality industry.

Land is an asset that is not depreciated. The depreciation on the building and furniture and equipment is computed on its cost basis, namely fair market value. The covenant not to compete creates a new intangible asset. The $1,500,000 is a factor in this transaction because it is expressly for the purchase of the assets. Goodwill, another intangible asset, is created because the purchase price of $1,500,000 exceeds the $1,100,000 FMV of the assets by $400,000.

Furthermore, if the transaction includes additional costs for the name of the business or trademarks, these new assets are also amortized.

Exhibit 5 shows a theoretical comparison made when a buyer purchased the assets of a business. The sole objective of the exhibit is to dramatize the effect of a change in depreciation. The seller's income statement of last year is used as a forecasting tool for next year. In this case, the $20,000 profit of the business turns into a loss of $10,000 because of the change in depreciation. This is not extraordinary because the seller will typically have purchased the assets at lower cost many years ago: since the seller has owned the business for many years, the assets are nearly fully depreciated.

Seller's Salary Versus Buyer's Needs

The ideal circumstance occurs when a business is paying the seller a lavish salary that a buyer would not consider essential for his or her personal needs and lifestyle. In such a case, the buyer can adjust the payroll costs downward and thus provide a buffer for paying back any financing.

Exhibit 6   Change of Ownership: Impact of Wages When a Family-Owned Business Is Purchased

	Seller (a)	Buyer (b)	
Sales	$500,000	$500,000	
Cost of sales	150,000	150,000	
Gross profit	$350,000	$350,000	
Payroll & Related:			
Owner's salary	40,000	60,000	(new owner's requirement)
Spouse & children	0	55,000	(replace unpaid family time)
Employee payroll	50,000	50,000	
Employee benefits (c)	18,000	33,000	(20% of paid wages)
Other expenses	194,000	194,000	
Total expenses	302,000	392,000	
IBIT	$ 48,000	$ (42,000)	

(a) Last year's data. Also represents typical operating year.
(b) Seller's sales and expenses, as modified, used to forecast buyer's first year of operations.
(c) Employee benefits include payroll taxes and insurance plans.

However, a seller may have been paid a salary that is less than satisfactory to the buyer. If the seller's salary has been limited by the capability of the business, there may be no remedy for the buyer because the profits of the business may not provide sufficient cash flow to pay the requisite salary.

Family-Operated Businesses

The purchase of a family-operated business calls for a careful examination of the staffing and related wages. It is not unusual for a husband-and-wife team to operate a facility while only one member is paid a salary or wage. Additionally, their children may render services and receive only a personal allowance. Unless a buyer can duplicate these free or lower-paid services, the wage expense in the seller's financial statements will need to be revised.

Exhibit 6 shows how payroll costs can affect profits when (1) the salary needs of the buyer are greater than those of the seller, and (2) the buyer will have to pay for services a family-operated business received at little or no cost. Notice that the family-operated business had a $48,000 profit last year. After making an adjustment for payroll due to a change in ownership, the business now has a *loss* of $42,000.

The Impact of Financing on Profits and Cash Flow

A change of ownership for any business usually means a change in the interest expense and cash flow of the business. The seller may own the business debt-free or may have originally financed its purchase with a smaller loan balance than

Exhibit 7 Loan Amortization Schedule

Amount: $200,000	Term: 120 Months			Interest: 12%
Monthly payments (119): $2869.47			Last Payment (120): $2857.68	
	Total Paid	**Interest**	**Principal**	**Balance**
				$ 200,000.00
Year 1	$ 34,433.64	$ 23,406.58	$ 11,027.06	188,972.94
Year 2	34,433.64	22,008.08	12,425.56	176,547.38
Year 3	34,433.64	20,432.20	14,001.44	162,545.94
Year 4	34,433.64	18,656.47	15,777.17	146,768.77
Year 5	34,433.64	16,655.53	17,778.11	128,990.66
Year 6	34,433.64	14,400.82	20,032.82	108,957.84
Year 7	34,433.64	11,860.16	22,573.48	86,384.36
Year 8	34,433.64	8,997.27	25,436.37	60,947.99
Year 9	34,433.64	5,771.30	28,662.34	32,285.65
Year 10	34,421.85	2,136.20	32,285.65	0
Total	$ 344,324.61	$ 144,324.61	$ 200,000.00	

Comment:
The use of manual amortization tables and dissimilar computerized amortization software might result in a difference of pennies in the calculated periodic payments shown in this exhibit.

the buyer can match. It is unlikely that the financing of the buyer and seller will be identical. Therefore, the buyer must modify the interest expense in the seller's financial statements.

Most loans require a monthly payment that includes two parts:

1. A portion to pay off (amortize) part of the loan balance. The loan balance is called the *principal*.

2. The interest computed on the unpaid balance.

Typically, in the early years of a loan, the largest portion of the monthly payment pays the interest on the loan. Exhibit 7 shows an amortization schedule for a $200,000 loan payable monthly over a period of 10 years bearing a 12 percent interest rate. Notice that it is not until midway through the loan that the borrower's payments start to favor the principal portion. The interest expense of $144,324.61 over the life of the loan is considerable when contrasted with the original $200,000 principal.

A buyer should remember two important points when forecasting the success of a hospitality business:

1. The interest expense reduces the profits of the business, which also affect its cash flow.

Exhibit 8   Change of Ownership: Impact of Financing on Profits

	Seller (a)	Buyer (b)
Sales	$400,000	$400,000
Cost of sales	120,000	120,000
Gross profit	$280,000	$280,000
Payroll & Related:		
Owner's salary	60,000	60,000
Employee payroll	65,000	65,000
Employee benefits	25,000	25,000
Interest expense	0	23,407
Depreciation	10,000	10,000 (c)
Other expenses	100,000	100,000
Total expenses	260,000	283,407
IBIT	20,000	$ (3,407)

Comment:

While an income statement contains the interest portion of loan payments, it does **not** show the principal portion of loan payments. The first year's principal payments required cash payments totaling $11,027.

(a) Last year's data. Also represents typical operating year.

(b) Seller's sales and expenses as modified are used to forecast buyer's first year of operations.

(c) The buyer purchased the common stock from the seller. If the assets only had been purchased, depreciation would change.

2. The principal portion of the payments does not show on the income statement; instead, the buyer must consider it when measuring the cash flow of the business.

Exhibit 8 shows the effect on profits for a business that is financed with a $200,000 loan at a 12 percent interest rate payable monthly over 10 years. While the seller enjoyed a $20,000 profit, the buyer would experience a *loss* of $3,407 in the first year of operations. A loss also affects cash flow, which is needed to pay the $11,027 principal portion of the loan that does not show on the income statement.

Selecting an Enterprise to Buy

A prospective buyer of any business spends a lot of time shopping for the "right" business. A prospective buyer visits many facilities before narrowing the choices down to perhaps two that seem most promising. The following example examines the process of determining which of two restaurants to buy. However, the same principles can be applied to any number of alternative choices.

This example is designed to emphasize the quantitative approach to decision-making. For this reason, the two restaurants have been designed with identical attributes to eliminate argument or confusion about qualitative considerations. Their locations are equally desirable. Each enjoys similar goodwill. The facilities and equipment are comparable. Each serves identical customer markets. The

Exhibit 9   Comparison of Two Restaurants

Last Year's Results:

	Restaurant X	Restaurant Y
Sales	$ 800,000	$ 800,000
VC	440,000 (55%)	320,000 (40%)
CM	$ 360,000	$ 480,000
FC	270,000	390,000
IBIT	$ 90,000	$ 90,000

Assuming a 10% Sales Increase:

	Restaurant X	Restaurant Y
Sales	$ 880,000	$ 880,000
VC	484,000 (55%)	352,000 (40%)
CM	$ 396,000	$ 528,000
FC	270,000	390,000
IBIT	$ 126,000	$ 138,000

Assuming a 10% Sales Decrease:

	Restaurant X	Restaurant Y
Sales	$ 720,000	$ 720,000
VC	396,000 (55%)	288,000 (40%)
CM	$ 324,000	$ 432,000
FC	270,000	390,000
IBIT	$ 54,000	$ 42,000

Which restaurant is the best buy?

restaurants are identical in sales volume and profit, as shown in Exhibit 9. Each restaurant had sales of $800,000 and profits of $90,000 last year. The purchase price is identical for each restaurant; the only differentiating factor is the combination of variable and fixed costs. Assume that current conditions indicate the trend will continue for this cost composition.

Exhibit 9 also shows what the operating results would be if sales increased by 10 percent. The variable cost percentage and fixed cost dollars did not change with volume. Note that, when sales are increased, Restaurant Y shows a better profit than Restaurant X. The profit of Restaurant X is lower because its higher variable cost percentage produces a higher variable cost at this sales level.

Exhibit 9 further shows what the operating results would be if sales decreased by 10 percent. This time, Restaurant X shows a better profit than Restaurant Y. In times of decreasing sales, the profit of Restaurant Y is lower because of its higher fixed cost dollars.

With all the intangibles being equal, the ultimate choice depends on an investor's personal constitution. Let's use last year as a basis of comparison: in times of increased sales, Restaurant Y is the better choice; in times of decreased sales, Restaurant X is the better choice.

A dynamic entrepreneur would likely select Restaurant Y because of its greater earnings potential.

Buying a Franchise

A **franchise** is a marketing right granting the use of a name, trademark, and the marketing of branded services and products. The *franchisor* grants this right by contract (franchise agreement) to a *franchisee*.

A franchise acquisition usually requires an initial one-time fee. Once in operation, the franchisee pays a royalty, a fixed periodic fee, or a combination thereof. The royalty is usually based on sales. A hotel franchise agreement might stipulate a franchise fee composed of a fixed fee based on number of rooms plus a royalty calculated on revenue.

A franchise is usually granted for only one location. Some franchisors may sell a franchise covering a large territory, allowing the franchisee to also become a franchisor for that geographic area.

Buying a franchise offers the following advantages to the franchisee:

1. A successful, established name that is easily recognized and acclaimed by consumers.

2. Technical services such as site selection and building, market research, business advice, training.

3. Financing advantage, either directly (by the franchisor) or indirectly, because the franchisor's reputation imparts credibility to outside financing institutions and creditors.

4. National and regional advertising, the cost of which is either nominal or included in the royalty fee. The franchise agreement may specify that the franchisee financially contribute to national and regional advertising, as well as pay for local advertising.

5. Access to national computerized reservation systems.

On the other hand, the disadvantages of buying a franchise for a franchisee are listed here:

1. The initial cost of the franchise and continuing royalties might become unacceptable cost factors in the long run.

2. The franchisor's mandated standards of operation might present a loss of freedom not acceptable to the franchisee.

3. Products required for purchase by the franchise agreement might carry an unreasonable mark-up.

Major reasons to buy a franchise are to procure an instantly recognizable name and a proven business system. These features offer a greatly reduced business risk to the franchisee, compared with the risk assumed by a buyer of an independent operation. Selecting a franchise requires a careful analysis of the franchise agreement and its requirements, rights, and specified time period. Also, a prospective franchisee can gain valuable information by talking with existing franchisees.

Leasing

Leasing arrangements involve a written contract called a **lease**. The renter is called a **lessee**, while the landlord (owner) is known as a **lessor**. A lease gives the lessee use of property or equipment under a rental agreement, and the lessee avoids the cash outlay and particular obligations of ownership.

There are two methods of accounting for leases, one for an **operating lease** and one for a **capital lease**. Stated very simply, an operating lease is a rental agreement, while a capital lease is a purchase disguised as a lease. Capital leases are treated as asset purchases and are not discussed in this chapter.

Leasing Realty

It is not uncommon for a successful hospitality business to be situated on rented property. When the business is sold, the lease for the site is usually transferable to the buyer. The leasing of real estate can also occur when a business is purchased; the seller of the business may retain ownership of the real estate, thereby becoming a lessor after selling his or her business.

The decision to buy or lease real estate is typically not an option; it is restricted by circumstances dictating the buy/lease outcome. For example, an owner of a particularly desirable site might refuse any sales offers for it, but instead make it available for use through leasing. Or a site for sale might be excluded from the buyer's decision-making process because it is too expensive or financing is not available.

Signing the Lease. Many lessors insist that the lessee sign the lease twice: first as an officer of the corporation, which makes the corporation liable for the lease; and then as an individual, which makes the lessee personally liable.

The terms of a realty lease should be closely examined before the lease is signed because the lease is a legal contract. The prospective lessee should examine the lease's time period and rental charge, as well as some other major issues, including the following:

1. Responsibility for maintenance and insurance

2. Escalation clauses for lessor's insurance and property taxes

3. Transferability of the lease (sub-lease) by the lessee

4. Restrictions on improvements

5. Definition of improvements made by lessee (leasehold improvements) that become the property of the lessor at the end of the lease

6. Renewal options

7. Termination clauses

A lessor may offer the choice of a variable lease, a fixed lease, or a lease with the characteristics of both types. The proper selection of one of these types is important to the profitability of a hospitality business.

Selecting a Variable or Fixed Realty Lease. A **fixed lease** is characterized by a set rental charge for a specified period of time. A **variable lease** is also for a specified period of time, but the rental charge is stated as a percentage, usually of the lessee's sales volume.

Because of the owner's escalating insurance costs and property taxes, any lease may contain a rental adjustment clause to cover these increases.

If given the choice of a fixed lease or variable lease, a lessee should compute the **indifference point** to aid in the decision-making process. The indifference point is the sales level at which rental expense is identical for a fixed or variable lease. The indifference point can be calculated with the following formula:

$$\text{Indifference Point Sales} = \frac{\text{Cost of Fixed Lease}}{\text{Variable Lease Percentage}}$$

Assume that a lessor offers the choice of a fixed lease at $4,000 per month or a variable lease calculated at 5 percent of monthly sales. The indifference point is calculated as follows:

$$\text{Indifference Point Sales} = \frac{\$40,000}{5\%} = \$80,000$$

At a sales level of $80,000, it doesn't matter which type of lease is chosen. The rent for a fixed lease is $4,000, and, at sales of $80,000, the rent for a variable lease is also $4,000 ($80,000 × 5%). Based on this analysis, if the sales are expected to exceed $80,000 monthly, the lessee should take the fixed lease; for sales under $80,000, the lessee will pay less under the variable lease.

Leasing Automobiles

Leasing an automobile is paying for the *use* of a car over a period of time. Leasing still involves negotiating the purchase price of the car just as you would if you were buying. However, you are not the purchaser; instead, a leasing company buys the car from the dealer. The dealer acts as an agent of the leasing company, quite often a subsidiary of the car manufacturer. Once the leasing contract is signed, the lease relationship is with the leasing company, not the automobile dealer.

Even if an auto is leased, it imposes some of the same responsibilities as ownership. A lessee must make monthly payments and pay for licenses, liability and property insurance, property taxes, and maintenance. Repairs are usually covered by a manufacturer's warranty.

Gap Insurance. If a leased auto is stolen or destroyed, the lessee is responsible for the difference (gap) between what is owed on the remainder of the lease and the insurance proceeds. Gap insurance is often provided to protect the lessee from this catastrophe. Gap protection is generally not available in purchase financing.

Potential End-of-Lease Charges. At the end of the lease, the car is returned to the leasing company, usually at a dealership, though not necessarily the original dealer. The lessee may purchase the car at the price specified in the lease agreement. If the lessee does not purchase the car, he or she may be charged for excessive mileage or excessive wear and tear.

Lease-Versus-Buy Decision. Rigorous number crunching and abundant examples may never yield a decisive answer in a lease-versus-buy decision because the results are seldom conclusive. The advantages and disadvantages of leasing are difficult to quantify. Leasing should be analyzed from a short-term approach versus a long-term one.

The short-term cost of leasing is similar to the cost of buying. In leasing, you essentially pay for the depreciation of the car during the leasing period.

The long-term cost of leasing is usually higher than the cost of buying. If a buyer keeps a car several years after the loan is paid off, the cost is spread over a longer term. Buying should be the choice if a long-term financial benefit is the objective rather than the opportunity to drive a newer, better car more often.

The advantages of leasing are as follows:

1. *Lower up-front cash outlay.* However, some leases require an up-front acquisition fee that is sometimes equal to a purchase down payment.

2. *Deferred sales tax.* In a purchase, the sales tax is due in full. Under a lease arrangement, the sales tax is usually based on the monthly payment and is payable over the life of the lease.

3. *Lower monthly payments.* The monthly lease can be significantly lower than a monthly loan payment. On luxury automobiles, the difference can be several hundred dollars per month.

4. *Fewer repair costs.* The leased automobile is usually new or a recent model covered by a manufacturer's warranty.

5. *More car, more often.* Because of the small initial outlay and lease term, a lessee can drive a better model or more expensive car. At lease expiration, the lessee may again lease a new car.

6. *No used-car selling hassles.* When the lease expires, the lessee simply returns the car to the dealer.

The disadvantages of leasing are as follows:

1. *No ownership equity.* However, a lease usually offers a purchase option at a predetermined price that may be exercised upon lease expiration. Even though the leasing company owns the car, the lessor usually allows the lessee and any qualifying dealer to negotiate the purchase price, if, at the end of the lease, the purchase option price is higher than market value.

2. *Mileage charges.* A typical lease allows 12,000 or 15,000 miles annually without penalty. Excess miles can carry a significant charge. If higher mileage is expected, this factor should be negotiated in the initial leasing contract.

3. *Excess wear and tear charges.* At lease expiration, the leasing company expects the car to be returned in the condition stated in the lease. For example, any body dents, broken glass, and other major damages are chargeable to the lessee.

4. *Early termination penalty.* Generally, early termination incurs a penalty charge, a disposition fee, and a charge for all remaining depreciation on the car, less its residual value. In essence, early termination is not practical and quite often is nearly equal to the remaining lease payments.

Leasing Terminology. A variety of terms are used in the context of leasing. The meanings of several such terms are listed below.

- *Acquisition fee*: A service charge for the lease. This fee may include gap insurance. Leases without any acquisition fee might have included these costs in the capitalized cost.

- *Capitalized cost (cap cost):* The negotiated price of the car, a significant number because it is comparable to a "selling price."

- *Capitalized cost reductions:* Down payment, trade-in, dealer incentives, and manufacturer's incentives.

- *Net capitalized cost (net cap cost):* Capitalized cost less capitalized cost reductions.

- *Lease period or term:* Usually stated in months; most leases are for 24, 36, or 48 months.

- *Residual value:* Value of the car at the end of the lease. The higher the residual, the lower the monthly lease payment.

- *Money factor or lease factor:* The leasing company's charge for "interest," similar to purchase financing. This interest charge is not readily comparable because it is stated as a reciprocal of 24 in decimal format. To equate the money factor to an annual interest rate *percentage*, multiply the money factor by 2400. For example, a money factor quoted as .00333 converts to an annual percentage rate of 7.992 percent (.00333 × 2400).

Calculating the Monthly Lease Payment. A lessee need not be concerned with the intricate calculation of the monthly lease payment; it is provided by the dealer and stated in the lease agreement. The calculation of the monthly lease payment can be complex because of the many variables a lease may contain. Monthly lease payments consist of a depreciation fee, a financing fee (money factor), and sales tax, if any. The exact procedure used to calculate a monthly lease payment will vary among leasing companies. Exhibit 10 illustrates one method used to calculate a monthly lease payment. Its procedure is as follows:

Step	Description
A	Enter capitalized cost
B	Enter capitalized cost reductions
C	(A − B) = net cap cost
D	Enter residual value
E	(C − D) ÷ lease period = depreciation fee
F	(C + D) × money factor = financing fee
G	E + F = monthly lease payment, excluding sales tax
H	Enter sales tax
I	G + H = monthly lease payment

Exhibit 10   Calculation of Monthly Lease Payment

Lease Data: Term 36 Months, Money Factor .003333

Step	Description		Fee
A	Cap Cost	$27,000	
B	Cap Reductions	5,000	
C	Net Cap Cost	$22,000	
D	Residual	$16,000	
E	(C − D)	= 6,000 ÷ 36 =	$166.67 Depreciation fee
F	(C + D)	= 38,000 × .003333	$126.65 Financing fee
G	(E + F)		$293.32 Total
H	6% Sales tax		$ 17.60
I	Monthly lease payment		$310.92

The above procedure was developed from a formula in Auto Lease Guide, www.leaseguide.com, ©1997 Albert D. Hearn.

Closed-End and Open-End Leases. There are two types of automobile leases: closed-end and open-end. **Closed-end leases** are the usual consumer leases and are sometimes called "walk-away" leases. If the vehicle is worth less than its contract residual value, the leasing company is the loser, not the lessee. Yet, if the vehicle is worth more, the lessee can buy it at the stated purchase option price.

Open-end leases are used more in commercial leasing contracts. However, they can also be used in consumer contracts. In this case, the lessee takes the market value risk, not the leasing company. If the leased vehicle's market value is lower than a stated contract residual value, the lessee is responsible for paying the difference.

Capital Budgeting

Capital budgeting is planning for the acquisition of land, buildings, furniture, equipment, and other long-lived assets. In addition to planning for new business acquisition and expansion of present facilities, the executive management of a hospitality business is usually inundated with numerous requests from all departments for the procurement of additional furniture, vehicles, and equipment, or replacement thereof.

All businesses have limited cash or financing capability; therefore, capital acquisition requests must be ranked by priority. The ranking of these requests is generally determined from three basic factors in the following order:

1. Governmental requirements

2. Quality of facilities and customer service

3. Financial return

Governmental requirements may mandate safety equipment and protective devices under the Occupational Safety & Health Administration (OSHA). Federal, state, and local governments also have regulations covering handicap access, smoking, food handling, and other health standards. Compliance with these regulations often requires significant expenditures, and financial return is not part of the decision-making process.

The quality of facilities and customer service must be maintained for the business to enjoy repeat business and new guests. Replacement of items such as worn-out china or wobbly tables and chairs are expenditures that cannot be measured on a financial return basis.

After the mandatory and essential expenditures are determined, the remaining asset purchase requests (projects) are then financially evaluated and ranked based on their contribution to profits or on when the cash flow generated by the asset justifies its expenditure. This ranking is performed by the use of capital budgeting decision-making tools.

Measuring the financial return of a capital purchase request usually requires the following information:

- Initial cost (cash outflow)
- Depreciation (tax deduction, not a cash outflow)
- Annual operating expenses (cash outflow)
- Revenue or savings (cash inflow)

This information is then used in capital budgeting methods that evaluate the financial return of a project. Two simple methods are the average rate of return (ARR) method and the payback method. While these methods ignore the time value of money, they are quick and simple to use. The more sophisticated methods (net present value and internal rate of return) incorporate the time value of money, but are complex and time consuming, and require the use of present value tables. The typical hospitality manager is usually not expected to perform these calculations. Instead, the accounting department generally provides them.

Average Rate of Return

The average rate of return (ARR) method measures the net annual return (net after depreciation and income taxes) compared to the *average* of the investment. The formula is:

$$ARR = \frac{\text{Net Annual Return}}{(\text{Investment} + \text{Salvage}) \div 2}$$

Net annual return may be annual savings, annual cash flow, or annual profit (after deducting depreciation and income taxes). *Investment* is the initial purchase cost. *Salvage* represents the residual or scrap value of the asset at the end of its useful life. Adding the total initial purchase cost to the estimated salvage value of the new asset, then dividing the total by two, gives an average investment.

Using the data in Exhibit 11, the ARR for this proposal is calculated as follows:

$$ARR = \frac{\$3,080}{(\$30,000 + \$0) \div 2} = 20.5\%$$

Exhibit 11   Proposal to Invest in New Dishwasher

New Dishwasher Data:

Purchase cost and installation	$30,000
Salvage at end of useful life	0
Estimated useful life	5 years
Depreciation method	Straight line
Annual depreciation	$6,000 ($30,000 ÷ 5 years)

Old Dishwasher Data:
Fully depreciated
No salvage value

Annual Expenses

	Old Dishwasher	New Dishwasher
Wages & Related	$27,600	$20,000
Power	4,000	3,000
Supplies	800	600
Repairs	2,000	400
Depreciation	0	6,000
Total	$34,400	$30,000

Annual savings before income taxes	$ 4,400 ($34,400 − $30,000)
Income taxes @ 30%	1,320 ($4,400 × 30%)
Net annual savings after income taxes	$ 3,080

A minimum average rate of return is generally used to determine whether a project remains in contention with other purchase requests. The surviving projects are finally determined by a combination of the following factors:

- Initial cash and financing requirements
- Urgency to the business
- Project risk
- Financial return

Payback Method

The payback method measures the estimated number of years a project will take to return its original cost (or pay for itself). The formula is as follows:

$$\text{Payback Period} = \frac{\text{Purchase Cost}}{\text{Net Annual Return} + \text{Annual Depreciation}}$$

The *purchase cost* includes delivery, installation, sales tax, and all expenditures to make the asset ready for use. *Depreciation* is not a cash outlay expense and is added back to the *net annual return*. Therefore, the denominator represents annual cash flow.

Using the data in Exhibit 11, the payback period for this proposal is calculated as follows:

$$\text{Payback Period} \;=\; \frac{\$30,000}{\$3,080 + \$6,000} \;=\; 3.3 \text{ years}$$

A predetermined maximum allowable payback period is generally used to determine if a project remains in contention with other purchase requests. The surviving projects are finally determined by a combination of the factors previously listed in the ARR method.

 # Key Terms ───────────────────────────────────

capital lease—A long-term financing arrangement that grants present or future ownership of the leased property to the lessor.

covenant not to compete—An agreement by a seller not to operate a similar business in a certain geographical area for a specified amount of time.

fixed lease—A lease that is characterized by a set rental charge for a specified period of time.

franchise—An agreement by which the franchisee undertakes to conduct a business or sell a product or service in accordance with methods and procedures prescribed by the franchisor; the franchise may encompass an exclusive right to sell a product or service or conduct a business in a specified territory.

indifference point—The sales level at which rental expense is identical for a fixed and a variable lease.

lease—A contract by which the use of property or equipment is granted by the lessor to the lessee.

lessee—The person or company that uses leased property or equipment under the terms of a lease.

lessor—The person or company that leases property or equipment to a lessee.

operating lease—A lease similar to a rental agreement that has no appearance of present or future ownership of the leased property by the lessee.

variable lease—A lease taken for a specified period of time with its rental charge stated as a percentage, usually of the lessee's sales volume.

Review Questions ───────────────────────────────────

1. What is the difference between quantitative and qualitative factors in financial decision-making?

2. What is the abbreviated Contributory Income Statement format?

3. What are some qualitative factors to consider when making an off-season open or close decision?

4. What is the most prominent quantitative factor in an off-season analysis?

5. What are some qualitative considerations to ponder when searching to acquire a business?

6. What is a covenant not to compete?

7. What is the largest problem in using a seller's financial statements for a small business?

8. What critical questions should a buyer consider when forecasting the potential profits of a seller's business?

9. What accounting and legal considerations should a buyer of a corporation keep in mind when purchasing the corporation's common stock?

10. What is the depreciable basis of assets when a company is acquired by the asset method?

11. What is the largest single concern a buyer should have when examining authentic records of a family-operated business?

12. What are the two components of a loan payment? Which one does not appear on the income statement?

13. What is the definition of the following terms: franchise, franchisor, and franchisee?

14. What are the advantages and disadvantages of being a franchisee?

15. What is the definition of the following terms: lease, lessor, and lessee?

16. What is the indifference point the lessee should compute when considering whether to sign a fixed or variable lease? How is it calculated?

17. What is the definition of the following terms: capitalized cost, capitalized cost reductions, residual value?

18. What are the advantages and disadvantages of leasing an automobile?

19. What is the major difference between an open-end and closed-end automobile lease?

20. What is capital budgeting?

21. What are the two most popular and simple evaluation methods used to financially evaluate a capital budgeting request? How are they calculated?

Internet Sites

For more information, visit the following Internet sites. Remember that Internet addresses can change without notice. If the site is no longer there, you can use a search engine to look for additional sites.

Cost/Benefit Analysis
www.mindtools.com/pages/article/newTED_08.htm

Decision Tree
www.mindtools.com/dectree.html

Covenant Not to Compete
http://business-law.freeadvice.com/trade_regulation/covenant_not.htm

Leveraged Buy-Out
www.valuebasedmanagement.net/methods_leveraged_buy-out.html

Business Combinations
http://home.att.net/~s-prasad/GW.htm
http://cpaclass.com/gaap/gaap-us-101.htm
http://cpaclass.com/gaap/sfas/gaap-sfas-142.htm

Franchising
http://money.howstuffworks.com/franchising.htm

Leasing
http://pages.stern.nyu.edu/~adamodar/New_Home_Page/AccPrimer/lease.htm
www.restaurantreport.com/departments/ac_lease2.html

Average Rate of Return
http://teachmefinance.com/Financial_Terms/average_rate_of_return.html
www.bized.ac.uk/virtual/bank/business/finance/investment/theories2.htm

Payback Method
www.toolkit.cch.com/text/P06_6510.asp
www.itssimple.biz/biz_tools/text/P06_6510.html

Capital Budgeting and Methods
www.netmba.com/finance/capital/budgeting/
www.studyfinance.com/lessons/capbudget/index.mv?page=01
www.studyfinance.com/lessons/capbudget/index.mv?page=09
www.studyfinance.com/lessons/capbudget/index.mv?page=10

Problems

Problem 1

Complete the in-season/off-season analysis for Mountain View Resort. State a conclusion from your analysis.

	Last Year (12 Months)	In-season (9 months)	Off-season (3 months)	If closed (For Off-season)
Sales	$900,000	$ 800,000	$_____	$_____
VC	585,000	_____	_____	_____
CM	315,000	_____	_____	_____
FC	180,000	_____	_____	_____
IBIT	$135,000	$_____	$_____	$_____

Problem 2

You are analyzing two hospitality businesses for acquisition. Complete the analysis below for the stated conditions. State a conclusion from your analysis.

| | Last Year's Data | | If Sales Increase 20% | | If Sales Decrease 20% | |
	A	B	A	B	A	B
Sales	$500,000	$500,000	$ _____	$ _____	$ _____	$ _____
VC	200,000	300,000				
CM	300,000	200,000				
FC	200,000	100,000				
IBIT	$100,000	$100,000	$ _____	$ _____	$ _____	$ _____

Problem 3

The following is a partial section of a balance sheet of an incorporated business you are considering as an acquisition target.

	Cost	Accumulated Depreciation
Land	$200,000	
Building	500,000	$400,000
Furniture & equipment	150,000	100,000

The depreciation methods employ a zero salvage value; the full cost can be depreciated. The seller's asking price is $1,200,000 for purchase of the common stock. In addition, the seller is asking $75,000 for a covenant not to compete. Calculate the allowable lifetime depreciation and amortization that would apply if you purchased the corporate stock.

Problem 4

The following is a partial section of a balance sheet of an incorporated business you are considering as an acquisition target.

	Cost	Accumulated Depreciation
Land	$200,000	
Building	500,000	$400,000
Furniture & equipment	150,000	100,000

The depreciation methods employ a zero salvage value; the full cost can be depreciated. The seller's asking price for the assets is $300,000 for the land and $900,000 for the other assets. In addition, the seller is asking $75,000 for a no-compete agreement. Calculate what the allowable lifetime depreciation and amortization would be if you purchase the business using the Asset Method.

Problem 5

A landlord is offering you a fixed lease at $6,000 per month or a variable lease at eight percent of sales. Calculate the indifference point and state your conclusions.

Problem 6

A dealer quotes a money factor of .004545 in an automotive lease offer. Translate this money factor to an annual interest percentage.

Problem 7

Calculate the monthly lease payment from the following data:

>Capitalized cost: $30,000
>Down payment: $2,000 (exclusive of security and advance deposits)
>Residual value: $13,000
>Term: 48 months
>Money factor: .002917
>Sales tax: 5%

Problem 8

Use the information in Problem 7. You have negotiated the capitalized cost down to $28,000 and the residual value up to $14,000. Calculate the monthly lease payment.

Problem 9

The purchase terms of a target acquisition are as follows:

Land	$ 50,000
Building	180,000
Equipment	80,000
Trade name	100,000
No-compete covenant	20,000

The company is a proprietorship. Its income statement is shown below.

Sales	$1,200,000
Cost of Sales	360,000
Gross Profit	840,000
Payroll & related	420,000
Depreciation	5,000
All other expenses	150,000
Income before taxes	$ 265,000

The owner has been withdrawing $70,000 each year, which is not reflected in the payroll costs since owner's withdrawals in a proprietorship are not salaries or wages. You will organize your new business as a corporation. Your salary needs are $50,000 annually. Related taxes and benefits are 20 percent. Your accountant has provided the following straight-line depreciable lives with zero salvage values for the purchased assets:

Building	30 years
Equipment	10 years
Trade name	25 years
No-compete covenant	5 years

Ignoring organization costs and income taxes, prepare an annual income statement as you would if you purchased this company. Assume sales and all other costs remain relative.

Problem 10

Calculate the average rate of return from the following information. Show the ARR as a percentage with one decimal. The company's income tax rate is 40 percent.

New Point-of-Sale System

Purchase cost and installation	$56,000
Salvage at end of useful life	0
Useful life	7 years
Depreciation method	Straight-line

Annual operating expenses:

Payroll & related expense	$35,000
Power expense	5,700
Supplies expense	2,000
Repairs expense	300

Old Point-of-Sale System
Fully depreciated, no salvage value

Annual operating expenses:

Payroll & related expense	$45,000
Power expense	7,500
Supplies expense	2,500
Repairs expense	2,000

Problem 11

Determine the payback period (to one decimal point) from the information given in Problem 10.

Case Study

Business Acquisition—An Entrepreneurial Endeavor

Your entrepreneurial dreams have become reality. After researching many investment opportunities, you have selected a very attractive hospitality business in a prime location. It has a long-time success record and was operated under one owner. Your accountant reviewed the financial statements of the business and found that they were in conformity with generally accepted accounting principles. Also, no material modifications to the statements were necessary before they could be relied upon as a basis for analysis.

The land and building are presently leased from another party. Negotiations with the landlord to purchase the facilities did not succeed. Because of the business's location and success record, you acquiesce and accept the existing lease situation.

You form a corporation by investing $65,000 as start-up capital. Ten thousand (10,000) shares of $1 par value common stock are issued to you as the sole stockholder. The first business check issued by your company is to your attorney for $2,000, paying legal and state incorporation fees.

The purchase cost of the business and its assets is $200,000. The assets at fair market value (FMV) are as follows:

- Furniture and equipment $80,000
- Trade name 40,000
- No-compete agreement from seller 20,000

The seller provides the financing with terms of a $40,000 down payment; the $160,000 balance is payable over 15 years at 12 percent interest.

Last year's income statement for the business was:

Sales		$300,000
Cost of sales		84,000
Gross profit		216,000
Payroll		
Owner	$60,000	
Staff	40,000	
Payroll taxes, fringes	20,000	
Total payroll and related		120,000
Rent		30,000
Other operating expenses (excluding depreciation)		30,000
Total expenses		180,000
Income before depreciation & income taxes (IBDIT)		$ 36,000

The seller did not have any advertising expense because the business relied upon its established goodwill for its sales volume. The business did not have any interest expense for the last several years because all loans have been paid off.

Based on your market analysis, a marketing game plan should increase sales 10 percent in Year 1 and 5 percent in Year 2. You have decided to implement a planned advertising program that you estimate will cost $10,000 for Year 1 and $5,000 for Year 2. The marketing program's goals are to attract new customers and retain old customers by increasing food portions and improving customer service.

The marketing strategy will increase food cost and staff wages. Due to portion size increases, food cost will be at 30 percent of sales. You budget a 5 percent increase in Year 1 and another 5 percent in Year 2 for staff wages; this level of wages should retain qualified staff and attract highly qualified new employees. To offset some of these wage increases, you have decided on a personal salary of $50,000 in Year 1 with a 5 percent increase in Year 2.

You have determined the business will have the following expenses:

- Payroll taxes and fringes will be 20 percent of total salaries and wages.

- The rent will remain at $30,000 for the next two years.

- Other operating expenses will increase by $5,000 in Year 1; thereafter, they will increase by 2 percent.

Your accountant has advised you that the $160,000 note payable to the seller bearing 12 percent interest will require a monthly payment of $2,000, consisting of principal and interest. The interest expense portion in Year 1 is $19,000, and, in Year 2, $18,000.

Challenge

1. Explain why you selected the corporate form of organization. Support your explanation by discussing the advantages and disadvantages of the corporate form of business organization.

2. Describe the prerequisite qualitative consideration that you, the purchaser, must make when taking over a leased facility.

3. Prepare forecasted income statements for Year 1 and Year 2 under your ownership.

   - Ignore depreciation and amortization expenses.

   - Round all amounts entered on the income statement to the nearest $100.

4. Prepare a classified balance sheet as of the date of purchase, including the check written to the attorney.

Chapter 17 Outline

Cash, Cash Flow, and Profit
Cash Management
    Developing Cash Management Data
    Cash Budget Demonstration
Cash Management Tools
    Cash Float
    Lockbox System
    Management of Excess Funds
Misleading Measures of Cash Flow
    EBITDA
    Free Cash Flow

Competencies

1. Define cash, cash flow, and cash flow analysis and explain the relationship of cash to profit. (pp. 456–458)

2. State the purpose and benefits of cash management and use cash management terminology accurately and effectively. (pp. 458–459)

3. Create a cash budget from appropriate data using the method appropriate to meet either short-term or long-term needs. (pp. 458–465)

4. Explain the uses of such cash management tools as float management, lockbox systems, and zero balance and sweep accounts. (pp. 465–467)

5. Describe two popular shortcut measures of cash flow and demonstrate why they can be misleading. (pp. 467–469)

17

Cash Management and Planning

A LARGE CORPORATION typically has a chief financial officer and an accounting department that perform cash management and planning. But there are many hospitality entrepreneurs who cannot afford to employ an accounting staff or to pay for costly professional accounting services. Such entrepreneurs must perform cash management and planning themselves if they are to succeed in a competitive hospitality environment.

Cash management is important in every phase of developing and operating a business. Managers often overlook cash management because they are preoccupied with profits, culinary requirements, front office activities, guest service, and the many other demands of any hospitality business. Some hospitality managers feel secure as long as the money coming in exceeds the money going out. Unfortunately, this kind of thinking exposes a business to unexpected cash flow demands that could seriously affect operations and even threaten the business's survival. Many profitable businesses (according to their income statements) have gone out of business because of cash flow problems.

A company can usually go without profit for some time, but it cannot meet its day-to-day operating needs without cash. Cash is the lifeblood of any business. Employees, suppliers, landlords, and creditors expect to be paid. A bad payment record can make applying for and receiving credit either very costly (because lenders will charge a significantly higher interest rate to cover their risk) or impossible.

This chapter will answer such questions as:

1. What is cash?

2. What is cash flow?

3. What is cash flow analysis?

4. What is cash management? What are its benefits?

5. How is cash management data developed?

6. How is a cash flow analysis performed?

7. How can a business wisely use its excess cash?

Cash, Cash Flow, and Profit

Cash is money in the bank that the business can use. It does not include inventory, accounts receivable, or property. Even though inventory and accounts receivable are converted into cash in normal business operations, new inventory and new accounts receivable take their place in an ongoing business; thus, they place a continuing demand on cash. Property—a business's necessary, integral fixed assets like land, buildings, and equipment—is not generally sold, because it is used in day-to-day operations.

Cash is a current asset on the balance sheet and may consist of a number of components that have varying degrees of **liquidity**, or the ability to be easily and readily converted into cash. For example, the current asset *cash* might consist of petty cash, a payroll checking account, a regular checking account, non-interest earning accounts, demand deposits, and temporary cash investments (that is, investments of a demand nature or those having a maturity within 90 days at purchase). A surplus of cash may be invested in various ways; however, some surplus cash must be put in liquid accounts so that it is accessible when the business needs it. (The investment of surplus cash is discussed later in this chapter.)

The amount of working cash required varies according to business type; businesses that extend credit or have large, expensive inventories must have more working cash on hand.

Cash flow is the movement of money into and out of a business. Exhibit 1 presents examples of cash inflows and outflows. If the money coming in (the cash inflow) exceeds the money going out (the cash outflow), the resulting condition is called a **positive cash flow**. If the money going out exceeds the money coming in, the result is a **negative cash flow**. The cycle of cash inflows and cash outflows determines the business's **solvency**, which is its ability to pay all of its debt and stay in business.

Monitoring cash flow is a major task for managers and entrepreneurs. During the cash budgeting process, cash management involves proper planning to avoid negative cash flow. When bills become due, dealing with a cash flow problem is a burden to both the company and the parties it owes.

A negative cash flow indicates the need to borrow money or to raise more equity. A company can borrow money from banks or vendors who want the company to stay in business. Vendors (suppliers) might also cooperate by increasing the company's line of credit or by postponing the due date for the company's payment of accounts payable.

Positive cash flow, while beneficial, also requires analysis. If more cash is in the bank than necessary for business operations, management should consider making investments or expanding the business.

Cash flow analysis is the study of the cycle of cash inflows and outflows with the objective of maintaining adequate cash to meet the requirements of the business. It involves examining the components that affect cash flow, such as accounts receivable, inventory, accounts payable, bank loans, sales, and expenses.

It is important to realize that profit and cash are not the same thing. The profit amount on an income statement has no direct relation to the cash balance amount. This is true for several reasons:

Exhibit 1   Examples of Cash Inflows and Outflows

Examples of cash inflows are:

1.   Cash receipts from operations
   - Cash sales to customers
   - Cash collections from accounts receivable

2.   Cash receipts from financing
   - Cash borrowings
   - Issuance of capital stock
   - Issuance of bonds

3.   Cash receipts from investing
   - Sale of property or equipment
   - Sale of short-term investments (marketable securities)

Examples of cash outflows are:

1.   Cash payments for operations
   - Payment of wages and benefits
   - Payment of taxes, rent, insurance
   - Payment of operating expenses

2.   Cash payments for financing
   - Payment of debt
   - Payment of dividends

3.   Cash payments for investing
   - Purchase of property or equipment
   - Purchase of short-term investments (marketable securities)

- The income statement is prepared on an accrual basis, meaning that the revenues and expenses are listed when incurred, regardless of when or even whether payment has actually occurred. Sales on accounts or credit cards may still be in accounts receivable, and expenses may not have been paid yet.

- The payment of the principal portion of loans does not appear on the income statement.

- The payment of prepaid items does not appear on the income statement. For example, an insurance policy might be paid in one sum that benefits a 12-month period; the payment is charged to a temporary asset (Prepaid Insurance on the balance sheet) and equally expensed each month over the 12-month period.

- Certain expenses, such as depreciation and amortization, are non-cash expenses that affect profit but not cash.

Businesses want both profits and positive cash flow. However, other combinations often occur. A business can show a profit even with negative cash flow or, at the other extreme, can have positive cash flow and still show a loss. In the long run, of course, consistent profits are necessary for business survival. However, if profits do not generate positive cash flow, the achievement of profits is of little value. A business spends cash; it does not spend profits.

No formal accounting statement exists for cash management. The balance sheet shows a historical cash position as of a certain date, but it does not forecast future cash balances or requirements. The income statement shows historical information, but ignores cash because revenue and expenses are recorded on the accrual principle. The statement of cash flows is the only financial statement that is truly cash oriented, but it is also a historical representation because it is prepared from the balance sheet and income statement and does not reflect future cash balances or requirements. Since cash management cannot rely on a standardized cash management financial statement, each business must design and use a format that effectively meets its needs.

Cash Management

It is important to know proper cash management vocabulary when dealing with banks and creditors. Exhibit 2 presents definitions of some key cash management terms.

Cash management is the process of monitoring and controlling cash to meet the needs of the business. Its major objective is to plan for a company's cash flow so that cash is available when the company needs it; a related goal is to invest any idle cash (excess cash not needed for current operations) to provide a maximum return.

The benefits of cash management are:

- Payment of bills when due

- Ability to take advantage of purchase discounts

- Ability to take advantage of special purchases

- Proper planning for upgrades of equipment, replacement, expansion

- Attainment of inventory demands for seasonal cycles or special events

- Good credit rating

The process of cash management begins with a **cash budget** that is used as an overall plan for a future period or a series of future periods. The cash budget is composed of projected cash balances developed from projected cash inflows and cash outflows.

Developing Cash Management Data

The *operations budget* is a useful place to start when gathering information for cash flow projections. Note that the operations budget is based on accrual accounting, but a cash flow projection deals only with cash received and cash paid. A cash flow projection ignores non-cash expenses appearing in the operations budget, such as depreciation and amortization.

Other modifications must usually be made to the operations budget because of the following:

Exhibit 2   Cash Management Vocabulary

- *Bearer*: The holder of a negotiable instrument.

- *Canceled check*: A check that has been cashed by the financial institution on which it was drawn. The back of the check is imprinted with the date paid, and the check amount is charged to the account holder.

- *Cleared check*: Another term for a canceled check.

- *Commercial paper*: An unsecured obligation issued by a corporation or bank. Maturity is usually from 2 to 270 days; can be bought or sold in secondary markets.

- *Demand deposit*: An account that can be drawn upon on demand (without prior notice). Examples are checking accounts and most savings accounts.

- *Liquid investment*: Any investment that is quickly and easily convertible to cash.

- *Liquidity*: A general measure of how quickly an asset can be converted into cash; the greater the liquidity, the faster it can be turned into cash.

- *Money market*: A market for short-term debt securities, such as commercial paper, certificates of deposit, and Treasury bills, with a maturity of one year or less, and often 30 days or less. Typically, these are safe, highly liquid investments.

- *Negotiable instrument*: A transferable document that promises to pay its bearer a sum of money at a future date or on demand. Examples are checks, Treasury bills, and promissory notes.

- *Primary market*: The market for new issues of securities such as stocks, debt instruments, and negotiable instruments. The issuer may sell new issues directly to investors or may use banks and investment brokers as its agent.

- *Return:* The interest rate generated by an investment.

- *Risk:* The probability of losing some or all of the value of an investment. Money-market funds have no risk and Treasury bills have no risk if held to maturity.

- *Secondary market:* A market in which an investor can purchase securities from another investor (rather than the issuer). These securities are bought and sold subsequent to the original issue. Banks and investment brokers act as agents for the buyers/sellers. Also called the *aftermarket*.

- *Treasury bills:* Negotiable debt obligations issued by the U.S. government, usually having a maturity period of one year or less, some as little as 13 weeks from original issue. The interest they earn is exempt from state and local income taxes. Can be bought or sold in secondary markets. Also called T-bills.

- *Venture capital:* A name for funds made available to new businesses and small businesses that have exceptional growth potential. Venture capital investors expect a voting share of the business and might also provide managerial and technical expertise.

- Sales might not be 100 percent cash sales (or bank credit cards).
- Purchases might have extended payment terms.

- Principal payments on loans do not appear in an operations budget or income statement, but require cash payment.

- Prepaid assets (insurance and property taxes) from the balance sheet are written off (transferred) to expense and appear monthly in an operations budget, but might be paid only once per year.

A study must be made of the accounting records and management plans to determine the following:

- The estimated percentage of sales that are cash sales or cash equivalent.

- The collection schedule of accounts receivable; for example, 90 percent might be collected one month after the sale, and the remaining 10 percent, two months after the sale.

- Cash inflows from bank loans.

- Cash inflows from the sale of fixed assets or securities.

- Planned expansions or purchases of fixed assets.

- Loan payment schedules to determine principal and interest.

- Dividend payments.

There are two approaches to preparing a cash budget. The *adjusted net income approach* and the *cash receipts and disbursements approach*.

The adjusted net income approach is a cash budget format used for long-term planning. It is an indirect approach because it starts with the income statement's net income and modifies it for non-cash expenses and changes to certain assets and liabilities. The two major sections of the adjusted net income approach format are the sources of cash and the uses of cash.

The logic used in the preparation of the adjusted net income approach cash budget is similar to the logic used in the preparation of the statement of cash flows (indirect method). Briefly, increases to assets such as accounts receivable or inventory are considered uses of cash since such increases require cash outlays. Increases to accounts payable are also increases to cash, since the use of credit allows the business to purchase inventory.

An easy way to learn the adjusted net income approach is to study a comprehensive statement showing the plus and minus functions of each line. Exhibit 3 provides a sample comprehensive statement for one year. (A worksheet can be formatted to forecast cash flow for several years, if desired.) Starting with beginning cash, the budget then lists net income from the budgeted income statement. (Gains or losses on the sale of fixed assets should be excluded from net income.) Net income requires adjustment through the adding back of non-cash expenses like depreciation and amortization. Next, the various other sources of cash are added. The total of all these items provides the *total cash available* before any usage of cash. From this total, the listed cash items are subtracted to arrive at the estimated cash at the end of a year. Then, any minimum amount required as a safety cushion for the business is subtracted to arrive at the cash excess or shortage for the year.

Exhibit 3   Cash Budget—Adjusted Net Income Approach

Cash beginning of year		$ _____
Add sources of cash:		
Net income	$	
Adjustments to net income:		
Add Depreciation		
Add Amortization		
Other sources of cash:		
Proceeds from bank loans		
Sale of investments		
Sale of fixed assets		
Sale of capital stock		
Sale of treasury stock		
Decrease in accounts receivable		
Decrease in inventory		
Decrease in prepaid assets		
Total sources of cash	_____	
Total cash available		_____
Less uses of cash:		
Reduction of long-term debt		
Purchase of investment		
Cash payment for fixed assets		
Purchase of treasury stock		
Payment of dividends		
Increase in accounts receivable		
Increase in inventory		
Increase in prepaid assets		
Total uses of cash	_____	
Estimated cash at end of year		_____
Minimum cash requirement		_____
Cash excess or shortage		$ _____

The very popular cash receipts and disbursements approach is especially useful for short-term planning and cash projections. This approach is relatively easy to use and understand because it shows the projections of cash inflows and cash outflows in an itemized format. Using this approach, it takes more time to gather the information needed for an accurate cash budget than to prepare the report itself. Once gathered, the information is entered on a working paper that follows a standard logic:

Beginning Cash + Cash Receipts − Cash Payments = Ending Cash Balance

The newly calculated *ending cash balance* becomes the *beginning cash balance* for the following month (or period).

The typical needs of a hospitality manager or entrepreneur (who is not an accountant) are met by the cash receipts and disbursements approach. Its format is also easier to read, explain, and use as a planning tool. Because it is especially suited for the non-accounting hospitality professional, it is used in the following demonstration case.

Cash Budget Demonstration

This demonstration looks at the step-by-step preparation of a cash budget. The sequence of steps is as follows:

*   Gather preliminary data.

*   Prepare a budgeted income statement.

*   Prepare the cash flow analysis.

Gather Preliminary Data. Certain preliminary data must be gathered before a cash budget is begun, such as the following:

*   The percentages of cash sales and accounts receivable sales for a given month and the date(s) the accounts receivable are collected. This information can be derived from historical data. (A new business would have to estimate.)

*   The percentages of cash purchases and accounts-payable purchases for a given month and the date(s) the accounts payable are paid. This information can be derived from historical data. (Again, a new business would have to estimate this information.) Cost of sales may be used to represent purchases if inventories do not significantly fluctuate.

*   Those expenses that are incurred and paid in the current month. For example, payroll can be considered paid in the month incurred.

*   The prior month's sales and purchases. For example, if the cash budget is to be prepared for May, June, and July, the sales and purchases for April are required so that the cash portions applicable to May can be computed.

*   Prepaid items (a current asset) allocated to expense on a monthly basis. For example, a one-year $12,000 insurance policy may be paid in February. The income statement will show a $1,000 expense each month, but that $1,000 expense is a non-cash expense except for February, which incurs a $12,000 cash payment.

*   Management plans for capital acquisitions.

*   Loan schedules showing the principal portion of debt repayment.

*   The beginning cash balance for the period the cash budget is being prepared.

*   The budgeted income statement for the period the cash budget is being prepared.

The demonstration cash budget will be prepared for the three-month period of May, June, and July. Assume the following information:

Exhibit 4   Budgeted Income Statement for May, June, July

	May	June	July	Comments
Sales	150,000	180,000	200,000	Collections = 70%/30%
Cost of sales	45,000	55,000	60,000	Payments = 40%/60%
Gross profit	105,000	125,000	140,000	
Payroll & related	50,000	56,000	65,000	Paid in month incurred
Marketing	5,000	6,000	8,000	Paid in month incurred
Administrative	15,000	17,000	19,000	Paid in month incurred
Supplies, maintenance	17,000	18,000	19,000	Paid in month incurred
Utilities	6,000	7,000	8,000	Paid in month incurred
Property insurance	1,000	1,000	1,000	*$12,000 paid in February*
Interest	5,000	5,000	5,000	Paid in month incurred
Depreciation	2,000	2,000	2,000	*Non-cash expense*
Total operating expenses	101,000	112,000	127,000	
Income	4,000	13,000	13,000	

- Sales for any month are 70 percent collected in the month of sale; the 30 percent accounts receivable is collected in the following month.

- Purchases (cost of sales) for any month are 40 percent paid in the current month; the 60 percent accounts payable is paid in the following month.

- Sales for April: $130,000.

- Purchases for April: $40,000.

- Insurance of $12,000 is paid in February and charged to expense each month.

- A mortgage is paid monthly. The principal portion is $2,000.

- The cash balance on April 30 was $20,000.

- There are no planned capital acquisitions.

Prepare a Budgeted Income Statement. Use the budgeted income statement shown in Exhibit 4, which was prepared with the preliminary data gathered in the first step.

Prepare the Cash Flow Analysis. The information listed in the "Comments" column of the budgeted income statement shown in Exhibit 4 reminds us to ignore the property insurance expense because it is paid in February, and therefore would be considered only in February. The "Comments" column also reminds us that depreciation is a non-cash expense and does not appear in a cash budget.

- The sales for April totaled $130,000; of this, 70 percent were cash sales in April, and 30 percent, or $39,000, were accounts receivable that will be collected in May.

- The purchases for April totaled $40,000; therefore, 40 percent of purchases were paid for in April, and 60 percent, or $24,000, were accounts payable that will be paid in May.

Exhibit 5   Cash Flow for May, June, July

	May	June	July	Comments
Beginning cash balance	20,000	22,000	33,000	Last month's ending balance
Cash receipts:				
April sales 30% to May	39,000			April sales = $130,000
May sales 70%/30%	105,000	45,000		May sales = $150,000
June sales 70%/30%		126,000	54,000	June sales = $180,000
July sales 70%/30%			140,000	July sales = $200,000
Total cash received	144,000	171,000	194,000	
Cash paid out:				
April purchases 40%/60%	24,000			April purchases = $40,000
May purchases 40%/60%	18,000	27,000		May purchases = $45,000
June purchases 40%/60%		22,000	33,000	June purchases = $55,000
July purchases 40%/60%			24,000	July purchases = $60,000
Payroll & related	50,000	56,000	65,000	
Marketing	5,000	6,000	8,000	
Administrative	15,000	17,000	19,000	
Supplies, maintenance	17,000	18,000	19,000	
Utilities	6,000	7,000	8,000	
Interest on debt	5,000	5,000	5,000	
Debt principal	2,000	2,000	2,000	
Total cash paid out	142,000	160,000	183,000	
Ending cash balance	22,000	33,000	44,000	

- Payroll and related, marketing, administrative, supplies, maintenance, utilities, and interest are paid in the month incurred.

The gathered information is now used to prepare the cash budget for May, June, and July. The resulting cash budget is shown in Exhibit 5. The logic used to prepare this cash budget is as follows:

- The beginning cash balance was $20,000.

- April sales receipts:
  Collected in April (70% × $130,000)   = $ 91,000
  Accounts receivable (30% × $130,000)   = $\underline{\quad 39,000}$ (collected in May)
  $130,000

- May sales receipts:
  Collected in May (70% × $150,000)   = $105,000
  Accounts receivable (30% × $150,000)   = $\underline{\quad 45,000}$ (collected in June)
  $150,000

- June sales receipts:
  Collected in June (70% × $180,000)   = $126,000
  Accounts receivable (30% × $180,000)   = $\underline{\quad 54,000}$ (collected in July)
  $180,000

- July sales receipts:

Collected in July (70% × $200,000)	=	$140,000
Accounts receivable (30% × $200,000)	=	60,000 (collected in August)
		$200,000

- April purchases:

Paid in April (40% × $40,000)	=	$ 16,000
Accounts payable (60% × $40,000)	=	24,000 (paid in May)
		$ 40,000

- May purchases:

Paid in May (40% × $45,000)	=	$ 18,000
Accounts payable (60% × $45,000)	=	27,000 (paid in June)
		$ 45,000

- June purchases:

Paid in June (40% × $55,000)	=	$ 22,000
Accounts payable (60% × $55,000)	=	33,000 (paid in July)
		$ 55,000

- July purchases:

Paid in July (40% × $60,000)	=	$ 24,000
Accounts payable (60% × $60,000)	=	36,000 (paid in August)
		$ 60,000

- Payroll and related, marketing, administrative, supplies, maintenance, utilities, and interest were paid in the month incurred.

- Insurance expense is ignored since it is a monthly accounting allocation of a prepaid expense. It is considered only in February when the policy premium is due.

- Depreciation is ignored because it is a non-cash expense.

- The ending cash balance equals the beginning cash balance + total cash received − total cash paid out.

- The ending cash balance becomes the beginning cash balance for the next month. That is, May's ending balance of $22,000 becomes June's beginning balance.

Preparing a cash budget requires considerable organization and data analysis. If the preliminary work is properly done, putting the cash flow components together is not difficult.

Cash Management Tools

Cash management involves more than monitoring cash flow to ensure that funds are available for normal business operations. A business owner who dwells only on operating profits loses out on other ways to maximize the opportunities available to the business. Returns from business ownership are improved through the acceleration of cash receipts and the opportune investment of idle cash. Clearly, cash is an important asset that can both contribute to the business's profits and maximize owners' wealth.

Many banks offer sophisticated cash management services to commercial accounts, no matter how big or small they are. Banks actively promote a full array of services designed to help reduce the time and effort required to accelerate cash flow and optimize returns on idle cash. Banks work with business customers to help them achieve a good return on excess funds. By providing this service, banks develop strong relationships with their business customers in hopes of retaining those customers' checking and investment accounts and meeting their bank loan requirements.

Cash Float

The term *float* in accounting refers to the time lag in processing checks. **Cash float** is the interval of time between when a check is issued and when it is paid by the bank. Business managers can measure cash float by analyzing cash available in the accounting records and in the actual bank account. Cash float is caused by:

- The amount of funds represented by checks written but not yet presented to the bank for payment.

- The time between when checks are deposited in a bank account and when the funds are made available after the bank's check-clearing process.

For example, suppose a check is issued and mailed. The writing of the check creates an immediate accounting entry that reduces the cash balance in the business's accounting records. However, the funds are not actually deducted from the bank account until the check is delivered, is deposited by the recipient, and has gone through the bank's check-clearing process. This type of float is called **payment float** or **disbursement float**.

Collection float is the period between when a business deposits a check in its bank account and when the bank actually receives those funds and makes them available. For example, suppose a business receives a check, enters it in its accounting records, increases the cash balance, and deposits the check in its bank account. Although the accounting records show the funds as deposited, the funds are not available until the deposited check goes through the bank's check-clearing process.

Net float is the difference between collection float and payment float. Someone very experienced in financial matters could "play the float" to maximize returns. To achieve the greatest benefits of cash float, a business should examine three areas: mail float, processing float, and clearing float. *Mail float* is caused by the time the mailed check spends in the postal system during its transit from its point of origin to its destination. *Processing float* is the time it takes for a business to process checks received and deliver them to its bank for deposit. *Clearing float* is the time lag caused during the bank's handling of the deposited checks with the check issuer's bank (the paying bank). Holidays or other periods when the banks are not open for business also affect clearing float.

Lockbox System

Depending on a business's size and credit rating, many banks will work with the business to help it collect cash on a timely basis. One popular method used to accelerate the collection of cash is a **lockbox system**. Under this system, customers mail their payments to the company's bank, which immediately enters the payments as deposits. The bank prepares a list of the deposited checks and sends it to the business, which can then update its accounts receivable records.

The mailing address given to customers does not reveal that customers are mailing their payments to a bank.

Management of Excess Funds

Excess funds should not remain long in a checking account because business checking accounts do not earn interest. Excess funds can be easily switched from a business checking account to a cash equivalent alternative, and replaced when necessary. Two popular bank accounts set up to manage excess funds are the zero balance account and the sweep account.

A **zero balance account (ZBA)** is a checking account for which the bank maintains a balance of zero for its business customer by automatically transferring funds between it and a master investment account. If deposits to the account exceed checks cleared, the excess funds are immediately invested in government securities or money market funds. Conversely, when cleared checks exceed deposits, the bank sells the business customer's securities or reduces its money market fund to cover the shortfall. A ZBA arrangement can minimize idle balances in non-interest-bearing accounts.

A **sweep account** combines a business checking account with an investment account, usually a money market mutual fund. Sweep accounts were devised as a way to get around a government regulation that prohibits banks from offering interest on commercial checking accounts. A sweep account is a bank account from which the bank automatically transfers funds that exceed a target amount to an investment account at the close of each business day. In other words, the bank "sweeps" excess funds from the checking account to an interest-bearing investment such as a money market fund. Sweep accounts were formerly restricted to large companies. However, banks now offer them to the fast-growing small-business and entrepreneurial markets.

Misleading Measures of Cash Flow

Many lenders, investment bankers, financial analysts, and others involved in evaluating a company's financial performance use shortcut methods to measure cash flow. These methods often have limitations because they fail to measure:

- Cash required for working capital

- Debt payments

- Capital expenditures

Part of the problem with these shortcut methods is that, while they effectively evaluate profitability, it is dangerous and misleading to use them to measure cash flow. This is because there is a significant difference between profitability and cash flow.

EBITDA

EBITDA is an acronym for Earnings before Interest, [income] Taxes, Depreciation, and Amortization. It is occasionally also referred to as EBITIDA, an acronym for Earnings before Income Taxes, Interest, Depreciation, and Amortization. EBITDA is computed by taking the net income figure from the income statement and adding back the deductions taken for income taxes, interest, depreciation, and amortization.

EBITDA first came into being during the leveraged buyout craze of the 1980s as a shortcut measure of a company's ability to service its debt; it still is popular, commonly quoted, and used in investment and financial circles. Some texts and financial analysts promote EBITDA as a shortcut method to determine cash flow, based on the fact that depreciation and amortization are non-cash expenses. However, it is incorrect to assume that EBITDA represents cash flow. It does not.

EBITDA ignores the effect of financing decisions and accounting standards. In essence, it fails to measure true cash flow because its computation ignores the balance sheet. Specifically, EBITDA fails to consider debt payments and capital expenditures.

Debt payments on principal can be substantial for financed property and equipment in asset-intensive operations like hotels and large restaurants. Rapidly growing companies and new ventures alike require huge amounts of debt or cash expenditures. Capital expenditures are funds a company uses to acquire assets, or improvements made to assets, that will benefit the company for more than one year. Because capital expenditures can be large, their cost is spread over the life of the asset. This requires the company to make ongoing installment cash outlays before the debt is retired.

A further shortcoming of EBITDA as it relates to cash flow is that the computation is based on information from financial statements that were prepared using accrual basis accounting rather than cash basis accounting. Customer sales on account, vendor purchases on account, prepaid expenses, and sales of assets might distort the computed cash flow result.

EBITDA is useful in evaluations of profit potential, but it can be quite misleading as a measure of cash flow.

Free Cash Flow

Free cash flow (FCF) is another measure of financial performance that is sometimes used to examine cash flow results from a company's business operations. FCF is important to measure a company's financial capability to expand its business operations, acquire other businesses, pay off debt, and pay dividends to its shareholders.

One simple and popular method of measuring FCF is to subtract capital expenditures from cash flow from operations. But the fact that this is just one method is the heart of the issue. The problem is that there is no single standard definition of FCF and there are a variety of methods for its computation. The many different ways of computing it create problems of uniformity and comparability. Depending on the formula used, the same data set can yield various FCF amounts. This is clearly not a consistent or reliable approach to cash flow measurement.

International Accounting Standard (IAS) 7 recommends that FCF should be recognized as "cash from operations less the amount of capital expenditures required to maintain the firm's present productive capacity." There are a variety of standards for defining capital expenditures, and some areas ignored by free cash flow computations are dividend payments and long-term debt payments.

Key Terms

cash budget—A budget composed of projected cash balances developed from projected cash inflows and cash outflows. Also called the *cash flow analysis*.

cash float—The interval of time measured by analyzing cash available in the accounting records and the actual bank account.

cash flow—The movement of money into and out of a business.

cash flow analysis—The study of the cycle of cash inflows and outflows with the objective of maintaining adequate cash to meet requirements of the business.

cash management—The process of managing cash to meet the needs of the business.

disbursement float—The interval between when a check is issued and recorded in the accounting records and when the check is actually deducted by the bank due to the mailing process, the time the recipient takes to deposit the check, and the bank's check-clearing process. Also called *payment float*.

EBITDA—An acronym for Earnings Before Interest, (income) Taxes, Depreciation, and Amortization.

liquidity—An asset's characteristic of being easily and readily convertible to cash.

lockbox system—A system in which customers mail their payments to the company's bank, and the checks are immediately entered as deposits. Customers are unaware the addressee is the company's bank.

negative cash flow—A situation in which the money going out exceeds the money coming in.

net float—The difference between *collection float* and *payment float*.

payment float—See *disbursement float*.

positive cash flow—The situation in which money coming in (cash inflow) exceeds the money going out (cash outflow).

solvency—The ability to pay all debt and stay in business.

sweep account—An account from which the bank "sweeps" any funds in excess of a target amount into an interest-bearing account.

zero balance account (ZBA)—A checking account in which a balance of zero is maintained through the automatic transfer of funds to and from a master investment account.

? Review Questions

1. Why are accounts receivable and inventory not equivalent to cash even though they are converted into cash during normal operations?

2. What is cash flow?

3. What are positive and negative cash flows?

4. What is solvency?

5. What is cash flow analysis? What is its major objective?

6. Why don't the income statement, balance sheet, and statement of cash flows present a projected cash flow analysis?

7. What is cash management? What is its major objective?

8. Why is there a difference between *profit* and *increase to cash*?

9. What are the definitions of *liquidity, Treasury bill, venture capital, demand deposit,* and *money market*?

10. What are the benefits of cash management?

11. What are two common non-cash expenses?

12. What is a popular approach to preparing a cash budget? Is it used for long-term or short-term projections?

13. What is cash float? How does it occur?

14. What are *payment float, collection float,* and *net float*?

15. What is a lockbox system?

16. What is a ZBA? What is its benefit?

17. What is a sweep account?

18. What is EBITDA? How is it computed?

19. Why is cash flow not accurately represented by EBITDA or FCF?

Internet Sites

For more information, visit the following Internet sites. Remember that Internet addresses can change without notice. If the site is no longer there, you can use a search engine to look for additional sites.

Adjusted Net Income Approach
www.hftp.org/members/bottomline/backissues/1999/june-july/cash_budget.htm//

Cash Flow Analysis Defined and Described
http://sbinfocanada.about.com/cs/management/g/cashflowanal.htm

Cash Flow, Understanding and Controlling
http://www.sba.gov/library/pubs/fm-4.pdf

Cash Management Basics
www.inc.com/guides/start_biz/20675.html

EBITDA
http://beginnersinvest.about.com/cs/investinglessons/l/blles4ebitda.htm

Sweep Account
www.investopedia.com/terms/s/sweepaccount.asp

Treasury Bills
www.treasurydirect.gov/indiv/products/prod_tbills_glance.htm
www.savingsbonds.gov/indiv/research/indepth/tbills/res_tbill.htm

Zero Balance Account
www.investopedia.com/terms/z/zba.asp

Problems

Problem 1

The beginning cash balance for a month is $50,000. Cash inflow for that month is $140,000, and cash outflow is $160,000. Compute the cash flow for the month, and state if it was positive or negative.

Problem 2

Compute the cash inflow and cash outflow from the following information:

Cash sales	$120,000
Collections on accounts receivable	50,000
Bank loan borrowing	80,000
Payment of wages and expense	120,000
Payment of debt	70,000
Down payment on new vehicles	20,000
Depreciation	5,000

Problem 3

A company has projected sales as follows:

April	$200,000
May	250,000
June	220,000

A historical analysis shows that 60 percent of sales are cash sales. The sales on accounts receivable are collected as follows: 35 percent in the month following the sale, and 5 percent in the second month following the sale. Compute the cash inflow for June.

Problem 4

A small entrepreneur must forecast his cash position for next month. Compute the estimated cash balance for next month from the following information:

Beginning cash balance	$ 8,000
Estimated cash sales	9,000
Estimated sales on account	3,000
Estimated cash purchases	2,000
Estimated purchases on account	3,000
Estimated all other cash expenses	12,000

Problem 5

You are analyzing the sales and cash receipts for a particular month. Determine the percentage breakdown according to cash sales and monthly collections of sales on accounts receivable. Classify the percentages as cash sales, month 1 after sale, month 2 after sale, etc. The following information is provided for the particular month:

Sales: $200,000

Journal entry increase to accounts receivable: $70,000

Selected aging of accounts receivable analysis:

30 days:	$50,000
60 days:	14,000
90 days:	6,000

Problem 6

Compute EBITDA from the following condensed income statement:

Sales	$1,000,000
Cost of sales	300,000
Payroll & related	320,000
Other operating expenses	100,000
Interest expense	40,000
Depreciation	10,000
Amortization	2,000
Income taxes	45,000
Net income	183,000

Problem 7

Prepare a cash flow analysis for October, and compute the accounts payable at the end of October from the following information:

- Sales are paid for with cash or with bank credit cards.

- Purchases are paid 20 percent in month of purchase and 80 percent in the following month.

- All other expenses are paid when incurred.

- The cash balance at close of August 31 is $12,000.

Operating Statement

	August (actual)	September (projected)	October (projected)
Sales	80,000	90,000	100,000
Food cost	26,000	30,000	32,000
Operating expenses	48,000	57,000	64,000
Depreciation	1,000	1,000	1,000
Rent	4,000	4,000	4,000
Income or (Loss)	1,000	(2,000)	(1,000)

Problem 8

Compute the net float, and comment on its usefulness from the following information:

Checks written, deducted from books, not yet cleared: $25,000
Deposits entered in books, not yet available: $20,000

Problem 9

Prepare a cash flow analysis for April, May, and June, based on the following information:

- Sales are estimated at 30 percent cash, and the balance is collected as follows: 60 percent in the month after sale, and 10 percent in the second month after sale.

- Purchases are paid 70 percent in month of purchase, and 30 percent in the following month.

- All other expenses are paid when incurred.

- The principal portion of an equipment loan is $2,000 per month.

- The cash balance at close of March 31 is $16,000.

- Sales in March were $40,000.

- Purchases in March were $15,000.

Budgeted Operating Statement

	April	May	June
Sales	60,000	53,000	74,000
Food cost	20,000	16,000	22,000
Operating expenses	35,000	28,000	42,000
Interest	1,000	1,000	1,000
Depreciation	3,000	3,000	3,000
Rent	4,000	4,000	4,000
Income or (Loss)	(3,000)	1,000	2,000

Problem 10

The following historical data is available:

Annual sales	$780,000
Average accounts receivable for any month	13,000

Compute the historical percentage of cash sales and sales on account.

Case Study

Budgeted Income Statement and Cash Flow Analysis

The owner of a new restaurant has engaged you to assist him with his financial planning and cash management. The business will open its doors for the first time next week. The owner provides the following start-up information:

- The checking account balance at the start of business operations is $10,000.

- On the first day of the first month of business, an insurance premium of $6,000 is due. The term of this policy is for one year.

The owner provides the following estimates for the first two months of business:

Sales: $40,000 in first month, and $60,000 in the second month
Cost of sales: 35 percent
Cost of labor: 30 percent
Costs related to payroll (payroll taxes, benefits): 25 percent of payroll
Supplies: 5 percent of sales
Advertising: $600 monthly
Depreciation: $1,000 monthly
Rent: $3,000 monthly
All other expenses: 12 percent of sales

The owner provides the following statistical information based on industry studies and personal estimates:

- Sales are estimated to be 80 percent cash and 20 percent accounts receivable. The accounts receivable are collected in the month following the sale.

- Cost of sales represents purchases. The purchases are estimated to be 90 percent on accounts payable and 10 percent cash. The accounts payable are paid in the month following the sale.

- All other expenses are paid in the current month.

A delivery truck is required for the second month of business. This vehicle will cost $25,000 and requires a $4,000 down payment. Payments on the note will start in the third month of business.

Challenge

1. Prepare a budgeted income statement for each of the first two months.

2. Prepare a cash flow analysis for the two-month period.

3. Compute what the accounts receivable and accounts payable balances will be at the end of the two-month period.

4. Explain the dependability of the cash flow, as well as any future considerations regarding cash management, to the owner.

Chapter 18 Outline

Competencies

1. Provide a brief history of gaming from ancient times to the present. (p. 478)

2. Provide casino industry statistics, including those for gaming associations, commercial and Indian casinos, and racinos. (pp. 479–480)

3. Provide basic information about the casino games baccarat, blackjack, craps, keno, roulette, and slot machines. (pp. 480–484)

4. Explain principles of money handling, accounting and internal control, and revenue accounting in casinos. (pp. 484–489)

5. Explain the principles of casino financial accounting, including those affecting gaming revenue, a casino's financial statements, complimentary items and allowances, and payroll and other expenses. (pp. 489–492)

18

Casino Accounting

Casinos form another segment of the hospitality industry providing rooms, food, beverage, and entertainment. Casinos in the United States are highly regulated by state and federal laws. They may be owned by public corporations or Indian tribes, or, to a significantly lesser extent, by a proprietorship or partnership. Many Indian casino operations are managed by public corporations, but are subject to Indian executive management.

This chapter will focus on more than accounting issues. A hospitality accountant or manager must know more about casinos than just their accounting systems and financial statements. A hospitality manager should have a basic understanding of casino history; the casino industry; popular casino games; casino operations, accounting, and regulations; and other pertinent information so as to make intelligent, effective management decisions.

A single chapter on casino accounting cannot examine in detail the diverse, complex revenue flows, exacting accounting procedures, and internal control systems in place in casinos' many revenue centers. Indeed, separate chapters could be devoted to table games, slot machines, and other casino revenue areas to adequately explain the related extensive accounting and internal control procedures required. Instead, this chapter will examine and describe the basic concepts of casino revenue accounting and the fundamental internal controls required, thus providing the reader with a useful knowledge base.

Note that the term *gaming* is today commonly used instead of *gambling* when referring to the casino industry and to the playing of casino games. This shift in terminology, propounded more by those who favor legalized gambling than by those who oppose it, has occurred at least in part as part of an effort to avoid the negative connotations of gambling in the minds of many. Another phrase used to soften the image of gambling refers to *games of chance*. Although gaming and gambling may have different connotations, the terms can be used interchangeably.

This chapter will provide answers to such questions as these:

1. What is the history of gambling? What is gaming's present status?

2. What are gaming associations? What is their purpose?

3. What are Indian casinos and racinos?

4. What governmental regulations oversee Indian gaming? What are Class I, Class II, and Class III distinctions?

5. What are the more popular casino games?

6. What role does accounting play in casinos?

7. What are the fundamental principles of casino accounting and internal control?

8. What are the principles of casino financial accounting?

9. What financial statements do casino accountants produce?

A Brief History

Gambling has been popular with at least some segments of societies throughout history. Other segments of those same societies have often viewed gambling as evil, immoral, and/or socially undesirable because of its perceived effects on communities. These very different viewpoints have often led to social conflict over gambling.

Gambling dates back at least to ancient times. Dice have been discovered in Egyptian tombs. History shows that the Chinese, Greeks, Japanese, and Romans gambled for entertainment as long ago as 2300 B.C.E.

In America, gaming began with dice and card games offered in roadside inns and nightclubs. After the Revolution, the original 13 colonies made use of lotteries to raise funds, particularly for building projects. As decades passed, casinos arose on land and on riverboats, especially in the lower Mississippi River area and in New Orleans. As these gambling centers drew more and more people, however, local citizens began to blame professional gamblers for crime and other social and civic ills. In time, citizens tired of the problems they ascribed to gambling and united to force professional gamblers out of the South.

The rise of railroads and the increasing governmental prohibition of gambling took its toll on gambling houses and riverboats. The California Gold Rush, which began in 1848, was instrumental in making San Francisco a major hub of gambling. Gambling thrived in California. The United States outlawed almost all gambling and gambling operations by 1910. Only three states allowed betting on horse racing. However, many gaming houses operated covertly, and their owners had to bribe police officers so they could stay in business.

Interestingly, the 1929 U.S. stock market crash factored into the rebirth of legalized gambling. Bingo, horse racing, and casinos were considered ways to raise funds for charitable and governmental purposes. When casino gambling was declared legal in Nevada in 1931, Nevada succeeded California as the center of gaming. Many Nevada casinos in the period were owned by mobsters; later, however, lawful parties bought them out.

Today, casino gambling is popular in Nevada and many other states. The Indian gaming industry is growing, with large casinos in New Jersey, Connecticut, California, Florida, and other states. The United States has many legalized forms of gaming in addition to casinos; the most notable are horse racing, dog racing, and state-run lotteries. Other popular forms of gaming are the bingo-style games played for charity, and the usually illegal but nonetheless popular sports pools organized by employees in offices and other workplaces.

Casino gaming remains an industry whose social acceptance varies. Casinos may be rejected by some based on social morals or behavior, yet be highly accepted by others because of their entertainment value and the jobs and revenue streams they generate for states and local communities.

Gaming Associations

There are today many national and state gaming associations in the United States, as well as many gaming associations in other countries. Two important associations are the American Gaming Association and the National Indian Gaming Association.

Formed in 1995, the American Gaming Association (AGA) is located in Washington, D.C. The following statements are derived from its website:

> [The AGA's fundamental goal is to] create a better understanding of the gaming entertainment industry by bringing facts about the industry to the general public, elected officials, other decision makers and the media through education and advocacy. The AGA represents the commercial casino entertainment industry by addressing federal legislative and regulatory issues affecting its members and their employees and customers, such as federal taxation, regulatory issues, and travel and tourism matters.
>
> In addition, the AGA has an aggressive public education program designed to bring the industry's message to target audiences both in the nation's capital and across the country. The AGA provides leadership in addressing newly emerging national issues and in developing industry-wide programs on critical issues such as disorders and underage gambling.
>
> The association also serves as the industry's first national information clearinghouse, providing the media, elected officials, other decision makers and the public with timely, accurate gaming industry data.[1]

The nonprofit National Indian Gaming Association (NIGA) was formed in 1985 and is located in Washington, D.C. It has a membership of 184 gaming nations, and non-voting associate members representing tribal gaming enterprises throughout the United States. The NIGA's commitment is "to advance the lives of Indian peoples economically, socially and politically." The NIGA provides educational information about gaming to tribes, the public, government, and the media.

Today's Casinos and Racinos

There are currently more than 445 commercial casinos in the United States. Nevada brings in the most gaming revenue, followed by New Jersey. The AGA website provides information by state showing gross gaming revenue, number of casinos, number of casino employees, and so on. The following data is summarized from the website.[2]

Gross gambling revenue (GGR) is basically equivalent to what other industries call "sales." It equals the amount wagered minus the winnings of players. GGR is the revenue total a gaming operation earns before taxes, salaries, and other expenses.

The tax rate for the casino industry ranges from a low of 6.75 percent in Nevada to a high of 70 percent in Illinois. In most states, the revenue from those taxes is used for education, public safety, economic development, and infrastructure improvements.

Indian Casinos. The Indian Gaming Regulatory Act, enacted in 1988 as Public Law 100-497 and now codified at 25 U.S.C. §2701, establishes the jurisdictional framework that governs Indian gaming. The Act establishes three classes of games with a different regulatory scheme for each.

Class I gaming is defined as traditional Indian gaming and social gaming for minimal prizes. Regulatory authority over Class I gaming is vested exclusively in tribal governments.

Class II gaming pertains to the game of chance known as bingo as well as similar games. Class II gaming also includes non-banked card games, which are played exclusively against other players, not against the house or bank. The Act specifically excludes slot machines and electronic facsimiles of games. Tribes retain their authority to conduct, license, and regulate Class II gaming, provided the state in which the tribe is located permits gaming. Tribal governments are responsible for regulating Class II gaming with the Tribal Gaming Commission's oversight.

Class III gaming includes all forms of gaming not included in Class I or Class II. Generally, Class III gaming is referred to as casino-style gaming. As a compromise, the Act restricts tribal authority for conducting Class III gaming.

The NIGA website provides such statistics as tribal governmental gaming revenue and number of jobs provided. The following information is from the NIGA Library and Resource Center website.[3]

There are nearly 600 federally recognized Indian tribes; more than 200 tribal governments in almost 30 states offer Class II or Class III gaming.

The Indian Gaming Regulatory Act (25 U.S.C. 2710 [Sec. 11]) states that net revenues from any tribal gaming must be used only to:

- Fund tribal government operations and programs
- Provide for the general welfare of the tribe and its members
- Promote tribal economic development
- Donate to charitable organizations
- Help fund local government agencies

Racinos. Racinos are horse racetracks or dog racetracks offering casino facilities. Racinos provide gamblers the opportunity to bet on live and simulcast races and to play computerized games such as slots, blackjack, poker, and keno. Regulations do not allow racinos to offer table games such as blackjack, poker, roulette, or craps. Racinos have been legalized by state governments because they provide a source of revenue.

Casino Games

There are many casino games available at most casinos. A hospitality manager should understand at least the basic elements of the most popular games. The following sections briefly describe what are arguably some of the most popular casino games.

Exhibit 1   Blackjack Table

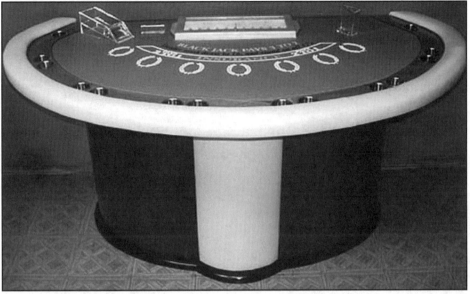

Courtesy of USA Gaming Supply.

Baccarat

Baccarat is a card game played with eight decks of cards. The player bets on any of three events: the player winning, or the house winning, or a tie result. To begin, each player gets two cards. The winner holds a hand of cards that totals 9 or is closest to 9. The value of a hand is counted as follows:

- Tens and face cards have a value of 0.

- Ace has a value of 1.

- Cards with numbers 2 to 9 carry their face value.

When the hand value is totaled, and the total has two digits, the first digit is omitted. For example, if a hand has a total value of 14, its playing value is 4.

The perfect hand has a total value of nine with the first two cards that were dealt; that hand is called a *natural*. A hand with a total value of eight is the second-best hand and is also called a *natural*. If any player or the dealer has a natural, the other players may not draw a third card.

Blackjack

Blackjack is a card game and likely the world's most popular casino game. The game is often simply called *21* because the object of the game is to get a number of cards to total 21, or as close to 21 as possible without exceeding it. Exhibit 1 shows a blackjack table typical in many casinos. The dealer stands at the center rear of the table, while the players are at the front of the table.

Exhibit 2   Craps Table

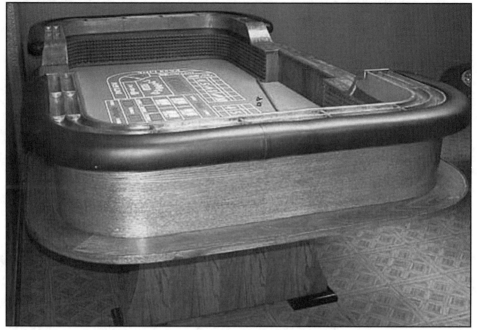

Courtesy of USA Gaming Supply.

In casinos, the blackjack player plays against the dealer. Several players may play at the same time; however, each player plays his or her hand only against the dealer's hand.

The cards are valued as follows: An Ace counts as a value of either 1 or 11; cards 2 through 10 are valued at their face number; the Jack, Queen, and King each has a value of 10. The suits of the cards do not affect the value. The winner is an individual with a hand value that is closer to 21 than that of the dealer, without going over 21. The players value the Ace as 1 or 11 to make the best hand.

Craps

Craps is a dice game played at a large table as shown in Exhibit 2. It is played with two dice. Skill and experience are not important in playing this game. Craps requires no complex calculations or strategies, yet the rules can be difficult for beginners to understand.

The first time a player picks up the dice and rolls them is called the *come-out roll*. Bets placed before the come-out roll are called *pass line bets*, which immediately win when a shooter's come-out roll is a 7 or an 11; and lose when the come-out roll is a 2 (snake eyes), 3 (cross eyes), or 12 (box cars). If the next roll results in a 4, 5, 6, 8, 9, or 10, that number becomes the point. The shooter then keeps rolling the dice until he or she rolls the point or a 7 to end the round. If the shooter rolls the point first, a pass line bet wins. If, however, the shooter rolls a 7 first (i.e., sevens out), a pass line bet loses.

Exhibit 3   Roulette Wheel and Roulette Layout

Courtesy of Simply Casino Supplies, Green Bay, Wisconsin.

Keno

Keno is a casino game similar to lotto and bingo. Basically, the player buys a keno ticket that determines the bet and payoff. The ticket is printed with the numbers 1 to 80; a player chooses from 1 to 20 numbers (as determined by house rules) and marks them on the ticket with a keno crayon. Each selection is called a spot; if the player selects 8 numbers, the player is playing an 8-spot game. The player presents the ticket with the wager to the casino and receives a duplicate ticket. The casino game has 80 balls, also numbered 1 to 80. For every game, the casino house draws 20 balls at random. The player wins based on (1) how many numbers match the ones he or she marked on the ticket, and (2) the wager he or she placed when purchasing the ticket.

Keno is usually played in casino lounges, but the game can be played elsewhere in the casino. Casino employees called *keno runners* take the player's winning ticket and deliver the winnings to the player after the casino verifies the ticket. Television monitors throughout the casino post the winning numbers. Keno tickets are available throughout the casino as well as in the casino's keno lounge.

Roulette

The European and French roulette wheels have 37 slots representing 36 numbers and one zero. The roulette wheel in the United States is slightly different: it has 38 slots, each designated with one of 36 numbers and two zeros. The numbers are not consecutively ordered, and the slots alternate between red and black. Exhibit 3 shows a roulette wheel and a roulette layout upon which bets are placed.

Before the game begins, each player buys uniquely colored chips so the bets can be identified with him or her. A roulette player wins when the roulette ball lands in a slot matching one he or she selected. Usually up to eight individuals may play roulette against the house. The dealer, or *croupier*, spins the roulette wheel, handles the bets, and pays the winners.

A player gambles on a particular number or numbers (0 included), or color (red or black), or a condition (odd or even). Other types of roulette gaming are not within the scope of this chapter.

Slot Machines

The "arm" and display window are easily recognized features of a slot machine. After entering a coin or coins, the player releases and pulls the arm to play the game. The slot machines of yesteryear had three reels displaying horseshoes, spades, diamonds, hearts, and bells. A player won when a particular combination of symbols appeared in the display window.

Today's casinos feature electronic slot machines offering many versions of games. Video poker, a poker card game in a slot machine, is very popular because the player has an opportunity for a large win. However, the player has to know and remember many playing rules and follow them exactly.

Basically, there are two kinds of slot machines: progressive and nonprogressive. They are essentially the same except for the jackpot payout. Progressive machines have a jackpot meter that is always changing; the jackpot increases each time the machine is played. Progressive machines usually pay off less frequently than nonprogressive machines, but pay off a bigger jackpot. A nonprogressive machine pays off a predetermined jackpot; the largest possible jackpot is displayed on the machine, but the machine usually pays out smaller jackpots to winners. The nonprogressive machines are sometimes referred to as straight slots, flat tops, or base slots.

Principles of Casino Accounting and Internal Control ———

While a casino may offer a hotel facility boasting thousands of guestrooms, and may operate many restaurant units, its major source of revenue comes from gaming. The hotel and its ancillary operations exist to serve the casino patron.

In any casino, the accounting department plays a key role in internal control. Internal control is a system designed to accomplish four major objectives:

1. Safeguard assets.
2. Ensure compliance with company policies.
3. Facilitate operational efficiency.
4. Ensure accurate financial information.

State casino licensing regulations demand that a casino have a highly effective, documented system of internal control in place before it grants the casino a license. Such an internal control system is imperative for a casino to operate efficiently and profitably. As in other industries, the casino's controller (who may also be called the chief financial officer, chief accounting executive, vice president, or another title) supervises a department that performs critical financial services for the organization and its employees. In some casino organizations, the following departments or functions report to the controller:

*   Internal auditing of gaming centers
*   Cage cashier
*   Vault supervisor

- The counting of money from gaming centers
- Payroll
- Financial accounting
- Data processing

The primary goal of a casino is to make a profit. Since large amounts of cash flow quickly into and out of casinos, refined internal control systems are essential. A key element of internal control is the separation of duties between operations staff and accounting staff. The separation of duties makes the staff of separate departments interdependent on one another, making it exceptionally difficult for individual employees to steal. Other precautions may be needed to prevent or discover cases involving employee collusion.

In a casino, chips are as good as cash. Casino employees from both the operations department and the accounting department handle chips and money. Operations employees who handle money serve in positions such as pit clerks and dealers, while accounting employees serve as cashiers in the cages and in the count rooms.

Money and chip handling and internal controls in a casino involve a number of terms and situations that are unique among hospitality businesses, including:

- Markers and foreign chips
- Cage cashiering
- Slot machine controls
- Table game controls
- Count room controls
- Vault controls
- Handle, win, and drop

Markers and Foreign Chips

Casino customers exchange cash for coins or tokens to play the slots, and exchange cash for chips to play table games. Players might also use house credit to pay for gaming. In addition, casinos may accept chips the player holds from any other casino.

A **marker** is a document that a player may use at the gaming tables in lieu of cash. A marker is the result of credit being granted to a customer. The customer must first get credit approval from the casino. Of course, casinos do not highly promote credit or easily grant it. In some cases, customers experience a delay in getting credit approval. Casinos may restrict credit to customers of status. Sometimes credit is granted only when the customer provides a signed negotiable instrument, such as a check. Once the casino approves credit, the customer is given a marker to use at the gaming tables, or a document that represents a check. Sometimes, instead of a marker, a customer receives special chips.

As a convenience, and to attract customers, some casinos allow customers to play with **foreign chips**, which are chips from other casinos. These chips are sent to the vault, where casino employees begin the chip exchange process with other casinos.

Cage Cashiering Controls

Cashiers operate in specified locations and enclosures called **cages**. Cashiers are accounting employees who perform the cage cashiering function and deal directly with the customer. Internal control in the cages is not complex because the cage funds are maintained on either the imprest system or the floating cage balance system. Under the **imprest system**, the cage fund is restored to its predetermined fixed amount at the end of a shift. This involves reimbursing the cage fund for any paid-outs and tokens, to restore the imprest amount. An internal audit of the cage fund is conducted daily. The disadvantage of the imprest system is its inflexibility: when gaming activity is especially high, cashiers must work hurriedly to meet player needs.

The **floating cage balance system** is almost identical to the imprest system, except that the cage fund balance may increase with a corresponding increase in gambling volume. This is accomplished when the cashier requisitions cash from the vault to temporarily increase the cage fund amount until customer activity returns to normal.

Cage cashiers are also responsible for *fills* and *credits* activity occurring between the cage and the gaming operations, especially with table games. A *fill* is a transaction giving cash to the table game, while a *credit* (to the table game) is given when the cashier receives cash from the table game.

Slot Machine Controls

Casinos are well aware of the importance of slot machine location and generally position them so the customer immediately sees them upon entering the casino floor. Slot machine activity plays a major role in casino revenues. Therefore, the casino's goal is to provide the ultimate in convenience to slot machine players by positioning floor personnel so they are close at hand and can quickly accommodate the players' coin and token requirements. Slot machine cashiering may take place between designated floor personnel and the customer or between a cashier and the customer.

The **slot hopper** in the slot machine contains a minimum number of coins necessary for operations. When there is a winner, the hopper automatically releases the won coins into a payout tray. The hopper is usually restored to its customary balance at the beginning of the operating day. Slot machines usually have two meters, a coin-in meter and a coin-out meter. The **coin-in meter** records the players' gaming activity, and the **coin-out meter** records the payouts to winners.

Table Game Controls

Each table game has its own dealer and a **table inventory** consisting of chips of various values. Chips are assigned to each table game using the **par method**, which means that the table starts its shift with a certain value of chips. The cashiering activity usually is conducted between the dealer and the player. The player

Exhibit 4   Fill Slip

SAMPLE
FILL SLIP

DATE			TIME
SHIFT	GYD	DAY	SWING

GAME	NUMBER	Denomination	AMOUNT
Craps			
21			
Roulette			
Baccarat			
TOTAL			
MEMO			

RUNNER	FLOOR MAN
CASHIER	DEALER-BOXMAN

F **3181**

"buys" chips with currency, markers, or other chips. The dealer instantly places the customer's money in a **drop box** secured to the table.

The casino predetermines the low limit for the table inventory, which is monitored by the dealer and the pit supervisor. If the inventory falls to this limit, a document called a *fill slip* (shown in Exhibit 4) is completed, taken to the cage, and exchanged for an additional amount of chips. Conversely, the table inventory may reach a high level that the casino has predetermined to be excessive. In this case, a document called a *credit slip* (shown in Exhibit 5) is completed. A casino employee called a *security runner* delivers the excess chips and a copy of the credit slip to a cage cashier for review and verification.

Casinos use various table accounting procedures when a shift change occurs. Regardless of the procedure used, the on-coming and off-going supervisory personnel perform a **table inventory**, which involves counting the chips and preparing an inventory form. The par method is the basis for restoring the table inventory; thus, players are not interrupted. The **table drop** procedure involves the supervised removal of drop boxes from the table; under custody, the drop boxes are then delivered to the count room.

Exhibit 5   Credit Slip

SAMPLE
CREDIT SLIP

DATE			TIME	

SHIFT	GYD	DAY	SWING

GAME	NUMBER	Denomination	AMOUNT
Craps			
21			
Roulette			
Baccarat			
Keno			
TOTAL			
MEMO		RETURN CHIPS ☐	

RUNNER	FLOOR MAN
CASHIER	DEALER-BOXMAN

C 3496

Count Room Controls

The **count room** receives the money and documents from the various games. The count room is under very intensive security using internal control measures such as camera surveillance, strict dress codes, and prohibiting personnel from bringing in any type of storage bag. Once the count begins, no one is permitted to leave the count room until the count is completed.

The counting activity includes the counting and reconciliation of money, fill slips, and credit slips. The money is recounted and sorted into various denomination bundles for further recounting by the vault. After the count is completed, the money, fill and credit slips, and count sheets are delivered under security to the vault.

Vault Controls

The vault operation plays a vital role in the casino's money-handling process. The vault receives money and documents from the count room, and operates under intensive security similar to that in the count room. The vault operation performs many functions:

- It verifies money and documents received from the count room.

- It reimburses cashiers for slips, checks cashed, and chips.

- It restores the cashiers' cash and chips to their imprest amount.

- It restores the casino **bankroll** (the minimum amount of cash the casino needs for daily operations).

- It stores foreign chips, or redeems them at the casinos from which they were issued. This exchange is called a **chip run**.

As in any business with systems of internal control, casinos should make bank deposits daily. Depending on the casino, the daily deposit procedures range from requiring a trusted employee to make the bank deposit to using an armored truck service. Casinos with large amounts of cash deposits typically do the latter.

Handle, Win, and Drop

Numerous accounting procedures are used to determine casino revenue. Recall that a basic accounting definition of the term *revenue* is "sales from operations." However, measuring revenue in a casino is not as simple as measuring it in other industries because neither invoices nor cash registers play a role in the revenue process. While cash is the basis of transactions in a casino, the total cash amount the casino receives cannot represent casino sales or revenue. Casinos use large amounts of cash to pay winners, and to replenish slot machines, table games, and other required operations.

Revenue for casinos is better understood if one thinks of gaming revenue as the winnings of the casino. Accounting for casino revenue requires the understanding of such industry-specific terms as the *handle, win,* and *drop.*

Handle is the *total amount of money gambled*. A slot machine can provide the handle since it has a meter that measures the betting activity. However, the handle for table games is indeterminable, since the manual recording of every table bet is not feasible.

Win is generally defined as *the total amount gambled less the amount paid to winners*. The win for a slot machine is the handle minus paid-outs minus refills. The win for table games requires a more lengthy computation involving dealer exchanges of cash for chips, as well as any fill or credit slips. While not complex, this procedure is beyond the scope of this chapter.

Drop is generally defined as *the money in a slot machine drop bucket or table game drop box*. The term does not refer to total amount gambled or to revenue.

Principles of Casino Financial Accounting ⎯⎯⎯⎯⎯⎯⎯⎯⎯⎯

The principles of accounting for a casino are almost identical to the principles of accounting for a hotel operation, except that the casino is the primary source of revenue. The casino is treated as the prime revenue center and is charged for its direct operating expenses.

The generally accepted accounting principles for casinos are similar to those applicable when hotels are the prime revenue centers. When a casino is the prime revenue center, some new accounts and terminology apply. This section explores the following financial accounting principles:

- Gaming revenue
- Financial statements
- Complimentary items and allowances
- Payroll and other expenses

Gaming Revenue

Gaming revenue represents the casino's winnings: the amount gambled by players minus the players' winnings. There are two methods of accounting for casino revenue: one that considers only gaming revenue, and a second that treats casino revenue as gaming revenue plus the retail value of the complimentary items given to players.

Certain games require special accounting treatment, especially slot machines, since the potential for jackpot winnings always exists. Slot machine revenue accounting depends on the type of slot machine involved. In addition to the progressive and nonprogressive slot machines mentioned earlier, there is a category known as participating slot machines.

Nonprogressive slot machines, which pay off set, predetermined jackpots, can have their jackpots deducted as they occur. If the expected payout for all machines is significant, the estimated jackpots may be deducted evenly over a period prior to any payout.

Progressive slot machines, which have jackpots that increase every time they are played until the jackpots are won, call for a different approach. Unpaid progressive jackpots are recorded as a liability and a reduction of slot gaming revenue.

Participating slot machines are slot machines owned by another party, not by the casino. These machines are operated under an arrangement in which the owner shares profits with the casino. Generally, the total winnings from these machines are recorded as the casino's slot gaming revenue, and the casino's payment to the owner is recorded as an expense.

Financial Statements

A casino's financial statement package includes the income statement, balance sheet, statement of cash flows, and departmental statements for each revenue and support department. The reporting package is similar to a hotel's financial statement package when the hotel is the prime revenue center. The balance sheet and statement of cash flows are identical to those used in most hospitality businesses.

The major difference is in the Casino Department's income statement (shown in Exhibit 6). The income statement to management would be accompanied by various supporting schedules explaining certain line items. For example, the line item Revenue would be accompanied by a supplementary schedule showing the various sources derived from slots, table games, and other games of chance. The slot machine schedule could show revenue by type and location of slots; the table games schedule could show revenue from blackjack, craps, baccarat, roulette, and

Exhibit 6   Casino Department Income Statement

Casino Department	
	Current Period
REVENUE	$
LESS COMPLIMENTARY ALLOWANCES (used only if above revenue includes complimentaries)	
NET REVENUE	
PAYROLL AND RELATED EXPENSES	
Salaries and Wages	
Employee Benefits	
Total Payroll and Related Expenses	
OTHER EXPENSES	
Complimentaries:	
Rooms	
Food	
Beverage	
Travel	
Special Events	
Other Amenities	
Contract Services	
Credit and Collection	
Gaming Taxes, License Fees, and Regulatory Costs	
Operating Supplies	
Postage	
Provision for Doubtful Accounts	
Telecommunications	
Training	
Uniforms	
Other	
Total Other Expenses	
TOTAL EXPENSES	
DEPARTMENTAL INCOME (LOSS)	$

Wheel of Fortune. The other gaming revenue might be from sources such as bingo, keno, race, and sports book.

Complimentary Items and Allowances

Giving complimentary or promotional goods and services to guests is a prevalent practice in the gaming industry. These allowances, which might include rooms, food, beverage, travel, and other amenities, are given as an incentive to gamble at the casino. The approximate retail value is used to account for these items. Other operating departments such as rooms and food and beverage generally provide these complimentary items; therefore, the retail value of these complimentary items is included in the sales of the operating departments that provided them.

The accounting procedure for complimentary items in the casino department depends on the revenue accounting method the hotel uses. The account called Complimentary Allowance on the casino departmental statement is used only if the hotel treats total casino revenue as comprising both gaming revenue and the retail value of complimentary items. Complimentary items are deducted from total casino revenue to arrive at the actual revenue from gaming operations. For example, assume that a casino department had $100,000 of gaming revenue and gave out $2,000 in complimentary items. The casino income statement would appear as follows:

Revenue	$102,000
Less Complimentary Allowances	2,000
Net Revenue	$100,000

Payroll and Other Expenses

Payroll, employee benefits, and most other expenses for the casino department are accounted for largely as they are in other operating departments. Of special interest are the following expenses:

- Credit and collection
- Gaming taxes, licenses, and regulatory fees
- Postage
- Complimentaries

The credit and collection costs associated with collecting on casino charge accounts are charged to the casino, unlike other operating departments where such costs are generally charged to the administrative and general department.

The specialized casino licensing fees are charged to the casino department, just as the beverage department is charged for its special beverage license fee.

Postage is generally charged to the A&G department. However, the casino postage expense is directly charged to the casino.

The complimentary items expense is similar to the amenities provided on a gratis basis in other major revenue centers. The free guest amenities given to casino customers appear as separate line items under Other Expenses on the statement for gaming operations. *This procedure is used regardless of the revenue method of accounting for the casino department.*

Endnotes

1. American Gaming Association, "About the AGA: AGA Overview" (Washington, D.C., 2003), available from http://www.americangaming.org/about/overview.cfm.

2. American Gaming Association, "Gaming Revenue: Ten Year Trends" (Washington, D.C., April 2007), available from http://www.americangaming.org/industry/factsheets/statistics_detail.cfv?id=8.

3. National Indian Gaming Association Library, "Indian Gaming Facts" (Washington, D.C., 2007), available from http://www.indiangaming.org/library/indian-gaming-facts/index.shtml.

📖 References

Roger Dunstan, "Gambling in California" (California Research Bureau, California State Library, Sacramento, Cal., January 1997), available at www.library.ca.gov/crb/97/03/Chapt2.html.

www.casinoratingcenter.com/history/gambling-history.html

www.casinoratingcenter.com/craps/craps-rules.html

www.blackjackinfo.com/

www.ildado.com/keno_rules.html

www.ildado.com/roulette_rules.html

www.win4real.com/tips/internet-casino/games/slot-machine.html

🔑 Key Terms

bankroll—The minimum amount of cash funds needed for daily operations. It is restored daily by the vault procedure.

cage—An enclosure in which the cashiers operate.

chip run—The exchanging of foreign chips with the issuing casinos.

Class I gaming—A governmental classification for Indian gaming that is considered social gaming for minimal prizes.

Class II gaming—A governmental classification for Indian gaming that includes bingo, games similar to bingo, and non-banked card games.

Class III gaming—A governmental classification for Indian gaming that includes all forms of gaming not classified as Class I or II gaming.

coin-in meter—A meter in a slot machine that records the monetary gaming activity.

coin-out meter—A meter in a slot machine that records the amount of the payouts (winnings by players).

count room—A highly secured location away from all activity where personnel open and count the lock boxes.

drop—The money in a slot machine drop bucket or table game drop box.

drop box—A locked box, attached to a gaming table, into which the table operator deposits all money during playing activity.

floating cage balance system—A system similar to an imprest system except that the funds are allowed to change as necessary to accommodate gaming demand.

foreign chips—Chips from other casinos brought in by players and used for gaming.

handle—The total amount gambled.

imprest system—A system in which funds are maintained at a fixed, predetermined amount.

marker—A document giving a form of credit to a customer to use for gaming.

nonprogressive slot machine—A slot machine that pays out predetermined jackpot amounts.

par method—A method of table inventory control in which a game starts with a predetermined value of chips.

participating slot machine—A slot machine owned by a party other than the casino; the casino and the owner share the profits.

progressive slot machine—A slot machine that has a jackpot that continues to grow with playing activity until there is a winner.

racinos—Racetracks with gaming facilities.

slot hopper—A mechanism in a slot machine that contains the minimum amount of coins necessary for operations.

table drop—A procedure in which the drop box is removed from the table and delivered to the vault.

table game drop—The money in the drop box of a table game.

table game win—A computation to determine the win amount of a table game. The formula is: Win = Drop + Credits − Fills − Beginning Cash.

table inventory—The monetary amount of chips at a table.

vault—A high-security location, away from activity, that receives money and documents from the count room. It performs various functions including restoration of cashiers' funds and preparation of the daily deposit.

win—The total amount gambled less the amount paid to winners.

 # Review Questions

1. Which state gained gambling prominence in the 1900s?

2. What is the American Gaming Association's fundamental goal?

3. What is the National Indian Gaming Association's commitment?

4. What three classes of games did the Indian Regulatory Act establish? How are they defined?

5. What is a racino?

6. Are baccarat, blackjack, craps, and roulette card games or table games?

7. What are nonprogressive slot machines? Progressive slot machines?

8. What department supervises the cage cashiers?

9. What is a marker?

10. What are foreign chips?

11. What is an imprest system?

12. What is a floating cage system?

13. What is a fill slip? What is a credit slip?

14. What are the functions of a coin-in meter and a coin-out meter?

15. What is a table par method?

16. What is a table inventory procedure?

17. What is a chip run?

18. What is the general definition of Win? Of Drop?

19. What is a table drop?

20. What is a participating slot machine?

21. What are the basic premises of the following casino games: baccarat, blackjack, craps, keno, and slot machines?

Internet Sites

For more information, visit the following Internet sites. Remember that Internet addresses can change without notice. If the site is no longer there, you can use a search engine to look for additional sites.

American Gaming Association
www.americangaming.org/

Canadian Gaming Association
www.canadiangaming.ca/english/home/index.cfm

Connecticut Casinos
www.americancasinoguide.com/conn.shtml

Connecticut Division of Special Revenue
www.ct.gov/dosr/

National Indian Gaming Association
www.indiangaming.org/

Nevada Casinos and Nevada Gambling
http://nevada.casinocity.com/

Nevada Gaming Commission
http://gaming.nv.gov/ngc_main.htm

New Jersey Casino Control Commission
www.state.nj.us/casinos/

New Jersey Casinos and Gambling
http://newjersey.casinocity.com/

State Gambling Agency Sites
www.gambling-law-us.com/Useful-Sites/State-Gambling-Agencies.htm

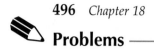

Problems ————————————————————————————

Problem 1

Describe a general internal control procedure for a table game's shift change.

Problem 2

Describe the general operation of the count room.

Problem 3

Describe the general operation of the vault.

Problem 4

The slot handle is $20,000; jackpots paid out were $16,000; and refills were $1,000.

    a. What is the amount wagered?

    b. What is the amount of the slot win?

Problem 5

Specify whether the craps player is a winner or a loser in each of the following:

    a. Player's first roll is a 12.

    b. Player's first roll is a 2.

    c. Player's first roll is a 4 and subsequent roll is a 4.

    d. Player's first roll is a 6 and subsequent roll is a 7.

Problem 6

Specify whether the blackjack player is a winner or a loser in each of the following:

    a. Dealer has 18 and player has an Ace and a King.

    b. Dealer has 18 and player has an Ace, an Ace, a Seven, and a Jack.

    c. Dealer has 20 and player has a Seven, a Four, and a Queen.

    d. Dealer has 16 and player has a Seven, an Eight, and a Ten.

Case Study ————————————————————————————

Casino Financial Accounting System

The Platinum Casino is a small casino incorporated in Nevada. It has applied for a gaming license and expects to get it.

Casino management is in the process of establishing internal controls and financial accounting procedures in the casino's prime revenue center, the casino. Management is examining and documenting similar procedures for the hotel and other ancillary departments.

The casino features nonprogressive and progressive slot machines. Free goods and services to players will be accounted for at retail and included in total casino revenue.

Challenge

Gaming revenue will be calculated by the controller's senior staff and recorded in the financial records. The controller has requested that you, a junior staff member, write up financial accounting procedures without any regard for equations, formulas, or internal control.

1. Select financial accounting procedures for the slot machines. Explain why you selected the procedures you did, justifying your choices and reasoning.

2. Illustrate and explain the presentation of gaming revenue and free goods and services on the income statement.

3. Explain the recording of expenses chargeable to the casino department.

Chapter 19 Outline

The Importance of Inventory Valuation
The Gross Profit Method
Approaches to Inventory Valuation
The Specific Identification Approach to
    Inventory Valuation
    The Specific Identification Perpetual
      Method
    The Specific Identification Periodic
      Method
The FIFO Approach to Inventory Valuation
    The FIFO Perpetual Method
    The FIFO Periodic Method
The LIFO Approach to Inventory Valuation
    The LIFO Perpetual Method
    The LIFO Periodic Method
The Weighted Average Approach to
    Inventory Valuation
    The Weighted Average Perpetual
      Method
    The Weighted Average Periodic
      Method
A Comparison of Cost Allocation Methods
LIFO Analyzed

Competencies

1. Describe how inaccurate inventory records can affect the financial statements. (pp. 500–502)

2. Explain the gross profit method of estimating inventory levels. (pp. 502–503)

3. Explain the basis of accounting for inventory, and differentiate between inventory valuation approaches according to their emphasis on product flow or cost flow. (pp. 504–505)

4. Describe the specific identification approach to inventory valuation. (pp. 505–508)

5. Explain the FIFO approach to inventory valuation and how it differs from the specific identification approach. (pp. 508–509)

6. Describe the LIFO approach to inventory valuation, and compare it with the FIFO approach. (pp. 509–511)

7. Describe the weighted average approach to inventory valuation and how it differs from the approaches previously discussed. (pp. 511–513)

8. Compare the three cost flow approaches to inventory valuation with respect to cost of sales and ending inventory. (pp. 513–514)

9. Summarize the benefits and drawbacks of the LIFO approach. (pp. 514–515)

19

Inventory Accounting

$\mathbf{A}$ HOSPITALITY OPERATION maintains inventories for both merchandise and operating supplies. Merchandise inventories include food, beverages, and other items primarily sold to guests. Operating supplies include cleaning supplies, office supplies, guest supplies, and other supply items consumed by a business in its day-to-day operations. While this chapter will concentrate on merchandise inventories, many of the concepts may be applied to supplies inventories.

Inventories influence the decision-making process in many areas of a hospitality organization. For example, food inventories are not just the concern of the food and beverage department. The marketing department is concerned that there be sufficient quantities of specific food items advertised as specials. The accounting department monitors food inventory costs related to financing, storage, insurance, and local inventory taxes.

Inventory accounting affects both the balance sheet and the income statement. The portion of inventory remaining at the end of the accounting period appears on the balance sheet as a current asset; the portion of inventory used during the accounting period appears on the income statement as Cost of Sales. Measuring the value of ending inventory and computing the cost of sales are significant tasks in merchandising operations. While taking a physical inventory is costly and time-consuming, the process is necessary to confirm the accuracy of the inventory amount reported on the financial statements.

This chapter addresses fundamental concepts related to inventory accounting by answering such questions as:

1. How do inventory errors affect reported income?

2. How is the gross profit method used to estimate ending inventories?

3. What is the distinction between product flow and cost flow?

4. How does the selection of an inventory valuation method affect the balance sheet and the income statement?

5. What are the advantages and disadvantages of the "last-in, first-out" approach to inventory valuation?

The purpose of this chapter is to present the concept of inventory valuation and its effect on the financial statements. The cumulative effect of inventory errors between two periods and the counterbalancing effect are explained. The gross profit method is demonstrated as a means of estimating ending inventories when a physical inventory is not available but financial statements must be prepared.

The discussion includes four approaches to **inventory valuation:** specific identification, first-in, first-out (FIFO), last-in, first-out (LIFO), and weighted average.

These approaches are discussed with respect to the perpetual and periodic methods associated with their application. The chapter concludes with a comparison of the effects of each method on the balance sheet and income statement, and with a critical analysis of LIFO.

The Importance of Inventory Valuation

Some companies adopt a perpetual inventory system and thus maintain perpetual records for all inventory items. Under this system, the acquisition of inventory is charged to an inventory account. During the sales period, the issues are costed and recorded by debiting a cost of sales account and crediting the appropriate inventory account. If a company adopts the perpetual inventory system, the general ledger inventory account reflects the inventory on hand at the end of an accounting period. However, the use of perpetual inventory cards is generally too time-consuming and expensive for a business to adopt this system on a universal basis.

If a company does not use a perpetual inventory system, the accounting department must use the periodic method to account for inventory in the financial records. Using the periodic inventory method, the acquisition of inventory is charged to a purchases account. Because there is no cost of sales account, no entry is made for cost of sales during the sales period. Since issues are not recorded by the storekeeper, this information is not available for accounting purposes. The inventory account is brought up to date only at the end of the accounting period through a physical inventory or an estimating procedure.

Of course, a company can use a combination of recordkeeping systems. Perpetual recordkeeping is often used for those items with high costs per unit. Items with low costs per unit might not require perpetual records, and would instead be accounted for using the periodic inventory method. The remainder of this section will focus on the periodic inventory method.

The measurement of inventory is a source of possible errors on the balance sheet. When inventory records are inaccurate, this not only affects the reporting of Inventory on the balance sheet, but also the computation of total current assets and total assets.

Inaccurate inventories also affect the income statement. Ending inventory is a primary factor in the cost of sales computation, which can be expressed in the following general format:

Cost of Sales = Beginning Inventory + Purchases − Ending Inventory

To perform this computation, a hospitality company must cost the items on hand at the end of an accounting period based on a physical inventory or an estimate. An inaccurate inventory measurement not only affects cost of sales on the income statement, but also distorts the net income on the statement. The distortion of net income will ultimately affect the equity section of the balance sheet.

Because the ending inventory of one period is the beginning inventory for the next period, an error in measuring ending inventory will affect at least two periods. This is best understood by studying the effect of inventory amounts in the calculation of gross profit.

Exhibit 1   Sample Report of Gross Profit

	Period 1	Period 2
Sales	$100,000	$90,000
Cost of Sales:		
Beginning Inventory	20,000	**30,000**
Purchases	42,000	26,000
Cost of Goods Available	62,000	56,000
Ending Inventory	**30,000**	22,000
Cost of Sales	$ 32,000	$34,000
Gross Profit	$ 68,000	$56,000

Exhibit 2   Computation of Gross Profit with Corrected Inventory

	Period 1	Period 2
Sales	$100,000	$90,000
Cost of Sales:		
Beginning Inventory	20,000	**27,000**
Purchases	42,000	26,000
Cost of Goods Available	62,000	53,000
Ending Inventory	**27,000**	22,000
Cost of Sales	$ 35,000	$31,000
Gross Profit	$ 65,000	$59,000

Gross profit on sales is calculated by subtracting cost of sales from the sales for the period. The gross profit must be large enough to cover payroll and other expenses. If gross profit is large enough to cover these expenses, the remainder represents income from operations; if gross profit is not large enough to cover these expenses, the difference represents a loss from operations. Exhibit 1 illustrates a calculation of gross profit on sales for two periods. Note that the ending inventory of Period 1 becomes the beginning inventory of Period 2.

Now assume that the reported ending inventory for Period 1 was erroneous; the ending inventory should have been reported as $27,000, not $30,000. Exhibit 2 shows the result of this correction in the calculation of gross profit on sales for Periods 1 and 2. Note that the corrected ending inventory becomes the beginning inventory of Period 2.

The effect of this inventory error on gross profit may be analyzed as follows:

	Gross Profit		
	As Reported	Should Have Been	Difference
Period 1	$ 68,000	$ 65,000	+ 3,000
Period 2	56,000	59,000	− 3,000
Total	$124,000	$124,000	0

Gross profit is the element in the income statement from which operating expenses, fixed charges, and corporate income taxes are subtracted to arrive at net income. Therefore, differences noted for gross profit also apply to net income. Due to the ending inventory error in Period 1, net income reported for Period 1 would be overstated by $3,000; net income reported for Period 2 would be understated by $3,000.

Assuming no further errors, the cumulative effect is self-correcting; when the differences for the two periods are totaled, the errors counterbalance one another. While the individual figures for gross profit of each period differ, the sum of gross profits for both periods are equal ($124,000) irrespective of the inventory correction.

The Gross Profit Method

If inventories are accounted for using the periodic inventory accounting method, the financial records do not readily provide inventory information as is the case with the perpetual inventory accounting method. Using the periodic inventory accounting method, ending inventory is nonetheless an integral part of computing gross profit. Therefore, the preparation of financial statements requires an inventory amount at the end of the accounting period.

Tax laws and generally accepted accounting principles require that a physical inventory be taken at least once in the business year. As part of its inventory control practices, a hospitality business will perform physical inventories more often to gauge spoilage, quality, and disappearance. Alcoholic beverages and other attractive inventory items may be inventoried weekly. Low-cost items may be physically counted less frequently.

If a physical inventory has not been performed and financial statements are to be prepared, an estimating procedure is necessary. One acceptable estimating procedure is called the **gross profit method.** The gross profit method is also useful in estimating inventory losses from fire, theft, and other casualties.

The gross profit method uses an estimate of the gross profit percentage on sales. The percentage is calculated by dividing gross profit by net sales, which are obtained from previous financial statements. The accuracy of the estimated ending inventory depends on the accuracy of the gross profit percentage used. The gross profit percentage represents an average on all inventory items sold.

The sales mix affects the gross profit percentage. As a result, the sales mix may affect the reliability of this method. If the gross profit percentage on the financial statements is 65 percent, it implies that the sales mix generates an average of 65 percent gross profit on sales. If the products composing the sales mix lack a relatively standard markup, or if the mix changes, the accuracy of this method may be affected. Gross profit percentages should be individually computed for food and beverages, and estimating procedures should be carried out separately for these two areas of inventory.

The gross profit method involves a number of basic assumptions and calculations. It assumes that the financial records provide the following information under a periodic inventory system:

Exhibit 3   Steps in the Gross Profit Method

Sales (net)	Known	100%
Cost of Sales:		
Beginning Inventory	Known	
+ Purchases	Known	
Cost of Goods Available	Addition	
− Ending Inventory	(C)	
Cost of Sales	(B)	(A)
Gross Profit	(D)	Known

(A)   Cost of Sales % = 100% − Gross Profit %
(B)   Cost of Sales = Cost of Sales % × Net Sales
(C)   Ending Inventory = Cost of Goods Available − Cost of Sales
(D)   PROOF: 1. Gross Profit = Net Sales − Cost of Sales
                 2. Gross Profit = Gross Profit % × Net Sales
                 3. Answers in 1 and 2 must be equal.

- Sales for the period
- Last period's ending inventory
- Purchases for the period

Having determined the gross profit percentage through an analysis of previous financial statements, one can work back to a figure for the cost of sales percentage, which relates cost of sales expense to net sales. Since net sales is the basis or common denominator for an income or expense analysis, net sales is always 100 percent. The procedure can be demonstrated as follows:

		If	Then
Sales (net)	=	100%	100%
Cost of Sales	=	− ?	−40%
Gross Profit	=	60%	60%

Using the cost of sales percentage, the cost of sales amount can be estimated. Net sales multiplied by the cost of sales percentage yields an estimate for cost of sales. This cost of sales estimate can, in turn, be used to solve for ending inventory.

Exhibit 3 demonstrates the steps involved in the gross profit method. This exhibit presents the basic procedure for estimating ending inventory.

Assume that a hospitality business's accounting records provide the following information:

Sales for the period	$50,000
Ending inventory of prior period	8,000
Purchases for the period	14,000
Estimated gross profit percentage	60%

Based on this information, Exhibit 4 shows how the ending inventory for the period is estimated as $2,000. It provides a proof of the calculation by comparing figures for gross profit determined two different ways.

Exhibit 4   Estimating Inventory by the Gross Profit Method

Sales (net)	$50,000	100%
Cost of Sales:		
Beginning Inventory	8,000	
+ Purchases	14,000	
Cost of Goods Available	22,000	
− Ending Inventory	2,000 (C)	
Cost of Sales	$20,000 (B)	40% (A)
Gross Profit	$30,000 (D)	60%

(A)   Cost of Sales % = 100% − Gross Profit %
     Cost of Sales % = 100% − 60% = 40%
(B)   Cost of Sales = Cost of Sales % × Net Sales
     Cost of Sales = 40% × $50,000 = $20,000
(C)   Ending Inventory = Cost of Goods Available − Cost of Sales
     Ending Inventory = $22,000 − $20,000 = $2,000
(D)   PROOF: 1. Gross Profit = Net Sales − Cost of Sales
                     $50,000 − $20,000 = $30,000
           2. Gross Profit = Gross Profit % × Net Sales
                     60% × $50,000 = $30,000
           3. Answers in 1 and 2 must be equal.

Approaches to Inventory Valuation

The primary basis of accounting for inventory is cost. Cost should include transportation charges unless such charges are not considered significant. In this case, their omission from inventory cost may be justified in the interests of convenience and economy in the accounting system. Purchase discounts do not enter into the computation of cost of sales or inventory. Under the *Uniform System of Accounts for the Lodging Industry,* purchase discounts are recorded as revenue.

The costs of inventory items, especially produce and other food items, change on a more or less regular basis. Produce prices may change from week to week. A category of items purchased at a particular price on one occasion may have a different price on another occasion. The effect of price fluctuations raises some important questions related to inventory valuation:

- What is the cost of inventory on hand?

- Should the value of items in inventory reflect their actual purchase cost?

- Should the value of items in inventory reflect the most recent purchase cost?

Answering these questions requires a knowledge of the various approaches to costing issues and accounting for inventories.

An important distinction between inventory valuation approaches is whether the approach emphasizes the flow of the physical product (product flow) or the flow of costs (cost flow). Of the four inventory valuation approaches presented here, only the specific identification approach emphasizes the flow of the physical product and its identified cost. The FIFO approach, the LIFO approach, and the weighted average approach emphasize the flow of costs.

For each of the four approaches, the inventory valuation process is explained for both perpetual and periodic inventory accounting methods. To use the perpetual method, perpetual recordkeeping cards must be maintained to record issues and ending inventory. The periodic inventory accounting method requires a physical count or estimating procedure to determine inventory at the end of the accounting period.

Examples of these inventory valuation methods will use the same basic illustrative case. We assume that transactions during the month of March are as follows:

Date	Inventory Transaction
3/1	Purchased 10 units at $1.00 per unit
3/2	Purchased 5 units at $1.02 per unit
3/3	Purchased 5 units at $1.05 per unit
3/6	Issued 3 units
3/10	Issued 11 units

These transactions will be processed for a new inventory item with a beginning balance of zero.

The Specific Identification Approach to Inventory Valuation

The **specific identification approach** uses the actual purchase cost of each unit of inventory as the basis for inventory valuation. In this approach, all items in the storeroom must be identified with their actual purchase costs. Thus, the specific identification approach is concerned with product flow, not cost flow. Supporters of this approach believe that the actual purchase price is the best measure for cost of sales and ending inventory.

Good inventory procedures require that the oldest products always be issued first. In other words, those products first in will be the products first out. This basic assumption underlies the FIFO approach to inventory valuation. The specific identification approach will produce the same result as the FIFO approach provided that the storekeeper always issues the oldest products first.

The specific identification approach to inventory valuation may be carried out by either of two methods: the specific identification perpetual method or the specific identification periodic method.

The Specific Identification Perpetual Method

Following the inventory procedures just described, the specific identification perpetual method produces the same result as the FIFO perpetual method. Therefore, it is possible to use a perpetual inventory card for the FIFO perpetual method (Exhibit 5) to explain the results of applying the specific identification perpetual method.

Exhibit 5   Example of FIFO Perpetual Inventory Card

Date	Ref.	PURCHASES			ISSUES			BALANCE ON HAND		
		Units	Unit Cost	Total	Units	Unit Cost	Total	Units	Unit Cost	Total
3/1		10	1.00	10.00				10	1.00	10.00
3/2		5	1.02	5.10				10	1.00	15.10
								5	1.02	
3/3		5	1.05	5.25				10	1.00	20.35
								5	1.02	
								5	1.05	
3/6					3	1.00	3.00	7	1.00	17.35
								5	1.02	
								5	1.05	
3/10					7	1.00	7.00	1	1.02	6.27
					4	1.02	4.08	5	1.05	
					11		11.08			
TOTAL		20		20.35	14		14.08	6		6.27

Note that, for each of the three purchases (March 1, 2, and 3), entries are made within the Purchases and Balance on Hand sections of the inventory card. In the Purchases section, purchases are recorded by number of units, unit cost, and total cost (number of units multiplied by unit cost). In the Balance on Hand section, number of units and unit cost are recorded on an ongoing basis, and the overall balance is updated as purchases are made. This same basic format for recording purchases is used in all of the inventory methods except the weighted average method, which will be discussed later.

The difference between the specific identification, FIFO, and LIFO approaches relates to the costing of issues. The specific identification approach uses the actual costs of individual groups or batches of items. When items are issued, the basis for costing will be the identified cost of the individual items. If similar items having different costs are received, they must be separately costed from existing items. Issues of the same items having different costs must be separately counted or weighed, and then costed.

On March 6, the storekeeper issues 3 items from the storeroom. Items from the oldest stock (purchased March 1) are issued first. These items had been purchased at a cost of $1.00 per unit. The 10 units at this cost are reduced by the issue of 3 units. The balance on hand is reduced by $3.00.

On March 10, the storekeeper issues 11 units. Seven of these units had been purchased at $1.00 per unit and 4 units had been purchased at $1.02. The balance on hand is adjusted to reflect this issue, leaving 1 unit on hand at $1.02 and 5 units at $1.05. The Balance on Hand section shows that the total cost of ending inventory is $6.27.

The mathematical accuracy of the ending balance on the perpetual inventory card may be verified by subtracting total issues for the period from goods available (beginning inventory + purchases) for the period. This procedure is as follows:

	Quantity	Cost
Beginning Inventory	0	$ 0
Purchases	20	20.35
Goods Available	20	20.35
Issues (Cost of Sales)	−14	− 14.08
Ending Inventory	6	$ 6.27

With respect to the costing of issues, the specific identification perpetual method would differ from the FIFO perpetual method only if products are issued out of order. In this case, the identified cost would be the basis for costing using the specific identification perpetual method.

The Specific Identification Periodic Method

The use of the specific identification periodic method does not require the maintenance of perpetual inventory cards, but still requires that goods in inventory be identified by their actual purchase cost. Using this method, inventory valuation is based on the identified cost of items on hand at the end of a period. Thus, both the perpetual and periodic variations on this approach match the flow of recorded costs to the physical flow of goods.

As a periodic method, however, the specific identification periodic method has labor-saving benefits; issues are not costed and inventory recordkeeping cards need not be maintained. When provisions are purchased, the Purchases account is debited. Issues are not recorded during the selling period. At the end of the period, however, a physical inventory is required.

A physical inventory using specific identification techniques involves counting the quantity on hand at each specific purchase cost, then totaling the amounts derived from the individual counts. For the inventory item in the previous example, a physical count would produce the following results:

Physical Count	Marked Cost	Ending Inventory Cost
1	$1.02	$1.02
5	1.05	5.25
Total		$6.27

This procedure is followed for each item in inventory. After all items have been counted and costed, the total of all the inventory items represents the ending inventory for financial reporting.

Any specific identification method emphasizes the flow of physical products and their identified costs. However, the use of a specific identification method requires considerable attention to detail since inventory items must be specifically identified at their actual costs.

If using a specific identification method is not possible or practical for a company, a cost flow method must necessarily be chosen. The question is whether to value the units in the ending inventory at the most recent costs (per the FIFO approach), the oldest costs (per the LIFO approach), or an average cost (per the weighted average approach).

The FIFO Approach to Inventory Valuation

As already stated, good storeroom procedures require that products be used in the order of their purchase. From a *product* flow perspective, this means that those items first in the storeroom will be those items first out of the storeroom. Inventory transactions may also be viewed from a *cost* flow perspective. If products first in are those first out, it follows that *costs* first in will be those first out.

FIFO is an acronym for **first-in, first-out.** This approach is not concerned with product flow, but instead concentrates on the sequence of costs in and out of inventory. The oldest cost in inventory will be the first to go out of inventory. Thus, FIFO produces results that approximate the physical flow of goods, although no effort is made to match an issued item with its specific cost as is required with a specific identification method.

Supporters of the FIFO approach emphasize that cost flow should parallel the typical flow of goods. Since the first-in (oldest) costs are used to cost issues, cost of sales will closely match actual purchase prices.

The FIFO approach to inventory valuation may be carried out by either of two methods: the FIFO perpetual method or the FIFO periodic method.

The FIFO Perpetual Method

Exhibit 5 is an example of a perpetual inventory card for the FIFO perpetual method. The same inventory transactions noted previously are the basis for purchases and issues represented on this card. The recording of purchases is identical to that described for the specific identification method under a perpetual system.

As issues are costed, the oldest cost represented within the Balance on Hand section is used first. The first issue of 3 items is costed at the oldest cost of $1.00 per unit. The second issue of 11 items allocates costs among the remaining 7 units on hand at $1.00 per unit and 4 units of the next batch at $1.02 per unit.

The Balance on Hand section reflects this costing process. After the first issue, the number of units at the oldest cost of $1.00 per unit is reduced by 3 units. After the second issue, all of the units costed at $1.00 per unit have been eliminated from inventory, and there is only one remaining unit at the next oldest cost of $1.02 per unit. All five units at the most recent cost of $1.05 per unit remain in inventory.

Whenever the total quantity issued exceeds the available balance on hand at the oldest cost, issues are costed for the remaining items at the oldest cost, then at the next oldest unit cost. This process is repeated until all of the units issued have been costed.

The mathematical accuracy of the ending balance on the perpetual inventory card may be verified using the procedure previously described for the specific identification perpetual method.

The FIFO Periodic Method

A company need not maintain perpetual inventory cards in order to take advantage of the cost flow features of the FIFO approach. Using the FIFO perpetual method just explained, the oldest costs in inventory are the first to go out of inventory. This process results in the most recent costs remaining in the inventory on hand. The FIFO periodic method costs ending inventory at these most recent costs.

To understand this, consider the previous inventory transactions:

Date	Inventory Transaction
3/1	Purchased 10 units at $1.00 per unit
3/2	Purchased 5 units at $1.02 per unit
3/3	Purchased 5 units at $1.05 per unit

A physical inventory of this particular item determines that 6 units are on hand at the end of the accounting period. The 6 units in ending inventory are costed at the most recent costs. The most recent purchase (March 3) was for 5 units at $1.05 per unit. One more unit cost is necessary, which may be obtained by referring to the March 2 purchase at $1.02 per unit. The cost of the ending inventory is computed as follows:

5 units $\times$ $1.05	=	$5.25
1 unit $\times$ $1.02	=	1.02
Total ending inventory	=	$6.27

The FIFO periodic method produces the same results for ending inventory as the FIFO perpetual method.

The LIFO Approach to Inventory Valuation

LIFO is an acronym for **last-in, first-out.** It assumes that those costs *last* in inventory will be those costs first out of inventory. Like the FIFO approach, LIFO is concerned with cost flow rather than product flow. Unlike the FIFO approach, LIFO uses the most recent costs as those first out of inventory.

Supporters of the LIFO approach believe that the cost of sales should reflect current replacement costs. Since the last-in (most recent) costs are used to cost issues, the cost of sales will more closely reflect the replacement costs compared to the FIFO approach.

The LIFO approach to inventory valuation may be carried out by either of two methods: the LIFO perpetual method or the LIFO periodic method.

The LIFO Perpetual Method

Exhibit 6 is an example of a perpetual inventory card for the LIFO perpetual method. The recording of purchases is identical to that described for previous perpetual methods. In costing issues, however, the LIFO perpetual method is strikingly different. The issues are costed at the last-in (most recent) costs rather than the oldest costs.

Note that the first issue of 3 items is costed at the most recent cost of $1.05 per unit. Costing the second issue of 11 items allocates costs among the 2 remaining

Exhibit 6   Example of LIFO Perpetual Inventory Card

Date	Ref.	Units	Unit Cost	Total	Units	Unit Cost	Total	Units	Unit Cost	Total
		PURCHASES			ISSUES			BALANCE ON HAND		
3/1		10	1.00	10.00				10	1.00	10.00
3/2		5	1.02	5.10				10	1.00	
								5	1.02	15.10
3/3		5	1.05	5.25				10	1.00	
								5	1.02	20.35
								5	1.05	
3/6					3	1.05	3.15	10	1.00	
								5	1.02	17.20
								2	1.05	
3/10					2	1.05	2.10			
					5	1.02	5.10			
					4	1.00	4.00	6	1.00	6.00
					11		11.20			
TOTAL		20		20.35	14		14.35	6	1.00	6.00

items at the most recent cost of $1.05 per unit, all 5 items at the next most recent cost of $1.02 per unit, and 4 items at the oldest cost of $1.00 per unit.

The Balance on Hand section reflects this costing process. After the first issue, the number of units at the most recent cost of $1.05 is reduced by 3 units. After the second issue, all of the units at $1.05 and $1.02 (the most recent and next most recent costs per unit) have been eliminated from inventory. The remaining units are costed at $1.00 per unit (the oldest cost).

Whenever the total quantity issued exceeds the available balance on hand at the most recent cost, issues are costed for the remaining items at the most recent cost, then at the next most recent cost. This process is repeated until all of the units issued have been costed.

The mathematical accuracy of the ending balance on the perpetual inventory card may be verified using the procedure previously described for the specific identification perpetual method.

The LIFO Periodic Method

A company that does not use perpetual inventory cards may still use the cost flow features of the LIFO approach. Using the LIFO perpetual method, the most recent costs in inventory are the first costs to go out of inventory. This process results in the oldest costs remaining in the inventory on hand.

Since the oldest costs remain in inventory, the ending inventory can be costed on this basis. The cost of the ending inventory is computed by starting with the beginning inventory and then working down through the purchases until enough units have been costed to cover the units in the ending inventory.

Consider the previous inventory transactions:

Date	Inventory Transaction
3/1	Purchased 10 units at $1.00 per unit
3/2	Purchased 5 units at $1.02 per unit
3/3	Purchased 5 units at $1.05 per unit

A physical inventory of this particular item determines that 6 units are on hand at the end of the accounting period. The 6 units in ending inventory are to be costed at the oldest costs going into the inventory. The oldest purchase (March 1) was for 10 units at $1.00 per unit. This purchase has enough units to cost the ending inventory of 6 units. The ending inventory can be costed at $6.00 (6 units × $1.00 = $6.00).

It should be pointed out that ending inventory values obtained under the LIFO periodic method may differ from those values obtained under the LIFO perpetual method. The LIFO periodic method may not be realistic if the ending inventory drops below the beginning inventory. This topic is best reserved for an upper-level accounting text.

The Weighted Average Approach to Inventory Valuation

Like FIFO and LIFO, the **weighted average approach** concentrates on cost flow rather than product flow. Unlike FIFO and LIFO, the weighted average approach uses an average unit cost for inventory valuation purposes. Cost of sales (issues) and ending inventory are costed at this weighted average.

The weighted average approach to inventory valuation may be carried out by either of two methods: the weighted average perpetual method or the weighted average periodic method.

The Weighted Average Perpetual Method

The weighted average method is based on the assumption that issues should be charged at an average unit cost, weighted by the number of units acquired at each price. Because a new average is computed after each purchase, the weighted average perpetual method is sometimes called the moving average method.

Computing a new average only after a purchase assumes that an issue from inventory does not affect the previous costs in inventory. If an average were to be computed after each issue, the average cost would not change with the exception of minor rounding differences. (Some users of the weighted average method compute a new average cost after every inventory transaction to resolve any rounding difference. For our purposes, a new average will be computed only after a purchase transaction.)

Exhibit 7 is an example of a perpetual inventory card for the weighted average perpetual method. The same inventory transactions noted previously are the basis for purchases and issues represented on this card. Since this is a new inventory item, the first purchase (March 1) is recorded at its actual cost of $1.00 per unit. However, after the second purchase (March 2), the inventory on hand represents a

Exhibit 7   Example of Weighted Average Perpetual Inventory Card

Date	Ref.	PURCHASES			ISSUES			BALANCE ON HAND		
		Units	Unit Cost	Total	Units	Unit Cost	Total	Units	Total	Unit Cost
3/1		10	1.00	10.00				10	10.00	1.00
3/2		5	1.02	5.10				15	15.10	1.007
3/3		5	1.05	5.25				20	20.35	1.018
3/6					3	1.018	3.05	17	17.30	
3/10					11	1.018	11.20	6	6.10	
TOTAL		20		20.35	14		14.25	6	6.10	

quantity of items purchased at different prices. Therefore, a new weighted average must be computed as follows:

$$\text{Weighted Average} = \frac{\text{Total Cost of Inventory on Hand}}{\text{Total Units in Inventory}}$$

After a third purchase on March 3, a weighted average must again be computed.

This weighted average cost becomes the basis for costing items issued. Notice that the first issue of 3 items is costed at the weighted average of $1.018 per unit. The second issue of 11 items is also costed at the weighted average of $1.018 per unit. If items are purchased after these issues, a new weighted average would be computed.

At the end of the accounting period, the perpetual inventory card reflects 6 units on hand. The Balance on Hand section shows that the total cost of ending inventory is $6.10. The mathematical accuracy of the ending balance on the perpetual inventory card may be verified using the procedure previously described for the specific identification perpetual method.

The Weighted Average Periodic Method

Under a perpetual recordkeeping system, the weighted average is a moving average because it is recomputed after every purchase. Under a periodic inventory system, however, the weighted average is computed on the total goods available for the period. Therefore, the results produced by the weighted average periodic method will be slightly different from those produced by the weighted average perpetual method.

Using the weighted average periodic method, a weighted average is computed by the same formula previously presented. However, instead of computing a new average after every purchase, the weighted average is computed only at the end of the accounting period. The procedure used to compute the weighted average and to cost inventory at the end of the accounting period can be summarized as follows:

1. List beginning inventory and purchases for the period and determine the total units and the total cost.

2. Using the total units and the total cost, compute a weighted average using the previous formula.

3. Multiply the ending inventory quantity by the weighted average to arrive at a value for the ending inventory.

For example, assume inventory valuation is to be accomplished using the weighted average periodic method. Transactions during the month are as follows:

Date	Inventory Transaction
3/1	Purchased 10 units at $1.00 per unit
3/2	Purchased 5 units at $1.02 per unit
3/3	Purchased 5 units at $1.05 per unit

In our example, no beginning inventory is carried over. Purchases are listed and totaled as follows:

	Unit Cost	Units	Cost
3/1 Purchase	$1.00	10	$10.00
3/2 Purchase	1.02	5	5.10
3/3 Purchase	1.05	5	5.25
Total		20	$20.35

Using the total units available during the period and the total cost of these units, a weighted average may now be computed:

$$\text{Weighted Average} = \frac{\text{Total Cost of Inventory on Hand}}{\text{Total Units in Inventory}}$$

$$\text{Weighted Average} = \frac{\$20.35}{20 \text{ units}} = \$1.0175$$

After a physical inventory on this particular item, it is determined that 6 units are on hand at the end of the accounting period. The ending inventory is costed with the following calculation:

$$\text{Ending Inventory} = \text{Number of Units} \times \text{Weighted Average}$$
$$\text{Ending Inventory} = 6 \text{ units} \times \$1.0175 = \$6.11$$

A Comparison of Cost Allocation Methods

Each of the cost flow methods previously discussed produces similar results using both perpetual and periodic inventory accounting methods. Therefore, the following discussion will compare results for the various perpetual methods discussed to this point. The comparison will demonstrate the effects of the various methods on the balance sheet and the income statement.

The previous examples used only one type of inventory item to demonstrate the costing of inventories. Ending inventory on the balance sheet is the result of costing and totaling all types of items on hand. For ease of presentation, our discussion is necessarily limited to one type of inventory product. This limitation is also true for the cost of sales comparisons.

Each of the cost flow methods will produce a different ending inventory amount on the balance sheet. Given our basic illustrative case involving a period of rising prices, the three cost flow methods produce the following values for ending inventory:

	Ending Inventory
FIFO	$6.27
LIFO	6.00
Weighted Average	6.10

During a period of rising prices, the FIFO method produces the highest ending inventory valuation on the balance sheet. Using the FIFO method, the most recent costs remain in inventory since issues are costed at the oldest costs. The LIFO method results in the lowest ending inventory on the balance sheet because the oldest costs remain in inventory. The weighted average method produces an ending inventory figure that is between those figures obtained using the FIFO and LIFO methods, as would be expected of any method using an average.

Each of the cost flow methods will produce a different cost of sales expense on the income statement. Based on the previous examples, the FIFO, LIFO, and weighted average methods produce the following amounts for cost of sales expense:

	Cost of Sales
FIFO	$14.08
LIFO	14.35
Weighted Average	14.25

During a period of rising prices, the LIFO method produces the highest cost of sales. Using the LIFO method, the most recent costs are the basis for costing issues. The FIFO method results in the lowest cost of sales because the oldest costs are used to cost the issues. Again, the weighted average method produces an ending inventory figure that is between those figures obtained using the FIFO and LIFO methods.

LIFO Analyzed

Unlike the FIFO approach or the specific identification approach, LIFO assumes a cost flow that is not compatible with typical storeroom procedures. If matching the physical flow of products with cost flow is an important criterion in choosing an inventory valuation method, LIFO would not be a satisfactory choice.

On the other hand, if the major concern is to closely relate cost of sales to current costs, LIFO is a better choice. Since the LIFO approach tends to produce a higher expense for cost of sales (assuming rising prices are typical), it has the advantage of deferring income taxes.

Generally, a company may use one method of accounting for financial reporting and another for tax reporting. For example, a company may select straight-line depreciation under generally accepted accounting principles and double declining depreciation for tax reporting. However, federal income tax laws require that, if a LIFO method is adopted for income tax purposes, it must also be used for financial reporting. Once a company elects to use a LIFO method for tax reporting, it must receive permission from the IRS to change valuation methods. Generally, a tax liability is created during the conversion.

Compared to the other inventory valuation methods, the major advantages of LIFO may be summarized as follows:

- LIFO provides a better measure of income. Because the most recent prices are used to cost issues, the cost of sales expense more closely reflects current costs.

- LIFO often has income tax benefits. A higher cost of sales expense reduces taxable income, resulting in a cash savings. A company may use these savings to produce revenue or to reduce debt and interest expense.

The disadvantages of using LIFO are not always obvious. Companies adopting LIFO sometimes realize too late the pitfalls of this method. Compared to the other inventory valuation methods, the major disadvantages may be summarized as follows:

- LIFO produces a lower figure for income. Investors and stockholders generally base their investment decisions on the net income of a company.

- LIFO produces a lower figure for inventory on the balance sheet. As a result, current assets, working capital, and the current ratio are all understated during periods of rising prices. This financial information is analyzed closely by investors, stockholders, and banks.

- The income tax benefits of LIFO are not guaranteed. Under certain circumstances, it is possible that LIFO will produce an increased tax burden.

- LIFO may not be practical for the hospitality industry, in which food and beverage inventories generally have a fast turnover. Compared to inventories maintained by manufacturing industries, hospitality inventories may never achieve significant levels. The increased costs associated with LIFO may not be worth the benefits.

Because of the added costs and potential problems associated with LIFO, serious and close scrutiny is necessary before selecting it as an inventory valuation method.

🔑 Key Terms

first-in, first-out (FIFO)—An inventory costing method that assumes the first costs incurred are the first costs issued. The result is that ending inventory consists of the most recent costs, and the oldest costs are in cost of sales.

gross profit method—A method of estimating the ending inventory based on the assumption that the rate of gross profit remains relatively constant.

inventory valuation—Refers not to market value but to the cost of inventory as determined by a costing inventory method such as FIFO, LIFO, or weighted average.

last-in, first-out (LIFO)—An inventory costing method that assumes that the most recent costs incurred are the first costs issued. The result is that ending inventory consists of the oldest costs, and the most recent costs are in cost of sales.

specific identification approach—A method of costing inventory by identifying the actual cost of the purchased and issued units.

weighted average approach—A method of costing inventory using an average cost per unit. The costing average is computed by dividing the total cost of goods available (cost of inventory on hand) by the number of units available (units in inventory).

? Review Questions

1. Which bookkeeping account is used to record the acquisition of food inventory under the following methods?
   a. The periodic inventory accounting method
   b. The perpetual inventory accounting method

2. How many monthly periods will be affected by an error in ending inventory? Why are cost of sales and gross profit affected by an error in ending inventory?

3. What are the cost flow assumptions of the following approaches?
   a. FIFO
   b. LIFO
   c. Weighted average

4. Which approach to costing issues will result in the highest ending inventory valuation in times of rising prices?

5. Which approach to costing issues will result in the highest cost of sales in times of rising prices?

6. What are the advantages and disadvantages of LIFO?

Internet Sites

For more information, visit the following Internet sites. Remember that Internet addresses can change without notice. If the site is no longer there, you can use a search engine to look for additional sites.

Beverage Cost and Inventory Adjustment
www.restaurantreport.com/features/ft_bevcost.html

Restaurant Receiving, Storage, Issuing, Inventory
http://web1.msue.msu.edu/imp/modtd/33300004.html

Cook-to-Inventory Kitchen
http://findarticles.com/p/articles/mi_m3190/is_49_32/ai_53382095

Periodic/Perpetual Inventory
http://retailindustry.about.com/library/terms/p/bld_periodicinv.htm
http://abcfinance.nase.org/abcInventory.asp

Perpetual Inventory & Ordering Template Download
www.restaurantowner.com/public/535.cfm

Gross Profit Method
www.accd.edu/sac/slac/ppointshows/acct/gross_profit_method%20.htm

Inventory Control: How Much Is Your Menu Costing?
www.computrition.com/Releases/Pub_3_24_00.html

Inventory Method Effect on Bottom Line
www.investopedia.com/articles/02/060502.asp

FIFO, LIFO, Average Cost Methods
www.wisegeek.com/what-is-lifo-and-fifo.htm
www.investopedia.com/articles/02/060502.asp

LIFO: IRS Frowns On
www.toolkit.cch.com/advice/113-99askalice.asp

Problems

Problem 1

A hospitality business uses the periodic inventory method. After reviewing the financial statements, the following determinations of gross profit were reported:

	Month of September	Month of October	Year-to-date October
Sales	$150,000	$130,000	$1,200,000
Cost of Sales:			
Beginning Inventory	18,000	17,000	15,000
Purchases	46,000	42,000	400,000
Cost of Goods Available	64,000	59,000	415,000
Ending Inventory	17,000	13,000	13,000
Cost of Sales	47,000	46,000	402,000
Gross Profit	$103,000	$ 84,000	$ 798,000

It is discovered that the ending inventory on September 30 should have been reported as $14,000. What are the corrected figures for gross profit in these periods?

Problem 2

Although monthly financial statements are due, management has decided not to take a physical inventory at the end of the month since several audits were performed during the month. The gross profit method will be used to estimate the ending inventory for financial statement purposes. Using this method, estimate the ending inventory for April 30 based on the following information:

Food inventory, March 31	$ 4,000
Food sales, April	31,000
Food purchases, April	12,000
Estimated gross profit percentage	64%

Problem 3

Purchases of a new inventory product during the month of April are as follows:

4/1	Purchased 15 units at $5.00 each
4/10	Purchased 10 units at $5.20 each
4/20	Purchased 8 units at $5.25 each

Since the facility uses a periodic inventory system, perpetual recordkeeping cards are not maintained and issues are not known. A physical inventory shows that 5 units are on hand at the close of business, April 30. Compute the dollar value of the ending inventory (to two decimal places) under the following valuation methods:

a. The FIFO periodic method

b. The LIFO periodic method

c. The weighted average periodic method (using a weighted average rounded to four decimal places)

Case Study

Inventory Management and Theft Deterrence

The Saturn Restaurant Chain has many large restaurants that carry extensive food and liquor inventories; all use the perpetual inventory record-keeping system. All locations have cost of sales and profits that meet corporate standards. All restaurants are equipped with advanced point-of-sale systems that have recipe and menu costing software, as well as inventory control software. The POS systems match the guest check with food from the kitchen to the cash register destination. These systems have proven both reliable and accurate.

Recently, the corporate office has instituted physical inventory audits without providing notice to restaurant managers. One restaurant is discovered to have a large discrepancy in its physical-versus-book inventory. The food physical inventory is $5,000 (at cost) below the book amount.

Challenge

1. Explain how the cost of sales and profits for this particular restaurant could be in line with corporate standards, yet have a $5,000 shortage in inventory.

2. Calculate the before-and-after effect on gross profit if the accounting records showed the following before the $5,000 inventory shortage:

Sales: $100,000
Beginning inventory: $15,000

Purchases: $28,000
Ending inventory per books: $18,000

3. Suggest how corporate headquarters could institute a simple, inexpensive audit procedure at each location that will quickly spot such shortages.

4. List some measures corporate management could take to effectively guard against internal theft.

Chapter 20 Outline

Competencies

1. Describe the purpose and typical content of a feasibility study. (pp. 521–524)

2. Identify undistributed operating expenses and fixed charges and use various methods to allocate those costs to one or more departments. (pp. 524–526)

3. Distinguish between historical cost and fair value accounting and explain why this distinction has recently become important. (pp. 526–529)

4. Define fair value and describe the FASB's three levels of fair value measurement. (pp. 527–528)

5. Determine when compound and present value calculations are required and perform those calculations. (pp. 529–532)

6. Apply compound and present value concepts to annuities and perform those calculations. (pp. 533–535)

20

Assorted Topics

THE BRANCH OF ACCOUNTING that deals with providing information to external users (stockholders, creditors, and governmental agencies) is known as *financial accounting*. The branch of accounting that deals with providing information essential to executives and managers for use in the decision-making process is known as *managerial accounting*. Financial accounting usually presents information to external users in the form of financial statements. Managerial accounting provides information to internal users in the form of reports and internal financial statements.

A number of important but unrelated topics concerning both financial and managerial accounting remain to be discussed at least briefly. This chapter will answer such questions as:

1. What is a feasibility study? What are its contents?

2. What methods allocate service department expenses and fixed charges to revenue centers to complete the concept of responsibility accounting?

3. What is fair value accounting?

4. What is compound value? How is it calculated for a lump-sum investment?

5. What is present value? How is it calculated for a lump-sum investment?

6. What is the compound value of an ordinary annuity or annuity due? How is the calculation performed?

7. What is the present value of an ordinary annuity with a series of payments? How is the calculation performed?

Feasibility Study

A **feasibility study** is a preliminary study made before a project is begun to determine the project's likelihood of success. It comprises financial information, statistics, conclusions, and recommendations. It can take many forms. Some are comprehensive studies investigating the location and building construction of a new hospitality business; other, less-involved studies may explore the potential of expanding present facilities. Feasibility studies use the present to predict the future. A feasibility study may reach a positive or negative conclusion. A positive conclusion does not guarantee financial success, since the feasibility study makes assumptions and estimates, and cannot anticipate unforeseen factors. However, regardless of these limitations, it is far better to have research results and prognosis in hand than not to have them at all, since the investment required to fund a new business or expand an existing business can be significant.

Feasibility studies providing meaningful results require the expertise of more than one professional: an accountant, a lawyer, a real estate developer, a hospitality consulting firm, and management. A single professional, usually representing a hospitality consulting firm, should be engaged to prepare the study and coordinate the expertise of the other professionals deemed necessary. The selected firm must be knowledgeable and experienced in marketing, operations, and finance.

A feasibility study should do more than provide a conclusion about the profitability or desirability of a project. It should also:

- Serve as a guide to planners and architects.

- Be instrumental in obtaining financing.

- Be a viable tool in negotiating franchising, leasing, management, or other prerequisites.

- Serve as a guide in preparing operating and marketing plans.

- Serve as a guide in preparing capital and operating budgets.

Feasibility Study Format

A feasibility study conducted for a hotel will have more content than that for a restaurant. However, a generalized discussion of a format is possible; the reader can pick and choose information critical to a particular business venture. Generally, any feasibility study should contain these sections:

- Proposal letter

- Opening section

- Description of market area

- Evaluation of area and project site

- Analysis of competition

- Demand analysis

- Recommended facilities and services

- Estimated income statement

Proposal Letter. The consultant prepares this letter to the client to clearly define the scope of the engagement. The proposal letter includes the reporting procedure, types of reports the consultant will prepare, and the consultant's fee and payment schedule. A feasibility study should not be initiated until the client accepts and signs the proposal letter.

Opening Section. The opening section of the feasibility report contains the following:

- Letter of transmittal

- Table of contents

- Introduction

- Summary and conclusions

The letter of transmittal describes the study's goal, qualifies the study's results, and describes any limitations. The table of contents lists the report's individual sections. The introduction explains the scope and methodology of the study. The summary and conclusions section summarizes the study's findings and the consultant's conclusions regarding market feasibility, facilities, services, financial performance, and other pertinent factors.

Description of Market Area. Part of this section defines market characteristics such as geographic, demographic, and economic indicators. Population, income, employment, retail sales, commercial/industrial activity, tourism, and transportation are all examined. The study also will discuss trends of these indicators and the diversification of the area's economy. Finally, the consultant provides an opinion about the economic strength of the market area.

Evaluation of Area and Project Site. A popular axiom says that the three most important considerations for business success are location, location, and location. The selection of a successful location is important in attracting the guest market the business wants to target, and the location must suitably serve that market segment. This section of the feasibility study should analyze:

- Site location, accessibility, and visibility
- The site's adaptability
- Zoning, licensing, and building codes
- Conclusion

The site location and accessibility discussion should pinpoint the site's location on a map; describe the site's physical boundaries and topographical features; discuss bus, train, and taxi services; and explain the site's relation to market generators such as amusement parks, theaters, museums, resorts, and other entertainment venues. Finally, it should address the ease of site ingress and egress. The site's adaptability to the proposed hospitality facility should be examined, with comments on noise, traffic, and other potential disturbances. The consultant may be capable of providing only summations regarding zoning, licensing, and building codes. More detailed information would require the engagement of a legal or real estate expert. The conclusion of this section might contain some uncertainty, because changes to location characteristics, roads, highways, and governmental regulations cannot be predicted over the long term.

Analysis of Competition. This section describes present and potential competition. It lists all present competitors, providing their location, size (number of seats or rooms), prices, hours of operation, type of service, facilities, chain affiliation, and reputation. A map showing all competitors provides a quick pictorial view of their proximity to the business. The section also describes any known potential competition to alert the reader to probable concerns.

Demand Analysis. This section is a critical element in any feasibility study; its goal is to estimate sales revenue. The other sections of the study serve as the basis for demand estimates. If the data used to estimate sales revenue is flawed, the final feasibility report will also be flawed, because sales is the basis for estimating cost of sales and operating expenses. This section investigates the success of existing competitors, department of commerce statistics, local/state sales tax figures (if available), industry reports, and other demand generators for the hospitality business. For a hotel, this section would estimate room night demand, price sensitivity, seasonality, and the need for health clubs, computer access, business services, conference rooms, and other guest requirements.

Recommended Facilities and Services. This section should recommend facilities and services that will satisfy the customer market researched in the demand analysis section. Unless the business is to be a franchise or chain-affiliated operation, an architect may be necessary to determine building design and capacity based on expected occupancy, as well as the type and size of the facility.

Estimated Income Statement. The format of the estimated income statement should be in accordance with the uniform system of accounts for the applicable hospitality industry (hotel or stand-alone restaurant). The income statement usually covers a period of several years, quite often five. In a feasibility study, it is acceptable to have the income statement terminate with the *income before income taxes* amount. Inflation factors are used for long-term projections, since inflation affects room rates, menu prices, and expenses. The statement should contain: (1) a description of the bases for estimates, (2) variables that might affect estimates, and (3) limitations of the estimates.

Allocating Service Centers and Fixed Charges

Under the *Uniform System of Accounts for the Lodging Industry* (both the Ninth and Tenth Revised Editions, which we'll call *USALI 9* and *USALI 10*), the summary income statement (*USALI 9*) and the summary operating statement (*USALI 10*) present undistributed operating expenses and fixed charges *after* the revenue center revenue and expenses. Notice that this approach does not reduce the income of each revenue center; instead, the service center expenses and fixed charges are deducted from the total income amount.

While this approach has its merits (it is, after all, the recommended format), managers might want to know what the results of operations would be if each revenue center were allocated the expenses of the service centers and fixed charges. All revenue centers would show less profit, and it is quite possible that some revenue centers might even show a loss instead of a gain.

Allocating service centers to the revenue departments is an extension of responsibility accounting. Even though revenue department managers cannot directly control the expenses of the marketing department, for example, the revenue centers receive a benefit from the marketing department, and should be allocated a share of that department's expense.

Bases for Allocation

In order for allocation to make sense and be fair, it must be based on something. There are various bases for allocation.

In some cases, allocation may be moot. If the total cost of a service center or fixed charge can be directly traced to a single revenue center, that revenue center will be charged for 100 percent of the allocable cost. For instance, if rent of $28,500 is paid just for storing rooms department furniture and equipment, the rooms department will be charged the total rent expense. However, in most cases, more than one revenue center enjoys the benefit of a service center or fixed charge. In these cases, the service center or fixed charge expense must be allocated to each revenue center that receives such benefit. For instance, total A&G expenses should be divided into portions attributable to the benefit received by each revenue center.

The *direct method* is commonly used to allocate the expenses of service centers and fixed charges. In this method, each service center and fixed charge is allocated to a number of revenue centers using an allocation basis such as:

- Percentage of payroll
- Percentage of square footage
- Percentage of total revenue
- Percentage of any basis determined to equitably allocate an expense

For instance, assume the following: management decides that the A&G expense is to be allocated as a percentage of total revenue; the A&G department's expense for the period is $164,181; management determines that only rooms, food and beverage, and the other operated departments will be charged for this service center; and the total revenue of these departments is $1,485,070, as broken out in the table below. This total becomes the divisor for the next step, which is determining what percentage of total revenue each department's revenue represents. The resulting percentages will be used to allocate the A&G expenses. The following table illustrates this example:

	Sales	Percentage	Allocation of A&G
Rooms	$ 897,500	60.4%	$ 99,165
F&B	524,570	35.3	57,956
Other operated	63,000	4.3	7,060
Total	$1,485,070	100.0%	$164,181

Note that the total of all computed percentages must equal 100 percent; if they do not (because of rounding), one amount must be forced up or down, usually not to exceed 0.1 percent or 0.2 percent. In this case, computation for the other operated departments was forced from 4.2 percent to 4.3 percent. Similarly, the dollar amounts must match the total being allocated. Because of rounding, the individual amounts may not add up to the target total; in this case, it might be necessary to force a dollar amount up or down, usually not to exceed $1 or $2.

The allocation computation is continued for each service center or fixed charge to be allocated. The completed income statement might take the format shown in Exhibit 1.

The direct method just described is a very popular, simple way to allocate service centers and fixed charges. Two additional methods are the *step method* and the *formula method*.

Exhibit 1   Income Statement Excerpt with A&G Allocations

	Rooms	F&B	Tel.	Other Operated Depts.	Other Income	Total
Reported department income	$692,261	$87,377	$(27,623)	$12,646	$61,283	$825,944
Less allocation of service centers:						
A&G	99,165	57,956		7,060		164,181
Marketing						
Property Operation						
Utility Costs						
Income before fixed charges	xxx	xxx	xxx	xxx	xxx	485,029
Less allocation of fixed charges:						
Rent						
Property Taxes						
Insurance						
Interest						
Depreciation						
Income before income taxes	xxx	xxx	xxx	xxx	xxx	66,138

Note: This is a sample presentation; not all entries are shown.

In the *step method*, undistributed expenses from one service department are allocated not only to revenue centers but also to other service departments benefiting from that department. One service center is first selected for allocation, then new totals are taken, and a second service center is allocated, until all have been allocated. As in the direct method, an equitable basis for allocation such as square footage or payroll must be selected before distributing an expense.

In the *formula method*, allocation of each department is made simultaneously to all other departments serviced by that department; this process is generally performed by a computerized application.

Fair Value Accounting

The traditional mandate in preparing financial statements according to generally accepted accounting principles (GAAP) was that land, building, equipment, and other assets should be shown at historical cost. This accounting treatment of fixed assets has long been subject to debate because it does not show assets at their fair or market value. For example, a building purchased years ago for $1 million will be shown today at that cost of $1 million, even though it may now have a true or fair value of far more.

One argument for showing assets (and liabilities) using fair value accounting is that historical-cost financial statements do not provide information about current values that are relevant to investors, creditors, and other readers of financial statements. Another argument is that historical costs are not comparable between companies and assets that were not purchased at the same time. For example, if an investor is analyzing two different hotel companies, the land and building prices on the balance sheets are probably not comparable; thus, comparing any asset-based financial ratios between the two companies may well be pointless.

The Financial Accounting Standards Board (FASB) has recently concluded that fair value is the relevant measurement attribute and has chosen to permit (or in some cases require) businesses to use the fair value option.

FASB Statement 157 is effective for financial statements issued for fiscal years beginning after November 15, 2007, and interim periods within those fiscal years. This Statement defines fair value and provides a basis for measuring fair value in accordance with GAAP, including disclosures about fair value measurements. The accounting definition of fair value, under GAAP, includes both assets and liabilities.

Statement 157 was issued because there were various definitions of fair value and only limited guidance for applying those definitions in GAAP; those differences created inconsistencies.

The fair value of an asset is defined as the amount at which an asset could be bought or sold in a current transaction between a willing buyer and seller, other than in liquidation of a business. The fair value of a liability is the amount at which the liability could be settled in a current transaction between willing parties, other than in liquidation of a business. If available, a quoted market price in an active market is the best evidence of fair value and should be used as the basis for the measurement. If a quoted market price or observable price is not available, an estimate of fair value is made using the best information or method available.

The use of a standard definition and basis for measuring fair value should enhance the consistency and comparability of fair value measurements. Disclosures about fair value should give financial statement readers information about:

- How fair value is used to measure assets and liabilities

- The inputs used to develop the measurements

- The effect of certain of the measurements on earnings (or changes in net assets) for the period

The International Accounting Standards Board (IASB) prefers fair value accounting for measuring assets. With the introduction of International Financial Reporting Standards (IFRS) in many parts of the world, including all publicly listed companies in the European Union, the application of fair value is becoming standard in financial statements.

Measurement of Fair Value

FASB Statement 157 states that the exchange price is the price in an orderly transaction between a seller and buyer in a principal or most advantageous market. Such a transaction may involve the sale of an asset or the transfer of a liability. Therefore, the focus is on the price that would be received on the *sale* of an asset or paid on the *transfer* of a liability (an exit price). Fair value is not the price that would be paid to acquire the asset or received to assume the liability (an entry price).

Fair value is a market-based measurement. Statement 157 establishes a fair value hierarchy, classified as Level 1, Level 2, and Level 3, for applying market-based assumptions to measure fair value. This step-by-step hierarchy is described as follows:

Level 1. The first and best measurement involves direct reference to *quoted prices in active markets* for *identical* assets or liabilities. The emphasis within Level 1 is on determining both of the following:

- The principal (or, failing that, most advantageous) market for the asset or liability considered from the standpoint of the reporting entity; and

- Whether the reporting entity can access the price in that market for the asset or liability at the measurement date.

Level 2. If a quoted market price is not available in Level 1, either a directly or an indirectly observable price is used for the asset or liability. This can be (1) a quoted price for *similar* assets or liabilities in active markets; (2) a quoted price for identical or similar assets or liabilities in markets that are *not active*; and (3) other observable market-corroborated inputs.

Level 3. Failing to obtain Level 1 and Level 2 inputs, an entity may use *unobservable* inputs for the asset or liability to the extent that they reflect the reporting entity's own assumptions about what market participants would use in pricing the asset/liability, including assumptions about risk. Unobservable inputs should be developed based on the best information available, which might include the reporting entity's own data.

Non-market-based fair values are subjective because they are based on estimates, assumptions, and measurement methods that management uses to determine fair value. However, subjectivity need not deter using fair value accounting, because the historical cost basis was neither comparable nor pragmatic.

Transition Adjustment

Switching from historical cost to fair value accounting will have potentially significant effects on financial statements. Adjustments will be needed to make the transition. The proper accounting treatment for the adjustment between cost and fair value is quoted from FASB Statement 157:

> The transition adjustment, measured as the difference between the carrying amounts and the fair values of those financial instruments at the date this Statement is initially applied, should be recognized as a cumulative-effect adjustment to the opening balance of retained earnings (or other appropriate components of equity or net assets in the statement of financial position) for the fiscal year in which this Statement is initially applied.

Limitations of Fair Value Accounting

Although fair value can provide better information than historical cost–based measurements, fair value reporting might make financial statements more susceptible to subjective decisions and assumptions. For example:

- *Reliability and Measurement*: Many assets and liabilities do not have an active market. In these cases, estimating their fair value is more subjective, very likely making the valuations less reliable. If management must use significant judgment in selecting market inputs when market prices are not available, reliability will be an issue.

- *Management Bias*: Because management uses significant judgment in the valuation process, especially for Level 3 estimates, management bias (intentional or unintentional) can adversely affect fair value measurements and result in misstatements of income and equity.

Compound Value

Compound value is the sum of the principal amount plus the compound interest amount. **Compound interest** is interest that is calculated both on the initial principal and on the accumulated interest of prior periods. Compound interest differs from simple interest, which is calculated as a percentage of the principal, ignoring interest earned. In compound interest calculations, the principal and interest of all prior periods become the new basis upon which new interest is calculated. The more frequently interest is compounded, the faster the principal grows. Yearly compounded interest is considered the norm unless specified otherwise.

The objective of the compound value calculation is to determine the future value of a known amount invested today.

It is common for banking institutions to pay interest more than once per year. Therefore, the stated annual interest rate must be converted to an effective period interest rate to calculate interest for a specific period. The formula is:

$$\text{Period interest rate} = \frac{\text{Annual interest rate}}{\text{Number of interest periods in the year}}$$

For example, an investment yielding 8 percent annually and paid four times in that 12-month period would have a quarterly (period) interest rate of 8 percent divided by 4 quarters, or 2 percent.

Using this example, if $1,000 is invested at the start of a year (and no other investments are added to it during the year), the value in the first year would grow as follows:

	Principal	Interest Earned	Compound Value
1st quarter	$1,000.00	$20.00	$1,020.00
2nd quarter	1,020.00	20.40	1,040.40
3rd quarter	1,040.40	20.81	1,061.21
4th quarter	1,061.21	21.22	1,082.43

When the period you wish to project is several years, the calculation of compound value can be tedious, time-consuming, and subject to error. Fortunately, the use of compound value tables, also called future value tables, greatly simplifies the calculation of compound value. Compound value tables are available for any number of periods and interest rates. Exhibit 2 presents a sample compound value table for a single investment made at the start of the first period. Note that the interest rates per period are listed at the top of the table and that the interest periods are listed down the left side of the table. The intersection of the per-period interest rates and the number of periods in the table provides a compound value factor to use in calculating the compound value at the end of the period.

Exhibit 2 Compound Value Factors for a Single Cash Flow

$FV_{n,k} = (1 + k)^n$

Number of Periods	1%	2%	3%	4%	5%	6%	7%	8%	9%	10%	12%	14%	15%	16%	18%	20%	22%	24%	26%	28%	30%	35%
1	1.0100	1.0200	1.0300	1.0400	1.0500	1.0600	1.0700	1.0800	1.0900	1.1000	1.1200	1.1400	1.1500	1.1600	1.1800	1.2000	1.2200	1.2400	1.2600	1.2800	1.3000	1.3500
2	1.0201	1.0404	1.0609	1.0816	1.1025	1.1236	1.1449	1.1664	1.1881	1.2100	1.2544	1.2996	1.3225	1.3456	1.3924	1.4400	1.4884	1.5376	1.5876	1.6384	1.6900	1.8225
3	1.0303	1.0612	1.0927	1.1249	1.1576	1.1910	1.2250	1.2597	1.2950	1.3310	1.4049	1.4815	1.5209	1.5609	1.6430	1.7280	1.8158	1.9066	2.0004	2.0972	2.1970	2.4604
4	1.0406	1.0824	1.1255	1.1699	1.2155	1.2625	1.3108	1.3605	1.4116	1.4641	1.5735	1.6890	1.7490	1.8106	1.9388	2.0736	2.2153	2.3642	2.5205	2.6844	2.8561	3.3215
5	1.0510	1.1041	1.1593	1.2167	1.2763	1.3382	1.4026	1.4693	1.5386	1.6105	1.7623	1.9254	2.0114	2.1003	2.2878	2.4883	2.7027	2.9316	3.1758	3.4360	3.7129	4.4840
6	1.0615	1.1262	1.1941	1.2653	1.3401	1.4185	1.5007	1.5869	1.6771	1.7716	1.9738	2.1950	2.3131	2.4364	2.6996	2.9860	3.2973	3.6352	4.0015	4.3980	4.8268	6.0534
7	1.0721	1.1487	1.2299	1.3159	1.4071	1.5036	1.6058	1.7138	1.8280	1.9487	2.2107	2.5023	2.6600	2.8262	3.1855	3.5832	4.0227	4.5077	5.0419	5.6295	6.2749	8.1722
8	1.0829	1.1717	1.2668	1.3686	1.4775	1.5938	1.7182	1.8509	1.9926	2.1436	2.4760	2.8526	3.0590	3.2784	3.7589	4.2998	4.9077	5.5895	6.3528	7.2058	8.1573	11.032
9	1.0937	1.1951	1.3048	1.4233	1.5513	1.6895	1.8385	1.9990	2.1719	2.3579	2.7731	3.2519	3.5179	3.8030	4.4355	5.1598	5.9874	6.9310	8.0045	9.2234	10.604	14.894
10	1.1046	1.2190	1.3439	1.4802	1.6289	1.7908	1.9672	2.1589	2.3674	2.5937	3.1058	3.7072	4.0456	4.4114	5.2338	6.1917	7.3046	8.5944	10.086	11.806	13.786	20.107
11	1.1157	1.2434	1.3842	1.5395	1.7103	1.8983	2.1049	2.3316	2.5804	2.8531	3.4785	4.2262	4.6524	5.1173	6.1759	7.4301	8.9117	10.657	12.708	15.112	17.922	27.144
12	1.1268	1.2682	1.4258	1.6010	1.7959	2.0122	2.2522	2.5182	2.8127	3.1384	3.8960	4.8179	5.3503	5.9360	7.2876	8.9161	10.872	13.215	16.012	19.343	23.298	36.644
13	1.1381	1.2936	1.4685	1.6651	1.8856	2.1329	2.4098	2.7196	3.0658	3.4523	4.3635	5.4924	6.1528	6.8858	8.5994	10.699	13.264	16.386	20.175	24.759	30.288	49.470
14	1.1495	1.3195	1.5126	1.7317	1.9799	2.2609	2.5785	2.9372	3.3417	3.7975	4.8871	6.2613	7.0757	7.9875	10.147	12.839	16.182	20.319	25.421	31.691	39.374	66.784
15	1.1610	1.3459	1.5580	1.8009	2.0789	2.3966	2.7590	3.1722	3.6425	4.1772	5.4736	7.1379	8.1371	9.2655	11.974	15.407	19.742	25.196	32.030	40.565	51.186	90.158
16	1.1726	1.3728	1.6047	1.8730	2.1829	2.5404	2.9522	3.4259	3.9703	4.5950	6.1304	8.1372	9.3576	10.748	14.129	18.488	24.086	31.243	40.358	51.923	66.542	121.71
17	1.1843	1.4002	1.6528	1.9479	2.2920	2.6928	3.1588	3.7000	4.3276	5.0545	6.8660	9.2765	10.761	12.468	16.672	22.186	29.384	38.741	50.851	66.461	86.504	164.31
18	1.1961	1.4282	1.7024	2.0258	2.4066	2.8543	3.3799	3.9960	4.7171	5.5599	7.6900	10.575	12.375	14.463	19.673	26.623	35.849	48.039	64.072	85.071	112.46	221.82
19	1.2081	1.4568	1.7535	2.1068	2.5270	3.0256	3.6165	4.3157	5.1417	6.1159	8.6128	12.056	14.232	16.777	23.214	31.948	43.736	59.568	80.731	108.89	146.19	299.46
20	1.2202	1.4859	1.8061	2.1911	2.6533	3.2071	3.8697	4.6610	5.6044	6.7275	9.6463	13.743	16.367	19.461	27.393	38.338	53.358	73.864	101.72	139.38	190.05	404.27
21	1.2324	1.5157	1.8603	2.2788	2.7860	3.3996	4.1406	5.0338	6.1088	7.4002	10.804	15.668	18.822	22.574	32.324	46.005	65.096	91.592	128.17	178.41	247.06	545.77
22	1.2447	1.5460	1.9161	2.3699	2.9253	3.6035	4.4304	5.4365	6.6586	8.1403	12.100	17.861	21.645	26.186	38.142	55.206	79.418	113.57	161.49	228.36	321.18	736.79
23	1.2572	1.5769	1.9736	2.4647	3.0715	3.8197	4.7405	5.8715	7.2579	8.9543	13.552	20.362	24.891	30.376	45.008	66.247	96.889	140.83	203.48	292.30	417.54	994.66
24	1.2697	1.6084	2.0328	2.5633	3.2251	4.0489	5.0724	6.3412	7.9111	9.8497	15.179	23.212	28.625	35.236	53.109	79.497	118.21	174.63	256.39	374.14	542.80	1342.80
25	1.2824	1.6406	2.0938	2.6658	3.3864	4.2919	5.4274	6.8485	8.6231	10.835	17.000	26.462	32.919	40.874	62.669	95.396	144.21	216.54	323.05	478.90	705.64	1812.78
26	1.2953	1.6734	2.1566	2.7725	3.5557	4.5494	5.8074	7.3964	9.3992	11.918	19.040	30.167	37.857	47.414	73.949	114.48	175.94	268.51	407.04	613.00	917.33	2447.25
27	1.3082	1.7069	2.2213	2.8834	3.7335	4.8223	6.2139	7.9881	10.245	13.110	21.325	34.390	43.535	55.000	87.260	137.37	214.64	332.95	512.87	784.64	1192.5	3303.78
28	1.3213	1.7410	2.2879	2.9987	3.9201	5.1117	6.6488	8.6271	11.167	14.421	23.884	39.204	50.066	63.800	102.97	164.84	261.86	412.86	646.21	1004.3	1550.3	4460.11
29	1.3345	1.7758	2.3566	3.1187	4.1161	5.4184	7.1143	9.3173	12.172	15.863	26.750	44.693	57.575	74.009	121.50	197.81	319.47	511.95	814.23	1285.6	2015.4	6021.15
30	1.3478	1.8114	2.4273	3.2434	4.3219	5.7435	7.6123	10.063	13.268	17.449	29.960	50.950	66.212	85.850	143.37	237.38	389.76	634.82	1025.9	1645.5	2620.0	8128.55
40	1.4889	2.2080	3.2620	4.8010	7.0400	10.286	14.974	21.725	31.409	45.259	93.051	188.88	267.86	378.72	750.38	1469.8	2847.0	5455.9	10347.	19427.	36118.9	*
50	1.6446	2.6916	4.3839	7.1067	11.467	18.420	29.457	46.902	74.358	117.39	289.00	700.23	1083.7	1670.7	3927.4	9100.4	20797.	46890.	*	*	*	*
60	1.8167	3.2810	5.8916	10.520	18.679	32.988	57.946	101.26	176.03	304.48	897.60	2595.9	4384.0	7370.2	20555.	56348.	*	*	*	*	*	*

*$FV_{n,k} > 99{,}999$

Again using the example of $1,000 invested at 8 percent annually, with interest earned quarterly, the procedure is as follows:

1. The interest rate per period is 2 percent.
2. The number of periods is 4.
3. The factor at the intersection of 2 percent and 4 periods is 1.0824.
4. $1,000.00 × 1.0824 = $1,082.40.

The amount differs by three cents from the manual calculation because the values in Exhibit 2 extend to only four decimal points. The same factor carried to a more accurate seven decimal points is 1.0824322, which accounts for the last three cents.

The preceding example covered one year, but compound value tables can easily be used to forecast investments over many years. Using the same example but changing the investment period to five years, the procedure is as follows:

1. The interest rate per period is still 2 percent.
2. The number of periods is 20 (4 interest periods per year × 5 years).
3. The factor at the intersection of 2 percent and 20 periods is 1.4859.
4. $1,000.00 × 1.4859 = $1,485.90.

Present Value

Present value is the value today of a known future amount. It is essentially the reverse of compound value, where we know the investment amount and wish to determine what it will be worth at a later date. With present value, we know what the future value is or must be, and from that amount we calculate what must be invested today to equal that amount in the future. Present value calculations are typically used to determine what must be invested now to meet a specific future goal.

As was the case with compound value, the use of present value tables makes it quick and easy to compute the amount needed now to achieve a goal at the end of a future period for an investment yielding a known percentage. A sample present value table for a single investment made at the start of the first period is provided in Exhibit 3.

Suppose the goal is to achieve a total of $2,000 at the end of a five-year period with an investment yielding 8 percent annually, and with interest compounded quarterly. The procedure to calculate the present value is as follows:

1. The interest rate per period is 2 percent.
2. The number of periods is 20 (4 interest periods per year × 5 years).
3. The factor at the intersection of 2 percent and 20 periods is 0.6730.
4. Goal of $2,000 × 0.6730 = $1,346.

If $1,346 is invested today under the assumed conditions, it will grow to the desired total of $2,000 by the end of five years.

Exhibit 3 Present Value Factors for a Single Cash Flow

$PV_{n,k} = 1/(1 + k)^n$

Number of Periods	1%	2%	3%	4%	5%	6%	7%	8%	9%	10%	12%	14%	15%	16%	18%	20%	22%	24%	26%	28%	30%	35%
1	.9901	.9804	.9709	.9615	.9524	.9434	.9346	.9259	.9174	.9091	.8929	.8772	.8696	.8621	.8475	.8333	.8197	.8065	.7937	.7813	.7692	.7407
2	.9803	.9612	.9426	.9246	.9070	.8900	.8734	.8573	.8417	.8264	.7972	.7695	.7561	.7432	.7182	.6944	.6719	.6504	.6299	.6104	.5917	.5487
3	.9706	.9423	.9151	.8890	.8638	.8396	.8163	.7938	.7722	.7513	.7118	.6750	.6575	.6407	.6086	.5787	.5507	.5245	.4999	.4768	.4552	.4064
4	.9610	.9238	.8885	.8548	.8227	.7921	.7629	.7350	.7084	.6830	.6355	.5921	.5718	.5523	.5158	.4823	.4514	.4230	.3968	.3725	.3501	.3011
5	.9515	.9057	.8626	.8219	.7835	.7473	.7130	.6806	.6499	.6209	.5674	.5194	.4972	.4761	.4371	.4019	.3700	.3411	.3149	.2910	.2693	.2230
6	.9420	.8880	.8375	.7903	.7462	.7050	.6663	.6302	.5963	.5645	.5066	.4556	.4323	.4104	.3704	.3349	.3033	.2751	.2499	.2274	.2072	.1652
7	.9327	.8706	.8131	.7599	.7107	.6651	.6227	.5835	.5470	.5132	.4523	.3996	.3759	.3538	.3139	.2791	.2486	.2218	.1983	.1776	.1594	.1224
8	.9235	.8535	.7894	.7307	.6768	.6274	.5820	.5403	.5019	.4665	.4039	.3506	.3269	.3050	.2660	.2326	.2038	.1789	.1574	.1388	.1226	.0906
9	.9143	.8368	.7664	.7026	.6446	.5919	.5439	.5002	.4604	.4241	.3606	.3075	.2843	.2630	.2255	.1938	.1670	.1443	.1249	.1084	.0943	.0671
10	.9053	.8203	.7441	.6756	.6139	.5584	.5083	.4632	.4224	.3855	.3220	.2697	.2472	.2267	.1911	.1615	.1369	.1164	.0992	.0847	.0725	.0497
11	.8963	.8043	.7224	.6496	.5847	.5268	.4751	.4289	.3875	.3505	.2875	.2366	.2149	.1954	.1619	.1346	.1122	.0938	.0787	.0662	.0558	.0368
12	.8874	.7885	.7014	.6246	.5568	.4970	.4440	.3971	.3555	.3186	.2567	.2076	.1869	.1685	.1372	.1122	.0920	.0757	.0625	.0517	.0429	.0273
13	.8787	.7730	.6810	.6006	.5303	.4688	.4150	.3677	.3262	.2897	.2292	.1821	.1625	.1452	.1163	.0935	.0754	.0610	.0496	.0404	.0330	.0202
14	.8700	.7579	.6611	.5775	.5051	.4423	.3878	.3405	.2992	.2633	.2046	.1597	.1413	.1252	.0985	.0779	.0618	.0492	.0393	.0316	.0254	.0150
15	.8613	.7430	.6419	.5553	.4810	.4173	.3624	.3152	.2745	.2394	.1827	.1401	.1229	.1079	.0835	.0649	.0507	.0397	.0312	.0247	.0195	.0111
16	.8528	.7284	.6232	.5339	.4581	.3936	.3387	.2919	.2519	.2176	.1631	.1229	.1069	.0930	.0708	.0541	.0415	.0320	.0248	.0193	.0150	.0082
17	.8444	.7142	.6050	.5134	.4363	.3714	.3166	.2703	.2311	.1978	.1456	.1078	.0929	.0802	.0600	.0451	.0340	.0258	.0197	.0150	.0116	.0061
18	.8360	.7002	.5874	.4936	.4155	.3503	.2959	.2502	.2120	.1799	.1300	.0946	.0808	.0691	.0508	.0376	.0279	.0208	.0156	.0118	.0089	.0045
19	.8277	.6864	.5703	.4746	.3957	.3305	.2765	.2317	.1945	.1635	.1161	.0829	.0703	.0596	.0431	.0313	.0229	.0168	.0124	.0092	.0068	.0033
20	.8195	.6730	.5537	.4564	.3769	.3118	.2584	.2145	.1784	.1486	.1037	.0728	.0611	.0514	.0365	.0261	.0187	.0135	.0098	.0072	.0053	.0025
21	.8114	.6598	.5375	.4388	.3589	.2942	.2415	.1987	.1637	.1351	.0926	.0638	.0531	.0443	.0309	.0217	.0154	.0109	.0078	.0056	.0040	.0018
22	.8034	.6468	.5219	.4220	.3418	.2775	.2257	.1839	.1502	.1228	.0826	.0560	.0462	.0382	.0262	.0181	.0126	.0088	.0062	.0044	.0031	.0014
23	.7954	.6342	.5067	.4057	.3256	.2618	.2109	.1703	.1378	.1117	.0738	.0491	.0402	.0329	.0222	.0151	.0103	.0071	.0049	.0034	.0024	.0010
24	.7876	.6217	.4919	.3901	.3101	.2470	.1971	.1577	.1264	.1015	.0659	.0431	.0349	.0284	.0188	.0126	.0085	.0057	.0039	.0027	.0018	.0007
25	.7798	.6095	.4776	.3751	.2953	.2330	.1842	.1460	.1160	.0923	.0588	.0378	.0304	.0245	.0160	.0105	.0069	.0046	.0031	.0021	.0014	.0006
26	.7720	.5976	.4637	.3607	.2812	.2198	.1722	.1352	.1064	.0839	.0525	.0331	.0264	.0211	.0135	.0087	.0057	.0037	.0025	.0016	.0011	.0004
27	.7644	.5859	.4502	.3468	.2678	.2074	.1609	.1252	.0976	.0763	.0469	.0291	.0230	.0182	.0115	.0073	.0047	.0030	.0019	.0013	.0008	.0003
28	.7568	.5744	.4371	.3335	.2551	.1956	.1504	.1159	.0895	.0693	.0419	.0255	.0200	.0157	.0097	.0061	.0038	.0024	.0015	.0010	.0006	.0002
29	.7493	.5631	.4243	.3207	.2429	.1846	.1406	.1073	.0822	.0630	.0374	.0224	.0174	.0135	.0082	.0051	.0031	.0020	.0012	.0008	.0005	.0002
30	.7419	.5521	.4120	.3083	.2314	.1741	.1314	.0994	.0754	.0573	.0334	.0196	.0151	.0116	.0070	.0042	.0026	.0016	.0010	.0006	.0004	.0001
35	.7059	.5000	.3554	.2534	.1813	.1301	.0937	.0676	.0490	.0356	.0189	.0102	.0075	.0055	.0030	.0017	.0009	.0005	.0003	.0002	.0001	*
40	.6717	.4529	.3066	.2083	.1420	.0972	.0668	.0460	.0318	.0221	.0107	.0053	.0037	.0026	.0013	.0007	.0004	.0002	.0001	.0001	*	*
45	.6391	.4102	.2644	.1712	.1113	.0727	.0476	.0313	.0207	.0137	.0061	.0027	.0019	.0013	.0006	.0003	.0001	.0001	*	*	*	*
50	.6080	.3715	.2281	.1407	.0872	.0543	.0339	.0213	.0134	.0085	.0035	.0014	.0009	.0006	.0003	.0001	*	*	*	*	*	*
55	.5785	.3365	.1968	.1157	.0683	.0406	.0242	.0145	.0087	.0053	.0020	.0007	.0005	.0003	.0001	*	*	*	*	*	*	*
60	.5504	.3048	.1697	.0951	.0535	.0303	.0173	.0099	.0057	.0033	.0011	.0004	.0002	.0001	*	*	*	*	*	*	*	*

*Rounds to zero

Compound and Present Values with Annuities

In the discussions of compound value and present value, the investment consisted of a lump-sum amount paid at the beginning of a period. In pragmatic investing programs, a *series* of investments is typically made over a period of time. At the other end of the spectrum, one could also receive a series of payments over a period of time. Various calculations may be necessary with regard to annuities.

An **annuity** is a cash flow stream for a finite number of periods where all of the cash flows are equal in amount. An **ordinary annuity** is a series of investments made at the *end* of a period. The period might consist of months, quarters, or years. An **annuity due** is a series of investments made at the *beginning* of a period. Note that the only difference between an ordinary annuity and an annuity due is *when* the investments are made in a period. For both of these types of annuity, it may be desirable to calculate the future value of the series of payments.

On the other hand, you may also wish to calculate the present value of an ordinary annuity. This calculation determines how much must be invested now to receive a known stream of payments for a stated number of years.

Calculations for any of the above may be performed manually or with the help of special present and future value tables. Manual calculations are very tedious, time-consuming, and prone to error. For pragmatic purposes, the use of tables is highly recommended. Tables may be purchased in booklet form or retrieved from the Internet. This discussion will focus on the use of tables.

The objective of an ordinary annuity calculation is to calculate the future value of a series of investments. In an ordinary annuity, a series of payments is made at the *end* of each period. Suppose $1,000 is invested at the end of each year over a five-year period at an annual interest rate of 6 percent. Using the ordinary annuity table shown in Exhibit 4, the calculation of future value is as follows:

1. The interest rate per period is 6 percent.

2. The number of periods is 5 (1 interest period per year × 5 years).

3. The factor at the intersection of 6 percent and 5 periods is 5.6371.

4. $1,000.00 × 5.6371 = $5,637.10.

An investment of $1,000 per year made at the end of each year for five years in an investment yielding 6 percent annually will grow to $5,637.10 at the end of the five-year period.

The objective of an annuity due calculation is identical to that of an ordinary annuity calculation. The major difference is *when* the series of payments is made. An annuity due investment is characterized by a series of payments made at the *beginning* of a period (unlike at the end of a period for an ordinary annuity). The table used to determine future value is again Exhibit 4. However, since the investment is made at the beginning of a period, the number of total periods is increased by one.

Using the same example of an investment of $1,000 per year, but made at the *beginning* of each year for five years, and earning 6 percent annually, the calculation is as follows:

Exhibit 4 Ordinary Annuity Table (Future Value Factors)

$$FVA_{n,k} = \frac{(1+k)^n - 1}{k}$$

Number of Periods	1%	2%	3%	4%	5%	6%	7%	8%	9%	10%	12%	14%	15%	16%	18%	20%	22%	24%	26%	28%	30%	35%
1	1.0000	1.0000	1.0000	1.0000	1.0000	1.0000	1.0000	1.0000	1.0000	1.0000	1.0000	1.0000	1.0000	1.0000	1.0000	1.0000	1.0000	1.0000	1.0000	1.0000	1.0000	1.0000
2	2.0100	2.0200	2.0300	2.0400	2.0500	2.0600	2.0700	2.0800	2.0900	2.1000	2.1200	2.1400	2.1500	2.1600	2.1800	2.2000	2.2200	2.2400	2.2600	2.2800	2.3000	2.3500
3	3.0301	3.0604	3.0909	3.1216	3.1525	3.1836	3.2149	3.2464	3.2781	3.3100	3.3744	3.4396	3.4725	3.5056	3.5724	3.6400	3.7084	3.7776	3.8476	3.9184	3.9900	4.1725
4	4.0604	4.1216	4.1836	4.2465	4.3101	4.3746	4.4399	4.5061	4.5731	4.6410	4.7793	4.9211	4.9934	5.0665	5.2154	5.3680	5.5242	5.6842	5.8480	6.0156	6.1870	6.6329
5	5.1010	5.2040	5.3091	5.4163	5.5256	5.6371	5.7507	5.8666	5.9847	6.1051	6.3528	6.6101	6.7424	6.8771	7.1542	7.4416	7.7396	8.0484	8.3684	8.6999	9.0431	9.9544
6	6.1520	6.3081	6.4684	6.6330	6.8019	6.9753	7.1533	7.3359	7.5233	7.7156	8.1152	8.5355	8.7537	8.9775	9.4420	9.9299	10.442	10.980	11.544	12.136	12.756	14.438
7	7.2135	7.4343	7.6625	7.8983	8.1420	8.3938	8.6540	8.9228	9.2004	9.4872	10.089	10.730	11.067	11.414	12.142	12.916	13.740	14.615	15.546	16.534	17.583	20.492
8	8.2857	8.5830	8.8923	9.2142	9.5491	9.8975	10.260	10.637	11.028	11.436	12.300	13.233	13.727	14.240	15.327	16.499	17.762	19.123	20.588	22.163	23.858	28.664
9	9.3685	9.7546	10.159	10.583	11.027	11.491	11.978	12.488	13.021	13.579	14.776	16.085	16.786	17.519	19.086	20.799	22.670	24.712	26.940	29.369	32.015	39.696
10	10.462	10.950	11.464	12.006	12.578	13.181	13.816	14.487	15.193	15.937	17.549	19.337	20.304	21.321	23.521	25.959	28.657	31.643	34.945	38.593	42.619	54.590
11	11.567	12.169	12.808	13.486	14.207	14.972	15.784	16.645	17.560	18.531	20.655	23.045	24.349	25.733	28.755	32.150	35.962	40.238	45.031	50.398	56.405	74.697
12	12.683	13.412	14.192	15.026	15.917	16.870	17.888	18.977	20.141	21.384	24.133	27.271	29.002	30.850	34.931	39.581	44.874	50.895	57.739	65.510	74.327	101.84
13	13.809	14.680	15.618	16.627	17.713	18.882	20.141	21.495	22.953	24.523	28.029	32.089	34.352	36.786	42.219	48.497	55.746	64.110	73.751	84.853	97.625	138.48
14	14.947	15.974	17.086	18.292	19.599	21.015	22.550	24.215	26.019	27.975	32.393	37.581	40.505	43.672	50.818	59.196	69.010	80.496	93.926	109.61	127.91	187.95
15	16.097	17.293	18.599	20.024	21.579	23.276	25.129	27.152	29.361	31.772	37.280	43.842	47.580	51.660	60.965	72.035	85.192	100.82	119.35	141.30	167.29	254.74
16	17.258	18.639	20.157	21.825	23.657	25.673	27.888	30.324	33.003	35.950	42.753	50.980	55.717	60.925	72.939	87.442	104.93	126.01	151.38	181.87	218.47	344.90
17	18.430	20.012	21.762	23.698	25.840	28.213	30.840	33.750	36.974	40.545	48.884	59.118	65.075	71.673	87.068	105.93	129.02	157.25	191.73	233.79	285.01	466.61
18	19.615	21.412	23.414	25.645	28.132	30.906	33.999	37.450	41.301	45.599	55.750	68.394	75.836	84.141	103.74	128.12	158.40	195.99	242.59	300.25	371.52	630.92
19	20.811	22.841	25.117	27.671	30.539	33.760	37.379	41.446	46.018	51.159	63.440	78.969	88.212	98.603	123.41	154.74	194.25	244.03	306.66	385.32	483.97	852.75
20	22.019	24.297	26.870	29.778	33.066	36.786	40.995	45.762	51.160	57.275	72.052	91.025	102.44	115.38	146.63	186.69	237.99	303.60	387.39	494.21	630.17	1152.2
21	23.239	25.783	28.676	31.969	35.719	39.993	44.865	50.423	56.765	64.002	81.699	104.77	118.81	134.84	174.02	225.03	291.35	377.46	489.11	633.59	820.22	1556.5
22	24.472	27.299	30.537	34.248	38.505	43.392	49.006	55.457	62.873	71.403	92.503	120.44	137.63	157.41	206.34	271.03	356.44	469.06	617.28	812.00	1067.3	2102.3
23	25.716	28.845	32.453	36.618	41.430	46.996	53.436	60.893	69.532	79.543	104.60	138.30	159.28	183.60	244.49	326.24	435.86	582.63	778.77	1040.4	1388.5	2839.0
24	26.973	30.422	34.426	39.083	44.502	50.816	58.177	66.765	76.790	88.497	118.16	158.66	184.17	213.98	289.49	392.48	532.75	723.46	982.25	1332.7	1806.0	3833.7
25	28.243	32.030	36.459	41.646	47.727	54.865	63.249	73.106	84.701	98.347	133.33	181.87	212.79	249.21	342.60	471.98	650.96	898.09	1238.6	1706.8	2348.8	5176.5
26	29.526	33.671	38.553	44.312	51.113	59.156	68.676	79.954	93.324	109.18	150.33	208.33	245.71	290.09	405.27	567.38	795.17	1114.6	1561.7	2185.7	3054.4	6989.3
27	30.821	35.344	40.710	47.084	54.669	63.706	74.484	87.351	102.72	121.10	169.37	238.50	283.57	337.50	479.22	681.85	971.10	1383.1	1968.7	2798.7	3971.8	9436.5
28	32.051	37.051	42.931	49.968	58.403	68.528	80.698	95.339	112.97	134.21	190.70	272.89	327.10	392.50	566.48	819.22	1185.7	1716.1	2481.6	3583.3	5164.3	12740.
29	33.450	38.792	45.219	52.966	62.323	73.640	87.347	103.97	124.14	148.63	214.58	312.09	377.17	456.30	669.45	984.07	1447.6	2129.0	3127.8	4587.7	6714.6	17200.
30	34.785	40.568	47.575	56.085	66.439	79.058	94.461	113.28	136.31	164.49	241.33	356.79	434.75	530.31	790.95	1181.9	1767.1	2640.9	3942.0	5873.2	8730.0	23222.
40	48.886	60.402	75.401	95.026	120.80	154.76	199.64	259.06	337.88	442.59	767.09	1342.0	1779.1	2360.8	4163.2	7343.9	12937.	22729.	39793.	69377.	*	*
50	64.463	84.579	112.80	152.67	209.35	290.34	406.53	573.77	815.08	1163.9	2400.0	4994.5	7217.7	10436.	21813.	45497.	94525.	*	*	*	*	*
60	81.670	114.05	163.05	237.99	353.58	533.13	813.52	1253.2	1944.8	3034.8	7471.6	18535.	29220.	46058.	*	*	*	*	*	*	*	*

*$FVA_{n,k} > 99,999$

1. The interest rate per period is 6 percent.

2. The number of periods is 6 (1 interest period per year × 5 years + 1 to convert to beginning-of-year investments).

3. The factor at the intersection of 6 percent and 6 periods is 6.9753.

4. $1,000.00 × 6.9753 = $6,975.30.

An entity investing $1,000 per year at the beginning of each year for five years in an investment yielding 6 percent annually will have $6,975.30 at the end of the five-year period.

Investing in an annuity that *pays out* a stream of cash flows will require a present value calculation. The *present value of an ordinary annuity* calculation deals with how much must be invested now (at the present) to receive a stated stream of payments for a stated number of years. Exhibit 5 presents a present value annuity table. To determine how much must be invested now in an investment yielding 6 percent annually to receive a stream of $1,000 annual payments over a period of 5 years, the calculation is as follows:

1. The interest rate per period is 6 percent.

2. The number of periods is 5 (1 interest period per year × 5 years).

3. The factor at the intersection of 6 percent and 5 periods is 4.2124.

4. $1,000.00 × 4.2124 = $4,212.40.

Given an annual interest rate of 6 percent, one must invest $4,212.40 now to receive $1,000 per year for five years.

 # References

Raymond Cote, *Business Math Concepts* (P.A.R. Incorporated, 1987).

A Practical Guide to Understanding Feasibility Studies (Lansing, Mich.: Educational Institute of the American Hotel & Lodging Association, 1985).

Uniform System of Accounts for the Lodging Industry, Ninth Revised Edition (Lansing, Mich.: Educational Institute of the American Hotel & Lodging Association, 1996).

Uniform System of Accounts for the Lodging Industry, Tenth Revised Edition (Lansing, Mich.: American Hotel & Lodging Educational Institute, 2006).

Statement 157 official pronouncement
www.fasb.org/pdf/fas157.pdf

Summary of Statement 157
www.fasb.org/st/summary/stsum157.shtml
www.nysscpa.org/cpajournal/2006/406/essentials/p37.htm

Exhibit 5 Present Value Factors for an Annuity

$$PVA_{n,k} = \frac{1 - \dfrac{1}{(1+k)^n}}{k}$$

Number of Periods	1%	2%	3%	4%	5%	6%	7%	8%	9%	10%	12%	14%	15%	16%	18%	20%	22%	24%	26%	28%	30%	35%
1	0.9901	0.9804	0.9709	0.9615	0.9524	0.9434	0.9346	0.9259	0.9174	0.9091	0.8929	0.8772	0.8696	0.8621	0.8475	0.8333	0.8197	0.8065	0.7937	0.7813	0.7692	0.7407
2	1.9704	1.9416	1.9135	1.8861	1.8594	1.8334	1.8080	1.7833	1.7591	1.7355	1.6901	1.6467	1.6257	1.6052	1.5656	1.5278	1.4915	1.4568	1.4235	1.3916	1.3609	1.2894
3	2.9410	2.8839	2.8286	2.7751	2.7232	2.6730	2.6243	2.5771	2.5313	2.4869	2.4018	2.3216	2.2832	2.2459	2.1743	2.1065	2.0422	1.9813	1.9234	1.8684	1.8161	1.6959
4	3.9020	3.8077	3.7171	3.6299	3.5460	3.4651	3.3872	3.3121	3.2397	3.1699	3.0373	2.9137	2.8550	2.7982	2.6901	2.5887	2.4936	2.4043	2.3202	2.2410	2.1662	1.9969
5	4.8534	4.7135	4.5797	4.4518	4.3295	4.2124	4.1002	3.9927	3.8897	3.7908	3.6048	3.4331	3.3522	3.2743	3.1272	2.9906	2.8636	2.7454	2.6351	2.5320	2.4356	2.2200
6	5.7955	5.6014	5.4172	5.2421	5.0757	4.9173	4.7665	4.6229	4.4859	4.3553	4.1114	3.8887	3.7845	3.6847	3.4976	3.3255	3.1669	3.0205	2.8850	2.7594	2.6427	2.3852
7	6.7282	6.4720	6.2303	6.0021	5.7864	5.5824	5.3893	5.2064	5.0330	4.8684	4.5638	4.2883	4.1604	4.0386	3.8115	3.6046	3.4155	3.2423	3.0833	2.9370	2.8021	2.5075
8	7.6517	7.3255	7.0197	6.7327	6.4632	6.2098	5.9713	5.7466	5.5348	5.3349	4.9676	4.6389	4.4873	4.3436	4.0776	3.8372	3.6193	3.4212	3.2407	3.0758	2.9247	2.5982
9	8.5660	8.1622	7.7861	7.4353	7.1078	6.8017	6.5152	6.2469	5.9952	5.7590	5.3282	4.9464	4.7716	4.6065	4.3030	4.0310	3.7863	3.5655	3.3657	3.1842	3.0190	2.6653
10	9.4713	8.9826	8.5302	8.1109	7.7217	7.3601	7.0236	6.7101	6.4177	6.1446	5.6502	5.2161	5.0188	4.8332	4.4941	4.1925	3.9232	3.6819	3.4648	3.2689	3.0915	2.7150
11	10.3676	9.7868	9.2526	8.7605	8.3064	7.8869	7.4987	7.1390	6.8052	6.4951	5.9377	5.4527	5.2337	5.0286	4.6560	4.3271	4.0354	3.7757	3.5435	3.3351	3.1473	2.7519
12	11.2551	10.5753	9.9540	9.3851	8.8633	8.3838	7.9427	7.5361	7.1607	6.8137	6.1944	5.6603	5.4206	5.1971	4.7932	4.4392	4.1274	3.8514	3.6059	3.3868	3.1903	2.7792
13	12.1337	11.3484	10.6350	9.9856	9.3936	8.8527	8.3577	7.9038	7.4869	7.1034	6.4235	5.8424	5.5831	5.3423	4.9095	4.5327	4.2028	3.9124	3.6555	3.4272	3.2233	2.7994
14	13.0037	12.1062	11.2961	10.5631	9.8986	9.2950	8.7455	8.2442	7.7862	7.3667	6.6282	6.0021	5.7245	5.4675	5.0081	4.6106	4.2646	3.9616	3.6949	3.4587	3.2487	2.8144
15	13.8651	12.8493	11.9379	11.1184	10.3797	9.7122	9.1079	8.5595	8.0607	7.6061	6.8109	6.1422	5.8474	5.5755	5.0916	4.6755	4.3152	4.0013	3.7261	3.4834	3.2682	2.8255
16	14.7179	13.5777	12.5611	11.6523	10.8378	10.1059	9.4466	8.8514	8.3126	7.8237	6.9740	6.2651	5.9542	5.6685	5.1624	4.7296	4.3567	4.0333	3.7509	3.5026	3.2832	2.8337
17	15.5623	14.2919	13.1661	12.1657	11.2741	10.4773	9.7632	9.1216	8.5436	8.0216	7.1196	6.3729	6.0472	5.7487	5.2223	4.7746	4.3908	4.0591	3.7705	3.5177	3.2948	2.8398
18	16.3983	14.9920	13.7535	12.6593	11.6896	10.8276	10.0591	9.3719	8.7556	8.2014	7.2497	6.4674	6.1280	5.8178	5.2732	4.8122	4.4187	4.0799	3.7861	3.5294	3.3037	2.8443
19	17.2260	15.6785	14.3238	13.1339	12.0853	11.1581	10.3356	9.6036	8.9501	8.3649	7.3658	6.5504	6.1982	5.8775	5.3162	4.8435	4.4415	4.0967	3.7985	3.5386	3.3105	2.8476
20	18.0456	16.3514	14.8775	13.5903	12.4622	11.4699	10.5940	9.8181	9.1285	8.5136	7.4694	6.6231	6.2593	5.9288	5.3527	4.8696	4.4603	4.1103	3.8083	3.5458	3.3158	2.8501
21	18.8570	17.0112	15.4150	14.0292	12.8212	11.7641	10.8355	10.0168	9.2922	8.6487	7.5620	6.6870	6.3125	5.9731	5.3837	4.8913	4.4756	4.1212	3.8161	3.5514	3.3198	2.8519
22	19.6604	17.6580	15.9369	14.4511	13.1630	12.0416	11.0612	10.2007	9.4424	8.7715	7.6446	6.7429	6.3587	6.0113	5.4099	4.9094	4.4882	4.1300	3.8223	3.5558	3.3230	2.8533
23	20.4558	18.2922	16.4436	14.8568	13.4886	12.3034	11.2722	10.3711	9.5802	8.8832	7.7184	6.7921	6.3988	6.0442	5.4321	4.9245	4.4985	4.1371	3.8273	3.5592	3.3254	2.8543
24	21.2434	18.9139	16.9355	15.2470	13.7986	12.5504	11.4693	10.5288	9.7066	8.9847	7.7843	6.8351	6.4338	6.0726	5.4509	4.9371	4.5070	4.1428	3.8312	3.5619	3.3272	2.8550
25	22.0232	19.5235	17.4131	15.6221	14.0939	12.7834	11.6536	10.6748	9.8226	9.0770	7.8431	6.8729	6.4641	6.0971	5.4669	4.9476	4.5139	4.1474	3.8342	3.5640	3.3286	2.8556
26	22.7952	20.1210	17.8768	15.9828	14.3752	13.0032	11.8258	10.8100	9.9290	9.1609	7.8957	6.9061	6.4906	6.1182	5.4804	4.9563	4.5196	4.1511	3.8367	3.5656	3.3297	2.8560
27	23.5596	20.7069	18.3270	16.3296	14.6430	13.2105	11.9867	10.9352	10.0266	9.2372	7.9426	6.9352	6.5135	6.1364	5.4919	4.9636	4.5243	4.1542	3.8387	3.5669	3.3305	2.8563
28	24.3164	21.2813	18.7641	16.6631	14.8981	13.4062	12.1371	11.0511	10.1161	9.3066	7.9844	6.9607	6.5335	6.1520	5.5016	4.9697	4.5281	4.1566	3.8402	3.5679	3.3312	2.8565
29	25.0658	21.8444	19.1885	16.9837	15.1411	13.5907	12.2777	11.1584	10.1983	9.3696	8.0218	6.9830	6.5509	6.1656	5.5098	4.9747	4.5312	4.1585	3.8414	3.5687	3.3317	2.8567
30	25.8077	22.3965	19.6004	17.2920	15.3725	13.7648	12.4090	11.2578	10.2737	9.4269	8.0552	7.0027	6.5660	6.1772	5.5168	4.9789	4.5338	4.1601	3.8424	3.5693	3.3321	2.8568
35	29.4086	24.9986	21.4872	18.6646	16.3742	14.4982	12.9477	11.6546	10.5668	9.6442	8.1755	7.0700	6.6166	6.2153	5.5386	4.9915	4.5411	4.1644	3.8450	3.5708	3.3330	2.8571
40	32.8347	27.3555	23.1148	19.7928	17.1591	15.0463	13.3317	11.9246	10.7574	9.7791	8.2438	7.1050	6.6418	6.2335	5.5482	4.9966	4.5439	4.1659	3.8458	3.5712	3.3332	2.8571
45	36.0945	29.4902	24.5187	20.7200	17.7741	15.4558	13.6055	12.1084	10.8812	9.8628	8.2825	7.1232	6.6543	6.2421	5.5523	4.9986	4.5449	4.1664	3.8460	3.5714	3.3333	2.8571
50	39.1961	31.4236	25.7298	21.4822	18.2559	15.7619	13.8007	12.2335	10.9617	9.9148	8.3045	7.1327	6.6605	6.2463	5.5541	4.9995	4.5452	4.1666	3.8461	3.5714	3.3333	2.8571
55	42.1472	33.1748	26.7744	22.1086	18.6335	15.9905	13.9399	12.3186	11.0140	9.9471	8.3170	7.1376	6.6636	6.2482	5.5549	4.9998	4.5454	4.1666	3.8461	3.5714	3.3333	2.8571
60	44.9550	34.7609	27.6756	22.6235	18.9293	16.1614	14.0392	12.3766	11.0480	9.9672	8.3240	7.1401	6.6651	6.2492	5.5553	4.9999	4.5454	4.1667	3.8462	3.5714	3.3333	2.8571

Key Terms

annuity due—A series of investments made at the beginning of a period.

compound value—The sum of the principal amount plus the interest compounded over the life of a lump-sum investment.

compound interest—Interest calculated both on the initial principal and on the accumulated interest of prior periods.

fair value accounting—The amount for which an asset could be bought or sold in a current transaction between willing parties, except in liquidation of a business; the amount for which a liability could be settled in a current transaction between willing parties, except in liquidation of a business.

feasibility study—A study made before a project is started to determine the likelihood of the project's success.

ordinary annuity—A series of investments made at the end of a period.

present value—A value in current dollars that will equal or grow into a known future value; a lump-sum amount that must be invested now to achieve a particular goal in the future.

Review Questions

1. What is a feasibility study?

2. What are the sections that might appear in a feasibility study?

3. Why might hotel management want to allocate service center expenses to revenue centers?

4. What bases of allocation might be used to allocate service centers under the direct method?

5. What is the definition of fair value accounting?

6. What prices are used in Level 1, Level 2, and Level 3 for purposes of measuring fair value?

7. What is the definition of compound interest?

8. What is the objective of a compound value calculation?

9. What is the objective of a present value calculation?

10. What is the objective of an ordinary annuity calculation?

11. What is the objective of an annuity due calculation?

12. What is the objective of a present value of an ordinary annuity calculation?

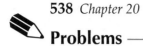

Problems ———————————————————————————

Problem 1

Two revenue centers have the following sales:

Rooms	$600,000
F&B	200,000

The Marketing department expense of $24,000 is to be allocated to each of these revenue centers. Calculate the amount allocated to the Rooms department and to the F&B department.

Problem 2

An investment yields 6 percent annually; the interest is earned semiannually. Calculate what the value of a $5,000 investment made today would be at the end of 10 years.

Problem 3

Calculate the lump sum that must be invested now to attain $5,000 at the end of 6 years in an investment yielding 4 percent annually, interest earned quarterly.

Problem 4

At the end of each year, $5,000 will be invested in an investment yielding 5 percent annually. Calculate what the value of the investment will be at the end of 15 years.

Problem 5

At the beginning of each year, $5,000 will be invested in an investment yielding 5 percent annually. Calculate what the value of the investment will be at the end of 15 years.

Problem 6

Calculate the amount that must be invested now to receive $2,000 per year for 10 years in an investment yielding 4 percent annually.

Index